For Isabelle, Mia, and Lydia May

NEW TO EDITION

New cases in this edition include:

Abercrombie & Fitch v Bordonaro (Case C-143/16) [2017] EU:C:2017:566

Achbita, Centrum voor Gelijkheid van kansen en voor racismebestrijding v G4S Secure Solutions (Case C-157/15) [2017] EU:C:2017:203

Adesokan v Sainsbury's Supermarkets Ltd [2017] EWCA Civ 22

Asda Stores Ltd v Brierley and Others [2016] EWCA Civ 566

Bellman v Northampton Recruitment [2016] EWHC 3104 (QB)

Bougnaoui and Association de défense des droits de l'homme (ADDH) v Micropole Univers (Case C-188/15) [2017] EU:C:2017:204

Cox v Ministry of Justice [2016] UKSC 10

Essop and others v Home Office (UK Border Agency) and Naeem v Secretary of State for Justice [2017] UKSC 27

Focus Care Agency v Roberts [2017] UKEAT/0143/16/DM

Gorka Salaberria Sorondo v Academia Vasca de Policia y Emergencias [2017] (Case C-258/15) (2017/C 014/10)

Graham v Commercial Bodyworks [2015] EWCA Civ 47

Grange v Abellio London Ltd [2016] UKEAT/0130/16/DA

Green v Bannister [2003] EWCA Civ 1819

Jackson v Murray and Another [2015] UKSC 5

Kennedy (Appellant) v Cordia (Services) LLP (Respondent) (Scotland) [2016] UKSC 6

Lock and Another v British Gas Trading Ltd (No. 2) [2016] IRLR 946 CA

Mohamud v WM Morrison Supermarkets PLC [2016] UKSC 11

Newcastle Upon Tyne NHS Foundation Trust v Haywood [2017] EWCA Civ 153

Novus Aviation Limited v Alubaf Arab International Bank BSC(c) [2016] EWHC 1575 (Comm)

O'Hare v Coutts & Co. [2016] EWHC 2224 (QB)

OCS Group UK v Dadi [2017] EWHC 1727 (Ch)

ParkingEye Limited v Beavis [2015] UKSC 67

Pimlico Plumbers Ltd v Smith [2017] EWCA Civ 51

Taylor v Ladbrokes Betting & Gaming Ltd [2016] UKEAT/0353/15/DA

Vaickuviene v J Sainsbury PLC [2013] CSIH 67

Various Claimants v Catholic Child Welfare Society [2012] UKSC 56

Wells v Devani [2016] EWCA Civ 1106

New legislation includes:

Equality Act 2010 (Gender Pay Gap Information) Regulations 2017
The Equality Act 2010 (Specific Duties and Public Authorities) Regulations 2017
The Intellectual Property (Unjustified Threats) Act 2017

PREFACE

The fifth edition of the textbook marks the 10-year anniversary since the publication of 'Business Law'. With this in mind it seemed timely to revisit its structure and format as both the law and pedagogy have evolved in this time. Following an extensive review and with the assistance of several anonymous business law experts, we decided that much greater emphasis should be placed on creating a book focusing on case authority and with an increase in visual aids. These are to enable the reader to rely on the book and not have to explore supplementary sources, and the diagrams and figures help to encapsulate and visualize ideas. We hope these features will add substantially to the readability and usefulness of the book as a single source of guidance. In particular, for those students who are kinaesthetic learners, these new and enhanced features sit alongside the flashcards available with the online resources and the problem questions used in each chapter to reinforce the application of the law. This creates an experience which is much less passive and, we hope, much more engaging.

We have also adopted the use of non-binary pronouns in our writing. As an increasing number of people do not identify as either gender, we wished to produce an inclusive environment for all learners.

In the two years since the last edition was published many changes have taken place. The law surrounding vicarious liability and the tests to establish an employer's potential liability have been refined, with older tests seemingly being considered redundant. Employment law has been as dynamic as ever. First with the removal of the fees to lodge claims to an Employment Tribunal and secondly with the increased number of individuals engaged in the 'gig' economy and how the laws on employment status deal with new forms of working. However, obviously the most significant changes are yet to come following the referendum result and the UK's decision to withdraw from the European Union (EU). This uncertainty has been difficult to accommodate and therefore we have decided for this edition to subsume information regarding the EU into the English legal system chapters. Once the future relationship with the EU is determined, we will incorporate further information in the updates available in the online resources.

This resource also hosts chapters on The Consumer Protection from Unfair Trading Regulations 2008; corporate manslaughter; the Legal Services Act 2007, and alternative legal systems (to contrast with the English legal system—on which this book is based). These chapters will further your understanding, provide a more holistic coverage of business law as it applies to consumers and corporations, and ensure that the requirements of professional bodies including the Chartered Institute of Management Accountants and the Association of Chartered Certified Accountants are satisfied.

We wish to express our thanks to our publishers at OUP for all their continued support and help in the development of the new edition. We would especially like to thank Felicity Boughton who was instrumental in the development of the fifth edition. Felicity sourced instructive reviews of substantial aspects of the book, she produced helpful and insightful suggestions to improve the content and presentation of materials, and continued to be a source of advice, enthusiasm, and inspiration. We would also like to thank our colleagues

Mark Edwards and Peter Griffith for their assistance with questions used in this edition. Their expertise and suggestions were invaluable.

We also want to acknowledge our daughters who help shape our understanding of learning, even at their tender age.

Finally, our hope is that this book helps you understand the legal principles surrounding the operation of businesses, introduces you to the fascinating study of the law, enables you to feel empowered to actively participate in class discussions, and enables you to successfully complete your assessment tasks.

Enjoy your studies.

James Marson and Katy Ferris, Sheffield.
December 2017

GUIDE TO USING THE BOOK

Put the law into its everyday context, understand how and why the law works, and approach the law with confidence.

The textbook includes the following features. They are designed to assist you in your understanding of the law:

BUSINESS SCENARIO

> **Business Scenario 6**
>
> Clive and Jane are friends. Clive is a plur
> house and install a new central heating
> completed by 10 April. The total cost was
>
> Having completed the job, Clive asked J
> short of money and would pay him the
> heard that Clive was in financial difficultie

These features provide some focus for the topic that is being presented. The scenario provides an example of a problem which could occur in real life and/or an assessment question. It demonstrates how the law applies to businesses, employers, and employees in everyday situations so that you get a contextual view of how the law operates in a working context and the 'Consider' boxes relate these issues to the content of the chapter.

CONSIDER

> **Consider**
>
> Can Jane pay £3,000 in full settler
> seeking the balance? No, part-payr
> of whether Clive agrees to this or
> and then bring proceedings to rec

The 'Consider' boxes appear throughout the chapters and relate the issues raised in the 'Business Scenarios' to the content of the chapters. They will help you make sense of the law and enable you to think independently about legal problems.

LEARNING OUTCOMES

> **Learning Outcomes**
> * Explain the meaning of the term 'tor
> * Differentiate between liability in con
> * Explain the three tests to establish l
> * Explain the facts and the court's reas
> * Identify the defences to a negligence
> * Identify the remedies available in cl

These are introduced at the start of each chapter to help you identify what you will be expected to gain from the chapter. They may act as a checklist to focus your attention on specific aspects of the topic. They are presented with the appropriate section(s) of the chapter identified for ease of navigation.

CASE SUMMARIES

> **Caparo Industries Plc v Dickma**
>
> **Facts:**
>
> Caparo had accomplished a takeover of
> directors of that company (Steven and R
> sentation, and an action against its audite
> in carrying out an audit of the company
> purchasing shares in Fidelity a few days

Throughout the chapters you will find summaries of the key case law pertinent to each topic. These boxes sum up the case facts and the impact that the case has had on the law to help you learn the importance of the leading cases.

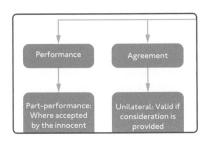

DIAGRAMS

Flow charts and tables are included to aid in your understanding of complex or difficult concepts. They offer an alternative method of learning and help you visualize important features.

SUMMARY OF MAIN POIN

Legal personality

- Natural persons and busin
  personality.
- The legal personality of a con
  out its functions.
- The legal personality of a con

SUMMARY OF KEY POINTS

A summary of the key points is included at the end of each chapter to act as a revision aid and to focus your attention on important concepts raised. They are an effective method of consolidating your learning and are particularly useful in the preparation and revision for examinations.

FURTHER READING

Books and articles

Anderman, S. (2000) 'The Interpre
  ployment' *Industrial Law Journal*

Boyle, M. (2007) 'The Relational P
  Vol. 27, No. 4, p. 633.

Brodie, D. (2004) 'Health and Safe

FURTHER READING

These suggestions are included at the end of each chapter and identify particular books and articles, and trusted and well-maintained websites, Twitter feeds and YouTube channels that are relevant to your studies. Once you have read this text and understood the underlying principles of the law, then use the sources of further reading to expand and deepen your knowledge of a particular point of law.

SUMMARY QUESTIONS

Essay questions

I. 'Employment law is one juris
  tion, continues to be underp
  true in relation to the doctri

  Assess the role played by im
  been developed by the judic

SUMMARY QUESTIONS

At the end of each chapter you will find sample problem and essay questions which enable you to self-test and reinforce what you will have learnt in the chapter. They are written in the style typical of seminar or exam questions and so will be a useful way to practice your technique for answering law questions. Once you have prepared an answer you can then compare this to the answer that is provided with the online resources.

Duress Compelling a party to enter a co
on the basis of a threat, which makes the
contract voidable.

Duty of care The rule that places an obl
to take reasonable care not to injure you
'neighbour' or damage property.

**Economic, technical, and organizationa
reason** Where there has been a transfer

GLOSSARY

At the end of the book you will find a glossary which simply defines the unfamiliar terms that you may come across in the chapters.

GUIDE TO THE ONLINE RESOURCES

Business Law is fully supported by a suite of online resources, which offers valuable student and lecturer materials to complement your textbook and enhance the learning experience. Go to www.oup.com/uk/marson5e/ to ensure you're getting the most out of your textbook.

STUDENT RESOURCES

The resources explained below offer innovative online tools which will support your learning, helping you to fulfil your potential in your business law assessments and exams. Visit www.oup.com/uk/marson5e/ to try the resources for yourself.

Multiple-choice questions: Use these questions to test your knowledge of the law covered within each chapter of the textbook. Immediate feedback on your answers makes it easy for you to assess your level of understanding.

Indicative answers to the end-of-chapter questions: Each chapter of the book contains sample problem and essay questions. Prepare your own answer, then check here for guidance on what an exemplary answer should include—ideal for exam preparation.

Flashcard cases: These interactive flashcards will help you to memorize important key cases and are ideal for revision.

Flashcard glossary: These interactive flashcards will help you to memorise important key terms and are ideal for revision.

Sample legal forms: Sample legal forms referenced in the book are available to download. Additional material: For those wanting to expand their knowledge, additional material on the courts and the Consumer Protection from Unfair Trading Regulations is featured.

LECTURER RESOURCES

Access to the following resources is limited to registered lecturers.

PowerPoint slides: Customizable PowerPoint slides covering key points from each chapter of the text for use in your teaching.

OUTLINE CONTENTS

DETAILED CONTENTS

TABLE OF CASES

TABLE OF LEGISLATION

TABLE OF STATUTORY INSTRUMENTS

TABLE OF EU LEGISLATION

TABLE OF INTERNATIONAL TREATIES AND CONVENTIONS

TABLE OF CODES OF PRACTICE

PART I
INTRODUCTION

Business law is a distinct topic from other modules on accountancy, business, and management courses. It requires an awareness of the law and legal principles which will give you an opportunity to think about business problems from a legal stand-point. This part of the book identifies strategies and good practice that will help with your studies. It provides a sample problem-type question, along with practical research and referencing instructions, and a sample answer to give you confidence when using the remaining substantive chapters of the book.

Chapter 1   Studying Law

1 STUDYING LAW

How would you feel if your company lost a lot of money because you made a mistake negotiating a contract? Or you were prosecuted for failing to meet health and safety standards? Understanding how the law affects business is absolutely essential to ensure those entering the profession can effectively manage the myriad legal implications to which businesses are subject. To be successful in a business career, you must thus have knowledge of the laws most commonly affecting undertakings, and the ability to apply these laws in business situations. Such skills will ensure you can make decisions correctly, quickly, and with certainty, whilst being able to readily identify when expert advice is required. This chapter begins by identifying why it is important to study law and goes on to identify strategies and good practice that will help you be successful in your studies. Business law is a distinct topic from other modules on accountancy, business, and management courses. You need to think about business problems from a legal standpoint and you must know the relevant laws—you cannot bluff knowledge of the law. This approach will ensure you answer legal questions with reference to the law, which is crucial to being successful in your business law module and, much more significantly, in your future business careers.

Learning Outcomes

- Identify why it is important, and indeed necessary, to study business law for your future business careers (1.2)
- Identify strategies and tactics that will assist you in being successful in your studies (1.3–1.3.3.3)
- Understand the features contained in this text and how they can assist you in your learning and development (1.4).

1.1 INTRODUCTION

It should be noted that whilst textbooks aim to provide the guidance and information required to pass courses (in respect of this book, the guidance and information relates to courses with business law as a component), it is your *understanding* of the topic that is essential. This means not just reading the textbook and regurgitating the material in an answer to a question, but thinking about how the law affects a business and how the law is applied in practical business scenarios. By reading and understanding the law, and gaining experience from answering questions in your classes, and those examples provided in this text, you will gain confidence in how to use your legal knowledge to tackle real-life business problems. Remember, regurgitating facts you have learned may be an effective short-term measure that assists in passing examinations, but this approach will likely lead to you making costly professional mistakes once in practice. Lack of knowledge is usually found out in business; it will be exploited by the other party, and will generally result in a competitive disadvantage. Your understanding of the law will be demonstrated through the feedback you receive in classes, and it can also be gauged by using the questions included in this text and the online resources (where indicative answers are included for your reference). Be aware that the feedback provided in each of your seminars/tutorials/discussions with tutors and colleagues is instructive, useful, and, if taken positively and engaged with, a significant help in developing your understanding of the law. Please do not think that feedback is limited to written comments following submission of a summative piece of coursework or provided following completion of an examination. You get feedback at every class in which you engage and participate—learn from it and use it in your development.

1.2 WHY STUDY LAW?

This is a question many students raise. Students who study business law are often undertaking courses in Accountancy, Business, Engineering, Information Management, Financial Services, and Management (to name but a few). The topic may thus not readily appear relevant to your chosen careers, and this is especially so when the topic becomes difficult. However, knowledge of the law is absolutely essential when you enter your business career. You will typically be involved in the recruitment of individuals and the termination of contracts of employment (therefore any number of elements of employment law will be applicable); as managers you will often have responsibility for the agreement of contracts that will bind the organization for which you work (contract law is applicable here); you may have responsibility for the health and safety of workers or be involved in situations where the public visit company premises (involving employment law and the law of torts); and for entrepreneurs, the formation of business organizations into sole traders, partnerships, limited liability partnerships, limited companies, and public limited companies requires an awareness of company law, including the performance of regulatory and compliance techniques.

Of course, it is correct to raise at this point that the issues raised above may necessitate the use of, or may be more suitable to consideration by, experts (lawyers). However, whilst legal experts are necessary at various times, there are day-to-day matters where advice from a lawyer may be unnecessary, time-consuming in waiting for a response, and potentially very expensive. It is not uncommon for a solicitor to charge £250 per hour for their time (and up to £700 an hour for a partner of a city firm), a barrister can charge several thousand pounds per day for appearances in court, and hence a business requires its management personnel or accountants to have an understanding of the law, in order to deal with more rudimentary issues, and also to be aware of when expert assistance is required.

1.3 HOW TO BE SUCCESSFUL IN YOUR STUDIES

An effective strategy to your studies must be adopted from the outset. Having purchased this text, you are on your way! Ensure that you attend your lectures and make notes wherever appropriate (I think this should be done after the lecture so you can concentrate on what the lecturer is saying, but this is a matter of personal preference). Where possible, prior to the lecture, read the relevant chapter(s) in the textbook. Finally, use the notes and the textbook to prepare answers for your seminar/tutorial questions and in-class debates. The seminars are where your learning can be greatly advanced, as you will be able to discuss the law and engage in legal arguments with your tutor and class colleagues.

1.3.1 How to Answer 'Law' Questions

I am often approached by students concerned that, as non-law students, they do not know how to answer a 'law' question. It is a necessary truth that few areas of law are 'black and white' in which an answer is guaranteed to be right or wrong, but by 'grounding' your answer with use of **case law** or statutory materials, you will be ensuring that your answer is based on a legal principle or **doctrine**, and the lecturer can identify how you have arrived at your conclusion. This text includes some of the most important case law and statutory materials that are necessary for your understanding of the topics included. There is a description of the law, and then an attempt to place this into context and explain how the law is used and why it is important to be aware of it. There are references to the actual case law contained in the **law reports**, and interested readers can find these 'primary' materials themselves. However, the value of a textbook is that the case summaries, and commentary regarding its importance and/or the point of law established, will save you the time in finding, reading, and interpreting these primary sources. Primary materials include sources of law such as cases and statutes before they have undergone some form of analysis or commentary. Textbooks and articles written in journals, for example, are known as 'secondary' materials.

In the following sections we discuss what lecturers will be looking out for when they mark assessments. We also include some tips about how to reference and cite sources successfully.

At 1.4 we introduce our technique for answering law questions and provide an example question and sample answer so you can see our method in practice.

1.3.2 What a Lecturer is Looking for in Assessments

There are certain generic characteristics that will be tested in most learning outcomes. You will need to adopt different styles for problem-based (scenario) questions, where a situation is outlined and you are asked to advise the parties as to their legal position, and essay-type questions, which require an analysis of a legal position or statement, but the following are useful guides for the collection of appropriate materials and their presentation:

- *The quality of research materials:* It is always good practice to demonstrate that you have found the appropriate case law and statutory materials, and incorporate these in a table to identify to the lecturer that the relevant law is included.

- *Use the legal materials:* **Statutes** and case law are widely available and are identified in this text, with commentary provided. Having identified the area of law being questioned, ensure you use the appropriate materials to assist you in providing a full and complete response. Your assessor will be looking for relevant references to statutes and case law (where appropriate) in your answer, but also the use of these materials— such as citing case law to 'ground' the legal point you are making. Remember, laws do not just appear. They are derived from case law, statutes, customs or treaties, and so on, so when a point of law is made (e.g. where an individual will be defined as an employee or an independent contractor), cite the law that proves your assertion.

- *Reference to literature:* In an essay-type question, it is important to utilize resources such as books, research reports, and journal articles to identify and analyse authors' comments on legal issues. In order to respond to these you will need to refer to the relevant literature to demonstrate that you have researched and understood the contribution that has already been provided on the topic by others; and this enables you to make a considered and meaningful response.

In problem questions reference to literature refers to citing and using the correct case law and statutory materials in your answer. An assessor will be looking for evidence that you can identify the area of law that is being examined, the relevant case law and statutory materials, and that you have applied the law to the problem in your advice to the parties. This ensures you demonstrate awareness of the relevant sources of law, and also that you can prioritize the most relevant facts from minor issues.

- *Presentation of sources:* When preparing answers for written assessments, the names of cases (case law) should be presented either as <u>underlined</u> or (as is used in this text) in *italics*. This immediately identifies when a case is being referred to and it is easier for the assessor to detect those cases used in an answer. The cases should also include the full references (year and where reported)—its 'citation' (see **1.3.3.2** for examples). Full citations for each case mentioned in this book are included in the table of cases. Books and journal articles that are used (mainly in essay-type answers) should include all the important referencing materials that would assist another reader in finding these resources (see **1.3.4.1** for examples). This text includes references to books and journal articles to enable you to undertake further research into particular topics and these may be used as a template for presentation in essays or other written work. Remember to include all your sources or you may find yourself accused of plagiarism. In examinations, the case name is usually sufficient (rather than the full citation) and the year of the case (although it is wise to ask your tutor as to the level of citation expected in any piece of assessed work).

- *Answer the question:* Any form of assessment will ask the candidate to do something— analyse a statement, advise parties, and so on. I am unaware of any form of assessment that has asked the candidate to state everything they know about a particular topic/area of law. Therefore, if you are asked to advise parties, having described the relevant law and discussed its application to the given facts, *advise* the parties. In the same way, if an essay question asks for an analysis of the usefulness of a particular statute, then conclude with this answer.

1.3.3 Presentation of Written Answers/Essays

This author does not presuppose to identify how each module/course leader/convenor for business law will want written work to be presented or the content that is required. However, by practising with the questions included in this book, and by preparing for your classes, you will gain the experience of how to produce answers to 'law' questions. Further, there are common features regarding the presentation of answers that may be indicative of good practice:

- Use formal language and avoid slang unless this is part of a direct quotation.
- Use correct grammar and punctuation, and make use of the spell check facility available in word processing packages.
- The assessed work should begin with an introduction that identifies what is included in the answer, and the main conclusions to be drawn.
- It should be presented in the third person (use 'the author' or 'it is contended' rather than 'I think') and the tense used should remain constant.
- Do not repeat the question in either an essay or examination answer. This merely gives the impression that you have nothing else to write, and it will not improve your grade.
- Always include a conclusion to your answer that summarizes your main arguments and answers the question set.

Following such simple guidelines makes assessed written work much easier to read and understand. The arguments are more likely to flow when you use a logical structure and this will certainly improve the presentation of your work. However, as always, content is more important than style—research the topic, be prepared, and do not attend examinations thinking your wit will help you pass. You either know case law and statutes or you do not, and law modules require the law to be used, so a lack of knowledge will severely damage your opportunities for success.

1.3.3.1 Include a bibliography

The bibliography contains the full list and references to books, journal articles, research reports, Parliamentary papers and proceedings, government publications, online resources, newspaper articles, and so on that have influenced the production of the assessed work (usually an essay or presentation that requires the submission of a paper copy). This is typically presented after the main body of work and, whilst there are various methods on how to present a bibliography or references list, the style adopted in this text is as follows:

- *Books:* Author Name(s); Year of Publication; Title (in quotation marks); Edition (if applicable); Publisher: City.

Steele, J. (2010) 'Tort Law: Text, Cases, and Materials' (2nd Edition) Oxford University Press: Oxford.

- *Journal articles:* Author Name(s); Year of Publication; Title (in quotation marks); Journal Title (in *italics*); Volume Number; Edition Number/Season; Page Number.

Craig, P. (2000) 'The Fall and Renewal of the Commission: Accountability, Contract and Administrative Organisation' *European Law Journal*, Vol. 6, No. 2, p. 98.

- *Chapters in edited works:* Author Name(s); Year of Publication; Title (in quotation marks); Author Name of Main Book; Year of Publication; Title (in *italics*); Publisher: City.

Prechal, S. (1997) 'EC Requirements for an Effective Remedy' in Lonbay, J. and Biondi, A. (Eds.) (1997) *Remedies for Breach of EC Law* John Wiley and Sons: Chichester, New York, Brisbane, Toronto, Singapore.

- *Parliamentary papers* (these may be used to discuss (for example) the meaning given to, or underlying purpose of, legislation when it was in the form of a Bill): The Speaker's Name; Volume of Hansard (since 1909 the House of Lords (HL) or House of Commons (HC)); Column Number(s); Date (in parentheses).

Lord Hailsham LC, 338 HL Debs, Col. 398–9 (29 January 1983).

- *Other materials* (such as government papers): Organization Name; Title (in *italics*); Date; Reference Number.
- Department of Health and Social Security, *Reform of the Supplementary Benefits Scheme* (1970) Cmnd 7773.
- *The bibliography:* This should be structured in alphabetical order, and then in reverse chronological order (the latest publication by the author listed first).

Where two or more works from the same author(s) are entered for the same year then the prefix of a, b, c, and so on should be used next to the year of publication.

Ellis, E. (1994a) 'The Definition of Discrimination in European Community Sex Equality Law' *European Law Review*, December, p. 563.

Ellis, E. (1994b) 'Recent Case Law of the ECJ on the Equal Treatment of Women and Men' *Common Market Law Review*, Vol. 31, p. 43.

1.3.3.2 Table of cases

Following the bibliography, a table with a list of all the cases cited in the assessed work, and their full references, should be included. These are presented in alphabetical order.

Chapelton v Barry UDC [1940] 1 KB 532.

Olley v Marlborough Court Ltd [1949] 1 KB 532.

Thornton v Shoe Lane Parking Ltd [1971] 2 QB 163.

1.3.3.3 Table of statutes

The table of statutes identifies each of the statutes that have been cited. These are presented in alphabetical order with the title and year.

The Consumer Rights Act 2015

The Equality Act 2010

The Unfair Contract Terms Act 1977

1.4 EXAMPLES OF ANSWERING LAW QUESTIONS

We advise our students to adopt a three-step approach when answering law questions (see **Figure 1.1**). At the end of each chapter in this book you will find example essay and problem questions that you can use to practice, and we include an example answer for every question (which employ the three-step approach) with the online resources. To help you visualize how it works we have included an example problem question and answer in this chapter.

1.4.1 Sample Question

Carl is a director of MediInternet plc and wishes to sell his 20 per cent shareholding in the company. His fellow director, Niall, would like to purchase them but does not have enough money, so Niall arranged a private bank loan, which is guaranteed by MediInternet plc, to obtain the shares. Additionally, MediInternet plc were provided marketing services by Ahmad, so they allotted him 20,000 shares in the company (of £1 nominal value) for this work. Ahmad then transferred all these shares to his new girlfriend, Isabelle. Another director of MediInternet plc, Nicole, is unsure as to the validity and implications of the transactions involving Niall and Ahmad respectively.

Using relevant legal authority, advise on the company law issues raised by the scenario.

1.4.2 Applying the Three-Step Process

In order to apply the three-step approach to this question we first have to identify the area of law that is most applicable to the problem. In this case it is company law, specifically maintenance of capital for corporations (see **Chapter 16**). Directors have great power in

Figure 1.1 How to answer 'law' questions

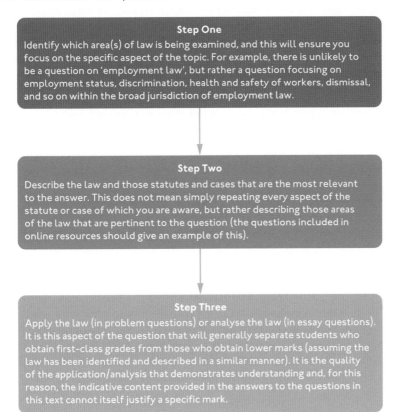

Step One

Identify which area(s) of law is being examined, and this will ensure you focus on the specific aspect of the topic. For example, there is unlikely to be a question on 'employment law', but rather a question focusing on employment status, discrimination, health and safety of workers, dismissal, and so on within the broad jurisdiction of employment law.

Step Two

Describe the law and those statutes and cases that are the most relevant to the answer. This does not mean simply repeating every aspect of the statute or case of which you are aware, but rather describing those areas of the law that are pertinent to the question (the questions included in online resources should give an example of this).

Step Three

Apply the law (in problem questions) or analyse the law (in essay questions). It is this aspect of the question that will generally separate students who obtain first-class grades from those who obtain lower marks (assuming the law has been identified and described in a similar manner). It is the quality of the application/analysis that demonstrates understanding and, for this reason, the indicative content provided in the answers to the questions in this text cannot itself justify a specific mark.

companies and changes they may propose to shares and their allotment are very carefully regulated—often leading to breaches and impacting on minority shareholders.

Once we have identified the area of law that applies, the answer should describe the most relevant statutes and case law. The most relevant statute that applies to this question is the Companies Act 2006 (CA 2006). As you will see in the example answer, there are a number of key cases that can be drawn on to answer the question.

Finally, to attain higher marks we must either apply the law (to answer a problem question) or analyse the law (to answer an essay question). The question we are answering is a problem question. We know this because we are asked to advise about the scenario rather than analyse or examine the law.

1.4.3 Example Answer

For the purposes of this question the following are the main laws relating to the scenario, a brief description of that law, and how they would apply to the individuals involved.

MediInternet plc's guarantee of Niall's loan to purchase shares

In a public company (denoted through the use of 'plc') it is unlawful for that company (or its subsidiary) to give financial assistance directly or indirectly for the purpose of the acquisition of its shares—CA 2006, s. 678(1).

Does the above situation amount to financial assistance as provided for under CA 2006, s. 677? That is, a gift, guarantee, security or indemnity, loan, or other agreement (here a guarantee under CA 2006, s. 677(1)(b)). Assistance must be for the purpose of the acquisition or to reduce or discharge a liability—see *Dyment v Boyden* [2004] EWCA Civ 1586. Niall is purchasing shares in MediInternet plc, so the financial assistance is given directly for the purpose of the purchase—therefore it is unlawful. However, exceptions do exist. Under CA 2006, s. 678(2):

• If the company's principal purpose is not share acquisition (a) or it is an incidental part of a larger purpose (b) and assistance is given in good faith.

Therefore, Niall must convince a court that the guarantee is given in good faith, it is in the company's interests and the principal purpose of the guarantee is not the share purchase, or is only incidental to it.

In *Brady v Brady* [1998] the House of Lords interpreted 'principal purpose' narrowly, distinguishing between a purpose and the reason why a purpose was formed.

Here it seems likely a court would say this is financial assistance as that is the primary purpose—so under CA 2006, s. 680(1)(a) and (b) this is a criminal offence by the company and every officer in default. They are liable to a fine and/or imprisonment (for a person) for a maximum of 12 months (ss. (2)).

Any director (especially Niall) who has authorized the financial assistance could be in breach of their duties under CA 2006, s. 171—the duty to act within powers (*Howard Smith Ltd v Ampol Petroleum Ltd* [1974]); CA 2006, s. 172—the duty to promote the success of the company (*Re Smith & Fawcett* [1942]), and possibly CA 2006, and s. 175—the duty to avoid a conflict of interest (*Aberdeen Railway Co v Blaikie Bros* [1854]). If so, they are liable to account for the full amount of the improper financial assistance (*JJ Harrison (Properties) Ltd v Harrison* [2001]).

Ahmad's allotment of shares

Under CA 2006, s. 580(1) shares must not be issued at a discount, but can be paid up in money or money's worth (including goodwill and know-how); CA 2006, s. 582(1).

There is a risk that shares paid for by non-cash consideration may be undervalued but at common law this is unlikely to be challenged unless it is illusory or manifestly inadequate—*Re Wragg* (1897).

However, whilst that may apply in private companies, a plc is subject to greater restrictions. First, it must not allot a share unless paid up to one quarter of its nominal value (and whole of any premium)—CA 2006, s. 586(1). Also, it must not allot shares otherwise than in cash unless it meets the conditions in CA 2006, s. 593(1), that is: (a)—the consideration (here Ahmad's services) has been independently valued; (b)—a valuer's report made during six months prior to the share allotment; and (c) a copy of the report has been sent to the allottee (Ahmad).

That valuation report must also be filed with the registrar of companies—CA 2006, s. 597(1).

There is no evidence this has been done so the company and every officer in default are guilty of an offence and liable to a fine—CA 2006, s. 607.

For Ahmad (the allottee) if he did not receive a valuer's report or knew/ought to have known some contravention of CA 2006, ss. 593 or 596 then he is liable to pay the company the nominal value of the shares and any interest—CA 2006, s. 593(3).

Furthermore, subsequent holders of the shares are jointly and severally liable (unless they are a purchaser for value without notice)—CA 2006, s. 605(1)(b). This would apply to Isabelle, who now owns the shares.

A court can grant relief from liability—CA 2006, s. 606(1)—if it considers it is just and equitable to do so having regard to all the factors in CA 2006, s. 606(2). The purpose of CA 2006, s. 593 is to ensure the company receives its capital. In CA 2006, s. 606(4) the overriding principle is that the company should receive money or money's worth equivalent to the nominal value (plus premium) of the shares. In *Re Bradford Investments (No. 2)* [1991], the company law regulations were not complied with and thus the court refused relief as it was not satisfied the business had any value when it was transferred. This may be compared with *Re Ossory Estates Plc* [1988] where relief was granted as there was clear evidence that the company received property equal to (and probably exceeding) the value of the shares. Ahmad has gained £20k effectively for his services, so only if he can show that the value of his work was at least this would he be granted relief.

CONCLUSION

This chapter has identified how to effectively study the law and what techniques may be incorporated to prepare for, and present answers in seminars and assessed work. If you incorporate these elements into your study pattern, you may gain more from your studies and achieve greater success for your efforts. You need to work hard in order to be successful, especially when you are studying so many legal jurisdictions, but spend your time reflecting on what you have read, ask yourself 'Why was it important that I read the case/statute?', and use the seminars and self-test questions in this text to assess your own understanding and develop your skills in responding to legal problems.

We wish you success in your studies and your future business careers.

FURTHER READING

The following may be useful for reference and expansion on the points raised in this chapter:

Finch, E. and Fafinski, S. (2017) 'Legal Skills' (6th Edition) Oxford University Press: Oxford.

Penner, J. E. (2008) 'The Law Student's Dictionary' (13th Edition) Oxford University Press: Oxford.

Strong, S. I. (2014) 'How to Write Law Essays and Exams' (4th Edition) Oxford University Press: Oxford.

Wacks, R. (2015) 'Law: A Very Short Introduction' (2nd Edition) Oxford University Press: Oxford.

ONLINE RESOURCES

www.oup.com/uk/marson5e/

For further resources relating to this chapter, including self-test questions, an interactive glossary, and key case flashcards.

PART 2
THE ENGLISH LEGAL SYSTEM

Many texts begin with an outline of the English legal system and the constitution of the State for completeness. Readers may feel that a descriptive account of how laws are made and the court structure is academically necessary, but perhaps irrelevant to their study of business- and accountancy-related subjects. In reality, the English legal system and the constitution involve the fundamental 'building blocks' and rules upon which are based the systems of creation and administration of law. As such, they form the bedrock of the other areas of law you will read throughout the rest of this book.

2

LAW, THE CONSTITUTION, EU MEMBERSHIP, AND HUMAN RIGHTS

Businesses are predominantly concerned with civil law (law between private parties), but an awareness of criminal law and the courts governing this jurisdiction is also necessary. By having an appreciation of Parliament's authority to make laws, and the underlying rules that govern the actions of those within Parliament; and by understanding key principles such as the 'separation of powers' and 'supremacy of Parliament', you will have a better understanding of English law. This in turn will make understanding the role of judicial decisions and precedent, and its impact in contract and torts, for instance, much more relevant, and will be invaluable when considering the implications for the United Kingdom's (UK) membership of the European Union (EU). Further, human rights laws are becoming ever more prominent in employment relations and the operation and regulation of businesses.

Business Scenario 2

Ms Betabita was employed by SecureCash Ltd as a receptionist. Betabita is a Muslim and her job involved dealing with customers from both the public and private sectors. Part of the contract SecureCash Ltd have with their employees is a prohibition of employees from wearing visible signs of their political, philosophical, or religious beliefs whilst in the workplace. This, they are told, is because the employer wants to maintain a position of neutrality in its contacts with customers. Betabita attended work wearing her Islamic headscarf and was informed this was against work rules and was asked to leave and come back wearing compliant attire. Betabita returned to work the next day wearing the headscarf, she again received the same warning about her behaviour and was suspended pending an investigation.

At the conclusion of the employer's investigation into the matter, Betabita was dismissed because of her continuing insistence on wearing her Islamic headscarf to work. Betabita wishes to challenge the legality of the dismissal according to her human rights and in accordance with European law.

Learning Outcomes

- Identify the sources that establish the constitution of the UK (**2.5.1–2.5.1.5**)
- Identify the essential features of the constitution (**2.5.2–2.5.2.4**)
- Explain the roles of the main institutions of the EU (**2.6.2–2.6.2.5**)
- Identify the sources of EU laws (**2.6.3–2.6.3.2**)

- Identify the rights protected through the European Convention on Human Rights (**2.7.1–2.7.1.2**)
- Explain the impact on the judiciary and legislature of the incorporation of the Human Rights Act (HRA) 1998 (**2.7.2–2.7.2.2**).

2.1 INTRODUCTION

Studies of the English legal system primarily consist of a description, and an evaluation, of the institutions and personnel involved in the practice and administration of justice. Therefore, the courts, tribunals, and the **judiciary** are discussed; their powers and the rationale for such authority are outlined; and the mechanisms of control and accountability identified. The aim of such study is to demonstrate how the mechanisms in the justice system work, and to give confidence in these or to outline aspects that require greater control. The English legal system exists to determine the institutions and bodies that create and administer a just system of law.

A just legal system incorporates principles including equality before the law, laws are accessible to all and are applied by an independent judiciary, a system of review of decisions is available, and a system of 'checks and balances' of State institutions are present. These are fundamental to a fair society. In the first three chapters of substantive law considered in this text, the English legal system is discussed, and each of these features is considered. This chapter begins by outlining what the law is and some important constitutional principles. Remember at this stage, the UK does possess a **constitution**, and it is uncodified not unwritten.

2.2 THE DEVELOPMENT OF ENGLISH LAW

The law consists of a body of rules, created through **Parliament**, the common law, and equity, whose jurisdiction extends to private and public bodies. The law provides for remedies and sanctions for transgressions, and establishes a system of rules to regulate behaviour at individual and State levels. Legal disputes may be initiated by individuals or an organization of the State, and these are heard in a relevant court or tribunal. Such a system of laws is necessary for the functioning of any society, and for these to be codified and developed in a representative democracy such as the one in the UK, ensures, as far as is possible, transparency and equity. It ensures, **inter alia**, that legislators are accountable to the electorate and have to answer questions on how taxes are raised and where they are spent, it ensures that the State provides a system of public order and safety for its citizens, it enables business relationships to be entered into on the basis that they will be respected and enforced when necessary, and it protects the vulnerable from abuse and provides fundamental rights that cannot be removed.

2.3 THE DIFFERING SOURCES OF LAW

The common law, equity, and Parliament have each helped to develop the English legal system. Whilst these sources are discussed more fully in **Chapter 3**, it is sufficient at this stage to remark that before Parliament became the supreme law-making body in 1688, the courts in the country had been deciding cases and, in this role, developing rules. Parliament respected the rules established through the common law and would only act to change them where necessary. Therefore, these three sources of law must be viewed as a system as a whole, each with a positive and important role to play in defining the laws of England and Wales.

The law is also separated into public and private jurisdictions. Public law is primarily concerned with the State and its interaction with private bodies in that State (including the State's interaction with other States in international treaties, challenges by private parties against, e.g., secondary legislation, and so on). Therefore, constitutional matters and the criminal laws are a concern of the State. It is important to note in such proceedings that the case is brought by the State as the offence is contrary to a law in England and Wales. This does not seek, necessarily, to compensate the victim (if any) in the matter but rather to punish the offender/protect the public from the offender. Only the State is permitted to take such action. However, this does not prevent the victim who has suffered a loss from seeking to recover any losses sustained through an action in private/civil law. This generally involves an action for damages (the legal term for monetary compensation) and does not allow the injured party to seek punishment of the offender, only to compensate them for any losses incurred. The majority of this text concerns itself with the civil law, although an incident may involve both criminal and civil law actions.

2.4 CRIMINAL AND CIVIL LAW

It is important to recognize that, as stated earlier, whilst the same situation may involve both civil and criminal liability, they are separate branches of the law and have different procedures and purposes. Criminal law seeks to regulate actions that contravene established laws, and it outlines actions that are 'against the law' rather than identifying what a person is entitled to do. The law and sanctions imposed can act as a deterrent to others, it may seek to protect the public from danger, and it may also seek to rehabilitate the transgressor and reintroduce them back into society. Above all, it acts as a punishment for the illegal act committed. The burden of proof in criminal cases is 'beyond reasonable doubt' and the protection afforded the accused in such cases is that it is the responsibility of the prosecution to find the defendant guilty; they do not have to prove their innocence.

In comparison, civil law regulates actions between parties in agreements they have voluntarily entered or where society has placed an obligation to take reasonable care not to cause damage or injury to others. It provides a mechanism to enable appropriate remedies to be available in such instances. There exist several courts and tribunals that consider civil disputes, specialist forums help to provide a settlement, and the cases are decided on 'the **balance of probabilities**'. The case begins with the **claimant** bringing an action against the defendant/respondent, and the claimant outlines the basis of this legal action, and quantifies the remedy they are seeking (usually damages, but other remedies may be involved depending on the nature of the claim).

2.5 THE CONSTITUTION OF THE UNITED KINGDOM

A constitution is a mechanism that outlines the rights and power of the State in relation to its citizens and indeed the whole system of regulation of the Government (all institutions of the State). As the State has ultimate power to establish laws and imprison its citizens, it is a requirement that specific rules are established to ensure tyranny is avoided. Many countries create a written document called a 'constitution' following a revolution, when they remove an unjust ruling monarchy (e.g. France removing its monarchy on 10 August

1792 during the French Revolution), when they overthrow an occupier (the American Patriots overthrew the British and in the political vacuum established the constitution of the United States of America (USA) on 17 September 1787), or when several countries unite to form a new union. It has often been stated that the UK has an 'unwritten' constitution because it does not possess a single document entitled a 'constitution' as do Canada, France, USA, and so on. In fact, the UK's constitution contains several written documents that collectively establish its constitutional underpinnings. In statutory form these include the Magna Carta, the Bill of Rights, the Human Rights Act (HRA) 1998, and the European Communities Act 1972. There is a contribution from case law that further adds to the constitution—see *Entick v Carrington* [1765] and *Malone v Commissioner of Police for the Metropolis (No. 2)* [1979] (see **2.5.1.3**). Therefore, it is more accurate to say that the UK has an uncodified constitution rather than it being unwritten.

Entick v Carrington (1765)

Facts:

Mr Entick had in his possession books and papers that the Secretary of State considered were seditious (treasonous) and sought to seize as evidence. Nathan Carrington and others, acting on the advice of the Secretary, entered Entick's premises relying on a warrant produced by the Secretary. Entick considered this action to be unlawful and brought proceedings against Carrington for the unlawful entry and for seizing property without authority. The Secretary of State insisted that the right to issue the warrant was within the State's power. However, the court held that the action amounted to a trespass and the Secretary of State did not possess the power to issue a warrant. There was no common law or legislative Act that granted to the Secretary the power to issue a warrant, and hence the action was illegal. If the court had provided the State with the power requested by the Secretary, that would have been to elevate its position to legislator, for which, clearly, the court did not have authority.

Authority for:

A State's right to exercise power must derive from some express authority—deriving from legislation or common law. Therefore, the State can only act when it has authority to do so. The reverse is true for individuals in the State. They are entitled to do anything (known as residual freedoms), unless such action is specifically denied by the State.

The significance of the UK having its constitution found in several documents and consisting of general Acts of Parliament (which like any other Act of Parliament can be repealed or altered with no special requirements necessary) is that it is very easy to affect the constitution (see s. 34(2)(d) of the Criminal Justice and Public Order Act 1994). Therefore, the constitution is continually changing and evolving to reflect society's views and needs, and such a 'flexible' constitution may be viewed as an advantage or disadvantage (depending on your point of view).

2.5.1 **Sources of the Constitution**

The sources of the constitution are relatively complex and a full account cannot be included in a text of this nature. However, the main features of these sources are identified in the following paragraphs.

2.5.1.1 **Statutory materials**

The statutory sources of the constitution include a plethora of texts, some of which have greater application than others, but each is entrenched in the legislative make-up of the UK. One of the first documents written on the constitution was the Magna Carta 1215, and supremacy to Parliament from the monarch was established through the Bill of Rights 1689. More recently, the European Communities Act 1972 not only formally led to the UK's membership of the Treaty but fundamentally changed the supremacy of Parliament by 'surrendering' parts of it to the EU. The HRA 1998 (in force in October 2000) gave legislative effect to the European Convention on Human Rights and provided rights for individuals against government/State bodies and the public services more generally. The constitution has been altered through devolving powers to the regions through the Scotland Act 1998, the Government of Wales Act 1998, and the Northern Ireland Act 1998, which established rights for their own Parliaments and Assemblies, and provide for certain changes in primary and secondary legislation to be adopted by these bodies. Further pieces of legislation that may be considered to be part of the constitution include the House of Lords Act 1999 and the Constitutional Reform Act 2005. This section does not intend to be an exhaustive list of the legislation establishing the constitution, but rather to demonstrate Acts that exist which have implications for State powers.

2.5.1.2 **Treaties**

The UK has a dualist constitution, establishing Parliament as the highest legislative authority, and international law as subordinate to this. The UK has held membership, among others, of the International Convention on Human Rights, the European Convention on Human Rights, and the International Labour Organization treaties. Each of these has had an effect on the impact of the State with its citizens and has often existed as an outward sign of a governmental commitment to the important rights detailed in these treaties. However, if a government considered aspects of these treaties to be against the public interest or contrary to its wider agenda, the offending article or provision may have been disregarded or repealed. The major distinction to the general rule of treaties and the effect of international law on domestic law is the EU. The European Communities Act 1972 gave effect to the EU as a body of law and rules, and has led to EU law taking primacy over inconsistent domestic law.

2.5.1.3 **Case law/the common law**

The common law has been a vitally important source in the establishment of constitutional rules. *Entick* established the judiciary's position to restrict the State from exercising powers without authority. This position was questioned in the following case:

Malone v Commissioner of Police for the Metropolis (No. 2) (1979)

Facts:

Mr Malone was on trial on suspicion of dealing in stolen goods. The prosecution admitted that it had intercepted Malone's telephone conversations under a warrant issued by the Secretary of State. Malone argued that the evidence was gathered through unlawful 'tapping' of his phone.

→

Authority for:

Whilst allowing the evidence and dismissing Malone's argument, Sir Robert McGarry remarked in relation to there being no statute that permitted the police to take the action of phone tapping: 'I am not unduly troubled by the absence of English authority: there has to be a first time for everything . . .' Essentially, this ruling purported to reverse the authority in *Entick* by allowing the State to take any action not prohibited by law.

2.5.1.4 Conventions/customs

Constitutional conventions may be referred to as 'soft law' and are not enforceable as is legislation or the common law. However, they establish important principles that are respected and followed by the State. Although mainly unwritten in nature, conventions are more frequently being transposed in written documents (such as codes of conduct) that are then distributed to (e.g.) Ministers and Members of Parliament to aid transparency and understanding. Conventions were established to make Ministers responsible for their actions and those of the department they lead, through **individual** and **collective ministerial responsibility**; they protect the public from abuse by the monarch by ensuring Royal Assent would be given to all the Bills presented by Parliament; they ensure the monarch will ask the leader of the party with a majority (or largest single minority) at a General Election to form a government; the Queen's speech at the opening of Parliament is prepared by her Ministers (the Government); and the Prime Minister will be selected from the House of Commons and not the House of Lords.

2.5.1.5 Prerogative powers

The necessity for constitutional powers (and the basis for Parliament's existence) has been in part because of the existence of prerogative powers. These were often referred to as the Royal Prerogative (as they were exercised by the monarch) but they are now provided to the Government for it to exercise. Prerogative powers are so called because of the power of the body that was empowered to wield them. The monarch, before 1688, held the power as the ultimate legislative authority and therefore held the right to sign treaties, declare war, appoint the judiciary, and so on. These rights have been provided to the Government, and are exercised by government Ministers (in consultation with the monarch). There exist prerogative powers that remain the remit of the monarch (dissolving Parliament, providing Royal Assent to Bills, and so on) but these are increasingly ceremonial in nature. As the Government has the authority to take the actions as listed above, without necessarily requiring the consent of Parliament, then abuse is possible, and whilst unlikely to take place as the UK is a democratic country, Parliament must remain vigilant to potential abuse through holding the Government to account. A system of checks and balances exists through the work of the House of Lords, the committee system, Parliamentary question times, debates, and votes of confidence.

2.5.2 Essential Features of the Constitution

There are underlying principles in which the constitution of the UK operates. These are important to identify and bear in mind, as they have implications for the UK's membership of the EU, and the State's power to legislate and provide a system of justice.

2.5.2.1 The rule of law

The theorist Dicey is credited as defining features of what is called the 'rule of law' and its importance to the constitution to ensure tyranny and abuse are avoided. The rule of law provides for fundamental features of a just and fair society, and whilst when critiqued these may be questioned as to their applicability in the modern era, the broad principles remain as the foundations for a just system of law. Essentially, Dicey identified the rule in three aspects:

1. No one can suffer a penalty except for a clear breach of the law, and there exists the absolute supremacy of regular law as opposed to the influence of arbitrary power. The powers of the State to impose sanctions against the population must exclude arbitrariness and wide discretionary power.

2. Everyone should be equal before the law, subject to the ordinary law of the land administered by the ordinary courts.

3. The rights of the individual are to be secured by the ordinary remedies in private law administered by the courts, rather than through a list of rights outlined in a formal (constitutional) document. The common law developed by the judiciary provides citizens with their rights and freedoms free from undue interference by the State.

Consider

Assume that national law prevents the discrimination against individuals on the basis of their race, religion, or religious beliefs (and non-beliefs). If an (older) EU law contradicts this rule by enabling an employer to maintain a rule of neutrality which applies to everyone, how should domestic courts interpret the national law?

2.5.2.2 Parliamentary supremacy

It has been asserted that the first Parliament was assembled in 1265 to provide counsel to Henry III and consisted of various representatives of the shires, cities, and boroughs in England. Parliament provides legitimacy for decisions that affect the country and achieves this through a system of representative democracy. Whilst the judiciary has made (and continues to make) significant contributions to the body of law, they are unaccountable to the public. Parliament is publicly accountable through direct elections, serving the will of the electorate, and therefore, compared with the common law, Parliament's laws are held to be supreme. Parliament has been, since 1688, the supreme law-making body in the country and as such has the power to 'make and unmake' any laws. Laws may be enacted, others may be repealed, but it is an essential feature of Parliament that it is free to legislate in the interests of the country. As such, old legislation may specifically be repealed, and hence removed from the statute books, but also, more recent laws may be passed that contradict the old legislation. On this basis, the older legislation is to be considered repealed by implication. Therefore, given two Acts of Parliament, the courts will apply and hold applicable the newer of the two if they are in conflict, even if the older legislation purported to be the definitive Act on the subject. This is the doctrine of 'implied repeal' that ensures that Parliament cannot bind successive governments from legislating in whatever way they see fit.

Vauxhall Estates Ltd v Liverpool Corporation (1932)

Facts:

The case involved provisions within the Housing Act 1925 and whether these prevailed over inconsistent laws within the Acquisition of Land Act 1919. The question arose because the latter Act appeared to prevent any change to it by the inclusion of a clause which provided that any future inconsistent provisions 'shall cease to have or shall not have effect'.

Authority for:

Per Avory J: 'I should certainly hold . . . that no Act of Parliament can effectively provide that no future Act shall interfere with its provisions . . . [I]f they [the two statutes] are inconsistent to that extent [so that they cannot stand together], then the earlier Act is impliedly repealed by the later.'

However, if it appears to the judiciary that Parliament could not have intended for newer legislation to repeal previous legislation, the judiciary may have the right not to give effect to the newer legislative provision.

Thorburn v Sunderland City Council (2002)

Facts:

Shopkeepers were convicted of breaches of regulations regarding foods to be sold in metric units (which some of the popular press referred to as 'metric martyrs'). The shopkeepers were required to identify goods in both metric and imperial measures as consistent with EU rules. They appealed on the basis that the relevant law (the Weights and Measures Act 1985) impliedly repealed the (earlier) European Communities Act 1972 (which required inconsistent national law to follow/be interpreted in accordance with EU law).

Authority for:

The nature of the EU Treaty was different than other international agreements in that it created a 'new legal order.' On accession, the UK surrendered its sovereignty in certain areas to the EU and the 1972 Act could only be overridden by express provisions. Hence, by enacting the 1972 Act, Parliament could not have intended it to be capable of implied repeal.

Supremacy of Parliament further has the power of ensuring the judiciary are subservient to Parliament and must apply legislation even if they disagree with it. If primary legislation has been lawfully passed, no court in the UK (even the Supreme Court) can call it unconstitutional, invalid, or refuse to enforce it (although hypothetical exceptions apply—see Lord Woolf of Barnes (1995) 'Droit Public—English Style' *Public Law*, p. 57). There is a mechanism available for the courts to review the decisions of public bodies (a government Minister, local authority planning department, and so on). These bodies are provided with powers and are governed as to the execution of this authority. Where an affected individual claims that the execution of these powers has been breached, or that the decision taken was beyond the powers bestowed on the body that took it, the courts may review the decision and provide a remedy. This system of 'judicial review' enables control of the administration of the power bestowed by Parliament, but this does not extend to reviewing the specific Act passed by Parliament.

2.5.2.3 The separation of powers

Separation of powers is an important facet of the constitution and seeks to establish a system of checks and balances between State institutions and to ensure a degree of separation between their functions. It has been criticized, and has been considered unrealistic and unachievable in reality, but the tenet of the principle is important in the public perception of fairness. The concept of placing too much power in one organ of the State without a means of ensuring accountability is alien to many countries, and those with a written constitution, including Australia, Germany, and the USA, have specific measures included in their constitutions to separate these powers. In the UK, whilst there is no written constitution comparable with the aforementioned countries, the concept of separation of powers is still maintained. This was noted by the French constitutional theorist, Montesquieu, who commented on the UK constitution in the eighteenth century and remarked, 'When legislative power is united with executive power in a single person or in a single body of the magistracy, there is no liberty. Nor is there liberty if the power of judging is not separate from legislative power and from executive power.' There are essentially three organs of the State that hold power: the executive (which is responsible for the administration of the country and for initiating legislation), the legislature (which is responsible for enacting laws and for holding the executive to account), and the judiciary (which has the role of interpreting and applying the law); and it is necessary that they have distinct domains in decision-making and the legal system. In this way, they can check on the decisions being made and ensure reviews are possible. To this end it is essential that the constitution provides for an independent judiciary to ensure the rule of law.

In conclusion of this section, it should be remembered that no system can have a true demarcation of the powers of the State as outlined earlier, and indeed in many areas the UK has 'transgressed' this constitutional doctrine (e.g. the role of the Lord Chancellor). However, by enabling interaction between these organs, as long as adequate independent 'checks and balances' exist, better government and administration is often the result.

2.5.2.4 No retrospective laws

The general principle is that citizens have a right to know the laws that affect them before any criminal sanctions may be imposed. For this reason, laws are made available through the Internet, in public libraries, and so on, and this is also the reason why ignorance of the law is no defence. As such, a lawful action today should not, retrospectively, be made unlawful by a subsequent Act criminalizing that action, passed tomorrow. However, there are exceptions, such as the War Crimes Act 1991, which covered crimes and illegal acts committed during the Second World War. Obviously, the general rule regarding the distaste for retrospective laws is understandable, and a point expressed through the European Convention on Human Rights Art. 7, but it can be deviated from if the nature of the legislation necessitates.

2.6 EU MEMBERSHIP

It is trite comment but EU law and its impact on the UK legal system, whilst currently still in force and applicable in its fullest form, will cease if the UK exits the EU as a consequence of the referendum result on 24 June 2016. The Conservative Government had sought to assure the electorate that 'Brexit means Brexit'. However, given the general election result of 8 June 2017 and the Conservative Party forming a minority government, whether there is a 'hard Brexit' (fully leaving the EU) or a 'soft Brexit' (some continued membership of the Single Market) remains unclear. At the time of writing it is also unclear if a further general election will be needed prior to the conclusion of the Brexit negotiations (March 2019). As such, this section of the book outlines the main laws of the EU and how they affect businesses, but the 'updates' included with the online resources will contain developments on the significant issue of future membership and on what basis that takes place.

2.6.1 Aims of the EEC

The aims of the original Treaty provided:

> By establishing a common market (now replaced as 'internal market' following the Treaty of Lisbon) and progressively approximating the economic policies of Member States, to promote throughout the Community a harmonious development of economic activities, a continuous and balanced expansion, an increase in stability, an accelerated raising of the standard of living and closer relations between the States belonging to it.

In order to achieve these goals, a customs union was created where the customs duties and equivalences of the Member States would be harmonized under European law to facilitate the Internal Market. Secondly, this Internal Market was extended to include free movements of goods, services, capital, and workers. The third element was an effective competition policy to ensure companies, markets, and cartels could not restrict the functioning of the Internal Market. These broad aims were established in the Treaty (and have been reviewed and extended in the subsequent treaties) and were given ever greater effect and definition through judgments of the Court of Justice of the European Union (CJEU) and the EU's secondary laws.

With regard to the free movement of goods, the main provisions of this source of law are contained in Arts. 28 (now Art. 34 TFEU), 29 (now Art. 35 TFEU), and 30 EC (now Art. 36 TFEU) concerning the abolition of quantitative restrictions, and all measures having an equivalent effect, on imports and exports (albeit with derogations permissible). It should also be noted that the CJEU has held Arts. 28 and 29 EC (now Arts. 34 and 35 TFEU) to be directly effective. A quantitative restriction may include a ban or quota on goods, or any measure that amounts to a 'total or partial restraint on import . . . or goods in transit'. The term 'goods' in the legislation is widely defined to include items of economic value such as food, clothing, and vehicles, but has also been extended to utilities such as gas and electricity. The free movement in this respect deals with actions taken at a State level to restrict the movement rather than private entities refusing to buy or stock EU-based products.

A measure having an effect equivalent to a quantitative restriction is not defined in the Treaty, but from the case law of the CJEU, this may include requiring an importer to possess a licence or permit, or certificate of origin; requiring goods to be stored in the Member State for a fixed period before being allowed to be sold (and is not applicable to domestic products); and to fixed national price controls on goods. These are merely a few examples, but they should serve the purpose of demonstrating the regulation of anti-competitive behaviour by Member States.

The free movement of workers (extended to self-employed persons) was a fundamental requirement of the common market to ensure that one of the key aspects to free up the factors of production, along with goods, services, and capital, was achieved. However, the EU did not see the worker as a mere source of labour or to be regarded as a commodity, but rather as a human being with the fundamental rights of the worker having prec-edence over the requirements of the Member States' economies. Whilst supplemented through Regulations and Directives, the main provision for this fundamental freedom derives from Arts. 39–42 EC (now Arts. 45–48 TFEU). Article 39 EC (now Art. 45 TFEU) is directly effective and seeks to abolish any discrimination based on the nationality of workers as regards employment, remuneration, and other conditions of work (subject to the derogations of public policy, public security, or public health). This gives the person the right to move freely within the territory of the Member States to take up work or search for work; reside in the State (according to domestic laws), and to remain in the State following employment. A worker is someone who works for another (and the defini-tion of the worker is subject to EU interpretation rather than that of a Member State), and can include a part-time worker, and a person who requires the use of their own savings (or State assistance) to supplement their remuneration if it is below the State minimum subsistence level. The requirement is that it is genuine and effective work, rather than being made for the purposes of the person taking up the work, and the motives of the worker are irrelevant in their decision to be a worker. The rights of workers are provided to citizens of the EU (in each of the 28 Member States) and once established as a worker, they are entitled to the same tax and social advantages as provided to citizens in the State, such as the same grants to students regardless of whether they are a domestic na-tional or EU national.

2.6.2 Institutions of the EU

2.6.2.1 The EU Commission

The Commission has had many roles in the EU but its main functions are to initiate legislation (working with the Council and the Parliament) and to enforce the laws of the EU. To achieve these it is divided into 44 Directorates-General and services. It has a right of initiative in the legislative process (to propose legislation for the Council and Parlia-ment to pass). It is also known by its title of 'Guardian of the Treaty' where it ensures that the Member States comply with their EU obligations—laws from the Treaty, Regulations, Directives, and Decisions. The Commissioners are selected by their Member States and those Commissioners meet at least once per week (in Brussels or in Strasbourg when the Parliament holds its plenary sessions), although these meetings are not held in public. At present each Member State supplies one Commissioner.

2.6.2.2 The Council of the European Union

The Council is one of the most powerful of the EU institutions and it is the main decision-making body in the EU. Its meetings are attended by the Ministers from the Member States and the EU Commissioners responsible for those areas. The Minister who attends is usually the Foreign Minister of the Member State, but as the Council is not a fixed body, the relevant Minister for whichever subject is being discussed will attend. The Council's role includes concluding agreements with foreign States, taking general policy decisions, and taking decisions based on the Commission's proposals. The Council meets in Brussels and Luxembourg and decisions are made by votes of the Ministers from the Member States. The method of voting depends upon the Treaty and the provisions laid down for dealing with the subject being voted on. These methods are: a simple majority; a qualified majority; and unanimity.

Each Member State takes the Presidency of the Council on a rotation basis for a six-month term (January–June; and July–December). During this Presidency the Member State provides a President who chairs the meetings of the Council, calls for votes, and signs the Acts adopted at the meetings. This Presidency also allows the Member State to control the political agenda of the Council and it will attempt to pass through as many measures as it can. The Council meets to decide on the future of the EU and is often represented by the leading Ministers of the Member States—typically the Prime Minister and Chancellor (or their counterparts in other Member States).

As the membership of the Council comprises Ministers who have full-time responsibilities in their own Member State, they are consequently in Brussels for a relatively short period of time. To ensure the continuity of the Council's work, this role is coordinated by a Permanent Representatives Committee (COREPER—Art. 240 TFEU), which is composed of permanent representatives of the Member States.

2.6.2.3 The European Parliament

The European Union has approximately 510 million citizens and these people, from each of the 28 Member States, have the ability to elect representatives to the European Parliament. The Parliament is elected every five years and its role is to contribute to the drafting of legislation which affects the Member States through Directives and Regulations.

There are 751 elected Members of the European Parliament (MEP) and every Member State decides on how its elections will be held. There are common rules which must be followed—the voting age is 18 (although in Austria it is 16) and there must be a secret ballot. The seats of the Parliament (for the 2019 elections) are shared out proportionately between the populations of the State (the maximum number of seats for any one State is 96 (Germany) and the minimum is six (Cyprus, Estonia, Luxembourg, and Malta)). The MEPs are expected to exercise their mandate independent of their Member State and are grouped by their political affinity (in one of seven Europe-wide political groups) rather than by their nationality. They divide their time between Brussels (Belgium), Luxembourg, and Strasbourg (France) in addition to their home constituencies, attending parliamentary committees and plenary sittings.

The Commission is the only body which is empowered to initiate legislation. It creates a legislative text, and an MEP, whilst working in one of the parliamentary committees, drafts a report which the committee votes on and can amend. The revised text may then be adopted and agreement can be made with the Council about the legislation and its subsequent implementation.

There are two forms of legislative procedure, depending upon the law to be passed. The ordinary process is called 'co-decision' and puts the Parliament on an equal footing with the Council in areas including transport and the environment. The second is a special legislative procedure where the Parliament only possesses a consultative role (e.g. in agriculture, visas, and immigration). The Parliament can present legislative proposals to the Council which may then become laws in the EU.

2.6.2.4 The Court of Justice

The CJEU is the body that considers the interpretation and application of EU law. It also has the role of enforcing the EU's laws. It is composed of 28 judges (each one selected from the Member States) assisted by eight Advocates-General who hold office for a renewable term of six years.

The Court may sit as a full Court, a Grand Chamber (of 13 judges in very important cases), or in chambers of three or five judges. Its role is completely independent of the Member States and it holds the responsibility of ensuring the application of EU law is maintained (enforcement function), and of interpreting the EU laws to assist the Member States in adhering to their obligations (interpretative function). These are the two main functions of the CJEU. It only has jurisdiction on matters and laws to do with EU law—it cannot (and will not) hear cases involving domestic national matters. It should further be noted that the CJEU is not an appeal court, nor is it in a hierarchy with domestic courts. It is deemed an equivalent to domestic courts and the cooperation between the CJEU and domestic courts is a crucial facet to the relationship between them.

2.6.2.5 The General Court

Following the Treaty of Lisbon, the Court of First Instance has been renamed the General Court. It is an independent court attached to the CJEU and consists of 28 judges (one from each of the Member States) who are appointed for a six-year term, which is renewable by the Member State. It was established in 1989 to relieve the pressure on the CJEU in its workload of cases. The General Court sits in chambers of three or five judges but occasionally may only consist of one judge and may even sit as a full court in very important cases. Its main role is to ensure the laws of the EU are observed through interpretation of the law, and the application of the law in the Member States.

2.6.3 Sources of EU Law

2.6.3.1 Primary law—EU Treaty Articles

The primary laws of the EU are found in the Treaty Articles (from the Treaty of Rome through to the Treaty of Lisbon), and through agreements and cooperative initiatives between the EU as a body and other international bodies and countries beyond the legislative scope of the EU's Member States. The important aspect to note about Treaty Articles is that they are the *highest form of EU law*, and as long as they satisfy the test of being *directly effective*, they have a similar legal effect to an Act of Parliament and must be given such an effect in the domestic court without any further action required by the Member State (they have **direct applicability**). They have horizontal and vertical effect (discussed later), which makes them accessible to all citizens in the Member States.

2.6.3.2 *Secondary laws*

The secondary laws of the EU are defined in the Treaty under Article 288 TFEU and outline what level of competence the laws have and the requirements imposed on the Member States. **Table 2.1** identifies on whom the laws are binding.

Secondary laws—Regulations

The laws created in the form of Regulations have general application to all Member States, they are the highest form of secondary legislation, and once passed, they are directly applicable in the Member States. The important element to remember is that these laws create uniformity in the States, and the Regulation's provisions are reproduced in the Official Journal. This, as a consequence, is a rather rigid and inflexible form of law, as the ability to create the same law in each of the languages of now 28 Member States in the Journal results in differing enforcement as lawyers argue as to the scope, nature, and applicability of the provisions.

A method of enabling the Member States to become involved to a greater extent in the legislative process and create laws which are more likely to be drafted in a form usually found domestically (and hence in theory to be more successfully enforceable) has been Directives.

Secondary laws—Directives

Directives are a tool frequently used by the EU to achieve its legislative goals. They enable the Member State to fulfil its EU obligations, but with a degree of flexibility as to how this may be realized. Directives require the Member States to transpose the effects of the law into their own legal system, in a method which is best suited for itself and its citizens, within a prescribed date (the date for **transposition**—the term is the process of taking the EU Directive and creating an implementing piece of legislation). Whereas Regulations produce uniformity in the laws of the EU, Directives seek harmonization of the laws (the spirit of the Directive is the same but the linguistic detail may be different).

Secondary laws—Decisions

The institutions of the EU have the ability to use Decisions as a method which allows a greater level of detail as to whom the laws will apply. The effect of using a Decision as a tool of law enables the EU to compel a particular Member State if it so chooses, or an individual, to perform or refrain from action. In addition, it can also confer rights or impose obligations on them.

Consider

SecureCash Ltd is attempting to rely on the Equal Treatment Directive (Council Directive 2000/78/EC) to defend its decision to ban the wearing of the headscarf. Would it be able to rely on this in a national court in a case against another private body (i.e. an employee)? Would it make any difference to your answer if the other party was in the public sector? Consider the horizontal and vertical direct effect of the Directive.

Table 2.1 The binding effect of EU laws

	Treaty Articles	Regulations	Directives
Who does the law bind?	The Member State and individuals	The Member State and individuals	The Member State
The extent to which the law binds	In its entirety	In its entirety	The result to be achieved (the Member State has discretion as to how it does this)
Need for domestic implementing measures?	No (not allowed)	No (not allowed)	Yes—the State has to implement (transpose) the law

2.6.4 **Direct Effect**

Direct Effect of EU law was developed by the CJEU to allow individuals and organizations to use the provisions of EU law within the Member States' domestic courts, and in the case of Directives, without having to wait for the Member State to fulfil some obligation that it had omitted to do. Direct Effect had been established for primary law (Treaty Articles) and the rationale of the CJEU developing this mechanism was that '. . . the useful effect (of an EU law) would be weakened if individuals were prevented from relying on it before their national courts and if the latter were prevented from taking it into consideration as an element of Community law.' (*Van Duyn v Home Office*). There has been controversy over the use of Direct Effect in primary law, but the doctrine was largely accepted by the Member States. It was further advanced to secondary laws (namely Directives) and this was to extend accessibility to EU rights, but this is where many problems began.

As Directives are a commonly used source of law, the application of Direct Effect would enable an affected individual to use a Directive's provisions in a domestic court after the date of transposition if the Member State had been guilty of either non-implementation or incorrect transposition. Direct Effect was considered permissible if the tests developed by the CJEU were satisfied. Tests were required as EU laws are often very general in scope and in order for any legislation to give rights to, or provide obligations on, individuals they must be sufficiently clear and precise to allow the affected parties to understand their scope. The tests to be satisfied for an EU law to have Direct Effect are:

1. the provision must be clear and unambiguous;
2. the provision must be unconditional; and
3. the provision must not be dependent on further action being taken by the EU or Member State.

Having established the tests, the application of Direct Effect came to the CJEU. It stated that so far as the tests were satisfied, Treaty Articles having general application would enable a claim using Direct Effect. The same provision applies with Regulations under the same rationale. However, when considering Directives, the CJEU had a major concern. EU laws, having application to individuals as well as the State acceding to the Treaty, resulted in individuals having obligations to follow EU law. This is what made the EU such an important aspect of law in the UK. No other international treaty had placed obligations on individuals in the Member State–they had only obliged the State to act in a certain way. The EU gave rights to individuals but also placed obligations on them. To ensure that individuals would comply with their obligations, it was only correct that they had access to any rights that they could benefit from. The CJEU, though, had to determine whether a Directive could be used between private parties as well as against the State. In this situation arose the concepts of Horizontal Direct Effect (HDE) and Vertical Direct Effect (VDE) (**Figure 2.1** on p. 30). HDE is so called because it involves using the provisions of an EU law directly against another private party (horizontal because both private parties have the same legislative power and obligations). VDE is so called because it involves a claim from a private party against the State or emanation of the State (vertical because the private party has no legislative power but the defendant (the State) is of a higher position in terms of legislative authority).

The issues of HDE and VDE are quite complex and do not require in-depth investigation in this text. It is, however, prudent to consider these issues briefly to appreciate their impact on the EU dimension to the protection and enforcement of rights. HDE of Directives is the use of the law between two private individuals where the court recognizes the EU law and

Figure 2.1 Horizontal and Vertical Direct Effect

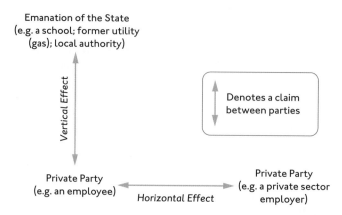

gives it effect as it would a domestic law. The CJEU therefore decided that the application of EU law domestically could only be enforced where the EU considered it had competence–via VDE. HDE has been considered to be beyond the scope of the CJEU because private parties have no legislative power so should not be held responsible when the Member State has failed in its obligations; if it did give the remedy of HDE this would almost be to elevate Directives to the power of Regulations which Article 288 TFEU did not allow; and if the Member State upheld its obligations then this remedy would not be necessary. The denial of HDE of Directives was demonstrated in the UK in the case of *Duke v GEC Reliance*.

Duke v GEC Reliance (1988)

Facts:

GEC Reliance had a policy of compelling women workers to retire at 60 years of age compared with 65 years for men (and this was applied to Mrs Duke). The House of Lords had held that the Sex Discrimination Act 1975 was not applicable to retirement ages, and instead had to consider whether Duke was able to claim directly under the relevant EU law (the Equal Treatment Directive—76/207/EEC). The Lords held that Duke could not use the Directive in her claim as her employer was not 'an emanation of the State', and the Horizontal application of Direct Effect of Directives was not possible.

Authority for:

The CJEU refused to recognize the Horizontal Direct Effect of Directives.

This case demonstrated that whilst EU laws have significant effects on the UK courts and Parliament, Directives themselves may not be used directly against parties in the private sector. This has implications in, for example, employment law where many of the advances in the law have derived from the UK's membership of the EU, and where most workers are employed in the private sector. A claim against their employer would be a claim against a person in the private sector and clearly if the Member State has not taken the correct action in transposing the EU law into domestic legislation, the employee has to look towards Indirect Effect to access their rights as there is no HDE of Directives.

As the CJEU did not consider that it could provide the enforcement mechanism of HDE it began to widen the concept of 'the State' to be of use in VDE claims. The State is no longer considered to be limited to the Government. Through case law, it has been applied by the CJEU to former nationalized utilities, schools, the police force, and hospitals. Essentially, any 'body' where the State possesses some direct control may fall under the remit of VDE. The consequence of this situation is that if the transgressor of an unimplemented EU Directive is an emanation of the State there may be a claim under Direct Effect through VDE; and if the transgressor in the same scenario is a private party there is no claim, as HDE is not allowed.

The CJEU recognized the problem of having two sets of rights depending on who the transgressor (defendant) was, and the perceived unfairness of this situation. It therefore wished to develop a remedy which was applicable to all in the EU and still ensured EU law was given effect and was respected—the doctrine of Indirect Effect was developed.

2.6.5 Indirect Effect

The CJEU was concerned at the problem posed by the lack of access to EU laws through a Member State not transposing a Directive, or doing so incorrectly, and hence how this denied access to rights. Member States were under a duty to give effect to EU laws and as such a method of statutory interpretation was adopted by the CJEU, under the doctrine of Indirect Effect. Hence the national law should be interpreted through the courts by reference to the EU law (such as a Directive), and this EU law would allow the judge to 'read into' the existing English law the provisions of the EU law, thus providing access to it.

Von Colson and Kamann v Land Nordrhein-Westfalen and Dorit Harz v Deutsche Tradax GmbH (1984)

Facts:

The first case involved two women, Von Colson and Kamann, who had applied for jobs as social workers at Werl prison. They were both unsuccessful (the positions were given to two male applicants) and claimed against the administrators of the prison that they were denied the posts due to their sex. In the second case Dorit Harz applied for a vacancy available to economics graduates but was refused an interview as she had been informed that the position was only available to male applicants.

In each of these cases Germany had not transposed the Equal Treatment Directive (Directive 76/207). The German court therefore referred questions to the CJEU, *inter alia*, establishing whether the Directive could be used directly in the claims. The CJEU held that instead of looking at the issue of Direct Effect and the potential application of that remedy, Member States had an obligation to interpret existing legislation to give effect to EU law and obligations: 'It is for the national court to interpret and apply the legislation adopted for the implementation of the directive in conformity with the requirements of Community law, in so far as it is given discretion to do so under national law.'

Authority for:

Directives may be used directly in domestic courts against a State or emanation of the State defendant (Vertical Direct Effect) but may not be used directly against a private-sector defendant (Horizontal Direct Effect). Therefore, where possible, a system of consistent interpretation of domestic law with EU law should be used (Indirect Effect).

Table 2.2 The extent of the applicability of EU law

	Primary law		Secondary laws	
	Treaty Articles	Regulations	Directives	Decisions
Directly effective	Yes (directly applicable)	Yes (directly applicable)	No	Yes (to whom they are addressed)
Horizontal Direct Effect	Yes	Yes	No	No
Vertical Direct Effect	Yes	Yes	Yes	Yes
Uniformity of laws	Yes	Yes	No (harmonization)	No

Indirect Effect of Directives is evidenced in the following ways;

1. Where legislation has been passed in the UK to implement a requirement derived from an EU Directive, then the UK courts are obliged to adopt a more purposive style of interpretation which seeks to read the obligations in light of the meaning and purpose of the Directive.

2. Where the law has not been passed to implement the requirements of a Directive, and its terms cannot be read so as to conform with the Directive, then the national legislation will be applied.

3. Where the law has not been passed to implement the requirements of a Directive, but the terms of the law are capable of being read in the spirit of an EU Directive, then the national law is capable of being read as though it had been so enacted.

Whilst being a rather contrived way of achieving effectiveness of EU law, it is a method of enforcement that would enable *all* those whose rights had been transgressed potential recourse to the EU law's provisions in the domestic court.

Table 2.2 provides an overview of the sources of law and their applicability.

2.7 HUMAN RIGHTS

The protection of human rights encompasses a wide range of liberties (including the social rights of accessible and competent healthcare, adequate housing, and the regulation of employment relationships through the prevention of abuses of managerial prerogative and discrimination). Whilst these are undeniably vital for the betterment of society, human rights and the subsequent legislative initiatives have focused on social and political rights, and therefore the European Convention and the HRA 1998 have sought to protect freedoms of assembly, religion, life, voting at elections, and so on. The UK has been signatory to the European Convention on Human Rights (ECHR—the Convention) since 1951, and incorporated these provisions through domestic legislation in 1998 (the HRA 1998, in force on 2 October 2000). However, it had been accepted that the UK respected human rights before membership of the Convention or enactment of the HRA 1998, and these principles were the cornerstone upon which the legal system was based.

Consider

Ms Betabita is arguing that her human rights are being infringed by not being able to manifest her religious beliefs. Which of these, if any, would you think applicable and are these rights absolute or subject to interpretation nationally?

2.7.1 The European Convention on Human Rights

The European Convention was signed in 1950 and ratified by the UK in 1951 (coming into force in 1953). Evidently, this was an international treaty and as such it governed the relations between those States that were signatories to it, ensuring respect for the human rights outlined in the Convention and providing for a system of accountability for abuses. **Table 2.3** sets out the Convention rights and corresponding Article numbers. Being an international treaty, the Convention protected individuals against actions by the State (rather than claims against other individuals), and sought to regulate the State in its legislative activities. It thereby restricted the State from enacting legislation that contradicted the Convention (although, as with other international treaties (including the EU Treaty), various derogations of these rights existed in areas such as war and national security). When the derogations were exercised by the State, it was the duty of the State to inform the Secretary-General of the Council of Europe of the measures (Art. 15).

Table 2.3 Convention rights

Article number	Convention right
2	The right to life
3	Freedom from torture or inhumane or degrading treatment or punishment
4	Freedom from slavery or forced or compulsory labour
6	The right to a fair trial
8	The right to respect for private and family life, his home, and his correspondence
9	Freedom of thought, conscience, and religion
10	Freedom of expression
11	Freedom of peaceful assembly and freedom of assembly
12	The right to marry and found a family
14	The enjoyment of the Convention rights without discrimination on any ground
Article 2 of the First Protocol	The right to an education
Article 3 of the First Protocol	The right to take part in free elections by secret ballot
The Sixth Protocol	The abolition of the death penalty

2.7.1.1 Convention rights

The Convention, and the subsequent extensions to the provisions through the various protocols agreed by the signatory States, ensured that the most significant civic and political rights were to be respected and protected. The rights included in the Convention are further to be enjoyed without discrimination on any ground including 'sex, race, colour, language, religion, political or other opinion, national or social origin, property, birth or other status' as identified in Art. 14.

2.7.1.2 Enforcement

Updated measures to deal with enforcement were effected through the Eleventh Protocol, which abolished the Commission and instead provided for a permanent court. The European Court of Human Rights (ECtHR) (based at Strasbourg) was established with judges from each signatory State who are selected by the Parliamentary Assembly of the Council of Europe from a shortlist by the State of three judges (Art. 22), and who remain in office for a six-year tenure (after which this tenure may be reviewed). A significant change from the original Convention is that enforcement of human rights now enables individuals to apply directly to have their case heard by the ECtHR. In order to do so, it is expected that the individual claimant has exhausted all domestic remedies and brought their claim within six months of the final decision in the State. The ECtHR then has to ensure that the claim is admissible and involves a point of law that it has not already decided.

The composition of the ECtHR is usually three judges sitting in a chamber who determine the admissibility of the claim. If the claim is determined to be admissible through a unanimous vote, then a chamber consisting of seven judges is convened to determine the merits of the case. In the most serious cases involving the provisions of the Convention and Protocols, a Grand Chamber of 17 judges is convened. The decisions of the ECtHR are final (Art. 29) and it is empowered to award 'just satisfaction' to the successful claimant (Art. 41).

2.7.2 The Human Rights Act 1998

The Labour Party and members of the judiciary had commented on the impact of the UK's membership of the European Convention and the difficulty in ensuring individuals had access to their human rights. Whilst it was undeniable that in most situations the UK had recognized human rights and built its legal system on ensuring respect for civil freedoms and political rights, underpinned through accountability, there were groups of people who were affected by powers or decisions of the State which they considered to be a breach of their rights. This was further compounded by the number of successful cases decided against the UK at the ECtHR. Under the UK's dualist system, alleged transgressions of these international laws did not enable the judiciary to provide any meaningful remedy. In order to seek 'justice', the individual had to travel to Strasbourg and have the case heard before the ECtHR. This gave the impression that individuals may not be able to get justice in the UK, and therefore a change in the legal system was necessary to empower the judiciary to hear claims of abuses of human rights and provide a remedy. Following enactment of the HRA 1998, cases involving European Convention rights can be heard by the UK courts and mechanisms are in place to provide for the application of effective enforcement measures. The HRA 1998 includes Arts. 2–12 and 14 of the Convention, Arts. 1–3 of the First Protocol, and Arts. 1 and 2 of the Sixth Protocol.

When enacting legislation, HRA 1998, s. 19 provides that the relevant Minister responsible for the Bill make a statement regarding its compatibility with the Act, or otherwise to declare to Parliament that they are unable to offer such a statement of compatibility, but the Government wishes to proceed with the Bill regardless. This ensures Acts that impact on human rights are considered in light of the HRA 1998 and the Convention, and also offers guidance to the judiciary in applying and interpreting the legislation.

2.7.2.1 Powers granted to the judiciary

One concern postulated in the consideration of enacting the HRA 1998 was that courts in the UK would be elevated to 'Supreme Court' status (in the USA model), whereby the court would be able to strike down legislation that transgressed the HRA 1998. This, evidently, would attempt to usurp the power of Parliament to legislate in whichever way it wished, and also would impact upon other constitutional principles such as the separation of powers. Therefore, in order to protect the constitution, the HRA 1998 identified and limited the extent of the powers of the judiciary in matters concerning human rights, and provided for strict rules on the powers of enforcement.

The judiciary has an obligation to interpret primary and secondary legislation, and the common law, consistently with the Convention (and through s. 2 of the HRA 1998 to take into account previous decisions and opinions of the ECtHR), to ensure that as far as possible human rights are given complete effect (s. 3(1)).

Ghaidan v Godin-Mendoza (2004)

Facts:

The protected tenant (under the Rent Act 1977) died and his same-sex partner, who had cohabited and shared a close and stable relationship with him for many years, sought a statutory inheritance of the tenancy. The Rent Act 1977 referred to a 'surviving spouse' of the tenant being entitled to succeed the tenancy, and this was extended in 1988 to include persons living together as husband and wife. The Act did not, however, specifically refer to same-sex couples and this led to the action.

Authority for:

In a previous case (*Fitzpatrick v Sterling Housing Association*) the House of Lords held a same-sex partner did not qualify under the law. This was based on interpretation of the law and that there was no explicit legal protection against discrimination on sexual orientation. When *Ghaidan* came to the courts, such a law (the Human Rights Act 1998) did exist. This allowed the Lords to interpret the national law in accordance with the European Convention on Human Rights (Arts. 8 and 14).

This generally results in courts providing a consistent interpretation of the law in light of the Convention, but exceptions do exist.

R v Horncastle and Others (2009)

Facts:

The appellants had been convicted of serious criminal offences. Evidence was presented at court in the form of witness statements. Statements came from a witness who had died before the trial and another who failed to attend the hearing due to fear of repercussions. The appeals against the convictions were dismissed by both the Court of Appeal and the Supreme Court.

Authority for:

Article 6(3)(d) of the European Convention on Human Rights guarantees everyone who is charged with a criminal offence the right 'to examine or have examined witnesses against him'. Further, the Human Rights Act, 1998 s. 2(I) requires national courts to take into account the jurisprudence of the European Court of Human Rights (*Al-Khawaja and Tahery v UK*). Whilst acknowledging the requirement of the UK courts to adhere to the Strasbourg Court, Lord Phillips explained that the current case was one of the '. . . rare occasions where this court has concerns as to whether a decision of the Strasbourg Court sufficiently appreciates or accommodates particular aspects of our domestic process. In such circumstances it is open to this court to decline to follow the Strasbourg decision, giving reasons for adopting this course.'

If a consistent method of statutory interpretation is not possible, then the HRA 1998, s. 4(2) enables the judiciary to issue a 'declaration of incompatibility.' The declaration has no legal force to change the legislation or affect its validity, but rather the incompatibility of the legislation with the HRA 1998 informs Parliament that there is a concern and Parliament may then choose to review the incompatible legislation. Following the review, the Government may amend the legislation that transgresses Convention rights through a 'remedial order' (s. 10 and Sch. 2 of the HRA provide for such an order, but it may also be made following a decision by the ECtHR).

2.7.2.2 Vertical effect of the Act

The HRA 1998, and the Convention upon which it is based, places an obligation on the State, including public authorities, to act in accordance with the rights established in those documents. Direct challenges can be made against public authorities, including local and central government, and the common law is also subject to the Act. HRA 1998, s. 7 allows a party with 'sufficient interest' in the matter to claim against an authority for breach of the Act, or to use it as a defence against an action. Following a successful claim, the court or tribunal is empowered to issue a remedy within its jurisdiction as it 'considers just and appropriate' (s. 8(2) and (3)), although there must be a civil action to be awarded damages. Therefore, the HRA 1998 regulates (in respect of human rights) what legislative action the State may and may not take, and enables a party who feels their rights have been adversely affected by legislation or the powers of a public authority, to bring a claim (effectively against the State (the 'vertical effect')).

As a consequence, the HRA 1998 affects the State in its enactment, amendment, and interpretation of laws with a human rights element, but it does not provide a clear right to use the provisions of the Act in proceedings between private parties ('horizontal effect').

X v Y (2004)

Facts:

The claimant had been dismissed from his job at a charity after he was cautioned for a public homosexual act and placed on the Sex Offenders Register. He appealed on the basis that under the Human Rights Act 1998, the State has a duty to protect individuals from private acts that breach their rights.

Authority for:

The claimant was unsuccessful. Attempting to use Convention rights (Arts. 8 and 14) in private proceedings involved its 'horizontal' application and this was beyond the scope of the tribunal. However, the Court of Appeal was critical of the approach in tribunals of the use of Human Rights law and suggested a framework for them to use:

1; Do the circumstances of the dismissal fall within the Convention? If not the Convention is not engaged and should not be considered. 2; If those circumstances do fall within the scope of the Convention, consideration should be made of the State's obligation to secure those rights between private persons. Where the State does not have such an obligation (i.e. on its horizontal direct effect), the Convention is unlikely to affect the outcome of an unfair dismissal claim against a private employer. 3; Where the State does have an obligation to secure the individual's rights, the justification for the interference with their right should be justified. (Where it is, the tribunal then proceeds directly to point 5). 4; If the State does not have such an obligation, did a permissible reason for the dismissal exist under national law which does not involve unjustified interference with a Convention right? Where not, the dismissal will be unfair for the absence of a permissible reason for its justification. 5; If an obligation does exist, the dismissal will be assessed for fairness according to national law but interpreting that in relation to HRA 1996, s. 3 to maintain compatibility with the ECHR.

Further, Dyson LJ remarked that from now the HRA 1998, s. 3 applies in its interpretation of national legislation to both public authorities and private individuals as it does between private parties.

It is also worthy of note that whilst a party *may not* rely directly on the HRA 1998 as a cause of action, they may use the Act to interpret existing laws to comply with it, or it may be used to extend existing rights provided through the common law. However, a significant extension to the direct use of Convention rights between private parties was evidenced in the following case:

Eweida and Others v UK (2013)

Facts:

Four cases were heard by the ECtHR in relation to Art. 9 of the ECHR (the right to freedom of thought, conscience, and religion, and a qualified right to manifest one's religion or beliefs) and the compatibility with English law. The four claimants were employees who wished to manifest their religious beliefs in the workplace.

→

1. Ms Eweida, employed by British Airways (BA), wanted to wear a crucifix—visible over her uniform. This was in breach of BA's dress code;

2. Ms Chaplin was a geriatric nurse who wanted to wear a crucifix—visible over her uniform. This was in breach of her employer's dress code;

3. Ms Ladele was a registrar who was required to perform civil partnership ceremonies and refused to do so for same-sex couples; and

4. Mr McFarlane was employed to provide counselling services for the organization Relate. He refused to provide sexual counselling for same-sex couples.

In relation to Ms Eweida, given that the crucifix was discreet and did not appear to have any negative impact on the BA brand, the UK, in not protecting Ms Eweida and thereby protecting her rights, had breached Art. 9. The fact that Ms Chaplin was not allowed to wear her crucifix over her uniform was justified on the basis of her working on a hospital ward and it was a matter of health and safety. Both Ms Ladele and Mr McFarlane's actions involved them treating people differently on the basis of their sexual orientation, which was unlawful, and the employers in each case were justified in taking remedial action.

Authority for:

Indirect effect cases are fact specific but the ECtHR has, in these cases, balanced the ability of an individual to manifest their religious beliefs through the protection which anti-discrimination provides the general population. The courts in the UK must interpret the Equality Act 2010 to conform with the spirit, and to give effect to, the Convention.

Consider

Given the *Eweida* case, how would you conclude? Does Ms Betabita have the right to manifest her religious beliefs in the manner presented and therefore would she likely succeed in a claim for unfair dismissal? The short answer is no. Read Chapter 22 for an explanation of the CJEU's reasoning on this issue in Case C-157/15 *Achbita, Centrum voor Gelijkheid van kansen en voor racismebestrijding v G4S Secure Solutions*.

CONCLUSION

This opening chapter of the English legal system has outlined some of the most significant constitutional principles protecting the UK and holding to account those who wield power in State institutions. Human rights are also playing an increasing role not only in establishing restraints on the actions of the State, but also in the relationships between private bodies. Having established these constitutional 'building blocks', the text continues by identifying the various sources of law, and how judicial decisions affect future cases through the doctrine of 'precedent'.

SUMMARY OF MAIN POINTS

- The laws of England and Wales are created through Parliament, the common law, and equity.
- The two jurisdictions of law, broadly speaking, are criminal and civil.
- Criminal laws regulate actions that contravene established laws.
- In civil law, the innocent party instigates the claim against the defendant and the case is decided on the 'balance of probabilities'.

The constitution

- A constitution is a mechanism to regulate the powers of the State, and its use of these powers.
- In the UK, the constitution was developed over many centuries and the UK has a written, but uncodified, constitution.

The sources of the constitution

- There are various sources of the UK's constitution.
- Statutory materials include the Magna Carta, the Bill of Rights, the EC treaties, the Human Rights Act 1998, and the Constitutional Reform Act 2005.
- Case law/the common law has been a mechanism where constitutional rules were developed by the courts. These sought to restrict the powers of personnel of the State from exercising powers that had not been granted.
- Conventions and customs are not enforceable in the way that legislation and the common law is, and as such it is often referred to as a form of 'soft law'. For example, conventions have established codes of practice for the conduct of Members of Parliament and the responsibilities they undertake.
- Prerogative powers empowered the monarch to exercise powers such as dissolving Parliament and declaring war (although most of these powers are now exercised by the Government).

Membership of the EU

- The original aims included the establishing of a common market. This was extended to incorporate the fundamental freedoms—free movement of goods, services, capital, and workers.
- The *Council's* roles include: concluding agreements with foreign States; taking general policy decisions; and taking decisions based on the Commission's proposals.
- The *Commission* has two main roles, it operates a legislative function taking the initiative from the Council and Parliament. Its other substantive role is of ensuring the Member States follow EU laws and as such is known as the 'Guardian of the Treaties'.
- The *Parliament* is elected every five years and its role is to contribute to the drafting of legislation that affects the Member States through Directives and Regulations. It does so through the co-decision procedure with the Council and Commission.
- The CJEU is a court of reference that assists the Member States through interpreting EU laws to apply in cases (under Art. 267 TFEU). It also hears the actions taken under Art. 258 TFEU when it is alleged that Member States have not adhered to their obligations under the Treaty.
- Primary law: The *Treaty Articles* which, if deemed to possess 'Direct Effect' are directly applicable in the Member State with no further action required by the State.

- The secondary laws are defined under Art. 288 TFEU. *Regulations* are the highest form of secondary laws, they are binding in their entirety, and have direct applicability. *Directives* are binding as to the result to be achieved upon each Member State to which it is addressed, but allows each State to decide how it will give effect to the aims of the Directive. A *Decision* establishes the scope of the legal provision and is binding in its entirety upon those to whom it is addressed (as opposed to *all* Member States).

Essential features of the constitution

- These features are important protections in the restriction of the State's exercise of power and the fundamental rights to which individuals are entitled.
- The rule of law established a set of principles to ensure tyranny and abuse of the State's power are avoided, and to establish fundamental rights that citizens are entitled to benefit from.
- **Parliamentary supremacy** was formed following the removal of James II as monarch and established Parliament as the supreme law-making body in the country (although the monarch still has to provide Royal Assent to legislation before it becomes effective).
- Parliament cannot bind successive Parliaments—therefore the new Parliament is entitled to repeal or change any previous Act regardless of attempts to entrench it.
- Newer Acts are deemed to implicitly repeal inconsistent prior Acts under the doctrine of Implied Repeal, unless Parliament makes an explicit notice to the contrary.
- Parliament's laws are deemed the highest form of law due to the election of members to this body, whilst the judiciary is not publicly elected. Therefore, the judiciary has an obligation to follow the laws of Parliament and does not have the right to challenge the enacted law as being 'unconstitutional' (as exists in other jurisdictions).
- Separation of powers instils a system of checks and balances where the three main organs of the State (the executive, the legislature, and the judiciary) are separated in an attempt to avoid abuse of power.
- As a general rule, legislation should not be introduced retrospectively. This ensures that citizens have the ability to be aware of laws that could make their actions unlawful.

Human rights

- The UK became signatory to the European Convention in 1951. This sought to regulate the actions of the State and provide a set of fundamental rights for individuals.
- The rights included freedom from discrimination based on sex, race, and religious and political views; the right to life; freedom from torture and inhumane punishment; the right to a fair trial; and freedom of expression.
- The Convention provided for enforcement through the ECtHR (based in Strasbourg).
- An individual with a claim based on the Convention's rights would exhaust all domestic remedies, and then proceed to the ECtHR. As this is an international treaty and the UK has a dualist constitution, the judges in the UK were limited as to the remedies they could provide for a breach of the Convention.
- This led to the UK enacting the HRA 1998, which came into force on 1 October 2000. This legislation provides, essentially, for the same rights as are contained in the European Convention. It enables the individual to have a remedy provided by a domestic court without having to travel to Strasbourg.

- The HRA 1998 must be interpreted in the spirit of the European Convention (using a purposive approach to interpretation) and the UK courts must also use the case law established by the ECtHR.

- When enacting new legislation that may have an effect on the HRA 1998, the Minister of the government department responsible for the Bill makes a declaration that the Bill either does or does not breach, or intend to breach, the HRA 1998.

- The HRA is used to interpret other rights. It cannot be used horizontally (a private individual against another private individual) but rather is used by an individual where the State (a concept that is broadly interpreted) has infringed their human rights.

- Following enactment of the HRA 1998, the judiciary may hear cases involving an alleged breach of the Act, and are empowered to issue a 'declaration of incompatibility' if the law, as interpreted with the HRA 1998, contravenes the claimant's human rights. There is no authority to strike down conflicting legislation.

- Following the declaration, Parliament may choose to change the offending statute to conform to the HRA 1998 through a 'remedial order' by the Government.

- If the individual is unhappy with the decision from the domestic courts, appeals are possible to the ECtHR.

SUMMARY QUESTIONS

Essay questions

1. 'The dualist constitution of the UK is a detriment to individuals as it provides the State with the choice of adhering to international agreements or not. Given this deficit of the constitution, international treaties are not worth the paper they are written on.'

   Critically assess the above statement. In your answer, give specific examples of international treaties which the UK has either repealed or disregarded.

2. 'The UK requires a formal written constitution if fundamental rights, evident in most democratic jurisdictions, are not to be abrogated by governments which rely on the apathy of the general public to remove essential protection against tyranny.'

   Discuss.

Problem questions

1. All Bright Consumables (ABC) Ltd operates a business involving the manufacture and sale of various electronic gadgets. The electronics division has seen rapid expansion in the past few months following the successful manufacture and sales of a new tablet computer. As such it wishes to reorganize the business and move to a seven-day production shift pattern.

   Edward was an employee of ABC and is a devout Christian. ABC asked Edward, as part of this expansion, to agree to work some Sundays as part of the shift rotation. He refused. Edward's religious beliefs prevented him from working on Sundays. As a compromise, ABC had offered Edward a different job within the organization which did not include working on Sundays, but he refused. ABC then offered Edward a generous redundancy package if he was unable to work the required Sundays, which he also refused. In light of this inability to work the required shift pattern, following the necessary dismissal procedures, ABC dismissed Edward.

   Edward has lodged an unfair dismissal claim and part of this legal action accuses ABC of breaching European Convention, Art. 9 (concerning freedom of thought, conscience, and religion).

Consider the likelihood of Edward being successful and how human rights legislation impacts on employment relationships.

2.   You have recently been appointed as the Human Resources Director of ABC Ltd. The company is aware of the requirements on the board of directors from the Companies Act 2006, s. 172, the Equality Act 2010, and the Human Rights Act 1998.

Write a briefing memo to the members of the board as to the most applicable human rights issues that will affect the company. Consider in your answer the obligations on the company to protect its workers against discrimination from colleagues and third parties. Further, explain the steps the board should take to govern its relationship with suppliers and manufacturers as part of its sourcing of products from the Far East and India.

 You will find guidance about how to answer these questions online at www.oup.com/uk/marson5e/.

 FURTHER READING

Books and articles

Clayton, R. (2007) 'The Human Rights Act Six Years On: Where Are We Now?' *European Human Rights Law Review*, p. 11.

Cohler, A. M., Miller, B. C., and Stone, H. (Eds.) (1989) 'Montesquieu: The Spirit of the Laws' Cambridge University Press: Cambridge.

Cohn, M. (2007) 'Judicial Activism in the House of Lords: A Composite Constitutionalist Approach' *Public Law*, Spring, p. 95.

Collins, H. (2006) 'The Protection of Civil Liberties in the Workplace' *Modern Law Review*, Vol. 69, No. 4, p. 619.

Cownie, F., Bradney, A., and Burton, M. (2013) 'English Legal System in Context' (6th Edition) Oxford University Press: Oxford.

Ewing, K. D. (1999) 'The Human Rights Act and Parliament Democracy' *Modern Law Review*, Vol. 62, No. 1, p. 79.

Ganz, G. (1992) 'The War Crimes Act 1991—Why No Constitutional Crisis?' *Modern Law Review*, Vol. 55, No. 1, p. 87.

Hunt, M. (1998) 'The 'Horizontal Effect' of the Human Rights Act' *Public Law*, p. 423.

Lord Irvine of Lairg (1998) 'The Development of Human Rights in Britain under an Incorporated Convention on Human Rights' *Public Law*, p. 221.

Marshall, G. (1998) 'Interpreting Interpretation in the Human Rights Bill' *Public Law*, p. 167.

Marson, J. (2004) 'Access to Justice: A Deconstructionist Approach To Horizontal Direct Effect' *4 Web JCLI*.

Phillipson, G. (1999) 'The Human Rights Act, 'Horizontal Effect' and the Common Law: A Bang or a Whimper?' *Modern Law Review*, Vol. 62, No. 6, p. 824.

Skach, C. (2007) 'The 'Newest' Separation of Powers: Semipresidentialism' *International Journal of Constitutional Law*, Vol. 5, No. 1, p. 93.

Stevens, R. (1997) 'The Independence of the Judiciary: The View from the Lord Chancellor's Office' Clarendon Press: Oxford.

Young, A. L. (2002) 'Remedial and Substantive Horizontality: The Common Law and *Douglas v Hello! Ltd*' *Public Law*, p. 232.

Websites and Twitter links

http://www.amnesty.org.uk
@amnestyUK/

https://www.youtube.com/user/HumanTV
Information from the campaigning organization whose purpose is to protect people wherever justice, fairness, freedom, and truth are denied. Many useful resources and links are provided on the website.

http://www.business-humanrights.org
@BHRRC
Resources focusing on the interaction between business and human rights. It has a global, rather than simply a UK perspective. It includes materials on corporate compliance and assessment with human rights, and contains various links to sources such as the United Nations and the International Labour Organization.

http://www.coe.int
@coe/

https://www.youtube.com/user/CouncilofEurope
Information resources from the Council of Europe with links to the European Convention on Human Rights and other treaties. They contain information on the work of the Council to protect human rights and fundamental freedoms.

http://www.echr.coe.int
@ECHR_Press/

https://www.youtube.com/user/EuropeanCourt
The website and up-to-date resources from the European Court of Human Rights. This provides details of the work and jurisdiction of the Court, and its case law.

http://www.equalityhumanrights.com
@EHRC

https://www.youtube.com/user/EqualityHumanRights
Information relating to the Equality and Human Rights Commission—containing advice and publications on all aspects of equality issues.

http://www.liberty-human-rights.org.uk/index.php/
@libertyhq

https://www.youtube.com/user/LibertyHumanRights
Liberty seeks to advance rights and freedoms through public campaigning, test case litigation, parliamentary lobbying, policy analysis, and the provision of free advice and information.

ONLINE RESOURCES

www.oup.com/uk/marson5e/

For further resources relating to this chapter, including self-test questions, an interactive glossary, and key case flashcards.

3
SOURCES OF LAW, STATUTORY INTERPRETATION, AND THE LEGISLATIVE PROCESS

An understanding of the sources of law governing individuals and organizations is required if one is to know where to find rules regulating conduct. Laws derive from Parliament, but the judiciary 'make law' through precedent, and laws have also been made through customs and conventions. Understanding the decisions from previous cases will enable disputes between businesses, or between the business and its workforce, to either be avoided due to the confidence of knowing how a case will be handled if it proceeds to court/tribunal (and this information can be relayed to the other party), or to be resolved without expensive legal advice. Government departments such as the Department for Business, Energy & Industrial Strategy (or BEIS) regularly invite opinions on draft Bills (proposed laws), and awareness of the progress of potential laws enables constructive dialogue between the State and businesses to occur. This can only strengthen the links between the two and help to produce legislation in the best interests of all in society.

To demonstrate how **statutory interpretation** will apply in a business scenario a hypothetical case study (based on the actual case of *Jones v Tower Boot Co. Ltd* [1997]) is presented in this chapter. The aim is not to discuss the content of the law here (it is a discrimination case) but rather how the parties, and then the courts, will interpret what the law means and how it should be applied.

Business Scenario 3A

Alan Robson, who is 16 years old, is employed at Bridge Boot Co. making shoes and boots. He is from mixed ethnic parentage and has, since joining the company, encountered substantial racial abuse. This has involved name-calling and most recently at a staff social event, Alan was subjected to physical abuse. Four weeks after joining the company he has decided he can endure the treatment no longer and has resigned. Alan wishes to make a complaint against his employer for the racial discrimination he has been subjected to. The Equality Act 2010 provides that an employer may be liable for actions of employees committed 'during the course of their employment'. Bridge Boot Co. deny liability as they say such discriminatory acts are not in the course of employment of their staff, and in any event, an interpretation of the law would not extend to actions occurring at social events.

Learning Outcomes

- Identify where the laws that govern England are located (**3.2–3.2.5**)
- Explain what is meant by the terms 'common law'/'case law', 'equity', 'legislation', 'customs' and 'conventions' (**3.2.1–3.2.5**)

- Identify and explain the use of the various methods available to the judiciary when interpreting statutes (literal, golden, mischief, and purposive approaches) (**3.2.1.3– 3.2.1.5**)
- Explain the process of how a Bill becomes an Act of Parliament (**3.3.4**)
- Identify the sources of delegated legislation and explain the uses of each of the three methods (**3.4.1– 3.4.4**)
- Explain the work of Committees in ensuring legislation is effectively considered (**3.5.1**).

3.1 INTRODUCTION

This chapter introduces elements of the administration of the legal system. The chapter begins by identifying the various sources of law in England and Wales. It continues with an examination of the roles played by the judiciary in interpreting and applying the **legislation**. It demonstrates the active and important role adopted by the judges in giving the full effect of the law. The law-making process is considered, along with the workings of the parliamentary system and the use of **delegated legislation** when expert knowledge is required or because of the pressures on parliamentary time. Sources of the law are initially considered to identify where laws may derive and their 'hierarchy' in the legal system. The law-making system is identified and the passage of a Bill (the intentions of future legislation) to its completion as a piece of legislation is considered, along with the protection afforded through scrutiny of these Bills by Parliament. The chapter concludes by identifying and critiquing the ability of Parliament to delegate the responsibility of passing legislation. It acknowledges the necessity for this method of law-creation, whilst also highlighting some of the perceived dangers in terms of accountability and scrutiny.

3.2 SOURCES OF LAW

In order to identify the law governing an area such as contract and employment relations, it is necessary to understand the sources of those laws and how they have impacted on the legal system. As the constitution of the UK has been developing over several hundreds of years, various sources have contributed to it.

3.2.1 Case Law/Common Law

Before an effective and united system of government existed in the UK, laws had been created through judges, on a regional basis, in deciding cases brought before them. These regions therefore established systems of law (Scotland being the most distinct from the others) which were known as the '**common law**'. The laws created from this source were very important to the regulation of activities and were to be respected by Parliament. As a consequence, Parliament did not legislate where the common law had already established a law that did not require any alteration, and Parliament would only legislate against the common law where necessary. The common law has the advantage of being created through reference to practical cases, and so the law has been created in real-life situations, it is flexible and can be adapted to reflect changes in society, and it is created by judges who have extensive experience in practising and applying the law.

Consider

The term 'course of employment' is used as part of the test to determine an employer/principal's vicarious liability—established and refined over many years by the courts in their judgments. However, sometimes using an interpretation developed in the common law may produce unintended consequences (such as a restrictive right or application of the law). Hence, in Alan's case, where a statute is created, simply because it uses similar terminology to that which exists in the common law will not result in the judiciary being similarly restricted if that would be to defeat the scheme of the legislation. Legislation is not just a higher law to inconsistent common law, it also enables the judiciary to use a range of statutory approaches to achieve the goal intended by Parliament.

The common law is so called where there was a law created by the judiciary and no statute existed. It is also sometimes referred to as case law (evidently because it was created through a court case), but this may be more applicable to a court giving an interpretation of a statutory provision. However, these terms are often used interchangeably and unless it is specified, they should be assumed to refer to the same judge-made law.

3.2.1.1 The binding force of precedent

At this stage it is important to realize that the rationale for the common law to be referred to as a 'source of law' is that, whilst established by judges, it has a binding effect on lower courts. This is known as **precedent** and works on a hierarchical structure, so the highest court will bind those below it, but importantly, precedent does not bind the court that established the rule (a distinction does exist with the Court of Appeal) and that court may reverse the decision in the next case it hears. This element of the law was created through the doctrine of *stare decisis* (which means 'stand by what has been previously decided'). Having established a precedent, judges in lower courts (hearing future cases) will follow the same decision if a similar case with comparable points of law is presented. A judge in a lower court may deviate from a precedent where some material difference between the precedent and the case before them exists. This is known as 'distinguishing' a precedent, and as long as the judge explains the distinction, making reference to the precedent and why they believe the facts are sufficiently different to allow a deviation from it, this is within their powers.

3.2.1.2 The *ratio decidendi* and *obiter dicta*

For a precedent to be established, the rule must have formed the ***ratio decidendi*** of the decision (this is the reason for the decision). This rule, consequently, must have involved a point of law rather than simply have been an aspect of the facts of the case. The court may also make a pronouncement ***obiter dicta*** ('something said by the way'), which, as it was not pertinent to the judgment provided in the case, will not form a precedent but may form a persuasive authority if a future case does come before the courts with a similar legal position. This means that the judges are not bound by *obiter dicta* as they are by *ratio decidendi*, but they may refer to the obiter and be influenced by it in their rulings in future cases.

3.2.1.3 Statutory interpretation

The legislature passes the Acts of Parliament and these are interpreted and applied by the judiciary. The judges therefore look towards the text of the legislation in their rulings, and if its provisions are uncertain or ambiguous, their task is to interpret and give it meaning. Despite the comprehensive drafting of legislation, following the debate and deliberation it receives in its passage through Parliament, there may be errors contained in the text or there may be aspects of the provisions that are challenged by the parties. In the interpretation of the legislation, the judges must follow the principles that are designed to assist them in understanding the meaning Parliament intended to give the legislation.

3.2.1.4 Aids to assistance in interpretation

To assist the judiciary in the correct interpretation and application of the legislation as enacted by Parliament, the following mechanisms may be used. Within the legislation, the courts may look to the 'long title' of the Act in instances of ambiguity to identify what the Act was designed to achieve. This is not a particularly useful mechanism in most cases, but it exists and has been used in judgments.

Royal College of Nursing v Department of Health and Social Security (1981)

Facts:

The Royal College challenged the legality of the power of nursing staff to conduct abortions. Whilst the Offences against the Person Act 1861 made it an offence for any person to carry out this procedure, the Abortion Act 1967 provided a defence for doctors where certain conditions were satisfied. However, medical advances meant that few surgical abortions were necessary and these had been replaced with hormonal abortions which could be administered by nurses.

Authority for:

The House of Lords held that abortions carried out by nurses were lawful. The title and intent of the 1967 Act was to broaden the grounds on which abortions could be carried out as part of ordinary medical care. Thus, nurses were protected under the Act.

The courts may also use the punctuation employed in the text where it would help to remove some ambiguity (*Director of Public Prosecutions v Schildkamp*), and many pieces of legislation contain examples of how the legislation should be interpreted (as utilized in the Consumer Credit Act 1974 in Sch. 2.). There are also aids that are not within the text of the legislation, but were included in the debates and consideration of its passage through Parliament, and the rules on the use of these materials have been somewhat relaxed.

Pepper v Hart (1993)

Facts:

A teacher at a private school was required to pay tax on a benefit received as part of his employment (here it was in the form of reduced school fees for his sons). An argument

→

regarding the taxation of this benefit ensued as to the application of the Finance Act 1976, s. 63(2). The House of Lords dismissed the appeal and ordered a rehearing of the case where the teacher attempted to rely on a statement made by the Minister at the time of the passing of the Act and reported in Hansard. This gave details of circumstances where tax would not be payable.

Authority for:

Sources such as Hansard can now be used if they would benefit the judges' interpretation of legislation. Per Lord Browne-Wilkinson '. . . courts have a duty to give effect to the intention of the Parliament. In most cases, reference to parliamentary materials will not throw any light on the matter of dispute. However, in a few cases, where the Parliament has considered the very problem will give a clear indication of their intentions. Therefore, in this kind of situation, the courts should not turn a blind eye and construe words in the way that they cannot bear.'

Three criteria were identified to be met to permit reference to Hansard:

1. Where the legislation is ambiguous/obscure, or its application would lead to absurdity;
2. The material/evidence on which the person relies consists of a statement by the relevant Minister/promotor of the Bill along with other parliamentary material as is necessary to understand that statement and its effect; and
3. The statement relied on and presented is clear.

As these were met in the case, the use of Hansard was permitted.

The judges may refer to dictionaries for definition of the text of a statute in the Literal method of interpretation, and the courts have also been permitted to refer to Reports of the Law Commission and White Papers when using the Mischief Rule (see *Davis v Johnson*). Further, the courts have developed guides for the correct construction of words that are used in legislation to ensure conformity and fairness:

1. *Ejusdem generis:* This guide has been developed to direct the interpretation of 'general' words used in legislation, that follow specific words, to be read in the context of those specific words.
2. *Expressio unius est exclusio alterius:* If one word or specific definition is provided in the legislation, then this is constructed to naturally and implicitly exclude all other things.
3. *Noscitur a sociis:* The interpretation of a word derives from the other words and the context in which they are used.

3.2.1.5 Methods of statutory interpretation

- *The Literal Rule:* This has been a method of interpretation traditionally used in the courts and, as its name suggests, involves the judges looking at the text of the legislation and giving it its plain and ordinary meaning. It is the most 'pure' form of interpretation as the intention of Parliament is sought through a direct examination of the text. There are many examples of the courts considering the interpretation of legislation, the most significant being provided by the Court of Appeal and the House of Lords (now Supreme Court).

R v Hillingdon London Borough Council, ex parte Puhlhofer (1986)

Facts:

The applicants were a married couple residing in one bedroom of a guest house with a young child and (later) a baby. There were no cooking or washing facilities in the accommodation, although the applicants were provided with breakfast. They argued against the housing authority's assessment, accepted at judicial review, that they were not homeless.

Authority for:

The Court of Appeal agreed with the housing authority. The issue was the suitability of the housing offered and this was for the authority itself to determine unless its decision was absurd: 'The plight of the homeless is a desperate one, and the plight of the applicants in the present case commands the deepest sympathy. But it is not . . . appropriate that the remedy of judicial review, which is a discretionary remedy, should be made use of to monitor the actions of local authorities under the Act save in the exceptional case. The ground upon which the courts will review the exercise of an administrate discretion is abuse of power—eg bad faith, a mistake in construing the limits of the power, a procedural irregularity, or unreasonableness . . . unreasonableness verging on an absurdity.'

Assistance has also been provided in this matter through Parliament enacting the Interpretation Act 1978, which enables judges to seek definitions of words beyond just the Oxford English Dictionary and similar materials—that may not provide the meaning Parliament had intended.

Consider

If the courts take a literal interpretation of the words 'course of employment' they may provide an artificially restrictive view of the concept. It was a term included in the Act to establish the liability of the employer where discriminatory acts took place whilst those individuals undertaking such action were under the control of the employer (and the employer failed to take reasonable steps to prevent it). *Fisher v Bell* is an example of the use of the literal method of statutory interpretation, which was appropriate as to extend the law in that case would have led to the criminalization of a shopkeeper. Here the law, through the Equality Act, is intending to protect fundamental principles and values whilst individuals are at work. This responsibility falls on the employer and they are required to comply with both the wording and the spirit of the law. A literal interpretation would be restrictive and inappropriate.

- *The Golden Rule:* This method of interpretation provides the court with the option of interpreting ambiguous legislation in a way that would otherwise lead to an absurd result if its literal meaning were given (as defined in *Grey v Pearson*). This, however, is only one use of the method of interpretation, and where the wording of the text is clear, yet its literal application would lead to a result that is against public policy, the Golden Rule may be used in preference to the Literal Rule.

Adler v George (1964)

Facts:

The case involved the application of the Official Secrets Act 1920, s. 3, which made it an offence to obstruct the actions of the armed forces 'in the vicinity of' a prohibited place.

Authority for:

The offence committed by the defendant was obstructing a member of Her Majesty's forces engaged in security detail at a Royal Air Force station. As such, the offence took place 'in' a prohibited place rather than 'in the vicinity', which the literal text of the legislation stated. As a literal interpretation would be absurd (and have led to the discharge of the defendant), the Golden Rule was used to give the true effect to the Act so it read 'in or in the vicinity of'.

In the second example involving public policy, it must be remembered that the Golden Rule is sparingly used so as not to abuse the judges' power and reinterpret what Parliament has already created.

Re Sigsworth (1935)

Facts:

The case involved the beneficiary of a dead person's estate. However, the beneficiary (the son) had murdered his mother (the victim), and under the relevant law (The Administration of Estates Act 1925), he was entitled to claim from her estate.

Authority for:

The strict, literal meaning of the Act clearly gave the murderer the right to be a beneficiary of his mother's estate, but such a result would have been against the public policy of allowing a murderer to profit from their crime. Consequently, the court would not interpret the legislation in accordance with its literal meaning, even though it was not unambiguous.

- *The Mischief Rule:* As the name suggests, this rule of interpretation looks to the mischief that the legislation was enacted to avoid, and interprets it accordingly. This rule was established in light of *Heydon's Case*, and has been applied by the courts in modern scenarios.

Smith v Hughes (1960)

Facts:

The Street Offences Act 1959 was passed to stop prostitution in the 'street or public place' (s. 1) and obviously to restrict the activities of this action. To circumvent the legislation, a prostitute solicited from inside her house and as such was not in a street or public place in accordance with the literal interpretation of the Act.

Authority for:

The court considered that the legislation had been enacted to stop the mischief of prostitution, whether the soliciting occurred in a street or in the person's own home (by tapping on the balcony rail or window pane to draw the attention of men passing in the street). Therefore, it was interpreted that 'street or public place' could include the person's home.

Consider

The courts may look to the mischief that the Equality Act was designed to remove and interpret the statute sufficiently broadly to meet this aim and the values that equality enshrines. The fact that the physical abuse suffered by Alan occurred at a social event would undermine the values of the Act if it was to facilitate the employer escaping responsibility. This was not, for example, a private birthday party to which some individuals, who have a relationship as work colleagues, attended. For instance, in December 2016 the High Court held that a fight following a work Christmas party where a manager suffered serious brain injuries was not in the course of his employment and hence the employer (and their insurers) were not liable—see *Bellman v Northampton Recruitment*. Had the fight occurred during the party, the court surmised that the employer may have been vicariously liable. In the present case, the actions took place during a work event and the law should be interpreted to stop the mischief of inequality (whether verbal or physical). Hence the 'course of employment' should be interpreted as including an assessment of the tortfeasor's (the person who committed the tort) 'field of activities' at work and determining whether their actions were part of an unbroken sequence of events.

- *The Purposive/Teleological Method:* Particularly following the UK's accession to the European Union (EU), the courts in this jurisdiction have an obligation to follow the Court of Justice of the European Union's decisions (when considering laws either emanating from the EU or with an EU dimension) to use a purposive approach to interpretation. As opposed to the previous rules of interpretation outlined, this approach looks to the spirit or intent of the legislation, and seeks to give effect to it in as wide a means as possible. A similar approach is used with the Human Rights Act 1998 following the European Convention on Human Rights and the case law of the European Court of Human Rights as sources of interpretation. The power of a purposive form of statutory interpretation can be seen in the seminal case *Marleasing*

SA v La Comercial Internacional de Alimentación SA. The facts of the case would not be particularly helpful but its implications are of great significance. In its judgment, the Court of Justice of the European Union permitted national courts to insert 'additional words . . . They could be taken out; they can be moved around' to ensure domestic law conforms with the EU parent law (at para. 49).

Consider

The courts may adopt a meaning to the words 'course of employment' which adhere to principles of EU law and seek, in accordance with various social policy directives, to provide clear legislative expression to the underlying purpose of the statute. The object of the Equality Act is to achieve the goal of equality (here in the workplace) and places a responsibility on realizing this through the activities of the employer. Alan would thus find the courts interpreting the term with the purpose of ensuring the fundamental principle of equality is not defeated by technical rules (which could happen if a literal interpretation was provided to the term 'course of employment').

3.2.2 Equity

Whilst an ordinary interpretation of the word 'equity' means 'fairness', the legal meaning is more complex. Equity was developed along with the common law, where civil actions were based on a document known as a 'writ' that identified the legal grounds for the action. Ever more writs were developed to include the increasing number of claims being made, but at some time in the thirteenth century the process of new writs was halted. The claimants in these new cases had to use the existing writs and if their particular claim did not fall into one of the existing writs, then they could not proceed with their action through the common law. There was a further problem with the common law, in that it was becoming increasingly prescriptive and the only remedy available was damages. In many cases this is what the injured party wanted, but there were situations where a monetary payment would not adequately compensate the claimant. In order for individuals in these circumstances to pursue their claims, they began petitioning the Chancellor, who could decide the cases following an investigation, but this was a very unsatisfactory method of achieving a settlement. The reasons for the dissatisfaction included the lack of oral testimony accepted as evidence; disclosure of documents was not a requirement; and there were no rules binding the actions of the Chancellor, therefore, a system of precedent was missing from the cases being decided. The solutions being provided by the Chancellor were welcomed and appeared to be a fairer means of providing a remedy beyond damages in the common law—equity offered injunctions, specific performance, rectification, and rescission (rectification provides for words in a document to be changed if they do not express the true intentions of the parties). The Judicature Acts 1873 and 1875 provided that equity, and the common law, could be provided by all courts (at their discretion in the case of equitable remedies), and there would not be different procedures to obtain each of the remedies available.

It must be noted that as equity provides a wider range of remedies than does the common law, it is based on underlying maxims that must be adhered to (note, there are other principles than the three listed here, but these are the most relevant in the context of this section of the text). The first is that parties to equity must 'come with clean hands'. This essentially means that a claimant who wishes to avail him or herself of an equitable remedy (such as an injunction) must not have acted in a wrongful manner. A second rule is that the claimant who wishes to seek an equitable remedy must act in an equitable manner, and thirdly, the claimant must bring their claim in a reasonable time, with no unreasonably long delays.

The power of injunctions can be seen in the following case. Injunctions are a court order and their breach can have serious effects.

OCS Group UK v Dadi (2017)

Facts:

Mr Dadi was an employee of OCS. He was alleged to have sent confidential information through his personal email account and was subject to an injunction to prevent further disclosures. Dadi breached the injunction several times including deleting approximately 8,000 emails and informing others of the injunction. These actions were performed in the absence of legal advice. Following his taking legal advice, Dadi admitted the breaches and attempted to recover the deleted emails.

Authority for:

For his breaches of the interim injunction, Dadi was sentenced to six weeks' imprisonment. This reflected what the court considered was the minimum term of imprisonment for each of the breaches. Imprisonment was necessary to ensure continued compliance with the order and to act as a warning to others.

3.2.3 Legislation

Legislation is created through Parliament, and came to the fore following the supremacy of Parliament through the 'Glorious Revolution' in 1688, where the ultimate authority to create legislation moved from the monarch to Parliament. Legislation is usually initiated by the Government and passed through Parliament in the form of general Public Acts. These laws have the power to apply to everyone in a country (such as England) or may have application to the entire UK. The legislation passed may be in the form of primary legislation (through Parliament) or through secondary legislation whose power has been provided through a government Minister (known as delegated legislation).

3.2.3.1 Parliamentary supremacy

Parliament became the supreme law-making body in England following what became known as the 'Glorious Revolution' in 1688 (whilst some have questioned whether a revolution occurred at all, it is termed 'glorious' in that, unlike other revolutions, this did not involve widespread bloodshed or civil war). Prior to this, the monarch held the power to create laws (and indeed still holds the constitutional role of granting the Royal Assent as the final stage in the legislative process). King James II, a Catholic, succeeded to the throne when his brother, Charles II, died on 6 February 1685. James II attempted to impose his religious views on the rest of the country, to the disquiet of the Anglican clergy and the majority of the population. He also attempted to remove power from Parliament, enabling him to pass laws without reproach. This led James' Protestant son-in-law (William of Orange) to intervene and when he arrived in Devon, England, with his troops on 5 November 1688, James exiled himself to France. This led to the Bill of Rights being established in December 1689, which held that Parliament was to be the supreme law-making body in the country, and a Protestant must occupy the throne.

Unlike the common law, which can be altered quickly by superior courts to reflect changes in society or the needs of the law, legislation can only be changed following a repeal of that law or it being superseded through a newer piece of legislation that contradicts it (implied repeal).

3.2.4 Customs

Custom is used in the law increasingly sparingly in the modern era, but had been used to provide for accepted practice such as the long-established rule that allowed fishermen to dry their nets on private land. In order for the custom to have the force of law, it must satisfy several criteria, including the 'time immemorial' clause, where it must be established that the claimed right has existed at least since 1189, and could have been exercised since that date (*Wyld v Silver*). The custom must have clear boundaries and be sufficiently precise to enable a court to enforce such a right, it must have been specific to a certain region or locality that the court can identify, and it must not conflict with legislation, otherwise it will fail to be established as an enforceable law.

3.2.5 Conventions

A convention is an accepted way in which something will be done and may be more coarsely referred to as 'playing by the rules of the game'. These are usually historical ways, derived from established practices, in which individuals will act. However, they do adapt to modern society and are subject to change and/or modification. They are part of the uncodified constitution of the UK, and sometimes are (re)produced in written forms to 'formalize' the rule. Examples include that the Prime Minister must be a member of the House of Commons and not the Lords, the monarch must accept the party with the largest number of seats in Parliament to form the government, and the monarch must give assent to legislation passed through Parliament. Consequently, conventions are more generally applicable to constitutional matters rather than the laws created by Parliament or the common law, but they have a significant impact as a source of law.

3.3 HOW LAWS ARE CREATED: THE LEGISLATIVE PROCESS

Business Scenario 3B

Fulldrilla plc is a drilling company which seeks to promote the use of a controversial process of energy generation called 'fracking'. A member of the House of Lords is the chairman of the company and has arranged a series of meetings between the company's senior management, lobbyists and ministers, and civil servants in the Department of Energy and

→

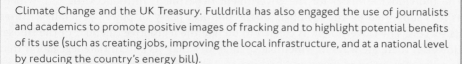

Climate Change and the UK Treasury. Fulldrilla has also engaged the use of journalists and academics to promote positive images of fracking and to highlight potential benefits of its use (such as creating jobs, improving the local infrastructure, and at a national level by reducing the country's energy bill).

Following the meetings and public media campaign, the government introduced the (fictitious) Independent Energy, Renewal and Infrastructure Bill in Parliament.

Parliament exists, along with other functions, to pass legislation that governs individuals, organizations, and institutions in the State. Legislation begins with a Bill that outlines the scope and intentions of the law, and this is debated and voted upon by both Houses of Parliament (the Commons and the Lords (the Upper Chamber)). Generally, the Bill begins the process at the Commons, and then, having proceeded through the various stages, it moves to the Lords to be debated in the same way. If both Houses agree, the Bill will be sent for Royal Assent and will become law. As the Lords is a second chamber and unelected, the Parliament Acts 1911 and 1949 impose restrictions on its ability to prevent the passing of legislation. Of course, legislation is not necessarily the product of the government and interested MPs' initiatives in isolation. Pressure groups lobby the government, identifying where legislation is required or expressing their concerns at new legislative proposals. This allows interested parties to get involved and positively impact on the legislation that will directly affect them, but may also lead to questions being raised about the level of influence such organizations can exert on the legislative agenda.

3.3.1 The House of Commons

The House of Commons is a body that enables citizens to elect individuals as MPs to represent their constituency and who are members of a political party. The party with the largest number of MPs may form a government that dictates the legislative calendar in Parliament and proposes Bills that may become Acts of Parliament.

3.3.2 The House of Lords

The House of Lords functions as a legislative body (to initiate Bills and to review the Bills sent to it by the Commons) although it is an unelected upper chamber.

The monarch selects individuals for membership to the Lords (following recommendation from the Prime Minister and through the Appointments Commission). The Lords fulfil the function of reviewing the legislative proposals sent from the Commons.

3.3.3 Types of Bill

Whilst it is true that the Government is elected to pass legislation and has a mandate to govern the country, this is not the only source of Bills to pass into legislation. It may be the most successful, but others exist and demonstrate the nature of the system that allows individual MPs and corporations to advance proposals for legislation.

3.3.3.1 Government Bills

The individual Minister for the government department introduces the Bill, which, as it is supported by the members of the political party in power, generally ensures its success. The Government is elected to dictate the legislative calendar of the House. However, there are ways in which backbench MPs may seek to initiate legislation that may pass the relevant stages and become an Act. These are through Private Members' Bills and six were successfully passed (there were 16 Government Bills that received Royal Assent) in the 2015–16 session of Parliament.

3.3.3.2 Private Members' Bills

An individual MP or private peer in the House of Lords may introduce a Bill that is, usually, of wider public moral/social concern. Without the support of the Government, due to the constraints of parliamentary time, such Bills are unlikely to be passed. However, MPs may also raise the issue in Parliament or the media, and bring the issue to the public's attention for debate and scrutiny.

3.3.3.3 Private Bills

Bills may also be presented by organizations from outside of Parliament (companies and local authorities) in areas that they have a specific interest, to obtain powers for themselves to take actions in excess of those provided by the law. Private Bills are not intended to alter the law for the country, but rather are focused on a specific locality or industry/individual, and are most commonly witnessed in additional powers being granted to local authorities.

3.3.3.4 Public Bills

These are the Bills that do affect the UK, unless it is specified that they are only to apply to certain regions. Much of the legislation that is discussed in this text refers to laws that began as Public Bills.

3.3.4 From a Bill to an Act: The Stages of a Parliamentary Bill

Figure 3.1 shows a diagram of the stages of a Parliamentary Bill.

Figure 3.1 Stages of a Parliament Bill

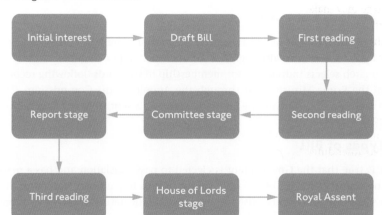

3.3.4.1 Initial interest

Before a Bill is formulated, the Government may produce documents that set out the nature of the legislation required and may do so in a Green Paper or a White Paper. The Government is increasingly moving towards producing draft and pre-legislative Bills so that interested parties (such as businesses) can comment on the proposals, and this provides an additional level of scrutiny.

3.3.4.2 The draft Bill

Having identified the nature and scope of the law the Government wishes to create (perhaps from a commitment made in the Queen's speech at the opening of Parliament), lawyers from the Parliamentary Counsel Office liaise with the relevant government department to draft a Bill that is presented to Parliament.

3.3.4.3 The first reading

On the first day of its presentation to Parliament, the Bill is allocated a number and The Stationery Office prints the Bill for the House (such Bills can begin in either the Commons or the Lords, but this section assumes they have begun in the Commons). Explanatory notes accompany the Bill for further detail.

3.3.4.4 The second reading

Having printed the Bill, it can proceed to this second stage where the real process of debating and considering the proposal begins. The House considers the nature and content of the Bill, its implications are discussed in rather broad terms, and these debates are reproduced in Hansard to form a permanent record of the proceedings.

3.3.4.5 Committee stage

A Standing Committee is established for each Bill presented to the House (and as there may be several Bills at any one time, each Committee is denoted through Standing Committee A, Standing Committee B, and so on.), which takes each clause and Schedule of the Bill and examines it, either agreeing with its inclusion, or deleting it from the subsequent document. This may lead to a wider discussion of the Bill and it is possible to include additional clauses and Schedules if the Committee feels this is appropriate.

3.3.4.6 The report stage

Having had the individual clauses and Schedules considered at the Committee stage, the Report Stage may make further amendments to the Bill, but will not consider any aspects of the Bill that were not considered by the Committee. This enables MPs who were not members of the Committee to forward amendments and allows for reflection of the Bill. At this stage the House may accept the amendments made by the Committee or reverse those made.

3.3.4.7 The third reading

The final stage of the Bill in the Commons is the Third Reading, which occurs directly following the Report. The House considers the Bill, which may have been amended by the Committee or at the Report Stage, and is somewhat of a formality with a very quick debate. No amendments are permissible at this stage.

3.3.4.8 The House of Lords stages

Having successfully passed through the Third Reading in the Commons, the Bill is sent to the Lords and follows a similar process to that which is followed in the Commons.

However, in the Lords, the Committee Stage is usually held by a Whole House Committee (as opposed to a Standing Committee), and amendments are permissible at the Third Reading.

If the Bill passes the Stages as outlined above, and the Lords make an amendment to it, the amendment(s) is printed and sent to the Commons for consideration. The Commons then has the option to agree with the amendment(s) and accept it; agree with the amendments along with amendments of its own (and ask the Lords to agree); or it may disagree and send the Lords reasons for this, requesting that it considers the matter further. Assuming the Lords has not amended the Bill, it informs the Commons of this fact and the Bill proceeds to Royal Assent.

3.3.5 Royal Assent

Once a Bill has been through the relevant stages and has been debated in the Houses to a situation where the Commons and the Lords agree on the content, it proceeds to the monarch for Royal Assent. No legislation is valid until it has been given this Assent, and once provided, the Bill becomes an Act of Parliament.

These stages of the progression of a Bill to an Act must be completed within one session of Parliament and if that does not happen then the Bill is to be presented again at the next session (completing each stage a second time). However, a possibility exists for the Bill to be 'carried-over' from one session of Parliament to the next, and since an agreement was concluded by the House on 29 October 2002, a Minister may move a Motion to have a Public Bill not completed in the current session of Parliament, resumed in the following session.

3.4 NON-PARLIAMENT LEGISLATION: SECONDARY LEGISLATION

The majority of laws passed are not through Parliament's primary legislation, but rather through secondary, delegated legislation. It is necessary to be aware of the sources and the controls that are available to scrutinize these measures. For example, if legislation is to be made through a by-law by a local authority, it may be wise for businesses affected by the proposal to share their views, or seek clarification on the issue from the Authority, before the legislation is passed. Where a Statutory Instrument is used that affects a business, the local Member of Parliament may be able to raise any questions regarding the measure on behalf of the business. Scrutiny assists in ensuring all points of view have been considered, and that the views of small businesses are valued and respected by Parliament.

Consider

It is possible that, in order to enable constructive dialogue with interested parties, or possibly to enable legislation to be passed without the publicity and full scrutiny of Parliament, rather than trying to pass the Independent Energy, Renewal and Infrastructure Bill, the government seeks to introduce its features by changing an

→

existing (fictitious) Energy and Land Act 1999. This could be achieved through a statutory instrument. This form of secondary legislation does not require a full debate in Parliament. However, even though such a fictitious law would raise significant interest in the immediate locality of any proposed fracking site, do Members of Parliament generally possess the skills and insight to identify any problems with the Act or to critique its full implications ahead of enactment?

As can be seen, passing legislation is a complex, time-consuming, and potentially difficult exercise. Parliament also does not have the necessary time to pass each piece of legislation itself and so may delegate such authority to other bodies.

3.4.1 Delegated Legislation

Not all the legislation that is passed and takes effect in this country is passed in Westminster. Delegated legislation refers to legislation that is passed by someone other than Parliament (under Parliament's authority). The authority that is provided is done so through an 'enabling' or 'parent' Act that establishes a framework of the law, and enables the delegated legislation to provide the detail. There are three types of delegated legislation—Statutory Instruments, Orders in Council, and by-laws.

3.4.2 Statutory Instruments

Statutory Instruments are a method of law-making that allows legislation to be subsequently brought into effect or changed without the necessity for Parliament to pass new legislation each time. The Bill is passed through Parliament as described earlier, but the legislation may omit the technical details of the legislation (such as the date on which different elements of the law will come into effect, or to change the level of fines or awards of compensation). A further specific example is the power for a 'remedial order' to be made where legislation, which has been found to be incompatible with the Human Rights Act 1998, can be altered through a Statutory Instrument (s. 10). This power is then provided to a Minister to complete the tasks necessary as outlined in the enabling Act. The legislation is drafted by the legal office of the relevant government department, is given a number, and is identified by 'SI' on the legislation to denote it has been passed through a Statutory Instrument (the full text of all Statutory Instruments since 1988 are available at http://www.opsi.gov.uk/stat.htm). Parliament passes approximately 2–3,000 Statutory Instruments a year.

Statutory Instruments are subject to control by Parliament through the method by which they must be laid before Parliament—*negative resolutions* and *positive resolutions*. There is also Parliamentary scrutiny available through the Joint Committees on Statutory Instruments, which is a Select Committee that may take oral and written evidence from the relevant government department. It should be noted, however, that these Committees do not consider the merits of the Statutory Instrument but seek to ensure that the Minister's powers have been exercised in accordance with the provisions of the enabling Act (the procedural rather than substantive aspects of the proposals).

3.4.3 Orders in Council

Orders in Council are issued 'by and with the advice of Her Majesty's Privy Council'. Again, an enabling Act is issued to identify the extent and powers that may be passed through this secondary (and in some situations, primary) form of legislation. Orders in Council may be used for emergency legislation (Civil Contingencies Act 2004) but in their ordinary function they provide legislation where an ordinary Statutory Instrument would be inappropriate. An example is where powers were transferred from Ministers of the UK Government to those in devolved assemblies, including the Scotland Act 1998 (Transfer of Functions to the Scottish Ministers Etc) Order 1999 (S.I. 1999/1750). It is also the mechanism used to give effect to the resolutions of the United Nations Security Council (United Nations Act 1946, s. 1).

3.4.4 By-laws

Local authorities and public corporations are given powers through enabling Acts such as the Local Government Act 1972 and the Public Health Act 1936 to create by-laws.

3.5 CONTROL OF DELEGATED LEGISLATION

Control exists through scrutiny by Standing Committees, debates in Parliament, and through the courts. The courts have reviewed Orders in Council in *R v Foreign Secretary, ex parte Bancoult*; and by-laws.

Kruse v Johnson (1898)

Facts:

Kent County Council created a by-law which permitted a police officer to require a person to stop making music or singing within 50 yards of a dwelling house in a public place or highway. The claimant was associated with the Salvation Army and was singing hymns. He was subject to such a request and refused. In a challenge to the reasonableness of the creating of the by-law and his fine, the claimant sought a judicial review to declare the by-law as void.

Authority for:

The court upheld the by-law, but remarked at its unease at the use of the Council's power in this way. The court demonstrated its benevolent interpretation and judicial restraint in interfering with the by-laws established by elected authorities.

3.5.1 Control Through Committees

Statutory Instruments subject to the affirmative/positive procedure are automatically referred to Standing Committee if a Minister puts in a motion to that effect. The Committees are established to consider the specific item of delegated legislation and, having completed their duties, are discharged. The Committee debates the Instrument, with a maximum time allowed of between 90 minutes and 2 hours and 30 minutes, and reports to the House on its findings. With Instruments subject to the affirmative resolution procedure, it is normal for formal approval to be provided the next day, without any debate.

Consider

The Secondary Legislation Scrutiny Committee (a Lords Select Committee which examines the policy merits of secondary legislation) may act as a review of the proposed changes to the (fictitious) Energy and Land Act 1999. Here the Committee would, within 12 to 16 days of the measure being laid before Parliament, enable any Member of the House to raise questions or issues (by tabling a motion for debate) within the 40-day 'prayer' window for rejecting negative Instruments.

3.5.2 Control Through Debates in Parliament

The precise method of control through Parliament is contained in the Statutory Instruments Act 1946, and is further defined in the enabling Act, but will generally fall into one of two categories: the negative resolution procedure or the positive resolution procedure. Increasingly, Statutory Instruments are debated on the floor of the House, although finding the Parliamentary time to ensure a successful debate can take place is difficult. These generally happen at the end of the day and may only be debated for up to one-and-a-half hours.

3.5.2.1 Negative resolution procedure

The function of the negative resolution is that the delegated legislation (Instrument) will become law unless there is an objection from the House.

The procedures under this resolution are:

1. The Instrument is laid before Parliament in draft form and cannot be made if disapproved within 40 days.
2. The Instrument is laid before Parliament after making, and is subject to annulment if such a motion is passed within 40 days.

The Instrument will become law on the date specified within it, unless there is a motion (called 'Prayers') for annulment by either the Commons or the Lords. The time period for the motion is usually 40 days including the day on which it was laid before Parliament, and no account is taken of time when Parliament is dissolved. Any MP may make this motion.

3.5.2.2 Positive/affirmative resolution procedure

The nature of the positive resolution results in the Instrument not becoming law unless approved by the House. This procedure accounts for approximately 10 per cent of such Instruments.

The procedures under this Resolution are:

1. The Instrument is laid before Parliament but cannot be made unless both Houses approve the draft.
2. The Instrument is laid before Parliament after making, but cannot come into force until it has been approved.

3. The Instrument is laid before Parliament after making, and will take effect immediately but cannot continue in force unless it is approved in either 28 or 40 days (as appropriate).

The very nature of this Procedure provides a more thorough control as it actively requires Parliament's approval for the Instrument to progress into law. The period for approval is generally 28 days, but can be 40 days. This time excludes when Parliament is dissolved or adjourned. The approval process does not enable a debate of the Instrument (unless the enabling Act expressly provides for this), but only an acceptance of it or a move to annul (depending on the type of procedure). Procedures exist where the Instrument is only published for information and does not require Parliamentary scrutiny. Further, procedures even exist where the Instrument does not need to be laid before Parliament.

The Instruments have to be identified through notice in the local press one month before publication, and they must be available for minimal cost and for public inspection (the most common form of access is through the Internet but they are also available from The Stationery Office).

3.5.3 Control Through the Courts

As the legislation is being passed by a body other than Parliament, the Instrument is subject to review by the courts. However, the merits of the Instrument are not subject to challenge but rather the measures taken by the body/Minister are. As such, the provisions in the Instrument may be quashed on the grounds of *ultra vires* (*Commissioners of Customs & Excise v Cure & Deeley Ltd*), inconsistency with Statutes (a Statutory Instrument will be considered void if it is created in conflict with EU laws as provided for under the European Communities Act 1972, s. 2(4)), unreasonableness (*Strickland v Haynes*), or uncertainty.

Percy v Hall (1996)

Facts:

Demonstrators were arrested many times for trespassing on military land. The relevant by-laws, created by the Secretary of State, had been previously declared as invalid. The argument presented by the demonstrators was that their arrest and imprisonment by the arresting officers was wrongful.

Authority for:

The Court of Appeal, reversing the finding of the trial judge, regarded the validity of the by-law as irrelevant and even were it void for uncertainty, the convictions would be set aside but the officers would still have acted lawfully. The officers were acting in the reasonable belief that the by-law was effective and took their actions accordingly. Per Brown LJ: 'Better . . . to treat the instrument as valid unless so uncertain in its language as to have no ascertainable meaning, or so unclear in its effect as to be incapable of certain application in any case.'

CONCLUSION

The chapter has demonstrated the various sources of law affecting individuals and organizations in England. It has also outlined the methods of legislating and the distinction between laws passed through Parliament and those passed under delegated legislation. Controls exist to ensure debate and accountability in the passage of these Bills into Acts of Parliament. However, it is open to question whether these mechanisms provide the robust system of scrutiny that would be expected.

The following chapter identifies the court structure in the UK and the increasingly important role played by alternative dispute resolution techniques. Arbitration, conciliation, and mediation are being used by businesses to avoid court actions when disputes occur, in an attempt to reduce costs and to maintain the business relationships that are normally killed when disputes involve lawyers and the courts.

SUMMARY OF MAIN POINTS

Sources of law

- There are various sources of English law that will have an impact on individuals and businesses.

The common law

- The judiciary had created a system of establishing laws before a united system of government was formed, and this is known as the common law.

- Judges spend time preparing a judgment that outlines previous case law authorities, and with reference to these, explain how they have arrived at the decision. From this detailed information the ratio may be found.

- The ratio is 'the reason for the decision' and requires lower courts to follow the rules established in previous cases. The system of precedent is hierarchical, and it is binding on 'lower' courts.

- The judgment may also include pronouncements that do not form part of the decision (the legal issue under consideration). This part of the judgment is *obiter dicta* and is not binding but rather is of persuasive authority.

Statutory interpretation

- When interpreting legislation, the judiciary is subject to rules on how such an interpretation may be given. Intrinsic and extrinsic sources may be used to assist them.

- The methods of interpreting statutes can be summarized in four categories—the literal approach, the golden approach, the mischief approach, and the purposive approach.

Equity

- Equity was developed along with the common law to provide more appropriate remedies beyond damages, available under the common law, which often failed to adequately compensate the injured party.

- Equitable remedies include injunctions, specific performance, rectification, and rescission. Being 'equitable' remedies, they are available at the discretion of the courts and they will not be awarded where the injured party has not acted equitably: they must have acted in an equitable manner, and they must seek the remedy in a 'reasonable' time.

Legislation

- Parliament's role, among others, is to legislate for the country.

- Parliament's law is supreme (above the common law and equity) because of the 'Glorious Revolution' in 1688, where Parliament superseded the monarch as the supreme law-making body.
- Parliament also has the power to delegate legislative authority to bodies such as Ministers, Local Authorities, and the Privy Council.

Customs

- Whilst little used, they have created laws that are respected if they satisfy the test of 'time immemorial'. They must also be sufficiently precise for the courts to enforce the right; be specific to a locality, region, and/or industry; and they must not conflict with statutes.

Conventions

- Conventions are known as 'soft' law and establish principles that are abided by. They are increasingly codified into codes of practice.

The stages of a Parliamentary Bill

- An Act begins life as a Bill.
- The Bill has its First Reading where its title is presented, it is issued with a number, and The Stationery Office prints it for the House.
- At the Second Reading, a debate is possible and the Opposition may defeat the Bill by tabling a 'reasoned amendment'.
- The Bill then proceeds to a Standing Committee, which debates and considers the Bill clause by clause. In the Lords, the Committee Stage is usually held by a Whole House Committee as opposed to a Standing Committee.
- The Report Stage will decide on the issues raised at the Committee Stage and allows for those Members not part of the Committee to forward amendments and reflect on the Bill.
- The Third Reading involves a quick debate on any changes made at the Committee and Report Stages.
- Where the Bill began in the Commons, the Lords may make amendments as they see fit and these are then sent back to the Commons for agreement or further debate.
- Having passed each of these stages and with agreement from both Houses, the Bill is sent for Royal Assent.

Control over the power of the House of Lords

- The House of Lords is the unelected second chamber that can stall legislation by making amendments with which the Commons may not agree. There is protection against this chamber stopping the Commons from having a Bill enacted, through the Parliament Acts 1911 and 1949.

Non-Parliament legislation: secondary legislation

- Legislation may be delegated from Parliament to another body due to the time constraints on Parliament, the need for expertise, the fact that legislation may be needed in an emergency, or because the changes may be so slight as not to warrant the passage of the Bill in the manner outlined earlier.
- The three types of delegated legislation are Statutory Instruments, Orders in Council, and by-laws.

Control of delegated legislation

- Standing Committees have been specifically established to review Statutory Instruments and European Union documents.

- Delegated legislation, generally, is subject to either a negative resolution procedure or a positive resolution procedure.

- The courts may also review the power to create the legislation, or to ensure that the requirements as established in the enabling Act were followed, but they are not empowered to consider the merits of the legislation.

SUMMARY QUESTIONS

Essay questions

1. 'Governments in the UK are elected to create legislation; however, this power may be abused if accountability is not ensured. The role of the Government in this respect therefore requires a system of checks and balances to be exercised to ensure public scrutiny.'

   Identify how Parliament can maintain accountability of the Government and critically assess its effectiveness in this role.

2. 'Delegated legislation is a necessary requirement for the effective functioning of the legislative process, it is a purposeful use of expertise, and it enables Parliament to concentrate on issues of national significance.'

   Discuss.

Problem questions

1. The planning department of Redmount Borough Council (RBC) has been given the power (through delegated legislation) to build a new road through parkland. This legislation will enable the compulsory purchase of farmland and privately owned parkland where necessary to facilitate the build programme. The enabling Act requires RBC to consult with local people regarding the impact of this proposal before a final decision is made. Further, the Council is required to consult with interested pressure groups when reaching its conclusion.

   The Council failed to consult with many of the local residents, instead restricting its consultation to three of the most powerful businessmen in the area. Having obtained their agreement (probably in part due to the purchase price of their property and the fact they do not live in the area), RBC sought to proceed with the build.

   Advise Hamish, a farmer who lives and owns property in an area proposed for the new road, who was not consulted, as to any mechanism available to him to challenge the decision. Further, explain who may be the most powerful groups involved in the decision-making in terms of the Parliamentary process, media campaigning, and gaining the support of other powerful groups.

2. The (fictitious) Police and National Security Act 2005 provides that, in relation to the increased security risks from terrorist activities in recent years, retailers may not offer for sale prohibited items. The list of prohibited items identified in the statute includes radio-based devices which may be used to hear communications between members of the police service. As Ron (an off-duty police officer) was walking past a retail outlet of ABC, he looked in the window and saw a newly developed police scanner displaying a price tag of £85. The information on the display box of the scanner lists as one of its features—'full access to police communications—listen to what they don't want you to hear'.

Ron knew of the Act, having attended a briefing session run by the police service, and reports ABC to the appropriate authorities. Consequently, ABC is charged with a breach of the 2005 Act.

In relation to the methods of statutory interpretation available to the judiciary, assess the potential liability of ABC in the above scenario.

 You will find guidance about how to answer these questions online at www.oup.com/uk/marson5e/.

FURTHER READING

Books and articles

Carney, G. (2015) 'Comparative Approaches to Statutory Interpretation in Civil Law and Common Law Jurisdictions' *Statute Law Review*, Vol. 36, No. 1, p. 46.

Harden, I. and Lewis, N. (1986) 'The Noble Lie: The British Constitution and the Rule of Law' Hutchinson: London.

Lord Devlin (1976) 'Judges as Lawmakers' *Modern Law Review*, Vol. 39, Issue 1, p. 1.

Page, E. C. (2001) 'Governing by Numbers: Delegated Legislation and Everyday Policy-Making' Hart: Oxford.

Watt, G. (2016) 'Cases and Materials on Equity and Trusts' (10th Edition) Oxford University Press: Oxford.

Websites and Twitter links

http://www.gov.uk/beis
@beisgovuk

https://www.youtube.com/channel/UCyGwamm_eoM69zCIwO9qVDg
Sources of information from the Government Department of Business, Energy & Industrial Strategy. They contain a wealth of material and access to various sources of information to achieve the Department's goal of building a dynamic and competitive UK economy.

http://www.judiciary.gov.uk/about-the-judiciary/advisory-bodies/cjc/
The website of the Civil Justice Council—an advisory public body with the responsibility for overseeing and coordinating the modernization of the civil justice system.

http://www.judiciary.gov.uk
@JudiciaryUK

Sources of information from the judiciary of England and Wales. It has information including case law and sentencing decisions, and the website has a very useful interactive learning suite with features such as 'you be the judge'. It is informative and easily navigable.

http://www.legislation.gov.uk
@legislation
@HouseofCommons
@UKHouseofLords

Sources of information on domestic legislation, where and how this has been amended, provisions which are not yet in force, how legislation has been amended for different jurisdictions (such as for England and Wales, and for Scotland), and links between affecting and affected legislation.

http://www.number10.gov.uk
@Number10gov
  Sources of information from the office of the Prime Minister.

http://www.opsi.gov.uk/legislation/about_legislation.htm
Legislation of the UK from 1988 to the present day.

http://www.parliament.uk
@UKParliament

https://www.youtube.co.uk/user/UKParliament
Details of the role of Parliament, its members, standards, and business.

http://www.parliament.uk/about
Details of how laws are made, the role and powers of committees, and the workings of the Commons and the Lords.

ONLINE RESOURCES

www.oup.com/uk/marson5e/

For further resources relating to this chapter, including self-test questions, an interactive glossary, and key case flashcards.

4 THE COURT STRUCTURE AND ALTERNATIVE FORMS OF DISPUTE RESOLUTION

The courts in the English legal system, and the increasing use of alternative dispute resolution mechanisms, are relevant to businesses as they are used either to settle disputes or for dispute avoidance. Businesses will, at least occasionally, become involved in disputes with suppliers, customers, or their workforce, and the following chapter outlines the mechanisms for seeking an outcome to such disputes. Knowing the appropriate court, or the mechanisms for non-legal action that exist to offer a settlement to disputes, may enable a more speedy resolution to business problems. Not all disputes will have a justiciable remedy or perhaps even require recourse to the courts, but the courts' position in the application of legal rules and administration of justice necessitates their discussion.

Business Scenario 4

Usman has worked in the accounts department of ABC Industries plc for five years. He is a Pakistani national who has a good understanding of the English language but can sometimes make mistakes, particularly when idioms are used. Usman's ex-girlfriend (Bea) also works for ABC Industries plc in another department and recently they had an argument at work. Usman was alleged to have threatened her, which other members of staff heard. However, Usman claims that whilst he accepts there was a heated exchange between the two, it was a misunderstanding and was not a threat. It seems that Bea and the other staff thought Usman used the expression 'I will cut your face' in the argument when he claims to have said 'I will shut your face.'

Following an investigation and gathering of all the relevant facts (which includes acceptance of Usman's level of spoken English and some evidence pointing towards Bea goading Usman into the argument) the employer has the choice of dismissing Usman or using other disciplinary measures.

Learning Outcomes
*   Identify the judiciary in the courts in both civil and criminal jurisdictions (**4.2.2–4.2.3.1**)
*   Explain the hierarchy of the court structure and its jurisdiction (**4.2.1–4.2.10.2**)
*   Critique the creation of tribunals and contrast their role with the courts (**4.3–4.3.4**)
*   Identify examples of alternative mechanisms to dispute resolution and where they may be most appropriately used (**4.4–4.4.4.3**).

4.1 INTRODUCTION

This chapter concludes the section on the English legal system with consideration of the court structure and the hierarchy of the courts. Having described the constitution and the sources of laws in the United Kingdom in the previous chapters, this chapter identifies where these laws are interpreted and utilized in the legal system—courts and tribunals. The jurisdiction of the courts and the personnel within them are described and a comparison is drawn between these forums for the administration of justice. It is important for those in business to be aware of the work of at least one tribunal—the Employment Tribunal, as many employment-related disputes ultimately progress here.

4.2 THE COURT SYSTEM AND APPOINTMENT PROCESS

It should be understood that the term 'court' is rather difficult to accurately define in any practical sense due to the variety of courts that exist in the English legal system, and those administered by the State and other non-State-administered bodies (e.g. Jewish law has the Beth Din and Muslim law has the UK Islamic Shari'a Council). What is easier to achieve is a description of the work undertaken by the courts (and for the purposes of this text the discussion is limited to the State-administered courts) and the role of the personnel within them.

4.2.1 An Overview of the Courts

Parliament provides the rules under which the various courts and tribunals in the legal system must work. This identifies the powers and jurisdiction of the court, and the role of judges/arbitrators in this process. Courts are a forum for disputes to be heard and judgments to be provided. They exist for disputes between parties to be considered (in civil law) and determine a defendant's guilt or innocence (in criminal cases).

The passage into law of the Legal Services Act 2007 has had a significant impact on the legal profession and opportunities for greater access to courts through, *inter alia*, increased rights of audience of lawyers. It also aimed to assist individuals in their relationship with providers of legal services (e.g. consumer legal complaints), through the creation of the Office for Legal Complaints. Given the word constraints of this text, the online resources include additional materials on this topic.

Some courts may hear both civil and criminal cases under their jurisdiction (such as the Court of Appeal and the **Supreme Court**, which both hear criminal and civil cases, but there is a clear demarcation between the two jurisdictions). The courts also exist under a hierarchical system where a decision of the higher court is binding as a precedent on those courts below it. These decisions are not (always) binding on the court that has provided the judgment (it can reverse the judgment in some later case) or on any court(s) above it. **Figure 4.1** on p. 70 demonstrates the structure of the civil court system and the arrows demonstrate how precedents bind lower courts.

As is evident from this diagram, the courts at the top are the superior courts and deal with appeals and/or the most complex and important cases (and they consider points of law applied in the case rather than the facts). The courts at the lower end hear the more simple cases or those that are just beginning and may need to be referred higher. As shown in **Figure 4.1**, tribunals sit at the bottom, yet it should be noted that whilst some are still referred to as tribunals, they are in fact courts and are specialists in that jurisdiction of law. Such an example is the Employment Appeal Tribunal, where appeals from decisions of an Employment Tribunal are heard.

Figure 4.1 The court structure in the Civil Division

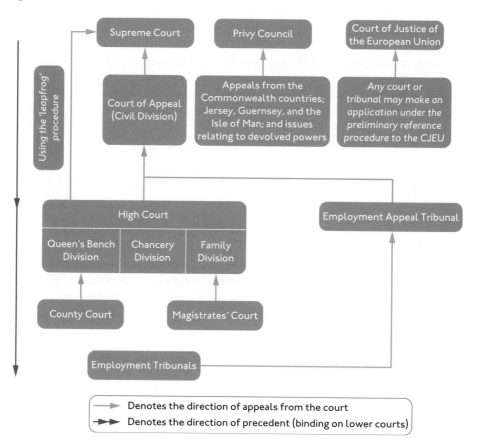

4.2.2 **Judiciary**

The judiciary refers to the judges who preside over the cases heard in the courts in the civil and criminal jurisdictions. There are a variety of judges, established on a hierarchical basis, who sit in the courts in the English legal system. The most senior of these is the Lord Chief Justice (the head of the Court of Appeal (Criminal Division) and the Queen's Bench Division of the High Court), whose responsibilities include representing the judiciary as a body to Parliament; the second most senior judge is the Master of the Rolls (the head of the Court of Appeal (Civil Division)); then there is the President of the Family Division and the Vice-Chancellor (Head of the Chancery Division of the High Court).

Next in the hierarchy are the Lord Justices, who, along with the Lord Chief Justice and the Master of the Rolls, sit in the Court of Appeal.

As of 2014 there were 106 High Court Judges in post: assigned between the Chancery Division, the Queen's Bench Division, and (predominately) to the Family Division.

The next level of the judiciary involves Circuit Judges and District Judges. In 2014 there were 142 District Judges in the Magistrates' Court who support the lay magistrates in the Court and consider the full range of cases before the Court, either sitting with the lay magistrates or sitting alone.

Justices of the peace (lay magistrates) are the volunteers who sit in the Magistrates' Court and are appointed by the Lord Chancellor on behalf of the monarch (with the exception of Greater Manchester, Merseyside, and Lancashire, where the appointments are made by the Chancellor to the Duchy of Lancaster). In the Magistrates' Court they sit in a bench of three, and when sitting in the Youth Court or Family Proceedings Court, there must be at least one man and one woman. When in the Crown Court, the justices sit with a judge to hear appeals and cases committed from the Magistrates' Court, for sentence.

The historical restriction to the position of a judge to persons previously engaged as a barrister was changed under the Courts and Legal Services Act 1990. The Act provided for solicitors to have the opportunity to become judges if they possessed the 'rights of audience' in the particular court, and it was to broaden the opportunities for those engaged in the legal services to aspire to the highest positions in the 'industry'. The right of audience is identified in s. 71(3) of the Act and includes the Supreme Court; High Court; Crown Court; County Court; Magistrates' Court; and a 'general qualification' covering rights of audience in the Supreme Court, County Court, and Magistrates' Court.

4.2.3　Appointment Proceedings

Part of a commitment to improving the transparency and openness of government led to the Constitutional Reform Act 2005. This piece of legislation was broad and included the development of the Supreme Court, which became the highest court. The function of the Lord Chancellor (the office with responsibility for the judges) was changed, as this office was largely responsible for the appointment of judges, which had been viewed with scepticism by commentators as being opaque. Consequently, there was little transparency in the selection of these judges. There was a disproportionately small number of judges representing the various ethnic minority groups in the country; few appointments were made of those with disabilities; and judges were frequently ridiculed as being out of touch with society. Therefore, the system of appointments was revised under the Act, with the creation of the Judicial Appointments Commission.

4.2.3.1　The Judicial Appointments Commission

The Commission is composed, in accordance with the Constitutional Reform Act 2005, and as amended by the Judicial Appointments Regulations 2013, of 15 members. This includes a chairperson, five 'lay' members, five members acting from a judicial capacity, two legal professionals, a tribunal member, and a lay magistrate (Sch. 12). The role of the Commission is to select the judges on the basis of the merits of their application, in discussion with the panel, with the need for accountability and transparency to remain a focus of the appointment process. The Commission also has a requirement to consider the current composition of the judiciary and have regard to increasing its diversity (Constitutional Reform Act 2005, ss. 63–64).

The judges to the Supreme Court are required to possess sufficient knowledge and practical experience of the law. The initial members of the Court were the 12 Law Lords (s. 27(8)). When a vacancy arises, the Lord Chancellor formulates a selection panel, which includes a member of the Commission, to select a person from the candidates and report this to the Lord Chancellor who may accept the decision, reject it, or require the panel to reconsider its decision. The Lord Chancellor then passes this information of the successful candidate to the Prime Minister, who makes the recommendation to the monarch for the appointment to the Supreme Court. For judges to the lower courts (High Court Judge, District Judge, and so on) the Commission makes the recommendation to the Lord Chancellor, who in turn makes the recommendation to the monarch.

4.2.4 **The Supreme Court**

The Supreme Court replaced the judicial function of the House of Lords from 1 October 2009. It is located in the old Middlesex Guildhall in Parliament Square, which is intended to provide the Justices of the Supreme Court (the new name of the 'Law Lords') with greater space to undertake their functions (than was available in the House of Lords).

The Supreme Court is the final court of appeal in civil cases for the courts of the UK, and is the final court of appeal for criminal cases for the courts of England, Wales, and Northern Ireland. The Supreme Court hears cases involving matters of general importance. It uses the case law and precedents developed by the House of Lords, and the Court is required to ensure its independence from the executive is maintained (Constitutional Reform Act 2005, s. 3).

The Law Lords who were present in the judicial branch of the House of Lords became the first Justices of the Supreme Court. There are 12 Justices, the President of the Supreme Court is Lady Hale. The Justices will, like other judges, retire at 70 (Judicial Pensions and Retirement Act 1992) so that they do not continue in office beyond useful service. Judges may sit part-time until 75 years old, and it was mooted whether the Justices of the Supreme Court should be able to continue full-time until this age (bearing in mind the length of service usually required before being chosen to serve at the Supreme Court). This was not accepted and the retirement age remains.

The qualifications required for appointment to the Supreme Court are governed by the Constitutional Reform Act 2005, ss. 25–31 (as amended by ss. 50–52 of the Tribunals and Enforcement Act 2007):

1. They must have held 'high judicial office' (which includes High Court Judges of England and Wales, and Northern Ireland; Court of Appeal Judges of England and Wales, and Northern Ireland; and Judges of the Court of Session in Scotland) for two years; or

2. They must possess a 15-year Superior Court qualification/or have been a qualifying practitioner for the 15-year duration.

4.2.5 **The Court Of Appeal**

The Court of Appeal hears civil and criminal cases in its two divisions and forms part of the Senior Courts of England and Wales with the High Court and Crown Court (under Supreme Court Act 1981, s. 1(1) (which, following the Constitutional Reform Act 2005, was renamed the Senior Courts Act 1981)). The Court of Appeal is composed of up to 38 'ordinary judges' (known as Lord (or Lady) Justice of Appeal), and judges including those from the Lords, the Lord Chancellor, the president of the Queen's Bench of the High Court, and similar qualified judges (Senior Courts Act 1981, s. 2(1) and (2)). To qualify for appointment to the Court of Appeal, they must have held a 10-year High Court qualification or have been a High Court Judge (Courts and Legal Services Act 1990, s. 71).

The Court of Appeal has a president—in the civil division the position is occupied by the Master of the Rolls, and in the criminal division by the Lord Chief Justice. In the civil division, the Court hears appeals from the High Court and the County Courts, although it is possible for the appeal to 'leapfrog' the Court of Appeal and move straight to the Supreme Court (Administration of Justice Act 1969, ss. 12–15). The Court consists, usually, of three judges, or cases may be heard by two judges in cases appealed from the High Court that could have been brought in a County Court. The law prevents a judge in the Court of Appeal from hearing an appeal from his/her own decisions, in the interests of natural justice and to give the public confidence in an appeals process (Senior Courts Act 1981, s. 56).

4.2.6 The Privy Council

The Privy Council holds two positions in the constitution: a legislative role, and a role as a court of appeal. Its historic roots date back to when the Privy Council would assist the monarch in matters of State. However, as with other institutions, it has evolved as the country evolved. The Privy Council consists of the Cabinet Ministers (the Right Honourable Members of Parliament) and a number of junior Ministers, who meet every month. Its role is predominantly concerned with the affairs of chartered bodies (those companies and charities incorporated by Royal Charter).

In its judicial role, the Privy Council (the Judicial Committee) consists of the Lord Chancellor (and previous Lord Chancellors), the Lords of Appeal in Ordinary, other Privy Council members who hold or have held high judicial office, and other judges in superior courts in other Commonwealth countries. It is the final court of appeal for UK overseas territories and the Commonwealth countries that have opted to retain appeals to the UK (Her Majesty in Council). It also has jurisdiction to hear appeals from Jersey, Guernsey, and the Isle of Man; from the Disciplinary Committee of the Royal College of Veterinary Surgeons; from certain Schemes of the Church Commissioners under the Pastoral Measure 1983; and it hears and determines issues relating to the powers and functions of the legislative and executive authorities established under the various devolution Acts for Scotland and Northern Ireland, and the competence and functions of the Assembly for Wales. The Judicial Committee hears 55–65 appeals per year, and sits in chambers of five judges for Commonwealth cases, usually with three judges for other matters. In civil cases, leave to appeal is usually obtained as of right, as it is in cases involving constitutional interpretation.

4.2.7 The High Court

The High Court is separated into three jurisdictions with specific areas of expertise: the Queen's Bench Division, the Chancery Division, and the Family Division. The trial will normally take place before a High Court Judge (or Deputy High Court Judge), who will also hear any pre-trial reviews or other interim applications. Generally, one judge hears each case, and appeals from the Court (that require permission) are heard by the Court of Appeal, with further appeals to the Supreme Court. Where a Master hears the case, an appeal is first heard by a High Court Judge, and then it may proceed as any other appeal.

The Divisional Court of the Queen's Bench hears the appeals from the County Court, and has jurisdiction to hear appeals from the criminal jurisdiction from cases started in the Magistrates' Court and those appealed from the Crown Court. These criminal issues are relevant in a business scenario due to the criminal liability imposed by legislation, including the Consumer Protection Act 1987 and the Consumer Protection from Unfair Trading Regulations 2008. When handling the criminal cases, the Court sits with two or three High Court Judges (one of whom will be the Lord Chief Justice or a Lord Justice of Appeal) and they have the power to uphold the decision, reverse it, amend it, or to send the case back to the referring court. An appeal from the Divisional Court is heard by the Supreme Court.

4.2.7.1 The Queen's Bench

The Queen's Bench is the division that considers cases involving contract (breach of contract), torts (personal injury, negligence, libel, and slander), non-payment of debts, and possession of land or property. The President of the Queen's Bench is the Lord Chief Justice and a Lord Justice of Appeal has been appointed as the Vice-President, along with the High Court Judges who preside over the cases. A judge is appointed to handle the Jury List, and another is in charge of the Trial List. Masters (junior judges) hear less serious cases.

The Division is further subdivided into the specialist courts of the Admiralty Court, the Technology and Construction Court, and the Commercial Court. Due to the specialism of each Court, they publish their own Guide or Practice Direction that modifies in certain circumstances the Civil Procedure Rules (CPR) 1999.

4.2.7.2 Chancery Division

The Chancery Division is based in the Thomas Moore Building in the Royal Courts of Justice and is subdivided into the Chancery Chambers and Bankruptcy and Companies Court. The Division considers claims including trusts, probate (when this is contested), companies, company liquidation, land, claims for the dissolution of partnerships, commercial disputes, revenue issues (such as appeals against taxation under VAT or Income Tax), and intellectual property issues in the Patents Court.

4.2.7.3 Family Division

The Family Division considers all matrimonial issues under the Children Act 1989, the Child Abduction and Custody Act 1985, and matters arising from Part IV of the Family Law Act 1996. It deals with cases involving family matters of a broad jurisdiction, and can include issues of domestic violence, wardship and adoption, and divorce and annulments. It is, however, of little significance in the study of business law.

Consider

If Usman is dismissed from his employment, he has the right to claim the dismissal is in breach of his contract (a wrongful dismissal). In certain circumstances, the claim will be heard in the County Court. The issue of court costs should form part of Usman's decision to proceed on this route.

4.2.8 The County Court

The County Court is the 'lowest' of the courts, but this does not reflect its significance in the English legal system or indeed its contribution to the administration of justice. The Court hears many cases with a business emphasis, and as such, it follows the High Court in possessing unlimited jurisdiction to hear contract and torts claims. The main distinction in whether the case is heard in the County Court or the High Court is the expected value of the claim (the figure that the claimant may reasonably expect to be awarded by the court). In the absence of a claim including personal injury, if the value of the claim is less than £25,000 then it will generally be heard in the County Court. If the claim involves a value of over £50,000 then it will generally be heard in the High Court.

The majority of the cases heard in the Court are undertaken by Circuit Judges, Recorders, District Judges, and Deputy District Judges. When reference is made to the 'small claims court' it is in reality the County Court using the 'Small Claims Track'.

The Court hears claims including breach of contract, faulty goods, goods not supplied, claims for bad workmanship, and personal injury. It will deal with many of the claims between a **consumer and a trader** and there exist mechanisms to assist in reaching a speedy resolution to a dispute. Cases in the County Court are heard by a District Judge when the issue is straightforward or the matter is uncontested. Where the issue is more complex, a Circuit Judge will hear the case, and appeals from the County Court will proceed to the High Court.

Judgments of the Court will be entered into the Registry of County Court Judgments, which is a public document and is often used by credit agencies prior to an offer of a loan or where goods are to be paid for over a period of time. Having settled the judgment, the party's name is removed from the Register. If this is completed within one month of the judgment, the name is removed immediately, but if it is completed after one month, the name will be held on the Registry and removed following a period of six years. This is very important for individuals and businesses who may wish to obtain credit in the future, and for those who would have to make such a declaration to a potential business partner under the duty of 'good faith'. Simply doing nothing when an action is initiated is not wise and seeking advice from legal and non-legal sources is always to be recommended.

4.2.9 The Tracking System

Having established that a dispute between businesses or within a business cannot be resolved informally and amicably, the 'last resort' of resolving the dispute may be to have a court determine the issue. When a claim is initiated, the courts will assign it to one of the following claims tracks—the small claims, fast, or multi-track, which has implications for costs, the value of the claim, the privacy available to the parties, and the time allowed (or considered necessary) to dispense with the claim.

4.2.9.1 The small claims track

The courts and the parties may decide that the case is most appropriately conducted under the small claims track. When a case is initiated, the parties are sent a questionnaire (called an 'allocation questionnaire') that identifies the most cost-effective and just method of dispensing with the case. If the claim involves a dispute with an amount of less than £10,000; if it involves a situation such as consumer claims (faulty goods, poor workmanship, problems with the sale or supply of goods and services, and so on), accident claims, and disputes between landlords and tenants; and it will involve minimal preparation, then it may be suitable for this track. Such claims will not normally involve many witnesses or any difficult or complex points of law, otherwise a different track may be more appropriate. The major benefits to a claim under this track are that legal costs are not generally awarded against the losing party and cases are dealt with much quicker than other types of claim.

4.2.9.2 The fast track and multi-track

The court will ask the parties for their views on the most appropriate track to use in the case, but will use the fast track if the claim involves a claim in excess of £10,000 but less than £25,000, and if the case will take no longer than 30 weeks to prepare and take no more than one day in court (assessed at five hours). If the case involves either a claim of more than £25,000 or will take longer than 30 weeks then the judge may allocate the case to the multi-track, where each case is allocated on the basis of its circumstances. In these cases, the party that wins the case will expect to recover some (or all) of the costs involved in their case from the losing party. When this involves the legal fees, and of course the losing party will have to pay their own expenses and legal fees, court action is something not to be entered into lightly.

Again, the parties complete an allocation questionnaire and it is expected that both parties cooperate and return the questionnaire to the court within 14 days of receiving it. The cooperation will involve the parties agreeing on the most appropriate track to use, the length of time the parties believe the trial will take, the time needed for preparation, and whether experts will be needed.

4.2.10 Criminal Courts

As stated earlier, the Supreme Court, Court of Appeal, Privy Council, and High Court have jurisdiction over criminal law matters in addition to their civil law responsibilities. The remaining courts specific to the criminal law are the Crown Court and the Magistrates' Court. The Magistrates' Court will refer a case to the Crown Court (usually) where the maximum possible sentence for imprisonment it has the power to impose is likely to be exceeded following conviction of the defendant, or where the maximum fine that may be imposed (£5,000) is insufficient. The power of imprisonment is limited to six months—however, note that the Magistrates' Court can impose two consecutive six-month prison sentences (hence a 12-month sentence) for offences triable 'either way.' If, following the trial the defendant is acquitted, insofar as no other offences are pending, they are free to leave court.

4.2.10.1 The Crown Court

The Crown Court handles the following types of cases:

- the more serious criminal offences, and these are tried before a judge and jury;
- appeals from the Magistrates' Court, and these are tried before a judge and at least two magistrates;
- defendants who have been convicted in the Magistrates' Court and are referred to the Crown Court for sentencing.

Offences heard by the Crown Court are divided into three categories of seriousness. Class 1 offences are the most serious and as such include murder, genocide, manslaughter, piracy, and so on. Class 2 offences include rape, and various other sexual offences. Class 3 includes all other offences not included in the first two classes. A Circuit Judge will generally hear cases at the Crown Court (such as class 3 offences). However, in cases of significance or complexity (such as in class 1 and 2 offences), the case will be heard by a High Court Judge. The cases involving a jury trial will involve the judge assessing the evidence, the application of the rules of the court, and so on, whilst the role of the jury is to consider the facts and the weight to be placed on the evidence heard. The jury will then decide whether they consider the defendant guilty or not guilty, and having found the defendant guilty, the judge passes sentence. Appeals on the basis of the conviction or sentence are possible from the Crown Court (see **Figure 4.2**) and these are heard by the Court of Appeal (Criminal Division).

4.2.10.2 The Magistrates' Court

The Magistrates' Court plays a key role in the administration of the criminal justice system, as the vast majority of cases begin at the Magistrates' Court and most are concluded there. There is a single head of the Court (the Senior District Judge—the Chief Magistrate) who has responsibility for the administration of the bench.

Figure 4.2 The court structure in the Criminal Division

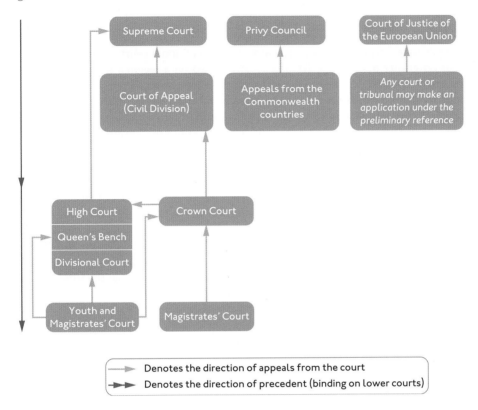

The Magistrates' Court hears both civil and criminal cases. Examples of the criminal aspects handled by the Court have been identified earlier, and the civil element includes licensing, betting and gaming, family issues, civil debts, complaints regarding council tax, and so on. The Court also has a division called the Youth Court, where three specifically trained magistrates hear cases involved with young people between 10 and 17 years of age. If the case involves an allegation of a particularly serious offence (in which an adult would be subject to imprisonment for a term of 14 years or more) then the Magistrates' Court can commit the accused for trial in the Crown Court. Appeals are available from a conviction at the Magistrates' Court, or against the imposition of a sentence, and appeals in criminal law are somewhat 'easier' than those in the civil law, but it must be considered that the Crown Court, upon the appeal (where the case is retried), may increase the sentence issued, although they may not exceed the maximum sentence that is available in the Magistrates' Court.

Consider

If the employer wishes to dismiss Usman but he feels this has been unfair given the circumstances or if he feels the investigation has been flawed, his case may be presented to an employment tribunal. What are the advantages of the tribunal system above the court system (which may be used if he claimed wrongful dismissal)?

4.3 TRIBUNALS

4.3.1 Introduction

Tribunals were established as an alternative to the traditional court system, with an emphasis on greater informality. Tribunals were created on a regional basis, with areas of local knowledge and expertise in matters such as welfare, immigration, and employment. Tribunals were so called because of the three members: a legally qualified chairperson, along with two independent wing (lay) members with expertise/experience in the area (in Employment Tribunals these offer expertise from an employer's perspective (e.g. from the Confederation of British Industry) and from an employee's perspective (e.g. from a trade union or Trades Union Congress)). From 1 December 2007, chairpersons of the Employment Tribunals are referred to as Employment Judges (Tribunals, Courts and Enforcement Act 2007, Sch. 8, para. 36). The tribunal does not provide a judgment but rather makes an award, and as the binding force of precedent moves downwards the tribunal is not bound by decisions made in other cases heard in tribunals, although they frequently look to such decisions when considering a case. If an appeal has to be made, then the case will progress to the High Court (although in employment matters this is to the Employment Appeal Tribunal). Appeals are established on the basis of a point of law, or that the tribunal came to a conclusion which no reasonable tribunal could have reached. This is a particularly difficult test to prove, and it operates on a similar basis to natural justice.

4.3.2 The Advantages of the Tribunal System

The following elements can be identified as the advantages that tribunals are supposed to have over courts:

- *Speed of cases:* Tribunals enable an effective balance to be established between the legality of the hearings and the formalities to which any 'real' hearing must adhere. To this effect, the chairperson of the tribunal is legally qualified and works within the rules established for each tribunal, and they have the ability to assist claimants in presenting their case if they attend unrepresented. The decisions of the tribunals are also provided more quickly than in the courts, with awards frequently being made within the day of the hearing.

- *Reduction in costs:* Tribunals were created to eliminate the necessity for legal representation, removing this very expensive aspect of the legal system. The less formalistic rules and procedures in tribunals removed the necessity (in theory at least) for lawyers.

- *Expert knowledge in jurisdiction and locality:* Employment Tribunals were established to hear claims on disputes between employers and employees. They would therefore begin to establish a body of expertise in these specific areas and this would assist in deciding future cases more expeditiously. A further benefit would be that as tribunals were regionally based, they would be able to establish an understanding and expertise of practices in the local region.

- *Informality:* There are various tribunals, and each has its own jurisdiction and methods of work. However, they are generally less formal and therefore, it is hoped, less intimidating than courts.

- *Reducing the workload of courts:* As cases such as disputes in employment are heard by Employment Tribunals, the courts would be free to hear other claims with the perceived result that it would assist in speeding up the judicial system by reducing their workload.

- *Reasoned hearings:* Tribunals are presided by a legally qualified chairperson (e.g. an Employment Judge), and work within the rules established by law. Therefore, when decisions are made, these are based on the rule of law and the parties can have confidence that justice was seen to be done. There is also an appeals procedure.

4.3.3 The Disadvantages of Tribunals

Given the advantages identified for the adoption and justification of the tribunal system, the disadvantages and limitations to the system must be considered.

- *Increased formality:* Tribunals were designed to be informal systems. However, they have increasingly become legalistic and barristers have begun to specialize in certain jurisdictions (such as employment law). The increasing competence of tribunals in legal jurisdictions, and the technical rules governing claims and the formalities of procedure, have lessened this distinct advantage.

- *Limitation in legal assistance:* Legal aid (a source of free legal advice and representation) has been governed since April 2013 by The Legal Aid Sentencing and Punishment of Offenders Act 2012. This assistance is not available for individuals in the presentation of claims at tribunal.

- *The complexity of the tribunal system:* The perception of the system of tribunals as being less formal and legalistic than courts is now increasingly unrealistic. Employment Tribunals are a very good example of this increasingly complexity. When they were first established (and known as industrial tribunals) their jurisdiction was unfair dismissal legislation. However, there are now well over 60 different jurisdictions.

- *No precedent in tribunals:* Tribunals are not bound by the decisions of other tribunals, and with reference to Employment Tribunals, as many of the decisions are determined with a strong emphasis on the facts of the case, then decisions can be made that appear to contradict cases with similar facts. This can be seen most clearly in Part 7 of this book.

- *Costs in Employment Tribunals:* Application to Employment Tribunals used to be free of charge but as of 29 July 2013, fees were introduced on the basis that parties to the tribunal system should be required to contribute to its running. The fees are explained later at **4.3.4**. Also, from 6 April 2014, Employment Tribunals have had the discretionary power to order employers that lose a tribunal case to pay a financial penalty where they have breached an individual's rights.

4.3.4 Employment Tribunals

As Employment Tribunals, above other tribunals, are likely to be of most interest to employers and businesses, they are selected for a brief description. These tribunals hear disputes between employers and employees/workers, and also claims based on EU laws (*Impact v Minister for Agriculture and Food (Ireland)*). Cases must be lodged on an approved form (ET1 or ET1A) available from the Employment Tribunals Service (ETS), and once this has been accepted by the ETS (as being on the correct form, within the correct time limits, and so on) the employer to whom the claim relates is provided with a response form (ET3) that must be completed and returned within 28 days (unless an extension is requested and supported with reasons for the request). As of April 2012, in cases of unfair dismissal, judges may sit alone—without the use of the two wing members (Employment Tribunals Act 1996 (Tribunal Composition) Order 2012, S.I. 2012/988).

McCafferty v Royal Mail Group Ltd (2012)

Facts:

The claimant was a postman who refused on several occasions to attend work on his day off. He claimed this was due to problems in getting in to work. The employer then provided him with access to an account to charge taxi fares to enable him to attend work. The employer claimed McCafferty began to abuse this system and after it was discovered, McCafferty was dismissed.

Authority for:

The tribunal members agreed that there had been a reasonable investigation into the circumstances before the decision to dismiss. However, the employment judge disagreed with the wing members of the tribunal regarding whether this allowed the employer to hold a reasonable belief in McCafferty's misconduct. Tribunal decisions were at this stage a group decision (now these cases are generally heard by the employment judge sitting alone). Therefore, the judge was outvoted by the two wing lay members of the tribunal.

At appeal, Lady Smith observed: 'It will not have escaped notice that this case is an example of the lay members of an Employment Tribunal reaching a different conclusion on the facts of the case—drawing in part on their valuable "common sense" and knowledge of what any employee could be expected to know—from that of the Employment Judge. Had this claim been one to which the new [employment laws] applied, it seems likely that it would have been heard and determined by an Employment Judge sitting alone, in which case the result would evidently have been rather different. Some may consider that to be a sobering thought.'

The judge will decide whether they wish to convene a pre-hearing review, and this decision may be made if either party requests the hearing. Typically, such reviews are used to determine whether the claim should be struck out at that stage. They may be used to determine entitlements to initiate or defend the claim; and they may be used to consider whether a deposit should be paid where a case is particularly weak. If the case passes this pre-hearing, it continues on to the full hearing. Costs for legal fees incurred are not normally awarded against the losing party in tribunal cases, however, the judge has the option to award up to £10,000 against a party that was legally represented where their claim had no reasonable prospect of success, or they behaved unreasonably or were abusive/disruptive in the proceedings.

4.4 ALTERNATIVE DISPUTE RESOLUTION

This chapter has identified the courts and tribunals in the English legal system. The text also discusses the law and its application in jurisdictions including company, competition, contract, employment, and torts laws. This includes a description of the relevant statutes and a discussion of the cases heard before the courts and tribunals. The courts and tribunals are often the forums for disputes to be adjudicated, and they too have been subject to the need for more effective means of resolving disputes. Further, other methods are being introduced that move away from the adversarial system of law that is necessary in the courts, to a more conciliatory means of dispute resolution.

Consider

Rather than dismiss Usman, the employer could choose to preserve the employment relationship and attempt some form of alternative dispute resolution. When reading through this section, consider which form would be of most use to the parties and how could its use be beneficial to all sides?

4.4.1 The Need for Alternative Dispute Resolution

ADR has several benefits for the parties, including some of the following features:

- *Cooperation v adversarial approaches:* Traditional court cases are based on an adversarial system where the parties attempt to 'win' rather than work cooperatively to establish a mutually acceptable resolution. For those in business, when such a system is applied internally (e.g. between the directors of a firm, or between management and the staff), the ramifications for a dispute that leads to court action could ultimately result in the firm being dissolved, or its adverse effects may impact on employee relations affecting morale, productivity, sales, and outputs. In all situations it is likely to be discordant between members of the business. It is disruptive and can exacerbate relatively minor issues into much larger, and unnecessary, problems.

- *Speed of resolution:* ADR reduces the congestion of the courts by removing disputes between parties to be heard through mediation or arbitration.

- *Costs:* The rationale for a perception of cost-savings in ADR as opposed to legal action is that many initiatives are being established by the courts, businesses, and organizations outside the court structure, that offer cost-effective, or free, services to the parties. Although for businesses a mediator or arbitrator may have to be paid to provide the ADR service, this is typically much cheaper than hiring a solicitor, or retaining legal counsel.

- *Expertise in resolution:* Disputes between businesses may involve a disagreement based on a technical difficulty or a dispute that requires expertise and knowledge of the industry and its practice. The courts do not always have this knowledge, but through ADR the dispute may be heard by an arbitrator with expertise in the industry, or who has specific knowledge of the area, and can facilitate a more speedy resolution.

- *Informality:* Even though lawyers may still be involved in the process, ADR is a more informal and less intimidating forum than the courts, and this encourages effective dispute resolution through a structured mechanism.

- *Compliance:* A legal judgment may be provided against the party having 'lost' a case, but actually enforcing the judgment may be more difficult. There is a higher success rate of compliance with orders when ADR is used.

- *Privacy:* Whilst most court cases are available to the public to attend and can lead, in some cases, to high-profile judgments, ADR is more confidential and allows a level of privacy not readily available in court. For parties that would rather have disputes dealt with in a more discreet environment, ADR offers significant improvements over court action.

4.4.2 Disadvantages of ADR

There are several advantages to parties using ADR to resolve their disputes, but these are context-specific, and may not be advantageous in all circumstances. Further, it should not be underestimated that some claimants want 'their day in court' and do not want to mediate a resolution.

- *Legal protection:* The courts are based on specific rules outlined in legislation regarding the choice of judge and the powers of the court. These are general protections that are lost when ADR is chosen, and to ensure that it is a valid means of resolving disputes, the decisions made in ADR may be binding on the parties.

- *Duplication of fees:* It is possible that ADR cannot resolve the dispute between the parties. In this scenario, there will have been costs in the ADR process, and then legal fees will also have to be paid to resolve the dispute in the courts.

Saigol v Thorney Ltd (2014)

Facts:

A minor dispute involving claim and counter-claim leading to awards to the parties (respectively) of £745 and £375, could not be resolved through mediation. It went to court and led to legal costs for both parties of £67,000 and £77,000—a total of £144,000.

Authority for:

As neither party made seemingly genuine and reasonable attempts to settle the claim, they were each liable for their own costs. Parties should be reminded to enter into ADR with a positive and proportionate attitude, and to enter into litigation with caution and having made sensible attempts to settle claims.

- *Legal expertise:* Whilst the mediators and arbitrators in ADR may be available to offer expertise in technical or industrial matters, they are not experts in law or legal procedures. Therefore, in the absence of judges hearing evidence, important points of law or statutory protections may be missed or not considered in the resolution process.

- *Lack of use:* In spite of the numerous advantages of ADR over the courts in resolving disputes, there is a proportionately low take-up rate.

- *Imbalance of power relations:* Mediation and negotiation may be successful if the parties are of even powers and may be able to negotiate on similar terms. However, in reality the parties do not have the same powers. For example, in employment disputes, frequently the employer will not mediate where they feel their position is strong, and individuals will often settle claims with a lesser settlement than may have been provided if the issue had gone to court/tribunal.

The use of ADR has to be carefully considered and its implications understood before it is used as a method for resolving disputes. It should not be viewed as a solution for all dispute resolutions.

4.4.3 Dispute Resolution in the Courts

There had been a growing desire from within and outside the judiciary and legal professions to establish a means for disputes to adopt some of the principles of ADR. Following the Woolf Report (1986), the emphasis was on settling disputes before they came before the courts. These are used more by parties involved in civil and family disputes, rather than between businesses, but they are still relevant to individuals' disputes (such as the sole trader and their client, and consumers).

Under the CPR 1999, courts are required to undertake case management including 'encouraging the parties to use an alternative dispute resolution procedure if the court considers it appropriate and facilitating the use of such procedure' (Rule 1.4(2)(e)). The courts are further empowered to stay (halt) the proceedings when the parties request or if the court identifies this as appropriate to enable a settlement through ADR (Rule 26.4). The courts may also make an order for costs against a party that has failed to utilize ADR when this would have been appropriate (Rule 44.5), but the parties cannot be compelled to use this method of dispute resolution (in *Halsey v Milton Keynes General NHS Trust* the Court of Appeal held that to impose ADR could amount to a breach of Art. 6 of the Convention). However, in *PGF II SA v OMFS Company 1 Ltd*, the Court of Appeal held that ADR (and not simply restricted to mediation) is a valuable mechanism to parties in dispute. A complete and unreasonable refusal to engage in the process by a party (as in this case) will lead to a sanction through the award of subsequent court costs incurred by the opposing party (similar to the *Saigol* judgment, see **4.4.2**).

4.4.4 Alternative Forms of Dispute Resolution

There are many approaches to ADR including internal dispute resolution techniques, negotiations, and the ombudsman scheme. Internal techniques may not involve third parties, utilize any procedures for the use of arguments or evidence in the dispute, or indeed produce enforceable solutions. However, they are informal and may produce a mutually acceptable resolution. They are also being increasingly used in employment disputes to prevent resort to tribunal. The ombudsman scheme is used in banking, public services, and central and local government. The process for using ADR will begin with some form of negotiation, then, unless there is an arbitration agreement in the contract (as often included in construction cases), the parties may attempt some form of mediation, and then possibly move towards conciliation and then arbitration in the event that the dispute cannot be resolved. This is a very broad topic and it is beyond the scope of this text to include all the facets of this form of dispute resolution; however, the most commonly used mechanisms include arbitration, mediation, and conciliation.

4.4.4.1 Arbitration

This is a voluntary system of ADR and involves the parties relying on the services of an arbitrator who is an independent, fair, and impartial third party (Arbitration Act 1996, s. 33(a)), and is often legally trained or is an expert in the subject matter of the dispute (a list of appropriate arbitrators is available from the Institute of Arbitration). The arbitrator and their employees or agents, are immune from liability unless they can be shown to have acted in bad faith (or had failed to act at all)—Arbitration Act 1996, s. 29. The process has the benefit of privacy and the arbitrator will decide the case on the basis of the evidence, with the application of the law, and the decision is legally binding upon the parties. The Arbitration Act 1996 provides for the dispute to be resolved according to rules of procedure similar to those used in the High Court, and as such, due to the 'legal' nature of this method of ADR, it may not prove to be less expensive than traditional court action, particularly as 'legal aid' is unavailable in arbitration. Section 1 identifies that the objective of arbitration is to produce a fair resolution of disputes by an independent tribunal without unnecessary delay or expense; and that the parties should be free to agree how their disputes are resolved.

Arbitration may be selected as a means of dispute resolution by the parties, the parties may be referred to it by the court, or an Act of Parliament may require it. The parties may apply to the court hearing the case to stay the proceedings if the matter involves an aspect of the dispute that they had agreed to be dealt with under arbitration (s. 9). Arbitration may also involve the entire case, or it may be selected as appropriate for one aspect of the dispute. As such, it has flexibility in approach. When it is selected, the parties should do everything in their power to ensure compliance with procedural and evidential matters, and to limit any delays in the proceedings (s. 44). The arbitrator provides their decision (an award) and this is binding on the parties, although an appeal process exists (to, and with the permission of the High Court) on a point of law, or with the permission of each party. Such appeals are, however, not commonplace. Whilst the hearings under arbitration are conducted in a judicial manner and are subject to the rules of natural justice, they have the benefit of being private and hence in business, a firm's actions, or its contractual dealings, financial records, and so on, are not subject to public scrutiny.

4.4.4.2 Mediation

Mediation may be 'evaluative' (where an assessment is made of the 'legal' issues of the subject forming the dispute) or it can involve a 'facilitative approach' (where the emphasis is on assisting the parties to resolve their differences in a mutually acceptable way). The parties appoint the mediator (as opposed to an independent body as is the case with arbitration or litigation) and where the process is successful in establishing a resolution, this may form the basis of a legally binding agreement between the parties, unless there is a provision between the parties that such agreements are not to be binding. The mediator will establish a set of 'ground rules' by which the dispute will be assessed, and they will gather information from each of the parties. This is where a specific concern of mediation has been identified. The gathering, and sharing, of information may be undertaken not to reach a settlement or compromise, but may rather be used surreptitiously to obtain information regarding the strength or weaknesses of the other party's claim. This form of ADR is a significant mechanism in attempting to resolve disputes and indeed is a feature considered by the European Union in a Directive transposed into domestic legislation on 20 May 2011 (Directive 2008/52/EC and The Cross-Border Mediation (EU Directive) Regulations 2011, S.I. 2011/1133).

Consider

Let us assume that the employer believes Usman's version of events and, after considering his length of service and good character during this time, decides to use an outside agency to resolve the dispute between him, them and Bea. How might the organization ACAS help? (Read Chapter 21 for a broader consideration of the role of ACAS in employment disputes).

4.4.4.3 **Conciliation**

This process is somewhat similar to mediation, and indeed is often considered to be inter-changeable with mediation. However, the conciliator adopts a more proactive role. Their role is to offer solutions and identify strategies for the successful resolution of the dispute. A very common example of the use of conciliation is in employment disputes, where ACAS intervenes with the parties to reach a settlement without recourse to the Employment Tribunal. The conciliation officer speaks with the parties and identifies their concerns, sharing evidence and identifying the likely success of any claims. This raises similar concerns regarding the use of this information as in mediation (see **4.4.4.2**).

CONCLUSION

The chapter has identified the courts and their hierarchy in the civil and criminal jurisdictions, the judges who sit in the various courts and their authority, and the forms of ADR available to the parties and how they may facilitate more effective dispute resolution. This chapter has concluded the specific examination of the English legal system, although the following two chapters consider the impact and effect of the UK's membership of the EU on the constitution, individuals, and businesses. This is of supreme importance to an understanding of the legal system, and has many practical implications for businesses that must be understood.

SUMMARY OF MAIN POINTS

The court system/tribunals

* The courts in the civil jurisdiction administer justice and seek to resolve disputes between parties.
* The courts in the criminal jurisdiction administer justice and consider charges made by the State against a defendant for breaches of the law (although some have civil functions).
* Whilst some courts have a dual role of hearing criminal and civil cases in their different divisions, there are courts that deal predominately with either civil disputes or criminal matters.
* The courts exist on a hierarchical basis, with the Supreme Court holding the position as being the 'highest' court in the country. This has implications for the system of precedent in case law/common law.
* The Supreme Court and Court of Appeal are singularly appellate courts, with the other courts hearing cases and providing judgments on the facts of a case.
* Tribunals specialize in many areas of law including immigration, employment, and data protection.
* There are many perceived advantages to tribunals over the traditional court structure, including the speed at which cases are heard and resolved, a reduction in costs, expertise in the nature of the claim, and increased informality. They also reduce the workload of the courts.
* The disadvantages to the tribunal system include the increasing use of law and formal procedures so that tribunals may be more akin to specialist courts, limitation in the availability of free legal assistance, the procedures in tribunals being increasingly complex, and there being no system of precedent in the tribunals (although precedent established in higher courts is applicable to tribunals).

The judiciary

* Judges and lay people play a significant role in the administration of justice, and there exists a hierarchy of judges, with the most senior having positions of heads of offices and/or sitting in the Supreme Court and Court of Appeal.

- The Government attempted to make the appointment of the judiciary more transparent through the creation of the Judicial Appointments Commission.

Assigning the case to a track

- The civil law cases are assigned to a 'track' depending upon the wishes of the parties and the views of the judge, the value of the claim, issues of privacy, and the time assessed for disposal of the case.

- The courts expect the parties to have considered the use of ADR rather than simply having decided to take their dispute to court. Any party having unreasonably refused to consider this may have to pay costs.

Alternative dispute resolution (ADR)

- ADR is a mechanism increasingly used in the court process to avoid courts having to resolve disputes that could be dispensed with in some other manner.

- It focuses on cooperation rather than the adversarial approach adopted in court cases, and can, in some cases, reduce costs and speed up the resolution of disputes.

- It does have disadvantages, including the possible duplication of fees if the ADR process does not resolve the dispute, and the legal protection afforded by the court process may be lost.

- The forms of dispute resolution include arbitration, mediation, and conciliation.

 SUMMARY QUESTIONS

Essay questions

1. 'Courts are intimidating, daunting and expensive ways of resolving disputes.'

   Critically assess the above statement with specific reference to the benefits provided by tribunals in the administration of justice.

2. 'There are various ways of looking at (the Supreme Court): as a change of place and name which was of major constitutional importance; as an interesting social experiment, which left it to the Justices to create a new set of rules and conventions to replace those that regulated their conduct in the House of Lords; as an ill-judged political exercise, which has cost a great deal of money and exposed the Court to pressures on its budget imposed by the Executive which the Lords of Appeal in Ordinary never encountered while they were in Parliament.' Lord Hope, Barnard's Inn Reading, 24 June 2010.

   Critically assess the above statement. Specifically comment on the rationale for the development of the Supreme Court and the perceived advantages its introduction has had over the judicial branch of the House of Lords.

Problem questions

1. Janet was recently shopping in a retail outlet of All Bright Consumables (ABC) Ltd. She asked the sales assistant to recommend a Personal Computer (PC) for her to purchase having given him the information he asked for. Janet was very clear that whilst she had little experience of computing, she required a computer to surf the Internet, run word processing, and have a camera for video chats. Finally, for entertainment she wanted to make sure it had a blu-ray disc player, and she had been told to ensure it had at least 4GB of RAM. Having received this information, the sales assistant obtained a PC from the store and Janet purchased it.

   When Janet's friend set up the computer at home, Janet was informed that the computer actually only had 2GB of RAM, it had a DVD disc player not the blu-ray as requested, and it did not have a video camera. Janet immediately returned to the store to complain and asked for a refund. The store manager refused as he said as soon as the PC was opened there could be no returns unless the PC was faulty (which it was not), and he did not believe that the sales assistant would get her order wrong. Rather, the manager suggests Janet was not clear about her requirements and could not obtain a refund just because she 'had second-thoughts' about the purchase.

Using your knowledge of the court system, explain to Janet which court(s) would hear any claim she made for a refund. Explain to her the tracking system used and how this would impact on her legal action for compensation.

2. ABC Ltd has experienced the following problem with one of its major customers and requires appropriate advice to ensure an effective resolution. ABC has a significant corporate customer, BigByte Ltd, which regularly places very large orders for PC components. However, while ABC provides BigByte with a standard trade credit period of 'full payment within 30 days', BigByte has got into the habit of paying late (sometimes as late as 90 days). ABC's concern is that if other trade customers get to know that they are relaxed about enforcing payment according to the terms of its trade credit agreement, the other customers may ask for similar extended credit periods. ABC has considered increasing the price of goods sold to BigByte so as to 'charge' the company for the additional credit but fear that any increase in price will merely result in this valued customer going elsewhere.

Advise ABC about alternative forms of dispute resolution (ADR) that could be used to resolve this situation. Specifically identify the advantages ADR may provide compared with traditional court action in relation to business relationships.

 You will find guidance about how to answer these questions online at www.oup.com/uk/marson5e/.

FURTHER READING

Books and articles

Adams, L., Moore, A., Gore, K., and Browne, J. (2009) 'Research into Enforcement of Employment Tribunal Awards in England and Wales' Ministry of Justice, Research Series 9/09.

Brown, H. and Marriott, A. (1999) 'ADR: Principles and Practice' (2nd Edition) Sweet and Maxwell: London.

Goldsmith, J. C., Ingen-Housz, A., and Pointon, G. (2006) 'ADR in Business: Practice and Issues Across Countries and Cultures' Aspen Publishing: New York.

Lord Mance (2006) 'Constitutional Reforms, the Supreme Court and the Law Lords' *Civil Justice Quarterly*, Vol. 25, p. 155.

Oliver, D. (2003) 'Constitutional Reform in the United Kingdom' Oxford University Press: Oxford.

Websites and Twitter links

http://www.cedr.com

The Centre for Effective Dispute Resolution, a non-profit organization that manages and facilitates dispute resolution services.

http://www.judiciary.gov.uk

@JudiciaryUK

The official website and Twitter account of the judiciary of England and Wales. They provide information including statistics, details of the roles of different judges, and various speeches given by higher members of the judiciary.

http://www.justice.gov.uk/tribunals/employment
Details the Tribunal Service that provides information, assistance, and online claims forms for employment actions.

http://www.justice.gov.uk/tribunals/employment-appeals
Details the cases heard by the Employment Appeal Tribunal, the grounds on which appeals may be made, and various publications and reports.

http://www.legalservices.gov.uk/civil.asp
Information from the Legal Aid Agency on topics such as ADR and human rights.

http://www.legislation.gov.uk
@legislation

This is the official list of statutes in force. The website is particularly valuable as it clearly indicates where the legislation is no longer in force or has been superseded through amendments or a more recent piece of legislation, and it shows where forthcoming changes (not yet in force) will affect the law being searched.

http://privycouncil.independent.gov.uk
The website of the Privy Council—it contains information of both the judicial and legislative branches of the Council.

https://www.supremecourt.uk
@UKSupremeCourt

http://www.youtube.com/user/UKSupremeCourt
Information, commentary, and the judgments from the Supreme Court (available from July 2009).

http://www.tribunals-review.org.uk
Leggatt Report, 'Report of the Review of Tribunals'.

ONLINE RESOURCES

www.oup.com/uk/marson5e/

For further resources relating to this chapter, including self-test questions, an interactive glossary, and key case flashcards.

PART 3
CONTRACTUAL OBLIGATIONS

Contract law is one of the most significant jurisdictions of law that businesses will face. Contracts will determine and regulate relations within the organization and with outside bodies, and will establish the dispute resolution mechanisms applicable when things go wrong. Contract law is largely based on common law and equitable principles, but increasingly statutory intervention has been necessary to codify and advance the law. This part of the book begins by identifying the elements necessary to establish a legally binding contract, before detailing the content of the contract and the consequences for breaches of the agreement.

PART 3

CONTRACTUAL
OBLIGATIONS

ESSENTIAL FEATURES OF A VALID CONTRACT 1: OFFER AND ACCEPTANCE

What makes an agreement a legally enforceable contract? When you contract on behalf of your business, will you have any rights against the other party if they fail to complete the agreed obligations? What is the legal status where an item is advertised in a newspaper or a shop window—is it an offer by the shopkeeper to sell the item? Can you force the sale of an item that displays an incorrect price on the tag? These are just a few questions the answers to which businesses must be aware of before trading, and this chapter and **Chapter 6** provide the answers.

Business Scenario 5

Alpha wrote to Beta offering to sell a 3D printer for £30,000—the letter arriving on Tuesday. Alpha and Beta had engaged in business transactions previously and consequently, even having received the offer by letter, Beta contacted Alpha by telephone to discuss the 3D printer and the offer, with an intention to accept. The conversation went well, but as part of the discussion, Alpha requested that due to the nature of the item, its value and for reasons of certainty, Beta would have to confirm the acceptance through written evidence. This evidence was required by 12pm on Wednesday and as such, Alpha agreed to keep the offer open until then.

Beta duly posted the letter of acceptance, along with a cheque for the full amount, at 6pm on Tuesday. This letter arrived with Alpha at 11.30am on Wednesday.

Shortly after the initial telephone call on Tuesday, Alpha received an offer of £35,000 for the 3D printer from Charlie, which it accepted immediately. At 7pm on Tuesday night, Alpha wrote to Beta informing it that the offer was no longer in existence due to the contract with Charlie, and was being revoked. This letter did not arrive with Beta until Friday morning at 9am.

How might your assessment of Alpha and Beta's position differ if Beta had heard from an officer of Charlie that it had completed the contract for the sale of the 3D printer from Alpha prior to Beta posting the letter of acceptance?

Learning Outcomes

- Identify the nature and essential elements of a legally enforceable agreement (**5.4–5.4.2.2**)
- Differentiate between an offer and an invitation to treat (**5.4.1–5.4.1.1**)
- Understand the implications of counter-offers terminating an offer (**5.4.1.2**)
- Identify when true acceptance has taken place (**5.4.2–5.4.2.2**).

5.1 INTRODUCTION

This chapter identifies the essential features necessary to establish a legally binding contract. It is important to note at the outset that most contracts need not be reduced in writing and indeed most of the contracts you have established today—buying a newspaper or cup of coffee—were not established in writing, even if you received a receipt. However, each of the essential features noted in this chapter and **Chapter 6** are present in forming those contracts. Before the essential features are considered, it is important to briefly note that contracts can be established by the parties exchanging promises, or by one party promising to perform an act in return for some action by the other. In this later scenario, the second party has no obligation to take any action unless they wish to enter the contract.

5.2 UNILATERAL AND BILATERAL CONTRACTS

It is important to identify whether the contract made is unilateral or bilateral. Bilateral contracts are those where one of the parties offers to do something in return for an action by the other party—they exchange promises. Each of the parties in this type of contract has an obligation to perform some action. For example, one person agrees to wash the other's car in return for having their lawn mowed. A unilateral contract is one where the first party promises to perform some action in return for a specific act, although the second party is not promising to take any action. *Carlill v Carbolic Smoke Ball Co.* is an example of a unilateral contract. There is no obligation on the person to buy the advertised smoke ball, but where they do and, as with Mrs Carlill, contracts influenza, they can claim the £100 advertised as the contractual obligations will have been completed. This case is fully discussed at **5.4.1**.

5.3 VOID AND VOIDABLE CONTRACTS

The main focus of this chapter and **Chapter 6** is to identify the essential features required to make an enforceable (valid) contract. Some contracts, however, do not obtain the status of a valid contract because the law will not recognize the agreement or it may miss one of the essential features and so not amount to a contract.

- *Void contracts:* A **void contract** is not a contract that the law will recognize and so has no legal effect. In law such an agreement was never a valid contract and consequently there are no obligations on either party.

- *Voidable contracts:* A **voidable contract** is one where the injured party has the option to affirm the contract (they can continue with the agreement and bring about an enforceable contract) or they can avoid the contract (and the contract is terminated). The key element here is that it is for the injured party to decide if they wish to proceed with the agreement or have it set aside. This must be performed within a reasonable time to be fair to each party (in contract and torts law the word 'reasonable' is often used. In the absence of specific instruction from legislation or a principle from case law this word is interpreted with regards to the facts of a particular case. In any respect, in this situation the party should act as quickly as is possible).

5.4 THE ESSENTIAL FEATURES OF A VALID CONTRACT

Having identified what a contract is, it is then important to establish how a legally enforceable contract is created. The term 'legally enforceable' contract is important because
in the absence of one or more of the following requirements the courts will not acknowledge that a legally recognizable contract is in existence. This text contends that the essential features can be subdivided into five categories, and once it is satisfied that the parties
have the legal capacity to contract, the following are the most relevant and important
features of a valid contract (**Figure 5.1**).

Figure 5.1. **The essential features of a valid contract**

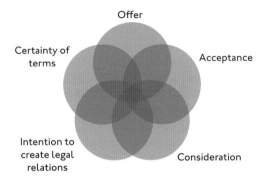

- *Offer:* The statement from the **offeror** to the **offeree** identifying the terms by which
  they are willing to be bound. This must be distinguished from an invitation to treat,
  which is a situation whereby offers are invited. Offers can be unilateral or bilateral.
- *Acceptance:* The full and unconditional acceptance by the offeree of the terms identified in the offer. If any other terms are included by the offeree then the response
  is said to be a counter-offer that terminates the first offer and will not constitute
  acceptance.
- *Consideration:* The legal element to ensure the contract is a bargain (the law will not
  enforce a 'bare' promise). The consideration only has to be sufficient, not adequate.
- *Intention to create legal relations:* The parties must intend that their agreement is to
  create legal responsibilities on both sides, resulting in possible legal consequences if
  one party fails or defaults on their obligations. This goes beyond the scope of 'social
  agreements' and intends to establish the availability of a legal remedy in the case of
  breach.
- *Certainty of terms:* The terms of a contract have to be sufficiently clear and certain to
  enable the courts to enforce the contract.

Consider

Alpha is writing to Beta with an offer to sell. There is no discussion needed here
between whether an offer is made or if this is the start of negotiations (an invitation
to treat). The key issue is about the rules of communication applicable.

5.4.1 Offer

An offer is simply an identification of the terms by which the offeror is willing to be bound. This offer is made to the offeree, who may be an individual, company, group of people, or even the entire world. The offeror is the party that establishes the terms by which they are willing to be bound and therefore they have the choice of what terms are contained and to whom the offer is made. Only the offeree may accept the offer and they must accept in the method expressed (if stipulated) by the offeror.

Carlill v Carbolic Smoke Ball Co. (1893)

Facts:

The defendants were proprietors of a medical preparation—the 'Carbolic Smoke Ball'. The company was so confident in its product that it advertised in newspapers that anyone who used the ball three times daily for a two-week period and contracted influenza would be rewarded with £100. It further identified in the advert that to demonstrate the company's sincerity, it had deposited £1,000 in a local bank to satisfy any claims. The claimant, Mrs Carlill, on the faith of this advertisement, bought one of the balls and used it as directed. However, she contracted influenza, and claimed her 'reward', although, as could be expected, the Carbolic Smoke Ball Company did not wish to pay the £100 and argued to the court why the advertisement did not constitute a contract.

The Court of Appeal held that there was a valid contract. The £1,000 being placed in the bank demonstrated the company's sincerity in paying the £100 identified in the advertisement. Carlill's acceptance was evidenced through her using the product (her conduct), and there was nothing in the advertisement that required a specific form of acceptance to be notified to the company. As such, the advertisement could be accepted by anyone who saw the advert and purchased and used, as directed, the product.

Authority for:

(In relation to this aspect of the case—as *Carlill* is authority for many propositions.) It is possible to make an offer to the entire world, and it may therefore be accepted by those persons.

5.4.1.1 Offer v invitation to treat

An 'invitation to treat' is the term used when a party invites offers (essentially the party with the goods/services to trade invites offers which they are able to accept or decline). In this context, the word 'treat' means to negotiate, hence it is an invitation to negotiate for a good or service. Cases that have established the general rule of where an invitation to treat exists did so in light of traders selling goods, advertisements, auctions, and negotiations. It should be noted that for businesses, it may be wise to sell goods under 'invitation to treat' rather than 'offers', as this provides the company with flexibility in its sales strategy.

- *Goods displaying price tags:* Goods displayed in shop windows or on the shelves in retail outlets, and those goods advertised in newspapers/on television, and so on may be offers to sell or invitations to treat. To identify which is applicable, the common law has developed the following precedents.

Pharmaceutical Society of Great Britain v Boots Cash Chemists (1953)

Facts:

Boots Chemists established shops that began to operate a 'self-service' system whereby customers could select items displayed in the shop, place them in their basket, and present these at the till to complete the purchase. On the shelves were various products, with a price marked on the packaging, and these products included various drugs and proprietary medicines that could only be sold in the presence of a registered pharmacist. The customer would select goods and present these to the cashier at a till-point, where the transaction would take place. At each till-point was a registered pharmacist who was in control of the department. The Pharmaceutical Society of Great Britain brought an action against Boots. It alleged that a 'sale' took place when a customer placed items from the shelves into their shopping basket (hence not in the presence of the pharmacist and contrary to the legal requirements). The Court of Appeal disagreed. The customer offered to purchase their selected goods at the till-point (in the presence of the registered pharmacist) where the retailer either accepted or declined the offer. Therefore, no infringement of the law had taken place.

Authority for:

Items displayed on the shelves of shops with a price tag attached are invitations to treat not offers to sell.

The Court of Appeal established the precedent that items in a shop with a price tag attached did not constitute an offer to sell, binding the shopkeeper to sell to whoever entered the shop and selected an item. This is necessary to prevent a shop from displaying goods with an incorrect price tag on and then being compelled to proceed with the contract on the basis of an innocent mistake. This precedent established in the *Boots* case was corroborated in *Fisher v Bell*.

These cases identified that the courts will generally consider goods advertised in shop windows or those with a price tag attached to constitute an invitation to treat. Whilst this is true in the widest sense, there have been instances where an item in a shop window with information regarding the price has constituted an offer, not an invitation to treat. The following case was heard in the USA (and because it is not in this jurisdiction it has limited authority as a precedent), but due to the similarities of the legal systems (the common law) it could provide evidence of how an English court may apply law in a case with similar facts:

Leftkowitz v Great Minneapolis Surplus Stores (1957)

Facts:

The company placed an advertisement in a Minneapolis newspaper regarding a sale that was to take place on a Saturday morning, 9am sharp, where two mink scarves and a stole were to be sold for $1 each (significantly below the usual retail price). Mr Leftkowitz presented himself at the appropriate counter in the store and demanded the item for $1

→

and was refused. He was informed that he could not avail himself of the special price due to a 'house rule' that stipulated the offer was only available to women. When Leftkowitz brought an action for damages the company contended that the advertisement was an invitation to treat, not an offer to sell, and hence it was within its rights to reject the offer to purchase the goods for $1. The court, however, stated that the circumstances in this case would constitute an offer to sell, which the customer was within his rights to accept.

Authority for:

An advertisement in a newspaper, or shop window, may be elevated from an invitation to treat to constitute an offer to sell if the offer is clear, definite, and explicit, and it leaves nothing open for negotiation.

This case demonstrated an alternative view to the general rule of advertisements being an invitation to treat, and demonstrates the importance of the correct drafting, and the legal significance, of advertising materials. It was the level of detail in the advertisement that established it as an offer rather than an invitation to treat. The more definite the detail and description of what is for sale and under what terms the sale will take place, the more likely the court will hold the advertisement as an offer.

Note that when prices are displayed, under the case law identified in this chapter, these are generally invitations to treat and so the trader has no obligation to sell at the displayed price. However, if a price is displayed and is done so where the trader is not prepared to sell (and in essence is deceiving the purchaser) then this is a breach of the Consumer Protection from Unfair Trading Regulations 2008 and the trader may face prosecution.

- *Advertisements:* Advertisements are a potentially problematic area often because the words used can lead buyers to assume an offer has been made. This is frequently not the case and you must exercise care to apply the law, not customer relations policies in such circumstances:

Partridge v Crittenden (1968)

Facts:

Arthur Partridge had placed an advert in the *Cage and Aviary Birds* magazine that read 'Quality British bramblefinch cocks, bramblefinch hens . . . 25s each'. Mr Thompson responded to the advert, sending payment, and he received a bird. The bramblefinch hen that was sent had a closed-ring around its leg identifying that it was bred in captivity and hence legal to sell, but it was possible to remove the ring and consequently Partridge was charged with unlawfully offering for sale a bird contrary to the Protection of Birds Act 1954. Partridge claimed the advertisement was not an offer to sell but an invitation to treat. The Divisional Court agreed.

Authority for:

Following the previous authorities, an advertisement in a newspaper, a magazine, a billboard, on television, and so on will be considered an invitation to treat.

The courts will often interpret advertisements in newspapers, magazines, and journals as an invitation to treat. With advertisements generally, whether these are through television, radio, or the Internet, the same rules apply.

- *Auctions:* The auction is a typical example of an invitation to treat. The auctioneer invites bids to the goods as advertised and can then decide to accept or decline, with completion being achieved on the fall of the hammer:

Payne v Cave (1789)

Facts:

Mr Cave made the highest bid for goods at an auction held by Mr Payne. However, before the fall of the auctioneer's hammer, Cave withdrew his bid. The question for the court was whether Cave possessed the right to withdraw a bid at an auction.

Authority for:

There was no contract. The auctioneer's request for bids is an invitation to treat. Therefore, a bid at an auction is merely an offer which may be withdrawn by the bidder at any time until acceptance.

There have also been cases concerning auctions which advertised the sale of particular items which were subsequently not included in the sale. Whether individuals who intended to offer on the (non-presented) items can claim their expenses back was considered in the following case:

Harris v Nickerson (1872–73)

Facts:

Mr Nickerson was an auctioneer who had advertised an auction (to include office furniture) to be held by him for three days. Mr Harris was a broker and travelled to the auction with the intention of bidding on the furniture. On the third day of the auction, when the office furniture was to be auctioned, all the lots were withdrawn without prior notice. Harris claimed breach of contract and attempted to recover his losses of time and expenses incurred (railway fare and his board and lodgings) as he contended the advertisement was an offer to sell those lots and as he had travelled to the auction to purchase and accept that offer. The High Court held that Harris could not recover his losses, as the advertisement was a mere declaration of intent that could not amount to an offer capable of acceptance.

Authority for:

Auctions are examples of invitations to treat. Simply advertising products in auctioneering literature does not create any obligations that those items will be included or that any subsequent offers will be accepted.

The case confirmed the previous rulings by the courts that an advertisement in the press will not, of itself, create any contract with a reader until the acceptance has been recognized in law. In the present situation, that would be that the highest, genuine, bidder at the auction makes an offer accepted by the auctioneer and forms a valid contract.

- *Tenders:* It had traditionally been considered that an invitation to tender is an invitation to treat. The party that submits the tender is making an offer and the party inviting the tender has the option to accept or decline. However, whilst this position provides the party inviting the tender with great power and seemingly little in the way of obligations to the party submitting the tender, those inviting tenders may have an obligation to 'consider' the tender:

Harvela Investments Ltd v Royal Trust Co of Canada Ltd (1986)

Facts:

Shares in the defendant company were to be sold through a sealed competitive tender (the shares being sold to the highest of two invited bidders). Harvela offered $2,175,000 and the second tender offered '$2,100,000 or $101,000 in excess of any other offer, whichever was higher.' The second tender was accepted (on the basis that it in effect constituted a bid of $2,276,000) and this led to Harvela's claim.

Authority for:

The House of Lords held that Harvela's bid had to be the one accepted. The nature of the tender, whilst only an invitation to treat, was based on fairness, and also on the basis of the reasonable expectation of the parties. The parties had invested time and effort in preparing the tender, they were invited to submit the tender, and it was reasonable for the decision to be made on the criterion described—that is, that the tenders were to be 'fixed bids.'

This element of reasonable expectation to consider a tender was followed in *Blackpool and Fylde Aero Ltd v Blackpool BC:*

Blackpool and Fylde Aero Ltd v Blackpool BC (1990)

Facts:

The company had operated flights from an airport under the control of the council. They were invited to bid for a new concession and submitted their tender on time. Despite it being the highest bid, it was not opened until after the deadline for submission had passed and because it was deemed late, it was not considered. The tender was offered to another bidder. When the council discovered this error, they argued for the bidding process to be reopened but this was objected to by the winning bidder. The Court of Appeal had to determine whether there was a legal requirement to consider all conforming tenders.

Authority for:

Whilst there is no obligation to accept a specific tender, a call for tenders does establish a collateral (separate) contract for it to be considered.

- *Negotiations:* Negotiations occur between parties in the contract process. Questions of item, price, quantity, and the terms surrounding any possible contract may come under consideration. This can lead to disagreements as to when an offer may have been made which is capable of acceptance. The courts have had to look to the parties' statements and other evidence to ascertain their true intentions:

Harvey v Facey (1893)

Facts:

Mr Facey and his wife owned a property named Bumper Hall Pen. They received a telegram from Adelaide Harvey which read: 'Will you sell us Bumper Hall Pen? Telegraph lowest cash price.' Facey responded with 'Lowest price for Bumper Hall Pen £900' and Harvey followed this with a further telegram: 'We agree to buy Bumper Hall Pen for £900 asked by you.' Facey did not reply or sell the property to Harvey who, as a result, brought an action for breach of contract and requested an order for specific performance (specific performance is a remedy (dealt with in **Chapter 10**) whereby the contract is ordered to be completed by the party in breach. Typically such an award is made where damages are not an adequate remedy and the subject matter of the contract is a unique item (land, property, antiques, and so on)). The Privy Council found that there was no contract established as no offer had been made to sell the property—only an offer to buy and acceptance of this had to be expressed and could not be implied.

Authority for:

There has to be a clear offer of a willingness from the offeror to be bound (a genuine offer to sell) for an acceptance to be possible and hence create a valid contract.

Mere negotiations between parties are insufficient to create a contract and the courts will not imply an offer in these situations. It is further demonstrated in the following case the necessity of distinguishing an offer to sell from an enquiry of an interest in purchase.

- *Request for information:* Requesting additional information with regard to a negotiation will not provide a valid acceptance of an offer nor defeat the offer through a counter-offer. Negotiations are an important element of forming a contract and the sharing of information is necessary to identify the scope of the obligations involved:

Gibson v Manchester CC (1979)

Facts:

Robert Gibson was a tenant and occupier of a council house under the control of Manchester City Council and had been actively interested in purchasing the house. In 1970 the Council undertook to offer for sale various Council-owned properties to sitting tenants and wrote to Gibson informing him that it may be prepared to sell the house to him for a price of £2,725 less 20 per cent (freehold). On 18 March 1971 Gibson wrote to the Council requesting the purchase of the house, but in May 1971 political control

→

of the Council changed, along with the policy of selling Council-owned properties, and only those houses where a legally binding contract had been established would be sold. The Council notified Gibson that the sale of the house would not be proceeding and he claimed breach of contract. The House of Lords held that as the Council had never offered to sell the property valid acceptance was not possible. All that had occurred in this case were the first steps towards negotiations for a sale which never reached fruition.

Authority for:

A request for information is not an offer capable of acceptance.

An invitation as to a willingness to enter a contract or a party's potential interest in forming a contract will not be considered an offer capable of acceptance. Negotiations have to proceed to a stage when a formal offer is made before a contract can be established:

Storer v Manchester CC (1974)

Facts:

The Council had sent the claimant information regarding the possibility of tenant's purchasing their Council-owned property. Storer completed the application form and the Council had replied with a letter requesting that the applicant sign an enclosed agreement for sale of the property and the Council would return the agreement as signed. Storer did complete and return the form but the Council did not reciprocate as promised before the control of the Council changed political parties.

Authority for:

The Court of Appeal held that a contract was formed as the letter from the Council was a firm intention to proceed with the sale when Storer returned the application form. As such, the Council was obliged to conclude the contract.

At this stage, it is possible to identify whether an offer or invitation has been created, or if negotiations are in progress rather than a formal offer having been established. However, for how long does the offer last—is it indefinitely or until acceptance has taken place? Or is some other method developed by the courts? In order for the offeror to have control over the length of time that the offer remains in existence, they may wish to incorporate methods of terminating an offer.

Consider

Alpha has communicated an offer to Beta, but following an offer from Charlie of an additional £5,000 on the asking price, Alpha wishes to retract the offer. If they wish to terminate the offer, they must communicate the termination before the acceptance has taken place.

5.4.1.2 **Termination of an offer**

It would not be prudent to make an offer and then have that offer last for an indefinite time. The offeror can incorporate whatever terms they wish into the contract, but because many contracts are not in writing (and contracts of sale need not be—see Sale of Goods Act 1979, s. 4) this 'time-scale' issue may not have been fully considered. Any offer which has been withdrawn before acceptance takes place stops any true acceptance. As a corollary, where an offer is accepted before it is withdrawn the other party must continue with the contract.

Termination can occur in a variety of ways, such as:

- *The death of the offeror:* If the offeror has made an offer that has not been accepted before their death, then the offer dies with them. If the offer has been accepted and then the offeror dies, where practicable the contract must still be performed (by the dead person's estate or executors). However, if the contract requires some element of personal service by the offeror (such as in contracts of employment) the contract will come to an end under the doctrine of frustration.

- *Expiry of a fixed time limit:* As stated previously, the offeror may incorporate any terms into a contract by which they are willing to be bound. This may include a time limit for acceptance which must be adhered to (as acceptance is full and complete acceptance of the offeror's terms). If the time limit for acceptance expires, then the offer dies and cannot be later accepted.

Consider

Alpha has informed Beta that the offer for the purchase of the 3D printer will remain open until 12pm on Wednesday, with a written answer to be provided. This is Alpha's offer and therefore they may identify the terms for acceptance. Note, however, that simply because Alpha has informed Beta of the offer remaining open until 12pm Wednesday does not oblige Alpha to keep the offer open. There is no consideration (see **Chapter 6**) from Beta to make this term enforceable.

- *Acceptance must be within a reasonable time:* The parties can incorporate terms into the contract, such as for time limits when an offer will expire, but where no such clause has been included, a reasonable time may be implied into the contract. What is reasonable, in this sense, is dependent upon the individual circumstances of a case:

Ramsgate Victoria Hotel v Montefiore (1865–66)

Facts:

Montefiore applied to purchase shares in the hotel in June but shares were not issued until November. Due to the time delay between his application and the issue of the shares, Montefiore refused to accept the shares and an action was raised for non-acceptance. It was held that whilst his offer of purchase did not contain any provision for expiry, the court considered that allotment must take place within a reasonable time, and this had not been achieved. As such Ramsgate's action failed.

Authority for:

In the absence of any specific provision for the expiry of an offer the court will imply one which is reasonable in the circumstances. This will vary depending upon the item being contracted for—for example shares will have a relatively short time for an offer to be accepted; perishable goods such as fruit and vegetables will possibly have an even shorter time.

- *If the offer is rejected:* The offeree can inform the offeror that they do not wish to accept on the offer made, which will reject the offer and destroy it. Rejection can be explicit in this manner and it can be through the actions of the party (such as making a counter-offer).

- *If a counter-offer is made:* In the negotiations of contracts the offeror establishes the terms by which they are willing to be bound, but where the offeree does not accept but alters the terms of the offer to suit themselves, this is a counter-offer. The positions of the parties (as offeror and offeree) are reversed. The legal significance of contractual negotiations is that any counter-offer destroys the original offer and means that the previous offer cannot later be accepted. The stages of offers/counter-offers can be seen in **Figure 5.2** in relation to the negotiations in *Hyde v Wrench:*

Hyde v Wrench (1840)

Facts:

On 6 June Wrench offered to sell land for £1,000 to Hyde. On 8 June Hyde replied, expressing 'acceptance' at a purchase price of £950. Wrench rejected the offer of £950 and later Hyde contacted Wrench stating he would accept the original offer and pay £1,000 for the land. Wrench declined to proceed with the sale. The court held that if Hyde had unconditionally accepted Wrench's offer to sell at £1,000 a binding contract would have been established that the court would enforce. However, by Hyde making his own offer of £950 he had (implicitly) rejected the first offer, which made it impossible to accept it at a later date.

Authority for:

A counter-offer terminates the original offer.

Care has to be taken when involved in negotiations. If a party attempts to obtain the best terms and reject an offer through their counter-offer, they will be unable to accept on that previous offer unless the other party offers it again.

- *Revocation of the offer:* The offeror has the right to revoke their offer at any time until acceptance has taken place. This is true even where the offeror has promised to keep the offer open for a specific period of time (*Dickinson v Dodds*, covered later). The exception to this general rule is where the offeree has provided some consideration for the 'benefit' of the offer remaining available. The stipulation to this rule is that the onus is on the offeror to inform those to whom they have made the offer that it has been revoked. As such, it is incumbent on the offeror to effectively communicate the revocation to the offeree (*Payne v Cave*, see **5.4.1.1**).

Figure 5.2 *Hyde v Wrench*

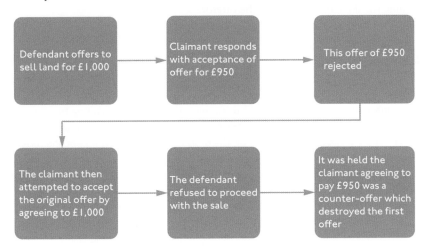

When communicating through the post, revocation is not effective until it has been communicated and hence received, by the offeree:

Byrne & Co. v Leon Van Tienhoven & Co. (1879–80)

Facts:

The case involved the sale of tin plates. An offer was sent to the claimant on 1 October with a revocation of this on 8 October. However, the claimant received the original offer on 11 October and confirmed its acceptance by telegram. It further sent a letter of acceptance on 15 October. On 20 October, the claimant received the defendant's letter of revocation and brought an action for breach of contract.

Authority for:

The postal rule differs when considered in relation to revocation. It is not sufficient to post a letter of revocation for it to be effective, it must be communicated.

This is unlike the postal rule on acceptance where acceptance takes effect on posting whether this is received or not.

Consider

Alpha's letter retracting their offer of the 3D printer to Beta would therefore only be effective when received (9am on Friday), not when posted. However, let us refer to the second element of the question about Beta's knowledge of the completed contract prior to Beta posting the letter of acceptance. Revocation must be communicated and if Beta knew before posting their acceptance of the 3D printer no longer being available for sale, this would satisfy the requirement of effective communication.

Revocation of an offer is also effective where this has been communicated to the offeree by a reliable third party rather than the offeror:

Dickinson v Dodds (1875–76)

Facts:

On 10 June 1874 Mr Dodds provided a document to Mr Dickinson stating that he would agree to sell his houses to Dickinson for £800 and the offer would remain open until 9am, 12 June. Dickinson had decided on the morning of 11 June to accept the offer but did not signify this to Dodds, as he believed he had until 9am the following day to communicate his acceptance. In the afternoon of 11 June Dickinson was informed by an agent for Dodds, that Dodds had agreed to sell the property to another person (and hence had implicitly revoked the offer to Dickinson). On hearing this news Dickinson sought to accept the offer through a formal letter. However, Dodds proceeded with the sale to the third party. Dickinson attempted to have this agreement rescinded and have his 'contract' enforced. The Court of Appeal held that the document sent to Dickinson was an offer that could be withdrawn at any time before it was accepted insofar as the revocation was communicated to the offeree.

Authority for:

Revocation of an offer can be effective through express words and also some act inconsistent with the continuance of the offer (in the present case selling it to another person).

In situations of 'unilateral' contracts (whereby one party makes an offer which can be accepted by a member of a class of persons to whom the offer has been made—for example *Carlill v Carbolic Smoke Ball Co.*, covered at **5.4.1**) the option to revoke the offer may be more difficult. In *Carlill*, it would be quite unrealistic to communicate the revocation to every person who may have seen the advertisement in a newspaper, but taking reasonable steps (such as another advertisement in the same newspaper revoking the offer) may be acceptable. Revocation can occur at any time *until* it has been accepted, but if the acceptance includes the performance of an act, once that act has been started (as acceptance through conduct) it may not be revoked:

Errington v Errington and Woods (1952)

Facts:

Mr Errington wished to provide his recently married son with a home and so purchased a house through a building society by paying a lump sum and leaving the balance on the mortgage to be paid by weekly instalments. The father kept the title to the house but promised that if his son and daughter-in-law paid the instalments he would transfer the ownership to them. The father died before the debt on the house was fully repaid and left all his property, including the house, to his widow. The widow brought an action for possession of the house against the daughter-in-law but this failed as the father had created

→

a contract and once this had been accepted, although incomplete of full performance, it could not be revoked. The father had made a promise to his son and daughter-in-law and only if the son and daughter-in-law had failed to continue with the payments on the mortgage (the acceptance) would revocation be possible.

Authority for:

Once acceptance has begun (albeit here incompletely) it cannot be subsequently revoked.

5.4.2 Acceptance

Having established that an offer has been made, the offeree has the option to accept or decline. This creates the agreement that will begin the process of substantiating the essential features of a legally binding contract. Agreement may be relevant when considering the issue of mistake to a contract and how this impacts on the enforceable contract.

5.4.2.1 Unconditional and full acceptance

The offeror establishes the terms by which they are willing to be bound, and as such, acceptance of those terms must be unconditional. In many cases this may constitute a 'yes' or 'no' reply to an offer made. There are situations where such a simple exercise may not be possible and it requires the courts to give direction as to how acceptance may be established:

- *The battle of the forms:* The 'battle of the forms' is commonly referred to when organizations use standard form contracts. The most common example of standard form contracts is where you purchase an item from a high-street retailer. The contract you receive has already been drafted and you must either accept these terms, or decline them and (usually) obtain the item elsewhere. This method is adopted to save time for both parties and to stop protracted negotiations at the store. When two businesses are trading and each has its own standard form contract then problems can arise. How can the courts settle disputes between them when there is disagreement as to which contract is to be used?

British Road Services v Arthur Crutchley Ltd (1968)

Facts:

The claimants delivered a consignment of whisky to the defendant's warehouse and the claimant's delivery driver handed the defendants a note to be signed that contained, among other things, the claimant's terms and conditions. This note was stamped by the defendants as 'received under Arthur Crutchley Ltd's conditions' and handed back to the driver. It had to be decided on which terms the contract was based as the consignment of whisky was stolen.

Authority for:

The court held that by stamping the delivery note, this established a counter-offer that was impliedly accepted by the driver delivering the consignment. Therefore, the contract had been made on the defendant's conditions.

The Court of Appeal was faced with a similar case, and established the concept of the 'first/last shot approach' to determining on which of the parties' standard terms a contract was based:

Butler Machine Tool Co. Ltd v Ex-Cell-O Corporation (England) Ltd (1979)

Facts:

In May 1969 Butler, sellers of machine tools, were contacted by Ex-Cell-O to supply a machine. Butler provided in the quotation for a price of £75,535 and delivery to be made in 10 months. The terms set out in the quotation contained a provision for a price variation clause whereby the goods would be charged at prices at the date of delivery. Ex-Cell-O replied with an order on its terms and conditions (including a 'tear-off' acknowledgement strip) that did not include a price variation clause. This was completed and returned by Butler. Various communications passed between the companies but none settled the 'dispute' over the acceptance or otherwise of the price variation clause. The machine was ready for delivery in September 1970 and Ex-Cell-O accepted delivery in November. Butler, when invoicing Ex-Cell-O, invoked the price variation clause and requested a further £2,892 in addition to the quoted price. It was held that the parties had established an agreement, but it had not been fully expressed. Hence, to determine which was the effective contract and thus the terms binding the parties, reference had to be made to whatever documents were present. As Ex-Cell-O had included an acknowledgement strip that Butler signed and 'accepted', the contract was based on these terms, without the price variation clause.

Authority for:

In agreements between businesses using standard form contracts, the 'first' or 'last shot' approach may be adopted by the courts when identifying the operative contract.

Butler v Ex-Cell-O identified the 'first/last shot approach' adopted by the courts. During the negotiations between the parties the issue of the incorporation of the price variation clause had not been settled. However, a machine had been produced and delivered to one party, and used by the other, and the courts had to determine which contract to use. It would be unfair of the courts to state that, having studied the facts, no contract was present. It would be very difficult to identify with any certainty the benefit gained by the party using the product to apportion and distribute that value. Consequently, the court had to determine which was the operative contract. As Butler had signed the 'tear-off' acknowledgement of Ex-Cell-O's order, and the terms of this order were to prevail, this 'first shot' was the operative contract.

Tekdata Interconnections Limited v Amphenol Ltd provided further evidence of the significance of the first/last shot approach. This ensures that the party which 'fires the last shot' in commercial transactions will have the contract established on its terms.

5.4.2.2 *Communication of acceptance*

Outward evidence of the offeree's intention to accept an offer has to be demonstrated and communicated in order for effective acceptance to occur. As such, where the offeror identifies silence as a means of acceptance, this will not be effective. The presumption is that if the offeree wishes to be bound by the contract, they will at least go to the trouble of making some outward sign/gesture to indicate the acceptance. Insofar as the rule on silence is adhered to, the offeror may insist on how acceptance is to be achieved. If included in the offer, then it must be complied with to provide effective acceptance:

Yates Building Co. Ltd v R J Pulleyn & Sons Ltd (1975)

Facts:

The defendant issued the claimant with an option to purchase land and stipulated that the response must be made through recorded or registered post. The claimant sent the acceptance through ordinary mail which the defendant rejected, referring the claimant to the requirements for acceptance. A claim was made for breach of contract.

Authority for:

There was no enforceable contract. As the offer established clear terms by which the manner of acceptance was to be made, even an equally effective method of acceptance was not sufficient.

The general rule, however, in the absence of specific forms of communication of acceptance is that where acceptance deviates from that stipulated in the offer but it is as quick, or quicker, than that required in the offer, this will generally be accepted as a valid method of acceptance.

Consider

Alpha has required acceptance to be through written evidence. A letter will be sufficient for this purpose and this was communicated by the expiry of the time limit imposed by Alpha.

The overriding element for acceptance to be established is that it must be communicated. Examples of the communication of acceptance may be through written reply, an oral statement, or implied through conduct. Conduct has already been demonstrated as acceptance in *Carlill*.

Alexander Brogden v Metropolitan Railway Co. (1877)

Facts:

The directors of the Metropolitan Railway Company (MRC) brought an action against Brogden & Co. for a breach of contract, a contract that Brogden denied was even in

→

existence. Brogden were colliery owners in Wales and had supplied MRC with coal and coke for use in their locomotives. A draft agreement was created to formalize the arrangement but no further action was taken on it, although orders continued on the basis of the terms stated in the document. Several orders passed between the companies and in these the document was frequently referred to. Problems began in the supply between the companies, including deficient supplies of coal and excuses for lack of orders, until December 1873 when Brogden declined to continue the supply of coal. This led to the breach of contract claim.

Authority for:

A long-term relationship between parties could amount to evidence of an agreement (although formal written acceptance of a contract was missing). The parties' conduct was evidence of acceptance of contractual terms.

The postal rule of acceptance also applies even where that letter never reaches the offeror (subject to certain rules—see *Re London and Northern Bank, ex parte Jones* [1900]):

Dunlop v Higgins (1848)

Facts:

An offer for the sale of pig iron was accepted through the posting of a letter. However, bad weather delayed the delivery of the letter and led the seller to reject the 'acceptance' as being out of time. A breach of contract claim was made.

Authority for:

The court held that the contract had been established on the posting of the letter. This applies even if the acceptance never reaches its destination due to outside factors (e.g. such as weather, the fault of the post office, and so on).

- *Acceptance through conduct:* The House of Lords had to decide whether a completed contract had been established in *Brogden*. There was an assertion that the document was merely an intention to create a contract that would have meant no contract was in existence. However, it was held that a valid contract had been established between the parties due to their actual conduct. A contractual document had been drafted by the principals of the relevant companies and was used in negotiations between the parties, and whilst it had not been signed, the intentions from the parties' actions enabled an agreement to be deduced. Therefore, the breach of contract claim was successful.

The case was important in that a formal, written contract is not required to establish a valid contract. The parties' intentions may identify a contract and if a period of time establishes a pattern of behaviour which may place obligations and expectations on the parties, then this may 'harden' an agreement into a contract:

Novus Aviation Limited v Alubaf Arab International Bank BSC(c) (2016)

Facts:

The parties were involved in discussions whereby Alubaf would provide funding for the purchase of an aircraft to be leased to Malaysian Airlines. A commitment letter and a management agreement were established before Alubaf pulled out of the deal—before the aircraft had been purchased. A space for signatures was included in the commitment letter, which Alubaf had signed but Novus had not, although the parties continued to advance the transaction evidenced by the incorporation of new companies, the opening of bank accounts, and the appointment of directors. Novus argued that a legally binding agreement had been established and Alubaf's withdrawal was a repudiatory breach.

Authority for:

The Commercial Court heard arguments from Alubaf as to why a binding contract was not established, including that its Head of Treasury and Investment did not have the authority to bind the company (through signing the commitment letter). The arguments were rejected and Novus was awarded damages. The case illustrated the acceptance of the contract through conduct. There was no express stipulation that the signature strip on the letter had to be signed and the parties' conduct was sufficient evidence of acceptance. More careful drafting of the documents could have avoided this problem—express stipulations will override inferences based on conduct.

- *Silence as acceptance:* The offeror may not have stipulated a specific form which acceptance must take, and consequently the courts may consequently decide a 'reasonable' method. It must be noted, however, that, as a general rule, the offeror cannot dictate the offeree's silence as a valid acceptance:

Felthouse v Bindley (1862)

Facts:

Mr Felthouse's nephew had placed several horses for sale by auction. Before the auction took place, Felthouse wrote to his nephew stating that he wished to purchase one of the horses and included the following in this communication 'If I hear no more about him, I consider the horse mine at £30.15s.' The nephew intended to sell the horse to his uncle, and made no reply. The nephew approached the auctioneer (Mr Bindley) and informed him that the horse was not to be included in the auction. The auctioneer, by mistake, did sell the horse and Felthouse attempted to stop the 'sale'. However, Felthouse only had the right to sue if he actually owned the horse and the court concluded that he did not as there had been no acceptance of his offer to buy the horse. The court held that the acceptance must be communicated clearly and could not be interpreted from the silence of the nephew.

Authority for:

Silence is not effective acceptance of an offer.

This case is relevant to the necessity for an outward sign of acceptance and for the offeree to positively communicate their acceptance. This is because the offeree should not be placed under the burden of a rejection every time an offer is forwarded to them and if the offeree does intend to accept an offer, they can make the effort to fulfil this requirement without undue inconvenience. However, it is possible to infer acceptance from silence between businesses, and it may be allowed if requested by the offeree. In the event that unsolicited (not requested by the recipient) goods are sent to a business, then s. 2 of the Unsolicited Goods and Services Act 1971 provides that a subsequent demand for payment constitutes a criminal offence. Protection is also given to consumers who are sent goods that they have not ordered through the Consumer Protection (Distance Selling) Regulations 2000.

Consider

Alpha have been communicating with Beta through the post and have asked for acceptance of their offer to be evidenced in writing. As such, if the postal rule of acceptance is applicable, did Beta's acceptance take place at 7pm on Tuesday (when the letter was posted) or 11.30am on Wednesday (when received)?

- *Acceptance by post:* A contract may be created through an exchange of documents via the post. Where offer and acceptance takes place through written communication rather than face-to-face negotiations, there exists the possibility that such communication may be lost, undelivered, or delayed through postal strikes or public holidays. The general rule established with the post (where it is a valid means of acceptance) is that acceptance is valid on posting:

Adams v Lindsell (1818)

Facts:

The parties were contracting for the sale of wool and were communicating by means of the post. In the course of these communications the defendant misdirected the letter of acceptance and it was subsequently delayed. Due to this delay, the acceptance was not received before the defendant, not receiving the anticipated acceptance by the due date, sold the wool to another party. The court held that as a matter of business efficacy, acceptance was effective when posted. This established the 'postal rule' of acceptance.

Authority for:

Where the post is a valid means of acceptance (usually because the offer has been made through the post or the offeror asks for the post to be the means of acceptance) then acceptance is binding upon posting, not upon the receipt of the acceptance.

The postal rule applies insofar as the correct address and postage were included in the sent letter:

Re London and Northern Bank, ex parte Jones (1900)

Facts:

Dr Jones made an offer in a letter and handed this to a postman to be delivered. The postman had no authority to receive letters, only to deliver them. Despite an attempted revocation later the same morning, the bank attempted to accept on the offer. Was there a contract?

Authority for:

The general rule of contract law—that acceptance of an offer is effective on posting, does not apply where that letter has been posted incorrectly (not posted in a postbox, handed to the post office, correctly addressed, safely sealed, postage paid and so on).

The court was adamant that this was fair. It hypothesized that if the offeror was not bound under a contract until the acceptance by the offeree had been received, then the offeree should not be bound until he received notification that the offeror had received his acceptance and assented to it. This system could not enable businesses to carry out their operations with any certainty and consequently the decision was based on business efficacy. Even if the letter was delayed, where this is not the fault of the offeree, there was still valid acceptance:

The Household Fire and Carriage Accident Insurance Company v Grant (1878–79)

Facts:

Mr Grant had applied to purchase shares in the claimant company. Whilst his application was accepted and his name added to the list of registered shareholders, his share certificates were not sent nor was any letter confirming the issue received by Grant. Grant did not pay for his shares but dividends were credited to his bank account. When the company went into liquidation the liquidator sought payment from Grant for his shares. Grant objected but the court held there was a valid contract and he owed the payment for his shares.

Authority for:

The postal rule was effective and despite a letter of acceptance not reaching Grant, the contract was effective on posting. The judges held there was value in the postal rule, and its advantages outweighed any disadvantages.

The postal rule is not effective, however, in situations where the express terms of the contract state that the acceptance must be received and in writing. Nor does it apply, per Lawton LJ in the following case, where the rule would 'produce manifest inconvenience and absurdity'.

Consider

Would *Holwell Securities v Hughes* alter your answer to the earlier 'Consider' point about when acceptance will be deemed to have been effective? If Alpha wants evidence of acceptance in writing, this would suggest it became effective when received at 11.30 on Wednesday.

Holwell Securities v Hughes (1974)

Facts:

Dr Hughes granted to Holwell a six-month option to purchase a property with notice to be provided in writing. Five days prior to the end of the six-month period, Holwell attempted to exercise the option through the posting of a letter. Hughes claimed this was not received and refused to proceed with the sale. Holwell argued the postal rule applied and acceptance was valid on posting.

Authority for:

The postal rule was still 'good law' but it did not displace the general principle of contract law of communication of acceptance. Where the parties required 'notice in writing,' this overrode the postal rule and required actual notice of acceptance.

- *Instantaneous forms of communication:* Compared with the postal rule and its 'business efficacy' decision, the courts have traditionally reverted to the common rule of acceptance being effective when communicated and received (in cases involving instantaneous forms of communication):

Entores v Miles Far East Corporation (1955)

Facts:

Entores, based in London, made an offer on 8 September 1954 to agents (based in Holland) of Miles Far East Corporation by telex for the purchase of 100 tons of copper cathodes. This offer was accepted on 10 September through telex received in Entores' offices in London. Entores claimed a breach of contract and sought to serve notice of a writ on Miles Far East but could only do so if the contract was created in England and therefore came under the jurisdiction of English law. Miles Far East alleged the contract was made in Holland and was consequently not within the jurisdiction of the court. The Court of Appeal held that due to the instantaneous means of communication in this case, acceptance was effective (and the contract concluded) in London—and within the jurisdiction of the English court.

Authority for:

With instantaneous means of communication, the 'postal rule' of acceptance is departed from and acceptance is effective when received, not when posted.

This ruling can be extended to other forms of instantaneous forms of communication such as a telephone or fax.

CONCLUSION

This chapter has sought to identify the importance of the common law in the development and evolution of the rules underpinning contract law. Offer and acceptance are essential features in the formation of an agreement, and these are furthered by the requirement of consideration, intention to create legal relations, and to have certainty of terms. These last three elements are considered in **Chapter 6**.

SUMMARY OF MAIN POINTS

- Offer and acceptance are the first stages in establishing an agreement that may form a legally binding contract.

Offer

- An offer is the statement of terms by which the party is willing to be bound.
- The offer can be made to a person, group, or even the entire world.
- An offer has to be distinguished from an invitation to treat (which is an invitation to negotiate).
- Items on display on the shelves in a shop, advertisements in newspapers, items displaying a price tag in shop windows, and information in auction catalogues have traditionally been held to be invitations to treat.
- Where detailed information is provided on the quantities of items and the time and date of their limited availability, the courts have been more willing to hold these as offers rather than invitations to treat.
- An offer may be accepted until it is terminated.
- Termination can occur by a party's express words, actions, through a counter-offer, lapse of time, or through some other consistent action.
- The offeror can revoke the offer at any time until acceptance takes place but this must be communicated and received by the offeree.

Acceptance

- Acceptance can only be made by the offeree or their agent.
- Where standard form contracts are used, the 'battle of the forms' is decided by the 'first' or 'last shot' approach.
- There must be outward evidence of acceptance. Silence, generally, will not constitute valid acceptance.
- The 'postal rule' establishes that where the post is a valid means of acceptance, acceptance is effective upon posting, not when the letter is received.
- With instantaneous forms of communication, the standard rule of acceptance being effective when received remains.

SUMMARY QUESTIONS

Essay questions

1. 'The "battle of the forms" when applied to businesses trading using their own standard term contracts may be resolved through the "first shot" or "last shot" approach. This is a wholly unsatisfactory situation and must be remedied through legislative action.'

   Discuss the statement with reference to case law and judicial pronouncements.

2. At what point does a display in a shop window become an offer to sell rather than an invitation to treat? Compare and contrast the cases of *Pharmaceutical Society of Great Britain v Boots Cash Chemists*, *Fisher v Bell*, and *Leftkowitz v Great Minneapolis Surplus Stores*.

Problem questions

1. Jack is considering selling his prized collection of comedy books to Diane. On Monday Jack writes to Diane offering to sell the collection for £100 and he further provides that he will keep the offer open until Thursday at 5pm. On Tuesday, following a change of mind, Jack sends a fax to Diane revoking the offer; however, Diane's fax machine is out of paper and she does not receive the message until Wednesday morning.

   On Tuesday, Diane had already posted to Jack her acceptance of the offer. Jack never received the letter of acceptance and as such at 6pm on Thursday Jack sold the collection to Bill.

   Advise the parties of any legal rights and liabilities.

2. Mortimer wished to sell his antique gold watch. He therefore sent his chauffeur with a note to Randolf offering to sell him the watch for £50,000 and asking Randolf to give his reply to the chauffeur.

   Being undecided, Randolf did not give his reply to the chauffeur and sent him back to Mortimer. One hour later Randolf posted a letter to Mortimer accepting his offer.

   Has a valid contract come into existence?

 You will find guidance about how to answer these questions online at www.oup.com/uk/marson5e/.

 ## FURTHER READING

Books and articles

Jackson, B. S. (1979) 'Offer and Acceptance in the Supermarket' *New Law Journal*, Vol. 129, p. 775.

Rawlings, R. (1979) 'The Battle of the Forms' *Modern Law Review*, Vol. 42, No. 6, p. 715.

Unger, J. (1953) 'Self-Service Shops and the Law of Contract' *Modern Law Review*, Vol. 16, No. 3, p. 369.

Twitter links

#contractlaw

@Contracts

A very useful link to debate, commentary, and analysis regarding all aspects of domestic and international contract law—note, this source is not regulated in the same way as are journals, books, and official law firm webpages. As such, exercise caution as to the veracity of the information presented.

 ## ONLINE RESOURCES

www.oup.com/uk/marson5e/

For further resources relating to this chapter, including self-test questions, an interactive glossary, and key case flashcards.

6 ESSENTIAL FEATURES OF A VALID CONTRACT 2: CONSIDERATION, INTENTION TO CREATE LEGAL RELATIONS, AND CERTAINTY OF TERMS

This chapter continues the discussion of the essential features of a valid contract. Of particular importance is the requirement that the contract be a 'bargain' as, without 'consideration' being present, the courts will not enforce what they deem to be a 'bare promise'. Contracts must also intend to be legally binding, and not just social or domestic agreements, and they must contain certain terms. Without an understanding of these crucial elements, agreements may be concluded but they will not create an enforceable contract.

Business Scenario 6

Clive and Jane are friends. Clive is a plumber who was asked to replace a boiler in Jane's house and install a new central heating system. This job was to start on 1 April and be completed by 10 April. The total cost was £5,000 with payment due in full on completion.

Having completed the job, Clive asked Jane for the payment, but Jane said that she was short of money and would pay him the following week. Jane did this because she had heard that Clive was in financial difficulties and his business may fail. When Clive returned for his payment, Jane informed him that she did not want to give him the full amount, but would pay him £3,000 in cash if he would take that as full payment and sign a contract to that effect. If he did not accept the £3,000 offer, Clive would have to take Jane to court and by this time his business would certainly have become insolvent.

In desperation, Clive agreed to accept the £3,000 and signed the contract that this was in full consideration of the work completed. Further, he agreed to refrain from seeking any further payment.

Learning Outcomes

- Identify and explain consideration in contracts (**6.2**)
- Explain the interaction between consideration and promissory estoppel (**6.2.3**)
- Explain privity of contract and how this affects who may enforce a contract or be sued on it (**6.3**)
- Ascertain how the courts establish when parties intend to create an enforceable contract (**6.4**)
- Explain the necessity of a legally enforceable contract containing definite and certain terms (**6.5**).

6.1 INTRODUCTION

This chapter continues identifying the essential features of a valid contract. Once an agreement has been established, consideration (what makes the agreement a 'bargain' and enforceable) must be present, the parties must intend that the agreement is to be legally binding, and its terms must be sufficiently certain to identify the rights and obligations of the parties. Further, a contract is enforceable by those parties to it (known as privity of contract), although this doctrine has been extended to provide rights for third parties where the contract has been made for their benefit. Having established that each of the features from **Chapter 5** and this one are present, the agreement 'evolves' into a binding contract.

6.2 CONSIDERATION

Consideration in a contract has frequently caused confusion for students, but this should not be so. Students are at an advantage when reading about, and applying legal principles of contract law because of their experience in regularly establishing contracts. Consideration is a necessary component of 'simple' contracts, and these are the contracts that are most common in consumer transactions. Certain contracts are required to be made by deed, and in these circumstances the absence of consideration does not make the contract unenforceable.

Consideration in contract law is merely *something of value* that is provided and which acts as the inducement to enter into the agreement. The definition that is most frequently used is from the seminal case on the issue, *Currie v Misa*, where Lush J stated:

> A valuable consideration, in the sense of the law, may consist either in some right, interest, profit, or benefit accruing to the one party, or some forbearance, detriment, loss, or responsibility, given, suffered, or undertaken by the other.

Despite that unwieldy definition, it is sufficient at this stage to recognize consideration as the bargain element of a contract—the price paid for a promise. Courts will enforce a 'bad' bargain (such as agreeing to sell something for a much lower price than its worth) but it cannot enforce a 'bare' (or gratuitous) promise. Consideration must be given in return of the promise made, and it must move from the **promisee** (therefore, the party who wishes to enforce the contract must provide (or have provided) the other party with consideration). The promisee may exchange promises with the **promisor**, or they may provide some act of forbearance, to establish good consideration.

An example of consideration may be seen in an agreement to mow someone's lawn. The promisor (A) agrees to mow the lawn of the promisee (B). The detriment to A is that they give up their time and effort to perform the task and the benefit is that they obtain pay or some goods/service in return for the act. The benefit for B is that they have their lawn cut (and therefore is given this service) and the detriment is either paying money, or providing goods or a service in return for the act of A. Therefore, consideration can be payment, or providing a service, or it can even amount to a future promise (so in the above example, if B agreed to wash A's car in return for the lawn being cut, that would be good consideration).

6.2.1 Executed and Executory Consideration

The two types of consideration are Executed and Executory.

- *Executed:* Executed consideration is often seen in unilateral contracts and involves one party making a promise in return for an act by the other party. The offeror has no obligation to take action on the contract until the other party has fulfilled their part. For example, A offers B £100 to build a wall, payment to be made on completion. B completes the building work and is entitled to the payment from A. If B did not want the work, or did not complete it, A would not have (taken action) and paid the £100.

- *Executory:* Executory consideration is performed after an offer is made and is an act to be executed in the future (hence *executory*)—it is an exchange of promises to perform an act. This form of consideration is frequently seen in bilateral contracts and may lead to a valid contract being established. An example may be where an order for an item is made with the promise that payment will be made in the future (e.g. when the item is delivered), and the other party promises to deliver the products ordered and receive the payment. The fact that consideration has not yet occurred but will take place in the future does not prevent it being 'good' consideration and in the event of, for example, non-delivery, this may lead to a **breach of contract** (assuming the remainder of the essential features are present).

- *Consideration must be sufficient (not adequate):* Consideration must have some legal, material value but it does not need to be adequate in relation to a 'fair' price for the contract.

White v Bluett (1853)

Facts:

Here a son complained to his father about not having as much money as his siblings. The father promised the son that he would lend him money if he would stop complaining. When the father died, his estate attempted to recover the debt from his son.

Authority for:

There must be valid consideration to establish a binding contract. The debt was repayable as the son was not giving anything in return for the father's loan.

In *Bolton v Madden* Blackburn J stated that 'the adequacy of the consideration is for the parties to consider at the time of making the agreement, not for the Court.' The courts are not in a position to assess what the value of a particular item or service is worth. Further, value may change rapidly or be whatever the parties consider it is worth, and also freedom of contract enters the equation. However, the consideration must have some value that can be assessed in financial terms. As the parties are free to negotiate terms, the courts do not believe it is their place to question the value of the bargain.

> ### Thomas v Thomas (1842)
>
> **Facts:**
>
> Executors of a deceased person's estate agreed for a house and its surrounding premises to be provided for life for the tenant. A sum of £1 per annum was to be paid towards the cost of the ground rent, and the house was to be kept in good repair.
>
> **Authority for:**
>
> In determining the existence of consideration, it must have some legal value and is not concerned with the motives of the parties. The £1 payment was a 'bargain' which created the binding contract and hence an enforceable contract, even though the value of the consideration was in reality not adequate for the benefit provided.

The courts have established that even if an item is of little value in itself, it may represent a benefit to one of the parties and therefore be good consideration, such as the submission of a chocolate bar wrapper in a sales promotion.

6.2.2 Good Consideration

What will establish 'good' consideration can be seen through the development of the case law, and this is underpinned by the rules outlined later. **Figure 6.1** provides an overview of what, from case law, constitutes good consideration.

> ### Chappell & Co. Ltd v Nestlé Co. Ltd (1959)
>
> **Facts:**
>
> Nestlé were manufacturers of milk chocolate products. Nestlé entered into a contract with Chappell where Nestle were permitted to sell copies of the song 'Rockin' Shoes' (Chappell owned the copyright). Purchasers duly paid 1s. 6d for each record and submitted three of Nestlé's chocolate wrappers with the application. The contract provided that Chappell was to be paid a proportion of the 1s. 6d for each copy of the song Nestlé sold, but it was silent as to the 'value' that each of the wrappers reflected. As Nestlé received a profit and benefited from each sale of its chocolate bars, Chappell considered that these should also form part of its remuneration. The House of Lords held that each of the wrappers amounted to good consideration, as the whole object of selling the record was to increase the sales of chocolate. This was so even if Nestlé was to discard the wrappers: they represented sales of its product.
>
> **Authority for:**
>
> Consideration must be sufficient, not adequate. As evidenced in this case, whilst the chocolate wrappers had no real value in themselves, they did represent three sales of packets of Nestlé's chocolate and hence provided a benefit to Nestlé.

The consequences of this case can be seen (e.g.) where vouchers are offered in magazines providing a discount on goods and services. The voucher/token will identify a stipulated value of (e.g.) 0.001p because such vouchers do have a legal value and will constitute consideration.

Figure 6.1 Good consideration

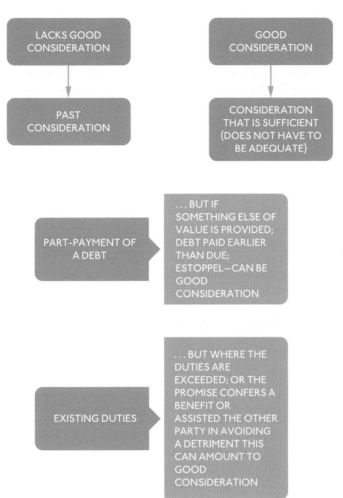

- *Consideration must not be past:* If a party performs an act and following the completion of the act the other party makes a promise, then the act will not have been sufficient to provide consideration. For example, if A gives B a lift to work in A's car and at the end of the journey B expresses his thanks and states that he will give A £10 for her trouble, there is no enforceable contract to enforce the £10 payment if none is received. This is because the lift was given voluntarily and not for gain. B did not agree to provide £10 for the lift and as the offer was made after the act, it did not amount to good consideration:

Re McArdle, Decd. (1951)

Facts:

Mr McArdle died in 1935 and left a bungalow that he owned to his wife. McArdle had four children and one of the four (Montague) and his wife, lived in the property.

➔

→

Montague's wife had been improving the property and had repaired it at a cost of £488. Later, Montague submitted a document to his brothers and sister in which they agreed to pay his wife the £488 for the improvements. However, there was a disagreement about whether the payment should be made and when Montague's wife attempted to enforce the agreement the Court of Appeal held that no contract had been established. The agreement to pay the sum was made after the work had been undertaken and there was no clear intention or expectation that payment would have been made.

Authority for:

Past consideration is not good consideration unless *Lampleigh v Brathwait* (see later) applies.

The decision rested on the fact that since all the repair work had been completed before the document had been agreed, the consideration was wholly past and the agreement to 'repay' the £488 was a **nudum pactum**. If the children had agreed before Marjorie McArdle's actions to pay £488 for the work being carried out, that would have amounted to a contract supported by consideration, and consequently would have been enforceable. Consideration has to be a bargain and the children in this case had already benefited from the work being carried out, so there was no bargain for the agreement. Beyond this general rule regarding past consideration, exceptions do exist:

Lampleigh v Brathwait (1615)

Facts:

Brathwait had killed another man and requested that Lampleigh seek from the King a pardon for his actions. This necessitated many days of following the King in attempting to raise and discuss this matter. Lampleigh was successful in obtaining the pardon and as a result, Brathwait made a promise to pay £100 for the service, but this payment was never made. It was held that Lampleigh was able to recover the £100 because the court felt that both parties must have contemplated that payment for the service would be made.

Authority for:

In comparison with *Re McArdle*, the following are necessary for an enforceable contract to exist when supported by past consideration:

1. the act that is the subject of the contract must have been requested by the promisor;
2. there must have been in the contemplation of both parties that payment would have been made;
3. all the other elements of a valid contract must have existed.

In a modern setting, if no price had been established for the act performed (such as the supply of a service), then the court would look to s. 51 of the Consumer Rights Act 2015 and determine a 'reasonable' price. Also, in most employment situations, where, for example, an employee has performed work or hours beyond what their contract stipulates, this may imply additional payment is expected and reasonable:

Re Stewart v Casey (Casey's Patents) (1892)

Facts:

Mr Casey was employed to promote the defendant's patents. When the majority of the work was completed the defendant promised to pay him for his service through a one third share of the patents. They later attempted to remove his name from the register of patents.

Authority for:

Despite the promise of payment (consideration) being made after the work had been completed, this was not a case of past consideration. The parties entered into the agreement on the understanding that remuneration would be provided.

• *Existing duties are not good consideration:* The courts have identified that consideration must be 'real and material' and as such, if the promisor is merely receiving what they are already entitled to, then there is no consideration furnished. For example, if you do some act, which you already have an existing duty to perform, then this will not provide a benefit for the promisor and hence a contract based on this will be unenforceable due to lack of consideration:

Collins v Godefroy (1831)

Facts:

The claimant was under a subpoena (an official order) to appear as a witness in a trial involving Godefroy, and whose evidence was to the benefit of Godefroy. To appease Collins, Godefroy offered to pay him a sum in respect of his trouble. Godefroy did not pay and this led to Collins' action to recover the money promised. In the judgment, the court acknowledged that Godefroy did make the promise, and received a benefit from Collins' attendance at court. However, Collins was already under a duty to give evidence (due to the subpoena) and this did not constitute real or 'good' consideration. Collins had done no more than what he already had a duty to do.

Authority for:

Performing an existing duty (and doing no more) will not constitute good consideration.

This rule seeks to ensure that improper pressure cannot be applied to renegotiate a contract on better terms for the promisee:

Stilk v Myrick (1809)

Facts:

The captain of a vessel on a voyage from London to the Baltic promised the existing crew an equal share of the wages of two seamen who had deserted (and who could not be replaced). On the vessel's return, the wages were not paid.

→

Authority for:

In the action to recover the wages, the court held that there was no consideration provided in support of the promise. The seamen were under an existing duty to 'exert themselves to the utmost to bring the ship in safely to her destined port.'

Exceeding an existing duty can establish good consideration for a promise:

Hartley v Ponsonby (1857)

Facts:

During a voyage half of the ship's crew deserted. The remaining sailors were promised additional money if they completed their voyage, but on their return the captain refused to pay the additional sum.

Authority for:

The court held the sailors were entitled to the extra pay as they exceeded their existing duties due to the significant risk of continuing the voyage with insufficient crew. They were therefore entitled to negotiate a new contract.

A more recent example of this rule can be seen in the following case:

Harris v Sheffield United Football Club Ltd (1987)

Facts:

The football club questioned whether they were required to pay South Yorkshire Police (represented by Harris) for the policing of the football matches held at its stadium. The argument presented was that the police force had a duty to protect the public and thus there was no consideration for requesting payment from the club.

Authority for:

The Court of Appeal held that supervision of the football matches went beyond protecting the public and maintaining law and order, and amounted to a 'special police service' that was good consideration.

Further, performance of an existing duty may be held as good consideration from the following case:

Williams v Roffey Bros & Nicholls (Contractors) Ltd (1991)

Facts:

Roffey Bros was a firm of building contractors that had entered into a contract with Shepherds Bush Housing Association Ltd in September 1985 to refurbish a block of flats. Roffey subcontracted various carpentry jobs to Mr Williams for a total price of £20,000. However, by the end of March 1986 it was common knowledge that Williams was in financial difficulty based on the fact that the price of £20,000 was too low to enable Williams to operate at a profit (at court, evidence was supplied by a surveyor, who stated a reasonable price should have been £23,783). Williams informed Roffey that he would be unable to complete the work. Roffey was concerned at this development because, in part at least, Roffey was subject to a delay clause in the contract that would have led to it being liable for substantial fees if the contract was not completed on time. Therefore Roffey agreed to pay Williams a further sum of £10,300 in excess of the original £20,000 for the work to be completed at the agreed date. When the additional payment was claimed, Roffey refused to pay on the basis that Williams had only performed an existing duty.

Authority for:

Where the promisee has actually conferred on the promisor a benefit or has assisted them in avoiding a detriment, and no unfair pressure or duress was used in the renegotiation, an existing duty may be good consideration.

The Court of Appeal held that the promise to pay the additional sum was binding. Despite Roffey's argument to the contrary, consideration was provided as Roffey did receive a benefit, or at the very least would avoid a detriment, through the completion of the work and the avoidance of the penalty fee and/or the difficulty in hiring a new subcontractor. The requirement of the benefit or avoiding a detriment factor of the decision in *Williams v Roffey* was confirmed in *Re Selectmove*:

Re Selectmove (1995)

Facts:

Selectmove had been subject to a winding-up petition by the Inland Revenue (IR) for arrears of tax under Pay As You Earn. Selectmove appealed on the ground that in October 1991 it held a meeting with the IR where it was agreed that due to Selectmove's cash flow problems, the tax owed would be paid in arrears of approximately £1,000 per month. The tax inspector who made the promise informed Selectmove that if it did not hear from the IR again, the plan outlined for the repayments would be acceptable. However, some time later, the IR did petition for the company to be wound up. The Court of Appeal held that the tax inspector who made the arrangement with Selectmove did not have the authority to bind the IR, and dismissed Selectmove's claim to have the petition set aside. The agreement was not enforceable as there was no consideration to support it.

Authority for:

Part-payment of a debt will not amount to good consideration, and where the promisee is merely performing an existing duty, this will not establish an enforceable contract.

Selectmove argued that in providing the payments, albeit late and over a longer period of time than required, there was a benefit to the IR. If wound up, the IR would be unlikely to receive the full amount of tax owed from the company, where the arrangement entered into would provide full repayment. However, the Court of Appeal distinguished *Williams v Roffey* as that case involved performing an act, whereas in the current case it was simply the repayment of money, and essentially could be considered the part-payment of a debt that is not, generally, good consideration.

Consider

Can Jane pay £3,000 in full settlement of her bill from Clive and prevent Clive from seeking the balance? No, part-payment of a debt is not good consideration regardless of whether Clive agrees to this or not. Clive would be advised to accept the £3,000 and then bring proceedings to recover to remaining £2,000.

- *Part-payment as consideration:* It is a general rule of contract law that part-payment of a debt will not prevent the party owed money from later claiming the balance. This is even if they have agreed to take the lower sum:

Pinnel's Case (1602)

Facts:

The claimant was owed the sum of £8 10 s and the defendant, through agreement, paid £5 2 s in full settlement. Could the claimant succeed in claiming the balance owed?

Authority for:

Despite the claimant accepting the lesser amount, the full amount could be recovered. The court held that there was no consideration in a part-payment of a debt unless the payment was made and accepted before the due date and/or the part-payment included some 'non-monetary' chattel.

Generally because there is no advantage for the party taking a lesser sum than that owed:

Foakes v Beer (1881–85)

Facts:

John Foakes owed £2,090 19s to Julia Beer but was in financial difficulties. He entered an agreement with Beer where she would not take any action to recover the sum owed if Foakes would agree to pay an initial sum of £500, and then £150 every six months until the full amount was repaid. Due to the financial difficulties suffered by Foakes, Beer further stipulated in the agreement that she would not claim any interest on the sum due. However, later Beer did sue Foakes for the interest that would have accumulated with the late payment.

Authority for:

The House of Lords held that Beer was entitled to the interest on the payment, even though she had agreed not to claim. The promise by Foakes to pay the money owed did not amount to sufficient consideration, as he was only doing what he was obliged to do, which was to pay the money, and there was no benefit to Beer for the agreement.

Consider

Would your answer differ if Jane offered £3,000 to Clive as well as a new spanner in full settlement? Remember, the courts will not assess the adequacy of non-cash consideration. If it has a legal value, the courts will uphold a bad bargain as readily as a good bargain.

A debt may be extinguished by proving something else of value other than money (a good or a service), whether this is to the value of the sum owed or not (as consideration need not be adequate). However, the general presumption of why a lower sum or part-payment cannot provide good consideration is that money is a constant factor (£1 is £1). Also, exceptions exist to this rule regarding part-payment. If the party has paid a lower amount, but has done so at an earlier date, then this may amount to consideration; or if there have been goods or another benefit provided along with the lower payment then this may also provide good consideration.

D&C Builders Ltd v Rees (1966)

Facts:

D&C Builders was in financial difficulties, and Rees owed the firm £482. Rees offered D&C a cheque for £300 'in completion of the account' or D&C may not get any payment at all. This was accepted by D&C, which then brought the action for the remaining money (£182).

Authority for:

The Court of Appeal held that D&C was entitled to claim the owed money as there was no consideration for the lesser amount and the financial pressure applied for the acceptance resulted in no true accord (agreement) being established.

The rule remains regarding the ability of the party who has accepted a lesser sum than owed to still claim the balance. The major exception to this rule, alongside the others noted earlier, is the doctrine of **promissory estoppel**.

6.2.3 The Doctrine of Promissory Estoppel

Whilst the rule of part-payment not being good consideration was established through the common law, the courts also created an equitable defence, which stops a party that has made a (gratuitous) promise from reneging.

Consider

Could Jane bring a counter-claim against Clive insisting that he made a promise not to recover the remaining money and she relied on this promise? No. Promissory estoppel will allow a promise lacking consideration to be legally binding, but it is only available as a defence (a shield) and not a cause of action (a sword).

Combe v Combe (1951)

Facts:

A husband promised to make maintenance payments to his wife following their separation. He never made the payments and the wife brought a claim for recovery of those sums arguing promissory estoppel.

Authority for:

The wife's claim failed. The court considered that promissory estoppel is only available as a 'shield not a sword' and as such can only be used in the defence of a claim against the party, not a cause of action.

For example, if a party makes a promise to accept a lower rent than that contracted for, and the other party relied on this promise, the promisor may be estopped (prevented) from reneging on this promise and claiming the balance owed if the court considers this unreasonable. This is a very interesting area of law, although not greatly developed through case law (and it is beyond the scope of this text to discuss it in any detail). Essentially, it seeks to suspend rights rather than to remove them (although this is a moot point in many instances).

Tool Metal Manufacturing Co v Tungsten Ltd (1955)

Facts:

Tungsten were infringing patents owned by Tool Metal. On discovery, Tool Metal offered to waive the rights to claim damages for this infringement in return for Tungsten paying a 10 per cent royalty and a further 30 per cent as compensation where Tungsten's sales exceeded 50kg in a single month. Tungsten considered these figures excessive, but agreed to them so as to avoid legal action for patent infringement. Tungsten had difficulties in making the payments, particularly during the years of the war, and Tool Metal agreed to waive the 30 per cent payments during this period.

Authority for:

Tool Metal were unable to claim the 30 per cent payments during the years of the war but were able to claim the payments afterwards. Promissory estoppel suspends legal rights, it does not extinguish them.

The seminal case on promissory estoppel is *High Trees* and the *obiter dicta* provided by Lord Denning.

Central London Property Trust v High Trees House Ltd (1956)

Facts:

High Trees House leased a block of flats at £2500 per annum from Central London Property Trust in 1937. With the outbreak of war, and the consequent bombings in

→

London, occupancy of the property was reduced. To limit the adverse effects, and to stop the property becoming unoccupied, High Trees entered into a new agreement in January 1940 with Central London Property under which the rent would be reduced by half. This period of reduced rent was not specified, but in the following five years High Trees paid the reduced rent. In 1945, the flats were full and Central London Property claimed for the full rent to be paid. The High Court held that when the flats became fully let, the (prior) full rent could be claimed.

Authority for:

Denning's statement (albeit obiter dicta) was that where the promisor makes a promise that is relied on by the promisee, they will be unable to renege on it due to the doctrine of promisory estoppel, even in the absence of consideration moving from the promisee.

Consideration is often linked with the concept of privity of contract, where the contract involves, or is for the benefit of, a third party. This is because the party whom the contract concerns has not provided any consideration and hence has no rights or obligations under the agreement.

6.3 THE DOCTRINE OF PRIVITY OF CONTRACT

The doctrine of privity of contract arose through the common law as a means of regulating the relationships between parties to a contract. The doctrine establishes that only parties to a contract may sue or be sued on it, and consequently provides rights and imposes obligations on those parties alone. This is important as many situations involve contracts where a right or benefit is to be provided for a third party. Even though the contract is for the benefit of this third party, they are unable to enforce it as they are not privy to the contract. The two elements necessary to enforce a contract are that the claimant must be a party to it, and there must be consideration provided by the promisee. These have become somewhat merged in the cases, although they remain legally separate.

- *'Only a person who is a party to a contract can sue on it' (Per Lord Haldane in Dunlop v Selfridge):* Only a promisee may enforce a contract as others are not privy to it:

Dunlop Tyre Co. v Selfridge (1915)

Facts:

Dunlop Tyre Company had contracted with a wholesale distribution company called Dew & Co. The contract provided that Dew would obtain an agreement from the retailers to whom it sold tyres that they would not sell them below the list price established by Dunlop. Dew obtained the agreements, and in a contract with Selfridge, it transpired that Selfridge sold tyres below this contracted price. Dunlop sought to obtain an injunction against Selfridge from continuing to sell the tyres at the price, and also initiated a damages action for breach of contract. The House of Lords held that there was no agreement between Dunlop and Selfridge. The contracts were between Dunlop and Dew, and Dew and Selfridge, therefore Selfridge was not party to the contractual agreement between Dunlop and Dew, and Dunlop could not enforce the contract. Selfridge was not the agent of Dunlop, and there was no consideration from Dunlop in return for Selfridge's promise to sell at the list price.

Authority for:

The common law rule established in the case was that only parties to a contract had obligations and rights on it.

- *Consideration must move from the promisee:* It is a necessary aspect of contract law that there must exist a bargain element to establish an enforceable contract:

Tweddle v Atkinson (1861)

Facts:

Mr Tweddle was engaged to marry Miss Guy and the fathers of the couple agreed to pay a sum of money when they got married. The contract stated that the husband should have the right to bring an action if either party failed in their obligations to pay the money. Mr Guy, however, died before the couple were married and hence before any money was paid. Following the wedding, Mr Tweddle attempted to enforce the contract from Mr Guy's estate; however, he had not provided any consideration to Mr Guy for the promisee to pay him. Mr Tweddle was merely a beneficiary to the contract and not a party to it.

Authority for:

The promisee must provide a good consideration to the promisor in order for a contract to be made. (Note, this rule is subject to the exceptions discussed at **6.3.1**.)

Having stated the tests that have developed the doctrine of privity, it must be observed that the doctrine could, in certain circumstances, produce unfairness and inconvenience to the parties. As a consequence the common law created many exceptions.

6.3.1 The Exceptions to Privity

Various exceptions to the general rule of privity have developed through the common law and examples of these are identified as:

- *Agency:* An agent is someone who has the authority to conclude binding agreements on behalf of someone else (known as the principal). This means that if an agent makes a contract with a third party, and the third party is aware that the person is acting as an agent with the authority of the principal, the principal can sue and be sued on the contract as if it were they who had agreed the contract:

Scruttons Ltd v Midland Silicones Ltd (1962)

Facts:

Scruttons were a company providing dock workers and were hired by a shipping company. The contract between Midland and the shipping company included a limitation clause that damage to goods through negligence would be restricted to $500 per unit. The dock workers damaged a drum containing chemicals and Scruttons attempted to rely on the limitation clause, despite Midland being unaware of the contract between the shipping company and Scruttons.

Authority for:

The House of Lords would not allow the dock workers to benefit from the limitation clause. Third parties may take advantage of a contract as agent where: the third party was intended to benefit from the term in the contract, the contracting party was also contracting as agent for the third party, the contracting party had authority to contract on this basis, and any problem with consideration to the agreement was overcome.

- *Collateral contracts:* A contract established between two parties may indirectly create another contract with a third party:

Shanklin Pier v Detel Products (1951)

Facts:

Shanklin employed a firm of contractors to paint its pier. Shanklin had negotiated with a paint manufacturer (Detel) about the suitability of its paint, and having received such assurances that it would last for seven years, included a term of the agreement with the contractors that they must purchase and use Detel's paint for the purpose of the job. However, when the paint was used it only lasted for three months before beginning to peel, therefore Shanklin brought an action for damages against Detel. Detel claimed that privity of contract stopped Shanklin from suing them.

Authority for:

The court held a collateral contract had been established between the two parties following the contract between Shanklin and the contractors. Further, consideration had been established for the promise through Shanklin's insistence that the contractors use Detel's paint.

- *Trusts:* A person may transfer property to a second person (known as the trustee) who maintains the property for the benefit of others (known as a beneficiary). The person who has created the trust identifies the rules by which the trust is to be administered, and if these terms are not complied with, the beneficiary may seek to enforce it:

> ### *Les Affreteurs Réunis v Leopold Walford (1919)*
>
> **Facts:**
>
> A broker negotiated a charter-party. The owner of the vessel promised to the charterer that payment of a commission would be made to the broker.
>
> **Authority for:**
>
> The court held the charterer to be a trustee of the promise to the broker and it was thus enforceable against the owner.

- *Insurance contracts:* A third party may be able to claim under an insurance policy that has been established for their benefit. This is despite the fact that they did not create the contract or pay the premiums, and can be most commonly seen in life insurance policies where the benefit is provided for the insured person's family.
- *Restrictive covenants:* Restrictive covenants are used to protect land and bind purchasers as to the provisions laid down which benefit adjoining owners and interested parties in the area:

> ### *Tulk v Moxhay (1848)*
>
> **Facts:**
>
> An owner of several houses in Leicester Square sold the garden in the centre of the premises to the purchaser, who covenanted to maintain the gardens in their present condition and enable individuals' access to, and use of, the gardens. This land was later sold and the purchaser (Moxhay) announced that he intended to build on the land, despite being aware of the covenant. Mr Tulk, who owned houses adjacent to the land, applied to the court for an injunction to restrain the action of building on the land.
>
> **Authority for:**
>
> The court held that the covenant would be enforced against Moxhay and all subsequent purchasers.

Note that in *Law Debenture Trust Corp. v Ural Caspian Oil Corp.* an injunction awarded by the court will be restricted to negative injunctions.

- *Contracts for interested groups:* A contract may be established by one party but for the interests of themself and others. Whilst the other parties have no right themselves to initiate a breach of contract claim, as there is no contract between themselves and the supplier of the good or service, the contracting party may seek that the court takes the losses of the other parties into account when determining damages:

> ### *Jackson v Horizon Holidays Ltd (1975)*
>
> **Facts:**
>
> The Court of Appeal considered a claim for damages from Mr Jackson for the disappointment he suffered at the lack of available facilities (as promised) in a holiday. The
>
> →

brochure for the holiday stated that there was a mini-golf course, an excellent restaurant, swimming pool, health salons, and so on, none of which materialized. Horizon Holidays accepted liability as to the sub-standard holiday, but Mr Jackson also wished to claim damages for his family's disappointment, and Horizon Holidays asserted that he was unable to do so.

Authority for:

The court awarded Mr Jackson £1,100 in damages for the breach of contract and disappointment for himself and his family, as Mr Jackson had entered the contract partly on their basis.

Subsequent to the case, the House of Lords criticized the decision in *Jackson* in the following case;

Woodar Investment Developments Ltd v Wimpey Construction UK Ltd (1980)

Facts:

Wimpey contracted for the construction of a development and, as part of the agreement, were to pay a third party £150,000 on completion. Wimpey ended the contract before paying the £150,000. Woodar brought the claim for the payment on behalf of the third party.

Authority for:

Woodar's action failed. In reversing the decision in *Jackson v Horizon Holidays*, the Lords affirmed the general rule of privity of contract which prevented the recovery for or on behalf of a third party.

It is therefore questionable whether a similar case would be decided in the same manner as *Jackson*. If the case did involve a package holiday, and there existed a loss of enjoyment, then the Package Travel, Package Holidays and Package Tours Regulations 1992 enables the person who entered into the contract to claim on behalf of the others in the party.

6.3.2 Reform of the Law

It had for many years been considered that the law on privity should be reviewed and this was articulated by an independent legal review body (the Law Commission published 'Privity of Contract: Contracts for the Benefit of Third Parties' (Cmnd 3329; Law Com. No. 242) in 1996, which recommended the rights for third parties to enforce contracts). The privity rule was considered unfair as it prevented those parties who had a genuine interest in a contract from being able to take any action on it, and many other countries (including those in Europe, Australasia, and North America) already had provision to allow such individuals to play an active part in the contract. This concern led to legislative action in the form of the Contracts (Rights of Third Parties) Act 1999. The legislation was not enacted to replace the common law that had been developed, but rather to add rights for the third party. It enabled a third party to enforce the terms of a contract if the contract expressly provided for it, or if the contract conferred on them some benefit (unless the contract did not intend that the relevant term should be actionable by the third party—s. 1). This involves the third party being named in the contract to enable them to claim under the Act.

Themis Avraamides v Colwill and Martin (2006)

Facts:

Themis Avraamides (TA) entered a contract with a company to renovate bathrooms. The company was later sold to Colwin and Martin (C and M) and a term of the contract of sale was that C and M would complete existing orders. The renovation of the bathrooms was not to the satisfaction of TA and, in the absence of a contract between TA and C and M, TA attempted to enforce their rights under the Contracts (Rights of Third Parties) Act 1999.

Authority for:

The Court of Appeal assessed the use of s. 1(3) of the Act and that as the contract between the company and C and M did not expressly identify third parties (including TA), the claim had to fail.

This Act further enables the third party to enforce the contract and seek damages as they would have been able to if they had been a full party to it (s. 1(5)). However, the third party will be unable to claim these damages if the injured party has already claimed (s. 5). The second section of the Act continues protecting third parties by preventing the parties from varying or cancelling the contract without the third party's permission unless this has been expressly stated in the contract. There are limitations to the Act such as preventing a contract being enforced by a third party against employees in contracts, or in contracts concerning the carriage of goods (s. 6).

6.4 INTENTION TO CREATE LEGAL RELATIONS

For the parties to be able to sue and be sued on a contract, they must **intend it to create legal relations**. 'Legal relations' means that the parties view the agreement as a legally enforceable contract and a breach of the contract could result in a remedy being sought. The courts have traditionally looked to the parties' intentions, which may be viewed in light of what a 'reasonable person' would have considered the intentions to be.

Consider

Is the agreement between Jane and Clive legally binding? Probably yes. They may be friends, but the nature of the work and the value of the job would likely mean that they intended this to be a legally binding agreement. There would have been a legitimate expectation that Clive expected payment.

In determining their intentions, the courts will look to the parties' use of words and the context in which they use them.

Parker v Clark (1960)

Facts:

Mrs Clarke wrote to her niece (Mrs Parker) inviting her to sell her property and for Parker and her family to live with Clarke. In the letter, Clarke also promised to leave this property to Parker on Clarke's death. Parker wrote back to Clarke accepting the offer. Later, and following an argument, the Parkers were asked to leave the property and they brought an action for breach.

Authority for:

It was held that whilst this was a social relationship, there was an intention for it to be legally binding. The sale of Parker's property and the changing of Clarke's will demonstrated its legally binding nature.

The presumptions of contract and the intention to create legal relations have fallen into one of two camps (as outlined in **Figure 6.2**). Those involving social and domestic arrangements are generally presumed as not intended to be legally binding, unless this is specifically established in the agreement. On the other hand, in business and commercial

Figure 6.2 Presumption of contract and intention to create legal relations

arrangement, the presumption is that the parties do intend to create legal relations, and if one of the parties wishes to rebut this presumption, they must produce evidence in support of this contention. Situations exist that sit somewhere between these two camps, where the parties have a social relationship but also negotiate an agreement that may be viewed as commercial. In such a scenario, the onus is placed on the party wishing to assert the contract to demonstrate tangible grounds that they intended to create legal relations (although this onus is less burdensome than if the relationship had been purely domestic).

John Sadler v George Reynolds (2005)

Facts:

Mr Reynolds agreed to have Mr Sadler ghostwrite his autobiography. However, Reynolds contracted another person to undertake the work.

Authority for:

There had been a contract between the parties. Whilst the meeting where the agreement was established was 'somewhere between an obviously commercial transaction and a social exchange' Reynolds knew Sadler was an experienced journalist who made money from ghostwriting. He met Sadler in this capacity.

In the first case dealt with in this section, it can be seen that the courts have viewed that agreements between a husband and wife will not generally be considered to have been intended to be legally binding.

Balfour v Balfour (1919)

Facts:

The parties were husband and wife. The husband was a civil engineer, employed by the Government of Ceylon as Director of Irrigation. Following their marriage, the couple lived in Ceylon together until they came to England when the husband was on leave. When the husband's leave was finished he returned to Ceylon while the wife remained in England and he agreed to contribute £30 per month for her living expenses. It transpires that some time later significant differences arose between the husband and wife. He agreed he would pay the £30 per month for her maintenance as agreed, and some time later the wife commenced divorce proceedings. The wife was seeking to recover the money agreed between herself and her husband that had not been paid. Her claim failed.

Authority for:

Arrangements between husband and wife will not presume to constitute a legally binding contract.

The case demonstrates the need for the parties to agree and confirm that the contract intends to be legally binding for an enforceable contract to be established. *Balfour* identifies that social or domestic arrangements will be deemed *not* to intend to create legal relations unless specifically identified by the parties. Note, however, that such a presumption is not made when the married couple are separated.

Merritt v Merritt (1970)

Facts:

The husband left his wife and went to live with another woman. The marital house was jointly owned by the husband and wife and the husband agreed in writing that he would pay her £40 per month so she could meet the repayments if she would pay the other charges relating to the mortgage. When the mortgage was fully repaid, he would transfer his share of the property to her. Following the repaid mortgage, the wife brought an action for a declaration that the house belonged to her.

Authority for:

The Court of Appeal held the agreement was binding. Spouses who are separated, unlike cohabiting married couples, generally intend their agreements to be legally binding. This was furthered by the evidence of a written agreement between the two.

The interpretation of the parties' intention to create legal relations in social arrangements has also been extended to friends and social acquaintances.

Hadley and Others v Kemp and Another (1999)

Facts:

Tony Hadley and the other claimants were members of the pop group Spandau Ballet, who brought an action against a fourth member of the group (Gary Kemp) and the Reformation Publishing Company Ltd. Hadley et al stated an oral agreement had been established in 1980–81 when the band were on the verge of being famous and successful, where Mr Kemp would share with the other members his 'publishing income' (Gary Kemp was credited as being the composer of the band's lyrics and music). However, following 1988 (when the relationship of the band members soured), no further payments were made. Hadley argued that this act constituted a breach of contract. The High Court decided that there was no contract (and hence no breach) because, inter alia, four of the band members had been at school in North London together (and the fifth member was the brother of one of the four), the band was established to play music together rather than make money, and as such the parties did not intend to create legal relations.

Authority for:

The presumption of parties not intending their agreements to be legally binding is applied to social acquaintances where there has been a prior history between the parties.

The parties in social or domestic arrangements must make clear, through express words or actions to the contract, or provide some positive outward sign to establish that they intend the agreement to be a legally binding contract.

Simpkins v Pays (1955)

Facts:

A grandmother (Pays), her granddaughter, and a lodger (Simpkins) regularly entered competitions in a newspaper. They each shared the costs of entering the competitions and had agreed to share in any prize money. When one of the competition entries won, the prize (£750) was claimed in the name of the grandmother and the lodger claimed one-third of the money. Pays refused to provide this money on the basis that this was a social arrangement and not legally enforceable.

Authority for:

The courts disagreed and held that the nature of sharing the costs of entry and the specific agreement elevated this beyond the typical social arrangement to one where the parties had intended to create legal relations.

Between commercial parties, intention to create legal relations is presumed unless the parties establish an agreement to the contrary.

Rose and Frank Company v JR Crompton (1925)

Facts:

Rose and Frank Company was an organization based in the United States trading in carbonizing tissue paper. Rose and Frank began trading with JR Crompton and later with a third company (Brittains Ltd). The three companies entered into an agreement under which the English companies agreed to confine the sale of all of their carbonizing tissue in the United States and Canada to Rose and Frank; and Rose and Frank confined its purchases of the tissues exclusively to the two English companies. This arrangement included a clause to the effect that the agreement was in honour only and not legally enforceable. When a disagreement occurred between the companies, a breach of contract claim was made. The House of Lords held that the arrangement had not created a binding contract because of the clause inserted that it was 'in honour' only and hence had removed this essential feature of a valid contract.

Authority for:

The presumption that business/commercial contracts intend to be legally binding may be reversed where the parties clearly identify an agreement to be binding in honour only.

The final element required in a valid contract is that the terms of the agreement are sufficiently certain for the courts to determine the boundaries of the agreement and by what terms the parties had accepted to be bound.

6.5 CERTAINTY OF TERMS

The terms of the contract must be certain if they are to be considered sufficiently precise to be enforced by a court. The courts will not rewrite a contract which has been incorrectly or negligently drafted. Of course, the courts may ignore a term of a contract which is meaningless:

Nicolene Ltd v Simmonds (1953)

Facts:

A contract was prepared on the basis that it was on one of the parties 'usual conditions of acceptance'. In reality there were no usual conditions of acceptance and the defendants attempted to escape from the contract on the basis that this was a meaningless term and the contract failed because of it.

Authority for:

The Court of Appeal held the term to be meaningless, but in this respect it could simply be ignored and the rest of the contract remained.

Further, the courts may look to particular customs in a trade/industry in an attempt to remove the uncertainty in the parties' intentions:

Shamrock SS Co. v Storey & Co. (1899)

Facts:

A contract was established for a vessel to load coal at Grimsby dock, but at the time a strike was affecting collieries in South Wales. This led to a backlog of other vessels attempting to use the dock, resulting in a delay in the vessel getting into the berth. An exclusion clause was included in the contract concerning actions of striking individuals which, beyond the control of the freighter, might prevent or delay the loading of the ship.

Authority for:

The court rejected the argument that this excused the delay as there was no strike at the place where the defendant's coal was procured. That this indirectly led to an increase in the use of the Grimsby dock was irrelevant to the parties' contract.

. . . and consideration of the previous dealings between the parties to ascertain any terms omitted in a contract may be required (consider in particular Lord Wright's comments in *Hillas & Co. Ltd v Arcos Ltd*). It is also worthy of note as to why such eventualities exist. Uncertainty may not be present simply due to poor drafting or some incompetence, but rather it may reflect changing conditions (where products have a 'lead time' before delivery can take place, and these are taken into consideration).

Consider

The terms of the agreement between Clive and Jane are sufficiently clear and certain to make them enforceable. However, if the price and dates by which the works were to be completed were not settled, or there were other elements of the agreement which were to be agreed in the future, the courts would likely consider these too speculative and uncertain to establish a binding contract.

There may exist situations where the parties establish 'an agreement to agree' that the courts may consider too vague.

Scammell and Nephew Ltd v HC and JG Ouston (1941)

Facts:

An agreement was reached between the parties for Scammell to supply a van for a price of £286 on hire purchase terms over a two-year period. As part of the deal, Ouston agreed to trade in an older vehicle for £100, however following a disagreement between the parties Scammell refused to supply the van.

Authority for:

There was no contract as there was a lack of certainty over important terms in the contract. Issues including the instalments to be paid and their frequency were missing from the agreement.

The agreement may fail due to uncertainty:

May & Butcher v R (1934)

Facts:

The parties agreed with a State body to purchase tents on terms which included 'a price to be agreed.' When the agreement broke down the court had to determine whether a contract had been reached.

Authority for:

There was no contract. The terms were too uncertain and an agreement to agree is not binding on the parties.

However, the courts will attempt to identify the legal effect of such terms.

Sudbrook Trading Estate Ltd v Eggleton (1982)

Facts:

As part of a lease, the tenant was provided with an option to purchase the freehold of the property at a price to be agreed between values of two surveyors, one appointed by each party. The tenant obtained a valuation and wished to exercise the option. The landlord refused to appoint a surveyor and argued there was no contract as the clause relating to the price was too vague and uncertain.

Authority for:

The clause was not uncertain as, whilst not identifying a purchase price, it did clearly outline the mechanism to determine it.

Parties must ensure that the terms contained within contracts are sufficiently precise and detailed to enable the parties, and indeed the courts if necessary, to identify the true intentions and responsibilities contained therein. As per Lord Wright 'It is a necessary requirement that an agreement in order to be binding must be sufficiently definite to enable the court to give it a practical meaning. Its terms must be so definite, or capable of being made definite without further agreement of the parties, that the promises and performances to be rendered by each party are reasonably certain.' Specifically, where a term is meaningless, then this term, if not the entire contract, may be considered as not forming a valid contract or contractual term. However, if this is simply a means to attempt to avoid the contract, the Court of Appeal has already limited the scope of such arguments. In *Nicolene Ltd v Simmonds* (see **6.5**) a contract was prepared on the basis that it was on one of the parties 'usual conditions of acceptance'. In reality, there were no usual conditions of acceptance and the defendants attempted to escape from the contract on the basis that this was a meaningless term and the contract failed because of it. The Court of Appeal held the term to be meaningless, but in this respect it could simply be ignored and the rest of the contract remained. A further example of a term in a contract which is meaningless and cannot be enforced is demonstrated in the following case:

Guthing v Lynn (1831)

Facts:

In the negotiations for the sale of a horse, a clause was inserted into the contract that a further £5 would be paid to the offeror if the horse 'proved to be lucky' for the purchaser. This clause led to a claim for the £5.

Authority for:

It was held to be ineffective as it lacked certainty as to what 'lucky' meant.

If the agreement has already begun, and the parties are performing obligations on the basis that a valid contract is in existence, the courts are much less likely to hold that there is no contract.

Percy Trentham Ltd v Archital Luxfer Ltd (1993)

Facts:

Percy Trentham was the main contractor of industrial units and Archital were walling sub-contractors. Quotations for the work, and offer and counter-offer, were exchanged between the parties without a formal contract ever being signed. The sub-contracted work was completed, but as this was late and led to the main contractor sustaining penalty payments, Percy Trentham attempted to recover this cost in damages. Archital argued there was no sub-contract in existence.

Authority for:

The Court of Appeal held there was a contract. An agreement was established between the parties and they were performing obligations on the basis that a valid contract was in existence.

The courts will also attempt to give effect to agreements between businesses where there was clear evidence of an intention to create legal relations.

> ### *Durham Tees Valley Airport Ltd v BMI Baby Ltd (2010)*
>
> **Facts:**
>
> The defendants agreed to operate two aircraft from the airport for a ten-year term. There was no identification in the contract of minimum passenger movement or flight details. As such, was there a contract?
>
> **Authority for:**
>
> The Court of Appeal held there was a contract capable of enforcement. The missing terms were implied on the basis of business efficacy.

CONCLUSION

This chapter has concluded the provisions required that establish a valid, enforceable contract. The agreement must contain each of the provisions, and the cases identified in this chapter and **Chapter 5** will assist in recognizing the factors the courts take into consideration when determining the existence of a contract. Having identified the essential features of a valid contract, the next step is to determine possible restrictions on individuals who may be party to an agreement or defects in the formation of a contract. These factors need to be appreciated as they can prevent an otherwise valid contract from having effect (and be legally enforceable).

SUMMARY OF MAIN POINTS

Consideration

- Consideration is the bargain element of a contract and may be referred to as the 'price paid for a promise'.
- Consideration must move from the promisee.
- Consideration must be legally sufficient but need not be adequate.
- The courts will not recognize a 'bare' promise.
- Consideration may be executed—one promise in return for an act by the other party (usually evidenced in unilateral contracts).
- Consideration may be executory—an exchange of promises (usually found in bilateral contracts).
- Simple contracts must be 'good' consideration.
- Performing an existing duty may not be good consideration.
- If the benefit provided exceeds an existing duty this may constitute good consideration.
- Past consideration is not good consideration unless the act was performed at the request of the promisor, there was a contemplation of both parties that payment would be made, and all the other elements of a valid contract exist.

- Part-payment of a debt will not prevent the innocent party seeking the balance owed. However, if something of value other than money is provided or if the part-payment has been provided at an earlier date than required, this may be good consideration.

- An exception to this general rule is the doctrine of promissory estoppel. This enables the court to prevent a party from reneging on a promise that was relied on by the other party if to do so would be unfair.

Privity

- The general rule in contract is that only those parties to a contract may sue and be sued on it.

- Exceptions exist where the contract is made by an agent for the principal, in collateral contracts, where property is transferred in trust to another party, where the contract has been made under an insurance agreement for the benefit of another, and where restrictive covenants are imposed on property.

- The enactment of the Contracts (Rights of Third Parties) Act 1999 has enabled third parties to enforce contracts conferring a benefit on them, or where the contract expressly permits the third party to enforce it.

Intention to create legal relations

- The parties must intend for an agreement to establish legal relations to create an enforceable contract.

- Social agreements are presumed not to intend to create legal relations (such as between husband and wife (unless they are separated) and social acquaintances).

- In commercial agreements, the presumption is that legal relations exist, unless the parties expressly state an agreement to the contrary.

Certainty of terms

- Terms of a contract must be drafted carefully and precisely if they are to be relied on by the parties.

SUMMARY QUESTIONS

Essay questions

1. 'The presumptions advanced in the assessment of whether parties intended an agreement to create legal relations are wrong. It provides for uncertainty and inconsistent judgments, and should be made more transparent (particularly necessary for vulnerable people).'

   Discuss.

2. 'Privity of contract is such an antiquated doctrine, resplendent with exceptions and caveats, that its practical effect is meaningless.'

   Discuss this statement in relation to business agreements.

Problem questions

1. All Bright Consumables (ABC) Ltd manufactures PC components. It runs this aspect of its operation from a factory that it leases from JJ Industrial Rentals Ltd (JJ), and the machines used in the production process are rented from iMachines and Tools Ltd (iMachines Ltd).

Given the economic crises in 2010, and increasing competition from the Far East, ABC is in financial difficulties. In March 2010 ABC wrote to JJ of its financial problems and stated 'We are suffering severe financial difficulties in these austere times. We both know you have factories that you are unable to rent, and unless you can reduce the rent on this factory we will have no choice but to cease trading and you'll be left with another unrented factory'. Following a discussion between the managing directors of both companies, JJ agree to accept half rent payment until such a time as ABC's business picks up.

ABC also informed iMachines Ltd in the same manner about its financial problems and it agreed to take a quantity of the PC components manufactured in lieu of its hire charges for the financial year 6 April 2010 to 5 April 2011.

In January 2011 JJ were suffering financial difficulties and demanded that ABC pay the full rent on the factory from February 2011. It also demanded payment of the rent owed from March 2010. It considers this part-payment of a debt and wishes to exercise its right to obtain payment. At this time, iMachines Ltd discovered that the PC components it had taken in lieu of hire charges were worth only half of the hire charges for the year. It has demanded that ABC pay the balance owed in cash.

Advise ABC as to whether the payments demanded have to be made.

2. Juana is the managing director of ABC Ltd. She arrived at the company's head office to discover the building was ablaze. She called the emergency services and when the firefighters arrived at the scene Juana told them that the contents of her office were extremely valuable and contained irreplaceable items. As such, if they could prevent the fire spreading there she would reward them with £100 each. The firefighters were successful in extinguishing the fire and it did not reach Juana's office.

Assess the likely success of the firefighters claiming the reward.

 You will find guidance about how to answer these questions online at www.oup.com/uk/marson5e/.

 FURTHER READING

Books and articles

Coote, B. (1990) 'Consideration and Benefits in Fact and Law' *Journal of Contract Law*, Vol. 3, p. 23.

Hedley, S. (1985) 'Keeping Contract in its Place: *Balfour v Balfour* and the Enforceability of Informal Agreements' *Oxford Journal of Legal Studies*, Vol. 5, No. 3, pp. 391–415.

Hird, N. J., and Blair, A. (1996) 'Minding Your Own Business—*Williams v Roffey* Revisited: Consideration Reconsidered' *Journal of Business Law*, May, p. 254.

 ONLINE RESOURCES

www.oup.com/uk/marson5e/

For further resources relating to this chapter, including self-test questions, an interactive glossary, and key case flashcards.

7

CONTRACTS, CONTRACTUAL CAPACITY, MISTAKE, MISREPRESENTATION, AND DURESS

Chapters 5 and **6** identified the essential features of a valid contract. Before the details of the terms of the contract, and its discharge are discussed, it is important to recognize that a contract may fail due to a party not possessing the capacity to establish a contract, it could involve a mistake by one or both parties, a provision may have been misrepresented in the negotiations, or the contract could have been concluded by using undue influence or placing the other party under duress. These factors have significant consequences on the validity of the contract and must be understood, in conjunction with the previous chapters, to ascertain whether the contract is void or voidable.

Business Scenario 7

Dewi is selling a plot of land in Derbyshire consisting of 200 acres. He is approached by Rahul who states that he is interested in purchasing, but only if he can be assured that the land is capable of sustaining his 200 herd of cattle.

Dewi provides this assurance despite the fact that he has no experience of this method of farming. Following the sale, Rahul discovers that the land is incapable of sustaining his cattle and they will have to be moved to another location (at great expense) and the land is worthless for his intended use.

Rahul's son, Minesh who is 15, recently took delivery of nine pairs of welted brogue shoes, four tweed jackets and three waterproof caps which he ordered from a local bespoke men's tailor shop. The total cost was £1,300 and payment was due following an invoice being sent to his home address. Minesh has no intention of paying the bill.

Later Dewi, an 88-year-old man, decides to sell his house to his grandson, Geraint. Geraint has been dealing with Dewi's financial affairs for some time and has control over his bank accounts and may make payments on Dewi's behalf. He informs Dewi that he will draft the contract of sale to save Dewi any trouble as he is very grateful to be receiving the house at a very competitive price. The agreement between Dewi and Geraint is that Dewi will remain in the house until he dies, and will pay Geraint a nominal rent.

Geraint drafts the contract as arranged but this does not include the agreement for Dewi to continue to reside in the property. Further, the agreement does not state that Geraint is to be the purchaser, but rather his business partner is the buyer. Geraint does not inform Dewi of these changes and presents him with the contract, informing him to sign it immediately and not to waste his time by reading the document or seeking legal advice. Geraint pressurizes Dewi to sign the contract before he leaves the property.

Geraint's business partner does not pay any money for the property, but has taken out a large mortgage on it and has not made any repayments. Subsequently, the mortgage company wishes to repossess the property to recover its money.

Learning Outcomes

- Identify how the law imposes restrictions on certain persons when forming a contract (**7.2**)
- Provide examples of illegal contracts (**7.3**)
- Explain the effect a mistake has on an agreement between the parties (**7.4–7.4.2**)
- Identify where a contract has been formed on the basis of misrepresentation, and the remedies available to the innocent party (**7.5–7.5.6**)
- Explain what effect the use of duress and undue influence has on the validity of a contract (**7.6–7.6.2**).

7.1 INTRODUCTION

Chapters 5 and **6** have identified the essential features of a valid contract. Once agreement, consideration, intention to create legal relations, and certainty of terms has been fulfilled, a contract may be established. However, problems may exist in how the agreement was concluded that could affect its validity. What if one of the parties induced the other into the contract by misrepresenting an important aspect of the contract? What if one of the parties was clearly in a drunken state and could not understand what they were agreeing to? What if one party was told to agree to the contract or they would be shot? Some of the reasons listed (naturally) are more common than others, but the emphasis of this chapter is to identify where problems may occur that could prevent the successful operation of the contract, despite fulfilling the essential features.

7.2 CAPACITY TO ENTER A VALID CONTRACT

For an enforceable agreement to be created the parties involved must have the capacity to create a contract. This is particularly so where the person is vulnerable.

7.2.1 Minors

A minor is a person under 18 years of age (Family Law Reform Act 1969, s. 1) and has the capacity to establish most contracts. However, whilst this is generally true, situations exist where the minor requires protection and in those situations the contract established may be voidable, hence allowing the minor the ability to avoid the contract. Typically, contracts involving the sale of shares, the leasing of property, and contracts of partnership have been held as voidable, rather than void.

Steinberg v Scala (Leeds) Ltd (1923)

Facts:

A minor had been allotted shares in Scala and had made an initial payment, but was unable to meet future payments. As such, she brought a claim to end the contract and recover the money already paid.

→

Authority for:

The court allowed Steinberg to end the contract (it was voidable by the minor) but she failed in her action to recover the money already paid.

The minor may avoid such contracts within a reasonable time, and until they reach the age of majority, but must satisfy any debts whilst party to the contract.

Circumstances exist where a minor is bound by the contract. If the contract is for necessaries, as defined under the Sale of Goods Act 1979, s. 3, then the contract will bind the minor.

Consider

Can the owner of the tailor's shop successfully recover the payment due for the clothes supplied to Minesh? Are they necessaries, and given the nature of the items ordered, would the courts be more likely to follow the ruling in *Nash v Inman* or in *Peters v Fleming* (both are covered below)?

Nash v Inman (1908)

Facts:

A tailor had supplied several waistcoats and other items of clothing, at a cost of £123, to an undergraduate studying at Cambridge. When payment for the items was not made, the tailor sought to recover the money.

Authority for:

The court refused to allow the defendant to recover payment. The goods supplied were not 'necessaries' as the minor had a sufficient quantity of clothes.

'Necessaries' is a broad term, and whilst this can include food and clothing, it has been assessed as including items reflecting the minor's social status.

Peters v Fleming (1840)

Facts:

Whilst a minor, Mr Fleming obtained several items of expensive and ornate jewellery. He would not pay for the items although he had the means to do so.

Authority for:

The jeweller brought an action for payment when Fleming reached majority, and it was held that items such as a gold ring and gold watch (as supplied) *were* necessaries for a rich young man. Designation of a necessary may depend on the status of the individual.

Where necessaries have been provided, the minor is liable to pay a reasonable price (Sale of Goods Act 1979, s. 3), rather than, necessarily, the price established in the contract. Further, where the contract is not unduly harsh or detrimental to the minor, it will be binding.

Clements v London and North Western Railway Co. (1894)

Facts:

A minor had been employed as a porter at a railway and had agreed to join an insurance society that was organized by the railway's employees. The effect of this membership was, in part, to waive rights against the employer as provided under the Employer's Liability Act 1880, as the society provided a more comprehensive package of protection. This protection was beneficial in some circumstances, but, importantly in this case, provided for sums to be paid out in claims at rates lower than would have been available under the Act. When the minor was injured due to negligence on the part of the employer, he sought to have his membership avoided to enable him to claim under the Act. The Court of Appeal held he could not. The contract was binding on him, as, when considered as a complete package, it was beneficial.

Authority for:

Where a contract is for the benefit of a minor, and does not place unfair responsibility on them, it is not voidable but rather binding and enforceable against the minor.

Conversely, where it places an unfair responsibility on the minor they may be able to avoid the contract.

Fawcett v Smethurst (1914)

Facts:

A minor had hired a car to help him move his luggage. The terms of its hire was for the minor to be liable for any damage to the vehicle regardless of whether this was caused by his negligence. The vehicle did cause damage through no fault of the minor and the court had to determine whether the contract could be enforced against him.

Authority for:

The court held the term was harsh and onerous and therefore the contract could be avoided.

Consider

The contract for Minesh's clothing would not be likely to be seen as unreasonable but they would also be unlikely to be seen as necessaries. We are not told about Minesh's social status so we can assume these are not exclusive items for a country gentleman (using the argument in *Peters v Fleming*), but having supplied the goods without payment or a guarantee of payment on delivery, the owner of the tailor's shop will likely be unsuccessful in recovering payment.

Despite the protection for minors, those entering into contracts with a minor are also afforded rights (under the Minors' Contracts Act 1987). The minor who, when reaching the age of majority, ratifies debts that were created during their minority, will have this ratification binding upon them (s. 1). Also, where a third party acted as guarantor for the minor in contracts that were unenforceable against them, this will not result in the contract being unenforceable against the third party (s. 2). Further, the Act consolidated the existing law allowing the remedy of restitution to be used to require the minor to return any property acquired under the contract, or any property representing this, in an unenforceable contract (s. 3).

7.2.2 Mental Incapacity

Persons who have been identified with a mental incapacity, and as such are defined under the Mental Capacity Act 2005 as a 'patient', are protected from entering contracts. The consequence is that any agreement made which purports to be a contract will be void. This is the situation even if the other party was not aware of the 'patient's' incapacity. There may be a different conclusion where the person is not considered to be a patient under the relevant legislation. In this scenario, there exists the ability for a contract to be established with a person suffering from a mental illness or some other form of mental incapacity. To avoid the contract, the mentally ill person must demonstrate that at the time of concluding the contract they did not understand the nature of the agreement, and the other party must or should have known of the mental incapacity present. The Sale of Goods Act 1979 has also provided guidance on how potential contracts may be viewed when they involve those without mental capacity. Under s. 3, if the contract is for necessities and the other party is unaware of the mental incapacity, the contract is valid and the price must be paid. If, however, the other party is aware of the mental incapacity, then only a 'reasonable price' must be paid. 'Necessities' is defined under the Mental Capacity Act 2005 as suitable to a person's condition in life and to their actual requirements at the time the goods/services were supplied (s. 7).

7.2.3 Intoxication

Persons who are drunk or under the influence of drugs when a contract is concluded are generally bound by the contract as it is presumed by the courts that they are aware of their actions. If the other party is unaware of the intoxication the contract is enforceable, but if the party is so intoxicated that they do not know the consequences of the agreement they are concluding, and the other party is aware, the contract is voidable.

7.3 ILLEGALITY

Illegality, in terms of contract law, refers to those contracts that will not be permitted (they are void) because they may be illegal in nature such as those contrary to statute (e.g. the Resale Prices Act 1976, where manufacturers conspire to regulate the price of goods), or against public policy. This includes a particularly wide range of scenarios, such as contracts that intend to prevent the prosecution by the State of an individual who is accused of some illegal act; and contracts that seek to promote immorality.

> ### Pearce v Brooks (1866)
>
> **Facts:**
>
> A woman was in the occupation as a prostitute and had hired a carriage for the purpose of carrying out this function.
>
> **Authority for:**
>
> When she refused to pay for the hire the owner could not recover the payments as the nature of the contract was illegal.

Such contracts have traditionally been held as void.

> ### Parkinson v College of Ambulance Ltd and Harrison (1925)
>
> **Facts:**
>
> A charity was provided with a donation of £3,000 on the basis that the donor would be given a knighthood.
>
> **Authority for:**
>
> Whilst this was not against the law, it was held that such a situation would be contrary to public policy as it may involve public officials being corrupted.

Further examples of contracts that will fall victim to illegality include those involving contracts of fraud or those where a crime is to be committed.

> ### Everet v Williams (1725)
>
> **Facts:**
>
> The case involved two highwaymen who entered into an agreement to share the proceeds of their activities from robberies committed together.
>
> **Authority for:**
>
> When these funds were not shared, the court would not allow the case to proceed for recovery.

It is also worthy of note that in this case the solicitors involved were fined for bringing the case to court and both highwaymen were hanged. Public policy arguments have also been used to restrict the post-contractual obligations placed on an employee through a restraint of trade clause (see **24.5**). Note, however, some illegal contracts may have legal effects.

> ### Tinsley v Milligan (1994)
>
> **Facts:**
>
> The parties were in a relationship where they purchased a property for the purposes of renting out rooms. However, the property was registered in the name of the claimant alone and this was to enable the defendant to fraudulently claim state benefits (the proceeds of which they would share). Following the breakdown of their relationship the claimant sought possession of the property whilst the defendant argued they both had equal shares in it.
>
> **Authority for:**
>
> The House of Lords held that the interest in the property be shared between the parties. Whilst the defendant had perpetrated a fraud, this did not prevent her action from succeeding as the claim did not rely on the fraud to be effective.

7.4 MISTAKE

Mistake is the area of law where the contract may be held void if the mistake was fundamental to the contract, as the parties did not have a true agreement. However, it is distinct from where the parties may have erroneously entered into a contract that is a bad bargain, or where one party later has 'second thoughts'. Also, mistake is not concerned with the attributes of a particular item, for example buying a printer for a computer under the misapprehension that it had a scanner facility as well. Unless this feature was misrepresented to the buyer, the buyer has no claim under their mistaken belief.

In order for the mistake to enable the contract to be made void, it must be fundamental, and 'operative', which prevents the **consensus ad idem** that is required for a contract to be established. A mistake can be a common mistake (where both parties make the same mistake), mutual (where the parties are at cross-purposes—also known as bilateral mistake), and unilateral (where only one party is mistaken).

- *Common mistake:* Here the parties have made the same mistake. Typical examples include contracts involving property which neither party is aware no longer exists:

> ### Couturier v Hastie (1856)
>
> **Facts:**
>
> Here the parties were negotiating for the sale of corn, but whilst the negotiations were proceeding, the carrier of the goods disposed of it.
>
> **Authority for:**
>
> It was held that there could be no contract as the goods being negotiated for were not available when the contract was concluded. However, being careless in a negotiation is not the same as an operative mistake and such a party may be liable for breach of contract.

Another example of common/mutual mistake is demonstrated in the following case:

Solle v Butcher (1950)

Facts:

The parties had entered into an agreement for the renting of premises that they both believed was subject to a controlled rent. The rent established between the two was, as a consequence, artificially low.

Authority for:

The Court of Appeal held that there should be a **rescission** of the contract, with the proviso that a new tenancy for the premises be offered on the normal, average rent.

The court decided the case on the basis of an equitable mistake. The ruling in *Solle* was changed (disapproved), and the original view of common mistake as provided in *Bell v Lever Bros Ltd* was followed by the Court of Appeal in the following case.

Great Peace Shipping Ltd v Tsavliris Salvage International Ltd (2002)

Facts:

The ship *Cape Providence* had sustained serious damage at sea. Tsavliris offered its salvage services and a contract was established. Tsavliris contacted a London broker to find a ship to assist and entered into the hire of the *Great Peace* (as the closest vessel) for a minimum of five days. However, the *Great Peace* was 400 miles away, and another available vessel was closer. Therefore, the brokers were informed to cancel the contract for the *Great Peace* and establish a new contract for this closer ship. Tsavliris refused to pay for the hire of the *Great Peace* on the basis that the contract was void for common mistake.

Authority for:

The case has removed the ability to grant rescission for common mistake as to quality (the contract is not voidable in equity). The remedy for common mistake is that the contract is void (where it involves a fundamental mistake).

It was held that there is no basis on which a contract is to be rescinded due to mutual mistake where, at common law, the contract is valid and enforceable.

- *Mutual mistake:* It is a possibility that in the negotiations for a contract, both parties are at cross purposes as to the nature of the contract or its subject matter. These instances are uncommon, but not without authority:

> ### *Raffles v Wichelhaus* (1864)
>
> **Facts:**
>
> The parties contracted for the sale of cotton, the cargo on the ship the *Peerless*, sailing from Bombay. However, in fact there were two ships called the *Peerless* sailing with cotton from Bombay, and the parties were referring to different vessels.
>
> **Authority for:**
>
> There could be no contract as the parties were mistaken as to the subject matter. If the court could have identified from the parties' evidence that one specific vessel was being referred to then a contract would have been established, but as this was impossible to deduce from the evidence, the contract was held void.

- *Unilateral mistake:* The more common form of mistake is where one party is mistaken as to the terms of the contract or the identity of the other party. This, by its nature, involves the mistake by one party and the cases described in **7.4.1–7.4.2** demonstrate its application.

7.4.1 Mistake in the Terms of the Contract

There may exist situations where the contract may be held void because the written contract contained contradictory information compared to the agreement established orally, and this is evident to the other party who attempts to rely on it.

> ### Consider
>
> The contract established by Geraint is different from the terms as explained by him to Dewi. The agreement for the purchase, but for Dewi to continue residing in the property until his death, is a significant aspect of the agreement which is missing from the written contract.

> ### *Hartog v Colin & Shields* (1939)
>
> **Facts:**
>
> The written contract provided that in the sale of hare skins, the price would be established on the basis of the weight of the items (price per pound). The oral agreement had previously concluded that the price would be established on the basis of the number of skins (price per skin), which was a more common calculation in the trade.
>
> **Authority for:**
>
> The buyer would have been at a great advantage if the written contract was allowed to proceed on this basis and it was clear that he must have been aware of the mistake.

Unlike in *Hartog*, the written contract may be signed, not necessarily as a record of oral negotiations, but simply as a method of contracting in this form. Where a person has signed a document without reading it, the courts will not readily provide a remedy just because they later discover the content of the contract and disagree with it. In the absence of a **misrepresentation** or some form of **duress** being applied for the signing, there may be no escape from the contract. However, the courts have allowed a defence to be raised of *non est factum* (it is not my deed). There are safeguards to the use of this defence and it will not be available where the signor has been careless or negligent in signing a document (such as signing a blank document and allowing the other party to complete it later—as in *United Dominions Trust Ltd v Western*). It may be of use where the signor is vulnerable and has had their vulnerability exploited by the other party.

Consider

Dewi is an older man and could be seen as being vulnerable. It could be argued that he was careless in signing a contract without first reading it but given the relationship between the parties, the *non est factum* defence may be available.

Foster v Mackinnon (1869)

Facts:

An elderly man with very poor eyesight was misled into signing a document that he was informed was a guarantee, but was in reality a bill of exchange.

Authority for:

Despite the 'narrow use' and availability of the doctrine, here the signor was under a disability, he signed a document whose terms were fundamentally or radically different from those which he thought he was signing, and he was not negligent (in this respect careless) in the signing. As a consequence the contract was void.

The requirement of a fundamental or radical difference to the nature of the contract is somewhat harsh but is in line with the narrow use of the plea.

Gallie v Lee (Saunders v Anglia Building Society) (1970)

Facts:

Here an elderly woman mistakenly signed a contract believing it was to assign her house to her nephew, but in reality was signing a sale to her nephew's business partner for £3,000. The business partner did not pay the money, nor maintain repayments on a mortgage he had placed on the property. When the mortgage company wished to repossess the house, the now deceased woman's family attempted to have the contract avoided due to mistake. The House of Lords would not allow the claim to succeed as the contract

→

she signed was not sufficiently different from the one she believed she was signing, and she had not exercised sufficient care in reading the document before signing.

Authority for:

Mistake as to the terms of a contract, in the absence of misrepresentation, will not enable the signor to avoid the contract where it is not fundamentally/radically different from what the signor believed they were agreeing to. The plea of *non est factum* will not generally be allowed of a person of full capacity.

Consider

The contract is very different from that which Dewi thought he was signing. Also, unlike in *Gallie v Lee*, Dewi has been pressurized to sign the contract without having the opportunity to obtain legal advice or even to read it. Thus, the authority in *Gallie v Lee* may be distinguished.

7.4.2 Mistake as to the Identity of the Party

Mistake in this area is linked with misrepresentation. Cases involve the rogue obtaining the possession of the victim's property and by doing so obtaining a voidable title. This title may be removed where the victim takes steps to avoid the contract before the rogue passes the goods on (which they generally will wish to do so as to realize any value in the goods obtained). If the goods are transferred to a buyer purchasing the goods in good faith, then the goods' title transfers to the buyer. There is no general principle of good faith included in contract law (as it appears in the law of agency, some employment relations, relationships involving fiduciary obligations, and so on); however, in *Yam Seng Pte v International Trade Corporation* a term of good faith and fair dealing was implied into the contract. Similarly, in *Mid Essex Hospital Services NHS Trust v Compass Group UK and Ireland Ltd (t/a Medirest)* the Court of Appeal considered the scope and extent of an express good faith clause. The court held that, unlike *Yam* where the good faith clause should be interpreted broadly, here it was interpreted restrictively and required the parties to work together honestly. It further considered that there was no need for the implication of good faith into the contract and hence declined to pursue the matter. Ultimately, the question of good faith in contract law generally will need further clarification by the appeal courts, but parties would be wise when using these and incorporating them into contracts (expressly) to clearly define and articulate their extent and what they will mean for the parties.

This is somewhat unfair but essentially the courts deal with the two innocent parties to the mistake, the victim of the rogue who has lost their property, and the innocent buyer who is subject to a claim for recovery of the goods from the victim (the rogue is unlikely to be found and hence subject to a claim against them). The courts have generally held in favour of the innocent buyer rather than the victim of the rogue's fraud. This is because the victim had the power not to allow goods to leave their possession without verifying the identity of the rogue and their attributes (or quality—essentially whether the rogue had sufficient funds to pay for the goods). The courts will then only allow a contract to be held void for mistake where the rogue's identity was crucial to the conclusion of the contract.

The mistake as to the identity of the parties occurs where one party believes they are negotiating with a particular person, when in reality they are dealing with someone else. The first examples given are where the parties have not met in person (face-to-face). This has often been an 'easier' case to prove of mistaken identity because the victim can more readily claim that they reasonably believed they were dealing with the person the rogue held himself out to be.

Cundy v Lindsay (1874–80)

Facts:

The case involved Mr Blenkarn, who purported to be a sales representative of a firm called Blenkiron & Sons. He previously hired property in the same street as the firm and had written to the claimants from this address seeking to obtain linen goods. Blenkarn entered into a contract through the post with the claimants for the purchase of a consignment of handkerchiefs, and sold these on without making payment. The claimant had to go beyond proving fraud by Blenkarn (fraud would render the contract voidable, and unless set aside before the goods are passed on, a bona fide purchaser would obtain a good title). The House of Lords held that the claimants had intended to deal with Blenkiron, and not Blenkarn, and as this was a fair mistake, the contract was void.

Authority for:

The Lords held that Lindsay was aware of the genuine and reputable firm (Blenkiron & Sons), and had provided the goods on credit due to the contract being, it believed, with this firm. Mistake as to identity was easier to find in this case as the parties never met in person, but rather communicated via the post.

This case was decided due to the mistake over the identity of the other party, but how would the courts determine situations where it is not the identity of the party in question, but rather their creditworthiness?

Kings Norton Metal Co. Ltd v Edridge, Merrett & Co. Ltd (1897)

Facts:

A company provided goods to a fraudster claiming to be a representative of a reputable firm. However, whereas as in *Cundy* the firm existed and was reputable, in *Kings* the firm did not exist.

Authority for:

The case demonstrated that mistake as to the attributes of the other party is insufficient to establish mistake, and the identity of the party was not crucial. The goods had been passed on to another buyer in good faith, and as there was no 'mistake' as to the rogue's identity, the claimants were not entitled to the return of the goods.

The previous cases considered mistaken identity where the parties had not met face-to-face. Where the parties have actually met in person, there is a strong presumption that it will prevent a claim for mistake as to identity.

Phillips v Brooks (1919)

Facts:

A rogue entered the claimant's jewellers shop. He purchased a number of items and presented a cheque as payment. The staff were uncomfortable at the man taking the products by merely leaving a cheque but he managed to convince them to allow him to take a ring. He identified himself as Sir George Bullough of St. James's Square. The jeweller was aware of a person of that name and checked that he lived at that address. The jeweller allowed the rogue to leave with the ring and, when the cheque was dishonoured at the bank, sought its return. However, the rogue had already sold the ring to a pawn broker and disappeared. The claimant argued for the return of the ring as there had been a unilateral mistake as to identity.

Authority for:

The claim failed. The contract was not void for mistake as, when parties transact in person, there is a presumption that they deal with the person in front of them, not with whom that person claims to be. Significantly, the jeweller could not convince the court that they would have only sold the ring to Sir George Bullough.

However, this line of reasoning has to be considered in light of the House of Lords decision in *Shogun Finance v Hudson*:

Shogun Finance Ltd v Hudson (2003)

Facts:

The case involved a rogue impersonating one Mr Patel. Mr Patel had no knowledge or involvement in the fraud, with the rogue producing documents of sufficient quality to convince the finance company of his assumed identity (a driving licence in Mr Patel's name). The court held that the rogue had not obtained a good title to the car and it belonged to the finance company, not the innocent third party (Hudson) who purchased it.

Authority for:

Contracts formed on the basis of mistaken identity, where adequate checks have been performed to ascertain the identity of the other party, will make the subsequent contract void—not voidable.

Innocent purchasers of goods are protected under Part III of the Hire Purchase Act 1964 and s. 23 of the Sale of Goods Act 1979, which provides innocent purchasers with good title against the owner where the contract is voidable. However, despite Hudson's arguments, the Lords held that this contract, involving mistake as to identity, resulted in the contract being void, and as such the Hire Purchase Act 1964 was of no use. The key element was the identity of the rogue. Here, the finance company believed it was dealing with Mr Patel, through the documentary evidence provided. The company only intended to deal with Mr Patel and would not have provided the seller of the car with the permission to allow anyone other than Mr Patel to take possession of the vehicle. The company had performed adequate checks to verify this information and as such the contract between the rogue and the finance company was void. As being void, rather than voidable, the title could not be passed on to Hudson.

7.4.3 The Remedy of Rectification

Rectification is an **equitable remedy** available in the case of mistake where a written agreement between the parties fails to reflect the actual agreement that was reached. The courts have an option, if they believe that a contract did not reflect the true intentions of the parties at the time of the agreement, to have the relevant terms changed. This is particularly relevant where one of the parties has deliberately intended, through false and misleading information, to induce the contract.

Hurst Stores and Interiors Ltd v ML Europe Property Ltd (2004)

Facts:

ML Europe made substantial changes to a draft contract with Hurst Stores before it was signed. Hurst was not informed, or aware, of these terms and signed the final contract on the basis that it contained the same terms as the previous draft.

Authority for:

It was held by the Court of Appeal that ML Europe must have known Hurst was unaware of the changes to the final contract and consequently ordered that the contract be changed back to the previous draft.

7.5 MISREPRESENTATION

Chapter 8 identifies the importance and significance of determining whether a statement made in the course of negotiating a contract will be determined as a term or a representation. A breach of a representation will not enable a breach of contract claim, but may, however, lead to a misrepresentation that makes the contract voidable. An action under misrepresentation is available if the untrue representation is considered 'actionable'. This means that there is a legal remedy available where a false statement of fact (not opinion) is made that induces the other party to enter the contract.

Therefore, to determine an actionable misrepresentation the elements outlined in **Figure 7.1** must be satisfied.

7.5.1 A Statement of Material Fact

Statements of fact are sometimes difficult to separate and distinguish from opinions. If the statement can be determined, objectively, as being true or false, this may assist in identifying whether it is a fact or opinion.

Figure 7.1 Actionable misrepresentation

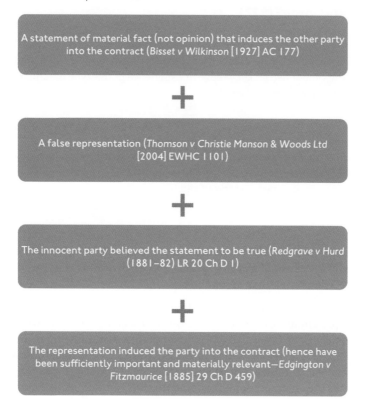

A statement of material fact (not opinion) that induces the other party into the contract (*Bisset v Wilkinson* [1927] AC 177)

+

A false representation (*Thomson v Christie Manson & Woods Ltd* [2004] EWHC 1101)

+

The innocent party believed the statement to be true (*Redgrave v Hurd* (1881–82) LR 20 Ch D 1)

+

The representation induced the party into the contract (hence have been sufficiently important and materially relevant—*Edgington v Fitzmaurice* [1885] 29 Ch D 459)

Consider

When Rahul enquires about the sustainability of the land on sale by Dewi, is Dewi's response an opinion or a statement of fact? Given that Dewi has provided his assurances, and if Rahul has no way of determining whether Dewi has knowledge of use of the land for this purpose, it would likely be considered a fact rather than opinion. This would be an important distinguishing of the rule in *Bisset v Wilkinson*.

Opinions cannot, by their nature, be objectively tested as true or false, whereas facts can be tested in this manner (although in *Smith v Land & House Property Corp.* a statement of opinion also contained a fact and hence enabled a claim for misrepresentation).

Bisset v Wilkinson (1927)

Facts:

A vendor's assurances of the suitability of land for sheep farming, when the purchaser was aware the vendor had no knowledge or experience of this type of farming, was held to be an opinion rather than a fact.

Authority for:

The statement was held as an opinion. However, in relation to a statement of law, the courts traditionally hold that such a statement is not a fact. This is due to the presumption that everyone has access to the law and everyone should be aware of the law and be in a position to assess if it is correctly stated.

Exceptions to this rule were evident in cases such as *Laurence v Lexcourt Holdings Ltd*, where a statement as to the extent of planning permission when dealing with the use of premises was held to be a fact rather than an opinion.

- *Silence as misrepresentation:* The general rule of contract is that silence cannot amount to a misrepresentation, even if the disclosure of such information would in all probability dissuade the other party from contracting. Naturally, there are exceptions, and if there is a material change in the circumstances, if remaining silent would make a statement misleading, if the parties had a fiduciary relationship, and in cases where the contract is one of good faith, then an actionable misrepresentation is possible.

- *Material change in circumstances:* There exists an obligation to provide (volunteer) information to the other party if the facts materially change between the issuing of the statement and the acceptance of the contract.

With v O'Flanagan (1936)

Facts:

A doctor who was selling his practice had a duty to disclose material changes between the agreement and the conclusion of the contract.

Authority for:

The information originally provided regarding the income from the practice (approximately £2,000 per annum) was correct, but in the time between the agreement and the sale, the doctor had become ill and his patient list substantially declined, along with the income.

Whilst silence generally will not be considered a misrepresentation, in this instance the court considered the doctor had a duty to disclose the information.

Spice Girls v Aprilia World Service BV (2002)

Facts:

An advertising campaign by a scooter manufacturer involved pictures of the pop group The Spice Girls including a member of the group (Geri Halliwell). However, at that time Halliwell had already decided to leave the group and the remaining members were aware of this decision.

Authority for:

It was held to be a misrepresentation as the group had an obligation to inform Aprilia and for it to take this into account when determining the advertising campaign.

- *Duty to answer questions truthfully:* If a person is asked a question during the negotiations, and an answer is offered (although there may be no legal duty to answer questions), there is an obligation that the answer is truthful. This places an obligation on the person issuing the statement to provide a full and complete answer, which does not mislead the other party.

Consider

As Dewi has offered an answer, and given he could have simply refused to reply or identified his lack of expertise in this area so as not to mislead Rahul but did not, his answer will likely be considered a misrepresentation.

Further, a true statement, but one that misleads the other party, can amount to a misrepresentation.

Nottingham Patent Brick & Tile Co. Ltd v Butler (1886)

Facts:

A solicitor, acting for the seller of land, was asked by the prospective buyer if there were any covenants applying to it. The solicitor replied he was unaware of any, which was true, but only because he had not looked at the documents. In fact, restrictive covenants did apply to the land.

Authority for:

Even though the statement was true, it still amounted to a misrepresentation.

- *Evidence of a fiduciary relationship:* A fiduciary relationship is one involving trust and can typically be seen in relationships of partners of an undertaking, solicitor and client, doctor and patient, and so on. In these situations, it is presumed that any material fact must be revealed to the other party and if this is not volunteered, then the silence can be held to be a misrepresentation.

- *Contracts of good faith:* In certain contracts, especially those involving contracts of insurance that require *uberrimae fidei*, 'utmost good faith', there must be a full disclosure of relevant factors that would influence a decision to enter an agreement or not. This includes volunteering information even if a question regarding the fact is not asked (*Lambert v Co-op Insurance Society Ltd*).

Hood v West End Motor Car Packing (1917)

Facts:

There was a failure to disclose the fact that goods were to be carried on the deck of a ship rather than covered from the elements, and as such enabled the insurance company to avoid its obligation to provide cover.

Authority for:

The court held that regardless of whether there was a negligent or intentional failure to disclose material facts, the fact of the failure to disclose was the relevant consideration in cases of misrepresentation.

7.5.2 **The representation was false**

In order to amount to a misrepresentation, it must be found by the court that the statement was in fact false.

Consider

Dewi's representation is false. He has no experience of using the land to sustain cattle and this is not a matter in which a reasonable person would hazard a guess.

Thomson v Christie Manson & Woods Ltd (2004)

Facts:

Christie's (a famous auction house) presented two vases which were represented as 'a pair of Louis XV porphyry and gilt-bronze vases'. The buyer argued this was false although it was agreed that Christie's had represented that it had grounds for holding its opinion.

Authority for:

The representation at issue here was not of the vases themselves (this would be an opinion) but rather of the identification and opinion of Christie's. This was not in issue and was therefore not false.

7.5.3 The Innocent Party Believed the Statement to Be True

The innocent party must have considered the statement to be true to enable them to proceed with an action for misrepresentation. This does not place an obligation on the innocent party to check the validity of the statement made, unless there are tangible reasons in which it would have proved necessary to question the validity.

Redgrave v Hurd (1881–82)

Facts:

A lawyer bought into a partnership having been told it had an income of £300pa. He had an opportunity to examine the accounts but he declined. It transpired that the actual income was £200pa.

Authority for:

The lawyer had relied on the statement. He was under no duty to verify the representation (even though he had the opportunity to do so) and was thus allowed to rescind the contract.

7.5.4 An Inducement to Enter the Contract

For a statement to amount to a misrepresentation it must have been of sufficient importance and materially relevant to induce the other party to have entered into the agreement. This does not necessarily mean that the statement was the only consideration in the innocent party's decision to enter the agreement, but it must have been an important factor and the innocent party must have relied on the statement.

Edgington v Fitzmaurice (1885)

Facts:

An investor in a company bought debentures on the basis of the incorrect details within the company's prospectus, and the investor's own research.

Authority for:

Even though the investor carried out his own research, he still relied on the details in the prospectus and this enabled the claim of misrepresentation.

! Consider

Rahul has entered into the contract on the basis of Dewi's assurances and he believed the statement to be true. The next stage is to determine which form of misrepresentation has been committed.

7.5.5 Three Types of Misrepresentation

Having identified that a misrepresentation has occurred, and this is established as action-able, the next stage is to identify which type of misrepresentation it is. This is important as it affects the remedies that are available.

* *Fraudulent misrepresentation:* This involves a false statement that has been made know-ingly or recklessly. This entitles the innocent party to claim rescission of the contract and/or damages, and sue in the tort of deceit. As the type of misrepresentation here is 'fraudulent' this goes beyond carelessness. Due to the problems inherent in establish-ing sufficient evidence to sustain such an allegation . . .

Long v Lloyd (1958)

Facts:

The claimant purchased a lorry from the defendant following his viewing of an advert. The advert identified the lorry as being in exceptional condition but, on inspection, there were evident defects with it. Undeterred, the claimant continued with the purchase. Problems began with the vehicle on the first journey and, following an offer by the seller to contribute half the costs of repair, the claimant accepted. A further journey saw the vehicle breakdown completely and the claimant sought to rescind the contract for inno-cent misrepresentation.

Authority for:

On accepting the offer of paying costs towards the repairs needed for the lorry, the claimant became aware of its defects and had affirmed the contract by taking it back.

. . . many claimants attempt to seek a remedy under negligent misrepresentation:

Derry v Peek (1889)

Facts:

The case involved Derry and other directors of the Plymouth, Devonport and District Tramways Company, which issued a prospectus stating it was to run trams by steam power (which was to be lucrative). It issued the claim on the assumption that such authority would be granted by the Board of Trade, which ultimately refused much of the permis-sion, save for limited sections of the tramway. This led to the company being wound up and the directors were sued for fraud. The House of Lords held the directors were not guilty of fraud as they genuinely believed the statement, and it was not made recklessly.

Authority for:

To establish fraud committed in a misstatement, the *defendant* must have known the statement to be untrue, or had no reasonable grounds upon which to maintain the belief that it was true, or have acted recklessly in making it.

- *Negligent misrepresentation:* This involves a false statement being made which induces the other party to enter a contract. However, it does not involve fraud, and so is easier to prove, as the party making the statement is unable to show that they believed the statement to be true, or held a reasonable belief that it was true.

Consider

Dewi made a representation with no knowledge of its truthfulness and would be unlikely to demonstrate reasonable grounds for him holding the belief in the assurance made. It is possible that it could be fraudulent, but it may be easier to prove a negligent misrepresentation and on this basis Rahul could seek a remedy for rescission (as he has no use for the land for his intended purpose) and damages (covering the costs associated with moving the cattle to a new location).

A finding of negligent misrepresentation entitles the innocent party to claim rescission and damages. The Misrepresentation Act 1967 s. 2(1) provides that once the claimant has demonstrated that a misrepresentation has been made, the burden then switches to the *defendant* to establish to the court's satisfaction that they believed the statement to be true, and also held reasonable grounds upon which this belief could be established. Further, as the Misrepresentation Act 1967, s. 2(1) provides a remedy for negligent misrepresentations, and the courts have held that this calculation should be made in the same way as for those awarded in cases of fraud, a claim for misrepresentation may actually provide the claimant with a 'better' monetary damages award than if a claim of breach of contract had been made.

- *Innocent misrepresentation:* This involves a false statement, but in the honest, albeit mistaken belief that it was true (see *Oscar Chess Ltd v Williams* in **8.2**). This entitles the innocent party to claim rescission as the contract is voidable, and if this is not possible, it may provide for a damages claim in lieu of rescission under the Misrepresentation Act 1967, s. 2(2). To demonstrate innocent misrepresentation the party needs to establish that they believed the statement that was made, and they had reasonable grounds upon which to hold this belief.

7.5.6 Remedies for Misrepresentation

The remedies available for misrepresentation depend upon the type of misrepresentation involved (fraudulent, negligent, or innocent).

- *Rescission:* The remedy of rescission is an equitable remedy where the party has the option to set the contract aside and the parties are returned to their pre-contractual position. In order for the parties to be placed back in their original position the court may order any money paid, or any property which has been transferred, to be returned to the relevant parties. The court, through s. 2(2) of the Misrepresentation Act 1967, has discretion as to whether to provide a remedy of rescission, and in practice this is often impossible. The remedy of rescission is available for all types of misrepresentation, and as in situations of misrepresentation the contract is said to be voidable, the innocent party is able to rescind (avoid) the contract but this right must be exercised within a reasonable time. The right to rescind the contract has to be communicated to the other party to be effective, and once this is chosen, the contract cannot be revived.

- In situations that involve fraudulent misrepresentation, it may be more difficult to communicate the intention to rescind. This is usually because by the time the fraud has been discovered, the rogue has disappeared. There is still a possibility of communicating rescission in this example through conduct such as seizing the goods that the rogue had sold; or by performing some act which is consistent with communication (e.g. informing the police).

- *Damages:* A simpler method of remedying the loss sustained due to a misrepresentation is through an award of **damages**. Here, an amount of money is awarded to the innocent party to compensate them for any losses sustained. In the case of fraudulent misrepresentation, the damages are intended to place the party in the position they would have been if the fraud had not been committed (reliance damages)—Misrepresentation Act 1967, s. 2(1) as applied in *Royscot Trust v Rogerson*. Damages can be awarded in contract and tort (such as fraud)—*Derry v Peek* (see **7.5.5**), and of course through statute.

For those who have been subject to an innocent misrepresentation, the courts have the discretion to award damages under s. 2(2) of the Misrepresentation Act 1967 in place of rescission. To be able to succeed in a claim for damages under this section:

1. the misrepresentation must have been such as to allow the innocent party to rescind the contract;

2. the claimant must prove that the contract has been (or ought to have been) rescinded;

3. the court must consider the award of damages, rather than awarding rescission, to be equitable.

Damages are rarely awarded under this section, and when they are, the assessment is based on the contractual remedy of damages that seeks to place the parties in the position they would have been had the representation not been untrue.

7.6 DURESS AND UNDUE INFLUENCE

Freedom of contract relies on the presumption that those who enter into contracts do so under their own free will. If a contract is established on the basis of violence (or a threat), or unlawful economic pressure, this may be considered a case of duress, whereas if a party has unfairly exploited its relationship with the other party this may amount to undue influence. In each of these situations the contract will be held to be voidable: duress on the basis of the common law, and undue influence in equity. Note that, as undue influence is based on equity, the courts may use other equitable remedies to prevent an unjust outcome.

7.6.1 Duress

There are two types of duress that may be exercised against a party—physical and economic.

- *Physical duress:* There are, in modern times, relatively few cases that involve claims of duress on the basis of violence, or the threat of violence. As one could imagine, this is common sense, as if the person was in such a state of fear that they would agree to enter the contract, they are unlikely to seek to have the contract avoided because of this act or threat. There have been examples of the use of this form of coercion and these are outlined below. Physical duress occurs when the party who has entered into a contract has done so on the basis of violence or the threat of violence.

Barton v Armstrong (1975)

Facts:

The managing director of a company based in Australia, Mr Barton, agreed to purchase shares from the chairman of the same company, Mr Armstrong. The price of the shares was very favourable to Armstrong because Armstrong had threatened to have Barton killed unless he entered the contract.

Authority for:

The Privy Council held that the contract should be voidable due to duress.

Consider

Dewi was pressurized into signing the contract created by Geraint. However, it is unlikely that the level of pressure exerted would be sufficient to establish duress. There was no threat of violence, it was his suggestion to pass on his property to his grandson, and there is no economic element to enable a successful claim of economic duress.

- *Economic duress:* It has proved very difficult in the past for the courts to set aside a contract for economic duress as difficulty exists in establishing where business pressure in commercial dealings becomes an actionable threat. Negotiations in commercial contracts are often based on exploiting financial weaknesses of the other party, or extracting the very best deal due to a need to sell goods quickly and raise funds immediately. These types of negotiation are quite legitimate, and hence criteria were necessary to give greater guidance as to the point where economic pressure amounts to duress:

  - illegitimate pressure (which need not be unlawful), such as exerting unacceptable levels of pressure which go beyond those normally expected in commercial negotiations:

R v Attorney-General for England and Wales (2003)

Facts:

The claimant was a member of the SAS and the Bravo Two Zero patrol. Various members had begun writing about its missions and publishing books. In some instances, this included distorting the truth (blaming dead and still serving colleagues) and in any

→

respect, the actions were seen as being motivated by commercial gain. These tactics were causing problems within the patrol and consequently, the Ministry of Defence introduced confidentiality clauses (preventing future publications) for those who wished to continue serving in the SAS. R was one of the members of the patrol who was required to sign the new agreement (failure to do so would result in a return to unit—widely seen as a punishment).

Despite signing the agreement, six months later he decided to leave the service and wished to write a book about his experiences. The State applied to the court for an injunction to prevent the publication and R argued the agreement should be set aside. He said he signed it under military orders and argued both duress and undue influence.

Authority for:

R's arguments failed. He was clearly acting under military orders, and the pressure this causes, but he still had a choice not to sign it. The State was entitled to introduce the clause and as this was reasonable, it did not amount to illegitimate pressure.

- whether the party claiming duress demonstrated protestations against the contract;
- whether the party had any alternative to proceeding with the contract, evidenced by the availability of independent advice that could have better informed the claimant:

Atlas Express Ltd v Kafco Importers & Distributors (1989)

Facts:

Atlas, a delivery firm, entered into a contract with Kafco to transport goods at prices determined on the size of the loads. However, the first load was considerably smaller than estimated, and it proved to be uneconomical to continue the service, therefore Atlas informed Kafco that it would refuse to make any further deliveries unless the price was renegotiated to include a minimum price. Kafco did not wish to do this (if for no other reason than it involved higher costs) but felt compelled as it had a dependency on a contract with a high-street retailer (Woolworths), and did not have time to arrange for a new delivery service. It was held that the contract was based on economic duress and therefore voidable. Kafco had been forced to renegotiate the terms of the contract that involved illegitimate pressure, and it had no real alternative but to agree to the change.

Authority for:

A contract established on the basis of economic duress will not be enforceable. Here, the defendant was performing an existing contractual obligation which was incapable of amounting to sufficient consideration to enforce the agreement.

7.6.2 Undue Influence

The party who has been subject to undue influence may have the contract set aside by the courts. It is the exploitation of the power one party has over another that will make the contract voidable, and this generally occurs when an individual's vulnerabilities are subjugated. The claimant merely has to demonstrate that they would not have entered into the contract except for the undue influence.

Williams v Bayley (1866)

Facts:

A father, an elderly man, entered into a contract with a bank to guarantee his son's debts. This action would prevent the son from being prosecuted for fraud.

Authority for:

The House of Lords held the contract voidable as the father had not entered the contract freely.

In situations where there is no fiduciary relationship between the parties, the party wishing to rely on undue influence must demonstrate that they would not have entered into the contract but for the influence. Alternatively, in situations where a fiduciary duty does exist (such as with a solicitor and their client or doctor and patient) insofar as the party claiming undue influence has been subject to a disadvantage as being party to the contract, undue influence is presumed. The onus is on the other party to disprove the allegation.

Consider

Dewi was dependent on Geraint for his financial arrangements and relied on his advice. Geraint therefore has a duty not to disadvantage Dewi in his financial dealings and this fiduciary relationship may enable Dewi to avoid the contract.

The courts have also extended the concept of a fiduciary relationship.

Goldsworthy v Brickell (1987)

Facts:

An elderly woman became dependent upon her neighbour to manage her substantial and valuable farm. The neighbour provided the woman with advice and eventually was given a tenancy of the farm on very favourable terms, without the woman having any other advice on the matter.

Authority for:

The Court of Appeal held that a fiduciary relationship existed between the parties and therefore the contract was voidable.

The courts had traditionally considered that no fiduciary relationship exists between a husband and wife. However, an important ruling was provided by the House of Lords:

Barclays Bank v O'Brien (1993)

Facts:

The case involved the husband persuading his wife to agree to a mortgage on their jointly owned house that he stated was for a maximum of £60,000 and for three weeks. This was a short-term loan to assist his business (which the wife had no ownership of). The reality was there was no limit on the mortgage or its duration. The bank had not followed the instructions of its head office that the parties should have been informed of the details of the mortgage.

Authority for:

It was held that the wife had no access to independent advice, and she had suffered undue influence in agreeing to the mortgage. The bank was aware of the possibility of abuse in this situation and hence the contract was deemed to be voidable. This has led banks, in particular, to be very careful with regard to informing clients about the consequences of contracts that are being signed and the importance of advice.

Information from the parties' solicitors is effective in this regard.

Royal Bank of Scotland v Etridge (No. 2) (2001)

Facts:

Mr and Mrs Etridge decided to buy a property but wished to purchase it in Mrs Etridge's name only. There were various sources to finance this, including the couple's former home. Mr Etridge was responsible for all the preparation for the financing—Mrs Etridge took no part in these proceedings. Two mortgages also formed part of facilitating the purchase—one being from the claimant company (RBS). RBS had its own solicitor who prepared the relevant paperwork which Mrs Etridge signed without reading (trusting her husband) and without asking any questions of its contents. Sometime after the purchase the bank sought to repossess the property and in attempting to avoid the action, Mrs Etridge claimed she was subject to undue influence by her husband.

Authority for:

The House of Lords held that Mrs Etridge had a responsibility to read the papers before signing them and she should have taken legal advice prior to committing to a loan secured on property. There was no undue influence. However, the Lords did say that reasonable steps to hold a private meeting between the solicitor and Mrs Etridge should have taken place where the risks can be clearly set out.

7.6.2.1 **Restriction of rescission**

In the event of undue influence being established, the courts have the option to rescind the contract. However, being an equitable remedy, it is a remedy that is provided at the discretion of the court, and the right to recession may be lost if the party is deemed to have affirmed the contract (such as not making any outward sign of protest against the contract), if they unduly delay in seeking to rescind, or if the contract involved property which has been sold on before the complainant brought their claim.

CONCLUSION

This chapter has outlined how contract law seeks to protect vulnerable groups, the impact of mistakes and misrepresentation on the contract, and the effect of unfair influence or duress applied in the formation of a contract. The book continues the examination of contract law by discussing the terms of the contract, representations made in negotiations, and the use of exclusion clauses in restricting a party's potential liability in contract and tort.

SUMMARY OF MAIN POINTS

Types of contract

- In unilateral contracts, only one party is promising to perform some action—in exchange for a specific act.
- In bilateral contracts, the parties share promises.
- A void contract is one which has no legal effect.
- A voidable contract allows the injured party in the proceedings to affirm or avoid the contract.
- Unenforceable contracts prevent the application of the contract.

Capacity

- Minors (those under 18 years old) may enter most types of contract. Restrictions exist in relation to forming and enforcing certain contracts.
- Mental incapacity can make an agreed contract void if the person is defined under the Mental Capacity Act 2005 as a 'patient'. In other situations the contract may be enforced against them, particularly when considering 'necessities'.
- Intoxication, whether through drugs or drink, generally has no consequence on the effectiveness of the contract unless the party is so intoxicated that they could not understand the consequences of their actions and the other party was aware of this.
- Certain contracts are illegal and are made void due to public policy or because they involve criminal actions.

Mistake

- The contract may be void due to an operative mistake.
- Where the parties are at cross-purposes as to the nature of the contract or its subject matter the agreement is void.
- A unilateral mistake involves the mistake of one party as to the terms of the contract or the identity of the other party.
- A party who has signed a contract on a misapprehension of its contents or effects may be able to claim non est factum and have its effects set aside.

Misrepresentation

- Misrepresenting a fact that is false that the innocent party believed to be true and inducing them into the contract enables the party to seek the remedy of rescission and/or damages depending on whether the misrepresentation is fraudulent, innocent, or negligent. It makes contracts voidable, not void.

- Damages are generally not awarded if the misrepresentation was innocently made. However, under the Misrepresentation Act 1967, the court may award this in lieu of an order for rescission (s. 2(2)).

- The option of rescission may be lost if the contract is affirmed. Affirmation may also be effective through lapse of time.

- Silence, as a general rule, cannot amount to a misrepresentation unless:

    - this would be misleading,

    - the contract is one of good faith where information must be volunteered,

    - there has been a material change in the facts between the agreement and the contract, or

    - where the parties are in a fiduciary relationship.

Duress

- Duress may consist of physical duress (violence or the threat of violence), and will result in the contract being held voidable.

- The House of Lords extended the concept of duress, beyond physical violence, to include unacceptable economic pressure where the other party had no option other than to proceed with the contract.

Undue influence

- As opposed to physical or economic threats, undue influence involves the exploitation of the other party's vulnerabilities. This can include exploitation of a fiduciary relationship.

- Relationships such as doctor and patient, parent and child, and solicitor and client generally have a presumption of undue influence if the contract cannot be explained by their relationship.

SUMMARY QUESTIONS

Essay questions

1. Assess the development of the rules in establishing an actionable misrepresentation. Focus on the parties' obligations to provide information and how this is interpreted in light of the general rule that silence cannot amount to a misrepresentation.

2. 'It is much better, when possible, to claim for a breach of a contractual term than to argue a misrepresentation has occurred.'

    Critically assess this statement.

Problem questions

1. Eric is searching for a residential property to rent. He views a flat being offered for rent by Fabulous Flats and Furnished Properties (FFFP) Ltd, a very commercially aggressive firm which attempts to sign residents to contracts as soon as possible. Following his viewing of this first flat, FFFP ask Eric to sign a tenancy contract that includes the following clauses:

    1. FFFP is not responsible for any damage or loss to individuals or their belongings as a result of any act of negligence by the company or its staff.

2. It is a condition of this contract that the tenant is responsible for the safety of all visitors to the premises and to ensure the flat is maintained in a good condition (i.e. it is at a minimum kept clean).

Eric, despite having not read the contract, signs it even though he smells strongly of alcohol and appears quite confused.

Sometime later, FFFP visits the property rented by Eric to ensure that all is well. Discovering that there are no fire extinguishers in the property, and having another person who has already expressed an interest in renting the premises, FFFP invoke clause 2 and seek to terminate Eric's contract for breach of the condition.

Advise the parties of their legal rights in this situation.

2. Mohammed runs a spa and healthcentre under the name Leisure, Endurance Gym in Oxford Street Ltd (LEGOs). Membership of LEGOs is available to members of the public following the completion of an application form and agreeing to a minimum 12-month contract. Membership costs £600 per year.

As part of its advertising campaign, Mohammed produces a leaflet to be distributed in the local area. The leaflet describes the features of the spa as including an extensive free weights area and a swimming pool of Olympic standard.

Siobhan reads one of the leaflets and visits LEGOs the following day where she signs the contract and pays £600 for membership. When she arrives at the spa later in the week she visits the free weights area to discover that this consists of no more than a rack of ten dumbbells. Disappointed, she decides to go to the swimming pool as Siobhan is a keen diver and intended to use the facility to work on her technique. However, the pool was only 7ft in depth and not suitable for diving.

Advise Siobhan on any misrepresentation claim she may have against LEGOs.

 You will find guidance about how to answer these questions online at www.oup.com/uk/marson5e/.

 ## FURTHER READING

Books and articles

Adams, J. and Brownsword, R. (2007) 'Understanding Contract Law' Sweet and Maxwell: London.

Alexander, T. [2006] 'Spilling the Beans' New Law Journal, Vol. 156, No. 7236, p. 1241 for an analysis of the duty imposed on partners, and the remedies available for fraudulent misrepresentation.

Allen, R. [2004] 'Caveat Emptor Beware?' Lloyd's Maritime and Commercial Law Quarterly, No. 4, November, p. 442.

Chandler, A. and Devenney, J. P. (2004) 'Mistake as to Identity and the Threads of Objectivity' Journal of Obligations and Remedies, Vol. 3, No. 1, p. 7.

McLauchlan, D. (2005) 'Mistake of Identity and Contract Formation' Journal of Contract Law, Vol. 21, p. 1.

 ## ONLINE RESOURCES

www.oup.com/uk/marson5e/

For further resources relating to this chapter, including self-test questions, an interactive glossary, and key case flashcards.

8 CONTRACTUAL TERMS

Chapters 5, 6, and 7 have identified the features of a binding contract. Contracts are made up of various terms that identify the rights and obligations of the parties. However, which are the most important terms, and which are of lesser significance? How can they be distinguished and what can the parties do to ensure the significance of a term is reflected in the contract? Is it important to differentiate important and lesser terms? These points will be considered in this chapter. Further, there may be a period of negotiation between the parties before a contract is established. Will all of the statements made during this period be held as terms of a contract? Some may be considered representations that will affect the injured party in seeking a remedy. Finally, imagine you run a store that offers free parking to its customers. Are you liable if the customer's car is damaged whilst parked on your premises? Can you restrict a customer who has parked their car on your premises from seeking damages if their car is damaged? Having established that a contract exists, this chapter explores the contract in more detail.

Business Scenario 8

Beta Ltd (Beta) and Aspen Ltd (Aspen) enter into negotiations for the sale of Beta's technology merchant business. Beta informs Aspen that its annual turnover is £300,000 and this figure can go as high as £450,000 but has never dropped below £250,000 in the previous five years. Its current stock of Point of Sale (POS) software systems is 500 units. Beta guarantees Aspen that these numbers are correct and there is no need to check their veracity.

The sale includes access to Beta's high street shop which is subject to a lease with restrictions imposed. Beta enthusiastically informs Aspen that the property has a second floor above the ground floor sales room which, although in disrepair, is a fantastic asset as it could be developed for residential purposes. There is also a shared car parking space to the rear of the property and Beta says that they intended to block a gateway in the space to increase their outside storage facilities. However, following the conclusion of the negotiations and when the written contract is presented to Aspen it transpires that the lease restricts the use of the property, or any part of it, as an individual dwelling.

Later Aspen intends to ship a consignment of POS systems from London to Mexico and requires a vessel to transport the goods to the destination. Due to the problems encountered in the past, Aspen inserts the following clause into its contract with Paragon World Shipping:

It is a condition of this contract that the vessel is seaworthy.

→

Learning Outcomes

- Distinguish between a term of a contract and a representation (**8.2**)
- Differentiate between express and implied terms (**8.3.1–8.3.2**)
- Explain how terms are implied into contracts from the courts, through customs, and from statute (**8.3.2**)
- Identify the status of a term and the implications of it being described as a warranty or a condition (**8.4–8.4.1**)
- Identify exclusion/limitation clauses and the rules of incorporation established through the common law (**8.5–8.5.4**).

8.1 INTRODUCTION

Having identified a contract, the details of the contractual agreement have to be considered due to the implications of what the parties intend to include in the agreement, what they did not mean to be included in the contract, and what significance different terms may have in the contract. This chapter therefore considers the distinction between terms of a contract and **representations**; whether, when a term has been identified as such, it is a 'condition' or a 'warranty'; and how terms are implied into the contract and how this affects terms that have been expressed. The chapter concludes by examining how parties may seek to exclude or limit a legal responsibility through the incorporation of an **exclusion clause**.

8.2 TERMS AND REPRESENTATIONS

During the agreement stage of the formation of a valid contract, the offeror identifies terms by which they are willing to be bound. This is where the details of these terms of the contract are expressed. Those included in a written document entitled, for example, a 'contract'/'agreement' would most likely be accepted as a term. However, contracts need not be in writing to be effective and the terms of the contract may therefore not have been reduced in writing. The parties may have negotiated the deal which involves statements being issued and these are either agreed to or subject to a counter-offer. Finally, an agreement is reached and the contract formed. However, not all the statements made will be considered to be terms. There are practical reasons for this. Suppose one party remarks to the other in the sale of a car, for example, that the car is 'a good runner that won't give you

Table 8.1 Distinguishing terms and representations

Term	Statement	Representation
	Made by a party with actual or reasonably expected lesser knowledge of the contractual subject matter	→
←	Reasonable reliance on statement made by the other party	
←	Stronger/more empathic statements (unless statement cannot establish a term)	
←	Statement made close to the agreement (inducing the contract to be concluded)	

any problems'. Is this a term? Does the statement have any legal meaning and obligation that could be enforced? Is it a fact or merely an opinion (and it may be considered that an opinion is as valuable as the cost of obtaining it)? Therefore, it is necessary to consider how the courts have addressed the question of whether a statement is a term or representation. **Table 8.1** outlines the indicators of where statements will be held terms or representations.

- *Significance for available remedies:* If the statement has been held to be a term and that term is breached, the innocent party has the right to claim damages and possibly end (repudiate) the contract. If the statement is considered a representation and it is breached, there is no breach of contract, but a remedy may exist for misrepresentation, although since the enactment of the Misrepresentation Act 1967, statutory remedies are available for untrue statements. There are no strict rules as to what will constitute a representation and a term, but guidance is available from case law.

- *Relative degrees of the parties' knowledge:* If one party has a better knowledge, or could be expected to have a better knowledge of the contractual subject matter than the other party, statements made by the party with the lesser knowledge will be more likely to be regarded as a representation.

Oscar Chess Ltd v Williams (1957)

Facts:

Mr Williams traded in a used Morris car for a new Hillman Minx from Oscar Chess (car dealers). Mr Williams described the Morris car as a 1948 model and produced the registration book as evidence. Oscar Chess checked the document and the first registration date, and gave £290 in part exchange. Approximately eight months later Oscar Chess discovered that the Morris car was not a 1948 model but was in fact registered in 1939. This was identified when the chassis and engine numbers were sent to Morris Motors Ltd. Had this been known when the part-exchange price was offered, Williams would have only received £175 for his car. Oscar Chess attempted to recover the overpayment but the Court of Appeal held that the statement of the age of the car was not intended to be a term but was instead a representation. Williams honestly believed the car was as he described and Oscar Chess, as car dealers (and therefore experts), should have the means to check the car's details more readily than the owner.

→

Authority for:

Statements made by a party with no special skill or knowledge, particularly with the other party who does possess this skill/knowledge, are likely to be considered representations rather than terms.

The case identified that if one party makes a statement and they have less knowledge on a particular topic or subject than the other party, such a statement will be more likely to be considered a representation than a term. The situation is reversed when a party making a statement has much greater knowledge. Each case is taken on its merits, but this is a good indication as to how the courts will view such negotiations.

Dick Bentley Productions v Harold Smith Motors (1965)

Facts:

Mr Bentley purchased a used motorcar from Smith on the representation that it had travelled only 20,000. After the purchase it was clear the vehicle had travelled many more miles than that stated by Smith (probably 100,000) and Bentley's action was to claim for this misrepresentation.

Authority for:

Bentley's action was successful and Smith's appeal dismissed. The representation when made in commercial dealings is presumed to act as a warranty and to be used as a way of inducing the contract. Smith was an experienced car dealer who should have been sufficiently diligent to identify the mileage of the vehicle, or at least he should not have made a false representation.

- *Reliance shown to be placed on the statement:* When the parties are involved in negotiations, if a party reasonably relies on the statement made by the other party without examining the truth, then reliance can elevate the statement to a term.

Consider

The actual contract for the lease of the shop includes restrictive covenants including a right of way through the car park area and a restriction on converting the property into residential accommodation. Thus, the statement made by Beta is contrary to the written terms of the contract. Given that this statement is said with force and is issued as an incentive to conclude the agreement, it is likely to be held as a term. As such, its breach would enable Aspen to pursue damages.

Buyers should be as specific as possible about the requirements of a product of a contract, and if assurances are made that induce the contract, the statement will likely be considered a term.

Bannerman v White (1861)

Facts:

A contract for the sale of hops stipulated that the purchaser intended these to be used in the production of beer. As such, the purchaser asked if the hops had been treated with sulphur and if so, they would be unsuitable for the intended purpose. The seller gave those assurances when in fact the hops had been so treated.

Authority for:

The statement was held as a term of the contract, not a representation. The significance of this aspect of the negotiations was clearly made and the seller relied on the statement provided. The action for breach of contract was successful.

- *Strength of the statement:* The stronger and the more emphatic that the statement is made, the more likely that the statement will be considered a term. The strength of the statement may be identified through stopping a person investigating the validity of a statement, providing a guarantee about the truth of the statement, and so on.

Consider

Imagine that the statement regarding the turnover of the business is incorrect and actually, the turnover has never been more than £150,000 per annum. Would this constitute a term of a contract and has the term been breached? Would this also be the case if the number of units held by Beta was incorrect? A term is a statement of fact whereas a representation is a statement of opinion (or cannot be verified). Is the number of items held and the income generated by a business an opinion?

Schawel v Reade (1913)

Facts:

In the sale of a horse, the claimant required the animal for stud purposes and was informed by the seller that it was 'perfectly sound.' Following the purchase it became clear the horse was not in such a condition.

Authority for:

The seller of the horse had specialist knowledge of the animal and thus the statement was a term rather than a warranty.

However, statements made with strength or presented emphatically will not be considered as terms where it is understood by the parties that statements cannot amount to a term.

Hopkins v Tanqueray (1854)

Facts:

A horse was to be sold at Tattersall's by auction and the potential buyer, when inspecting the horse, was told by the seller not to inspect the animal as it was 'perfectly sound'. On the basis of this statement the inspection was halted and the horse was subsequently purchased. When it was later discovered that the horse was not sound, the purchaser attempted to claim damages for breach.

Authority for:

It was held that this was not possible due to a rule at Tattersall's that all horses were sold without any warranty as to soundness.

- *The time at which the statement was made:* When the parties are negotiating, the courts will take into account the timing of any statements (in relation to when the contract was agreed). If a statement is made which causes the other party to agree to conclude a contract, this will be more likely to be considered a term. This is because the court may view the statement as being of such importance to the other party that it made them agree to the contract. The longer the delay between the statement and the conclusion of the agreement, the less likely the statement will be held as a term; this is particularly so where the written agreement does not include the statement made orally. Cases involving the timing of the statement are decided largely on the facts, rather than some application of the law, and attempts to second-guess how the court will determine the status of a statement are very difficult.

- *Was the statement reduced into writing:* If a statement is made during the course of negotiations, and the agreement is subsequently reduced into writing, statements made prior to the contract will be viewed as representations. The rationale is the **parol evidence** rule, where outside factors cannot be introduced into a contract or used to vary the written document. Generally, important terms will be included in the contract by the parties, and those other statements that were made, but not included, are by their nature of lesser importance.

Routledge v McKay (1954)

Facts:

The claimant had acquired a motorcycle with the registration documents identifying the vehicle as a 1942 model. When selling it, he used that date although in reality the motorcycle had been registered in 1936. The purchaser inspected the vehicle and when returning some days later, a written agreement was produced without the date being included.

→

Authority for:

The statement was a representation. Neither party was an expert on the subject matter, there was a delay between the statement (of the year of the vehicle) and the conclusion of the deal, and the year of the vehicle was not included in the written agreement.

Note, however, that if the written agreement has been incorrectly drafted so as to exclude certain elements of the statement made in the negotiations, or where this may have been an intentional act to exclude statements that had been made, it may be held that these should still be part of the written contract terms. Further, oral statements made in the negotiations but not included in the written document may themselves establish a separate (known as collateral) contract that is enforceable.

Remember that these are merely guidelines to identify a term or representation and the courts can place importance on whatever factors are present in each case to determine the status of the statement. Indeed, Moulton LJ in *Helibut, Symons & Co. v Buckleton* stated that all of the factors that led to the contract have to be considered to identify terms from representations, and whilst the previous authorities are good guides, not one can be universally true in every case.

Terms of a contract are not simply those that are expressed. It would be unrealistic to attempt to include all of the terms applicable and hence some may be implied into the contract. It is vital you understand where terms derive, and how they may be implied, to appreciate the full implications of the contract being agreed.

8.3 TERMS OF THE CONTRACT

Imagine you are drafting a contract, for example, for the employment of a member of staff. You are going to include the most important points—the hours to be worked, duties, to whom the individual must report and take directions from, what rate of pay is being provided, when and how payment is made, and so on. These terms are fundamental to the contract and hence are expressed. However, what about overtime duties? What if the business has to reorganize its production due to changes in delivery, new technology, or a change in legislation? If you hire a person in a management capacity for a multinational company will they be expected to move to new branches in different cities if their expertise is needed? These are aspects of the contract that are included, often, through implied terms. They still form part of the contract, they are terms, and may be enforced, but by their very nature they will not have been expressed orally or in writing. Therefore, express and implied terms in all contracts have to be understood, as their effects are far-reaching.

8.3.1 Express Terms

Express terms are, naturally, those that have been expressed in some form. Terms may be outlined in a written form (perhaps in the contractual document, in correspondence between the parties, or (in an employment law context) through a works handbook) or they may be identified from the oral negotiations between the parties. Being expressed in such an overt way, they are often the most important terms and contain key elements to the contract (the item to be sold, the price to be paid, and so on).

8.3.2 Implied Terms

Whilst terms are expressed in a contract, it would be impossible to include every element of the contract in a written document or an oral negotiation. Some terms may be necessary to make the contract work, some may be so obvious that they do not need to be expressed, and, importantly, Parliament has introduced implied terms in business, consumer, and employment contracts to regulate the behaviour of the parties. As such, terms are implied into contracts by the courts, through customs and statutes that must be appreciated to understand the obligations on parties, and their rights under the contract.

Wells v Devani (2016)

Facts:

Mr Wells had developed residential flats. Following a discussion with his neighbour, Wells was alerted to the fact that an investment company may be interested in purchasing the remaining seven flats. Being receptive to the proposal, the neighbour contacted the investment company and Devani, an estate agent. Later, Wells and Devani agreed, subject to contract, the purchase of the flats by a Housing Association. After the acceptance of the offer, Devani sent Wells an email seeking payment of his fees and attaching terms of business. A dispute arose over the content of the conversations between the pair prior to the email and the terms of business. Had the parties reached the stage of a legally binding contract given that the written terms were issued after the agreement with the Housing Association?

Authority for:

The Court of Appeal would not imply terms for the purposes of establishing a contract which would otherwise not exist. Per Lewison LJ: '... it is wrong in principle to turn an incomplete bargain into a legally binding contract by adding expressly agreed terms and implied terms together.' The parties should ensure that important contract terms have been agreed even if the complete contract has yet to be ascertained.

- *Terms implied by the courts:* Courts imply terms into a contract as a matter of fact or a matter of law. This is undertaken to help make sense of the agreement between the parties, or to make the contract work. Courts have also allowed terms not expressed in the contract to be implied because of the custom in a particular industry or market. Be aware, however, that whilst the courts may be willing to imply terms, they will not rewrite a poorly drafted contract and essentially perform the task that should have been undertaken by the parties. The two main reasons for the courts implying terms as a matter of fact have been due to **business efficacy**; and secondly, because the term was so obvious each party must have assumed it would be included.

The Moorcock (1889)

Facts:

The owners of a wharf on the River Thames entered into a contract to allow the owner of a steamship (named the *Moorcock*) to moor the vessel at the jetty for the purpose of discharging cargo. Whilst the *Moorcock* was discharging her cargo the tide ebbed and she hit the bottom of the riverbed and sustained damage. The owners of the *Moorcock* claimed damages, but in its defence the owner of the wharf stated the agreement had not provided assurances with regards the safety of the vessel or the suitability of the wharf. The Court of Appeal considered that the ship could not be used in the manner envisaged without it resting on the riverbed, and hence this must have been implied as the intentions of the parties. Esher LJ considered that an implied term existed (on the basis of business efficacy) and therefore the damages action would succeed.

Authority for:

The courts may imply a term where it is necessary to produce an intended or anticipated result in the contract.

- The second scenario where a court may be willing to imply a term is where it is so obvious that the parties clearly intended it to be included.

Shirlaw v Southern Foundries (1939)

Facts:

Southern Foundries entered into an agreement with Mr Shirlaw employing him as managing director for a term of 10 years. Two years later a company called Federated Foundries Ltd acquired Southern Foundries and it was decided that Shirlaw should be removed from the board of Southern Foundries and this in effect resulted in Shirlaw's employment being terminated. Shirlaw, in response, brought an action for wrongful dismissal. The Court of Appeal held that Mr Shirlaw should not have been dismissed. Mackinnon LJ used what has become known as the 'officious bystander' test when considering the parties' negotiations and held that they must have agreed, implicitly, to ensure that Mr Shirlaw was bound to complete the term of the contract for 10 years, and Southern Foundries were bound not to remove or replace him in the same period.

Authority for:

The courts may imply a term which is so obvious that it goes without saying. Hence, if, while the parties were making their bargain, an officious bystander were to suggest some express provision for it in their agreement, they would testily suppress him with a common 'Oh, of course!'

When considering implied terms in a contract, the courts can adopt the 'business efficacy' route as established in the *Moorcock*. The alternative route was created in *Shirlaw* that established that if the term is so obvious that it 'goes without saying' then the term will be implied into the agreement. This officious bystander test is very important as it considers what a hypothetical officious bystander would have thought should be included in a contract. If the bystander was to make an observation of a clause to be inserted and the parties were to respond that 'of course the term was included in the agreement' (essentially that it was so obvious that it need not be stated) then this would amount to a term implied into the contract. Further, unlike the previous examples of terms being implied due to the facts of the case, in *Liverpool CC v Irwin* the House of Lords held that contracts such as those involving the lease of apartments in a tower block could have terms implied as a matter of law.

- *Terms implied through customs:* Customs can be used if they are very widely known and accepted by the general population (such as the term 'baker's dozen' which refers to 13 of a particular item rather than 12 which the term 'dozen' generally refers to—see *Smith v Wilson*, where the court implied the local custom that '1,000 rabbits' actually meant '1,200 rabbits'). Customs are mainly used in commercial or business transactions where the parties have not identified an express term to the contrary, and could be held to have intended to be bound by the business/industry practice (insofar as it is consistent with that type of contract). The custom may also be common to businesses in a particular geographical location. The courts will look towards the custom being notorious, certain, commonplace, reasonable, and legal to comprise an implied term. The term may also be implied on the basis of the previous dealings between the parties.

Spurling J Ltd v Bradshaw (1956)

Facts:

The defendant used a warehouse on a regular basis. When goods were delivered to the facility he signed an agreement containing an exclusion clause. The invoices came after these agreements were signed. On the occasion of the storage of orange juice, and the consequent spoiling of the consignment, the defendant refused to pay for the storage. The claimant's action was for the recovery of the owed sum—relying on the exclusion clause as to any potential for damage to the goods. The defendant argued that the exclusion clause had not been incorporated into the contract.

Authority for:

The clause was incorporated into the contract due to the previous dealings between the parties and that the defendant had been aware of its existence.

- *Terms implied through statutes:* Protection of consumers and those entering contracts has been significantly enhanced through the actions of Parliament. The Sale of Goods Act 1979, for example, has been particularly prominent in this area. Such statutes will be considered in detail in **Chapter 9**.

Finally, it is important to remember that the courts may imply terms because the contract is silent on the particular issue. However, where an express clause is included, then a contradictory term will not be implied (unless as required by law).

8.4 CLASSIFICATION OF TERMS

Consider

Aspen includes a clause in the contract that the seaworthiness of the vessel is a condition. Are the parties permitted to conclusively designate clauses in the contract as terms and conditions?

8.4.1 Types of Terms

It is important to identify how the courts will determine what classification is to be given to each term of a contract. This is specifically relevant in the event of a breach of the contract. The breach will occur when a term(s) of the contract is not adhered to by a party, and the remedy available will depend upon whether it is a warranty or a condition. Also note a third classification of term was introduced in the *Hongkong Fir* (discussed later in this section) case called **innominate terms** (where the parties cannot identify a term as a warranty or condition in advance of a breach).

• *Warranty:* A warranty is a lesser term of a contract. As stated by Denning LJ in *Oscar Chess Ltd v Williams* (see **8.2**), 'During the last 50 years … some lawyers have come to use the word "warranty" … to denote a subsidiary term in a contract as distinct from a vital term which they call a "condition".' If breached the remedy of damages for any loss may be claimed but the injured party is not entitled to repudiate the contract (they must continue to fulfil their obligations in the contract).

Bettini v Gye (1876)

Facts:

Mr Bettini was a professional singer who had agreed with Mr Gye, the director of the Italian Opera in London, to perform as first tenor during his engagement. Bettini agreed that he would attend rehearsals in London at least six days prior to the commencement of the engagement. However, he became ill and could not travel to London for the rehearsals. He did arrive two days before the engagement, ready to perform, but Gye considered this a breach of contract and terminated the agreement. The High Court held that the stipulation for attendance at the rehearsals was not a condition of the contract. Also, as the contract was not for a small number of performances (the contract was for 15 weeks), which may have led to the requirement of attendance at rehearsals, Blackburn J held that this was a warranty. As a warranty, Gye was entitled to claim damages for Bettini's breach (not paying Bettini when he was not present) but Gye had to continue with the contract.

Authority for:

Lesser terms will generally be considered a warranty and will not enable the injured party to end the contract, although they may still claim damages in the event of a breach.

Bettini has implications for the effective drafting of contracts, and as noted by Blackburn J in the case, if Gye had required attendance at the rehearsals as a condition and essential to the contract, this could have been drafted into the agreement enabling the contract to be ended. However, simply because the parties have used the word 'condition' will not oblige the court to interpret it as such.

L Schuler AG v Wickman Machine Tool Sales Ltd (1973)

Facts:

Schuler, manufacturers of tools, entered into a contract with Wickman, a sales company, for Wickman to have exclusive rights to sell certain tools produced by Schuler. A term in the contract required Wickman to send a sales person to named companies once a week (comprising of 1,400 visits). This term was identified as a condition. When Wickman failed to make some visits, Schuler both terminated the contract and claimed damages.

Authority for:

The House of Lords considered the term a warranty. It was not open to a court to take into account post-contractual conduct when determining the meaning and effect of the contract.

This does not prevent a party from identifying a term that they consider essential and insisting that it is a condition due to its significance.

Lombard North Central Plc v Butterworth (1987)

Facts:

The defendant had entered into a hire purchase agreement for the purchase of a computer which provided for prompt payment (time of the essence) of the instalments. When the defendant got into arrears, the lessor took possession of the computer, sold it to recover some of the owed money, and claimed the rest in damages.

Authority for:

The nature of the term requiring prompt payment was held as a condition of the contract. Per Mustill LJ: 'A stipulation that time is of the essence in relation to a particular contractual term, denotes that timely performance is a condition of the contract. The consequence is that delay in performance is treated as going to the root of the contract, without regard to the magnitude of the breach.'

Also, where statute has implied 'conditions' into contracts, these will be interpreted as such (e.g. the Sale of Goods Act 1979—see **Chapter 9**).

- *Condition:* A condition is an important term of the contract. It is often described as a term that goes to the 'heart of the contract' or it is 'what the contract is all about'. Due to its fundamental status, a breach of a condition enables the injured party to claim damages *and* they have the option to bring the contract to an end. If the choice is made to end the contract this must be acted upon quickly and within a reasonable time (reasonableness is based on the facts of the particular case and will vary on the basis of the subject matter of the contract).

Poussard v Spiers (1876)

Facts:

Madame Poussard was a professional singer engaged to appear in an operetta for a period of three months. The contract required Poussard to be present for the opening night. However, before the opening night, Poussard became ill and could not attend the performances and Spiers engaged a replacement to cover her role. One week later Poussard returned and wished to begin her performance in the show. Spiers refused and Poussard brought an action for breach of contract. The High Court held that the requirement to be present for the opening night was a condition, predominantly on the basis that Poussard's illness was serious and its duration was uncertain. Spiers could not be expected to stop the opening of the show until Poussard became available and so was entitled to appoint a replacement.

Authority for:

The failure of Poussard to be available at the commencement of the contract went to the root of the contract and consequently discharged the defendant (a breach of a condition).

The performer had to be available and present at the opening night as an essential feature of the contract. When compared with *Bettini*, Poussard was not available for the opening show while Bettini was. As the 'heart of the contract' for acting and operatic performances is to be available when the public are present at the opening night, and where the contract expresses this requirement as a condition, failure to satisfy this will result in the term being considered a condition.

- *Innominate/intermediate terms:* As conditions and warranties have such implications for the parties, and the courts do not like to have their time wasted with disputes identifying the status of terms, the courts consider that parties define the terms themselves. The rationale for this is that the money spent on the correct drafting of the contract will save the parties future expenses, and enable disputes to be settled without recourse to the courts. Whilst this 'term-based' approach, focusing on whether the term is a condition or a warranty, is commonly used, a court may be persuaded to use a 'breach-based' approach. The focus here is on the seriousness of the consequences of the breach. A better description of innominate terms is that they are intermediate terms and where the consequences of the breach are held to be serious, the effects of the breach will be treated as if a condition was broken, with less serious breaches being regarded as breach of a warranty. Therefore, innominate terms have not replaced conditions or warranties, but are simply a means of looking at the consequences of a breach, rather than the traditional method of looking at the parties' intentions in drafting the contract.

Consider

Would Aspen's repudiation of the contract be justified or would it amount to a breach of contract? With reference to *Hongkong Fir v Kawasaki*, does Aspen have to complete the balance of the contract?

Hongkong Fir Shipping Co. v Kawasaki Kisen Kaisha (1962)

Facts:

The vessel the *Hongkong Fir* was chartered to Kawasaki for a period of 24 months. The ship was to be fitted for 'ordinary cargo service' and the owners were to maintain the ship during its service. The ship was delivered in a reasonable condition. However, due to its age, it required expert maintenance by engine room staff. The staff were incompetent and too few in number, and due to these facts there were serious breakdowns in the machinery. The ship was at sea eight-and-a-half weeks, off hire for five weeks and when it reached its first destination it required an additional period of 15 weeks in repair. Due to the reliability problems, Kawasaki ended the contract. The owners of the *Hongkong Fir* brought an action for breach of contract, and Kawasaki claimed in response that the owners were obligated to provide a seaworthy vessel and had failed in this respect. Diplock LJ stated that the obligation of seaworthiness was neither a condition nor a warranty but in effect could constitute both dependent upon the consequences of the breach. The Court of Appeal held that Kawasaki had no legal entitlement to end the contract, although it was entitled to damages for any breach of the contract by Hongkong Fir Shipping Co as to delays when the vessel was being repaired and in port.

Authority for:

The courts may adopt a 'breach-based' assessment in the identification of terms of a contract. A breach of a term that has deprived the innocent party of substantially the whole benefit of the agreement will be held a breach of a condition.

The contract had been established but the condition that the ship be fitted for ordinary cargo service was so broad that it could not be used by Kawasaki in the manner attempted. A range of scenarios could have made the ship unseaworthy, some being a condition (such as a hole in the hull) and others a warranty (insufficient life-jackets). Therefore, as the businesses could have better drafted a contract to protect themselves if required, the breach had to be interpreted on the basis of the agreement and the benefit available in the contract. The 20 weeks being unavailable was a relatively small time in the balance of the two-year contract. The owners took responsibility for the repairs, and any losses incurred could have been reclaimed in damages.

This case has identified the importance of correct and technical drafting of contracts and the effect and importance applied to significant terms. Identifying 'conditions' and 'warranties' will save time in future disputes between the parties but there exist situations, as in *Hongkong Fir*, where it is the effect of the breach which will determine whether a breached term is a condition or warranty. Further, the courts have stated that if there is an established commercial practice regarding the status of terms used in commercial contracts, these should be interpreted as such to ensure certainty, which is good for public policy, between the parties.

The Mihalis Angelos (1970)

Facts:

Owners of a ship let it to charterers identifying that it would be ready for use on 1 July and if it was not ready to load by 20 July the charterer would have the option to cancel the contract. The charterer could not get their cargo ready by 17 July and thereby, on that date, cancelled the contract (arguing frustration). The ship was ready by 23 July and the owners sought to enforce the contract.

Authority for:

It was held the charterer had breached the contract on 17 July, however they were only entitled to nominal damages. The charterers would have cancelled the contract on 20 July as per the contract and losses should be restricted to this.

8.5 CONTRACTUAL TERMS EXEMPTING/ EXCLUDING LIABILITY

8.5.1 Exclusion/Exemption Clauses

An exclusion clause is a term of the contract whereby one party seeks to exclude or restrict a liability or legal duty that would otherwise arise. Rules have been developed through the common law and through statutes to regulate how exclusion clauses may be fairly used in contracts. Typically, the exclusion clause will be made known to the other party through a notice, written in the contract itself, or expressed in the negotiations between the parties. Further, an exclusion clause can be a non-contractual notice. The clause has to be incorporated into the contract at the offer and acceptance stage (i.e. when it is created), it must be reasonable, it must be specific as to what liability it purports to exclude, there must be a reasonable opportunity for the other party to be aware of the existence of the term (although it is not the responsibility of the party who is relying on the exclusion clause to ensure the other party has read the clause), and it cannot exclude liability where Parliament has provided specific rights.

There are numerous reasons why exclusion clauses have been allowed in contracts. These include that the courts have the ability to strike out unreasonable clauses; statutes have provided greater protection against unreasonable terms; exclusion clauses often result in cheaper services (such as the price paid for parking, which would be significantly higher if it included insurance for damage and/or theft); and unlimited exposure to any number of claims in numerous situations is of itself unfair and unrealistic to the contracting parties. However, the main rationale for the ability for one party to exclude its liability is because of the freedom of contract. Freedom of contract had developed through the market forces argument whereby the State would not seek to regulate contracts if the market could do so adequately. No one can be forced into a contract against their will, therefore if the terms of the contract are not acceptable by the other party, either the offeror will have to change the terms (which may be the exclusion clause), or the market will provide another party who will offer the terms required. This system works in a perfect market but the reality is that there is relatively little choice for consumers (see the price similarity for televisions, games consoles, and so on) and different high-street stores are often owned by the same multinational corporations. There is also an unequal power relationship between the parties. It was in response to these concerns that the State began to restrict the ability for certain terms to be excluded from contracts.

8.5.1.1 Incorporation (the common law approach)

The following cases demonstrate the courts' approach to how an exclusion clause may be incorporated into an agreement. It should also be noted that, whilst this section considers the common law approach, exclusion clauses have to be construed in light of the statutory requirements following the Unfair Contract Terms Act (UCTA) 1977 and the Consumer Rights Act 2015 (considered in more detail in **Chapter 9**).

* *Signing the contract binds the parties:* If a party had signed a document held to be a contract, provided they had been given an opportunity to read it, they are bound by the terms.

L'Estrange v Graucob Ltd (1934)

Facts:

Miss L'Estrange was the owner of a cafe in Llandudno who entered into an agreement to buy an automatic slot machine for cigarettes. The machine did not work correctly and engineers had to be called out several times, but each time the machine failed to work shortly after being repaired. Later L'Estrange wrote requesting that Graucob remove the machine, as it had not worked for one month. Graucob, however, refused to terminate the contract. The contract contained an exclusion clause that all express and implied terms and conditions were excluded. The High Court held that by signing the document, even though she did not read it, she was bound by it. There was no misrepresentation or fraud, and consequently L'Estrange could not reject the contract.

Authority for:

A general rule exists that a party who signs a contract is bound by it, even though they failed to read it. (But this rule is subject to many exceptions.)

This is the situation insofar as the other party has not lied or misrepresented the contents of the contract.

Curtis v Chemical Cleaning and Dyeing Co. (1951)

Facts:

The claimant used the cleaning services of the defendant to clean her wedding dress. The form she was asked to sign contained a number of exclusions. The claimant asked the assistant about the form and was told it referred to the exclusion of liability for damage

→

to any beads on the dress. However, it went much further and excluded all damage, however so caused. The dress was returned to the claimant having been badly damaged.

Authority for:

The assistant had misrepresented the contents of the form to the claimant and could therefore not rely on it to exclude liability for the damage. This was despite the fact that the claimant had signed the form. Per Denning LJ: 'When one party puts forward a printed form for signature, failure by him to draw attention to the existence or extent of the exemption clause may in some circumstances convey the impression that there is no exemption at all, or at any rate not so wide an exemption as that which is in fact contained in the document.'

Standard form contracts frequently contain exclusion clauses, minimum periods for the life of the contract, and outline the remedies in the event of a breach. Parties should familiarize themselves with the terms and obligations before agreeing to be bound, as not having read the document will not exclude the party from its provisions.

- *The clause must be included at the creation of the contract:* For a valid exclusion clause, the term must have been included at the offer and acceptance stage. Once the parties have agreed the terms of the contract, future terms may not be inserted unless supported by fresh consideration.

Olley v Marlborough Court Ltd (1949)

Facts:

Mrs Olley stayed as a guest in the Marlborough Court hotel. She paid a deposit and proceeded to the bedroom where, behind a door, was a notice excluding the proprietors from responsibility for articles lost or stolen, unless these had been handed to the manageress for safe custody. Mrs Olley returned to her room where she discovered some of her possessions had been stolen. She brought a claim for damages but the hotel denied responsibility and referred to the exclusion clause displayed in the hotel room. The Court of Appeal held that as the notice was displayed in the hotel room this was seen after the contract had been established at the reception. Therefore, it was not included in the contract and could not prevent Mrs Olley's claim.

Authority for:

An exclusion clause must be incorporated into a contract at the offer/acceptance (agreement) stage to be effective. Attempts to include further terms after this stage in the formation of a contract must be supported by fresh consideration.

Similarly, in the following case, the terms binding the parties must be incorporated at the agreement stage. It is a requirement of the party attempting to rely on the term to ensure it is part of the contract.

Thornton v Shoe Lane Parking Ltd (1971)

Facts:

Mr Thornton was attending an engagement at the BBC. He drove to the city and went to park his car in a multi-storey, automatic-entry, car park where he had never been before. At the entrance to the car park was a notice that read 'All Cars Parked at Owner's Risk'. Thornton approached the entrance, took the ticket dispensed by the machine, and parked the car. The ticket included, in small print, a term that it was issued subject to 'the conditions of issue as displayed on the premises'. This included a notice displayed within the car park excluding liability for any injuries sustained by persons using the car park (the case was heard before the enactment of UCTA 1977, where contracts purporting to exclude liability for death or personal injury due to negligence were held void). Thornton returned to the car park three hours later and was severely injured in an accident, the responsibility for which was shared between the parties. Thornton claimed for his injuries and Shoe Lane Parking considered the exclusion clause protected it from liability. It was held that the ticket was nothing more than a receipt and once issued, further terms could not be incorporated into the contract. Only those terms included at the entrance were effective (excluding liability from theft or damage to the vehicle) and not those displayed within Shoe Lane's premises.

Authority for:

A party subject to an exclusion clause is bound (insofar as it satisfies the test of reasonableness) by the terms identified to them at the agreement stage. Further, there must be a reasonable opportunity for that party to be aware of the existence and extent of the term(s).

An important element was that Mr Thornton had not been to the car park before. If he had, and thereby presented with the opportunity to have seen the exclusion clause, he would have been bound by it (as per the previous dealings between the parties).

- *Implying exclusion clauses through prior dealings:* An important feature of the court's decision in *Thornton* was that the exclusion clause did not apply, in part, because Mr Thornton had not visited the car park before. Reasonable opportunity to be made aware of the clause is all that is required, and therefore, previous dealings where an exclusion clause is present may imply this term into future agreements.

    1. *Between businesses:* If businesses have a history of trade where exclusion clauses have been included, these are likely be accepted by the courts as forming part of subsequent agreements. Further, if the clause is used and is commonplace in an industry or between businesses, it may be implied into the contract.

British Crane Hire v Ipswich Plant Hire (1974)

Facts:

The two businesses were involved in hiring plant and earth-moving equipment. Ipswich Plant Hire contacted British Crane for the hiring of a crane, but this was required immediately and the contract was concluded through an oral agreement conducted on

→

→

the telephone. As such, the conversation did not include the conditions under which the contract would be based, and failed to identify the exclusion clause. This clause required the hirer to indemnify the owner for any expenses that would be incurred in connection with the crane's use. It was included in the written copy of the contract that was forwarded to Ipswich Plant Hire, but before this could be signed and returned the crane sank into marshland. British Crane argued that the exclusion clause was effective and sought to be compensated for its losses. It was held that the exclusion clause was implied into the contract because of a common understanding between the parties that standard terms as used in the industry would form part of any agreement between them.

Authority for:

Exclusion clauses commonplace in a particular industry or in particular business agreements will be implied into those contracts and are therefore effectively incorporated.

2. Private *consumers:* Private consumers are granted protections by the courts against exclusion clauses that, if implied into contracts, may produce unfairness. The first case noted here demonstrates the necessity for the party wishing to benefit from the exclusion clause to bring it to the other party's attention.

McCutcheon v David MacBrayne Ltd (1964)

Facts:

Mr McCutcheon requested that his brother-in-law transport his car using the services of David MacBrayne Ltd (McCutcheon had used the firm several times previously). MacBrayne occasionally required customers to sign a 'risk note' that included an exclusion clause for losses or damage to the vehicles shipped. On this occasion no note was provided or signed. The car was shipped but the vessel never reached its destination as it sank due to negligent navigation and the car was a total loss. Mr McCutcheon attempted to recover the value of the car but MacBrayne referred to the exclusion clause that had been previously included in its business dealings with McCutcheon. The House of Lords held that the exclusion clause was not present in this contract, and its previous use was so inconsistent so as not to be implied into further dealings.

Authority for:

Previous dealings between the parties are only relevant if they identify a knowledge of the terms of the contract (such as an exclusion clause) and these dealings can demonstrate assent (acceptance) of them.

Previous dealings with contracts involving exclusion clauses will bind a party if they have had an opportunity to be aware of the terms and there is a history of previous dealings. In this case, however, the contract with the exclusion clause present had not been agreed and McCutcheon was entitled to assume a different agreement was being concluded than those previously agreed. It may take many contractual dealings where an exclusion clause was present for the courts to later imply one. *Hardwick Game Farm v Suffolk Agricultural Poultry Producers Association* involved more than 100 situations of the exclusion notices forming part of the agreement; this was considered indicative of prior dealings enabling the clause to be implied.

- *The clause must be brought to the other party's attention:* For an exclusion clause to be effective, it must be provided in the contract, through a notice, prior dealings between the parties, or expressed in the negotiations between them. If it is hidden in some document in which the party would not reasonably expect contractual terms to be included, it may be ineffective.

Chapelton v Barry UDC (1940)

Facts:

Mr Chapelton visited a beach, under the control of Barry Council. Beside a café, on the beach were deck chairs owned by the Council available for renting through payment to an attendant. Chapelton took two chairs, one for himself and one for his friend, and received two tickets from the attendant, which he placed in his pocket. Importantly, the tickets contained conditions on the back disclaiming liability for injury when using the chairs. Chapelton used the chair, but when he sat down he went through the canvas and sustained injury to his back for which he had to seek medical attention. He claimed against the Council for the injury he sustained. The Court of Appeal held that the attempted exclusion clause was not effective as it had not been incorporated into the contract. It was not identified on the notice displaying the price for the hire of the chairs and the ticket provided could be considered only as a voucher and a reasonable man would think of a ticket as proof of purchase (relying on a precedent established in *Parker v South Eastern Railway Co.*).

Authority for:

To be effectively incorporated into a contract, an exclusion clause must have been reasonably brought to the other person's attention and not hidden in some document where a term of a contract would not be expected.

Where a person would normally not expect a ticket to include terms and conditions that may restrict or bind them, such terms will not be considered as having been incorporated. However, where it was reasonable that a ticket contained terms and conditions, exclusion clauses included in such a document will be effective.

- *Unusual terms must be brought to the other party's attention:* Not only must the party wishing to gain protection from the exclusion clause give the other party a reasonable opportunity to be aware of the term, if such a clause would be unusual (such as to provide a significantly increased sum of damages) this must be identified to be effective.

> ### *Interfoto Picture Library v Stiletto Productions (1988)*
>
> **Facts:**
>
> Stiletto had ordered 47 photographic transparencies from Interfoto. A note accompany-
> ing the delivery was included identifying terms and conditions, the most onerous of which
> provided that a 'holding fee' of £5 per day, per transparency, was to be paid if they were
> not returned within 14 days. Stiletto failed to return the transparencies as required and the
> resultant holding fee amounted to £3,783. The Court of Appeal held that such a clause had
> not been incorporated into the contract as it was unusual practice in the industry, it appeared
> to be unreasonable, and Interfoto had failed to adequately bring it to Stiletto's attention.
>
> **Authority for:**
>
> Where a condition of a contract is particularly onerous or unusual, it is for the party attempt-
> ing to rely on this to demonstrate that they fairly brought it to the other party's attention.

8.5.2 Misrepresentation May Restrict the Operation of an Exclusion Clause

An exclusion clause which has satisfied the tests as noted at **8.5.1** will generally be held by
the courts to be effective, even if the injured party has been ignorant of it. An exclusion
clause which was otherwise lawful will fail if it was misrepresented to the other party.
Such misrepresentation can be through words or conduct, but the key element is that it is
sufficient to mislead the injured party about the existence or extent of the exclusion clause
(see *Curtis v Chemical Cleaning and Dyeing Co. Ltd* in **8.5.1.1**).

8.5.3 Interpretation of the Clause

Having satisfied itself that the exclusion clause had been validly incorporated into the
contract, the clause must be considered to ascertain whether its scope includes the nature
of the event which has led to the loss/injury. The courts have traditionally interpreted
such clauses **contra proferentem**, and thereby against the party wishing to rely on it. Of
course, this section must be read in light of the restrictions on contractual clauses through
UCTA 1977, which has strengthened protections against the use of exclusion clauses.

* *The purpose of the contract:* The courts will look at the nature of the contract and ascertain if the exclusion clause attempts to contradict the purpose of the underlying
  agreement or the intentions of the parties.

> ### *Evans Ltd v Andrea Merzario Ltd (1976)*
>
> **Facts:**
>
> The parties had contracted for the importation of machines from Italy by sea. The stand-
> ard form contract contained an exclusion clause, upon which the defendants attempted
> to rely when the goods were lost in transit. The machines had been stored in a container
>
> →

→

on the deck of the ship, but the claimants had been given an oral assurance that the machines would in fact be stored below deck. The container in which the machines were housed was lost when it slid overboard during the voyage. The Court of Appeal held that the defendants were not able to rely on the exclusion clause in the standard form agreement as this was contrary to the assurance given, and this assurance was to override the exclusion clause.

Authority for:

The oral assurance provided to the claimant was a term of the contract (a collateral contract was established) and overrode the inconsistent provisions of the written agreement. Hence, the written exclusion clause was ineffective against the collateral contract.

• *The* contra proferentem *rule:* Whilst an exclusion clause is permitted under the freedom of contract, as its effect is to restrict or limit a liability that would otherwise exist, the courts will interpret it *contra proferentem* (against the party who wishes to rely on the clause). Therefore, the party wishing to rely on the clause must ensure it is correctly and precisely drafted to cover the event that led to the claim.

Houghton v Trafalgar Insurance Co. Ltd (1953)

Facts:

The claimant had insured his five-seat car through the defendant insurers. The policy included an exclusion clause that the insurers would not accept liability for any damage caused whilst the car was 'conveying any load in excess of that for which it was constructed'. Mr Houghton was involved in an accident in which his car was a total loss, but at the time of the accident there were six passengers in the car. Under these circumstances, the defendants relied on the exclusion clause that six people in the car constituted an excess load. The Court of Appeal held that there was ambiguity in this clause, as the 'excess load' would have been more likely to cover situations of excessive weight rather than number of passengers. Due to this uncertainty, the exclusion clause could not be relied upon.

Authority for:

The courts will interpret exclusion clauses *contra proferentem* and any ambiguity will probably result in the clause, and its application, being limited in effect.

The requirement for precision in the drafting of the clause, and its effect thereafter was demonstrated in the following case:

Baldry v Marshall (1925)

Facts:

The case involved the purchase of a car. The claimant informed the defendant motor dealers that he wished to purchase a car suitable for touring. They recommended and supplied him with a Bugatti car, and a clause in the contract stated that the defendants would not be liable for any 'guarantee or warranty, statutory or otherwise'. The car was unsuitable for its purpose and the claimant rejected it and sought to recover his payment.

Authority for:

The Court of Appeal held that the claimant's stipulation of a car suitable for touring was a condition of the contract, and as, under an exact reading of the exclusion clause, it did not seek to exempt liability for a breach of condition, it could not be enforced in this case.

Similar reasoning as to interpreting exclusion clauses in light of the main purpose of the contract was seen by the House of Lords decision in *Glynn v Margetson*.

8.5.4 **Limitation Clauses**

Where exclusion clauses attempt to exclude a claim for loss or damage, and exempt liability for breach, **limitation clauses** seek to reduce exposure to claims by limiting liability to (e.g.) a monetary claim for damages, to a fixed sum, and for any consequential losses. Following UCTA 1977, the courts have been more willing to accept limitation clauses in contracts (since unreasonable clauses may be disregarded under the Act), and in *Photo Production v Securicor Transport Ltd* it was held that such clauses should be given their ordinary, natural meaning, and not construed differently from other clauses in the contract. Like exclusion clauses, the courts, in assessing the viability of the clause, will begin by assessing whether the limitation clause forms part of the agreement, whether it covers the breach in question, and finally whether it uses the *contra proferentem* rule of interpretation.

8.5.5 **The Statutory Position**

Particularly since the enactment of UCTA 1977, consideration of the validity of an exclusion and limitation clause has included statutory measures. UCTA 1977 was designed specifically to regulate the use of exclusion clauses, and the Consumer Rights Act 2015 has extended the powers to the entire contract. These statutes are of great significance in this area and are considered in **Chapter 9**.

 CONCLUSION

The chapter has identified the factors that help to distinguish between terms and representations. Further, it has demonstrated the distinction between the terms in a contract and the significance of the status of warranty and condition. Exclusion clauses, their validity, and methods of incorporation, have been discussed, and the reader should be in a position to recognize the common law rules established for the effective incorporation of such clauses. The book continues by examining the effect of statutory involvement in the regulation of contracts.

SUMMARY OF MAIN POINTS

- The provisions of the contract may be viewed as a term or a representation.
- Terms are the most significant aspect of an agreement and failure to fulfil the agreement enables a claim under breach of contract.
- A representation is not a term under the contract and the injured party must seek a remedy under misrepresentation.

Representations

- A statement made by a party with greater knowledge, and relied on by the other, will generally be held a term.
- If the statement is made with strength it will be more likely to be regarded a term, unless it is implicitly/explicitly agreed that it cannot be held as such.
- A statement that induces the other party to enter the contract will be more likely to be held a term.
- Statements made in the negotiations, but that do not appear in the final written contract, will be held to be a representation (although a collateral contract may have been created).

Terms: expressed and implied

- Terms may be expressed orally or in writing and these will form part of the contract.
- Due to the problems in attempting to include every term into a written or oral contract, or deduced from conduct, terms are implied.
- Terms may be implied by the courts as a matter of fact or a matter of law.
- Customs established by the parties' previous trading relationship, the industry, or the conduct of business in that locality may form part of the contract.
- To form a custom the term must be notorious, certain, commonplace, reasonable, and legal.
- Many terms are implied into contracts by statutes—such as the Sale of Goods Act 1979 and UCTA 1977.

Terms: warranties and conditions

- A warranty is a lesser term, breach of which enables the innocent party to seek damages although they must continue with the contract.
- A condition forms the most important aspect of the contract, breach of which enables the innocent party to seek damages, and they may end the contract or affirm it.
- Warranties and conditions are determined on a 'term-based' approach. However, the courts may also adopt a 'breach-based' approach. Here, it is the seriousness of the consequences of breach that will identify the term as a condition or warranty (referred to as 'innominate terms').

Exclusion/limitation clauses

- These clauses seek to limit or exclude a liability that would otherwise exist.
- To be effective the clause must be incorporated into the contract at the agreement. Incorporating an exclusion clause after this time requires fresh consideration.
- The clause must be reasonable (assessed using UCTA 1977) and not contrary to statute.
- The clause must be specific to the liability being excluded.

- It must have 'reasonably' been brought to the other party's attention.

- This obligation is even more strictly applied if the exclusion clause involves a particularly unusual term.

- Exclusion clauses may be implied through previous dealings between the parties.

- The *contra proferentem* rule applies so that any ambiguity in the exclusion clause will be interpreted against the party attempting to rely on it.

 ## SUMMARY QUESTIONS

Essay questions

1. 'Employment law is one jurisdiction of law that, whilst dominated by statutory intervention, continues to be underpinned by ordinary contractual principles. This is particularly true in relation to the doctrine of implied terms.'

   Assess the role played by implied terms in employment relationships and how they have been developed by the judiciary.

2. How have the statutory developments regulating the use of exclusion clauses altered and restricted their use?

   Compare how the cases pre-1977 would be decided in the courts today.

Problem questions

1. A Ltd and Z Ltd are negotiating for the charter of a ship on an 18-month contract. A Ltd is concerned that the goods to be shipped in the vessel reach the customers on time or it will face penalties and may also lose business. Therefore A Ltd has inserted the following clause in the contract:

   'It is a condition of this contract that the ship is seaworthy in all respects.'

   Following the signing of the charter, when the ship is at sea there are continued problems with its maintenance as the crew supplied by Z Ltd are very inexperienced and the chief engineer has an alcohol problem. In part due to this, the ship is in the dock with engine problems for the first three months in the initial eight months of the charter.

   A Ltd fears for the probable negative consequences of the ship and now wishes to end the contract and claim damages from Z Ltd.

   Advise A Ltd accordingly.

2. Sarah works for a local school and travels to work each day by car. She usually parks on a nearby piece of waste ground, but was unable to do so last week because of flooding. Instead, she parked her car in the multi-storey car park. A notice just inside the entrance to the car park states:

   'The company will not be responsible for death, personal injury, damage to vehicles or theft from them, due to any act or default of its employees or any other cause whatsoever.'

   Reference to this notice is also contained on a ticket which Sarah received when entering the car park. On her return to collect the car, Sarah discovers that it has been stolen. She goes to report this to the attendant and is injured when he negligently allows the barrier to fall on her head.

   Advise Sarah.

 You will find guidance about how to answer these questions online at www.oup.com/uk/marson5e/.

FURTHER READING

Books and articles

Lawson, R. (2014) 'Exclusion Clauses and Unfair Contract Terms' (11th Edition) Sweet and Maxwell: London.

Lewis, M. and Hinton, C. (2004) 'No Room for Ambiguity' *New Law Journal*, Vol. 154, 7138, p. 1128.

ONLINE RESOURCES

http://www.oup.com/uk/marson5e/

For further resources relating to this chapter, including self-test questions, an interactive glossary, and key case flashcards.

9 STATUTORY REGULATION OF CONTRACTS

Contracts between businesses, and those between businesses with consumers are regulated increasingly through statutory intervention. These statutes control the use of terms, whether exclusion of liability is void or permitted insofar as being reasonable, and other statutes imply or guarantee terms into contracts. Sellers of goods in particular must have an awareness of these laws and ensure they do not negligently or knowingly transgress the provisions. Knowledge of the content and application of the legislation is necessary, as some rights impose strict liability on the seller, whilst others involve negligence liability.

Business Scenario 9

Ghirardelli Curator Ltd is an independent, bespoke chocolatier based in Soho, London. Due to its reputation for extravagant designs and celebrity customers, and because of the recent appointment of Michelin star winning chef Christophe Dupain-Cheng, it has seen a rapid rise in its popularity.

In July, Ghirardelli was contacted by a representative for the company Amelia Barnes Inc, a well-known international banking company, to create a chocolate sculpture of a yacht as the centrepiece for one of its holiday parties for its most important staff and clients. Amelia Barnes Inc was insistent that the sculpture was made from Belgian chocolate with Teja chillies to provide the flavour most suited to its guests. However, following delivery, Amelia Barnes Inc has complained to Ghirardelli that the chocolate used was actually Ghanaian milk chocolate and it contained salted caramel 'walls' within the sculpture which proved to be far too intense, making it inedible.

One week later, Meghan Willis, an American country-singing star, bought a box of custom and handmade couture chocolates from Ghirardelli's shop in Soho. However, Meghan had to cancel her performances in London as she was hospitalised after suffering anaphylactic shock after eating two of the chocolates. It transpires that some of the chocolates contained dry-roasted peanut extract to produce the multisensory effect sought by Christophe, but this was not identified on the packaging or by the retail staff. The costs associated with the cancelled performances are anticipated to be in the region of £1 million.

Learning Outcomes

- Explain the protection afforded to buyers in contracts for goods and services, through statutory intervention (**9.2–9.3.5**)

- Explain the protection for consumers concluding contracts through distance selling, on- and off-premises, and through digital downloads (**9.4–9.4.11.4**)

- Demonstrate how statute restricts the use of exclusion clauses in contracts (**9.5–9.5.4**)
- Explain the effects of the Consumer Rights Act 2015 on the regulation of consumer contracts (**9.1–9.3.5**).

9.1 INTRODUCTION

This chapter continues to explore the contract in greater detail by examining how the terms of a contract are regulated through statutory intervention. Such legislative measures have been provided due to the unequal bargaining positions of the contracting parties in business to consumer contracts, and the State regarding some aspects of laissez-faire to be contrary to public policy and fairness (such as certain exclusion clauses). For example, statutes, such as the Sale of Goods Act 1979, imply terms into contracts, the Consumer Rights Act 2015 guarantees certain rights, and the Unfair Contract Terms Act 1977 regulates the parties' use of exclusion clauses. This particularly protects the weaker party to a contract from exploitation and provides minimum rights that may not be waived.

From 1 October 2015 the Consumer Rights Act (CRA) came into effect and has changed the statutory sources of protection in business-to-consumer (B2C) contracts, and to business-to-business (B2B) contracts (albeit to a lesser extent in this second category of contractual relationships). The CRA 2015 formed part of the government's initiative to reform consumer rights, in some instances simplifying the current range of legislation, and in other areas seeking to codify and establish a consistent application of the law.

The CRA is comprised of three parts:

- Part 1 is concerned with consumer contracts for goods, digital content, and services;
- Part 2 deals with unfair terms; and
- Part 3 considers miscellaneous provisions such as investigatory powers, enforcement mechanisms and collective redress, and other private actions relating to anti-competitive behaviour in competition law.

Given the overlap between the previous statutory regulation of contracts (which are likely to continue to have effect for several years into the future) and the rights provided specifically to consumers through the CRA 2015, the relevant provisions of the CRA 2015 are incorporated in this chapter in conjunction with existing legislative provisions.

9.2 THE SALE OF GOODS ACT 1979 AND THE CONSUMER RIGHTS ACT 2015

Contracts concluded prior to 1 October 2015 between consumers and a trader are protected by the Sale of Goods Act (SOGA) 1979. Therefore, if, for example, when shopping at a high-street department store you see a sign reading 'No refunds provided for unwanted goods. This does not affect your statutory rights' the store is identifying that it will not provide a refund for a good that is not faulty and is simply unwanted. This approach is lawful and in accordance with statutes including SOGA 1979, but businesses involved in retail must be aware of the implications of SOGA 1979, to adhere to its requirements, recognize its application to contracts involving consumers, and also the effects of this being replaced in business-to-consumer (B2C) contracts by the CRA 2015. SOGA 1979 continues to be applicable in B2B contracts. Remember, under the CRA 2015, the consumer is protected when contracting with a trader.

For years, the common law and legislation have afforded protection to consumers and businesses (in fact most of the case law on the subject involves B2B disputes). SOGA 1979 was revised and updated from the original Act of 1893 but the main provisions remain remarkably similar to this legislation. Further, whilst case law has provided 'flesh on the bones' of the legislation, it is also worthy of note that protections for those involved in buying and selling goods had been developed through the common law; indeed, the 1893 Act was actually a codification of these rights into one Act of Parliament. From its inception, SOGA 1979 offered protection to 'buyers'. This Act implies the terms into contracts and, in certain circumstances these cannot be removed through waiver or a contractual term to the contrary.

- *Definition*: For protection to be provided through SOGA 1979, a sale must take place (s. 2(1) and s. 5 of the CRA 2015). Whilst this may appear obvious (if for no other reason than the title of legislation) its effect is that barters (exchanging items) and loans are not protected unless a transfer of the ownership has occurred. SOGA 1979 includes contracts of sale (where the goods purchased are taken into the possession of the buyer immediately) and agreements to sell (where the contract becomes a contract of sale when the goods exist and the ownership passes to the other party—s. 2(5)). This second scenario may be evident where a product is sourced/manufactured with a lead-time before delivery is made.

- *The meaning of 'goods'*: The transfer of 'goods' invokes the provision of SOGA 1979. Goods are defined as 'all personal chattels other than things in action and money . . . ; and in particular 'goods' includes emblements, industrial growing crops, and things attached to or forming part of the land which are agreed to be severed before sale or under the contract of sale and includes an undivided share in goods' (s. 61(1)).

As such, items ordinarily used by consumers including televisions, tables, mobile telephones, and cars will be considered 'personal chattels' and covered by the Act. 'Things in action' is a historical expression for something, unlike personal chattels which involves a tangible good, which must involve the exercise of a legal right in order for it to 'materialize'. A most obvious business example of this would be a guarantee provided when a good is purchased. The paper that the guarantee is written on is not what the guarantee is, but rather provides evidence that a guarantee can be exercised and pursued through the courts if necessary. Things in action are not covered by SOGA 1979. In B2C contracts 'goods' means any tangible moveable items—including water, gas and electricity if, and only if, they are put up for supply in a limited volume or set quantity (CRA 2015, s. 2(8)).

- *Who is protected:* The significance of SOGA 1979 is that certain terms are implied into the contract that offer a level of certainty, and security, for the goods contracted. These place obligations on the seller of the goods to ensure that SOGA 1979, ss. 12–15 are adhered to. These implied terms are held as conditions of the contract and hence allow an injured party to repudiate the contract within a reasonable time if they are breached. Further, after this reasonable time, the terms are held as warranties and allow an injured party to seek damages (but they will not be in a position to repudiate the contract). The other major advantage of SOGA 1979 is that the liability is strict and hence it does not matter how the good fell below the standard required: the seller has responsibility. Sections 12, 13, and 15 apply to all sales contracts. Section 14(2) and (3) applies to contracts made by a consumer with a seller acting in the course of business (prior to contracts concluded on or after 1 October 2015).

The CRA 2015, s. 2 provides important definitions applicable to qualification to protection under the Act:

- *Trader*—this term refers to a person (both natural (human) and artificial (corporation)) acting for purposes relating to their trade, business, craft, or profession. The term trader applies whether they are acting personally or whether another person is acting in the trader's name or on their behalf.
- *Consumer*—this term refers to an individual acting for purposes that are wholly or mainly outside of that individual's trade, business, craft, or profession. The significance of this definition is that it provides certainty and consistency between consumer protection legislation. Any trader who claims that the individual was not a consumer for the purposes of this law has the obligation to prove it. Such definitions remove the confusion present in the current/previous legislation relating to consumers and traders. The Unfair Contract Terms Act 1977, s. 12 sought to define what 'dealing as a consumer' and acting in 'the course of business' meant in real world scenarios.

R & B Customs Brokers Co. Ltd v Union Dominions Trust Ltd (1988)

Facts:

R & B was a two-person shipping broker company which bought a used car from Union Dominions. R & B intended that the vehicle would be used by its managing director but when delivered, it was discovered that there were problems with the car. This included a leaking roof and R & B attempted to use s. 14(3) of SOGA 1979 in pursuit of a remedy. However, the contract of sale excluded any implied terms relating to fitness for purpose. This would be permitted in business-to-business contracts, but contrary to the Unfair Contract Terms Act 1977 in business to consumer sales. Thus, if R & B was held as a business for the purpose of the sale, the exclusion clause would be permitted and the claim would fail.

Authority for:

R & B was held as having acted as a consumer for the purposes of this sale. This purchase was incidental to the running of R & B's shipping business and not 'in the course of' its business. It was an irregular activity and a degree of regularity is required before such activities can be called an integral part of the business.

Business—includes the activities of any government department or local or public authority.

9.2.1 SOGA 1979, ss. 12–15

For sellers and buyers, significant protections are provided through SOGA 1979, ss. 12–15. Section 12 is applicable to all sales and cannot be waived. Sections 13–15 may be waived in B2B sales where it is reasonable. Similar provisions are available in B2C sales (with distinctions drawn where appropriate between the statutory provisions).

- *Section 12—title to goods:* A fundamental aspect to a contract of sale is that in order for a 'true' sale to take place, one party must be free to transfer ownership (good title) to the other. The buyer is then able to enjoy 'quiet possession of the goods'. In order to achieve this, the first party must possess the title to transfer or have the owner's consent to dispose of the good.

> ### *Rowland v Divall* (1923)
>
> **Facts:**
>
> Mr Divall purchased an 'Albert' motor car and he later resold it for £334 to Rowland. Rowland, a motor car dealer, sold it to a Colonel Railsdon for £400, but the car had been stolen before Divall bought it and it was repossessed by the police. Rowland returned the £400 purchase price to Railsdon and brought an action against Divall to recover the £334 he had paid for the vehicle. SOGA 1893 had implied into every contract of sale 'a condition on the part of the seller that . . . he has a right to sell the goods', and if this is not satisfied the buyer has the right to have the purchase price returned. Only a person who holds 'good title' to a property has the right to transfer or convey this, and if the property is in fact stolen, then no passage of title may occur. The Court of Appeal held that Rowland was entitled to have his money returned.
>
> **Authority for:**
>
> Section 12 provides that in every contract of sale, there exists an implied condition that the seller has the right to sell.

In this case, as the parties had purchased the stolen vehicle in good faith, there was no criminal element to the proceedings, but the seller did not have good title to the goods and hence the contract failed. Colonel Railsdon could claim the return of the price paid to Rowland (despite having use of the vehicle for several months), Rowland had the right to claim the purchase price from Divall, and Divall had the right to pursue the seller from whom he purchased the vehicle and have the money returned (albeit in reality it may be very difficult to find the seller of the stolen goods to pursue the return of the money paid).

Whilst this situation regarding stolen goods appears to be straightforward, the seller has no right to sell the good so cannot pass on good title and the original owner will have the good returned to them, this is not strictly so. In this scenario, the loss would fall on the innocent buyer, as in *Rowland* above, who would have to recover their losses from the rogue who sold the stolen good. There are mechanisms that enable an innocent buyer to obtain good title when they purchase goods in good faith and lacked knowledge of the rights of the owner/seller.

In *Rowland*, the sale was said to be void (did not exist) because the car that was sold had been stolen. If, however, the transfer of ownership is 'voidable' then SOGA 1979, s. 23 is important. It states: 'When the seller of goods has a voidable title to them, but his title has not been avoided at the time of the sale, the buyer acquires a good title to the goods, provided he buys them in good faith and without notice of the seller's defect of title.' Such a situation may occur when the sale is agreed with the rogue on the basis of a misrepresentation (e.g. taking possession of the goods through providing a cheque in payment that fails to clear), and hence the rogue now possesses a voidable title to the goods that can be transferred. This 'title' can be lost where the true owner takes action to avoid the contract—either through contact with the rogue or through some other means (such as reporting the incident to the police). However, SOGA 1979, s. 25 provides a further hurdle for the owner. Even where steps have been taken to avoid the contract with the rogue, where the rogue 'buyer' has taken possession of the good (although not ownership of the title) and they sell the good to another buyer who is acting in good faith, the buyer will obtain title to the goods. Sales of goods can occur through the actions of an agent with possession of the owner's good passing on the title to a buyer acting in good faith, and in situations where the owner allows the buyer to believe the seller of the goods has the owner's permission to sell.

It is important to recognize that when the title to goods has passed, this is effective even before the payment has reached the seller (however, payment must have been intended). This may occur where one business transfers goods to another business and payment is made, for example, at the end of each month. If ownership has transferred, but the other party fails to pay for the goods and those goods have been resold, or the party is liquidated, the seller may have difficulty in obtaining payment. As such, a contract may incorporate a reservation of title clause whereby the seller has the ability to recover the goods for non-payment. The reservation of title clause is effective where the contract states that the goods remain in the possession of the seller until payment is made (at which point the title to the goods will transfer), the goods are still in the buyer's possession, and the goods are readily identifiable (hence the goods have not been joined with other goods and they can be identified).

Borden v Scottish Timber Products Ltd (1981)

Facts:

Resin was supplied to a chipboard manufacturer on retention of title terms. The resin was used, and thereby incorporated into the chipboard, thus changing its identity with the manufacture of a new product.

Authority for:

The supplier's claim of the retention of title was defeated.

These clauses are referred to as 'simple' but it may not be realistic or in the best interests of the seller to incorporate such a clause that may prevent the buyer using the goods. Hence, a particularly important judgment was made in the following case.

Aluminium Industrie Vaasen v Romalpa Aluminium Ltd (1976)

Facts:

The sellers of aluminium wanted protection against possible non-payment and therefore contracted with the buyers on the basis that the goods supplied were to be maintained separately from the buyer's other goods, the sellers would have ownership of the buyer's products that had been made with the seller's goods, these products must be stored separately from other goods, and the proceeds from any sales of the goods were put into a separate bank account so the sellers could be assured of payment when requested. When the buyer's business failed and it was wound up the sellers were successful in obtaining its goods supplied, but unused, and the money it was owed.

→

Authority for:

The case was decided largely on its facts so its application may be limited. 'Romalpa clauses' effectively provide the seller with a charge over the goods supplied. However, due to the restrictions on how charges can be made over a company's property, and to circumvent possible legal issues with the effects of this case, the buyers were considered as bailees of the seller's goods.

• *Section 13—description of goods (B2C contracts see s. 11 of the CRA 2015):* Goods that are sold by description must correspond to that description. This may be evidenced in situations involving the sale of products where it may be particularly difficult or time-consuming for the buyer to verify the claims. It enables sales to take place with the protection for the buyer that the item possesses the features that they were assured.

Consider

Amelia Barnes Inc has requested a specific type of chocolate to be used in the production of the sculpture and this is agreed. Hence the product is being bought according to the description provided by Ghirardelli Curator Ltd. As such, a remedy may be available for breach of s. 13 SOGA. However, as the chocolate itself is of satisfactory quality and fit for its intended purpose, there is no breach of ss. 14(2) or 14(3) SOGA.

Section 13 allows the buyer protection when they rely on the description provided, but it does not where the buyer has not relied on the description and has taken the responsibility for verifying the good.

Harlingdon and Leinster Enterprises v Christopher Hull Fine Art (1990)

Facts:

The claimant bought a painting described in an auction catalogue as by a German painter 'Munter' for £6,000 from the defendant. The defendant sellers were not experts in paintings of this type and the claimant sent his own experts to inspect the painting. Following the purchase, the claimant discovered the painting was not by this artist and was actually worth less than £100. The buyer claimed a breach of s. 13 of SOGA as the painting was not as described.

Authority for:

The claim was rejected. The court held that to use s. 13, the claimant must have relied on the description and by using their own experts resulted in this not being a sale by description.

The protection of s. 13 also applies to advertisements and sales materials that the buyer relies on (see the Unfair Commercial Practices Directive). It is important to note that whilst the sections of the Act are separated, they may work independently of each other or in unison. For example, s. 13 is not concerned with the quality of the product, which may be perfectly fine in terms of its quality and fitness for purpose, but not as described. This would still allow a remedy under SOGA 1979.

Arcos v Ronaasen (1933)

Facts:

An agreement for the sale of wooden staves to be used in the making of barrels iden-tified the staves as being of half an inch thickness. However, when delivered, some of the staves were of slightly different thicknesses (although they were still usable for the intended purpose). The buyer attempted to reject the staves as not being as described.

Authority for:

The court held there was a right to reject the goods. They were not as described.

The significance of the overlap of the provisions can be seen in relation to the seller. Section 14 requires the good to be of a satisfactory quality, but this is only an implied term in sales in the course of business (i.e. the buyer has to possess the status of a consumer as noted earlier). Where goods are sold privately the buyer has no protection unless a warranty is provided (and usually this is not—*caveat emptor*).

Beale v Taylor (1967)

Facts:

A private seller sold a car that was described as a Triumph Herald, but in reality was two cars welded together (with only one half of the car corresponding to the description).

Authority for:

The Court of Appeal held, whilst the buyer could not rely on s. 14 as to the car's quality, an action was permitted under s. 13 (as it applied to all sales).

- *Section 14(2)—quality of goods (B2C contracts see s. 9 of the CRA 2015):* Section 14(2) incorporates a term in sales established in the course of business requiring the goods to be of a satisfactory quality. Note, this will not prevent a business from seeking protection under the Act where the sale is not part of the 'course of business' and in essence the buyer is acting as a consumer.

Stevenson v Rogers (1999)

Facts:

The defendant was a fisherman who sold his fishing boat to the claimant. The claim-ant considered the boat not to be of satisfactory quality and thus a breach of s. 14. The

→

defendant argued that s. 14 did not apply as the boat was not sold in the 'course of business'. The fisherman's business was in catching fish, not selling boats.

Authority for:

The Court of Appeal held s. 14 did apply. The buyer was acting as a consumer.

'Quality' will vary between products depending on issues such as whether the good was brand new or used. Section 14(2) is applicable in each scenario, but the interpretation of the word will differ. If the item is sold as new, it should have such a condition (free from scratches, in its new and original packaging, and so on).

Clegg v Anderson (2003)

Facts:

The contract involved the purchase of a yacht. The keel of the vessel was to be built to the manufacturer's standard specification but when installed, it was heavier and the claimant rejected the yacht. The defendant argued that the rejection of the yacht was unreasonable given the manufacturer had offered to rectify the defect.

Authority for:

The right to reject had not been lost despite the offer of a repair. There is no requirement that the right to reject is subject to consideration of reasonableness.

If the good is used, some general 'wear and tear' must be expected but it must still be of 'satisfactory' (formerly known as merchantable) quality.

Thain v Anniesland Trade Centre (1997)

Facts:

The claimant bought a used Renault car. It had an automatic gearbox, had approximately 80,000 miles on the odometer and was priced just below £3,000. Ms Thain was offered the opportunity to purchase three months' warranty with the vehicle but declined. After a couple of weeks' use, the vehicle made droning noises which was later diagnosed as a failing gearbox. Thain continued using the vehicle for more weeks until it broke down. The cost of replacing the gearbox was uneconomic and Thain tried to reject the car as not being fit for purpose and recover her purchase price.

Authority for:

The court held that the car made no noise when it was bought and as such was fit for its purpose when supplied. A used car, and one with such high mileage, could fail at any time and the reasonable person accepts this risk.

For the purposes of SOGA 1979, goods are of satisfactory quality if they meet the standard that a reasonable person would regard as satisfactory, taking account of any description of the goods, the price (if relevant), and all the other relevant circumstances (which may include the precautions the reasonable person would undertake in the use of a good).

Heil v Hedges (1951)

Facts:

The claimant brought a claim against a butcher on the basis that pork chops that had been sold to the claimant were not fit for purpose. When eaten, the claimant contracted a tapeworm infestation due to parasites in the meat.

Authority for:

The court held the meat was fit for its intended purpose. The claimant had not properly cooked the meat to kill the parasites and it was generally known that pork had to be cooked for a substantially longer time than other meats. It has been suggested, however, that given the risks involved in some foods, it is incumbent on the seller to warn customers of potential dangers.

The issue of quality extends from the good itself, to include the packaging in which it is contained, and to 'external factors' that would make the good fall below the quality required.

Wilson v Rickett Cockerell (1954)

Facts:

The claimant purchased a bag of coalite from the defendant. When it was lit, the coalite exploded as it contained detonators. The claimant argued the coalite was not of satisfactory quality.

Authority for:

The defendant argued that it was the detonators that were not of satisfactory quality, but the coalite was. However, the court considered that as the coalite was sold in a unit (in a bag), the contents of the bag were to be determined on the basis of satisfactory quality. Therefore, damages were awarded for a breach of s. 14(2).

Features to be considered when assessing the quality of a good include:

1. fitness for all the purposes for which goods of the kind in question are commonly supplied;
2. appearance and finish;
3. freedom from minor defects;
4. safety;
5. durability.

This last aspect—durability—may also assist buyers when considering the life span of the goods. For example, if you purchase a television, you may receive a one-year manufacturer's warranty. However, under SOGA 1979, it may be considered that it should last much longer, and if used correctly, would provide the owner with the right to have the item repaired or replaced if a defect appears within six years (after a reasonable time the term will be considered a warranty—again, general 'wear and tear' or damage caused other than a defect will not enable a claim under the Act). Hence, even though replaced in consumer contracts on 1 October 2015, the SOGA 1979 will remain significant for consumers (and traders who will be responsible for claims made under this legislation) for several years into the future.

The main value of s. 14(2) is that the liability is strict and hence it does not matter how the defect in the good was created, as many businesses simply resell goods bought along the supply chain: if there is a defect, protection is granted under s. 14(2).

Consider

The statutory implied terms contained in s. 14(2) of SOGA requires the relevant good to be of satisfactory quality. This imposes a strict liability where the contract applies between businesses as is the case between Amelia Barnes Inc and Ghirardelli Curator Ltd. Section 14(2) imposes a basic obligation, whilst s. 14(2A) introduces an objective element into judging whether satisfactory quality is present or not. The fact that the wrong chocolate is used in such a contract would be a sufficiently serious breach to affect the quality of the goods in the entire contract.

Whilst these protections exist, defences are available to sellers against what could be considered as 'unfair' claims. Section 14(2C) outlines situations where protection under s. 14(2) will not extend. For example, if a product is purchased and a defect has been pointed out, particularly where an incentive has been provided in 'compensation' for the defect, the buyer cannot later rely on s. 14(2) for this specific problem.

Bartlett v Sidney Marcus Ltd (1965)

Facts:

Sidney Marcus was a car dealer specializing in the sales of Jaguar and Ford motor cars. Sidney Marcus sourced a car at the request of Mr Bartlett and whilst its sales executive travelled in the car to show Bartlett, he noticed the oil pressure gauge was defective and the clutch was not operating perfectly. These defects were identified to Bartlett and hence he was offered the car for £575 (with the car repaired), or for £550 and Bartlett could have the repairs completed by his garage. Mr Bartlett agreed with the latter offer as he believed he could get the repairs necessary completed for between £2–3. When the car broke down and it was sent for repair, Bartlett was informed the cost of repair would be over £84, and he initiated his claim for damages for the cost of the repair. Bartlett's claim was based on a breach of s. 14(1) and (2) SOGA, but the Court of Appeal held that there was no breach of SOGA 1979, and Mr Bartlett could not claim damages.

→

Authority for:

Where defects have been brought to a buyer's attention before the sale, any subsequent claim on this basis for breach under s. 14(2) will fail due to the application of s. 14(2C).

Likewise, if the buyer had examined the good themself before the purchase, and that examination ought reasonably to have revealed the defect, then this will be a defence to the seller (s. 14(2C)(b)). This does not require that the buyer should identify every defect, but very obvious defects where it could reasonably have been expected that the buyer would have seen and could have taken action on, may provide a defence against holding the term as a condition.

Satisfactory quality, in the CRA 2015, adopts a similar standard as under previous legislation. The standards of quality should be what a reasonable person would agree would be satisfactory. Used/second-hand goods will have evidence of wear and tear and they are not likely to be expected to be as durable as a new item (but then this would presumably be reflected in the price). Goods which are advertised and sold at a considerably lower price than comparable goods would likely not be deemed to be unsatisfactory if they did not match the same standards of quality as much more expensive goods (items such as televisions, watches, computers can have 'similar' features, but the price charged may be markedly different. Such differences may reflect the quality of components used in these devices and thereby affect the experience of them—speed, durability, etc.).

- *Section 14(3)—fitness for purpose (B2C contracts see s. 10 of the CRA 2015):* The Act continues regulating the quality of goods by providing that the item should be fit for its intended purpose. If the item purports to provide some function, it must do so.

Grant v Australian Knitting Mills Ltd (1936)

Facts:

Dr Grant brought an action against Australian Knitting Mills claiming damages on the grounds that he contracted dermatitis from woollen underpants sold under the name 'Golden Fleece'. Australian Knitting Mills had been negligent in failing to remove a chemical used in the manufacture of the underpants (free sulphate—which, when combined with sweat, produces successively sulphur dioxide, sulphurous acid, and then sulphuric acid). As such, Grant claimed the underpants were sold but were not 'fit for their purpose'. The presence of the chemicals in the garment was a hidden and latent defect, and could not be detected by any examination that could reasonably be made.

Authority for:

In the case of implied reliance on the quality of the good, the buyer can gain protection from either implicit or explicit reliance on the relevant term.

Products sold for a particular purpose must be suitable and 'fit' for that purpose. In the case of Dr Grant, these were underpants that would be worn against the skin. Due to the chemicals present, this was impossible and hence the garment failed under s. 14(3).

Consider

Section 14(3) of SOGA requires the relevant good to be fit for its intended purpose. Again, this imposes a strict liability between Amelia Barnes Inc and Ghirardelli Curator Ltd. The use of salted caramel which has rendered the sculpture inedible would clearly mean that this good, which is intended to be eaten, would not be fit for its intended purpose and would breach this section of the Act. With regards to Meghan Willis, as an individual consumer her claim would be for a breach of s. 10 of the CRA 2015. The use of nuts, especially dry-roasted peanuts which are widely considered to elicit the most severe reaction in allergy suffers, would make the chocolates unfit for their intended purpose for a person with such an allergy. However, for persons without an allergy the goods would be fit. Hence, should Ghirardelli have been under a duty to identify the use of nuts, or should Meghan have identified her allergy prior to purchase?

Protection is provided where the buyer seeks assurances from the seller as to the suitability of a particular good for a specific task. In this case the buyer is relying on the judgement of the seller, and if this is reasonable, then even if this request is beyond what would normally be associated with a reasonable use of the good, the law will still protect the buyer.

Ashington Piggeries Ltd v Christopher Hill Ltd (1971)

Facts:

The buyers were manufacturers of animal feeds and had contracted for herring meal to be used in mink food. The sellers knew of the purpose of the herring meal but had no experience of making food for mink. The herring meal had become contaminated so as to make it poisonous to all animals that it was fed to, but would be fatal if given to mink.

Authority for:

The House of Lords held that there was a breach of s. 14(3) as the buyers had relied in part on the judgement of the sellers to sell them appropriate materials.

The CRA 2015 also provides consumers protection in a contract to supply goods by reference to a model of the goods that is seen or examined by the consumer before entering into the contract. A term is thereby guaranteed to the effect that the goods will match the model. An exception is provided to the extent that any differences between the model and the goods are brought to the consumer's attention before the consumer enters into the contract (s. 14).

* *Section 15—sale by sample (for B2C contracts see s. 13 of the CRA 2015):* If a sale of goods takes place through a sample of a larger consignment the bulk of the consignment must correspond to the sample (in practical terms, this section is of most use to businesses). The goods should also be free from defects that would make their quality unsatisfactory that would not have been apparent on a reasonable inspection.

Godley v Perry (1960)

Facts:

A young boy bought a plastic catapult from a local retailer. When used, the elastic band on the catapult snapped and severely injured his eye. Damages of £2,500 were awarded. Further, the retailer refused to sell any more of the catapults. He had purchased a consignment of the catapults from the wholesaler and wished to reject them all.

Authority for:

Following a reasonable inspection, where a sample of a consignment proves to be of poor quality, the purchaser may treat the remaining items as of equally poor quality.

SOGA requires that in a sale by sample, the bulk must correspond to the sample. This means that if the sample is of a good quality, the buyer can expect the remaining items to be of a similar standard. This also works in reverse: where the sample is of a poor standard the bulk can be considered as being of a similar quality.

Figure 9.1 identifies the consequences for breach of SOGA 1979.

Figure 9.1 Consequences for breach of SOGA 1979

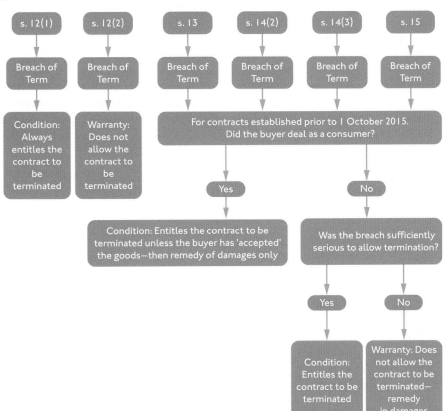

9.2.2 Remedies for Breach of the Sale of Goods Act

The terms implied through ss. 12–15 are conditions that allow the injured buyer to claim damages and repudiate the contract. The buyer must act within a reasonable time to allow the term to be treated as a condition. After this reasonable time, the term will be considered a warranty and the buyer will not be able to repudiate, but they may seek damages/ the goods to be repaired or replaced.

9.2.2.1 Buyer's remedies—SOGA

As has been noted at **9.2.2**, a breach of the various sections of SOGA will entitle the buyer to reject the goods and have the price paid returned, or to have the good repaired. These rights are dependent upon the terms of the contract which have been breached and when this has occurred.

- *The right to reject goods:* Rejection is permissible where the seller has breached a condition such as by delivering the wrong quantity of goods, where the seller has repudiated the contract, and where the goods are not of satisfactory quality. The injured party can reject the goods and refuse to pay the sum agreed, or to claim for any money paid. Conditions of SOGA include ss. 13–15 and enable the buyer acting not in the course of business to reject. However, such rights are lessened in B2B sales (s. 15A) and the defect in those situations has to be reasonable to allow a rejection. This further involves a partial rejection under s. 35A, where the buyer can accept those goods that correspond with (e.g.) s. 14(2), and reject the rest of the consignment. In order to reject the goods, s. 35 lays down a requirement for quick action and any delay may result in the buyer losing the right. There was a statutory extension to this provision through s. 35(5) which enabled the buyer a reasonable time to inspect the goods before it was determined that they had 'accepted' them, but the reality was the courts had generally included this element in their deliberations in deciding the case. The decision of the court in respect of 'quick' action is based on the individual facts of the case, and clearly each case will differ, but it appears that the price of the good and the corresponding expectations will be factors considered by the courts.

Rogers v Parish (1987)

Facts:

The claimant purchased an as-new Range Rover vehicle that was very unreliable and had suffered various mechanical problems. It was replaced but the replacement proved to be equally unsatisfactory and spent much of its existence from purchase in the garage being remedied. Despite the fact that it was seven months old, and having travelled some 5,000 miles, the claimant attempted to reject the car.

Authority for:

The Court of Appeal enabled the good to be rejected under s. 35. An unreasonably delayed rejection will prevent the buyer from rejecting the good, but here the cost of the vehicle allowed for higher expectations of the buyer than for someone buying a cheaper vehicle.

Consider

The implied terms of ss. 13, 14(2), and 14(3) SOGA 1979 and s. 10 CRA 2015 have been breached. As implied terms, they are each regarded as conditions and thus Amelia Barnes Inc and possibly Meghan Willis can repudiate the contract as well as claiming damages. Of course, the right to repudiate the contract only applies where the goods have not been accepted under s. 35 SOGA.

The buyer also has the right to have the goods repaired instead of rejecting the goods. This may be a route taken because the buyer is unaware of their rights under SOGA 1979, s. 35(6), which enables the buyer to have the good repaired without any inference from this action that they have accepted the good. Therefore, it preserves their right to later reject the good if it is unsatisfactory.

- *The right to claim damages:* As with any breach of a condition of the contract, the injured party (the buyer) is entitled to claim damages and to end (repudiate) the contract at their discretion. Under SOGA, the right for damages usually involves the non-delivery of goods (s. 51) where there is a difference in price between the cost of the goods at the time of the contract and the cost when the good has not been supplied. As always with damages (which is covered in **Chapter 10**) it is designed to place the injured party, as far as possible, in the position they should have been before the breach.

Consumer's rights to enforce terms about goods (s. 19 of the CRA 2015)

The protection afforded to B2B contracts through implied terms is similar in many respects to those terms guaranteed in B2C contracts. Existing/previous legislation sought to categorize contractual terms as either conditions (which go to the heart of the contract) or warranties (lesser terms), breach of which determined whether the consumer could reject the contract (a right only allowed for a breach of a condition) or to affirm the contract and seek damages. There was some distinction between the remedies for breach of the terms depending on the legislative instrument which provided the right, and as such the CRA 2015 seeks to add a consistency to the approach of remedies (see **Table 9.1** on p. 214).

Right to reject (s. 20)

The right of rejection is exercised if the consumer indicates to the trader that they are rejecting the goods and treating the contract as at an end. This indication may be something the consumer says or does, but it must be sufficiently clear to be understood by the trader.

Once the right to reject has been invoked, the trader has a duty to give the consumer a refund, and the consumer has a duty to make the goods available for collection by the trader or (if there is an agreement for the consumer to return rejected goods) to return them as agreed. Regardless of whether or not the consumer has a duty to return the rejected goods, the trader must bear any reasonable costs of returning them, other than any costs incurred by the consumer in returning the goods in person to the place where the consumer took physical possession.

Table 9.1 CRA 2015 rights and remedies

The right	Available remedy
Section 9 (goods to be of satisfactory quality) Section 10 (goods to be fit for particular purpose) Section 11 (goods to be as described) Section 13 (goods to match a sample) Section 14 (goods to match a model seen or examined) Section 16 (goods not conforming to contract if digital content does not conform)	(a) the short-term right to reject (ss. 20 and 22) (b) the right to repair or replacement (s. 23); and (c) the right to a price reduction or the final right to reject (ss. 20 and 24)
Section 12 (other pre-contract information included in contract)	The consumer has the right to recover from the trader the amount of any costs incurred as a result of the breach, up to the amount of the price paid or the value of other consideration given for the goods
Section 15 (installation as part of conformity of goods with contract)	(a) the right to repair or replacement (s. 23) and (b) the right to a price reduction or the final right to reject (ss. 20 and 24)
Section 17 (trader to have right to supply the goods etc.)	The consumer has a right to reject (subject to s. 20)

Time limit for short-term right to reject (s. 22)

A consumer who has the short-term right to reject loses it where this is not exercised according to the limits outlined below (unless the trader and the consumer agree that it may be exercised later—which must not be a shorter timeframe than the minimum established in law).

The short-term right to reject is the end of 30 days, beginning with the first day after these have all happened:

(a) ownership or (in the case of a contract for the hire of goods, a hire purchase agreement or a conditional sales contract) possession of the goods has been transferred to the consumer,

(b) the goods have been delivered, and

(c) where the contract requires the trader to install the goods or take other action to enable the consumer to use them, the trader has notified the consumer that the action has been taken.

Note; in the event that the goods are of a kind that can reasonably be expected to perish after a shorter period than the right to reject above would give, the time limit for exercising the short-term right to reject is the end of that shorter period.

Where the consumer requests or agrees to the repair or replacement of goods, the periods outlined above stop running for the length of the waiting period.

Right to repair or replacement (s. 23)

Where the right to repair (making the goods conform to the required standard) or replacement of the goods applies, and where the consumer requires the trader to perform this task, the trader must:

(a) do so within a reasonable time and without significant inconvenience to the consumer, and

(b) bear any necessary costs incurred in doing so (including in particular the cost of any labour, materials or postage).

The consumer cannot require the trader to repair or replace the goods if that remedy is impossible, or is disproportionate compared to the other of those remedies. 'Disproportionate' involves the imposition of costs on the trader which, compared to those imposed by the other remedies, are unreasonable, taking into account:

(a) the value which the goods would have if they conformed to the contract,

(b) the significance of the lack of conformity, and

(c) whether the other remedy could be effected without significant inconvenience to the consumer.

Questions as to what is a reasonable time or significant inconvenience are to be determined taking account of the nature of the goods, and the purpose for which the goods were acquired.

> **Consider**
>
> Given that Ghirardelli sold chocolates to Meghan Willis which contained nuts, and this was not identified to her as a customer, they are in breach of s. 10, and arguably ss. 9 and 11 too. Hence, Meghan is entitled to the remedies to reject, repair, or replacement, or to a price reduction or a final right to reject. It would appear that given the nature of the product and that it could not be repaired, and a replacement may not be what Meghan would like after the reaction she has suffered, a rejection under ss. 20 and 22 of the CRA 2015 may be most appropriate. Also, note that remedies under contract and the sale of goods deal with the contract itself—that is, the sale of the chocolates. Refer to Chapters 10 and 11 regarding remoteness of loss and the implications of a negligence action for the recovery of damages for the cancelled performances.

9.2.2.2 Seller's remedies—SOGA

As the buyer has remedies under SOGA, so does the seller for a breach by the buyer. This may occur if the buyer refuses to pay for the goods ordered (s. 49) or if they refuse to accept the supply of the goods (s. 50). These rights are typically used when the seller is selling the goods to another business, which may become insolvent and therefore not have the means to pay for the good. In the event of the buyer refusing to accept goods under the contract, the seller may claim damages. The assessment of damages is based, if an available market exists at the time for the goods subject to the contract, on the difference between the contract price and the market price at the time of non-acceptance. Damages will also be available for other reasonably foreseeable losses incurred due to the buyer's breach. However, it is possible that the parties may wish to exclude liability for potential losses (although this is most often seen in commercial contracts rather than between a private individual and a business).

Glencore Energy UK Ltd v Cirrus Oil Services Ltd (2014)

Facts:

Glencore contracted to sell oil to Cirrus which Cirrus intended to sell to a third party. When the third party refused to accept the oil from Cirrus, Cirrus refused to accept the oil from Glencore. Glencore brought its action against Cirrus for breach of contract, but Cirrus argued that an exclusion clause in the contract restricted any claim for loss of profits and Glencore's claim was for loss of anticipated profits rather than repudiation of the contract.

Authority for:

The court held that Glencore was entitled to damages in excess of $2.5 million on the basis of its 'loss of a bargain' rather than loss of profits. The exclusion clause did not extend to loss of a bargain and, in relation to non-acceptance of goods, SOGA requires that this is calculated on the basis of 'how much worse off the seller would be, if at the time of the breach, he had sold the goods to a substitute buyer.'

This case relates closely with the use and extent of exclusion clauses and demonstrates the need for careful drafting and review to ensure the clause protects the parties in the way and to the extent they expect.

A further right is for the seller to retain possession of the goods until payment has been made (s. 41), unless the seller waives the right or the price is paid (s. 43); the seller may stop the goods in transit and therefore restrict the physical passing of the goods to the buyer (where the buyer is insolvent—s. 44); and the seller may resell the goods to another buyer to mitigate any potential losses (where the goods are perishable or the seller has notified the buyer of the intention to sell if payment is not received—s. 48).

9.3 **THE SUPPLY OF GOODS AND SERVICES ACT 1982**

Note; for B2C contracts, this Act's provisions are replaced by the CRA 2015.
The Supply of Goods and Services Act is amended so that it covers B2B contracts and consumer to consumer contracts only.

The legislation governs the supply of services, and the supply of faulty goods and materials provided with the services in B2B contracts. It requires that a supplier of a service, acting in the course of business, provides that service with reasonable skill and care, within a 'reasonable' time (unless there is an express agreement to the contrary), and make a reasonable charge for the service. Part I of the Act provides protection by implying terms into contracts involving the transfer of property in goods, and into contracts for the hire of goods. The Act complements the rights provided in SOGA 1979.

9.3.1 Transfer of Property in Goods

A contract under this part of the Act includes any contract where the title to the goods passes to another, and is not a contract for the sale of goods, or contracts under hire-purchase agreements (as other statutes offer protection). An example of such a contract would be for a boiler to be installed in a house.

The Act gives protections as outlined in **Table 9.2**:

Table 9.2   Protection provided by the Supply of Goods and Services Act 1982 (relevant for consumer contracts prior to 1 October 2015)

Protection	Condition or warranty
The right to transfer the property (s. 2(1))	A condition
Quiet possession and freedom from encumbrances (s. 2(2))	A warranty
Correspondence with description (s. 3(2))	A condition if the buyer deals as a consumer
Satisfactory quality (s. 4(2))	A condition if the buyer deals as a consumer
Fitness for purpose (s. 4(5))	A condition if the buyer deals as a consumer
Correspondence with sample (s. 5(2))	A condition if the buyer deals as a consumer

9.3.2 Contract of Hire

Here, the title to the goods is not passed (transferred) to the other party, but a temporary possession is provided.

The Act gives the protections as outlined in **Table 9.3**:

9.3.3 Supply of a Service

Part II of the Act covers the very important protections afforded where a service is supplied. These terms are implied into contracts and are not included in SOGA 1979.

Table 9.3   Rights provided by the Supply of Goods and Services Act 1982 (relevant for consumer contracts prior to 1 October 2015)

Protection	Condition or warranty
Right to hire (s. 7(1))	A condition
Quiet possession and freedom from encumbrances (s. 7(2))	A warranty
Correspondence with description (s. 8(2))	A condition if the buyer deals as a consumer
Satisfactory quality (s. 9(2))	A condition if the buyer deals as a consumer
Fitness for purpose (s. 9(5))	A condition if the buyer deals as a consumer
Correspondence with sample (s. 10(2))	A condition if the buyer deals as a consumer

- *Section 13—duty to exercise reasonable care and skill:* There is an implied term that a supplier (who is acting in the course of business) will exercise reasonable care and skill. The protection is different from the implied term as to quality in s. 14 of SOGA 1979, which imposes a strict liability standard, in that the test as to reasonable care and skill is based on the test established in torts law (see **Chapter 11**). With the supply of a service, an outcome cannot be guaranteed as easily as with the sale of a good.

- *Section 14—performance within a reasonable time:* Where a supplier, acting in the course of business, provides a service but the time for the service to be carried out and/or completed is not identified in the contract, s. 14 provides that this must be achieved within a 'reasonable' time. The section of the Act, when read in conjunction with s. 14(2), provides that what is reasonable is for the courts to decide when investigating the facts of each case.

- *Section 15—the obligation to pay a reasonable price:* This section provides that, regardless of whether the supplier is acting in the course of business or not, there is an implied term of a reasonable price to be paid. Note that the section is not implied where the price has already been agreed in the contract, or has been agreed between the parties in the course of their dealings with each other. It is also relevant to be aware that a quotation is generally determined as a price at which the contract is to be performed. If the section is implied into the contract, s. 15(2) states that a reasonable price is to be determined on the facts of the case.

9.3.4 Consumer Contracts for Services—The CRA 2015

The CRA 2015 guarantees various terms into contracts for the supply of a service. The main provisions are included in ss. 49–52 which provide:

9.3.4.1 Service to be performed with reasonable care and skill (s. 49)

Every contract to supply a service is to be treated as including a term that the trader must perform the service with reasonable care and skill. This, consequently, no longer requires such a term to be referred to as being 'implied' into the contract. Further, the CRA does not provide a definition for 'care and skill' although it will likely follow that used in the previous applicable legislation (the Supply of Goods and Services Act 1982 s. 13) and case law identifying that this will differ between industries, and 'reasonable' will also be a variable concept, determined presumably with reference to the price paid for the service.

9.3.4.2 Information about the trader or service to be binding (s. 50)

Every contract to supply a service is to be treated as including, as a term of the contract, anything that is said or written to the consumer, by or on behalf of the trader, about the trader or the service. This becomes effective where the information is taken into account by the consumer when deciding to enter into the contract, or where it is taken into account by the consumer when making any decision about the service after entering into the contract.

This is an entirely new provision in the legislation (not previously incorporated in the Supply of Goods and Services Act 1982) and operates where promises/statements are made by a trader or on their behalf which induce the consumer to enter into the contract.

Further, given the Consumer Contracts (Information, Cancellation and Additional Charges) Regulations 2013 and the requirement imposed on traders to supply certain information to consumers, where such information is provided, s. 50 allows the consumer to use that information as forming a term of the contract.

Table 9.4 Rights and remedies for services in the CRA 2015

The right	Available remedy
Service to be performed with reasonable care and skill (s. 49)	The right to require a repeat performance (s. 55), and if that is impossible, or not done in a reasonable time or without significant inconvenience the right to a price reduction (s. 56)
Information about the trader or service to be binding (s. 50)	The right to a price reduction in price (s. 56)
Service to be performed within a reasonable time (s. 52)	The right to a reduction in price (s. 55)

9.3.4.3 Reasonable price to be paid for a service (s. 51)

This section applies to a contract to supply a service if the consumer has not paid a price for the service, the contract does not expressly identify/establish a price, or the contract is silent on how the price is to be reached (see **Table 9.4**). In such circumstances, s. 51 holds that the contract is to be treated as including a term that the consumer must pay a reasonable price for the service, and no more. What is a reasonable price is a question of fact for the courts to determine in the specific circumstances.

9.3.4.4 Service to be performed within a reasonable time (s. 52)

Where a contract to supply a service does not expressly fix the time for the service to be performed, it does not identify how it is to be fixed, and the information that is to be treated under s. 50 as included in the contract does not fix the time either, the contract is to be treated as including a term that the trader must perform the service within a reason-able time. Reasonableness, as with s. 51, is determined on the basis of a question of fact.

9.3.5 Remedies and Implications

In the event that a trader seeks to exclude their liability for breach of these guaranteed terms, such as that relating to the exercise of reasonable care and skill or information about the trader or service to be binding, s. 57 establishes that such a clause will not be binding on the consumer. Further, the consumer will always possess the right to seek a refund of the price of the service where there has been a breach of the terms as identified above. Any term or clause inserted into a contract which seeks to restrict their liability to an amount which is less than a contract price, will not be binding or enforceable. Note also that where the restriction in liability in the contract relates to a price above or in excess of the contract price, such a clause may be accepted where it satisfies the test of fairness (s. 62).

9.4 THE CONSUMER CONTRACTS (INFORMATION, CANCELLATION AND ADDITIONAL CHARGES) REGULATIONS 2013

The Regulations affect retailers in their relations with consumers and are part of a broader move by the EU and the Government to reform consumer laws. The Regulations took effect on 13 June 2014 and they replace and revoke the Distance Selling Regulations 2000 and the Off Premises (Doorstep) Regulations 2008. These Regulations form a minimum standard and traders are within their rights to offer more favourable terms if they so wish (and indeed may use this as a unique selling point through which to gain custom).

9.4.1 The Focus of the Regulations Includes:

- identifying information which a trader must give a consumer before or after making a sale, including how that information should be given;
- delivery times for purchases and information regarding the passing of risk;
- rights of consumers, when buying at a distance or off-premises to change their minds (cooling-off periods) and cancel orders; and
- prohibitions on consumers having to pay additional sums in excess of the basic rate of post-contract helplines, or in any additional payments which appear as a default option.

9.4.2 Contracts Affected

The Regulations may be applicable to contracts which are concluded on-premises—hence these are made in person and at the traders' business premises; they also apply to contracts agreed to off-premises—such as doorstep sales and any sales where the trader and consumer are not physically together and the contract is concluded at a place which is not the business premises of the trade. Note that a business premises can include a movable business structure such as the use of market stalls or vehicles in so far as the trader carries on their business there on a usual basis. They apply to distance contracts, which are typically those concluded online or through a telephone sales system. However, some contracts, such as for package travel are excluded from the scope of the Regulations.

The Regulations recognize three forms of contract:

1. sales contracts;
2. service contracts;
3. contracts for digital content supplied through downloads/streaming services.

A sales contract may include the sale of a tangible good such as a DVD but, importantly from the provisions included in these Regulations, it further includes digital content. Given the increase in purchases of digital media, especially in the advent of iTunes, and streaming services such as Netflix and so on, the increase in protection for consumers in this medium is particularly important and was not, arguably, protected sufficiently through previous consumer protection legislation. Further, sales contracts cover contracts for the supply of goods alone, and they also cover mixed contracts for the supply of goods and the fitting of appliances.

9.4.3 Contracts Excluded from the Regulations

The Government's practice guidelines give details on the implementation and application of the Regulations. These details also include contracts to which the Regulations will not apply (they are exempted):

- gambling contracts as provided through the Gambling Act 2005;
- package travel contracts;

- timeshare contracts;
- most financial services contracts (with the exception of warranties, credit agreements, and insurance offered as part of an ancillary contract);
- purchases from vending machines;
- construction and sale of immovable property such as new buildings;
- contracts for the letting of residential properties;
- single telecom connections (payphones and so on);
- the supply of consumables by regular roundsmen (e.g. milkmen and their deliveries).

9.4.4 Contracts Partially Covered

- items dispensed on prescription are exempt from the information and cancellation provisions;
- contracts with a value of less than £42 (identified as low value) and agreed off-premises contracts are exempt from information and cancellation provisions. They are, however, subject to the additional payments, charges, delivery, and risk elements of the regulations;
- passenger transport contracts are exempt from the cancellation rights and from most of the information provision requirements.

9.4.5 Cancellation Rights for Distance and Off-Premises Contracts

The cooling-off period, whereby a consumer may change their mind and revoke an acceptance, and hence a legally binding contract, extends from the current provision of seven calendar days for contracts concluded off-premises; and seven working days in relation to distance sales, to a period of 14 calendar days in respect of both types of contract. The cooling-off period exists for consumers to cancel a contract without having to provide the trader with any explanation or justification. Where the consumer exercises the right to revoke acceptance, they have a 14-day period to return any items contracted for (where applicable) and the trader must refund within 14 days of the cancellation of the service contract or receipt of goods (or evidence of the consumer having the goods) monies paid. Traders are protected during this period by being able to withhold any refunds until the goods are returned, or suitable evidence of this is provided. Provision is also made for traders to reduce any amount of money refunded where goods returned show evidence of handling beyond that necessary to ascertain whether the goods are as expected.

Finally, in the event of the consumer cancelling the contract, any ancillary contract (which relates to a type of contract to which a consumer would be unlikely to enter without the existence of the main contract) such as a credit agreement or any warranty which is provided as part of the sale is automatically cancelled. Two conditions are required to be met for a contract to be considered ancillary. The first is that an ancillary contract must be related to the main contract and secondly, it must be provided by either the trader to the main contract or by a third party with whom the trader has such an agreement. Where the consumer purchases, for example, a warranty independently although related to the purchase of the good or service from the trader, this will not satisfy the definition of an ancillary contract which will automatically be cancelled following the cancelling of the main contract.

Traders using the distance or off-premises method of selling will be required to provide a model cancellation form where the consumer has a right to cancel the contract. However, the consumer will be under no obligation to use this form: its existence is for the ease and benefit of the consumer.

9.4.6 Contract Excluded for the Cancellation Rights

The following online and off-premises contracts do not attract cancellation rights, however, as this is a statutory right for the protection of consumers, the consumer *may not* waive their rights to cancellation—they are allowed, however, not to exercise the right:

* customised/build-to-order goods (although this is unlikely to apply to computers which are made from standard component parts);
* goods which by their nature will perish/deteriorate rapidly;
* contracts established at public auctions (including ebay auctions);
* purchases of periodicals (newspapers and so on but not where a subscription has been entered into);
* contracts entered into by the consumer to effect emergency household repairs;
* sealed software/audio visual products which have been unsealed;
* goods which by the nature of being mixed with other products after delivery cannot be retrospectively separated;
* certain investment products which are subject to market variations/price fluctuations;
* goods sealed for hygiene or health protection reasons which have been unsealed;
* contracts of service where the service has been performed;
* contracts for the rental of accommodation, vehicles, or services related to leisure activities where the contract provides for specific dates/periods in which performance will occur (e.g. the hire of a wedding venue).

9.4.7 Delivery Times and the Passage of Risk

With the exception of a specific agreement between the trader and the consumer, delivery of goods should be made without undue delay, which in practical terms will be assumed to be within a 30-day period.

Risk in the goods will pass from the trader to the consumer when the goods are delivered. However, consumers should be aware that if they choose a courier personally, or privately arrange for a courier delivery of the goods, risk passes to the consumer when the item is delivered to the courier.

9.4.8 Additional Payments and Post-Contract Helplines

Prior to the Regulations it was sometimes common practice for traders to use pre-ticked boxes to tie consumers to additional payments. Here, consumers had to 'un-tick' the relevant box or would find an additional payment being added to the cost of the goods or service that was being ordered. Consumers must now give their express consent before a trader may take additional payments and consumers will not be liable for costs of which they have not been informed, prior to the contract being formed.

A further problem faced by consumers was the use of telephone helplines in relation to an item they had bought and were having technical difficulties or issues with. These telephone helplines often charged premium rates and hence dissuaded some consumers from their use. The Regulations require that where traders offer a telephone helpline for consumers for this purpose, the cost of the call should be no greater than set at the basic rate.

9.4.9 Online Payment Buttons

To avoid any confusion to the consumer, online retailers are required to identify clearly, through the use of appropriately labelled buttons, where a step in the online purchase process will result in an obligation to the consumer to pay for the goods.

9.4.10 Providing Information

It is important that traders are aware that the information to be provided to the consumer must be made on a durable medium. 'Provided' for the purposes of the Regulations includes the sending of a letter, a DVD, email, text message, and placing information in a consumer's personal account (e.g. when applying to a personal account used by a telephone service company for online billing). A 'durable medium' may include the letter, DVD, email, text message, and personal account as highlighted above, but be careful not to include information in links to websites which may change. The Regulations require the trader to provide the information; there is no duty imposed on the trader to ensure that the consumer has read/accessed it. The nature of a durable medium means that the information is addressed personally to the consumer; is accessible by them in an unchangeable format; but does not need to be unique to them as it can incorporate, for example, standard terms and conditions of sale.

9.4.11 Examples of the Application of the Regulations

Similar examples to those provided in the following sections exist in the guidance as outlined earlier from the Government's implementation document and may vary slightly depending on the method of contracting.

9.4.11.1 On-premises sales

Let us assume that an individual runs a coffee shop on a local high street. In order to comply with these new Regulations, the steps to be taken or to ensure are satisfied include:

1. Ensure the goods or services provided by your business are not in the exempt or partly exempt category.
2. Identify that the information that should be provided to the consumer purchasing items is available. Where the information required is obvious, then the nature of the information has already satisfied this requirement—for example the address of the business may not necessarily have to be expressly provided if it is obvious from the location of the shop from where you trade. Note further that where the purchases made in the shop are classified as day-to-day transactions and hence are completed immediately, which would include the sales of coffee at a coffee shop, these transactions are exempt from the information requirements for these Regulations. This does not stop the application of other consumer protection legislation

such as the Consumer Protection from Unfair Trading Regulations which require information relating to the nature and price of products.

3. Ensure your process of delivery of any items ordered, where applicable and unless agreed specifically to be alternative with the consumer, is provided without undue delay and certainly within 30 days.

4. If you provide a dedicated phone line for post-contract queries (unlikely in relation to a coffee shop but it is included here for completeness) at least one number should be provided for this purpose at a charge not exceeding the basic rate.

9.4.11.2 Distance sales

Distance selling has been regulated through statute since 2000 by the Consumer Protection (Distance Selling) Regulations and these Regulations continue to be applicable. What is important about the 2013 Regulations is the protection in relation to downloaded digital content. To ensure compliance with the 2013 Regulations it would be advisable (where you are the trader) to go through the following checks:

1. Identify that the goods or services being provided are not within the full or partial exemption of the Regulations.

2. Ensure that the information required is available; where the right to cancel in the contract exists, ensure a model cancellation form is provided (such as by the use of a hyperlink) and that the relevant information relating to consumer rights when selling by distance is provided in an understandable form.

3. Ensure that all the costs which will be incurred by the consumer, and this is especially important where potential costs that may occur in the future are relevant, are clearly identified and their calculation is provided prior to the consumer clicking on the purchase button or making their agreement when through a telephone-based distance sale. A further important point to highlight to the consumer is in regards to returning goods as the nature of distance sales will require the consumer to pay for the delivery (unless you as the trader are willing to absorb that cost—if so make sure the consumer is aware of this). Where possible, provide an indication as to the likely cost to the consumer of returning the item.

4. During any online sales, clearly identify and highlight the button which will oblige the consumer to pay for the goods. There is no prescription on the nature or wording of this button but it must be clear to the consumer that that button will conclude the contract. Consider using expressions such as 'pay now', 'obligation to pay', 'final payment', and so on. Further, the total price to be paid by the consumer should be clearly identified before they click the purchase button or agree to the contract if by telephone sale.

5. Review your website to ensure any additional payment checkboxes are not pre-ticked for the consumer, hence requiring the consumer to untick the box to avoid the charge. The consumer must be in a position whereby they have to make an active and outright choice to tick the box to incur any additional charge or payment.

6. Deliver goods within 30 days at a maximum, but without undue delay generally, unless an agreement to the contrary has been reached between you and the consumer.

7. Provide, before or with the delivery of the goods and/or services, the relevant information to be issued to consumers in a durable medium.

8. Where you are selling a service to the consumer and the consumer wishes for the service to commence within the 14-day cancellation period, it is incumbent upon you to gain their explicit consent and to advise them that in the advent of them later cancelling the contract within the 14-day period, they will have to pay for any services delivered during this period. This is part of the general information requirements and the Regulations impose burden of proof on the trader when establishing information has been provided. As such it is important to maintain records and have these available for inspection as and when required.

9. Consumers have the right to cancel the contract for whatever reason within 14 days of the contract being agreed and this need only be communicated to the trader; there is no requirement for the consumer to provide this in writing. Remember, the sample form that you provide to the consumer is optional for them to use, it is not a requirement or precursor to ending the contract.

10. Check your relationships with any third parties and where any specific agreement is in place for ancillary contracts as part of the services or goods you provide, ensure communication is provided to these third parties and, where appropriate, ensure refunds are provided upon cancellation by the consumer. Again, it is your responsibility to ensure the cancellation and refund is communicated with the third party, not the consumer's.

11. Where the consumer invokes the cancellation provision, the refund of all monies must be received within 14 days of either the cancellation of the services or where the goods have been returned by you. Where the consumer provides proof of the return prior to you receiving the goods, the 14-day period should apply to you on receiving the proof. The money to be refunded includes any payment of outbound delivery costs. This figure is to be returned to the consumer rather than necessarily the full cost of delivery where the consumer has chosen a more expensive option rather than the cheapest standard delivery provided. You also have the right to deduct money from a refund where the goods show evidence of unreasonable use—this relates to wear and tear rather than the removal of packaging to inspect goods.

12. If you provide a telephone line for post-contract queries, this number should be provided to consumers and the charge for the calls must be no more than the basic rate.

9.4.11.3 Downloaded digital content

The same requirements as related to information, confirmation, and issuing of confirmation of a contract on a durable medium and provided within a reasonable time, and the provision for telephone helplines apply to downloading digital content as they do for distance sales (**9.4.11.2**). However, consumers should be informed where the trader (if they wish to invoke this provision) will not allow consumers to cancel a contract once the download has started. Obtain the consumer's consent regarding this exclusion where it applies and maintain this information in case of any queries.

9.4.11.4 Off-premises sales

The 2013 Regulations replace the previous legislation protecting consumers (the Cancellation of Contracts made in a Consumer's Home or Place of Work etc. Regulations 2008). The requirements for such contracts follow points 1, 2, and 5–12 identified earlier in relation to distance selling contracts. Additional requirements in extension/comparison to those are:

1. As a trader, you should ensure all costs, including those potentially effective in the future, are explained and consented to in advance of the contract being agreed. Where this is not possible due to variables, you should clearly demonstrate how the final cost figure and its calculation has been reached. With any returns, you must explain to the consumer their responsibility for any costs of returning delivered items if you do not intend to accept these costs yourself.

2. Where goods are given to the customer and their nature means these cannot be returned through the post (e.g. large furniture), you as the trader are responsible for the costs of their collection and this cost must not be placed on the consumer.

3. As with point 7 earlier in relation to distance selling contracts, information must be provided to the consumer, but where this occurs off-premises you must provide a signed copy of the contract, or evidence of its confirmation, and this must be provided on paper (or another durable medium if the consumer agrees), not later than the delivery of the goods or by when the service is provided.

4. Finally, where a consumer has called the trader out to their home to effect an emergency repair, the consumer does not have a right to cancel—although the right to cancel continues in relation to any non-urgent services, or goods contracted for whilst you were on their premises, other than the replacement parts you used for the emergency repairs.

9.5 THE UNFAIR CONTRACT TERMS ACT 1977

> **Note;** in respect of B2C contracts the Act's provisions are replaced by the CRA 2015. UCTA is amended so that it covers B2B contracts only.

As its name implies, the function of the Unfair Contract Terms Act (UCTA) 1977 is to ensure that certain terms that may be unfair (under this Act, i.e. exclusion clauses) are removed or held invalid by the courts. However, it is also important to note that UCTA 1977 also regulates the use of non-contractual notices attempting to restrict liability for negligence. Certain exclusion clauses will automatically be considered void under the Act (such as excluding liability for death or personal injury due to negligence) and those remaining have to satisfy the test of 'reasonableness'. UCTA 1977 is primarily concerned with business liability (s. 1(3)) in contract and tort, and hence the liability for breach of obligations or duties occurring in the course of business.

9.5.1 Liability in Contract

UCTA 1977 provides protection when exclusion clauses are included in standard form contracts. These were typically used by businesses and the consumer was in a weak position in attempting to decline their use—it was often a 'take it or leave it' scenario.

- *Exclusion of rights under the sale of goods legislation:* Section 6 of UCTA 1977 is very important to SOGA 1979. The implications of s. 6 of UCTA 1977 is that s. 12 of SOGA 1979, and the Sale of Goods (Implied Terms) Act (SGITA) 1973, s. 8 cannot be excluded from any contract. Sections 13, 14, and 15 of SOGA 1979, and ss. 9, 10, and 11 of SGITA 1973 cannot be excluded from contracts where the buyer acts as a consumer with a seller in the course of business, but they may be excluded in non-consumer (course of business) contracts, as far as they satisfy the tests of reasonableness.

The following provisions of the CRA 2015 may not be excluded from a consumer contract, nor may the trader restrict a liability relating to them. Such a term of a contract which purports to do so is not binding on the consumer:

- Section 9 (goods to be of satisfactory quality);
- Section 10 (goods to be fit for particular purpose);
- Section 11 (goods to be as described);
- Section 12 (other pre-contract information included in contract);
- Section 13 (goods to match a sample);
- Section 14 (goods to match a model seen or examined);
- Section 15 (installation as part of conformity of goods with contract);
- Section 16 (goods not conforming to contract if digital content does not conform);
- Section 17 (trader to have right to supply the goods etc.);
- Section 28 (delivery of goods);
- Section 29 (passing of risk).

A term of a contract to supply goods is not binding on the consumer to the extent that it would:

1. exclude or restrict a right or remedy in respect of a liability under the provisions listed above;
2. make such a right or remedy or its enforcement subject to a restrictive or onerous condition;
3. allow a trader to put a person at a disadvantage as a result of pursuing such a right or remedy; or
4. exclude or restrict rules of evidence or procedure.

9.5.2 Liability in Negligence

UCTA 1977 specifically voids attempts through contractual terms or through notice to exclude liability for death or personal injury caused through negligence. Negligence in torts law imposes a duty to take reasonable care not to injure others or damage property. However, under this Act, the term 'negligence' is given a broader interpretation to incorporate negligent performance of a contract and the concept of negligence in breaching a statutory duty (see **Chapters 11** and **13**). Negligence causing loss or damage to property may only be excluded or restricted where it satisfies the test of reasonableness. Simply because a person has agreed to, or was aware of, a term or notice that purports to exclude or restrict the other party's liability in negligence will not, of itself, be indicative of a voluntary acceptance of risk.

9.5.3 Liability under Misrepresentation

Section 8 of UCTA replaced s. 3 of the Misrepresentation Act 1967 and prohibits any term in a contract that purports to restrict or exclude a liability for a misrepresentation made before the contract was agreed; or attempts to restrict or exclude a remedy the other party would have in the event of such a misrepresentation, unless the party seeking to rely on the clause can demonstrate its reasonableness under s. 1(1) of UCTA 1977. Note that this protection applies to both consumers and non-consumers.

9.5.4 **Reasonableness of the Exclusion Clause**

UCTA 1977 contains provision for how the reasonableness or otherwise of an exclusion clause will be determined. This has caused considerable problems when the case law is examined.

SAM Business Systems v Hedley and Co. (2002)

Facts:

Here a software supplier was entitled to rely on an exclusion clause that enabled it to supply an inadequate product, and the term was considered 'reasonable'. (Note that this case was between two businesses. The courts assume businesses should be in a better position to protect themselves than consumers dealing with a business).

Authority for:

The obligation on demonstrating that the clause is reasonable rests with the party relying on the clause, and it will have to show that in all the circumstances the clause was reasonable and was brought to the other party's attention, or it should have been in their 'reasonable contemplation.'

Schedule 2 outlines the tests that the courts will use in determining the reasonableness of an exclusion clause:

(a) the strength of the bargaining positions of the parties relative to each other (the most important statutory consideration).

Where the parties are of equal bargaining strength, the courts are more likely to accept exclusion clauses than if the contract was between a consumer and a business.

Watford Electronic Ltd v Sanderson CFL Ltd (2001)

Facts:

The claimant had entered into a contract with the respondent for the supply of a computer system. When the system failed, the claimant sought damages and the respondent attempted to rely on a limitation clause.

Authority for:

An otherwise unreasonable exclusion/limitation clause will be allowed unless the term is so unreasonable that the court must move to restrict it. In this case, involving the supply of computer equipment, an exclusion clause limited liability to £104,596, and this was considered reasonable even though the actual losses sustained were £5.5 million.

(b) whether the customer received an inducement to agree to the term, or in accepting it had an opportunity of entering into a similar contract with other persons, but without having to accept a similar term;

(c) whether the customer knew or ought reasonably to have known of the existence and extent of the term (having regard, among other things, to any custom of the trade and any previous course of dealing between the parties);

(d) where the term excludes or restricts any relevant liability if some condition is not complied with, whether it was reasonable at the time of the contract to expect that compliance with that condition would be practicable; and

(e) whether the goods were manufactured, processed or adapted to the special order of the customer.

The practical use by the courts of a consideration of the reasonableness of an exclusion clause has been addressed in the academic literature.

George Mitchell v Finney Lock Seeds (1983)

Facts:

Seeds were sold between businesses, but an exclusion clause restricted any claim for loss to the cost of the seeds, not the potential harvest (which naturally would have been substantially greater).

Authority for:

The House of Lords rejected the clause as unreasonable. When the farmers placed the seeds in the ground it was not possible to identify the quality or type of the seed, and the seller could have obtained insurance at a cheap price.

Perhaps one of the most problematic areas when considering exclusion clauses is in assessing what amounts to 'unreasonableness'. Despite the guidance provided through the statute as noted earlier, the courts still maintain discretion as evidenced in the case law presented. This discretion can lead to unusual results, and, as stated in *George Mitchell*, appeal courts will not interfere with the decision in the original case unless the judge had made their decision based on an 'erroneous principle or was plainly and obviously wrong'.

Beyond the guidance provided in UCTA 1977 with regard to what amounts to reasonableness when attempting to exclude a potential liability, the House of Lords offered further assistance in the following case.

Smith v Eric S Bush (1990)

Facts:

The claimant purchased a house on the basis of the defendant's negligent valuation report. The report had been produced and issued incorporating an exclusion clause disclaiming any liability for negligence. The surveyor of the property had not identified serious defects in the property, but soon after the purchase had been completed, the chimney collapsed, causing significant damage. When the claimant sued the defendant

→

for the damage, the exclusion clause was relied upon but the House of Lords held it to be unreasonable under s. 2(2) of UCTA 1977. It would be unfair and unreasonable to place potential risk of loss on a buyer for the negligence and incompetence of a surveyor providing a valuation.

Authority for:

The Lords identified factors that would be used in determining the reasonableness of an exclusion clause:

1. whether the parties were of equal bargaining power;

2. in situations involving advice, whether it was practicable (in costs and time) to obtain alternative advice;

3. the level of complexity and difficulty in the task which was subject to the exclusion of liability;

4. which of the parties was better able to bear any losses and should insurance have been sought.

CONCLUSION

The chapter has discussed the regulation of contract terms through legislation. These provisions offer certainty and protection to the parties against, among other things, the use of unfair terms. The next chapter discusses how contracts are discharged and the availability of remedies in the event of a breach.

SUMMARY OF MAIN POINTS

Sale of Goods Act (SOGA)

* There must be a 'sale' involving the transfer of title to the goods.

* Goods are defined as including all personal chattels (essentially goods that would typically be used in personal/domestic situations).

* Sections 12–15 are very important and ensure the seller has legal ownership of the good; the good corresponds to its description; the good is of a satisfactory quality and is fit for its intended purpose; and, in sales involving samples, that the bulk corresponds to the sample.

* Breach of SOGA will entitle the buyer to reject the goods (within a reasonable time), have the goods repaired/replaced, and claim damages depending on the nature of the breach.

* The seller has rights under the Act if the buyer refuses to pay for the goods or if they refuse to accept them.

The Supply of Goods and Services Act

* The legislation governs the supply of services, and of faulty goods and materials provided with the service.

* The supplier must demonstrate reasonable care and skill in providing the service and provide the service within a reasonable time.

* The Act includes the hire of goods (which was not included in SOGA).

Sale and Supply of Goods to Consumers Regulations

- Goods that are provided with a guarantee enable a consumer to obtain a remedy established in this document. This could include a repair or replacement and is particularly useful when, for example, the seller of the good has ceased trading and no claim is therefore available under SOGA.
- Claims are often available as a guarantee is provided by the manufacturer of the good.

Consumer Contracts (Information, Cancellation and Additional Charges) Regulations 2013

- Consumers must, in certain circumstances, be given information regarding the terms of the contract and important practical issues (e.g. delivery times and the passage of risk).
- It provides cooling-off periods for consumers to cancel orders when buying at a distance or off-premises.
- Helpline charges are subject to much greater controls, as are any additional payments forwarded by the retailer.

Unfair Contract Terms Act (UCTA)

- This Act specifically governs the use of exclusion clauses in contracts.
- It prohibits the exclusion of liability for death or personal injury due to the other party's negligence.
- Any other exclusion clause is subject to test under the Act's assessment of 'reasonableness'.

Unfair contract terms and the Consumer Rights Act

- A term or notice will be held as unfair if, contrary to the requirement of good faith, it causes significant imbalance in the parties' rights and obligations under the contract, and this is to the detriment of the consumer.
- Terms must be transparent. This requirement is satisfied where it is expressed in plain and intelligible language and (in the case of a written term) is legible.
- Terms must be prominent. This will be satisfied where it is brought to the consumer's attention in such a way that an average consumer would be aware of the term.

SUMMARY QUESTIONS

Essay questions

1. 'Consumers have always been in a poor bargaining position with traders and those running businesses. Parliament was right to equal the balance of power through its intervention with various protective statutes.'

   Critically discuss the above statement with reference to the legislation passed and how it protects consumers.

2. Given that many of the cases involving the statutory protections in the sale of goods are disputes between businesses, how fair has the application of the reasonableness test been in UCTA?

Problem questions

1. Jessica and her family were shopping for various goods and have experienced the following:

Jessica's son Buzz broke his mother's bone china vase. He visited a DIY shop and explained to the store assistant what had happened and how he needed to fix the vase before his mother returned home. The assistant sold Buzz a special clay adhesive which he said would fix the vase, but it fails to do the job.

Jessica's son Buzz bought a catapult from the corner shop to use to hit tin cans off the wall of his garden. He used the catapult, hit three tin cans and the next time he used it the elastic broke striking his eye. Buzz subsequently lost the sight in that eye due to the trauma.

Jessica bought a new washing machine from the local high street electrical retail outlet. It stopped working the first time Jessica used it to wash the blood out of the shirt worn by Buzz following the accident with the catapult.

Jessica purchased a new pair of training shoes for use at the gym. She selected the pair described as having 'gel-filled soles' and being suitable for running on a treadmill. When Jessica used the trainers they begin to fall apart during the first session at the gym and she discovered the soles are not 'gel-filled' as advertised.

Jessica's husband Woody decided to purchase a barbeque cooker for the garden. He selected a gas barbeque from the DIY shop which was priced at £25. Woody used the barbeque during much of the summer, but when he used it for a party in the last week of August it failed to produce sufficient heat to thoroughly cook the pork chops he was preparing for his family and friends. As a consequence of this, the guests who ate the pork chops sustained food poisoning as the parasites inside the food had not been destroyed during the cooking process.

Advise the parties as to their rights and liabilities.

2. Larry wishes to purchase a van for his domestic use of transporting equipment for his hobby of surfing. He visits Vans and only Vans Ltd (a company specializing in selling used vehicles) and views a white van with a notice in the window reading:

'1990 Ford Escort Van. 100,000 miles; 1.8 litre engine; one previous owner and good little runner.'

Larry discusses the van with the salesman who informs Larry that the vehicle is in very good condition, however, it has a defective clutch (but it will drive with no problems for at least two months). The company will fix the clutch before purchase or Larry can take the van in its present condition and can have a £70 discount if he wishes to have the clutch fixed himself. Larry thinks he can get the clutch fixed for a cheaper price and therefore purchases the van minus the £70 discount.

In his first week of ownership the clutch fails and Larry has to have the van towed to his local garage where he is informed of the following facts:

- The van is in fact stolen and does not belong to Vans and only Vans Ltd
- Larry checks the logbook, which identifies that there have been five previous owners of the vehicle.
- Previous MOT certificates demonstrate that the van has travelled over 250,000 miles.
- The van has a 1.4 litre engine.
- The clutch will cost £300 to fix.

Advise Larry of the legal consequences of these issues.

 You will find guidance about how to answer these questions online at www.oup.com/uk/marson5e/.

FURTHER READING

Books and articles

Adams, J. and Brownsword, R. (1988) 'The Unfair Contract Terms Act: A Decade of Discretion' *Law Quarterly Review*, Vol. 104, p. 94.

Brown, L. and Chandler, A. (1993) 'Unreasonableness and the Unfair Contract Terms Act' *Law Quarterly Review*, Vol. 109, p. 41.

Macdonald, E. (2004) 'Unifying Unfair Terms Legislation' *Modern Law Review*, Vol. 67, No. 1, p. 69.

Websites, Twitter links, and YouTube channels

https://www.youtube.com/user/thefcatv
The Financial Conduct Authority, the body that regulates the financial services industry in the UK. The website details its remit, and powers, and provides general advice.

https://www.gov.uk/government/organisations/competition-and-markets-authority
@CMAgovUK
  The Competition and Markets Authority promotes competition for the betterment of consumers and, along with the Financial Conduct Authority, undertook many of the responsibilities of the Office of Fair Trading, which was closed on 1 April 2014.

http://www.legislation.gov.uk/ukpga/1979/54
The Sale of Goods Act 1979.

http://www.legislation.gov.uk/ukpga/1977/50
The Unfair Contract Terms Act 1977.

http://www.legislation.gov.uk/uksi/1999/2083/schedule/2/made
The Unfair Terms in Consumer Contracts Regulations 1999.

ONLINE RESOURCES

www.oup.com/uk/marson5e/

For further resources relating to this chapter, including self-test questions, an interactive glossary, and key case flashcards.

10 DISCHARGE OF CONTRACT AND REMEDIES FOR BREACH

A contract establishes the rights and duties of the parties and where successfully completed, the parties will be considered to have discharged their responsibilities. However, this is not the only way in which the contract may be discharged and this chapter aims to discuss these other ways, and importantly, identify the remedies when a party has breached the contract. For example, suppose you were to agree to sell a piece of land, fulfil the essential features of a valid contract, and then decide not to proceed. If you return the deposit paid then would you merely be responsible for the costs incurred by the other party? Read *Mountford v Scott* (see 10.3.2) and you will appreciate why it is vital to appreciate the implications of contractual obligations and the remedies that are available to the innocent party.

Business Scenario 10

High Performance Construction Industries (HPCI) operates a manufacturing and services business for large and smaller construction projects. The first part of its business is designing, manufacturing, and installing building solutions. Salma approaches HPCI to prepare and install a 350-square foot garage which is 11 feet high and to be constructed of steel with a base of bright orange coloured bricks (to a height of four feet). This is important to Salma as she is very particular about the aesthetics of her property. The contract is agreed with a completion date of five weeks and a cost to Salma of £27,000.

The contract price includes the groundwork, external materials, fitting, and erection of the structure and an expensive climate control and smart hub. This system centrally controls the doors, lights, and the heating, whilst also allowing further functionality such as identifying where the doors are opened and closed, motion sensors, and whether vehicles are in the garage. This system has amounted to £4,500 of the overall cost of the garage and Salma has insisted that HPCI identify its inclusion as a condition of the contract.

Later HPCI wish to expand the business by producing building materials and pre-fabricated structures based on an augmented reality app. This will significantly simplify and speed up the process of customers ordering complex structures which can be erected in only a matter of weeks (compared with the several months' lead-time as is the current timeframe). To achieve this, HPCI need specialist machinery. They order this machine from Bechtel Ltd with delivery to be made on or before 1 January. A clause in the contract provides that for every day that Bechtel Ltd is late with delivery, a payment of £1,000 will be due as a pre-estimate of loss. Bechtel Ltd are aware that HPCI is a commercial business in the construction sector, but have no further knowledge of the use of the machine that they are supplying nor of any of the profits that HPCI generally make.

Learning Outcomes

- Discuss the methods in which a contract may be discharged (10.2–10.2.4)
- Explain the development, through the common law and statute, of the doctrine of frustration (10.2.3)
- Identify the remedies available for breach of contract (10.3–10.3.2)
- Explain the implications and effects of the equitable remedies available for breach of contract (10.3.2).

10.1 INTRODUCTION

This chapter concludes the analysis of the law of contract. Having established in **Chapters 5–9** the essential features in the formation of a contract, the different types of terms and their significance, the method of inclusion of terms, and a consideration of the protection afforded through implied statutory provisions, this chapter considers how a contract will be discharged. Discharge through performance and agreement, how contracts may become frustrated, and the consequences and remedies following a breach of contract are each examined.

10.2 DISCHARGE OF CONTRACT

Under the normal rules of contract, a party is only **discharged from a contract** when they have completed their obligations under it (complete performance). Having completed the contract each party is free of further obligations. A failure to complete the contract may lead to a breach of contract claim, although situations exist where the parties may release each other from further obligations (discharge by agreement) or the contract may have been partially or substantially performed. Further, the contract may have become radically different from that envisaged, or impossible to perform. In these last examples, the contract will not have been performed but there is no breach as it has been **frustrated**. The methods of **discharge of contract** are identified in **Figure 10.1** (p. 236).

10.2.1 Discharge Through Performance

The most obvious form of discharge is through the parties' completion of their obligations (the contract being performed). Where complete performance has not been achieved, the courts have had to develop rules on what implications such a situation will have for the parties.

Cutter v Powell (1795)

Facts:

Captain Powell engaged Cutter as part of his crew in a voyage from Jamaica to Liverpool. The contract stipulated that the contract was only fulfilled when the entire contract was performed and payment was only due when the voyage was completed. Mr Cutter died 19 days before the vessel arrived in Liverpool and his widow claimed for his owed wages.

→

→

Authority for:

It was held that the claim must be denied as it was a condition of the contract that payment would be made on completion of the voyage, and this had not been complied with.

Figure 10.1 Discharge of contract

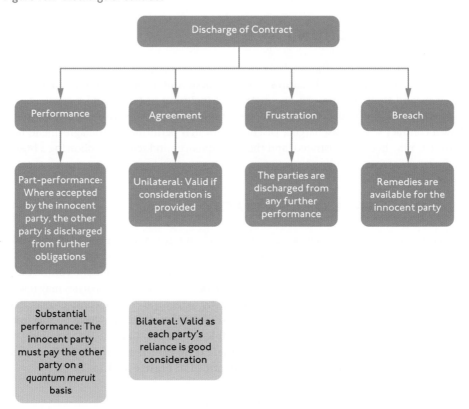

This rather harsh application of the rules of contract has been changed where the contract, as opposed to being an entire contract as in *Cutter*, may be divisible (contracts of employment are often examples of divisible contracts). This means that the contract is broken down into smaller units.

Ritchie v Atkinson (1808)

Facts:

Here a contract for the shipment of cargo was agreed at a price of £5 per ton. Not all of the cargo was delivered, therefore the owners claimed a breach. Further, they asserted they were not obliged to pay any amount as all of the contract had not been completed.

→

Authority for:

It was held that there was a breach, but as this was a divisible contract, payment was due on the basis of the number of tons of cargo actually delivered.

- *Part-performance:* There may exist situations where a contract is not fully completed, and the other party voluntarily accepts the partial performance. It must be noted at this stage that the acceptance *must* be undertaken voluntarily for it to be valid. Where the innocent party has no choice but to 'accept' the part-performance the party in breach is not entitled to payment for the work completed on the contract.

Sumpter v Hedges (1898)

Facts:

The parties contracted for the erection of two houses and stables for the defendant, with payment on completion. During the construction, and having completed approximately half of the work, the claimant ran out of money and could not complete the work. The claimant sought approximately half of the contract price as the defendant had completed the works himself and had thereby accepted partial performance (whilst also preventing the claimant finishing the work).

Authority for:

The claim failed as the defendant had no choice but to 'accept' the performance as he was left with a half built house on his property.

The acceptance of the partial performance discharges the party from any further obligations under the contract and the innocent party must pay an appropriate proportion of the price.

- *Substantial performance:* If, on the other hand, a substantial proportion of the contract has been completed, the innocent party has an obligation to pay, taking into account the shortcomings of the contract.

Hoeing v Isaacs (1952)

Facts:

A contract was established for the decorating and furnishing of a flat for a fee of £750. Whilst the decorating had been substantially completed, there were minor aspects still to be completed to furnishings.

Authority for:

It was held that as the contract had been substantially performed, the claimant was entitled to be paid, with £55 being deducted to reflect the outstanding work uncompleted.

However, the obligation to pay is only where there has been 'substantial' performance.

Bolton v Mahadeva (1972)

Facts:

The claimant agreed with the defendant to install a central heating system in the defendant's house for the fee of £560. When the claimant had completed the works, the defendant refused to pay, citing that the work was defective. When tests were carried out, it was discovered that the flue had been incorrectly installed, which resulted in fumes remaining in the room, and the heat through the radiators was irregular, resulting in differing temperatures in each room. The cost of rectifying these defects was £174.

Authority for:

The Court of Appeal held that as a result, the claimant was not able to recover the amount due as there had not been substantial performance.

There is also a claim for a partial or substantial performance of the contract if the full and complete performance of the contract was prevented through the other party's actions.

Planche v Colburn (1831)

Facts:

A book was commissioned (for a fee of £100) and the author had partially completed this when the contract was cancelled.

Authority for:

It was held that £50 was to be paid to the claimant for the work already completed (known as *quantum meruit* assessment).

* *Time limit for performance:* Unless the parties have otherwise agreed (through express or implied terms), time limits for the performance of the contract are not strict. Therefore, if a party is late in performing their obligations this will not, of itself, enable the other party to reject the performance when it occurs. This is the general rule insofar as there is no unreasonable delay. Where a delay does occur, the innocent party may identify a (reasonable) time for the contract to be completed.

Charles Rickards Ltd v Oppenheim (1950)

Facts:

A contract was entered for the construction of a motor chassis by a given date. That date passed and a later date of four weeks' time was agreed (time being of the essence). This date for delivery of the chassis was missed and some time afterwards the claimant

→

sought to deliver the chassis, but the defendant would not accept delivery. An action for breach of contract was heard by the court.

Authority for:

It was held that the defendant was entitled to cancel the contract and not accept delivery. It would have been unjust to approach the case on the basis that, having been lenient with regards the first deadline for delivery, the defendant was thereby barred from requiring a quick delivery of the goods, albeit subject to reasonable notice.

A similar argument could be made under the doctrine of promissory estoppel (see **6.2.3**).

10.2.2 Discharge Through Agreement

The parties may agree between themselves that they no longer wish to continue with the contract, and therefore release each other from their obligations. As this is in effect a new contract, and varying a contract requires the formalities as identified in **Chapters 5** and **6** to make it valid, the elements of agreement (referred to as accord) and consideration (referred to as satisfaction) are necessary. There may be a unilateral or bilateral discharge of the contract.

- *Unilateral discharge:* If one party has completed their part of the contract and the other party wishes to be released from their obligations which are outstanding, such an agreement will be allowed, but is only legally binding if consideration (a benefit) is provided.

- *Bilateral discharge:* If both parties have obligations outstanding under the contract, then if both agree to release each other from further obligations, the contract will be discharged by these mutual exchanges of promises. That both parties release each other will be good consideration and stop any legal rights under the contract.

10.2.3 Discharge Through Frustration

Frustration was a doctrine developed by the courts in order to offer relief in circumstances whereby a contract could not be performed or had become radically different from that contemplated (and this was the fault of neither party).

The effects of frustration result in the parties being discharged from any further performance of the contract and any money paid is returned (at the discretion of the court). It should be noted at the outset that this is known as a doctrine of 'last resort' and will therefore only be used where the parties have not made their own arrangement for a frustrating event. The courts encourage parties to draft contracts in as detailed a manner as possible to include for eventualities and the method of resolution to be adopted (***force majeure*** clauses).

There are several examples of what may amount to frustration and, whilst each case is decided on its own merits, there are common themes that aid in identifying what may be held to be frustration.

- *The subject matter of the contract ceases to exist:* In a situation where the subject matter of the contract has ceased to exist before the contract has been performed, and it is neither party's fault that this has occurred, then the courts consider this frustration.

Taylor v Caldwell (1863)

Facts:

Taylor and Caldwell had entered into a contract on 27 May 1861 where Caldwell had agreed to let Taylor have the use of the Surrey Gardens and Music Hall at a rate of £100 per day. This hire was to take place for four days for the purpose of giving a series of grand concerts. The contract was established, but before the first performance the Music Hall was destroyed by fire and therefore the concerts could not take place. Taylor claimed damages for the money spent on the advertising and preparation for the concerts. The decision of the High Court was 'the Music Hall having ceased to exist, without fault of either party, both parties are excused, the plaintiffs from taking the gardens and paying the money, the defendants from performing their promise to give the use of the Hall and Gardens and other things.'

Authority for:

Where the entire subject matter of a contract is destroyed before the contract is performed, and this is the fault of neither of the parties, the contract is impossible to perform and is held to be frustrated.

Where the sole purpose of the contract has not been destroyed or is not unable to be completed, and the benefit of the contract remains, the contract will not be considered to have been frustrated.

Herne Bay Steam Boat Company v Hutton (1903)

Facts:

The defendant hired a steamship from the claimant for the purpose of taking paying passengers around a Naval Review which was occurring during King Edward VII's coronation. Due to an illness affecting the King, the coronation celebrations, including the Naval Review, were cancelled. Consequently, the steamship was not used and the defendant argued frustration of contract.

Authority for:

It was held the contract was not frustrated. The Naval Review was not the only commercial activity that could have taken place and thus the defendant was not deprived of the sole purpose of the contract.

- *A person engaged under a contract of personal service becomes unavailable:* If a person has personally agreed to perform a contract and subsequently they become unavailable then this may constitute frustration. Whether it will invoke frustration depends upon the length of time the person is unavailable. If it is a temporary situation (such as a short illness as part of a sufficiently long or open-ended contract) then this will not be frustration, but if the person is dead or is permanently unavailable then this will frustrate the contract.

Condor v The Barron Knights (1966)

Facts:

The Barron Knights was a pop group who hired Condor, a 16 year old, as their drummer. His five-year contract required him to perform shows seven nights per week. Soon after he began work, Condor became ill and the band was informed that if he continued to work under the terms of the contract, Condor would become permanently ill. Condor's doctors suggested he could work four nights per week but as the band did not want a part-time drummer, they terminated the contract.

Authority for:

Condor claimed he was wrongfully dismissed, but it was held that as he could not complete the contract without sustaining permanent injury, the contract was frustrated and not breached.

- *An event central to the contract has not occurred:* If parties contract for a specific event, and for some reason this event does not take place, the contract will be frustrated.

Krell v Henry (1903)

Facts:

Mr Krell left instructions with his solicitor to rent out his suite of chambers located at 56a Pall Mall. On 17 June 1902 Mr Henry responded to an advertisement for the hire of the flat (from which it was possible to view the procession of the King's coronation). Henry agreed to take the suite, and paid a deposit, but the King became ill before the coronation and hence the procession was cancelled. Henry refused to pay the balance due and Krell began this action to recover that sum. It was argued by Krell that the contract could still continue as the flat was still in existence, and Henry could still have the use of it for the days identified in the contract. The Court of Appeal held that the contract was frustrated. It took a broader view that the entire purpose of hiring the flat was to view the coronation (evidenced from the price paid to hire the premises). The King's illness was the fault of neither party but its effect was to make the contract radically different from what was agreed. Hence the contract was frustrated.

Authority for:

Where, due to the fault of neither party, a contract becomes radically different from that agreed, the contract is frustrated.

- *The contract cannot be performed in the manner specified:* If the contract is specific about the manner in which it must be performed, and this cannot be complied with, the contract will fail due to frustration.

Nickoll & Knight v Ashton, Edridge & Co. (1901)

Facts:

The parties contracted for the shipping of a cargo of cotton seed from Egypt to England on the ship The Orlando. However, before the contract could be fulfilled, The Orlando was damaged at sea and was unavailable to be used.

Authority for:

The contract was frustrated. The vessel was damaged at sea due to the fault of neither party and as this specific vessel was named in the contract, its unavailability to satisfy the contract frustrated the contract.

- *If the contract becomes illegal to perform:* If the parties have agreed a contract, but before the contract is due to be performed it subsequently becomes illegal, then the contract is frustrated.

Fibrosa Spolka Akcyjna v Fairbairn Lawson Combe Barbour (1943)

Facts:

Fairbairn, based in England, could not legally supply goods to Fibrosa, based in Poland, as Germany had occupied Poland in 1939 and England had declared war with Germany. There was a provision preventing British companies from supplying, *inter alia*, machinery to an enemy-occupied country, and consequently the contract was frustrated.

Authority for:

Any attempt to deliver the goods under the contract would result in supervening illegality.

- *The contract becomes radically different:* The previous examples have demonstrated where the contract could not be completed due to some event or circumstance. It is also the case that if the contract was to be radically different from that which was envisaged when the contract was formed, then this may constitute frustration.

Davis Contractors Ltd v Fareham Urban DC (1956)

Facts:

A contract was established for the erection of a building that was to be completed in eight months. However, due to shortages in labour, completion was not achieved until 22 months later. The contractors claimed frustration in part as the contract became significantly more difficult than the one that had been agreed. The House of Lords disagreed and stated that the shortage of labour is something that could have been expected, and if not provided for by the parties, then they are assumed to have accepted the risk.

→

Authority for:

Simply because a contract involves greater expense or hardship, or the contract becomes a bad bargain, will not amount to frustration.

- *The limits to frustration:* The previous examples have demonstrated that there may be many reasons why a contract may be frustrated, but an essential factor is that it must not be the fault of either party. Simply because the contract cannot be performed will not result in it being frustrated. If one of the parties has deliberately or negligently led to the contract failing, they must accept the loss and/or compensate the innocent party.

Ocean Trawlers v Maritime National Fish (1935)

Facts:

Ocean Trawlers owned a steam trawler (the *St Cuthbert*), which was chartered by the Maritime National Fish company; both companies were based in Halifax, Nova Scotia. A contract was entered into in July 1932, subject to the legislative requirements which made it a punishable offence to leave or depart from any port in Canada, with the intent to fish, with an unlicensed vessel that used an otter or similar trawl. The *St Cuthbert* could only operate with an otter-trawl and Ocean Trawlers also operated four other vessels, each fitted with otter-trawling gear. In March 1933 Maritime National Fish Ltd applied for licences for the five trawlers, but only three of the five trawlers were so issued. Maritime National Fish informed the Department of the vessels the three licences should be applied to, excluding the *St Cuthbert*. Maritime National Fish Ltd then asserted that through no fault of its own the charter became impossible to perform and consequently the contract was frustrated. The Privy Council held that this was not a case of frustration and Ocean Trawlers were entitled to recover damages.

Authority for:

In the absence of a contract being radically different from that contracted for, or impossible to perform, it will not be frustrated.

Here, Maritime National Fish Ltd was aware of the relevant legislation requiring licences for the vessels and as it gambled on securing licences for all five vessels, it had to accept any subsequent losses if these were not issued. It was possible for the company to insert a clause into the contract making the hire of the vessels dependent upon the successful granting of licences, but it had not done so. Just because this was a different contract to that anticipated by Maritime National Fish Ltd (i.e. it could not use the *St Cuthbert* as anticipated), it was neither radically different from that contracted for, or impossible to perform.

- Force majeure *clauses:* To 'protect' themselves against a frustrating event ending the contract, the parties may establish a *force majeure* clause that makes provision for the frustrating event. This clause involves some level of forseeability as to the possible frustrating event that was in the contemplation of the parties at the time of contracting. Examples may include provisions for bad weather and difficulties in supplies of labour. Such clauses are valid and will be accepted by the courts if 1) it is the true intention of the parties and 2) the clause is not designed to limit one of the parties' exposure to liability for breach.

- *The effects of frustration:* When the court has determined that a contract has been frustrated, the contract ceases to exist as soon as the frustrating event occurs. As this typically affects businesses more than consumer contracts, the courts have encouraged the parties to make provisions in the contract on the basis of such eventualities. If no provisions are contained in the contract, assistance has been provided through the Law Reform (Frustrated Contracts) Act 1943. This statute provides:

  - all money still owing under the contract ceases to be due (s. 1(2));

  - all money paid is recoverable (at the court's discretion—s. 1(2));

  - the money returned includes deposits (pre-payments) and expenses that, before the case law and statutory interventions, resulted in such loses 'lying where they fell'. (The harshness of the application of losses in this respect can be seen in *Appleby v Myers*, where a contractor's expenses for labour and materials lost following a fire were not recoverable as the contract stipulated payment on completion. Section 1(2) codified the law to enable the return of expenses.);

  - any valuable benefit which has been gained has to be compensated for (s. 1(3)).

These provisions do not apply if the parties make their own provisions for the effect of frustration (s. 2(3)).

Where, before the frustrating event, one of the parties received a valuable benefit (other than a payment of money), the other party may claim (a return of) its value. This assessment is made somewhat more difficult in the absence of statutory definition of 'valuable benefit'. However, its effect may be seen in the following case.

BP Exploration Co. (Libya) Ltd v Hunt (No. 2) (1982)

Facts:

In December 1957 the Libyan Government granted Hunt a concession to explore for oil, and to extract it, from a specified area of desert. In June 1960 Hunt entered into an agreement with BP for it to drill and extract the oil, and the concession would be shared between Hunt and BP. BP was to assume all risks in the extraction of the oil. In 1971 Libya nationalized the oil industry and stopped BP's oil extraction, causing a loss of $35 million. Hunt had been provided with compensation from Libya (in the form of oil) and BP claimed damages from Hunt as the contract had become frustrated under the Law Reform (Frustrated Contracts) Act 1943. The House of Lords held that under the Act, the contract had become frustrated, and as a consequence BP was entitled to a share of Hunt's profits as a value/benefit received.

Authority for:

Where one party has received a valuable benefit other than money prior to the frustrating event, and where it is just, some or all of that benefit may be recovered from the other party.

10.2.4 **Discharge Through Breach of Contract**

If one of the parties breaches their obligations under the contract, then the other party must ascertain whether the breach of the term was due to a condition or warranty. A breach of a condition gives the injured party the option to both end (repudiate) the contract and claim damages. In some instances it may be advantageous for the injured party to claim damages but also to continue with the contract. In the case of a warranty, as it is a lesser term it entitles the injured party to damages, but they must still continue with the obligations under the contract.

In the event that the full contractual obligations owed by one of the parties is not fulfilled, or the performance is substantially less than could be expected, the innocent party may treat this as a complete breach of the contract. Situations may also arise where one of the parties recognizes that the other party is not going to fulfil their contractual obligations, or the party informs the other of this situation (although this must be clear and unequivocal, but it may be retracted before accepted). This is referred to as an anticipatory breach.

Hochester v De La Tour (1853)

Facts:

A contract was agreed for the claimant to be hired by the defendant as a courier for a term of three months. Before the contract was due to be performed the defendant informed the claimant that his services would not be needed.

Authority for:

The court held this was a case of anticipatory breach and the claimant was able to bring proceedings before the date of the performance of the contract. The injured party did not have to wait until the actual breach occurred before seeking to recover.

However, it may not be a particularly good tactic to seek damages ahead of the actual date of the breach (see **10.3.1**).

Where anticipatory breach occurs, the innocent party can accept this as a breach immediately and treat the contract as repudiated (and presumably make other provisions to lessen the negative effects of the breach). Or they can wait for the time when performance was due, and when the contract is breached, and then seek a remedy.

Shaftesbury House (Developments) Ltd v Lee (2010)

Facts:

In 2007, Ms Lee paid a deposit to secure a property being built on a new development. However, when the property was completed (in 2009) she refused to pay the balance owed to complete the purchase. In so doing, she sought to rely on representations made by an estate agent at a property developer's premises regarding the anticipated increase in its value. There was a clause in the contract which prevented Lee from relying on any matter in the agreement unless this had been dealt with between the parties'

→

solicitors prior to the establishing of the contract. Lee argued that she informed the claimant in 2007 that she intended not to proceed with the contract and they had an obligation to mitigate their losses by selling the property to another buyer.

Authority for:

The defendant's actions were inconsistent with her repudiating the contract and there-fore the claimant could not exercise an action on the basis of anticipatory breach. Further, the standard rule of contract continues that a party does not have to accept an anticipatory breach. They are within their rights to wait until the performance of contract is due and it is not unreasonable for them to do so.

There is no obligation on the innocent party to accept the anticipatory breach, but as soon as they do, reasonable steps must be taken to mitigate losses.

Clea Shipping Corporation v Bulk Oil International (1984)

Facts:

In 1979 the parties entered into a 24-month agreement for the charter of a vessel named the Alaskan Trader. This was an old vessel and one year into the charter the vessel suffered a serious breakdown that would take several months to repair. The charterer informed the owners that they had no further use for it but the owners continued with the repairs at a cost of $800,000. Approximately six months later the repairs had been com-pleted and when the owners informed the charterer that the vessel was again available for their use, they would not use it as they considered the contract had come to an end.

Authority for:

An innocent party has in general an unfettered right to elect whether to accept repudia-tion of a contract. However, it is possible for a court, in the exercise of its general equi-table jurisdiction, to refuse to allow an innocent party to enforce their full contractual rights if they have no legitimate interest in performing the contract rather than claiming damages.

The damages available for breach and anticipatory breach are the same.

However, at what point would the 'innocent' party know and be able to take action on an anticipatory breach? In *SK Shipping Pte Ltd v Petroexport Ltd* the Commercial Court identified the following as reasons enabling the innocent party to take action on an an-ticipatory breach:

1. where the other party acted in a sufficiently clear manner to demonstrate it would not perform its obligations;

2. the words or conduct of the other party were sufficiently clear, to a reasonable person, of this intended breach when considered in light of the circumstances of the case;

3. the innocent party held a (subjective) belief that the other party would breach the contract.

10.3 REMEDIES FOR BREACH OF CONTRACT

In the event that a contract is not performed, or obligations under the contract are not fulfilled, the innocent party may be entitled to compensation. Under the common law, this is usually in the form of damages (a money payment), but may also involve equitable remedies of specific performance, injunctions, and rectification.

10.3.1 Damages

Any breach of contract entitles the injured party to damages. This is irrespective of whether the term is classified as a 'condition' or 'warranty'. Damages (a money payment) exist to compensate the injured party for any losses sustained under the breach of the contract. Damages can be either **'liquidated'**, meaning the parties have anticipated the consequences of the breach, determined the level of damages to be paid and included this in the contract; or they can be **'unliquidated'**, which are more frequent and determined by the court. The purpose of damages is not to punish the transgressor, or put the injured party in a better financial position than they would have achieved through the completion of the contract. They are used to either place the injured party in the position they would have been had the contract been completed (expectation losses) or place the injured party in the position they were before the contract had begun (reliance losses). In order for the courts to assess damages, there are underlying principles that are applied to ensure fairness. The first principle is that the damages must not be too remote, they must be quantifiable by the court, they must be recognized as damages in English law, and the injured party must have sought to **mitigate** their losses as far as is reasonable.

- *Remoteness of damage:* Remoteness is a vital aspect of the contract as it provides that the defendant will not be liable for damages that are deemed too remote. The general rule is that remoteness is assessed at the time of establishing the contract, rather than when the breach occurred.

Jackson v Royal Bank of Scotland Plc (2002)

Facts:

The claimant and their main customer held business bank accounts at the Royal Bank of Scotland (RBS). The claimant provided services to the customer for which they obtained a profit. Unfortunately, RBS revealed some of the claimant's invoices to the customer which identified the level of profit they obtained from that relationship. This was a breach of contract (and of the confidence between the claimant and RBS) and, being appalled at the level of profit being made from them, and that they considered the claimant was seeking to hide this amount, the customer ceased trading with the claimant. The customer was the main source of income for the claimant and when this was lost they soon were forced to cease trading. They claimed against RBS to recover their losses.

Authority for:

The original decision was for the claimant and the RBS were forced to pay damages on the basis of these lost profits for a four-year period. The Court of Appeal reduced the damages to only a one-year period. The House of Lords, identifying that damages should be determined according to the contract not when the breach occurred, reversed this decision and restored the award made by the court at first instance.

Further, in the following case the House of Lords considered that damages awarded could be restricted.

Golden Strait Corporation v Nippon Yusen Kubishka Kaisha (The Golden Victory) (2007)

Facts:

The case involved a charterer of a ship who wrongfully repudiated a charter party. The innocent party accepted the repudiation, but the House of Lords restricted the award of damages.

Authority for:

The reasoning for the decision was because the contract contained a clause that the charterers would be allowed to cancel the contract in the event of war with Iraq (which was a possibility when the contract was formed). It was further known to both parties that this option would have been exercised had war broken out. The contract was repudiated before the outbreak of war, but the war was effective before the term of the contract was completed. As such, the Lords held that with this knowledge, as opposed to only assessing damages at the time of the breach, a more accurate assessment could be achieved along the lines of 'fair compensation'. Hence the assessment of damages was altered from the 'traditional' approach.

The general rules for assessing damages include the following considerations:

1. Do the damages arise naturally in the normal and ordinary course of the contract?
2. Are the damages within the 'reasonable contemplation' of the parties (which depends on the probability/forseeability of loss, and the knowledge of the defendant)?

Consider

HPCI have ordered a machine for the expansion of their business. Imagine that the delivery deadline of 1 January is missed and that the machine will not be ready until 1 May, what damages would HPCI likely receive? How might your answer change if HPCI wanted the machine to not only expand the business but to fulfil a lucrative, and secret, contract with the Federation of Master Builders to become their preferred contractor for new Augmented Reality projects? The secrecy of this contract would mean it was not in the reasonable contemplation of the defendant and thus this element of a damage claim would likely be unsuccessful.

Hadley v Baxendale (1854)

Facts:

Hadley owned a flourmill and in May the mill was stopped due to a breakdown of the crankshaft (the only one it had). Hadley was to send the crankshaft to a third party for

→

➡

it to be replaced, and Baxendale was the carrier used for the transportation. Baxendale informed Hadley that delivery would be made on the following day. However, delivery was delayed for seven days and this led to a loss of profits that Hadley attempted to recover. Baxendale argued that it had no knowledge that Hadley would have sent the only crankshaft and hence a delay would have completely stopped production. The court concluded that there had been a breach of contract, but damages should be based on what may fairly and reasonably be considered arising naturally from the breach. A complete cessation of work due to the delay would have not been reasonably foreseeable by Baxendale.

Authority for:

In assessing quantum of damages, the award should be based on what may fairly and reasonably be considered arising naturally from the breach. This involves assessment of what should have been in the contemplation of both parties at the time they established the contract, as a probable result of the breach.

As Hadley sent its only crankshaft to be delivered by Baxendale, it had an obligation to inform Baxendale of this fact and a delay would have prevented any work being completed. With such information, Baxendale would have realized the consequences of any delay—a total loss of business and the consequent loss of profits. This legal reasoning was continued in the following case:

Victoria Laundry v Newman Industries (1949)

Facts:

The claimant purchased a large, commercial boiler from the defendant which it knew would be put to immediate use. The boiler was situated in the defendant's premises and they were to remove it and to install it in the premises of the claimant. In the removal process, the defendant damaged it and this caused a delay in breach of contract. A claim for damages was made for the loss of profits during the period of the delay but also for losses associated with a secret, lucrative contract which they lost due to the delay.

Authority for:

The losses as a consequence of the delay were reasonably foreseeable (in the reasonable contemplation of the parties) and were recoverable. Those associated with the loss of the secret contract were, by their nature, not in the (defendant's) reasonable contemplation and therefore could not be recovered.

Reasonable expectation can be seen in the following case:

> ### Koufos v C. Czarnikow Ltd (The Heron II) (1967)
>
> **Facts:**
>
> A cargo of sugar to be delivered to Basrah was delayed (and nine days late) due to voluntary deviations in the route. During these nine days, the price of sugar dropped and Czarnikow sought to recover these losses, but Koufos claimed it was unaware of Czarnikow's intention to sell the sugar at Basrah, but was aware that there was a market for the sugar. It was reasonable for the defendants to be aware that the cargo would have been sold in a recognized commodities market, and prices were liable to fluctuate, therefore the ship owners should reasonably have contemplated the serious possibility or real danger that, if delayed, the value of marketable goods on board the ship would decline.
>
> **Authority for:**
>
> This wrongful delay in the delivery of the goods led the House of Lords' assessment as to the measure of damages to be the difference between the price of the goods at their destination when they should have been delivered and the price of the goods when they were in fact delivered.

Having established whether the damages claimed were reasonable in the circumstances of the case, the next issue for the courts is how to quantify the losses.

- *Quantum of damages:* There are two methods a court may use to assess the measure of damages—reliance damages and expectation damages. Reliance loss is designed to prevent the injured party from suffering financial harm and returning them to the position before the contract had been established. The second type of damages is expectation loss. This identifies what the injured party would have achieved from the successful completion of the contract, and seeks to place them, as far as money can, in that position.

  In assessing the quantum of damages the courts will consider any loss of a bargain which the injured party has suffered, whether the parties have identified any 'agreed' damages in advance in the contract, and the duty on the injured party to mitigate their losses. The courts also have to ensure, when determining the quantum of damages, that the injured party is not unjustly enriched. For example, the usual remedy for a breach in a building contract is for the court to award the cost of reinstatement (i.e. to correct the defect). However, *Ruxley v Forsyth* (see later) provided an interesting interpretation of this rule.

- *Loss of opportunity damages:* If the injured party has not received what was contracted for under the agreement, damages is a remedy which is designed to award the cost of rectifying the loss, and provide compensation for any other foreseeable, consequential losses.

Consider

What would be the remedy if HPCI had constructed the garage but had used tangerine coloured bricks instead of the bright orange as requested by Salma? Would the courts grant damages for the costs of demolition of the steel structure to enable the bricks to be replaced before another structure is added? Perhaps not, especially if the costs of rectifying the damage is unreasonable.

Loss of opportunity damages is limited to where the courts see the award as being reasonable and the following case demonstrates where the courts did not provide 'adequate' damages following a breach.

Ruxley Electronics and Construction Ltd v Forsyth (1995)

Facts:

Ruxley was engaged to build a swimming pool for Mr Forsyth in his garden. The contract specified that the swimming pool should have a depth at the diving end of 7 feet, 6 inches. However, upon completion, the depth of the swimming pool was only 6 feet. Whilst this did not have any adverse affect on the value of the property, it did result in Mr Forsyth not having the depth of pool contracted for. It was estimated that it would cost £21,560 for the pool to be rebuilt to the required depth. It was held in the first case that this constituted a breach of contract, but Forsyth was awarded £2,500 for loss of amenity, not the cost of rebuilding as this would be an 'unfair enrichment' and unreasonable in the circumstances. There had been no consequential loss to the owner of the pool. The House of Lords agreed with this judgment.

Authority for:

In the event of a breach of contract where the contract was to provide the innocent party with something of value, if there is no other reasonable way of providing compensation, the damages should represent the extent of that value.

Lord Jauncy stated: 'Damages are designed to compensate for an established loss and not to provide a gratuitous benefit to the aggrieved party from which it follows that the reasonableness of an award of damages is to be linked directly to the loss sustained. If it is unreasonable in a particular case to award the cost of reinstatement it must be because the loss sustained does not extend to the need to reinstate. A failure to achieve the precise contractual objective does not necessarily result in the loss which is occasioned by a total failure.' Common sense may have prevailed here, and there exists an argument that the decision was correct. However, Mr Forsyth did contract with Ruxley for a swimming pool at a specific depth and this was not complied with. Mr Forsyth wanted that depth to enable him to dive into the pool and the one built did not provide this. A sum of £2,500 will not provide the pool contracted for, and would hardly recompense Forsyth for the inconvenience suffered. This may be seen as a judgment of 'rough justice and convenience'.

- *Reliance damages:* Reliance damages are most applicable where the parties cannot, with any certainty, identify what would have been achieved on the successful completion of the contract. It therefore attempts to place the parties in their pre-contractual positions.

Anglia Television v Reed (1971)

Facts:

Anglia Television entered into an agreement with an American actor, Robert Reed, to play a part in a TV play. Later, Reed claimed to have been booked to appear in a play in the United States and informed Anglia that he would not be able to complete the contract. Being unable to find a substitute, Anglia claimed damages for the lost profits associated with the breach of contract.

Authority for:

Damages are usually awarded to place the parties in the position they would have been had the contract been performed. However, whilst the injured party may claim expectation losses (here that would be the lost profits from the play) or reliance losses (the costs incurred until the breach) they cannot recover both. As expectation losses in this case would be too speculative, reliance losses for costs such as script writers, location fees etc. (amounting to £2,750) could be recovered.

* *Damages for injured feelings:* The traditional view of the courts when determining the level of damages applicable in a case has been to ignore any injured feelings or loss of enjoyment suffered.

Addis v Gramophone (1909)

Facts:

The claimant was a manager engaged by the defendant who breached the contract when replacing the claimant with a new manager. The claim for damages included the manner in which he was dismissed; his difficulty in obtaining alternative, suitable employment; and the damage to his reputation.

Authority for:

The House of Lords held that the purpose of damages in contract law was to put the injured party in the position they would be had the contract been performed. It did not include exemplary damages or damage to reputation. It would be limited to losses such as the loss of wages and commissions available due in the contractual notice period (six months' notice).

The reasoning for the decision is due to the problems inherent in quantifying such damages and the potential of opening the floodgates for claimants. However, exceptions to this rule have been developed in various cases (e.g. in *Malik v Bank of Credit and Commerce International* (see **19.6.2**) and *Perry v Sidney Phillips*, where the Court of Appeal held that distress following the negligence in a survey of a property which subsequently required the execution of substantial repairs, did entitle the injured party to damages) but can be seen most succinctly in the following:

Jarvis v Swans Tours (1972)

Facts:

Mr Jarvis was a solicitor, aged 35, who booked a 15-day Christmas winter sports holiday with Swans Tours. The brochure described the venue, in Switzerland, as a 'house

→

party centre' in very attractive terms. Mr Jarvis paid £63.45 for the package holiday; however, the holiday was very disappointing. Only 13 people were at the venue in the first week, with no other guests in the second week. Neither the owner of the house nor the staff could speak English; in the first week there were no full-length skis for Jarvis to use, and in the second week the skis were available but the boots supplied were of no use; the live entertainment consisted of a yodeller from the locality, who arrived in his working clothes, sang four or five songs very quickly, and then left; and the bar was only open one evening—located in an unoccupied annexe in the house. As such, Jarvis sought to recover the cost of the holiday and his salary for the two weeks spent on holiday. The Court of Appeal held that Jarvis was entitled to be compensated for his disappointment and distress at the loss of entertainment and facilities that he had been promised in Swans Tours' brochure. Damages should recognize the nature of this type of contract, and as it was specifically for enjoyment, if the contract does not provide what was promised then damages could be extended to account for that.

Authority for:

Damages awards should conform to the general rules of remoteness of damage. As such, the loss should be in the reasonable contemplation of the parties. Whilst damages for mental distress are not usually awarded in commercial contracts, they are applicable to non-commercial contracts.

• *Mitigation of loss:* The injured party in a contract has an obligation to limit the losses which they incur as a result of the breach. This is known as the duty to mitigate and means the injured party cannot lie back idly and allow the damages to amass. The background to the duty is one of economic efficiency, avoiding undue hardship to the defendant.

Consider

HPCI informs Salma that, due to supply chain problems, they are unable to supply the smart hub system as promised in their original quote. An alternative system, available from X-Wave Industries, would provide the same functionality, but costs £6,000. HPCI are unwilling to pay the additional amount for this as it would reduce their profits from the contract. Can Salma reject the contract if the smart hub system is not included? If Salma bought the X-Wave system, would such action amount to reasonable mitigation of loss?

The duty to mitigate loss is not absolute and an element of reasonableness is introduced whereby the injured party does not have to take unnecessary steps to reduce loss. This may be witnessed most obviously in contracts of employment where the worker has been unfairly/wrongfully dismissed and they must take steps to find alternative, but appropriate, employment (in relation to factors including locality, seniority, and pay).

Brace v Calder (1895)

Facts:

Mr Brace had entered a two-year contract in December 1892 with Calder (a firm of Scotch whisky merchants consisting of four partners). In May 1893, before the two years had expired, two of the partners retired, with the other two continuing to carry on the business. As a result, Calder offered Brace to serve the new firm for the remainder of the contract and on the same terms as the original agreement. Brace stated that he had not agreed to serve the new firm and declined the offer, claiming wrongful dismissal. The Court of Appeal held that there was a wrongful dismissal on the dissolution of the partnership, but Brace was only entitled to nominal damages (£50). This was because he was offered alternative work with the new partnership, which was fair and reasonable in the circumstances, and he could not wait for the court case and claim the remainder of the two years of the contract. Brace had failed to mitigate his losses.

Authority for:

Nominal damages may be awarded where an innocent party has failed to mitigate their losses following a breach.

In this situation, as the contract had been breached, but an alternative, suitable, offer was made and would have left Brace suffering no real loss, he was only entitled to nominal damages. The award of nominal damages essentially reflects that the claimant has 'won' the case, but they may not have acted reasonably in the circumstances.

- *Agreed/liquidated damages:* Businesses, particularly, may wish to consider the possibility of a contract not being completed on time or being breached, and the parties may seek to agree beforehand the amount to be paid in relation to this. This allows for greater certainty in the contract and the parties can determine how best to proceed without necessarily relying on the courts to determine such issues. This pre-determination of the damages payments is known as 'liquidated damages', whereas those determined by the court are referred to as unliquidated damages. For liquidated damages to be accepted, it must be a genuine pre-estimate of the loss rather than a penalty clause. A penalty clause is a threat against breaching the contract and will not be enforceable. However, simply because the contract uses the word 'penalty' will not necessarily make it a penalty clause.

Cellulose Acetate Silk Co. v Widnes Foundry (1933)

Facts:

The defendant entered into a contract to build for the claimant a chemical plant with a lead time of 18 weeks. On the basis that this deadline slipped, a 'penalty' payment of £20 per working week would be incurred. When the defendant completed the contract 30 weeks late, the claimant sought £5,850 in damages as the lost profit due to the breach. The defendant argued that, under the terms of the contract, they were only liable for £600 in damages.

Authority for:

The court held the term regarding the £20 per working week was not a penalty clause. Whilst it did not reflect the actual losses which a delay would cause the claimant, as it was lawful it would be interpreted as a limitation of liability.

There are tests that may help to distinguish liquidated damages from a penalty clause, and the following case provides useful instruction from the House of Lords:

Dunlop Pneumatic Tyre Company v New Garage and Motor Company (1915)

Facts:

Dunlop, manufacturers of tyres, covers, and tubes for motor vehicles, entered into a contract with a third party to supply them with goods under a contract that would only allow resales at prices established by Dunlop. The third party supplied New Garage with Dunlop's goods subject to a clause that it could not sell or offer the goods to any private customer or cooperative society at less than Dunlop's current list prices. Breach of the agreement would lead to liability of £5 by way of liquidated damages for each item. New Garage did breach this agreement and Dunlop sought to recover the damages as agreed; however, New Garage considered the term a penalty clause rather than liquidated damages.

The House of Lords held that the clause should be considered liquidated damages and not a penalty. Lord Dunedin referred to factors that point towards a penalty clause or liquidated damages.

Authority for:

Resultant to this case, the following are indicative in establishing liquidated damages and penalty clauses:

1. The use of the words 'penalty' or 'liquidated damages' may illustrate the nature of the clause but this is not conclusive.

2. The essence of liquidated damages is a genuine pre-estimate of damage.

3. The question whether a sum stipulated is a penalty or liquidated damages is a question to be decided on the terms and circumstances of each contract, and judged at the time of the making of the contract, not as at the time of the breach.

4. To assist this task of construction, various tests have been suggested, which may prove helpful:

   a. It will be held to be a penalty if the sum stipulated for is extravagant and unconscionable in amount in comparison with the greatest loss that could conceivably be proved to have followed from the breach.

   b. There is a presumption (but no more) that it is a penalty when 'a single lump sum is made payable by way of compensation, on the occurrence of one or more or all of several events, some of which may occasion serious, and others trifling, damage.'

The tests established in the case are applicable as a guide to determine scenarios when the courts will hold a term that purports to be liquidated damages as a penalty clause. These will not, in all cases, be rigidly followed. They exist as a guide as to features indicative of contractual clauses that may be penalty clauses but which, in reality, necessitate complex enquiry.

Consider

Given that Bechtal Ltd has informed HPCI that the new machine ordered will not be delivered until 1 May, could HPCI invoke the clause requiring payment of £1,000 per day as unliquidated damages (£120,000)? Assess this carefully in light of the *Cavendish Square Holding BV v Talal El Makdessi (El Makdessi)* and *ParkingEye Ltd v Beavis* [2015] ruling and whether such a sum is 'exorbitant or unconscionable.'

A significant clarification of the use and applicability of penalty clauses was provided by the Supreme Court in 2015, and this has seemingly broadened the provision of pre-estimates of loss.

ParkingEye Ltd v Beavis (2015)

Facts:

The case involved Mr Beavis who, whilst using a car park in Chelmsford, was issued with a parking fine of £85 by the management firm ParkingEye Ltd for overstaying the two-hour time limit. Beavis argued the clause and the amount charged for its breach amounted to a penalty clause and was thus unenforceable. Notices at the car park identified the parking regulations and the charge liable for a failure to comply. In the Court of Appeal, Moore-Bick referred to *El Makdessi v Cavendish Square Holdings BV* [2013] EWCA Civ 1539 when determining the fairness of such clauses: '[T]he modern cases thus appear to accept that a clause providing for payment on a breach of a sum of money that exceeds the amount that a court would award as compensation . . . may not be regarded as penal if it can be justified commercially and if its predominant purpose is not to deter breach.'

Authority for:

The Court of Appeal, with which the Supreme Court agreed, considered that the purpose of the £85 charge was to deter motorists from staying in a bay for longer than two hours. Despite its commercial purpose (to facilitate the turnover of shoppers in using the car park), the court allowed the charge. Insofar as such a charge is not extravagant and unconscionable, it will be allowed as a pre-estimate of loss.

10.3.2 Equitable Remedies for Breach of Contract

As stated at **10.3.1**, the courts will generally provide damages as a remedy for breach of contract wherever possible (as this is usually the simplest form of a remedy as it is a money payment). However, there are occasions where money would not provide an appropriate remedy, or would be unjust due to the nature of the breached contract. This has led to the development of the equitable remedies, but remember that as they are 'equitable' remedies, they are awarded at the court's discretion.

- *Specific performance:* Specific performance is a remedy that is available when monetary damages are insufficient and do not adequately compensate the injured party for their loss. This is a court order compelling the party in breach to perform their contractual obligations. As the remedy is only available where monetary damages are inadequate, it is an order generally where the subject matter of the contract is unique—such as the sale of land or antiques which by their nature cannot be replaced (although those examples are not guaranteed to be awarded specific performance). Specific performance cannot be ordered in contracts for personal services, or contracts requiring constant supervision by the courts. In *Rainbow Estates v Tokenhold*, specific performance was granted compelling a tenant to carry out repairs to the landlord's premises (as identified in the contract) as once the repairs were completed, no further supervision would be necessary. Finally, as an *equitable remedy*, it must also be available (potentially) to both parties and would not cause unreasonable hardship.

Co-op Insurance Society v Argyll Stores (1997)

Facts:

The Co-op Insurance Society was landlord of a shopping centre in Sheffield consisting of 25 outlets and provided Argyll Stores with a 35-year lease. This lease was granted for the purpose of operating a supermarket and contained a covenant that the supermarket would operate during usual business hours. Approximately 16 years later Argyll Stores decided to close all of its stores, including the supermarket in Sheffield, as it was trading at a loss. Co-op applied for a remedy of specific performance to prevent the closure of the stores in the fear that it would have a detrimental impact on the other businesses in the shopping centre.

Authority for:

The House of Lords refused to order specific performance. To make such an order would have been to punish Argyll Stores and this was not the purpose of remedies in contract law. Per Lord Hoffman: 'The purpose of the law of contract is not to punish wrongdoing but to satisfy the expectations of the party entitled to performance. A remedy which enables him to secure, in money terms, more than the performance due to him is unjust.'

Specific performance is a very powerful remedy, but may also be perceived as harsh and at times unfair.

Mountford v Scott (1975)

Facts:

Mr Mountford and his wife were members of a small property development company called H. & L. Cronk Ltd who were interested in purchasing properties with a view to building a new development. The new development could only be considered as viable if the appropriate planning consents were provided. Cronk Ltd sought to obtain options to buy the houses in the area of the proposed development, consequently obtain, if possible, the consents, and to proceed with the sales or to decide not to exercise the option.

→

> Mr Scott was a gentleman of West Indian origin who had lived in England for approximately 20 years, and although he spoke and understood English well, he was illiterate. Scott's house was one of the properties Cronk Ltd obtained an option on purchasing. The agreement allowed for Cronk Ltd to purchase his house for the price of £10,000, to be completed within six months of the agreement, with £1 being paid to Scott in consideration for the option. It transpires that later Scott did not want to continue with this arrangement and requested that Cronk Ltd release him, which it would not do. Cronk Ltd decided to exercise the option to purchase Scott's house.
>
> **Authority for:**
>
> On the decision of Mountford to refuse to continue with the sale, the court ordered specific performance of the contract. The Court of Appeal held that the agreement was valid and hence constituted an irrevocable offer to sell. The agreement was entered into freely and consideration (of the £1) established a valid contract. Russell LJ remarked that specific performance, rather than damages, should be the appropriate remedy in the case: 'If the owner of a house contracts with his eyes open, as the judge held that the defendant did, it cannot, in my view, be right to deny specific performance to the purchaser because the vendor then finds it difficult to find a house to buy that suits him and his family on the basis of the amount of money in the proceeds of sale.'

Mountford demonstrates the practical use of the remedy of specific performance and provides evidence of its effectiveness in ensuring compliance with the contract. Specific performance is restricted in use, as outlined earlier, and complements the other equitable remedy of injunctions as ensuring fairness is achieved in breaches of contract.

- *Injunctions:* There are two main types of injunction available to the courts—mandatory injunctions and prohibitory injunctions (although interim injunctions may be granted prior to a full hearing to prevent injury to the claimant—these may be seen in cases of infringement of intellectual property—see **Chapter 24**). Mandatory injunctions require the party compelled to perform the contract, whilst the more common type is a prohibitory injunction, which stops a party from breaching the contract. Failing to follow the order of an injunction will result in the transgressor being guilty of contempt of court—a potentially very serious charge. It is a valuable mechanism in ensuring that a party does not breach the contract although, as with specific performance, it will only be used where damages would be inadequate and the issuing of the injunction must be reasonable.

Warner Brothers v Nelson (1937)

Facts:

The case involved the actor Bette Davis who entered an exclusive contract with Warner Bros where she agreed not to undertake any other work without their permission. The contract had two years to run when Davis complained about a number of issues including not getting a role in a particular production. In response to the dispute she travelled to the UK to take up work for another organization (in breach of contract). Warner Bros applied to the court for an injunction to prevent her taking up this work.

Authority for:

The injunction was awarded against the organization attempting to get Davis to breach her contract rather than preventing her from actually working.

• *Rectification:* The remedy of rectification enables a written document (e.g. a contract) to be changed (e.g. including/removing of clauses) to more accurately reflect the terms that were identified in the oral agreement subsequently reduced in writing.

A Roberts & Co. v Leicestershire CC (1961)

Facts:

The claimant was a firm of building contractors who had entered into an agreement with the defendant for the erection of a school building. The contract identified a period of 30 months whilst the original tender was for a period of 18 months, and the claimants believed this tender was for the same period. It transpires the defendants were aware of the misunderstanding on the part of the claimant as to the period of the tender and failed to inform the contractors.

Authority for:

The contract was rectified and the clause identifying the term of 30 months was replaced with a period of 18 months. The defendant knew of the mistake in the written contract compared with the original agreement and understood the consequences of its error.

In order for a claim for rectification to succeed, the parties must have established an oral contract that identified the terms of the agreement, these terms did not change from the oral agreement until it was written, and the written contract does not accurately provide what was stated in the oral agreement. The remedy allows the written document to be altered to reflect what the parties agreed orally, but this will only allow the document to reflect this oral agreement, not what one of the parties wanted to have included. In *Re Sigma Finance Corporation (in administrative receivership)* the Supreme Court reversed decisions of both the High Court and Court of Appeal with the effect that a contract was rewritten to give effect to the context/meaning of the words used in an agreement, even though the natural wording of the agreement was correct. The court considered that a literal interpretation of the words would have been to distort the commercial intentions of the parties.

Rectification may be available where one of the parties believes that the contract reflects the intentions of the parties, but it does not, and the other party is aware of this mistake. This must go beyond the negligence of the party in reading the agreement and not spotting the error, and whilst it may involve 'turning a blind eye' rather than demonstrating actual knowledge, 'unconscionability' will be required.

Commission for the New Towns v Cooper (GB) Ltd (1995)

Facts:

The defendant's predecessor (as tenant of commercial premises underlet by the claimant's predecessor) had made three agreements with the underlessor. When the defendant acquired the remaining and unexpired lease, it wished to end the contract but wanted to avoid a penalty payment. Therefore, it pretended to be negotiating for one of the options in the relevant contract when in reality it had no intention of using that option. Rather, it intended to use another of the options which would provide it with scope to achieve its aims—but did not inform the other party of this in negotiations. It was agreed that the new contract would be on the same terms as those enjoyed by the predecessor. As soon as the agreement was reached, the defendant attempted to exercise the option and the claimant sought rectification of the agreement.

Authority for:

An order for rectification was made due to the defendant having deliberately attempted to mislead the claimant into making the relevant mistake. Cooper had, according to the Court of Appeal, attempted to put up a 'smokescreen' and intentionally omitted to bring to the Commission's attention the issue of the option.

The Court of Appeal held in *Daventry District Council v Daventry & District Housing Ltd* that a contract may be rectified in instances of common mistake. However, this decision has been criticized due to the emphasis on whether the parties have objectively made a common mistake, rather than a subjective assessment being applied.

There exist limits by when a claim for breach of contract must be made. Under the Limitation Act 1980, an action under a simple contract must be made within six years from when the right to the action arose (s. 5). In the case of contracts made under deed, the claim must be established within 12 years (s. 8(1)).

There is no statutory provision for time limits to claim under the equitable remedies, but as these are equitable, they must be sought within a reasonable time.

CONCLUSION

This chapter has concluded the topic of the law of contract. These chapters have identified the essential features of a valid contract; the terms within a contract, and their source; the legislative impact on contracts; and the discharge of contracts. This chapter has identified how the courts will ascertain the level of damages, if any, to be awarded in various situations, and the equitable remedies available. The book now proceeds to a further element of the wider topic of obligations; investigating torts applicable to businesses.

SUMMARY OF MAIN POINTS

Discharge

- Contracts may be discharged through performance, through part-performance (if accepted by the other party), and through substantial performance.

- Contracts may be discharged through the parties' agreeing to release each other from their further obligations (this can involve unilateral or bilateral discharge).

- The contract may become radically different from that which was agreed or impossible to perform. If this is neither party's fault then the contract is discharged through frustration.
- Discharge is effective through a breach of contract if the innocent party chooses to accept the repudiation.

Remedies for breach

- Damages are available as the primary remedy in breach.
- Damages may be based on expectation losses (that seek to put the innocent party into the position they would have been had the contract been completed) or reliance losses (that put the innocent party back to the position they were in before the contract was established).
- Damages must not be too remote: they must derive from the breach and have been in the reasonable contemplation of the parties when the contract was formed.
- Damages are not designed to penalize the party in breach and hence they must be quantified to reflect the losses sustained by the innocent party.
- The innocent party must proactively (albeit reasonably) attempt to mitigate their losses rather than wait for the losses to accrue.
- Damages may be agreed in advance (called liquidated damages) but these must not amount to a penalty clause.

Equitable remedies

- Specific performance may be ordered to compel the fulfillment of the contract. This, as with each of the equitable remedies, is available at the discretion of the court and is awarded when damages would not adequately compensate the innocent party. They are generally used in contracts involving unique items.
- Injunctions can be awarded to prevent a party from breaching the contract.
- The courts may also order rectification of the contract so that the written contract is changed to accurately reflect the parties' intentions.

SUMMARY QUESTIONS

Essay questions

1. 'The equitable remedy of specific performance is harsh, unfair, and it exposes vulnerable people to potentially unsound contractual obligations. It should be abolished and replaced with a common law damages assessment.'

   With reference to case law, critically assess the above statement.

2. Identify the methods in which contractual obligations may be discharged. Specifically comment on the differing approaches taken by the judiciary in relation to discharge through frustration.

Problem questions

1. In June 2016 Tariq entered into a contract with Wagner Brothers Ltd to write a script for an intended play that Wagner Brothers Ltd was to provide to Apollo's Theatres Ltd. Apollo's intended to use this for several performances it had scheduled for November 2017. The contract provided that Tariq was to submit the completed script on or before June 2017.

   It transpires that Tariq did not have time to write the script as he was busy with other projects and had taken on too much work. On 25 April 2017 Tariq wrote to Wagner Brothers

Ltd with notice that he would not be able to complete the script as promised and had no intention of attempting to do so. By this stage, Wagner Brothers Ltd and Apollo's Theatres Ltd had incurred substantial expenses on the basis of this project. Wagner Brothers Ltd had also entered into preliminary contractual agreements with several television production companies for a mini-series of the script.

Advise Wagner Brothers Ltd and Apollo's Theatres Ltd of any action they can take for damages.

2. Stephane books a holiday with Super Skiing Holidays Plc who specialize in holidays for single people. Stephane books for a two-week vacation to a resort in Switzerland. The brochure describes the resort as hosting a 'house party' where live entertainment will be provided every night and there will be several people to meet and enjoy the resort with.

When Stephane arrives he is unhappy with the quality of the room and the food is of a very poor standard. The only ski boots available are too small for his feet and the skis were designed for children—there were no adult sizes. The entertainment consists of a local plumber who provides his Elvis Presley impersonation for 30 minutes each night on his way home from work. Stephane is joined at the resort by three other guests, each of whom are French and do not speak English, and they leave after five days—leaving Stephane the only person at the resort for the remainder of the holiday.

When Stephane returns home he complains to Super Skiing Holidays but they state it was not their problem and he cannot claim damages for the loss of enjoyment of his vacation.

Advise Stephane.

 You will find guidance about how to answer these questions online at www.oup.com/uk/marson5e/.

 FURTHER READING

Books and articles

Davies, P. S. (2012) 'Rectifying the Course of Rectification' *Modern Law Review*, Vol. 75, No. 3, p. 412.

Nicholson, A. (2016) 'Too entrenched to be challenged? A commentary on the rule against contractual penalties post Cavendish v Makdessi and Parking Eye v Beavis' *European Journal of Current Legal Issues*, Vol. 22, No 3.

 ONLINE RESOURCES

www.oup.com/uk/marson5e/

For further resources relating to this chapter, including self-test questions, an interactive glossary, and key case flashcards.

PART 4
TORTIOUS LIABILITY

Torts law forms the second element of the law of obligations. Unlike contractual liability where the parties enter into agreements on a voluntary basis, tortious liability may be imposed as a matter of law. Businesses in particular need to be aware of their responsibilities when producing and selling goods and services; the extent of their liability to visitors and trespassers; their responsibilities to their workforce; and their potential liabilities for the torts of their employees. Adequate insurance can mitigate against aspects of these responsibilities but it would be unwise to begin operating a business without a knowledge of torts law.

11 NEGLIGENCE AND NUISANCE

Whilst the civil law places obligations on those parties who wish to undertake duties freely and agree to be legally bound via contracts, torts law imposes the obligation without, necessarily, prior agreement. The duty is to take reasonable care and not intentionally or negligently cause harm or damage. 'Torts' derives from the French word 'wrong' and is essentially a civil wrong that entitles the injured party to the remedy of compensation. This remedy has the aim of placing the victim back into the position they were (as far as money can) before the tort was committed.

Business Scenario 11

The straight boundary at Middleshire County Cricket Club's ground is 85 yards from the wicket. The fence between the ground and an adjoining road, 5 yards beyond the boundary, is 4 feet high. Cricket balls have been struck into the road over the fence on 19 occasions in the last 10 years.

Vihaan, a visiting player from the West Country, who has never played on the ground before, but who is renowned for his big hitting, strikes the ball into the road. The ball hits Mavis off her bike, causing her minor cuts and bruises. She lands on the recently-sprayed grass at the roadside and contracts a serious skin infection as a result of contact with weed killer to which she is allergic.

Learning Outcomes

- Explain the meaning of the term 'tort' (11.1–11.4)
- Differentiate between liability in contract and liability in tort (11.4)
- Explain the three tests to establish liability in negligence (11.5–11.5.3.2)
- Explain the facts and the court's reasoning in *Donoghue v Stevenson* (11.5.1)
- Identify the defences to a negligence claim (11.6–11.6.4)
- Identify the remedies available in claims of tortious liability (11.7)
- Assess where a business or individual may commit an act of nuisance and available defences to such actions (11.8–11.8.2.3).

11.1 INTRODUCTION

One of the most important torts is negligence (which may be commonly seen in instances of personal injury) and this tort is considered first in the chapter before acts of private and public nuisance are addressed.

11.2 FAULT LIABILITY

The law imposes a duty to take reasonable care to not negligently or intentionally cause damage. Many claims of negligence involve fault liability: someone is at fault and this enables the injured party to seek compensation for the resultant loss/injury. As such, situations of damage that are determined 'acts of God' will generally not be compensatable as there is no party from which to claim. This is in contrast to liability in contract that is strict (e.g. the retailer is responsible for goods not being of a satisfactory quality despite the fact that, often, they would have no way of knowing this or have been personally responsible for the (lack of) quality).

Note also that in other situations relevant to this topic, tortious liability may be imposed in the absence of fault. Under the doctrine of vicarious liability, one person may be held liable for the torts of another (such as an employer being held liable for the torts of their employees, or the principal being liable for torts of their agent). Fault is also removed in claims under the Consumer Protection Act 1987 where the liability is strict.

11.3 TIME LIMITS

There exists a limitation period in which claims of negligence must be brought against the perpetrator of the tort (the **tortfeasor**). Under the Limitation Act 1980, s. 2, actions in tort must be brought within six years of the date giving rise to the right of action. Claims for personal injury, however, must be brought within three years of either the date on which the tort was committed, or from when the injury attributable to the tortfeasor became known (s. 11).

In the case of a death, where the deceased person's representatives wish to bring an action on their behalf, the claim must be brought within three years of the date of the death, or three years from the date on which they obtained this knowledge (ss. 11(5) and 12).

Protection is also afforded to minors (under the age of 18), and the time limits above do not apply until the claimant becomes 18. There is also protection to claimants who are suffering a mental disorder, as provided for in the Mental Capacity Act 2005, and who are incapable of managing their affairs. In such a situation the time limits do not apply.

11.4 THE DISTINCTION BETWEEN CONTRACTUAL AND TORTIOUS LIABILITY

Tortious liability differs from contractual liability in that the obligations undertaken in contracts are entirely voluntary. No one can be forced into a contract against their will and consequently the parties have the ability to be aware of the extent of their liability, and the possible consequences in the event of breach. In contrast to this, tortious liability is imposed on persons and organizations (sometimes) without their knowledge or the awareness of the potential extent of this liability. The law sometimes requires compulsory insurance to protect against claims of liability in negligence or other torts (e.g. employers' liability and public liability), but it may be prudent for businesses to carry insurance for their property and possessions in the event of claims against them. Do remember that there may be several claims involving the same scenario, such as a breach of contract claim *and* a negligence action (e.g. in *Grant v Australian Knitting Mills*—see **9.2.1**); and the scenario may involve a criminal action and a tort claim (such as an employee in a factory being injured through the use of dangerous and faulty equipment). Where the claimant has suffered a loss and injury, as in *Grant*, it is for the claimant to elect to pursue each element of their claim.

11.5 NEGLIGENCE

The law requires that those who are deemed to owe others a **duty of care** act responsibly and take necessary precautions to avoid injury and loss to others. The remedy primarily provided by the law is a damages payment to put the injured party back in the position they were before the tort had taken place—this can prove very expensive for businesses. Fundamentally to those in business, knowledge of the law and of responsibilities enables positive steps to be made to minimize the risk of negligence claims. When reading through the cases and judgments that follow, consider whether you would have acted as the business did, and whether you would have considered that liability would be imposed by the courts.

A definition of negligence is the breach of a duty to take care, owed in law by the defendant to the claimant, causing the claimant damage. In order to establish a successful claim in negligence, three tests must be satisfied. Each of these will be discussed in turn (**Figure 11.1**).

Figure 11.1 Negligence liability: an overview

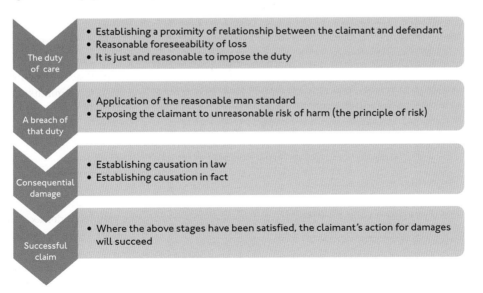

The duty of care
- Establishing a proximity of relationship between the claimant and defendant
- Reasonable foreseeability of loss
- It is just and reasonable to impose the duty

A breach of that duty
- Application of the reasonable man standard
- Exposing the claimant to unreasonable risk of harm (the principle of risk)

Consequential damage
- Establishing causation in law
- Establishing causation in fact

Successful claim
- Where the above stages have been satisfied, the claimant's action for damages will succeed

> **Consider**
>
> For Mavis to be successful in her claim she must establish that Vihaan (the cricketer) owes her a duty of care. In each sub-test mentioned in the following section, consider the facts of the case, its authority, and which of these are met in the case of Mavis or which authority may be distinguished.

11.5.1 The Duty of Care

Before proceeding to identify each of the 'three tests' necessary to establish a duty of care, it should be noted that these are separated, somewhat artificially, to demonstrate how they appear in the facts of the case and are identified by the courts. To establish liability in negligence, it must first be determined that the respondent owed the claimant a duty to take reasonable care.

11.5.1.1 Proximity of relationship

Here the claimant and defendant must have a closeness (proximity) of relationship.

Donoghue v Stevenson (1932)

Facts:

A friend and Mrs Donoghue visited a café in Paisley, Glasgow on 26 August 1928, where the friend purchased a bottle of ginger beer for Donoghue. The drink was served in a dark, stone, opaque bottle and, unknown to the purchaser, the retailer, or Donoghue, contained the remains of a snail. This only became apparent when the greater part of the contents of the bottle had been consumed and the remainder was poured into a glass. At the sight of the snail, Donoghue claimed she suffered from shock and severe gastro-enteritis. On the basis of this illness Donoghue brought her action for damages against the manufacturer of the ginger beer (David Stevenson). Donoghue contended that the claim should be made against the manufacturer as the ginger beer was bottled by Stevenson, labelled by him, and he sealed the bottle with a metal cap.

A key element in establishing negligence is the proximity between the parties, which led Lord Atkin to state: 'You must take reasonable care to avoid acts or omissions which you can reasonably foresee would be likely to injure your neighbour. Who, then, in law is my neighbour? The answer seems to be—persons who are so closely and directly affected by my act that I ought reasonably to have them in contemplation as being so affected when I am directing my mind to the acts or omissions which are called in question.'

Authority for:

In establishing that the defendant owes the claimant a duty to take care, there must be proximity of relationship between them. This is identified through Lord Atkin's 'neighbour principle'.

Donoghue v Stevenson is the seminal case in the establishment of the tort of negligence. The House of Lords determined that the claimant must establish that the defendant owes the claimant a duty of care, and in establishing this there must be proximity between the parties. 'Proximity' is the closeness of relationship between the parties that creates the duty to take care. Here, the manufacturer of a product was held liable for damage sustained by anyone who could have used, and consumed, its product. The case established that proximity is not restricted to a physical 'closeness' but can be extended to anyone who may reasonably be seen as being likely to be affected by the defendant's actions.

Consider

Mavis has been struck by the cricket ball whilst standing outside of her house. It would seem that there is a proximity of relationship between her and Vihaan. The next sub-test is of reasonable foreseeability. Should a cricketer have reasonably foreseen that by striking the ball in the manner he did, it may leave the ground and cause damage?

11.5.1.2 Reasonable foreseeability of loss

Having established the proximity between the parties according to the authority in *Donoghue*, the next stage in demonstrating the duty of care is whether the defendant's action could reasonably have been foreseen to cause the loss or damage.

Bourhill v Young (1943)

Facts:

Mr Young had been riding his motorbike and collided with a motorcar on 11 October 1938, in which accident he died. Mrs Bourhill (a 'pregnant fishwife') was a passenger on a tram. At the stop she alighted and was in the process of removing her fish-basket when the accident occurred. It was discovered that Young had been travelling at an excessive speed and was thrown onto the street as a result of the collision, where he died. Bourhill did not witness the crash (her view being obstructed by the tram), but became aware of it on hearing the noise of the impact (she was some 45–50 feet away). Young's body had been removed from the scene, and when Bourhill approached the point of the crash she observed the blood left on the roadway. In her evidence she claimed to suffer damage to her back and 'very severe shock to her nervous system', although she acknowledged that she did not fear for her own personal safety. The House of Lords held that a motorcyclist owed a duty of care to other road users and those he could reasonably foresee might be injured by his failure to take reasonable care, but Bourhill did not fall into this category as she was not in any area of potential danger. Young did not owe her a duty of care as it was not foreseeable that she may be injured in the incident, and there was a lack of proximity between the parties.

Authority for:

For a duty of care to be established, the defendant must have reasonably foreseen that their actions may cause injury or loss to the claimant.

The case demonstrated how the courts will deal with the issue of proximity of relationship and the link with forseeability. As the courts find one single definition of 'proximity' unrealistic (as noted by the Lords in *Caparo*) the examples provided in the cases presented in this chapter enable common features to be drawn and considered for application in similar scenarios.

Consider

Once a cricketer strikes a ball and it leaves the confines of the venue where they are playing, do they have any control over it? It is common sense that the ball will land beyond the cricket ground. Given that the cricketer and the owner of the ground have little control over the movement of pedestrians and vehicles, and there is only five yards between the fence and the road, the ball will strike something when it lands— perhaps just the ground, but it is reasonable that it could be a person or property.

11.5.1.3 Fair, just, and reasonable

The final element in the duty of care test was extended from a case involving economic loss. *Caparo v Dickman* established the threefold test of proximity; foreseeability; and whether it was fair, just, and reasonable to impose a duty of care (albeit that this case was largely decided on its facts rather than a 'true' application of legal principle).

Caparo Industries Plc v Dickman and Others (1990)

Facts:

Caparo had accomplished a takeover of Fidelity Plc and it began an action against the directors of that company (Steven and Robert Dickman) claiming a fraudulent misrepresentation, and an action against its auditors (Touche Ross & Co.) claiming it was negligent in carrying out an audit of the company. The basis of Caparo's claim was that it began purchasing shares in Fidelity a few days before the annual accounts had been published and made available to the shareholders. In reliance on these accounts, it made further purchases of the shares in order to take over the company, and claimed the auditors owed a duty of care to the shareholders and any potential investors. The audit had projected Fidelity's profits unrealistically high, which Fidelity should have realized; and the share price had fallen significantly, causing substantial financial loss to Caparo. The House of Lords had to consider whether the auditors did in fact owe Caparo a duty of care. The Lords held that this case involved a negligent misstatement, but protection in such cases was limited to those who had obtained specific advice and used it for a reason made known to the provider of the information. The audit was a requirement of the Companies Act 1985 and therefore did not impose a duty of care on the auditors to the shareholders or potential investors. Consequently, Caparo's claim failed as there was a lack of proximity between the auditors and Caparo.

Authority for:

The imposition of liability for negligence should only take place where it is 'just and reasonable' to do so. Importantly, as this was a novel case, the law should develop liability in such cases incrementally and restrict/limit the imposition to those whom a duty is owed.

The issue of proximity has been addressed in *Donoghue*; foreseeability has been demonstrated in *Caparo* as a similar test to that used in contract of whether it should have been foreseeable to the defendant what the consequences of their action would be and the possible results; and 'fair, just, and reasonable' is an argument based on public policy. It enables the court the discretion to consider the wider implications of establishing liability and has been referred to as the 'floodgates' argument. If establishing liability would 'open the floodgates' to numerous claims, then the court may decide that the liability should not be imposed. The courts also use this requirement to protect potential defendants such as public bodies (the emergency services, local authorities providing education services, and so on) from excessive claims and a diminution of public funds (compare the judgments in *John Munroe (Acrylics) Ltd v London Fire Brigade & Civil Defence Authority*) and *Kent v Griffiths and Others*).

The House of Lords later held in *Marc Rich & Co. v Bishop Rock Marine* that the requirement of establishing this 'threefold' test would be applicable to novel claims (such as in *Caparo*). However, where an accepted duty that had been previously held to exist (such as the duty imposed on drivers to other road users from carelessly causing injury), it was unnecessary to subject these claims to the *Caparo* threefold test when the question of duty has already been determined.

11.5.2 Breach of the Duty

Having established that the defendant owed the claimant a duty of care, the next step in determining liability is to establish the defendant's breach of this duty. Essentially, this means that the defendant fell below the standard required by law. The tests outlined in the following paragraphs, like the tests to prove the existence of a duty of care, are guidelines that have been developed through the courts, rather than an attempt to establish a single set of criteria that will or will not establish a breach of the defendant's duty of care. They will often overlap and each draws on elements of the other, but they are used to demonstrate the issues the courts will consider in attributing liability.

Consider

If we believe the cricketer owes Mavis a duty of care, the next stage is to determine if he has acted in breach. Think about the nature of the cricket ground, the distance of the boundary fence, its height, whether it is well maintained and so on. What would be the standard expected of the reasonable cricketer and the reasonable ground owner?

11.5.2.1 The 'reasonable man' standard

When determining if a breach of the duty of care has occurred, it is important to note that the courts will apply the 'reasonable man' test objectively. This means that whilst the defendant must take into account the shortcomings of others (e.g. vulnerable people such as children), there is no allowance to be made for lack of experience/intelligence.

> ### Nettleship v Weston (1971)
>
> **Facts:**
>
> Mr Nettleship gave driving lessons to Miss Weston, who was a careful learner. However, on the third lesson Weston failed to straighten following a left turn and drove into a street lamp, which led to Nettleship breaking his kneecap. Weston was convicted of driving without due care and attention, and Nettleship brought an action for negligence due to his injuries.
>
> **Authority for:**
>
> The Court of Appeal held that the fact that the driver was a learner was no defence to the negligence action; the test applied to a learner was the same, objective test, as applied to a careful driver.

Breach of the defendant's duty of care will often follow their failure under the 'reasonable man' test. In *Blyth v Birmingham Waterworks Co.*, Alderson B commented that 'Negligence is the omission to do something which a reasonable man, guided upon those considerations which ordinarily regulate the conduct of human affairs, would do, or doing something which a prudent and reasonable man would not do.' There is an obligation to display appropriate (professional) levels of skill.

> ### Bolam v Friern Hospital Management Committee (1957)
>
> **Facts:**
>
> Mr Bolam sustained fractures of the acetabula during the course of electroconvulsive therapy treatment administered whilst he was a voluntary patient at the defendants' hospital. Bolam initiated a damages action against the hospital alleging that the defendants were negligent in failing to administer any relaxant drug prior to the passing of the current through his brain, and they had failed to warn him of the risks involved in the treatment. The hospital produced expert witnesses who each agreed that there was a firm body of medical opinion opposed to the use of relaxant drugs. Further, it was the practice of the defendants' doctors not to warn their patients of the risks of the treatment (which they believed to be small) unless asked.
>
> **Authority for:**
>
> The High Court held that even if a warning as to the result of the treatment was provided, this would not have affected the outcome of the case, and the hospital had complied with professional standards. Therefore, the claim failed and the hospital was not negligent.

11.5.2.2 Actual breach committed

The claimant, in asserting that the defendant has breached their duty of care, will, as a general rule, have to demonstrate to the court's satisfaction that the defendant committed a breach. This places the burden of proof on the claimant.

1. *The principle of exposing the claimant to unreasonable risk of harm:*

The nature of the 'unreasonableness' of the risk of harm is demonstrated in the following cases.

Bolton v Stone (1951)

Facts:

A woman, standing outside her house, was struck by a cricket ball hit from an adjoining cricket club. She sought to recover damages for her injuries but the House of Lords refused.

Authority for:

The club had reasonably minimized the risk of harm through erecting a fence some 17 feet high at the perimeter of the ground. The fact that balls had only ever been struck over the fence six times in 28 years led to the judgment that the claimant had not been exposed to an unreasonable risk of harm.

The case reflected on the main elements to consider when assessing a breach of duty of care. Those are:

- the 'reasonable man' standard;
- the principle of risk (exposure to unreasonable risk of harm);
- the social utility and desirability of the defendant's actions;
- the cost/practicality of the measures to reduce the risk of harm.

The failure of Miss Stone to establish a breach of duty that prevented her successful claim can be compared with the case of *Miller v Jackson*.

Miller v Jackson (1977)

Facts:

The case involved a cricket ground (the Lintz Cricket Club) in County Durham, whose Chairman, Mr Jackson, was sued for negligence (and another tort action under nuisance) by Mr and Mrs Miller. Mr Miller had bought his house in the summer of 1972, and the garden was only 102 feet from the centre of the cricket ground. Miller claimed that cricket balls were struck from the club into his garden, which had caused damage to his property, and were so intrusive that he and his wife spent time away from the property during matches, and would not enter the garden for fear of being hit by stray cricket balls. This was despite a six-foot concrete wall at the end of the garden, and the cricket ground erecting a fence of 14 feet 9 inches (the fence could not be made higher due to stability problems). In 1975, six balls went over the fence into the neighbouring houses; in 1976 nine balls went over the fence.

Authority for:

In the first case the court held that there had been a breach of the cricket club's duty to take reasonable care.

Consider

The facts of the cases above allow the breach of the reasonable man standard to be determined in accordance with appropriate authority. The fence in the question is only five feet high and balls are leaving the ground approximately twice a year. Unless there is a satisfactory reason why the owners of the ground cannot raise its height they will have failed to do something the reasonable man would have. Further, even if a satisfactory reason is present, the owners of the ground would be expected to inform the cricketers to modify their play to minimize the risk of balls passing the boundary fence.

The more likely it would be that the defendant's action would lead to injury or loss, the more likely it would be that they had breached their duty to take reasonable care.

Brett v University of Reading (2007)

Facts:

Mr Brett died as the result of contracting mesothelioma attributed from working with asbestos. A claim was brought against one of his former employers, as during his employment as a Clerk of Works, he oversaw the demolition of the old library, which it was considered in evidence, probably caused asbestos to be released, despite the university hiring competent contractors to undertake the works. The claimant could not demonstrate that the university was negligent in the hiring of the contractors or that the university had breached any statutory duty.

Authority for:

The Court of Appeal held that it could not be proved that this employer, rather than others, had led to Brett contracting the disease, and as it had taken reasonable precautions to ensure his safety, the claim for damages had to fail.

Risk is accepted as part of most day-to-day activities (such as merely getting up in the morning and travelling to work), but it is in the unreasonable exposure to risk that will establish a potential breach.

Paris v Stepney BC (1951)

Facts:

The Council employed Mr Paris to undertake inspection and repairs of its vehicles. Paris had already lost an eye and was working on a job that was not considered by the employer to be sufficiently serious to warrant the use of safety goggles. During this job, when Paris hit a bolt with a hammer a piece of metal struck his good eye and he was blinded as a result.

Authority for:

The House of Lords held that due to the potential for injury, the employer did owe Paris a duty of care to provide the correct safety equipment, and due to this failure, he was entitled to succeed in damages for his injury.

2. *The social utility and desirability of the defendant's actions:* Of course when considering the risk the claimant was exposed to, the courts have to perform a balancing act between this risk and any benefit or valuable objective that the defendant was attempting to achieve. If an action is desirable and of social importance, the risks that correspond with the actions may be acceptable, whereas in other situations it would have led to unreasonable levels of risk (and damages in negligence).

Watt v Hertfordshire CC (1954)

Facts:

A fireman was injured by a jack that was not correctly secured in the lorry that was used to transport it to the scene of an emergency. The lorry had not been designed to carry such a large piece of equipment. However, the jack was required as it was used to save the life of a woman who had been trapped following an incident with a motor vehicle.

Authority for:

Per Denning LJ: 'It is well settled that in measuring due care you must balance the risk against the measures necessary to eliminate the risk. To that proposition there ought to be added this: you must balance the risk against the end to be achieved.' Consequently, the Court of Appeal held that there was no finding of liability on the Council because of the wider implications of the risk undertaken.

---

3. *The cost and practicality of measures to minimize the risk of harm:* Likewise, in point 2 above, the courts will assess the risk faced by the claimant in terms of the defendant's actions and the costs involved in attempting to minimize or remove these altogether.

Latimer v AEC Ltd (1953)

Facts:

A factory had suffered flooding following a period of heavy rain with the consequent mixing of the water with oil that was present on the factory's floor. In response, the owners of the factory (AEC) spread sawdust on the floor. However, Mr Latimer slipped on a patch of oil that had not been covered and sustained injury. Latimer claimed damages under negligence for his injuries but the claim failed as AEC had taken all reasonable precautions to minimize the risk of injury. Latimer had argued that the floor was unsafe and AEC should have closed the factory down until it could be made safe.

Authority for:

The House of Lords felt the argument for the closure of the factory would have been disproportionate to the inherent risk.

Consider

The balancing for the court will be, on the one hand, the cricket ground provides a social function, and this allows young people to take part in the sport and to bring the

→

community together. However, the costs of raising the fence may not be sufficiently significant nor impractical to warrant the owner adapting the fence to reduce the risk. Therefore the court is likely to hold that the duty has been breached as the cricketer and owner are aware of the risks and have not taken appropriate, reasonable, measures to minimize these.

Situations also exist where the most likely explanation for an accident/injury to the claimant is that the defendant must have been negligent. Here, the burden of proof is reversed and the onus is on the defendant to demonstrate that they were not negligent. This is known as *res ipsa loquitur* ('the facts speak for themselves'), and it will apply where the event that had caused the claimant loss was within the control of the defendant; and the event would not have occurred had the defendant exercised proper care and attention.

Drake v Harbour (2008)

Facts:

The claimant sought damages for the alleged negligent rewiring of her property that had led to fire damage. Albeit that the claimant did not have positive or scientific proof that the poor rewiring had led to the fire, the Court of Appeal held that what was required was a matter of judgement in each case having considered all of the available evidence. The evidence provided by the defendant, on the balance of probabilities, regarding alternative causes of the fire were improbable and where, as in this case, it was demonstrated that the defendant was negligent and the loss sustained was consistent with such negligence, it was not necessary for the claimant to positively prove the exact and technical reason.

Authority for:

The court is entitled to infer the loss as caused by the proven negligence.

A private duty to take reasonable care is not derived from a wider, statutory duty.

Gorringe v Calderdale MBC (2004)

Facts:

Calderdale Council had a statutory obligation to maintain the roads and ensure safety under the Highways Act 1980. The claimant in the case had caused an accident whilst driving along a country road by driving too fast towards the brow of a hill and, when she could not navigate the turn, colliding with a bus, as a consequence suffering severe injuries. The claimant's argument was that the Council had the responsibility for protecting the users of the highway and in this respect, it should have highlighted the danger of the particular road through signage such as marking the word 'slow' on the road before the hill. As such, the claimant contended that this public duty created a private duty to the users of the road, enabling her claim to succeed.

→

Authority for:

The court held that this did not impose such a duty on a local authority, as a private duty could not in this sense 'emerge' from a wider public duty. The Council had not taken any positive action in the accident and hence the claim failed.

The Compensation Act 2006 has had the effect of restraining the 'compensation culture' that was alleged to have crept into the English legal system. The courts would expect claimants to have been vigilant in protecting themselves and to appreciate obvious risks. This is not to say that it removes the legal obligations imposed on the defendant, but it has, particularly since the Compensation Act 2006, attempted to introduce a balance between the ability of claimants to seek damages for losses, and protection of those involved in providing desirable activities.

11.5.3 Consequential Damage

An essential component for a successful negligence claim is that the claimant has suffered loss, this loss must be of a type recognized by the law, and there must be a causal link between the breach and the loss suffered (consequential loss). For example, where an out-of-town shopping mall is built, the effects of this may be to cause economic damage to shops in the local town (as occurred when the Meadowhall development was built in Sheffield). However, despite this damage to their business through lost profits, the law does not allow the injured shop owners to bring a claim for damages against the developer of the shopping mall/the shopkeepers for any financial losses. Other torts exist that may enable a claim where the claimant has not suffered any damage. In claims of trespass, for example, the court will often award nominal damages even where no losses have been sustained.

11.5.3.1 Causation in fact

The court will examine the facts of the case and ascertain whether the defendant had caused or contributed to the claimant's injury or suffering. A test developed by the Court of Appeal in the case of *Cork v Kirby Maclean* is the 'but for' test. This test was defined in the following way: 'If the damage would not have happened but for a particular fault, then that fault is the cause of the damage—if it would have happened just the same, fault or not fault, the fault is not the cause of damage.'

Barnett v Chelsea and Kensington Hospital Management Committee (1969)

Facts:

A watchman sought medical attention following a bout of vomiting at work. He attended hospital where the on-duty nurse consulted a doctor, who advised the watchman to go home and seek advice from his own doctor the following morning if his symptoms had not improved. However, later in the day the watchman died, which was attributed to arsenic poisoning. A claim was brought against the hospital for the negligence of the doctor in failing to examine the watchman, but this failed. The watchman had such a high

→

concentration of arsenic in his system that he would have died regardless of any inter-vention, such as administering an antidote, even if his condition had been diagnosed in a doctor's examination.

Authority for:

Despite the existence of a duty to take care, and this had been breached, as the damage sustained was not a consequence of the breach, the claim failed.

Consider

'But for' Vihaan striking the ball outside of the ground, Mavis would not have been hit and injured. There is causation in fact.

11.5.3.2 Causation in law

The defendant is not liable for every consequence of their wrong. If there is some inter-vening act that causes the damage to the claimant then the (first) defendant will not be held responsible in negligence. If the damage sustained was too remote, then it would be unreasonable to hold the defendant responsible.

- *Remoteness of damage:* Remoteness of damage involves the test of reasonable foresee-ability. If the reasonable man could not foresee the consequences of the action, then the claim will be defeated.

Overseas Tankships (UK) Ltd v Morts Dock & Engineering Co. Ltd (The Wagon Mound) (1961)

Facts:

The defendants were the owners of a ship named the *Wagon Mound* and had been negli-gent in allowing oil to spill from the ship into Sydney Harbour. There was welding taking place in the Harbour at the time, and the oil had spread into the wharf owned by the claimant. The claimants stopped the welding, due to the potential risk of a fire, and sought clarification as to the danger, but were informed it was safe to continue their welding activities. Floating in the Harbour at the time was refuse, including cotton, onto which the molten metal from the welding fell and which caught fire causing the oil on the water to ignite. This fire quickly spread, resulting in substantial damage to the claimant's property, and led to the action against the owners of the *Wagon Mound*.

Authority for:

The Privy Council held that the defendants were only liable for the oil that had spilled into the Harbour and not the fire that had been caused. It could not be reasonably fore-seen that the oil would have caught fire due to its high ignition point (compare this deci-sion with *Hughes v Lord Advocate*).

When the claim involves the negligence of the tortfeasor, the causal link is vital to impose liability. This link (or chain of events) may be broken by a new act (a *novus actus interveniens*). If a new act, independent of the defendant's action, occurs and is sufficiently independent, it may stop the imposition of liability on the (first) defendant. If, however, the action occurs as a consequence of the initial breach by the defendant, and the actionable event was foreseeable, the defendant will still be liable. Foreseeability can be seen in the following case.

Lamb v Camden London BC (1981)

Facts:

The Council had caused damage to the water main that had led to Lamb's house being flooded. The house was uninhabitable and was vacated by Lamb whilst remedial work was carried out. When the house was left empty, squatters moved in and caused damage. Lamb brought an action against the Council for its negligence that resulted in this increased damage.

Authority for:

The Court of Appeal held that the Council was not liable as it was not foreseeable that the damage would have occurred, and the Council was under no obligation to secure the property whilst the repairs were being undertaken.

Attempts to mitigate losses will not, in most cases, result in the chain of causation being broken.

Corr v IBC Vehicles Ltd (2006)

Facts:

The claimant was the wife of a man who had committed suicide following injuries sustained during an accident at work. The employer had agreed that it had breached its duty of care (and statutory duty) towards the employee, and the employee had suffered post-traumatic stress and depression, leading to his suicide six years after the accident.

Authority for:

The Court of Appeal held that the depression suffered by the employee was foreseeable, and that it was further foreseeable that severe depression may result in suicide. Therefore, the claim was successful as the employee's suicide did not break the chain of causation between the defendant's negligence and the consequences of the suicide. In 2008, the House of Lords subsequently upheld this decision.

---

* *The eggshell skull rule:* There exists an obligation to take appropriate care to avoid causing damage that may lead to a negligence claim. However, there is also an obligation to 'take your victim as you find them'. This principle is known as the 'eggshell skull' rule and means that if the victim has a pre-existing condition that is exacerbated by the act of negligence, insofar as the damage is one which the law recognizes, there is no defence to claim that another person would not have been so badly injured. This can be seen in the case of *Smith v Leech Brain & Co.*

Smith v Leech Brain & Co. (1962)

Facts:

A workman employed by Leech Brain had been hit on his lip by molten metal whilst welding work was taking place. He suffered a relatively minor burn, which was expected and clearly foreseeable. However, he had a pre-cancerous skin condition. This was not known to anyone but was triggered by the burn he received, and he died three years later of the cancer. Smith's widow claimed against the employer.

Authority for:

Even though the burn would not have caused the death of most victims, the eggshell skull rule was invoked and consequently Leech Brain were held liable in negligence.

Consider

Mavis has a condition which would be unknown to the tortfeasor. However, the eggshell skull rule means that they will be liable for her skin condition requiring treatment (which presumably would not have been an issue for someone without the allergy). Vihaan struck the ball which hit Mavis, the owners of the ground did not incorporate a sufficiently high fence to prevent the balls from leaving the ground and without these actions Mavis would not have fallen from her bike and onto the treated grass. This is why the tortfeasor must take their victim as they find them.

The concept has also been applied to cases of psychiatric injuries. If the reasonable man would have suffered nervous shock, and the claimant's disposition exacerbates the injury they have actually suffered, then they will be able to claim for this greater injury, and not be reduced to the injury that would have been suffered by the reasonable man. Lane J in *Malcolm v Broadhurst* described it as the 'eggshell personality'.

11.6 DEFENCES TO A CLAIM OF NEGLIGENCE

In the event of a claim of negligence being made against a business, the business may wish to mount a defence. Defences to negligence claims may be complete defences whereby the business asserts it has no liability at all, or they may be partial defences where the business accepts some liability for what occurred, but asserts that the claimant was also partially responsible (the defendant will still have to pay a percentage of the award). Avoiding negligence actions in the first instance appears to be the best solution.

Consider

Imagine an extension to the question presented at the start of the chapter. If a cricketer seeing the danger had yelled a warning, but Mavis, wearing her stereo headphones, had not heard, would this affect your answer as to liability?

In order to avoid the legal responsibility that a successful negligence claim may provide, the defendant may attempt to raise a defence, the choice of which depends on the nature of the action. The most common forms of defence are:

1. illegality;
2. consent (*volenti non fit injuria:* no actionable injury/no injury is done to a consenting party);
3. contributory negligence;
4. necessity.

11.6.1 Illegality

Where the claimant has committed an illegal act they may be prevented from raising a negligence action (this is specific to the circumstances of the case).

Ashton v Turner (1980)

Facts:

The claimant was unsuccessful in seeking damages against the co-participant who drove the getaway car following a burglary. The car crashed and the claimant was seriously injured.

Authority for:

It was held that public policy would not allow the perpetrator of a crime to claim compensation against a co-participant for any injuries sustained in the course of the criminal activities.

However, illegality is a difficult defence to successfully rely upon, especially when involving companies rather than individuals.

Moore Stephens (a firm) v Stone & Rolls Ltd (in liquidation) (2009)

Facts:

A company's liquidator alleged that its auditors had been negligent in failing to identify that the company had been used to perpetrate a fraud. The claim failed, and was struck out by the court, as it was being made by the company itself (through the liquidator) and was relying on its own illegal act when seeking damages. This was, in part at least, because the fraudulent director was the 'controlling mind and will' of the company and hence it would be unfair to allow a claim to succeed where a fraudster would benefit by claiming against auditors who failed to detect their own deception.

Authority for:

The House of Lords, in a split 3 to 2 majority, agreed with the Court of Appeal's decision to strike out a claim for damages and accepted an illegality defence.

II.6.2 **Consent**

Consent is a complete defence to an action in tort but is closely linked with the partial defence of contributory negligence. The defence is available where there has been an express agreement to the particular risk of damage or it may be implied from the conduct of the claimant due to the actions of volunteering (such as acting as a rescuer) or by accepting entering into a situation involving risk (*Morris v Murray*). Examples of express and implied consent may be seen where a patient is undergoing surgery and they sign a consent form. This express agreement allows the surgery team to perform the procedure without committing the tort of trespass to the person.

Implied consent may be demonstrated in the context of sporting pursuits such as playing contact sports like rugby, or photographing sporting events in close proximity with the participants. However, merely participating in a regulated, physical sport such as rugby does not necessarily mean that the participant agrees to suffer injury and not seek a remedy.

Condon v Basi (1985)

Facts:

The claimant played football for a lower league club and during a match suffered a broken leg in the course of a tackle with an opponent. He claimed damages as a result of this injury.

Authority for:

The defendant player was in breach of his duty due to the recklessness of the tackle. Whilst a physical contact sport naturally involves the participants accepting a risk of injury, this does not extend to risks of injury which occur outside of the rules of the game. The court continued that the standard of care required of the participants is objective, but the objectivity will depend upon the circumstances. Thus, a higher degree of care is required of a player in the higher league divisions than those in lower league matches.

Recklessness is a test also applied in horseplay with friends.

Blake v Galloway (2004)

Facts:

Horseplay between four teenage friends led to the claimant suffering injury when a piece of bark struck his eye when the friends were throwing twigs at one another.

Authority for:

The Court of Appeal held that for the defendant to breach their duty of care in unregulated horseplay the defendant's conduct must amount to recklessness or sufficient carelessness or error of judgement.

The defence of consent is not available simply because a party (typically, in a business context, an employee) is aware of the risk of injury at the workplace, and continues to carry out their duties.

Smith v Baker & Sons (1891)

Facts:

The claimant was injured whilst at work. Next to his work space, other workers were engaged with placing stones into a crane which happened to swing above the head of the claimant. During the course of this activity a stone fell from the crane and struck the claimant on the head, causing him injury. The employers attempted to avoid liability by claiming *volenti*—the claimant knew the workplace was dangerous and he continued his work regardless.

Authority for:

The House of Lords held that whilst the claimant may have been aware of the danger, this did not mean he consented to the employer's lack of care for his safety. The claimant was entitled to recover damages.

The courts will not imply consent in such circumstances but will require an outward sign of consent in relation to the inherent risk. The defence is also unlikely to be successful in situations where the claimant has taken action to prevent harm or perform a rescue and has been injured in the process, particularly when this involves some psychiatric injury.

Chadwick v BRB (1967)

Facts:

Mr Chadwick was at the scene of the Lewisham train disaster of 1967 and attempted to provide care to the victims. He suffered a psychiatric injury (commonly referred to as nervous shock) and this, claimed his widow, eventually led to his own death.

Authority for:

The claim for damages succeeded. The court considered that where a rescuer is involved in the immediate aftermath of a particularly upsetting incident, it may be reasonably foreseeable that the rescuer will suffer some form of psychiatric injury.

The defence requires the claimant to have acted reasonably in the circumstances.

Haynes v Harwood (1935)

Facts:

The defendant had left his horse-drawn vehicle untethered in a crowded street. The horses bolted after a child threw a stone at them and in order to protect pedestrians on the street, an off-duty police officer attempted to stop the horses. In so doing he was injured and attempted to recover damages.

→

Authority for:

The horses were a source of danger and the owner had breached his duty of care by leaving them unattended on a busy street. It was reasonably foreseeable that a loose horse in an area with members of the public could cause injury. Further, it was also reasonable to expect a police officer to protect the public by intervening (therefore a *volenti* defence was unavailable) and he may get injured as a result.

Volenti may be a defence in employment situations where a deliberate act has been undertaken against the express orders of the employer.

ICI v Shatwell (1965)

Facts:

The claimant and a colleague, qualified shot-firers, made a test of an electrical circuit for firing explosives without taking the appropriate cover. They were injured and a claim was made for damages.

Authority for:

The House of Lords held that *volenti* enabled a complete defence by the employer, on both vicarious liability by one claimant and breach of a statutory duty by the other. The individuals had agreed to take this action knowing the danger and the action was contrary to the employer's instructions and statutory regulations. Therefore the claim had to fail.

11.6.3 **Contributory Negligence**

Section 1(1) of the Law Reform (Contributory Negligence) Act 1945 provides:

> Where any person suffers damage as the result partly of his own fault and partly of the fault of any other person or persons, a claim in respect of that damage shall not be defeated by reason of the fault of the person suffering the damage, but the damages recoverable in respect thereof shall be reduced to such extent as the court thinks just and equitable having regard to the claimant's share in the responsibility for the damage.

Contributory negligence is a partial defence to a claim where injury has been caused and the claimant seeks damages. It is not only applicable to claims of negligence but is applicable where there is 'fault' (with the exception to the torts of conversion and deceit). Contributory negligence is only applicable where the claimant was (at least in some part) responsible for their damage. A most common example of the defence of contributory negligence is where a person has been involved in an accident whilst driving, and they were not wearing a seat belt, or had failed to secure a crash helmet whilst riding a motorcycle (in *Capps v Miller* the claimant's damages were reduced by 10 per cent by the Court of Appeal). In the event that the courts hold the damage was the other driver's fault, the injured party who has suffered substantial injury, when they would not have sustained such a level of injury had they been wearing a seat belt, will have contributed to their own injury. This provides the court with an option to determine at what level of contribution the claimant was responsible, and can reduce any damages awarded. Guidance was provided in *Froom v Butcher*. Where injuries would have been altogether prevented by wearing the seat belt, the damages should be reduced by 25 per cent. Where the injuries sustained would have been 'a good deal less severe' the reduction should be 15 per cent.

In contributory negligence, the claimant is referred to as having 'contributed to their own misfortune' and if they have been at fault in any activities that have led to their injury, then the court will reflect this in the damages awarded.

Jackson v Murray and Another (2015)

Facts:

The Supreme Court had to consider the contribution of a 13-year old schoolgirl who was hit by a speeding motorist. The judge at first instance considered that the driver had demonstrated a lack of regard for the possibility of the danger of school children crossing his path when they alighted from a school bus. However, the judge considered the principal cause of the accident was the girl's recklessness of attempting to cross the road in the manner she did and held her 90 per cent responsible. At appeal, this contribution was reduced to 70 per cent due to her age and the consequent lack of experience she would have as to the danger, and the court's failure to fully assess the actions of the driver. The girl appealed this decision to the Supreme Court arguing there should be no imposition of contributory negligence. Whilst the court rejected the submission, on a majority decision, the girl's contribution was reduced to 50 per cent as the judge at first instance had failed to fully explain the reasoning for the apportionment of fault and that the driver must have been at least equally at fault as the girl.

Authority for:

The significance of the case lies in the different views on the facts of the case by the appeal courts. It is generally thought that appeal courts do not interfere with the court at first instance's assessment of the facts as it has the benefit of examination of all the facts and the witnesses. However, here appeal courts were willing to arrive at different conclusions than the first court, and also to reduce the victim's contribution to the damage sustained on two occasions. Perhaps, in similar circumstances, parties may be inclined to appeal future cases where they feel a decision is unjust and gamble on the prospect of an appeal court challenging the factual decision-making of the court at first instance.

Consider

Mavis was wearing her stereo headphones and therefore limited her capacity to hear a warning call about the imminent danger of being struck by the ball. As such, the court may reduce the compensation awarded to her to take into account her contribution to her own misfortune.

11.6.4 Necessity

A defence may be available to an action for negligence where the tortfeasor had acted in a way so as to prevent a greater harm occurring. To be successful the defendant must demonstrate that there was imminent danger to a person or to property and the actions taken were reasonable in the circumstances. These are subjective tests that will be assessed by the court.

Esso Petroleum Co. Ltd v Southport Corporation (1955)

Facts:

The defendant's oil tanker had run aground due to its heavy load, mechanical failures, and the weather conditions. The person in charge of the vessel discharged 400 tonnes of oil in order to free the tanker. This oil caused damage to the claimant's land and a lake which had to be closed until it had been cleaned—at substantial cost to the claimant.

Authority for:

The defendant argued the discharge of the oil was for reasons of necessity. Had the vessel not been moved, the rough seas could have driven it into the coastline wall. The defence was accepted, however, necessity cannot succeed as a defence where the situation leading to the emergency arose of the defendant's own causing.

11.7 REMEDIES

The remedies that may be awarded for successful claims of tortious conduct include damages and injunctions. The aim of damages is to place the injured party, as far as money can, in the position they were before the tort was committed (i.e. compensatory). Damages for personal injury suffered may incorporate any direct losses incurred such as loss of earnings, medical expenses, and travel expenses (such as not being able to drive and having to make alternative travel arrangements). Further losses that may be compensatable include damages for pain and suffering, and loss of amenity. These damages are not subject to taxation. Where the tortious act involves no real loss to the claimant (such as in trespass to land where no loss or damage has occurred) the court may award nominal damages.

Where the injured party has died as a result of the tort the claim for damages is different from those above (Law Reform (Miscellaneous Provisions) Act 1934). If the deceased had been financially supporting their family, then the dependants may claim for the lost earnings. The claim will also incorporate the funeral expenses. Further, the Fatal Accidents Act 1976, s. 1A(3) provides that spouses, and the parents of a deceased minor, may make a statutory claim of £11,800.

In terms of damage to property, the damages awarded will be to compensate the claimant for loss, and this will involve the cost of restoration and may involve an element of compensation where a replacement of the goods/property was difficult to achieve. Awards of damages are subject to a requirement for the injured party to mitigate their losses where this is reasonable (even where the mitigation leads to an increase in the losses sustained).

Injunctions may be awarded at the discretion of the court and will involve a court order requiring the subject to stop committing the tort. There are a number of tools to provide injunctive relief, which will be awarded depending upon the requirement of the particular tortious act. A prohibitory injunction requires that the defendant ceases the action that is causing the tort; and a mandatory injunction requires the defendant to act to prevent the tort being committed. The claimant may also wish to obtain an interim injunction to prevent a tort being committed and any (further) damage being sustained until the case comes to court. The power of an injunction, as was outlined in the contract chapters, is that it is a court order, and failure to comply constitutes a contempt of court that may lead to a fine or imprisonment.

11.8 NUISANCE

When a person unlawfully interferes with another's land, or the quiet enjoyment of the land, then the innocent party may have a claim under the tort of nuisance. In this respect, the claim is of private nuisance as it is concerned with private parties. The reason why this is important for businesses is because the nature of the offence is in creating a nuisance to those affected by it. By way of example, a business may have a manufacturing plant that produces rubber tyres. The business is not unlawful, the activity of producing rubber tyres is not unlawful, but if it makes unreasonable noise, smoke, vibrations, and so on, then these may be considered unlawful as they could affect another's use of their land. In order to bring a successful claim of nuisance the following features must be present:

- The interference affects the enjoyment of land/premises. This action may be brought by a person with an equitable interest in it, a tenant (*Hunter v Canary Wharf*), or a person with exclusive possession of land but with no title to it (*Foster v Warblington UDC*).

- There must be an element of damage associated with the nuisance. The term 'damage' in this area of law is not restricted to physical loss or damage, but can amount to the claimant losing their enjoyment of the premises (*Leeman v Montagu*). The law has to balance competing interests when dealing with claims of nuisance, the right for the owner/occupier of land to quiet enjoyment of the property, and the business that has to make some noise/disruption in the processing of the product. The courts will attempt to strike this balance by looking at the unreasonableness of the defendant's behaviour, taking into account such factors as the position of the premises that is causing the nuisance, when it is being conducted, for what duration the nuisance is caused, and what steps have been taken to minimize the disruption. For this reason, many such businesses have located themselves in industrial estates where their activities are unlikely to cause a nuisance in the same way that they would do in a residential area or in the centre of a busy city.

- It must be noted that the motives of the defendant are often relevant considerations in assessing nuisance, and as such, where the defendant has deliberately acted to cause a disturbance, the court will be more likely to hold this action as a nuisance.

Christie v Davey (1893)

Facts:

The claimant was a music teacher who provided lessons at her own home. She lived in a semi-detached house adjoining the defendant's property who complained on several occasions about excessive noise. The complaints went unanswered and the defendant resorted to banging on the walls, shouting, and beating trays to create noise in retaliation.

Authority for:

An injunction was granted to restrain the defendant's actions as they were motivated by malice and therefore constituted a nuisance.

- The court will look towards the reasonable foreseeability of the defendant's action in determining whether a nuisance has been committed.

Cambridge Water Co. v Eastern Counties Leather (1994)

Facts:

During the course of the defendant's leather tanning business, small quantities of solvents seeped through the floor of the building and into the ground beneath. From there the solvents found their way into a borehole owned by the claimant and this contaminated water supplying local residents. Consequently the claimant had to stop using the borehole and brought an action for damages in nuisance and negligence.

Authority for:

The House of Lords held exercising all reasonable care not to cause a nuisance may not, of itself, remove liability from the defendant. However, the defendant was not liable as the damage was too remote and not reasonably foreseeable.

- Unusually sensitive (hypersensitive) claimants will not generally succeed in an action for nuisance where another person would not have been adversely affected.

11.8.1 Defences to a Nuisance Claim

Defences exist where a claimant has alleged a nuisance and the defendant can point to a statutory authority, the consent of the claimant, or where the act has continued for over 20 years.

11.8.1.1 Statutory authority

Where a statute authorizes an act that is then subject to a claim of nuisance, the courts will assess whether the claim of nuisance is able to proceed.

Allen v Gulf Oil Refining Ltd (1981)

Facts:

A statute was passed to build an oil refinery on land to ensure a supply of oil was available, and this was in the public interest. In the building of the refinery, and its operation, local residents complained of the noise and smell arising from these activities.

Authority for:

The House of Lords held that no nuisance had been caused as the statute required that the oil refinery be built and operated, rather than merely giving the right for the erection and operation of such a venture.

However, simply because a statute gives a right to perform some action, does not remove potential liability of the defendant.

> **Barr v Biffa Waste Services (2012)**
>
> **Facts:**
>
> The claimants, a group of local residents, brought the action against the defendant for nuisance as a result of odour being emitted from one of its landfill sites. The defendant had previously been prosecuted by the Environment Agency for breaches of its operating permit with regards to such emissions.
>
> **Authority for:**
>
> The Court of Appeal held that merely because the defendants were carrying out activities in a manner consistent with the terms of their licence did not, of itself, provide a complete defence. The court held that there was no principle of law that meant compliance with a statutory scheme curtailed common law rights to seek damages.

11.8.1.2 Consent

If a party consents to a nuisance, they are unlikely to succeed in an action. This is a complete defence if the defendant can establish that the injured party had accepted the danger of the noise, smell, vibration, or other nuisance, having been aware of its existence. This is a grey area, as merely occupying land in the knowledge of a nuisance will not establish an effective defence of consent. It is the willingness to accept the possibility of the nuisance that is the key element.

11.8.1.3 Prescription

Here, a defence is available where the nuisance has been committed for over 20 years without complaint.

> **Sturges v Bridgman (1879)**
>
> **Facts:**
>
> The defendant operated the business of a confectionery shop which involved the use of a pestle and mortar that caused significant noise. This function had been conducted for over 20 years without complaint. However, this was because during its operation there had been no neighbouring property. Afterwards, the claimant built a consulting room adjacent to the shop and brought an action in nuisance to prevent the continuation of the noise. The defendant attempted to defeat the claim for an injunction on the basis of the Prescription Act.
>
> **Authority for:**
>
> The defence failed. For it to be accepted, it is important that the nuisance has been committed for 20 years, rather than simply the carrying out of that activity for the period of time.

11.8.2 Remedies in Nuisance

The main remedies provided in claims of nuisance are a damages action, and an injunction to prevent the nuisance being committed in the future.

11.8.2.1 **Damages**

The claim in nuisance, as opposed to negligence where damage/loss has been sustained, may not have actually caused any physical loss. As such, the claim is generally concerned with the loss of the enjoyment of the land that the claimant has suffered, or in terms of any devaluation of the land. That is not to say that there will be no claim for physical loss (see *Cambridge Water Co. v Eastern Counties Leather* above). Therefore, as long as the damage is of a type recognized in law, and it was foreseeable, then damages may be awarded for losses suffered.

11.8.2.2 **Injunctions**

These are a particularly effective mechanism to prevent the defendant from continuing the nuisance. Injunctions are equitable remedies, used at the discretion of the courts, and in cases of nuisance, may be used in addition to, or instead of, a damages award. When an injunction is granted, it is usually suspended to provide the defendant with an opportunity to refrain from further acts of nuisance.

11.8.2.3 **Abatement**

This is an (exceptional) remedy enabling the injured party to take action to stop the nuisance. It is allowed where to initiate a legal action may be inappropriate, or where immediate action is required. This is commonly seen where an owner of land lops the trees on a neighbour's property. As long as the injured party does not have to go onto the neighbour's land, and they, in this example, cut only the trees interfering with their land, and returns the trees that have been cut, then this will be an acceptable remedy.

CONCLUSION

The chapter has considered the torts of negligence and nuisance. Claims of negligence involve the three tests of duty of care, breach of that duty, and consequential damage. Having established these, the courts will then consider the level of damages to be awarded, having taken into account any defences asserted, and the vulnerability of the victim. Nuisance protects the claimant from unlawful interference with their property and is a significant factor for businesses running manufacturing/industrial processes. The next chapter discusses equally relevant and important torts to businesses (that can involve very significant claims), including liability for economic loss in negligence, negligent misstatements, and the liability for psychiatric losses.

SUMMARY OF MAIN POINTS

Tortious liability

- Liability is imposed through the civil law and requires, in certain circumstances, the party to take reasonable care not to negligently or intentionally cause harm.

- Many torts involve establishing 'fault' liability (blame) in order for a claim to proceed. Exceptions to this general rule include vicarious liability and claims under the Consumer Protection Act 1987.

- The Limitation Act 1980 outlines the time limits within which actions must be initiated. Generally, tort actions must be brought within six years of the date giving rise to the action and personal injury claims must be made within three years. The time limits do not begin until a minor reaches the age of majority (18), and further protection is given to those suffering mental disorders.

Negligence

- Negligence involves a breach of a duty to take care, owed in law by the defendant to the claimant, causing the claimant damage.

- The three elements to substantiate a claim consist of a duty of care, breach of that duty, and consequential damage.

- Where a duty of care has previously been held to exist, the threefold test from *Caparo* is unnecessary. In other circumstances, the three sub-tests establishing a duty include proximity of relationship between the parties; foreseeability of loss; and whether it is fair, just, and reasonable to impose the duty.

- A breach of duty involves falling below the 'reasonable man' standard and exposing the claimant to unreasonable risk of harm.

- The third element in establishing negligence is assessing the consequential damage suffered by the claimant.

- There must exist a causal link between the injury suffered and the breach of duty.

- The damage suffered must be one that is recognized by law.

- Not all claimants have to demonstrate loss/damage. Claims under trespass, for example, will often involve the award of nominal damages as no 'real' loss has been sustained.

- To assess causation of damage, the courts will use the 'but for' test—if the damage would not have occurred but for the actions of the defendant, then their action is the cause of the damage.

- Not every consequence of a defendant's wrongful action will lead to liability. Intervening acts may remove responsibility if the damage is too remote.

- The 'eggshell skull' rule provides that the defendant must take the claimant as they find them. Hence, if the claimant had a pre-existing condition exacerbated by the defendant's actions, the defendant cannot escape liability by asserting that another person so affected would not have experienced the same level of damage.

Defences

- The most common defences to tort actions are illegality, consent, contributory negligence, and necessity.

- Illegality may prevent a claim of negligence where the claimant suffered loss or damage during the course of performing an illegal act.

- Consent provides a complete defence where the injured party has consented to a risk, either expressly or through implication.

- Contributory negligence is a partial defence where the claimant who has been partially at fault for their injury (with the defendant being partly at fault) will have any award of damages reduced according to their level of responsibility.

- Necessity may provide a defence where the tortfeasor acted to prevent a greater harm, insofar as there was imminent danger and their actions were reasonable in the circumstances.

Remedies

- Remedies include damages and injunctions.

- Damages awarded for personal injury include compensation for direct and indirect losses. The aim is to place the injured party in the position they were in before the tort had been committed (insofar as money can).

- Injunctions are used to prevent the commission of a tort (available at the discretion of the courts). Injunctions are issued on the basis of the particular tort and the injunction may be prohibitory, mandatory, or interim.

Nuisance

- Private nuisance involves unlawful interference with another person's enjoyment of their land/property.
- The claimant must have suffered some form of loss/damage due to the nuisance.
- Where the defendant intended to cause the disturbance, the courts will be more inclined to hold that action as nuisance.
- It must have been reasonably foreseeable that loss/damage would have been the result of the defendant's action to enable a damages claim.
- There are several defences to a nuisance action including statutory authority, consent, and prescription.
- The remedies available are damages, injunction, and abatement.

 SUMMARY QUESTIONS

Essay questions

1. Cases such as *Bolton v Stone* and *Miller v Jackson* provide examples of the different approaches taken by the judiciary in relation to determining whether a defendant has breached their duty to take reasonable care. Describe the tests used to establish the negligence of a defendant and explain how the law has developed to make the exercise of these tests more relevant in the modern era.

2. Critically assess the defences available to a claim of nuisance. Do you feel they are fair or at least adequate and what suggestions could you make for improvements? Justify your answer through a critique of the case law.

Problem questions

1. All Bright Consumables (ABC) Ltd has recently diversified its business into supplying and fitting quality kitchens and bathrooms. Part of this business involves the company manufacturing its own tiles and furniture to offer the full bespoke service that it believes customers want. Dora is employed by ABC Ltd as a wood machinist operating a bench mounted circular saw. Today, while operating the circular saw Dora caught her right (dominant) hand in the saw's blade, severed four fingers and sliced the top off her thumb. On the day in question, she had worked a 12-hour shift and for the last six hours of her shift, her supervisor, Abe, asked her to lend her push stick (which she had been told she should use for feeding small pieces of wood into the machine) to a colleague. At the time of the accident, she was working on an urgent job which had to be completed that day for fitting by ABC's bathroom firm the next. Dora admitted that while working she had been distracted and had been chatting animatedly to another colleague.

   Consider the negligence liability (if any) of ABC Ltd

2. Alain is employed by Tasty Butchers (TB) Ltd to deliver meat to various retailers. Alain is expressly told not to race or drive dangerously in his company vehicle. However, today Alain ignores this instruction and decides to race against the driver of their rival company, Crusty Butchers Ltd, when the two drivers meet each other at traffic lights.

During the race Alain damages the car of Delia, which further causes the sealed door on the refrigeration unit of his company vehicle to be broken and the meat begins to thaw. At the end of the day Alain returns to TB Ltd's base and is told about cases of sickness being reported by customers at the shops he has delivered meat to. The view is that the meat has gone bad and caused food poisoning.

The manager of TB Ltd has also seen the damage to the company vehicle and been contacted by Delia who blames Alain for causing damage to her car.

Outline the potential liability of the parties in the above situation.

 You will find guidance about how to answer these questions online at www.oup.com/uk/marson5e/.

 FURTHER READING

Books and articles

Bermingham, V. and Brennan, C. (2016) 'Tort Law: Directions' (5th Edition) Oxford University Press: Oxford.

Collins, L. (1967) 'Interaction between Contract and Tort in the Conflict of Laws' *International and Comparative Law Quarterly*, Vol. 16, p. 103.

Herbert, R. (2006) 'The Compensation Act 2006' *Journal of Personal Injury Law*, Vol. 4, p. 337.

Moran, M. (2003) 'Rethinking the Reasonable Person: An Egalitarian Reconstruction of the Objective Standard' Oxford University Press: Oxford, New York.

Morgan, J. (2006) 'The Rise and Fall of the General Duty of Care' *Professional Negligence*, Vol. 22, No. 4, p. 206.

Mullender, R. (2006) 'Negligence Law and Blame Culture: A Critical Response to a Possible Problem' *Professional Negligence*, Vol. 22, No. 1, p. 2.

Neyers, J. W., Chamberlain, E., Stephen, G. A., and Pitel, S. G. A. (Eds.) (2007) 'Emerging Issues in Tort Law' Hart Publishing: Oxford.

Patten, K. (2006) 'Limitation Periods in Personal Injury Claims—Justice Obstructed?' *Civil Justice Quarterly*, Vol. 25, July, p. 349.

 ONLINE RESOURCES

www.oup.com/uk/marson5e/

For further resources relating to this chapter, including self-test questions, an interactive glossary, and key case flashcards.

12 ECONOMIC LOSS, THE LIABILITY OF PROFESSIONAL ADVISORS, AND PSYCHIATRIC INJURY

Loss may have been incurred due to a negligent act, but where this is in the absence of physical damage (merely economic loss), recovery of the loss from the tortfeasor has been restricted. Such instances can include the negligent statements made by professionals. As businesses may be involved in providing professional advice (lawyers, accountants, and so on) this is particularly relevant. Further, there has been an increase recently of imposing liability on employers for the stress and associated health problems suffered by their employees. One or all of these matters may affect a business and it is important to identify where responsibility and potential liability exist.

Business Scenario 12

Jing inherited £40,000 on her father's death. In the course of a conversation in her office with Imran, a financial journalist, Imran asked her what she intended to do with her inheritance. Jing replied that she had not made up her mind and was seeking ideas. Imran then said 'Of course it is not really my business to give investment advice, but if I were you I should invest in Graphica Ltd, a new computer design company. Although their shares are low at the moment, they are tipped to rise dramatically as they have developed a new software package'.

Acting on this advice, Jing invested all her money in Graphica Ltd. Unfortunately, Imran had confused Graphica Ltd with Graphs Unlimited; the former company was on the verge of bankruptcy, the latter had developed the new software package. Shortly after Jing invested, Graphica Ltd went into liquidation and Jing lost her entire investment.

Before Imran's mistake had become apparent, Jing had passed on his advice to David, a friend, who had invested £10,000 in Graphica Ltd.

Advise Jing and David who wish to claim damages from Imran.

Learning Outcomes

- Identify how liability for pure economic loss is established (12.2)
- Explain the nature of liability for negligent misstatements and how such liability may be restricted (12.3)
- Explain the difference between 'primary' and 'secondary' victims in claims of psychiatric damage and negligence (12.4).

12.1 INTRODUCTION

This chapter continues from the discussion of liability in negligence for physical damage to consider the potential liability businesses and individuals may have when they provide advice in the nature of their business, when they cause economic losses not associated with physical damage, and where the claimant suffers a psychiatric injury/nervous shock due to the acts of the tortfeasor. Restrictions are placed on the imposition of liability for **pure economic loss**, although such loss has been widened to include damages for negligent misstatements. It is of crucial importance that businesses are aware of the implications of providing information in the course of their professional activities that may cause an investor/client loss through negligence.

12.2 PURE ECONOMIC LOSS

Chapter 11 identified liability in negligence, and how this was linked with some form of physical loss or damage. In part, this limits the possibility of 'opening the floodgates' to many claimants and, as stated by Cardozo J in *Ultramares v Touche*, expose defendants to a potential liability 'in an indeterminate amount for an indeterminate time to an indeterminate class'. In cases of psychiatric injury, for instance, the courts have produced rules that restrict the possibility of many claims, particularly to those identified as '**secondary**' victims.

Consider

Jing and David have suffered economic loss due to advice provided by a third party. As this is not associated with physical loss they must establish that the law recognizes the third party owed them a duty of care and had breached this duty. The extent of their loss is foreseeable, yet whether there exists a special relationship between the parties to hold the third party liable for these loses is important.

Turning to liability where the claimant has 'only' suffered economic loss (as opposed to situations where it is linked to physical damage such as loss of income following a car accident) the recovery in damages of such losses is very limited. Clearly, if the economic losses have been sustained due to a negligent act and the parties had entered into a contract, then damages are recoverable. However, the parties have to agree to be bound by the terms of a contract and tortious liability is established on the basis of a civil wrong, often in the absence of any contractual agreement. This is not to say that pure economic loss is not important, but it is rather difficult for the courts to identify where the liability in such instances will extend, or be limited. This can be seen in the following case:

Weller v Foot and Mouth Research Institute (1966)

Facts:

The defendants negligently allowed the foot and mouth virus to escape from their research laboratory and the consequences were that cattle had to be destroyed and restrictions were imposed on the transport and trade of the cattle in the affected area. The claimant was an auctioneer who had lost profits in sales due to the restriction, and brought an action to recover the losses due to this negligent act. It was held that as this was a case of pure economic loss, the claim must fail.

Authority for:

Actions for losses attributed to pure economic loss are not compensatable as they are not linked with economic losses associated with physical damage/loss (e.g. lost wages (economic loss) following a car accident (physical damage)).

The sense of the judgment may be seen in a wider discussion of the issue of liability, and the rights to limit or restrict liability. For example, this claim was by an auctioneer whose trade was affected due to the outbreak. However, what about local butchers in the area that may have lost sales due to the limit in supplies of beef? Would consumers have a claim if the outbreak had limited the supply of this meat and they were 'forced' to purchase some other meat product? Clearly, there had to be a limit to claims in this respect, unless an aspect of physical damage was involved.

Spartan Steel v Martin & Co. Contractors Ltd (1973)

Facts:

Contractors who were digging in a public road had negligently cut an electricity cable and the claimant's factory lost power, damaging some furnaces that had molten steel in them, which cooled and hardened due to the loss of power.

Authority for:

It was held that the claimant could recover for the damage to these furnaces and the loss of the molten metal, but were prevented from successfully claiming for losses to further work that it was unable to carry out due to this power-cut, as this was pure economic loss.

The general rule preventing claims based on pure economic loss is subject to exceptions. This is particularly so where a special relationship exists between the parties that elevates the defendant's responsibility to the claimant.

Ross v Caunters (1980)

Facts:

A firm of solicitors had sent a will to their client to be signed and witnessed, but they failed to inform the client that the witness should not be a beneficiary or spouse. The will was returned, and not checked by the solicitors, and when the testator died, it was discovered that one of the witnesses was the spouse of a beneficiary and hence could not claim under the will. A damages action was brought against the solicitors.

Authority for:

It was held that the claimant could succeed. A special relationship was established and it was reasonably foreseeable that a beneficiary could be affected by their negligence.

Commissioners of Customs and Excise v Barclays Bank Plc (2006)

Facts:

The House of Lords had to consider the liability of the bank that had been instructed, through a court-ordered injunction, to freeze accounts of two companies that owed significant sums of money to Her Majesty's Revenue and Customs (HMRC). The aim of the injunctions was to prevent access to the money that, it was argued to the court, would be taken out of the country and thus make it very difficult/impossible for HMRC to recover. The bank, following the injunction, sent a letter stating it would abide by the order, but negligently allowed withdrawals (within hours of the injunction being served) to remove large quantities of money from the accounts, and this money was not recoverable by HMRC. As such, the claim was brought against the bank for the loss.

Authority for:

It was held that no liability was established. Barclays had no choice as to whether it would be involved in the injunction that froze the accounts in question. Liability for pure economic loss will only be recoverable where the person has a responsibility, or has assumed a responsibility for their statement to the claimant; a duty of care can be demonstrated to exist between the parties; and the tests as established in *Caparo v Dickman* are satisfied.

Business specialists and advisors may, in the course of providing advice, cause their client loss due to negligence. The seminal case outlining such liability is *Bolam v Friern Hospital Management Committee.*

Bolam v Friern Hospital Management Committee (1957)

Facts:

The claimant was suffering a mental illness and part of his treatment required him to undergo electroconvulsive therapy. The doctor failed to administer relaxant drugs and the claimant consequently suffered serious injury. Evidence was admitted to the court demonstrating the divided opinion amongst professionals whether the drugs should be used (associated with a limited risk of death) or not (associated with a limited risk of fractures).

Authority for:

In finding the doctor not in breach of the duty of care, the House of Lords established what became known as the 'Bolam test:' A medical professional will not be guilty of negligence where they have acted in accordance with practice accepted as proper by a reasonable body of medical practitioners skilled in that particular art.

The 'Bolam test' of professional advice refers to whether the advisors were acting in accordance with a practice of competent respected professional opinion. The court held the test continues to be appropriate and, when applied to the present case, the advice of the defendant satisfied this test. The court did find the defendant failing in the communication between the parties, although this dimension to the case was not subject to the Bolam test. The defendant was required to clearly articulate the risks to the client, which ultimately, having had a history for over a period of ten years, the defendant satisfied. Holding for the defendant, the court may have implicitly broadened the Bolam test to include the level of communication of risk involved when providing financial advice.

O'Hare v Coutts & Co. (2016)

Facts:

The claimant had been provided with investment advice from the defendant private bank on the basis of proceeds they obtained following the sale of a chemical engineering business. However, the claimant was unhappy with the level of communication between them and the defendant's employee. Further, they alleged that the products recommended were unsuitable, having no capital protection, and therefore exposed the claimant's wealth to significant risk of loss. The claimant accepted the investment advice, but argued that this did not mean the advice was correct.

Authority for:

The High Court clarified the distinction between the adoption of sales techniques in persuading a client to take a financial risk from offering competent advice.

Losses can be suffered in cases where business professionals make statements that a person relies on, but the statement turns out to have been negligently made, and this leads to pure economic loss. Can claims be made for such negligent misstatements?

12.3 NEGLIGENT MISSTATEMENTS

In some cases businesses provide expert advice that clients and others rely on when investing money, making financial/investment decisions, and so on, and when these have been negligently made, the recipient may suffer losses. For example, advice may be provided on where to invest money, which shares to buy, and whether credit should be advanced to a firm. Claims on the basis of a statement having been negligently made, prior to case law in 1964, had to be made in the tort of deceit and required that the defendant had acted dishonestly, rather than just negligently. This position was changed in *Hedley Byrne & Co. v Heller*.

Hedley Byrne & Co. v Heller (1963)

Facts:

Hedley Byrne was an advertising company and its bankers approached the bank of Heller regarding the financial stability and credit history of one of Heller's clients, a third party, Easipower Ltd. Hedley Byrne required this information as it intended to enter into contracts with the third party and wanted to ensure the company was creditworthy. Heller provided a reference as to the third party's creditworthiness, but further added that the information was intended for private use and did not impose any liability or responsibility on the provider of the reference. However, despite the reference in favour of the third party, the truth was that the firm was not of sound financial standing, and following the advance of credit, the claimants lost several thousands of pounds and brought the claim against the bank that had provided the negligent misstatement.

Authority for:

The House of Lords held that this case involved a 'special relationship of proximity' (beyond the 'standard' level of proximity established in *Donoghue v Stevenson*) between the parties and this would enable a claim (in theory). The problem (for the claimant) in this particular case was the bank's exclusion clause, disclaiming responsibility for any losses due to the statement, which prevented the damages action succeeding (although the point of law regarding the possibility of claims remained). However, such a disclaimer if used today would have to satisfy the requirements of the Unfair Contract Terms Act 1977 as being reasonable. So a business may not always be able to evade liability by the inclusion of a disclaimer.

A further, very important case demonstrating where liability may or may not be imposed was in *Caparo Industries Plc v Dickman and Others*. The case was raised in **Chapter 11** (**11.5.1.3**) but to briefly recap, the claimants owned shares in a company and relied on accounts prepared by the defendants to purchase more. The accounts were negligently prepared. However, the accounts were prepared as a requirement under the Companies Act 1985 and not on the basis of providing financial advice for any third party, including shareholders. The House of Lords determined that no duty of care existed between the claimant and the defendant. To hold the auditors liable would be to have enabled too many claimants possible recourse to claims for negligence for publicly produced documents. Lord Oliver remarked on the issue:

> The opportunities for the infliction of pecuniary loss from the imperfect performance of everyday tasks upon the proper performance of which people rely for regulating their affairs are illimitable and the effects are far reaching. A defective bottle of ginger beer may injure a single consumer but the damage stops there. A single statement may be repeated endlessly with or without the permission of

its author and may be relied upon in a different way by many different people. Thus the postulate of a simple duty to avoid any harm that is, with hindsight, reasonably capable of being foreseen becomes untenable without the imposition of some intelligible limits to keep the law of negligence within the bounds of common sense and practicality.

The Lords would not impose liability on the auditors. They stated that a 'special relationship' must exist between the parties and this was not evident in the case. Importantly, in terms of liability for a negligent misstatement, the Lords established four factors that had to exist to determine when liability would be imposed. These were:

1. the advice is required for a purpose which is made known, either actually or inferentially, to the advisor at the time when the advice is given;

2. the advisor knows that his advice will be communicated to the advisee, either specifically or as a member of an ascertainable class, in order that it should be used by the advisee for that purpose;

3. it is known that the advice so communicated is likely to be acted upon by the advisee for that purpose without independent inquiry;

4. it is so acted upon by the advisee to his detriment.

Consider

Applying the tests to Imran we can see that he was enjoying a conversation with an acquaintance and provided some information based on his knowledge of the financial market. Imran certainly communicated the advice to Jing, although it may seem strange that a person would invest a significant sum of money on the basis of a conversation without seeking verification or professional advice before proceeding. Jing did act on the advice and has suffered a loss as a result. However, as Jing apprised David of this information, Imran would have had no knowledge that this would be passed on (and actioned) and hence could not be liable to David.

Such an example of the application of this test was demonstrated a year after *Caparo* in the case of *James McNaughten v Hicks*.

James McNaughten v Hicks (1991)

Facts:

Accountants were asked to prepare information and draft accounts to be used for the basis of negotiations in the takeover of the firm. The accounts had been negligently produced, and led to the claimant's suffering financial loss. It was held that no liability arose, as the defendants were not aware of the precise use of the information prepared by them. As these were draft accounts, it was fair to assume that further investigation would be made before a financial decision was taken.

→

Authority for:

The case demonstrated the necessity of the defendant being aware of the claimant's use of the information that was being provided. Therefore, the following points should be considered:

1. the purpose for which the statement was made;
2. the purpose for which the statement was communicated;
3. the relationship between the advisor, advisee, and any relevant third party;
4. the size of any class to which the advisee belongs;
5. the state of knowledge of the advisor;
6. reliance by the advisee.

This case may be compared to *Yorkshire Enterprise Ltd v Robson Rhodes.*

Yorkshire Enterprise Ltd v Robson Rhodes (1998)

Facts:

The claimants had invested significant sums of money into a company that soon went into liquidation. They made the investment following accounts and correspondence between the claimants and the negligent accountants. It was held that liability would be imposed as the accountants were aware of why the claimants wanted the information, and what they had intended to do with this information. Further, to impose liability in these circumstances was considered reasonable.

Authority for:

When considering whether liability will be imposed in cases of negligent misstatement, the following points should also be considered:

1. there must have been negligence when the statement was made;
2. the statement must be given by an expert acting in the course of their expertise;
3. there must be a duty of care owed to the person who acts on the statement—an assumption of responsibility;
4. there must be reliance on the statement by the persons to whom it was addressed;
5. there must be foreseeable loss arising out of the reliance;
6. following *Caparo*, it must be fair, just, and equitable to impose the duty.

Consider

Applying the tests from *James McNaughten v Hicks* and *Yorkshire Enterprise Ltd v Robson Rhodes* it appears that no liability will be established between the parties.

Note; however, that the Lords stated in *Commissioners for Customs and Excise v Barclays Bank Plc* (see **12.2**) that the tests established in the previously noted cases were correct and had led to justice being served, but they are specific to the cases to which they relate, and sweeping statements regarding the application of tests are not possible. The cases have to be considered on their facts.

12.4 **NON-PHYSICAL (PSYCHIATRIC) DAMAGE**

An element of negligence that may affect businesses is where physical injury has not occurred to a claimant, but rather there is an element of psychiatric damage. Recently, this issue has become important to businesses where an employee suffers from stress at work, and the employer takes no action to remedy the situation. Given high pressure targets people often work under, not only will stress-related illness cost the employer in terms of sick leave and lack of productivity, it may now also lead to tortuous liability. The following cases demonstrate where liability may be imposed, and hence identify how businesses may seek to minimize the risk of such claims.

There are increasing situations where liability is imposed for non-physical injuries, such as employees being placed under stresses at work, or where rescuers (such as those employed in the emergency services) suffer through the traumatic nature of their job. Whilst injuries suffered in such situations may not involve physical damage, their effects are no less serious, no less debilitating, and no less important to the imposition of liability. Despite the wider issue of psychiatric injury, employers/managers in particular need to be aware of their responsibilities and be proactive in reducing the possibility of injury resulting from exposure to unreasonable stress.

Whilst in an employment relationship it is incumbent on an employer (at common law and through legislative measures) to protect an employee's health and safety; negligence in this respect may also lead to a damages claim against the employer. As such, an employer's obligations transcend many jurisdictions of law and it is necessary to view the law in its entirety, rather than how it is artificially presented in textbooks. Claims for psychiatric injuries have increased for businesses with the increased stress and burdens placed on employees, and where it is reasonable for an employer to be aware of this, and they do not take positive and sufficient action to remedy the problem, they may be held liable.

Intel Corp. (UK) v Daw (2007)

Facts:

Mrs Daw suffered stress due to unreasonable workloads placed on her from several managers at the firm. She had raised her concerns to her employer over the workload and how it was adversely affecting her health, and she was found in tears by one of her line managers, but the employer failed to take immediate action. Daw became clinically depressed and this led to a breakdown. The original trial awarded her £134,000 for her injury and loss of earnings and the Court of Appeal agreed.

Authority for:

An employer's offer of access to a short-term counselling service would not have reduced the risk of the employee's injury. Further, employers have a duty to protect the health and safety of their employees and the employer failed in its duty to provide a safe system of work.

A similar line of reasoning was used in *Barber v Somerset County Council.*

Barber v Somerset County Council (2004)

Facts:

The case involved a teacher who alleged to have suffered a stress-induced illness caused by an unreasonable workload. The teacher returned to work but the workload had not been reduced (albeit the employer stated this was due to the constraints of resources).

Authority for:

The House of Lords held that the employer had not taken any steps to reduce his workload or provide him with support, and therefore it was reasonably foreseeable that the employee, already known as being vulnerable in this regard, would suffer some form of injury. (This is one of the reasons why the Government introduced the 'family-friendly' employment policies—to assist in creating an acceptable work–life balance.)

It should be noted that employers are entitled to expect employees to withstand the 'normal pressures of the job'—*Sutherland v Hatton*—but despite the difficulties in determining when pressure leads to stress, and stress to injury to health, there will be signs that enable a reasonable employer to identify these and take action. Indeed, the Advisory, Conciliation and Arbitration Service has produced a guide for employers on how to identify signs of depression in the workplace, along with a booklet on health and wellbeing that includes checklists and policies to avoid breaching their duty to protect the employees' health and safety.

There may also exist situations where persons are exposed to situations where they are not necessarily employees, but liability for psychiatric injury is imposed. *Bourhill v Young* has already been discussed in **11.5.1.2**. Mrs Bourhill's claim failed, *inter alia*, due to the lack of proximity between the claimant and defendant, but raised the interesting element of whether to hold a defendant liable in cases of psychiatric harm. Negligence so far has dealt with some form of physical damage or injury and the application of rules to determine whether liability should be imposed. When the harm involves what is referred to as 'nervous shock', the claimant must demonstrate that the type of harm they sustained was reasonably foreseeable. This is particularly so in light of the judges' comments in *Bourhill* that the person must exhibit 'phlegm and fortitude' in the event of witnessing acts that may be upsetting. As in *Bourhill* where the pregnant fishwife had witnessed the aftermath of an accident, this did not place her in direct and immediate danger. Those persons who have experienced injury, even psychiatric injury, from having been placed in fear of personal danger are referred to as **'primary victims'**. The other type of claimant who suffers psychiatric injury after witnessing an event involving injury to others comes under the heading 'secondary victims'. It should be noted that the expression 'nervous shock' is important in identifying that the claims in this matter relate to sudden events which are distressing, rather than a protracted event or series of events (such as seeing a relative die slowly from a disease) which, whilst equally distressing, do not, generally, amount to a claim under this area of law.

The law determines a claimant, having suffered a psychiatric injury, as a primary or secondary victim. This is a somewhat harsh distinction and has led to claims that the word 'secondary' implies 'less deserving', and may imply that physical injury is 'superior to, or morally more entitled to compensation than, psychiatric illness' (see Jones in the Further Reading section at the end of this chapter). A case that demonstrates potential problems in determining whether a claimant is to be considered a primary or secondary victim was seen in *Macfarlane v EE Caledonia Ltd*.

Macfarlane v EE Caledonia Ltd (1994)

Facts:

The claimant was an oil rig painter in the North Sea and was in a support vessel some 550 metres from the Piper Alpha oil rig when it exploded. Due to the traumatic scenes (including having fire balls come within 100 metres of the vessel), and being aware of Macfarlane's friends being on the oil rig, he developed a psychiatric injury for which the first court awarded him damages.

Authority for:

The Court of Appeal rejected his claim as a rescuer as his activities in this regard were insufficient (moving blankets and helping the walking wounded), and further there was a lack of proximity between the defendant and Macfarlane. It was not reasonably foreseeable that he would suffer psychiatric harm or that a person of reasonable fortitude would have been affected as Macfarlane was. Therefore, Macfarlane was not considered a primary victim, and there was insufficient 'close relationship of love and affection between the plaintiff [the old term for a claimant] and victim' to establish him as a secondary victim.

12.4.1 Primary Victims

These are claimants who assert they have suffered some form of psychiatric injury as a result of being in the zone of physical danger of fearing for their own safety. This is tested on the basis of the reasonable forseeability of the defendant's actions.

Dulieu v White and Sons (1901)

Facts:

The spouse of a publican suffered from severe shock and distress when a horse-drawn carriage crashed into the public house where she was working at the time.

Authority for:

The claimant had not suffered physical injury, but the court found there to be sufficient evidence for him to reasonably believe that she may be injured and this enabled the claim to be successful.

More recently, the House of Lords considered the issue of foreseeability.

Page v Smith (1995)

Facts:

The claimant had been involved in an accident with a car driven by the defendant, but whilst not suffering any physical injury, a pre-existing condition of ME (myalgic encephalomyelitis) was worsened. A claim for damages was made.

Authority for:

It was still necessary to distinguish between primary and secondary victims in actions involving psychiatric injury, but where the claimant is a primary victim and it can be demonstrated that the defendant owed to them a duty of care not to cause physical injury, then it is sufficient to ask whether the defendant should have reasonably foreseen that the claimant may suffer personal injury as a result of the defendant's negligence. It is unnecessary to question whether the defendant should have foreseen the injury by shock.

12.4.2 Secondary Victims

Secondary victims have a more difficult task in proving that they have the right to damages. Reasonable forseeability is again the test to be invoked, but this is on the basis of the proximity of relationship. There must exist some direct relationship between the injured party and the claimant that would enable a claim (as no physical injury has been sustained, and the claimant was not in fear of their own safety). Such a close relationship may exist between siblings, or between spouses.

Hinz v Berry (1970)

Facts:

A woman who observed her husband being severely injured, leading to his death, and seven of their children injured in a car accident was entitled to recover damages for nervous shock (£4,000).

Authority for:

The Court of Appeal held, beyond the award made, no damages could be properly awarded for the grief and sorrow caused by a person's death or the subsequent worries for the remaining family.

Two cases that demonstrate how the courts may infer liability in respect of proximity were decided as a result of the football disaster at Sheffield Wednesday F.C.'s ground, Hillsborough, in 1989 where 96 people lost their lives.

Alcock v Chief Constable of South Yorkshire (1991)

Facts:

The case arose at the FA Cup semi-final match between Liverpool and Nottingham Forest held at Hillsborough in April 1989. The facts involved a policing error where too many of the Liverpool supporters were ushered into an enclosure that was incapable of holding so many fans. Some of the fans were late, and the match had already started, and there was a consequent surge of the fans to gain entry to view the match. The match was played when there existed metal barrier fencing around the perimeter of the fans' standing areas, and there was no seating in the area to restrict numbers. Due to the volume of fans directed into the enclosure, many at the front were unable to escape and crushed against the fencing. When the extent of the disaster was recognized and assistance was provided, 96 people were dead, and more than 400 more required attention at hospital.

The negligence action was initiated by those affected by the disaster including friends and relations of the 96 dead. These people had suffered psychiatric injury, rather than physical injury, and claimed under nervous shock. Most of the claimants in the action claimed as 'secondary victims' who had witnessed the disaster at the football ground, on television, and on the radio. The House of Lords held that none of the claimants satisfied the requirements to hold the police liable in negligence.

Authority for:

The House of Lords identified the following tests to establish liability as a secondary victim:

1. there must exist close proximity between the claimant and the person suffering harm (such as a close tie of love and affection);

2. the claimant must have been present at the scene of the accident or there in the immediate aftermath;

3. the claimant must have perceived directly the events of the accident or the immediate aftermath.

The case demonstrated the rules that courts must adopt when claimants bring an action for negligence as secondary victims. Further, it demonstrates the problems and practical difficulties in establishing a successful claim where the claimant has not suffered any direct harm, or fear of harm, personally. The claim failed despite the claimants including brothers and sisters of the people who had died, and a sister who had to identify the body of her dead brother (being eight hours after the event was not considered by the Lords to be in the 'immediate aftermath'). The decision has been criticized as being too harsh and being founded on the 'floodgates' argument. This line of legal reasoning was continued in *White v Chief Constable of South Yorkshire*.

White v Chief Constable of South Yorkshire (1998)

Facts:

Four police officers, who were present at the disaster and had provided assistance, including resuscitation and carrying the dead and dying over the fences, claimed for their psychiatric injuries as primary victims. The House of Lords determined, reversing the decision of the Court of Appeal, that the police officers could not succeed in their claim for compensation.

Authority for:

Even though the claimants were in direct contact with the injured people, the Lords stated that only those who were physically injured or in danger of being physically injured could bring a claim, and if not the secondary victims had to establish their claim under the rules laid down in *Alcock*. It was held that rescuers, professional or not, and employees, who had witnessed such distressing events had no claim as primary or secondary victims unless they satisfied the tests above.

The Court of Appeal has identified criteria necessary when attributing liability in cases of psychiatric injury. In *French v Chief Constable of Sussex* the claimants were police officers who had been involved in events leading up to an armed robbery that resulted in a fatal shooting, although none of the claimants had witnessed the event. In assessing the employer's liability, Lord Phillips CJ summarized the main criteria in establishing liability (summarizing the duties set out in *Rothwell v Chemical & Insulating Co. Ltd*):

1. there exists a duty to exercise reasonable care not to cause psychiatric injury or to place the claimant in fear for their physical safety (*Dulieu v White*, see **12.4.1**);

2. the defendant that breaches the duty not to endanger the physical safety of the claimant will be liable if the breach causes not physical but psychiatric injury, even if it was not reasonably foreseeable that psychiatric injury alone might result (*Page v Smith*, see **12.4.1**);

3. there is no general duty to exercise reasonable care not to cause psychiatric injury as a result of causing death or injury of someone (the primary victim) which is witnessed by the claimant (the secondary victim)—*Alcock v Chief Constable of Yorkshire Police* (see **12.4.2**);

4. point 3 applies equally where the claimant is employed by the defendant (*Frost v Chief Constable of South Yorkshire*, see **12.4.2**);

5. as an exception to point 3 there is a duty not to cause psychiatric injury to the claimant as a result of causing the death or injury of someone loved by the claimant in circumstances where the claimant sees or hears the accident or its aftermath (*McLoughlin v O'Brian*).

The previous case law had dealt with the common law right to seek damages.

> ### *Rabone v Pennine Care NHS Foundation Trust (2012)*
>
> **Facts:**
>
> The claimants were parents of a young woman who committed suicide following a hospital Trust's breach of its duty of care towards her and obtained damages for their anguish.
>
> **Authority for:**
>
> It was held that the Trust breached Art. 2 of the European Convention on Human Rights and s. 7(1) of the Human Rights Act 1998. Further, following the case law established by the European Court of Human Rights (*Kats v Ukraine*), the family members of the deceased were entitled to bring a claim in their own right. The parents were awarded £5,000 each. The Supreme Court has made it possible for claimants, who would not otherwise be able to seek damages under the common law, as not being a (secondary) victim, to obtain damages.

CONCLUSION

This chapter has identified where liability may be imposed for pure economic loss (in the absence of associated physical injury). The wider implications of liability for businesses and individuals where they provide advice or information in their professional capacity and situations where the claimant has sustained psychiatric injury have also been addressed. Businesses have to appreciate where risk exists and be proactive in establishing mechanisms that limit/restrict resultant damage or loss. The use of exclusion clauses or paying 'lip service' to complaints of stress from employees will not remove liability in these areas—effective mechanisms need to be in place. The text continues by considering employers' potential liability for torts committed by their employees and for breaches of statutory duties.

SUMMARY OF MAIN POINTS

Pure economic loss

- Liability in cases of pure economic loss is restricted by the courts.
- Where economic loss is linked to physical damage/loss then the economic losses are recoverable.
- Actions will be allowed where a special relationship of proximity exists between the parties.

Negligent misstatements

- Liability requires a special relationship to exist between the parties. Liability is imposed where the person providing the information was aware of the purpose of their advice, it was provided specifically to the advisee, the person providing the information knew that the information would be acted upon without any further advice being sought, and acting on the advice was to the detriment of the advisee.

Psychiatric injury

- A person who is not physically injured by the defendant's negligence, but has experienced trauma due to the consequences of the action, may be able to claim for their psychiatric injury (sometimes referred to as nervous shock).

- Claims for psychiatric injury will define the claimant as either a 'primary' or 'secondary' victim.

- Primary victims are persons who were not physically injured by the defendant's actions, but they were in reasonable fear for their personal safety (being in the zone of physical danger).

- Secondary victims are persons who also were not physically injured, and who were not in fear for their own safety. However, where they have a close proximity with the victim of the accident and they were present at the scene or in the immediate aftermath, they may succeed in their action for damages.

SUMMARY QUESTIONS

Essay questions

1. To what extent is a professional advisor liable in civil law for their misstatement and how does the law seek to regulate their activities and liabilities?

2. 'The case of *Alcock v Chief Constable of South Yorkshire* identified the rules to be satisfied before a successful claim as a secondary victim could be made. The judgment demonstrates the problems and practical difficulties in successfully establishing a claim where the claimant has not suffered any direct harm, or feared personal harm. As such, liability for psychiatric damage in such cases is rarely held and for all practical purposes should be abolished.'

   Critically analyse the above statement.

Problem questions

1. Rayan runs a firm of estate agents who provide a service of surveying and valuing properties, including domestic dwellings.

   Henry approaches Rayan and states that he would like a house valued at £500,000 to have a full survey before he decides whether to proceed with the purchase or not. Rayan accepts the contract and instructs an employee of his (Brian) to perform the survey. Brian visits the property, carries out the survey but is more interested in speaking with his friend on his mobile phone than performing his task diligently. Brian negligently performs the survey and misses very important defects in the property such as dry rot, and that the house is built on the tracks of a disused mine and may be subject to subsidence.

   Based on the favourable report produced by Brian, Henry purchases the property and later discovers these faults. The house, due to the defects, is actually only worth £300,000 and as a consequence Henry has lost a large amount of his investment.

   Advise Henry on any rights he may have to claim for the (potential) professional negligence of Rayan and the estate agencies.

2. Esteban and Jerry are commuters. They regularly caught the same train together. In this way they had become friends socially. One Monday morning, Esteban, a stockbroker, remarked to Jerry that British Bailout Ltd were an extremely attractive proposition on the stockmarket. Being a teacher, Jerry knew little about the state of the market, but expressed interest in the company's shares. Esteban assured him that the investment would 'make money hand over fist'. As a result, Jerry invested £1,000 in the company, which has just gone into liquidation. Jerry has lost his investment.

   Explain the potential liability of Esteban for Jerry's economic losses.

 You will find guidance about how to answer these questions online at www.oup.com/uk/marson5e/.

FURTHER READING

Books and articles

Allen, S. (1997) 'Rescuers and Employees—Primary Victims of Nervous Shock' *New Law Journal*, Vol. 147 , No. 6778 , p. 158.

Barker, K. (2006) 'Wielding Occam's Razor: Pruning Strategies for Economic Loss' *Oxford Journal of Legal Studies*, Vol. 26 , No. 2, p. 289.

Barrett, B. (2008) 'Psychiatric Stress—An Unacceptable Cost to Employers' *Journal of Business Law*, No. 1 , p. 64.

Case, P. (2004) 'Secondary Iatrogenic Harm: Claims for Psychiatric Damage Following a Death Caused by Medical Error' *Modern Law Review*, Vol. 67 , No. 4 , p. 561.

Griffiths, N. (2004) 'Shock Induced Psychiatric Injury: Damage Limitation' *Personal Injury Law Journal*, Vol. 24 , April, p. 18.

Hilson, C. (2002) 'Liability for Psychiatric Injury: Primary and Secondary Victims Revisited' *Professional Negligence*, Vol. 18 , No. 3 , p. 167.

Jones, M. (1995) 'Liability for Psychiatric Illness—More Principle, Less Subtlety?' *Web JCLI*, No. 4.

Mullender, R. (1999) 'Negligent Misstatement, Threats and the Scope of the Hedley Byrne Principle' *Modern Law Review*, Vol. 62 , No. 3 , May, p. 425.

ONLINE RESOURCES

www.oup.com/uk/marson5e/

For further resources relating to this chapter, including self-test questions, an interactive glossary, and key case flashcards.

13 VICARIOUS LIABILITY AND STATUTORY DUTIES

An employer will engage an individual to perform some function for their business and may give specific guidance as to how the tasks are to be completed. An employer, however, would be unlikely to engage the individual to commit a tort, but if this occurs in the course of employment, and they have the employment status of an employee, the employer may be jointly liable with the tortfeasor. This is referred to as the vicarious liability of an employer. The chapter identifies the doctrine of vicarious liability and its potential impact on employers. It also considers liability of those producing, supplying, marketing, and importing goods that contain defects and cause damage/loss. Many businesses will be involved in some form of trading in this capacity and hence they may be subject to a claim for damages as the liability in this jurisdiction of law is strict (it does not require the claimant to prove negligence). Businesses also occupy land and premises and must ensure that visitors (and even trespassers) are safe from injury, and various statutory duties are imposed that may lead to those in business being subject to claims where a person has been injured or suffered loss. As such, the extent of these areas of the law will require most employers/managers and those in business to have a knowledge of the principles underlying the imposition of liability, and to develop strategies to avoid tort actions.

Business Scenario 13

Aki, a milkman, drives a milk-float for Curdles Dairy Ltd. He is an employee of the firm. The dairy make it clear to all their employee that no-one, especially children, is to be allowed to help them in delivering milk. Aki, however, regularly allows Arthur, aged 10, to assist him in his delivery round. The delivery round includes the house of Aki's sister Sayo. One day, whilst doing his round accompanied by Arthur, Aki stops the milk-float outside Sayo's house, and Sayo calls Aki and asks him to help her move a heavy piano. Arthur offers to move the milk-float a few doors down the road whilst Aki is in Sayo's house. Aki agrees, but when Arthur releases the brake, he is unable to stop the milk-float from running down the road. The vehicle collides with Tori's brand new Porsche motor car, injuring Tori and her husband.

Advise Tori. In the event of Curdles Dairy being found liable, what action might they take against Aki?

Learning Outcomes

- Offer a definition of the doctrine of vicarious liability (13.2)
- Identify the rationale and justification for the development of the doctrine (13.3)
- Apply the tests to establish vicarious liability (13.5–13.5.2.4)

- Explain, with common law examples, how the courts identify 'course of employment' (13.5.2–13.5.2.4)
- Demonstrate the extension of vicarious liability to independent contractors (13.6–13.6.2)
- Explain the protection to the consumer through legislation (13.7–13.7.4)
- Identify the obligations imposed on the owners and occupiers of land under the common law and through statute (13.8–13.8.4)
- Explain potential liability established through a breach of a statutory duty (13.9–13.9.2.3).

13.1 INTRODUCTION

Vicarious liability occurs where one party has responsibility for a wrong committed by someone else. In a business context, vicarious liability is a doctrine where an employer will be held liable for the torts of their employee. The employer may have to compensate the injured party for any damage sustained to property or injuries suffered by the wrongful or negligent actions of their employee. The doctrine was developed, through the courts, to ensure that injured persons are compensated for losses sustained as a result of a negligent or wrongful act, and the obligation be placed on the employer to compensate and, further, to prevent any future torts being committed. These tests begin with the employment status of the worker (who generally must be considered an 'employee') and require that the tort was committed in the course of their employment. As concepts such as 'course of employment' are broad, common law examples are considered.

Further, the chapter considers the protection afforded consumers when defective products cause them injury. The Sale of Goods Act 1979 and other statutory protections provide remedies where goods fall below the required standard; however, they do not compensate where an individual suffered loss (such as damage to themselves or their property) due to the defect in the product itself. The Consumer Protection Act 1987 enables claims on such a basis.

Obligations are also placed on the occupiers of land and property that are accessible by the public (including, of course, shops and factories—pertinent to businesses). These obligations extend to visitors and non-visitors (such as trespassers) and identification of the potential liability in this area, and which mechanisms may reduce the instances of breaches are significant in a business context. The chapter concludes by considering statutory duties and how these may enable claims when the duty is breached.

13.2 VICARIOUS LIABILITY—A DEFINITION

Vicarious liability was succinctly defined by the Court of Appeal in the case of *Hudson v Ridge Manufacturing*) as 'a doctrine whereby an employer will be held liable for the torts of his employees'. The doctrine does not require that the employer has actively participated in the commission of the tort, only that there is some relationship between them and the tortfeasor that will enable the law to hold the employer responsible. Whilst the employer is held jointly liable with the employee tortfeasor, if a claim is successfully made against the employer they may in turn bring an action to recover from the employee under the Civil Liability (Contribution) Act 1978. As such, it is important to remember that even though vicarious liability involves the employer being held accountable, this does not remove the liability or fault from the employee who committed the tort.

Consider

Aki has allowed a child to move a works vehicle under his control, against the rules of his employment, and this has caused loss to a third party. The question identifies an expensive vehicle as being damaged to illustrate the point that a milkman will typically be unable to satisfy Tori's claim for the cost of repair and any injury to her and the occupants of her car. Employees also do not generally carry their own insurance for accidents that may occur at work (they rely on insurance of their employer). Therefore the question is of the potential vicarious liability of the employer.

13.3 RATIONALE FOR THE DOCTRINE

As vicarious liability is a doctrine that holds an employer liable for the torts of someone else (i.e. their employee), the theoretical justification and rationale for imposition of the liability has been the subject of controversy and academic comment for many years. One overriding explanation for the doctrine has been that the *employer had expressly or impliedly authorized the employee's action* (as identified in *Tuberville v Stamp*) and therefore should satisfy any claims on the basis of damage or injury as a consequence. The employer may have *employed a negligent employee* or have *failed in their duty to adequately control* the employee and hence 'set the whole thing in motion' (as stated by Brougham LJ in *Duncan v Findlater*). Further arguments to justify the doctrine have been that as the *employer derives financial benefit* from the work of the employee, they should be responsible for losses (referred to as 'enterprise risk'). The employer also has 'deeper pockets' than the employee and as such is in a better financial position to satisfy claims, as increasingly, the employer is no longer an individual but a corporation. It also avoids the situation where the employee is made the 'scapegoat' for any injuries/losses sustained due to the tort. A corporation may be *able to distribute any losses* more successfully than would a private individual, where a claim could lead to significant financial losses. A corporation may be able to reduce dividends to shareholders, reduce payments to staff or management, and so on, to generate the revenue to pay any claim. Private individuals do not have such options. *Compulsory insurance* is also required of employers. This ensures damage caused to employees will be compensatable. Again, private individuals may possess house and car insurance, but are unlikely to carry insurance in the event of their causing any damage or injury whilst in the course of employment. Therefore, it appears logical, if perhaps a little 'unfair' to hold an employer liable.

A major rationale for vicarious liability's justification has been the concept of *accident/ tort prevention*. In both *Limpus v London General Omnibus* and *Rose v Plenty* (see **13.5.2.1**), the employees were authorized to perform an act, but performed this act in an unauthorized way (although see Lawton LJ's dissenting opinion in *Rose v Plenty* regarding the act of the employee being the performance of an act which he was not employed to perform and as such the employer should have borne no responsibility for the injury). In so doing, they caused injury or damage through their negligence. As the courts in each case held the act had been committed in the course of their employment, the employer was held liable. However, the option for the employer in such instances is to consider the action as a fundamental breach of the contract of employment and dismiss the employee. Further, it would have been prudent following these judgments for the employer to conduct 'spot-checks' to ensure no other employee was breaking the rules and if they did, to apply whatever sanction necessary to prevent further breaches and potential negligent acts.

Holding an employer financially liable for the torts of an employee provides an effective incentive for their proactive approach to ensure safe systems of work are in place and the employees are controlled to an extent that will limit, as far as possible, any torts being committed. However, despite the justifications forwarded for the doctrine, it continues to be quite restrictively applied—'I accept that the court should not be too ready to impose vicarious liability on a defendant. It is, after all, a type of liability for tort which involves no fault on the part of the defendant, and for that reason alone its application should be reasonably circumscribed.' (Lord Neuberger in *Maga v Archbishop of Birmingham*, see **13.5.2.3**).

13.4 FOR WHAT IS THE EMPLOYER LIABLE?

For the employer to be held liable for the torts of their employee, the tort must have been committed whilst 'in the course of employment'. Evidently, this will cause consternation to rational thinking people, as no employer would engage a person to commit a tort. Course of employment, in the legal sense, is a term that establishes the liability an employer will have if the employee has acted in one of the following ways:

1. the employee acted negligently in an act that they were authorized to do with care;
2. the act was necessarily incidental to something that the employee was engaged to do;
3. the employee acted in a wrongful way that was authorized by the employer.

Such examples can of course be difficult to identify in the abstract and hence it is important, as an aid to understanding, to review case law that has created and exemplified these principles.

13.5 THE QUALIFICATIONS TO ESTABLISH VICARIOUS LIABILITY

For an employer to be liable for the torts of their employees two conditions are required:

1. the worker must be considered an *'employee'*;
2. the tort must have been committed in the *'course of employment'*.

Consider

The question has identified Aki as an employee. Therefore we know the first test of vicarious liability is satisfied with no need for further consideration. However, the existing common law must be examined to determine whether his actions will be held as occurring during the course of his employment.

13.5.1 Employee Status

The tests to establish a worker as an employee or an independent contractor are considered in **Chapter 19** and therefore this chapter will not replicate the discussion provided there. Note, however, that in vicarious liability, it is increasingly evidence of control exercisable by the employer, rather than the existence of a contract of employment, that will lead to an employer's liability.

Most recently, the Supreme Court has developed the law on what constitutes 'course of employment'. It demonstrates the evolution of the test when relating to, first, the action of a non-employee but the application of liability to an employer, and secondly, of the criminal actions of an employee when this was beyond the scope of their employment.

Cox v Ministry of Justice (2014)

Facts:

The claimant, a catering manager at a prison, was injured when an inmate working in the kitchen dropped a sack of food on her. She brought an action for damages against the Ministry of Justice. The accident was caused by the negligence of a prisoner, but the court agreed that the law of vicarious liability had moved beyond the confines of a contract of service—the prisoner was, generally speaking, under the control of the employer (akin to an employment relationship).

Authority for:

It was held that the prisoner's work was done on behalf and at the request of the Ministry, and this established a sufficiently close relationship to create the employer's vicarious liability. An important aspect of the case was that, when reviewing the five factors which determine whether a relationship will give rise to vicarious liability, the control test (so crucial in determining employment status) is increasingly seen as less relevant and almost a remnant of the past.

13.5.1.1 Liability for 'loaned' employees

Employers may at times loan an employee to another business where, for example, the other business has a temporary increase in demand or the loan is through an agency. Where this occurs, and the loaned employee commits a tort, which employer retains the responsibility (and may be held vicariously liable)? In *Mersey Docks & Harbour Board v Coggins and Griffiths (Liverpool) Ltd* the House of Lords held that the control exercisable by the employer is the determining factor. This, in most cases, will rest with the original employer. However, where it can be demonstrated that the control is actually exercised by the employer that has taken the loan of the employee, they will assume responsibility.

Hawley v Luminar Leisure Ltd (2006)

Facts:

The employer operated a nightclub and had hired a 'bouncer' from another business, under a contract to provide security services. The bouncer was directed by Luminar in

→

the tasks to be performed and the way that they were to be carried out. The bouncer assaulted a customer in the course of his duties.

Authority for:

For the purposes of liability, the employer was held to be Luminar. When the bouncer assaulted a customer, Luminar was vicariously liable for the tort as his 'temporary deemed employer'.

These cases identified where either the original employer, or the employer the employee was loaned to was held vicariously liable for the employee's tort. There may further be situations where both employers have to share responsibility, for example where both employers were held liable for the tort of the employee as each could have prevented the employee's action (see *Viasystems (Tyneside) Ltd v Thermal Transfer (Northern) Ltd*).

13.5.2 Course of Employment

To hold an employer liable for the torts of their employee, the employee must have been employed in the employer's business and be performing their job. As evidenced in *Joel v Morison* 'the servant must be engaged on his master's business and not off on a frolic of his own'. To identify how the courts will conclude what amounts to the course of employment it is necessary to examine the common law. Note that the following are examples and do not seek to establish a comprehensive list.

Consider

Aki was helping his sister to move a piano and at this point the accident occurred. Was this a 'frolic of his own' or an act incidental to employment?

13.5.2.1 Authorized acts conducted in unauthorized ways

- *Express prohibitions:* In an attempt to limit potential liability, employers may specifically instruct their employees to act in a certain way, or seek to prohibit certain actions that may likely lead to torts being committed. The employer is seeking to limit their exposure to risk of harm to property and persons, but the success or failure of such instruction may be viewed from the perspective of whether the employee had been expressly told not to do something and contradicted this instruction (no vicarious liability); or whether the employee is told not to perform an authorized task in an unauthorized way (liability may be established). These two instances may be seen in the following cases:

Limpus v London General Omnibus (1862)

Facts:

Limpus was injured in an accident involving one of London General Omnibus's vehicles. The driver of the defendant's bus was, at the time of the accident, racing with a driver from a rival bus company to reach a bus stop, and drove across the road in an attempt to block the other driver's route. There had been previous acts of such reckless actions between rival bus companies and as a consequence London General Omnibus had instructed its drivers not to engage in racing. When Limpus was injured, the claim was brought against the bus company rather than the driver of the vehicle. The defence raised against the vicarious liability action was that London General Omnibus had expressly instructed the drivers not to take the action that led to Limpus's injury, and hence the driver acted outside of the 'course of his employment'. The court rejected this argument as the driver was acting for his employer in an unauthorized manner.

Authority for:

An employer merely instructing an employee to refrain from action will not enable the employer to escape liability. Insofar as the employee is performing an authorized task, albeit in an unauthorized manner, the employer will remain vicariously liable.

The ruling can be contrasted where the employee does act outside their employment.

Iqbal v London Transport Executive (1973)

Facts:

A bus conductor was expressly forbidden by the employer to drive buses, and was informed that he should request an engineer to move a bus. However, he moved the bus himself and as he did, committed a tort. The injured party attempted to recover damages from the employer.

Authority for:

The claim failed as the conductor was not employed to drive buses. In order for the test of 'course of employment' to be satisfied the employee must be performing the obligations for which they were employed, and in this case driving buses was outside of the conductor's responsibilities.

- *Providing lifts:* It is important to identify when an employer may be held liable for an employee's tort when giving lifts as part of their driving responsibilities. This is particularly relevant when the employer has informed the employee not to provide lifts or carry passengers in works' vehicles. The first case discussed (*Twine v Bean's Express*) demonstrates the courts' reluctance to impose liability on an employer in such situations, but when compared with the second case (*Rose v Plenty*), the courts may be willing to hold an employer liable. In doing so, they ensure employers proactively reduce the possibility of negligent acts by their employees (accident prevention) and ensure their workers, and the public, are more effectively protected.

Twine v Bean's Express Ltd (1946)

Facts:

The defendants provided a commercial van and a driver (Harrison) to be used by a bank with the condition that the driver remained the employee of the defendants. There was a further agreement between the defendants and the bank that the defendants accepted no liability for any persons, other than their own employees, riding in the van. The driver of the van had been expressly told that no one was to be allowed to ride with him in the van, and there was also notice to this effect on the dashboard. The driver allowed an employee of the bank to ride with him, at his own risk, and in the course of this journey the employee died in an accident caused by Harrison. The employee's widow brought a claim for damages against the defendants. It was held by the Court of Appeal that only the defendants' employees were permitted to travel in the van and the deceased man was not one of these persons. Harrison, in giving the lift, was not acting in the course of his employment, and hence the defendants were not liable for the actions of the driver.

Authority for:

An unauthorized act performed by an employee will allow the employer to escape liability.

It is necessary to look to the judgment of Lord Greene MR for the rationale for the decision:

> [The driver was] employed to drive the van. That does not mean that because the deceased man was in the van it was within the scope of his employment to be driving the deceased man. He was in fact doing two things at once. He was driving his van from one place to another by a route that he was properly taking when he ran into the omnibus, and as he was driving the van he was acting within the scope of his employment. The other thing that he was doing simultaneously was something totally outside the scope of his employment, namely, giving a lift to a person who had no right whatsoever to be there.

This case can be compared with *Rose v Plenty*. The difference between the decisions may be due to the nature of the employee's action. In *Twine*, the employee was providing a lift to the bank's employee that was of no use to the employer and could in no way be associated with acting in the course of employment. However, in *Rose v Plenty*, the action of the milkman and the child assistant was to carry out the task required by the employer, albeit again, in an unauthorized manner.

Rose v Plenty (1975)

Facts:

The case involved a milkman who had employed a 13-year-old child to assist him on his milk round, despite a direct order from his employer that no one was allowed to ride on the milk float with the delivery drivers. The child was assisting the milkman when there

→

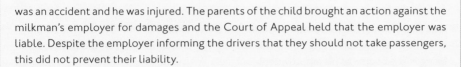

was an accident and he was injured. The parents of the child brought an action against the milkman's employer for damages and the Court of Appeal held that the employer was liable. Despite the employer informing the drivers that they should not take passengers, this did not prevent their liability.

Authority for:

An employer may be held vicariously liable for a tort committed by their employee who is performing an authorized task in an unauthorized manner.

If, by providing an express instruction not to commit a tort, the employer's potential liability could be circumvented, the protection the doctrine sought to provide would be removed. The milkman was 'doing his job' when the accident occurred, and the employer should have been more proactive in ensuring the employees adhered to the work rules. However, Lawton LJ dissented and considered that this case fell into the same category as *Twine v Bean's Express*, where the employee was not 'doing his job' albeit in an unauthorized manner, rather they were doing something completely different. This may be an example of vicarious liability being a doctrine of 'rough justice'. Mechanisms exist through employment law to take action against employees who fail to follow work rules, and it is in the enforcement of these rules that such accidents (and their consequent tort actions) will be prevented.

Consider

Aki's actions are very similar to those in *Rose v Plenty*. Whilst the employees were not supposed to give lifts to anyone or accept help in the course of their duties, the employer was not controlling Aki with sufficient care. Employers are not allowed to disregard their duties by merely instructing employees to behave in a given way. They must actively ensure employees correctly follow lawful instructions to ensure they are not carried out in a wrongful way.

13.5.2.2 Acts incidental to the employment

The courts have had to determine whether an employer should be liable for an act by their employee that is not what they were engaged to perform, but rather is incidental to their employment.

Crook v Derbyshire Stone Ltd (1956)

Facts:

A lorry driver had stopped at a lay-by near to a café. He crossed one section of the dual carriageway on foot to get to the café when a collision occurred between the driver and a motorcyclist, due to the driver's negligence, in which the motorcyclist was injured.

Authority for:

It was held that as the tort occurred during the driver's hours of employment the employer was liable. The tort being committed during the employee's 'break' did not stop him being in the course of his employment.

In *Smith v Stages* the House of Lords established rules that would identify where journeys incidental to the employment would create liability for an employer:

1. when an employee was travelling between his ordinary residence and work by any means of transport whether or not provided by his employer he was not acting in the course of his employment unless contractually obliged to do so;

2. travelling between workplaces was in the course of employment;

3. when an employee was paid for travelling in his employer's time the fact that the employee could choose the time and mode of transport did not take the journey out of the course of his employment;

4. when an employee was travelling from his ordinary residence to an unusual place of work or to an emergency the employee would be acting in the course of his employment;

5. a deviation or interruption of a journey would for that time take an employee out of the course of his employment.

Consider

Using the rules outlined in *Smith*, would you consider the dairy to be liable for the loss to Tori?

A particularly infamous case when considering the extent of vicarious liability and the responsibility of employers occurred in *Century Insurance Co. Ltd v Northern Ireland Road Transport Board*.

Century Insurance Co. Ltd v Northern Ireland Road Transport Board (1942)

Facts:

Mr Davison was employed to deliver 300 gallons of petrol in a tanker. At the garage he inserted the nozzle of the delivery hosepipe into the manhole of the garage's tank and turned on the stopcock of the tanker. Whilst the petrol was flowing into the tank

➡

Mr Davison lit a cigarette and threw away the lighted match igniting material on the floor of the garage, which caused a fire. The proprietor of the garage used a fire extinguisher in an attempt to put out the fire and instructed Mr Davison to turn off the stopcock. Instead, he began to drive the tanker away from the garage, stopping when he reached the street. Mr Davison exited the tanker and whilst the fire had been extinguished at the manhole, it had travelled up the delivery hose, into the tanker where a 'very violent' explosion occurred. The explosion destroyed the tanker, the motorcar of the proprietor of the garage, and several houses in the vicinity were also damaged.

Authority for:

The House of Lords held that Mr Davison was employed to deliver petrol and as such his tort was committed in the course of his employment. He was careless in discarding the lighted match, but he was performing his duties and consequently the employer had to accept the liability.

13.5.2.3 Deviation from a task

Having demonstrated where the tort of an employee, whilst committed during their working hours or travelling to and from work, may lead to the vicarious liability of the employer, a further area of import is where the employee has deviated from their employment. It is the extent to which the employee has deviated from their task that will establish liability.

Storey v Ashton (1869)

Facts:

Storey (a six-year-old child) was injured when delivery drivers for Ashton ran him over. Ashton was a firm of wine merchants that had sent their delivery driver and clerk to deliver a consignment of wine at Blackheath, and bring back empty bottles from the drop point. Having delivered the wine and picked up the bottles the driver was returning to Ashton's offices as instructed. However, about a quarter of mile from the destination, instead of returning to the offices, he was persuaded by the clerk to drive in another direction on the business of the clerk. It was on this journey that the accident occurred. The High Court held that the employer was not liable for the injury to Storey. The driver had been negligent, but he was not acting in the course of his employment as he was driving in a different direction, taking a different route, than where he was instructed.

Authority for:

For an employer to escape being held vicariously liable, the employee must have sufficiently deviated from their task for the tort not to have occurred in the course of employment.

Consider

Was Aki's deviation from his task sufficient for the authority in *Storey* to apply? He was on his route and delivering milk (as was his job) but he did go into his sister's house. Does it matter that he went to help her move a piano?

13.5.2.4   Criminal acts

It is very important to identify whether an employer will be held liable for the criminal acts of their employees that are committed during their employment. Where the employee's act was outside of their duties and employment, there has been no liability for the employer.

Heasmans v Clarity Cleaning Ltd (1987)

Facts:

A cleaner unlawfully used the phone of a client to make international calls (at a cost of £1,411). This was held by the Court of Appeal to be a criminal act wholly outside of the scope of their employment.

Authority for:

Merely because the employer provided the 'opportunity' for the commission of the act did not make them vicariously liable for the loss.

However, when the employee's action was taken in the course of their employment, the employer has been held jointly culpable (*Lloyd v Grace, Smith & Co.*).

Daniels v Whetstone Entertainments and Allender (1962)

Facts:

A steward (bouncer) employed at a dance hall assaulted a customer within the dance hall. The persons involved in this disturbance were removed to outside of the premises and the steward was informed by his employer to remain inside the dance hall and continue his duties. Instead, he proceeded to go outside in an attempt to find a second man involved in the disturbance, found the original victim of the steward's assault, and assaulted him again.

Authority for:

It was held that the first assault was within the steward's course of employment, but the second assault was not.

When determining if an employer should be held vicariously liable for the torts of their employees, the test of establishing whether the employee's act was a wrongful or unauthorized method of performing an authorized act is not always of use when assessing intentional torts. Rather, it is more apt to consider the closeness of the connection between the wrong committed by the employee and the nature of their employment, and to determine whether it is just and reasonable in those circumstances to hold the employer vicariously liable (*Bernard v The Attorney General of Jamaica*). A very significant judgment was provided by the House of Lords in *Lister v Hesley Hall*.

Lister v Hesley Hall (2001)

Facts:

Lister and two others brought an action against the employer of a warden at a residential school for boys with behavioural problems, of which they had been resident. In 1995, the warden was convicted of several sexual offences (including physical abuse) against children in his care, including the claimants. They brought an action for personal injury, alleging the employer was vicariously liable for these acts.

Authority for:

Lord Steyn followed the reasoning from judgments of the Canadian Supreme Court (*Bazley v Curry* and *Jacobi v Griffiths*) where, in determining an employer's vicarious liability in such actions, there must be a 'close connection' between the act and the employer's authorization. In essence, an employer is liable for acts which they have not authorized, provided they are so connected with acts which they have authorized that they may rightly be regarded as, albeit improper, modes of doing them. The employer should have been aware of the possibility and risk of sexual abuse by employees in positions of authority (but not perhaps of other employees) and hence it had not taken sufficient precautions to avoid the act(s).

This aspect of an employer's liability has also been applied in relation to a statutory right.

Majrowski v Guys & St Thomas' NHS Trust (2006)

Facts:

A clinical audit coordinator who had been bullied and subject to rude and abusive behaviour by a departmental manager was successful in claiming against his employer under the Protection from Harassment Act 1997, s. 3. The House of Lords held that where there had been a close connection between the course of conduct of the employee and the circumstances of their employment, it was no defence for the employer to claim that they did not authorize the conduct, or the consequences of the actions were not foreseeable (a point confirmed in *Jones v Ruth*—the statute does not require proof of foreseeability).

Authority for:

The implications of this statutory right offer an 'easier' route for employees to claim damages for bullying and stress-related claims against their employer as the claimant does not have to establish a psychiatric injury but rather distress/anxiety.

In the case *Maga v Trustees of the Birmingham Archdiocese of the Roman Catholic Church* the Court of Appeal determined the extent of the vicarious liability of the Roman Catholic Church for sexual abuse by a priest.

Maga v Trustees of the Birmingham Archdiocese of the Roman Catholic Church (2010)

Facts:

The appellant (M) alleged that when he was about 12–13 years old a Roman Catholic priest sexually abused him over a 6–12-month period. The issue of whether the Archdiocese (the Church) was vicariously liable for the acts of the priest centred on whether those actions could constitute a sufficiently close connection to his employment. The first court held there was no sufficiently close connection to make the imposition of liability fair and just (according to *Lister v Hesley Hall Ltd*). Neither M, nor his parents, were of the Roman Catholic faith or participated in its activities, the priest had not attempted to convert them to Catholicism, and the sexual abuse was (of course) not part of the priest's duties. The employment undertaken by the priest merely provided him with the opportunity to come into contact with young boys. The case was appealed.

Authority for:

The Court of Appeal held that there was sufficient evidence that M had been sexually abused, but it disagreed with the first court holding that the Church was not vicariously liable for the priest's actions. On reflection, it found there were a number of factors that established a sufficiently close connection between the priest's actions and his employment (seven factors were outlined by Lord Neuberger MR).

What is most interesting, and equally perplexing in this case, is that the court did not give any further detailed broad instruction which could help in establishing the boundaries (and thereby limitations) of the doctrine. In *Lister* (which significantly extended the close connection test), the abuse occurred at a residential home and the actions were essentially authorized in some misguided sense of discipline. Here, no such instruction or relationship existed, such as would be the case had M been an altar boy. The priest and M entered the relationship through M attending discos and other events arranged by the priest in his role of working with local children, and later by M undertaking additional paid work for the priest. The outcome of the case appears to be the extension of the scope of vicarious liability, and hence employers need to be ever more vigilant to control the actions of their employees, and have a structure/policies in place to effectively supervise their activities. Indeed, Lord Neuberger expressly noted in the judgment the 'inappropriately casual' approach taken by the priest's superior in relation to two complaints that the priest had been involved in sexual abuse.

A detailed review of the law on vicarious liability was recently provided by the Supreme Court:

Mohamud v WM Morrison Supermarkets PLC (2014)

Facts:

The case involved a customer, visiting the petrol station of a branch of the supermarket chain, who was seriously assaulted by an employee of Morrison. The court at first instance and the Court of Appeal held against the claimant, deciding that the actions of the employee were beyond the course of his employment. However, the Supreme Court, having reviewed the doctrine, focused on two issues: 1) the functions/activities which the employer had entrusted the employee with; and 2) the existence of a sufficient connection between the employee's position at work and his wrongful conduct (compare this decision with the judgments of the Court of Appeal in *Graham v Commercial Bodyworks* and of the Inner House in *Vaickuviene v J Sainsbury PLC*).

The key issue for the Supreme Court was that the employee was issuing an instruction for the customer to stay away from the employer's premises, and he furthered this instruction with a violent attack. This was an abuse of the job he was instructed to perform, but it was connected with the job as the employee did have dealings with customers.

Authority for:

The claimant had urged the court to replace the 'close connection' test with one of 'representative capacity'—that the question to be asked was whether a reasonable observer would have thought the employee was acting in the capacity of a representative of the employer whist carrying out the tortious act. The Supreme Court would not change the test but here found the employee's actions in the 'field of activities' of his role and employment. As the employer entrusted the employee with this role, it was also responsible for the potential for the employer to abuse the position.

13.6 LIABILITY FOR INDEPENDENT CONTRACTORS

Whilst the general rule exists that an employer is liable for the torts of employees but not of independent contractors, as the latter have their own insurance to satisfy claims and there does not exist the same level of control exercised over their actions as the former, the law provides for exceptions. In the following examples, an employer may still be held liable for torts committed by an independent contractor if they authorized the tort, or in situations where responsibility cannot be delegated. In **non-delegable duties** the employer is liable for negligent acts whether committed by an employer or independent contractor. The imposition of liability may involve a degree of public policy where the employer should not be allowed to remove their responsibility for health and safety (e.g.) of workers or the public, or where statute has imposed a specific responsibility on the employer.

13.6.1 The Fault of the Employer

An employer may be held liable for the torts of an independent contractor where the tort was ratified or authorized by them. In such a situation, both the employer and the independent contractor may be held liable as joint tortfeasors.

Ellis v Sheffield Gas Consumers Co. (1853)

Facts:

The defendants employed a contractor (without authority) to excavate a trench in the street for the purpose of accessing gas pipes. The trench was dug but the contractors negligently left the rubble from the trench in a heap on the footpath over which Ellis stumbled and sustained an injury. In attempting to avoid potential liability, the employers stated the contractors were at fault and as they were not employees any claim had to be made against them.

Authority for:

The court held that the agreement with the contractors amounted to an illegal act, and the employer could not delegate its responsibility to a contractor. As a consequence the employer was responsible for the damage sustained.

13.6.2 Non-Delegable Duties

The term 'delegated' duty is meant in the sense that the task required of the employer has been delegated to an independent contractor who is competent to perform the task. Consequently, the employer has a lower duty to take care in these situations of 'delegable duties' rather than the higher duty to take care in non-delegable duties. There are no definite rules to establish when an employer will be held liable for torts committed by an independent contractor, but examples include:

1. if the duty on the employer involves some extra-hazardous act (*Dodd Properties v Canterbury City Council*);

2. where the employer owes a duty for the health and safety of their employees (in *Wilsons and Clyde Coal Co. v English* the House of Lords held that an employer had a duty to provide competent staff, adequate material, a safe system of work, and effective supervision);

3. if the law imposes a duty on the employer (such as through statute), this cannot be delegated (*Smith v Cammell Laird & Co.*);

4. if substances are brought onto land which are dangerous (e.g. explosive materials) and would be likely to cause damage if allowed to escape (known as the rule in *Rylands v Fletcher*).

Rylands v Fletcher (1866)

Facts:

The case involved strict liability and is a form of private nuisance. The defendant occupied land near to the claimant's coal mine, whose mines extended below the defendant's land. These mines had been cut off and had become disused and the defendant obtained permission to construct a reservoir to provide water for his mill. Fletcher had employed

→

competent contractors. However, during their work they discovered the mineshaft, and that it was connected to another mine, but did not inform Fletcher or attempt to block it. When the reservoir was put into action the water entered the old mine shafts and consequently flooded Rylands' mine, who successfully claimed for the damage caused. The defendant was liable even though not vicariously liable nor negligent in his actions.

Authority for:

As per Blackburn J, 'the person who for their own purpose brings onto his lands . . . anything likely to do mischief if it escapes, must keep it at his peril and is *prima facie* answerable for all the damage which is the natural consequence of its escape'.

Whilst this is not an exhaustive list, these situations demonstrate that a tortious act by an independent contractor may still be the responsibility of the employer, who will have to satisfy any claims.

An important clarification (and arguably an extension) to the law on non-delegable duties was established in the following case.

Woodland v Essex County Council (2013)

Facts:

The appellant, a child aged 10 at the time of the incident, was a pupil at Whitmore Junior School. The school, through the local authority, engaged an independent, external, contract to provide swimming lessons—Direct Swimming Services. During a lesson, the child got into difficulties and, whilst attended to at the scene by the on-duty lifeguard and resuscitated, had suffered a serious brain injury. A claim was brought against the local authority in charge (and swimming teacher and lifeguard) under negligence. The key issue in respect of this aspect of the case was the argument by the appellant that the local authority had a non-delegable duty of care to the child and hence was liable for the damages sustained. In both the High Court and the Court of Appeal, it was held that no delegable duty existed in relation to the (negligent) actions of an independent contractor (unless of course the selection of that contractor was itself negligent). Unlike vicarious liability (which was not part of this claim) where liability can be imposed on a person on the basis of acts or omissions of others, liability in negligence is fault-based and the responsibility of the tortfeasor alone. Therefore, the appellant was seeking an exception to this general rule of law.

Lord Sumption explained in the judgment that the expression 'non-delegable duty' had become a conventional way of describing situations where the duty extends, beyond merely taking care, to procuring the careful performance of work delegated to others. Lord Sumption identified five features which would typically justify the fault-based limitation of liability being departed from and give rise to the existence of a non-delegable duty:

1. the claimant is a patient/child/prisoner or some otherwise vulnerable/dependent person;

➡

2. an antecedent relationship exists between the claimant and defendant which places the claimant in the care of the defendant and from which it is possible to assign a duty (and positive obligation) for the defendant to protect the claimant from harm;

3. the claimant has no control over the defendant's performance of this obligation;

4. the defendant has delegated this function (or some part of it) to a third party—which has assumed care (involving control) of the defendant;

5. this third party has been negligent in the exercise of the delegated power/function (at para. 23).

Evidently, had the Supreme Court followed the rules as stated above, there would have been no liability of the local authority due to the traditional interpretation of point 4 and the lack of control by the defendant (local authority) through the outsourcing of the function to the third party (Direct Swimming Services). However, significantly, Lord Sumption provided that the interpretation of control here was related to control over the claimant for the purpose of performing a function for which the defendant had assumed responsibility. Essentially, liability will only be imposed where public authorities have assumed a duty to perform a function, and this function, which has traditionally been performed by members of its own staff, has been outsourced—thereby re-establishing a form of vicarious liability to protect the claimant.

Authority for:

Providers of a public service are faced with an additional burden when choosing to outsource functions to third parties. However, a non-delegable duty will only be imposed where it is 'fair, just, and reasonable' to do so. Public authorities undertake the personal responsibility to ensure that tasks generally under its responsibility are performed with care.

13.7 THE CONSUMER PROTECTION ACT 1987

Where a business produces goods, and those goods contain a defect which results in damage/injury being sustained, unless a defence as identified under the Consumer Protection Act (CPA) 1987 is available, the producer, importer, marketer, or supplier will be liable. Proof of negligence is not required; simply the existence of the defect and the damage (over £275 in value) will allow the claimant to succeed. As such, knowledge of CPA 1987 is crucial to businesses that produce, import, market, or supply goods.

CPA 1987 was enacted to fulfil the requirements of the EU Product Liability Directive (85/374/EEC) and sought to assist consumers when claiming against defects in products. CPA 1987 enables claimants to seek damages if they were injured through the property, or if it had caused damage, and it adds to existing common law rights. Claims for injuries or damage to property would generally be made under the tort of negligence (see **11.5**), but this is fraught with difficulties and CPA 1987 makes such claims much easier in relation to products. Part I of CPA 1987 imposes a civil liability that enables a claim for injuries due to an unsafe product, Part II was repealed, and Part III (misleading prices) was superseded by the Consumer Protection from Un-fair Trading Regulations 2008 (see the online resources for additional content on the Regulations).

13.7.1 Protection Through the Act

CPA 1987 protects those individuals who may have suffered injury as a result of the product they purchased, or where the product caused damage to their property. The Sale of Goods Act (SOGA) 1979 enabled those with a contractual relationship with a retailer to have their money returned, or be provided with a repaired item or a replacement in the event of a product failing one of the sections (ss. 12–15). However, what if the defective product purchased caused injury to the buyer, or had damaged their property? The law of contract entitled the claimant to protection against a faulty product *not* for any losses attributed to this (as part of the concept of remoteness of damage). In such an event, the injured party would have to sue the defendant under negligence. Proving a breach of the duty of care owed to a consumer may be very difficult and expensive, and may dissuade potential claimants from seeking redress. Therefore, the legislation was drafted to provide a justiciable remedy.

13.7.2 The Strict Liability Under the Act

The importance of CPA 1987 in assisting claimants is by establishing the **strict liability** of the manufacturer. The claimant does not have to prove intention or negligence on the part of the defendant, only that there is a causal link between the product and the damage sustained by the claimant. This liability is only removed if a defence can be made under CPA's provisions.

13.7.3 Claims Under the Act

To be successful the claimant must bring their claim within three years of the awareness of the damage or defect in the product (Limitation Act 1980, s. 11A), and they must establish the following criteria:

1. the product contained a defect;
2. the claimant suffered damage;
3. the damage was caused by the defect;
4. the defendant was either a producer, a marketer (own-brander), an importer, or a supplier into the European Union (EU) of the product.

   - *The claimant:* Section 5 defines a claimant as any person who suffers injury to themselves or damage to their private property (CPA 1987 does not extend to business property).
   - *The product:* Section 1 defines a 'product', as the item itself, the packaging, and any instructions; therefore it covers a broad range of claims. However, it must be a product that is ordinarily used for private consumption.
   - *Manufactured products:* This definition includes the components of other products.
   - *Substances won or abstracted:* The products under this section include electricity, water, and gas.
   - *Industrial or other processes:* This includes agricultural products that have been subject to some industrial process.

13.7.3.1 Damage

The types of damage that are included in CPA 1987 are death, personal injuries sustained, and any damage to property that the claimant uses as part of their private consumption. However, CPA 1987 also requires that the damage must exceed a value of £275, which does not include the damage to the product itself. This is to ensure that the courts are not over-whelmed by voluminous cases, and there is a restriction on claims for pure economic loss.

13.7.3.2 The defect in the product

The defect in the product must make it unsafe ('not such as persons generally are entitled to expect'—s. 3) and thereby causes damage to the claimant or their property.

Abouzaid v Mothercare (UK) Ltd [2000]

Facts:

The case involved a child of 12 attempting to fasten a child's sleeping bag to a pushchair manufactured by Mothercare. In attempting to fasten the sleeping bag, Abouzaid had let go of one of the straps (which had a metal buckle on the end) and this caused the strap to retract and the buckle to hit him in the eye. The resulting injury caused him to lose his sight in the eye due to severe damage to his retina. Mothercare attempted to defend the claim on the basis that technical knowledge in the form of accident reports were unavailable at the time, but the Court of Appeal held that this lack of knowledge was irrelevant, and Mothercare was liable.

Authority for:

A defect in a product, for the purposes of s. 3, will be present where there is an identifiable risk, and the defendant could have discovered the danger and the lack of safety of the product before the victim's injury.

In order to be unsafe the product must fall below the standard which a reasonable man would be likely to expect and can be demonstrated in the following:

- *The ordinary use of the product:* The nature of products clearly result in their use being intended, perhaps, for a specific group of the population and the nature of it being unsafe is consequently tested against what may be expected from this group. For example, toys designed for young children would have to include safety considerations of non-toxic paint, sharp edges, and whether the toy contains parts that may be placed in the child's mouth and hence be dangerous. These considerations would be different for products aimed at the adult market, and therefore manufacturers may place age groups on the packaging to limit their potential liability. By stating that a product is intended for '3 years and above', if the product is given to a child below that age and some harm is caused, the manufacturer has a potential defence. If, for example, a child is allowed to have access to dishwasher powder, and they ingest this, then save for a fault with the packaging (such as the child-resistant cap on the bottle), then there is unlikely to be a successful claim under CPA 1987. An adult, who the product is marketed at, would appreciate that the item was not to be eaten, and the adult with responsibility for the child would have to bear the responsibility of enabling access to this material. In *Tesco Stores Ltd v Pollard* the Court of Appeal considered the failures of a claim made under CPA 1987 and the forseeability test where the claim is made through negligence.

- *Packaging and warnings:* Products in isolation may be safe, but if used incorrectly or joined with other products, have the potential to cause injury. An example may be provided through the use of medicines which if used when the claimant is taking other medicines may react badly and cause harm, or if used by a claimant with an allergy to the medicine could lead to serious consequences. Therefore, the defendant will have needed to include instructions and warnings with the product to ensure the claimant was sufficiently aware of any risks or dangers.

- *The issuing of the product:* If the product was issued when it was safe, but it later becomes known that the product is unsafe (such as with drugs which are later known to cause injuries), then the manufacturer will have a defence that at the time of issue the product was deemed safe. It is also the case where products are sold and a shelf life or 'best before' date is included. Using or consuming the product after this date may be at the claimant's own risk.

13.7.3.3 Supply of the product

The product may be supplied through a sale, hire, or gift, or through barter. The supplier must have been acting in the course of their business when doing this, but CPA 1987 clearly extends protection further than the remit of SOGA.

13.7.3.4 The defendant

Section 2 outlines that the following persons may be liable for injury or damage caused wholly or partly by a defect in a product:

- *The producer:* The manufacturer of the product, or the person responsible for the abstracting of the product will constitute a defendant under CPA 1987.

- *The importer:* An importer is the party who has initially imported the product into the EU.

- *The marketer:* An organization that has produced goods with its company name on the label will be treated as a producer of the good.

- *The supplier:* A supplier of a product will be liable if they fail when requested to identify the manufacturer, producer, or importer.

13.7.4 Defences Under CPA 1987

Section 4 outlines the possible defences that can be raised in the event of a claim under CPA 1987:

- *compliance with the law:* if the product complies with the relevant safety standards established in English and EU law, and the defect can be attributed to the standards;

- *non-supply of the product:* if the defendant did not supply the product in the course of their business (if making a product for sale was, e.g., a pastime or hobby);

- *the defect did not exist at the time of supply:* if at the time of the supply of the product the defect did not exist then there will be no liability on the part of the defendant;

- *acceptable risks in development:* there exists a special defence for those defendants who release new products onto the market, and who have used all available research and expertise to minimize any potential risk to the claimant. If, despite these safety standards, the claimant is still injured or property is damaged, the defendant will be able to raise this defence to the action. The rationale for the defence is to allow the producer/manufacturer the ability to develop innovative products which may be of benefit to the public/economy, who would otherwise be dissuaded to do so in fear of a liability action. It remains, however, a very controversial defence, as drugs (e.g.) have entered the market and caused significant health problems for the users, who, if this defence were accepted, would have no recourse under CPA 1987.

13.8 THE OCCUPIERS' LIABILITY ACTS

The Occupiers' Liability Act(s) 1957 and 1984 provide that the occupier of premises owes a duty of care to visitors and to trespassers. Injuries sustained to these visitors due to the failure of the occupier to protect their safety may lead to liability. As most businesses will occupy some premises, the legislation is particularly relevant to them.

There exist obligations (duties to take reasonable care) for occupiers of premises to both lawful visitors and to trespassers. The duty of care (which is a statutory duty rather than in negligence) is to ensure, as far as is reasonable, that the visitor will be safe in using the premises for the purposes for which they are invited to be there. Therefore, the premises have to be reasonably safe, and any claim against the occupier based on this legislation will be assessed in light of the danger that they were exposed to at the premises. In determining this danger, the test of reasonable foreseeability of the risk of injury to the (specific) claimant in the (reasonably expected) use of the premises is adopted (see *Simonds v Isle of Wight Council*).

The legislation relevant to occupiers of premises in this regard is the Occupiers' Liability Act(s) (OLA) 1957 and 1984. The 1984 Act was more restrictive than the 1957 Act in providing that the duty of care to those other than the occupier's visitor was restricted to a danger that the occupier of the premises knows of, or ought to know exists. Further, the occupier must know or ought to know that the trespasser is likely to come onto their land.

13.8.1 The Occupier

The definition of an occupier is provided in OLA 1957, s. 1(2), 'as the persons who would at common law be treated as an occupier'. The common law provides that it is the person who has control over the premises that will be considered the occupier. Lord Denning stated in *Wheat v Lacon* that the occupier may be any person with a degree of control over the state of the premises.

Section 1(3)(a) of OLA 1957 further provides that liability may also be imposed on the occupier of a fixed or moveable structure, and this extends to vessels, vehicles, and aircraft. The liability under this section applies to the danger involved with the structure itself rather than activities associated with the structure. In the event that injury is sustained in the course of activities associated with the structure, then the claim should be made through negligence.

13.8.2 Occupiers' Duties to Visitors

OLA 1957 requires that the occupier of premises takes reasonable care to ensure that a visitor to their premises will be reasonably safe. A visitor is a person who comes onto premises with the express or implied permission of the occupier. Express permission is determined on a question of fact, and simply because the person has been invited onto the premises does not mean that they are invited to all parts of the premises. The lawful visitor may also become a trespasser if they wrongfully use the premises. As expressed by Scrutton LJ in *Owners of SS Otarama v Manchester Ship Canal Co.*: 'When you invite a person into your home to use the staircase, you do not invite him to slide down the banisters, you invite him to use the staircase in the ordinary way in which it is used.' Implied permission may be provided to persons such as those who need access (e.g. reading utility meters) and others, such as postmen, have permission whether expressly invited or not.

The duty to take care provided through OLA 1957, s. 2(2) is 'to take such care as in all the circumstances of the case is reasonable to see that the visitor will be reasonably safe in using the premises for the purposes for which he is invited or permitted by the occupier to be there'. The duty of care required by OLA 1957 and 1984 is tested in accordance with the Compensation Act 2006, ss. 1 and 2. Therefore, the duty is taken with regard to the activities that the visitor is permitted to be on the premises to perform. Examples of the reasonable use of premises have been demonstrated in *Tomlinson v Congleton BC*, and a key feature of the recent judicial decisions has been an expectation of the person to exercise common sense and to take care of their own safety (*Lewis v Six Continents Plc*).

Clearly, the obligation to protect the safety of children visiting premises is greater than adults (s. 2(3)(a)), and the occupier has a duty to ensure that warning notices and barriers offer a sufficient deterrent against danger (s. 2(4)(a)). Where the visitor to the premises does so as part of their job, such as tradesmen (builders, electricians, and so on), they are deemed to have a better understanding of the inherent risks in the pursuit of that activity, than would an ordinary visitor. In *Roles v Nathan (t/a Manchester Assembly Rooms)* two chimney sweeps were killed by carbon monoxide poisoning from a sweep-hole that they were sealing. The sweeps had been warned by the occupier of the premises and an expert employed by him, of the danger from the gas. They had been told not to stay in the hole for too long, and were even physically removed by the expert, but despite this, they sealed the hole while the fire was alight, and subsequently died. The widows of the sweeps brought an action against the occupier, but it was held by the Court of Appeal that they had been given sufficient warnings as to the danger, and this was a danger that they could have been expected to guard against. The occupier may also escape liability where they have reasonably entrusted work to an independent contractor and in the execution of this work the contractor's actions led to the danger that caused loss (s. 2(4)(b)).

Claims under OLA 1957 may be made in respect of personal injury, losses, or damage to property (insofar as it satisfies the requirement of reasonableness). The occupier may raise the defence of contributory negligence (as it is fault-based liability) and *volenti* to an action, but simply because the claimant agrees to a notice or contract term that purports to exclude the defendant's liability will not amount to acceptance of the inherent risk (UCTA 1977, s. 2(3)).

13.8.3 Occupiers' Duties to Non-Visitors

A major extension through the enactment of OLA 1984 was to broaden the common law duty owed to trespassers. It imposes a duty of care on the occupier to trespassers and persons entering land without the permission or consent of the occupier. These are known as non-visitors. This protection is restricted to those exercising a private right of way rather than a public right. The rationale for the legislative protection is that trespasser or not, persons entering land require protection from the hazards and dangers on it, and common humanity required the occupier of premises (who knew or ought to know that trespassers would enter the land) to ensure that the trespassers would not be injured due to the condition of the premises.

The obligation on the occupier is to take reasonable care to ensure that the non-visitor is not injured due to any danger on the premises (s. 1(4)). The obligation may be removed through adequate warnings (s. 1(5)) and protective measures being taken to identify (and minimize) the risk. The occupier owes the duty where:

* they are aware of the danger, or ought reasonably be aware that a danger exists;
* they must be aware, or have reasonable grounds to believe, that the non-visitor is in the vicinity of the danger and may enter the premises (regardless of any lawful right to be in the area);
* the danger must be of a type that it is reasonable to expect the occupier to protect against (s. 1(3)).

The last stage in this list provides the most difficulty in establishing liability and will be tested on the circumstances of each case. The occupier may seek to avoid liability through *volenti* where the injured non-visitor willingly accepts the risks of their actions (s. 1(6)), and s. 1(8) expressly prevents actions for liability in respect of loss or damage to property.

13.8.4 Reducing the Risks

A breach of the legislation may lead to prosecution and, as with breaches of health and safety legislation (of which this may also be a facet), there may be a consequent damage to the reputation of the owner of the premises. As such, the owner of the premises should conduct risk assessments and identify any specific dangers, and the preventative measures that have been taken. For example, the workplace may display notices/signs warning of risks to visitors such as hot water, slippery floors, and low ceilings (marked with highlighting tape).

Depending upon the severity of the defect or the immediacy of the danger, it may be advisable to section off the area to prevent visitors using the affected area(s) and placing themselves in danger. Notices and/or guards could be utilized to prevent accidents (and also it is important to be aware of any visitors to the premises who may suffer a disability and hence the most appropriate measures to protect their safety must be implemented). Examples of mechanisms that could be invoked include the following:

* *Warnings:* The type of danger and the risks can be brought to the attention of visitors through warning signs and notices. These should be clearly displayed and impart the relevant information as simply as possible.
* *Provide information to all workers:* An employer is responsible for the health and safety, not only of their employees, but also any independent contractors who are working at the premises.
* *Maintain buildings:* Ensure that buildings are in a good state of repair, that floors leading into buildings that may become slippery during damp weather have mats/carpeted areas to dry the feet of visitors, that outside routes are kept clear. Keep indoor and outdoor areas suitably lit, provide hand-rails where appropriate, maintain access and exit routes, and so on.

- *Consent:* OLA 1957 enables an occupier to restrict or exclude their duty through an 'agreement or otherwise'. Section 2(1) reads 'An occupier of premises owes the same duty, the "common duty of care", to all his visitors, except in so far as he is free to and does extend, restrict, modify or exclude his duty to any visitor or visitors by agreement or otherwise.' Other exclusions of liability, for example restricting liability for damage to property, may enable the exclusion of liability insofar as it satisfies the requirements of UCTA 1977, s. 2(2).

13.9 BREACH OF STATUTORY DUTY

Whilst it has been identified that the claimant may establish an action in damages against an employer for negligent acts or omissions, and in cases of vicarious liability, they may also have a right to base a claim if the defendant (e.g. an employer) breaches a statutory duty. A typical example of a statutory duty is to protect the health and safety of employees. The employer, under a statutory duty, has an obligation to take actions (such as the duties outlined in the Health and Safety at Work Act (HSWA) 1974) and their failure will enable the employee to establish a plea. It may be possible for a claim by an employee of both **breach of statutory duty** and negligence for breach of the employer's general duty of care, and to claim damages for consequential losses.

13.9.1 Establishing a Claim

The tests to establish a claim of breach of statutory duty are quite similar to those used in negligence:

- the statute places an obligation on the defendant that they owe to the claimant(s);
- the defendant has breached this duty;
- the claimant has suffered a loss as a consequence of the defendant's breach;
- the damage suffered was of a kind contemplated by the statute.

For a claim to succeed, the statute has to provide the right for the claimant to seek damages under the civil law (e.g. the Congenital Disabilities (Civil Liability) Act 1976 enables a child, born disabled as a result of an occurrence before their birth, to bring an action in damages against the person(s) who caused the occurrence). Breaches of health and safety regulations generally allow a claim for breach of a statutory duty. However, HSWA 1974, s. 47 outlines breaches of duties, such as the general duties identified in ss. 2–8, that do not allow a civil law claim for damages. Previously, regulations such as the Provision and Use of Work Equipment Regulations 1998 created a strict liability (Reg. 5) but this has since been removed through the enactment of the Enterprise and Regulatory Reform Act 2013.

An example of these rules impacting on a claim of breach of statutory duty was addressed in *Gorringe v Calderdale MBC* (see **11.5.2.2**). It was held that in a road traffic accident the defendant Council had a statutory obligation to maintain the roads (under the Highways Act 1980) and whilst this was applied to all road users, it could not be used to impose a private duty (from the existing wider public duty) for a specific individual. There was no obligation under the statute that placed a duty on the Council to the claimant, and as such the Council's lack of action could not amount to a breach.

13.9.2 **Defences Available**

As with any claim for damages, defences may be available to reduce any compensation awarded or defeat the claim in its entirety.

13.9.2.1   **The defendant was not negligent**

Facing a claim for compensation, the defendant may raise the defence that they were not negligent and had performed the duties as required by law. The most obvious example of this defence was seen in *Latimer v AEC* (see **11.5.2.2**).

13.9.2.2   **Contributory negligence**

This defence involves the defendant being at fault, but further that the claimant also acted in a way that placed themself in danger (and as such they contributed to the negligent act). For example, an employer has an obligation to protect the safety of employees, but the employee also has a duty to protect their own safety at work. Employees have to use their common sense so as not to injure themselves or others, or place themselves in unnecessary danger (see *O'Reilly v National Rail and Tramway Appliances*). If the employee has contributed to any accident at work, the employer may seek to have any award of compensation reduced. This reduction will be assessed to reflect the claimant's responsibility for their injuries/damage.

13.9.2.3   **Consent**

The defence of *volenti non fit injuria* may be raised in claims of breach of statutory duty, as it may be raised in cases of negligence. If a claimant consents to the risk of being injured, they may not be permitted to claim if they do actually sustain an injury. This defence is available in 'general' negligence cases, but is less available in employment relationships where the employee is required to perform duties at work (see *ICI v Shatwell* discussed in **11.6.2**).

CONCLUSION

This chapter concludes the topic of torts law and demonstrates the importance of an employer being aware of their responsibilities for actions taken during work of employees and even independent contractors engaged for a specific task. Further, employers/managers must have knowledge of their obligations when producing or distributing goods, and their obligations to persons visiting or coming on to business land/property. Substantial claims may exist under the law of torts and a sound understanding of the employer's obligations are required to insure against, and as far as possible limit, such damages actions.

Part 7 of the book moves the discussion to the regulation of the employment relationship and has links with vicarious liability, in defining employee status and how courts have identified the key criteria in determining this issue.

SUMMARY OF MAIN POINTS

Vicarious liability

- Vicarious liability involves a party's responsibility for the torts committed by another.
- In torts law, this generally refers to an employer being held responsible for the torts of their employees.
- An employer is liable for:

- an employee acting negligently in an act that they were authorized to do with care;
- an act necessarily incidental to something that the employee was engaged to do;
- an employee acting in a wrongful way that was authorized by the employer.
- Employers have also been held liable for overtly criminal acts committed by the employee.
- Specific rules identify where vicarious liability will be effective:
  - where the tortfeasor has 'employee' status; and
  - so long as the tort was committed in the employee's 'course of employment'.
- 'Course of employment' has been held to include:
  - providing lifts in works' vehicles;
  - smoking whilst delivering petrol;
  - committing a fraud wholly during employment.
- There is generally no vicarious liability for the torts of independent contractors.
- Exceptions to the rule include:
  - where the employer authorizes or ratifies the tort of the independent contractor;
  - where the employer may not delegate their duty.

Consumer Protection Act

- This Act imposes a strict liability on producers, importers, marketers, and suppliers of goods that are faulty and result in loss or damage.
- That the product has a fault establishes a prima facie case and the defendant has to demonstrate a defence under the Act to avoid liability.
- It establishes much greater protection for consumers than attempting to claim through negligence.

Occupiers' Liability Acts 1957 and 1984

- Occupiers of land owe a duty to take reasonable care to ensure visitors and non-visitors will be safe and not exposed to unreasonable danger.
- The visitor must use the premises for the purposes for which they are invited and must have regard for their own safety.
- Owners/occupiers must ensure that material does not leave their premises that could cause loss/damage (such as smoke obscuring the visibility on the highway).
- Owner/occupiers should use warning signs, physical restrictions, and so on to prevent danger to visitors and non-visitors.

Breach of a statutory duty

- Employers may face claims for damages where they have breached a statutory duty.
- Claims have to satisfy the following tests to be successful:
  - the statute places an obligation on the defendant that they owe to the claimant(s);
  - the defendant has breached this duty;
  - the claimant has suffered a loss as a consequence of the defendant's breach;
  - the damage suffered was of a kind contemplated by the statute.

- Defences to such an action include:
  - that the defendant had performed their duties as required by law (a complete defence);
  - contributory negligence (a partial defence);
  - consent.

SUMMARY QUESTIONS

Essay questions

1. With specific reference to case law, explain the rules establishing the doctrine of vicarious liability. Identify the justifications for the doctrine and assess how many are still appropriate to businesses in the modern era.

2. 'Owners/occupiers of land have unfair responsibilities when it comes to trespassers. If an adult trespasses on land, they take responsibility for their own action and the owner/occupier should not be placed under additional duties to seek their protection.'

   In relation to the duties imposed on owners/occupiers of land by statute and the common law, critically assess the above statement.

Problem questions

1. Nigella wishes to develop her cooking skills and consequently decides to purchase a microwave oven. She visits the Electrical Superstore and purchases a new microwave, which she uses successfully for the first time to cook a meal for her family. The second time she uses the microwave she uses the timer feature. Nigella puts on the timer for 30 minutes, as per the manufacturer's instructions, and leaves her home to visit a friend. When she returns the microwave has set on fire destroying the oven and the food. The fire has also badly damaged the kitchen units on which the microwave oven was placed and her flat screen television (worth over £800). The kitchen is also going to require redecorating due to the smoke from the fire.

   Advise Nigella as to her legal position.

2. Wanda works as an employee at Crazy Hair—a hairdressing salon owned by Jason. Alec comes into the salon to have his hair cut and styled by Wanda. As Wanda begins to dye Alec's hair she accidentally puts too much peroxide in the solution and as it is applied to Alec's hair his scalp is burned, which causes him pain and discomfort. Alec later has a severe reaction to the solution used by Wanda and is hospitalized, which results in Alec missing several days of work as a consequence of the expensive medical treatment he requires.

   Advise Alec of his rights. Advise Wanda and Jason of their liability and any action Jason may take against Wanda.

 You will find guidance about how to answer these questions online at www.oup.com/uk/marson5e/.

FURTHER READING

Books and articles

Brodie, D. (2007) 'Enterprise Liability: Justifying Vicarious Liability' *Oxford Journal of Legal Studies*, Vol. 27, No. 3, p. 493.

Chapman, S. (1934) 'Liability for the Negligence of Independent Contractors' *Law Quarterly Review*, Vol. 50, p. 71.

Faure, M. and Van den Bergh, R. (1989) 'Essays in Law and Economics: Corporations, Accident Prevention and Compensation for Losses' Maklu: Antwerpen.

Howes, V. (2007) 'Liability for Breach of Statutory Duty—Is there a Coherent Approach?' *Journal of Personal Injury Law*, No. 1, p. 1.

Laski, H. J. (1916) 'The Basis of Vicarious Liability' *Yale Law Journal*, Vol. 26, No. 2, p. 105.

McAllister, R. (2006) 'Child-Resistant Bottle Tops and the Consumer Protection Act 1987' *Health & Safety Law*, Vol. 6, No. 2, p. 22.

Netto, A. M. and Christudason, A. (2000) 'Of Delegable and Non-delegable Duties in the Construction Industry' *Construction Law Journal*, Vol. 16, No. 2, p. 88.

Stevens, R. (2007) 'Vicarious Liability or Vicarious Action?' *Law Quarterly Review*, Vol. 123, January, p. 30.

Waite, A. J. (2006) 'Deconstructing the Rule in *Rylands v Fletcher*' *Journal of Environmental Law*, Vol. 18, No. 3, p. 423.

Williams, G. L. (1956) 'Vicarious Liability: Tort of the Master and Servant' *Law Quarterly Review*, Vol. 72, p. 522.

Websites and Twitter links

http:www.legislation.gov.uk/ukpga/Eliz2/5-6/31/contents

The Occupiers' Liability Act 1957.

http:www.legislation.gov.uk/ukpga/1984/3

The Occupiers' Liability Act 1984.

http://www.legislation.gov.uk/ukpga/1987/43

The Consumer Protection Act 1977.

ONLINE RESOURCES

www.oup.com/uk/marson5e/

For further resources relating to this chapter, including self-test questions, an interactive glossary, and key case flashcards.

PART 5
COMPANY LAW

Businesses may trade under various guises. In some instances an individual will operate a business as a sole trader, perhaps they will join with others to form a partnership. Further, the individual may 'incorporate' the business which will then become a company. In each form of trading structure are advantages, disadvantages, and consequences for all involved. It is important to recognize the significance of each trading structure before selecting the most appropriate one in the circumstances. The bureaucracy and regulation of the business is greatly increased when it is incorporated, as are the duties of the personnel involved. This section of the book outlines and discusses the implications of the trading structure selected and through which the business operates.

14 TRADING STRUCTURES AND FORMING THE BUSINESS ENTERPRISE

You are going to start your own business. What form will your business take? Will you operate as a sole trader, go into partnership with others, or form a corporation? Each of these forms of business organization will impact on the responsibilities and duties of the personnel involved, it will have tax implications, and the administration of each will vary. It is only by understanding the advantages and disadvantages of these forms of organization that an informed choice can be made.

Business Scenario 14

In 2014, Abebi established a business specializing in computer repairs and began operating as a sole trader. In January 2016, she incorporated the business and formed IT-Fixers Ltd with a share capital of 10,000 £1 shares. Abebi was issued with all 10,000 shares in consideration of the transfer to the company of her business and its assets.

Abebi continued to insure the business assets in her own name as she had done prior to the incorporation of IT-Fixers Ltd.

In January 2018, following a fire at IT-Fixers Ltd's premises, the building was substantially damaged and the equipment within it was destroyed.

Later, and following the winding up of IT-Fixers Ltd, Abebi intends to start a new business based on her experience in IT by selling biometric door locks. This, Abebi considers, will be the next big thing in home technology and security. After some initial success, Abebi speaks with a lawyer about establishing a limited company under the name Eyesecure Ltd. During this time, Gaagle plc announces the release of its latest biometric locking system with 3D retina scanning to add even more security. Abebi wants to acquire several of these systems as this latest technology will be sought after by her clients. She does not feel able to wait until her new company Eyesecure Ltd is incorporated and enters into an agreement with Gaagle plc for the purchase of 100 systems on the following terms:

> This agreement is entered into on and behalf of Eyesecure Ltd.

During the initial board meeting of Eyesecure Ltd, Abebi ratifies the contract with Gaagle plc. However, later, Gaagle plc refuses to supply the systems as promised as demand has been so high that Gaagle believes it can sell them for a higher price than that agreed with Eyesecure Ltd.

Learning Outcomes

- Explain how a company has its own legal personality (**14.2**)
- Identify the advantages and disadvantages of the various forms of business organization (defined throughout the chapter and in the Summary)

- Explain the process of forming various business organizations (14.3.1; 14.3.2; 14.3.3; 14.3.7–14.3.8.6)
- Compare and contrast a simple partnership and a limited liability partnership (14.3.2–14.3.3)
- Compare the different types of limited company and explain the implications of forming the business organization as a public and private limited company (14.3.5–14.3.6).

14.1 INTRODUCTION

This part of the text considers the various forms of business organization that are available to those who trade. There are many forms that organizations can take, from sole traders, to working in partnerships with others, and the organization may wish to become incorporated and operate as a limited liability partnership (LLP), private limited company, or a public limited company (PLC). Each of these provides advantages and disadvantages to the members of that organization and those who deal with it, and there are implications for a business such as taxation, succession, and regulation.

This chapter focuses on the types of trading structures available, and how they are established. This will provide an overview of the implications of each form of business organization. It will enable an initial assessment of which is most appropriate for the individual/group that wishes to begin trading or who want to vary their existing organizational structure. It should be noted that there is no one model that will suit everyone or every business model. It is very much the decision of the individual, having assessed their business, what they wish to do with the business and how they see it continuing in the future, to determine the form of enterprise chosen. Being aware of the consequences for the business organization is crucial in making this decision.

14.2 LEGAL PERSONALITY

The law recognizes persons having a **legal personality**, which provides them with rights and also subjects them to duties. This enables persons with the appropriate capacity to enter contracts, be subject to criminal laws, and so on. Every human has a legal personality and is known as a natural legal person. Companies, on the other hand, are artificial legal things that are known as **corporations** (when they are incorporated). When incorporated they are recognized in law as having their own legal personality and the most common example of such bodies is a limited company.

Consider

Abebi was running a business as a sole trader before establishing IT-Fixers Ltd. On incorporation, IT-Fixers Ltd becomes the legal owner of the assets of the business transferred to it. Abebi has no legal ownership to these and, as such, cannot insure the assets in her name (she has no insurable interest in the assets).

- *Separate legal personality:* It is essential to recognize that an LLP and limited company have their own legal personality (as recognized at law). The company may enter into contracts, sue, and be sued, and these are rights and duties that are independent of the members of the company (shareholders and directors). This is despite the fact that, clearly, the directors/partners will be performing the actual duties of the corporation in its relations with the outside world. The issue of a company possessing a legal personality was established in the following seminal case.

Salomon v Salomon & Co. Ltd (1897)

Facts:

Mr Salomon had been successfully trading as a sole trader for many years as a leather merchant who produced and sold goods such as shoes and boots. It was then decided that he would change the status of the business and register as a company, and then sell the business to this newly formed company. He duly registered the business and it became incorporated, providing him with a payment of £39,000 for the sale of this business to the company. From this payment, Salomon left £10,000 in the company as his personal loan, and it was intended that this would be paid back to him, therefore he established himself as a secured creditor by taking out a mortgage debenture. Some time later the company had problems in meeting its debts and went into liquidation owing money to Salomon and other creditors. The company only had assets remaining of about £6,000 and Salomon claimed that as a secured creditor. Following an action by the liquidator as to the legality of Salomon establishing himself as a secured creditor, the House of Lords held that he was entitled to the remaining money. As the company had been correctly registered, and there was an agreement between Salomon and the company regarding the loan, as a secured creditor he was entitled to the money before unsecured creditors.

Authority for:

When correctly formed and registered (therefore in accordance with the statutory requirements) a company possesses its own legal personality. This is legally recognized and is separate from the members/directors of the company.

This case established the importance of the limited company, limiting the liability of the members of the company to the shares/money owed to the company. Whilst it may have appeared unfair, the company was correctly registered, and the creditors had been informed of the new status and hence the potential implications for trading with a limited company.

The element of the separate legal personality of the corporation, and its separation from those persons 'running' the business, was demonstrated in *Macaura v Northern Assurance Ltd*.

Macaura v Northern Assurance Ltd (1925)

Facts:

The owner of a timber mill sold his timber to a company of which he and his nominees were the only shareholders. The company owed him money, and he took it upon himself to insure the company's assets, but did so in his own name (rather than through the company). When the timber was destroyed in a fire and Macaura attempted to claim on the insurance policy, he was informed that he had no insurable interest in the company's assets and was thus ineligible to claim.

Authority for:

The company and he were separate legal entities and the insurance should have been made through the company rather than him personally.

Consider

Abebi has insured IT-Fixers Ltd's assets in her own name. Whilst Abebi as the sole proprietor of the company is allowed (*Salomon v Salomon*), the effects of the *Macura* judgment is that the insurance company would not be responsible for the losses of the assets damaged and destroyed in the fire. Abebi stopped having an insurable interest in the premises and assets when they were transferred to IT-Fixers Ltd and Abebi should have transferred the insurance to the company's name and responsibility.

Whilst it is true that companies have a separate legal personality, and this is somewhat similar to a human (a natural person) as regards the ability to form contracts, sue and be sued, and be subject to criminal offences, it does not extend to rights such as rights to vote, or to suffer human emotions (such as suffering injured feelings).

Collins Stewart Ltd v Financial Times Ltd (2005)

Facts:

Following the publication of an article regarding High Court proceedings brought against them, Collins Stewart Ltd sought damages for defamation. The losses claimed for the damage to the company's market capitalization value amounted to over £230 million.

Authority for:

The court refused to award damages on this basis. Beyond the speculative nature of a possible market capitalization value as a basis for the award of damages, the nature of the defamation claim here was regarded by the judge as misconceived and untriable.

- *The veil of incorporation:* Separate legal personality affords a distinction between the corporation as an entity and its directors and shareholders. Further, limited companies have a particular feature: the shareholders have limited liability. The metaphor of the 'veil' identifies a cloak of secrecy/shield of the people behind it—the members of the company are protected from liability for the company's debts. Further, it transpires that due to the company's separate legal personality, the courts have often been unwilling to 'lift the veil' and find out what the directors actually did in running the business (what decisions were taken, and by whom, and so on). Due to this demarcation, it has been said that the veil of incorporation protects the members of the company. Whilst the veil is effective, to continue the metaphor, it has been 'raised' by the courts where it has been deemed relevant. The courts have been notoriously unwilling to establish clear rules as to when the veil will be lifted, and they have stated that they will not do so 'merely' in the interests of justice. Further, where one company owns shares in another (subsidiary companies), insofar as the companies are legally distinct then the courts will not seek to lift the veil.

Adams v Cape Industries Plc (1991)

Facts:

Cape Industries was an English company and the head of a group of companies which mined asbestos in South Africa. It had a subsidiary called Capasco, which itself had a marketing subsidiary based in the United States (US). Claims were brought against the US subsidiary for personal injury associated with working with asbestos and these claims were settled. Later, following a reorganization, there were no assets in the US company and the claimants sought damages from Cape in the UK courts. The Court of Appeal identified that Cape could only be subject to the US jurisdiction if the corporate veil was pierced. This would only occur if Cape was treated as a single economic unit; that it had been established as a façade; or the US subsidiary were the legal agents of Cape.

Authority for:

The rationale for the court refusing to pierce the corporate veil was that the use of corporations with independent subsidiaries to protect the remainder of the group was a legitimate use. The companies had separate boards (and were not a single economic unit); there was no evidence that the subsidiary was established as a sham or a façade; and an agency relationship could not be implied. Thus, the veil would not be lifted to see the workings of the companies.

However, the company must not be established to commit some fraud:

Jones v Lipman (1962)

Facts:

The defendant had entered into a contract for the sale of land but later changed his mind. To avoid the contract, he formed a company of which he was the owner and transferred

→

the land to the company. In refusing to complete the sale, the defendant argued that the land now belonged to the company—a separate legal entity.

Authority for:

The court held the company to be a sham, having been created to avoid the contract for the sale of land. As such, specific performance was made against the owner to compel the sale to be completed.

. . . or to attempt to circumvent contractual agreements:

Gilford Motor Co. Ltd v Horne (1933)

Facts:

The defendant was a managing director of the claimant company and was subject to a restraint of trade clause preventing him soliciting Gilford's customers on leaving the business. When his employment was terminated, Horne formed a company and he stated this company employed him, and he began soliciting the customers of Gilford in breach of the restraining clause. He argued the clause was binding upon him rather than the company, but the Court of Appeal granted an injunction to restrain him from breaching the clause. It lifted the veil to identify the true nature of Horne's role in the company. The court considered the formation of the company to be a sham.

Authority for:

The veil of incorporation separating the company from its members (with regard to the company's separate legal personality) will be lifted by the courts where the company's formation is a device/stratagem to evade the effects of a contractual term. The veil may be lifted where the company is a 'sham' or has been established to perpetrate a fraud.

. . . or the veil will be lifted to identify the true nature of the undertaking (e.g. a 'sham' company).

14.3 TYPES OF BUSINESS ORGANIZATION

Consider

Abebi has initially established a business as a sole trader. What is the extent of her personal liabilities and what risks are present when operating this trading structure?

14.3.1 **Sole Traders**

A sole trader is the simplest business organization due to the ease of establishing and dissolving the business. The person carries on their business as an individual; they personally own the property and assets; they generally perform the work, unless they employ others or subcontracts; and, very importantly, they have unlimited liability for any acts or omissions of the business. They may have a business name, but this does not create a separate legal person as it does for a limited company.

They must conform to the Companies Act (CA) 2006, Part 41, which prohibits, for example, a business name suggesting a connection with central or local government or its agencies without the approval of the Secretary of State (CA 2006, s. 1193).

The sole trader is merely responsible to their customers and the State (such as registration with Her Majesty's Revenue and Customs (HMRC), and registration for Value Added Tax (if applicable)). This ensures the appropriate taxes are paid and the business can be regulated in conformity with the law (such as that presented in this text regarding employment, torts, contract, relevant insurance coverage, and so on). Therefore, there is relatively little external regulation of the business. The sole trader, as a self-employed person, is responsible for their end-of-year taxes being prepared on the basis of a self-assessment form submitted in arrears at the end of January each year (unless otherwise agreed). The taxation of earnings is subject to the provisions of the Income Tax (Earnings and Pensions) Act 2003, whilst the taxation of trading income is subject to the Income Tax (Trading and Other Income) Act 2005.

* *Forming the sole trader business:* As stated above, there are no formal rules regarding the steps to be taken to form such a business enterprise. Insofar as no regulatory requirements exist (such as in professions, including lawyers and accountants) the sole trader may begin to trade immediately. The sole trader may also operate the business in whatever way they wish, as they do not have to ask the permission of partners or seek to change the nature of the business that may have been included in a memorandum of association (as with a corporation).

* *Bringing the sole trader business to an end:* There are very few formalities when ending the sole trader business. Assuming that tasks as contracted to undertake have been completed, and creditors have been paid (along with any associated taxes/duties owed), the sole trader need only inform the relevant authorities of their action to cease trading. Clearly, where the sole trader cannot pay debts associated with the business, there are formalities to do with bankruptcy proceedings (but these are not discussed in this text).

14.3.2 **Partnerships**

A person may wish to form a business enterprise, and may seek to achieve this by forming a partnership with others. There may be many reasons why a partnership may be sought. The partners may complement each other by each offering expertise in some area, they could establish new markets (such as a builder, plumber, and electrician forming a partnership to build houses), new partners may be brought in to introduce capital without obtaining a bank loan, or partners may be able to offer additional help in running the business. As such, they may decide to establish a 'simple' partnership. The most common type of partnership is an unlimited partnership, where the partners are responsible for the debts/liabilities of the firm and must satisfy these from their own assets if required. The partners simply have to agree to form the partnership (hence it need not be in writing (although this may be wise) and it may be formed through verbal agreements or implied through conduct).

A partnership may also trade as a limited partnership under the Limited Partnerships Act 1907. This simply requires one of the partners to agree to accept full liability for any debts if the partnership is unable to satisfy its obligations (while the other partners' loss is restricted to any capital/property invested). The 'limited' partner must also not have any part in the management of the firm or they will lose the 'limited' status and be liable with the other partners for any debts or liabilities. These types of partnerships are not often used as a form of business organization but are more likely to be seen in the formation of collective investment schemes. Since 2000, a firm can be established as a Limited Liability Partnership (LLP):

- *Types of partner:* Generally, there are four types of partner in a partnership:
  - Under the Partnership Act 1890, s. 24 the 'typical' partner is one who has the right to take part in the management of the firm (unless specifically agreed to the contrary).

  - A 'silent'/dormant partner may come into the firm who, by their nature, invests money into the partnership but who does not take an active role in the management.

  - A firm may usually require a partner to join in the partnership by making some investment and 'buying into' the firm. However, it is possible, and used by some professional firms such as lawyers and accountants, for a person to join the partnership as a salaried partner. They do not have the rights and obligations of the other partners, and is essentially treated as an employee, but appears on the firm's letterheads.

  - Where the partner allows their name to be used by the partnership, such as on the letterhead of the firm to add to its credibility with outside bodies, the partner may be a partner by estoppel. The Partnership Act 1890, s. 14 provides that where a person, through their words (spoken or written) or conduct, either represents themselves as, or knowingly allows themselves to be represented as a partner of the firm, they are liable as if they were a partner of the firm to anyone who contracted with the firm (such as providing credit/money).

Similarly with sole trader business organizations, a partnership is simple to create and to dissolve (there are no specific formalities or registration), there is little external regulation (although HMRC must be informed that the self-employed person is a partner rather than a sole trader) other than that already identified for sole traders, and partnerships can commence trading immediately. The partnership is restricted in the choice of business name, and whilst a partnership may use the word 'company' in its business name, it must not identify itself as a limited company or use the initials 'Ltd' and 'Plc' as these are restricted to those organizations that have followed the appropriate registration requirements. The tort of passing-off is also applicable to the business name of the partnership.

Partnerships are two or more persons who come together, and act in common, to form (or with a view to form) a business 'with a view of profit'.

Khan v Miah (2001)

Facts:

The individuals involved agreed to set up a restaurant business. They engaged in pre-
paratory activities including opening a joint bank account, they obtained a loan, bought
premises and equipment, and advertised the new venture. However, before they began
trading, one individual no longer wished to continue with the business. The other continued and when they obtained profits, the first individual attempted to obtain a share
in the business capital and profits. The question for the court was whether there was a
partnership in existence?

Authority for:

The House of Lords concluded that parties to a joint venture became partners in the firm
when it engaged in activities that were part and parcel of what the parties had agreed
to do. It did not have to actually begin trading for the partnership to become effective.

This is of crucial importance in that whilst the Act states that the partner joins with a view
to a profit, this does not mean that having not shared in any profits they do not qualify
as a partner.

M Young Legal Associates Ltd v Zahid (2006)

Facts:

A solicitor in a law firm was paid a fixed amount, but had no entitlement to share in the
firm's profits. A question was raised as to his status as a partner.

Authority for:

The solicitor was a partner of the firm. There was no minimum threshold as to a person's
rights to receive profits or their involvement in management before they can be considered a partner. The test is whether, in accordance with their actions, the parties had
meant a partnership was to be created.

- *Identification of partners:* The names of the partners must be shown on the letterheads
  (and when a business name is used which is different from the true surnames of the
  partners). This is a requirement identified in CA 2006, and applies in the same way
  as to all business organizations with regard to the choice of business name, and the
  correct identification of the partners/members.
- *Partnership property:* When a partnership is formed the partners each own the property of the partnership. The Partnership Act 1890, ss. 20 and 21, identifies that, in
  the absence of any agreement between the partners to the contrary, property will
  be considered partnership property where it had been purchased with partnership
  money, the partner who brought property into the firm had been credited with its
  value, or where it is treated as an essential part of the firm's property. Hence, when

the business is dissolved, the partners will take back the property they brought to the firm. However, if the firm is dissolved owing money to creditors, the creditors have the right to realize partnership assets before the partners can 'take back' property introduced into the business.

- *Partnership ratio:* It is worthy of note that where, for example, two people are intending to join together to form a partnership, it is wise not to arrange it on a 50/50 ratio split. Where the two partners have an equal share of, and right to manage, the firm, inevitably a situation will arise where one of the partners wishes to follow a route (e.g. expanding the business), whilst the other partner is more cautious and does not agree with the strategy (and potential risks). As neither partner has the power to force the decision, the partnership may come to an end with such a disagreement (with the consequent problems entailed).

- *Partners as agents:* Partners are considered agents of the organization under s. 5 of the Partnership Act 1890 for the purpose of the partnership's business (this means that the organization is bound by the actions of the partner if the partner has acted in a way that is consistent with the kind of business normally carried out by the organization). This enables the partners to manage the organization, contract on behalf of the firm, and obligate the other partners as a result of this action (as agents). Such authority enables a partner to obligate the firm in the sale of the firm's goods, to purchase goods that would normally be purchased on behalf of the firm, to pay the debts of the firm, and to hire workers. They, therefore, will bind the other partners and the firm in (lawful) agreements that they have concluded. This means that even if a partner does not have the actual authority to perform such actions, they may still bind the partnership under 'apparent' authority (see **18.3.2**). The reason why partners may be held liable for the actions of another partner is to protect the public, who may not be aware of the internal power relations within the organization. It is generally accepted that partners can buy and sell goods, take money on behalf of the firm, and issue receipts for transactions in the name of the partnership. These rights regarding transactions of this type are more 'securely' granted on partners in a firm that trades as its object, rather than professional firms (such as accountants) whose partners may not readily exercise such authority.

- *Liability of partners:* A crucial aspect of partnerships is of joint and several liability. Section 9 of the Partnership Act 1890 includes such liability for debts or contracts (as extended under the Civil Liability (Contributions) Act 1978), and s. 10 applies the liability for torts committed in the normal course of business (outside of the normal course of business the individual partner is held responsible (*Hamlyn v Houston and Co.*)).

Hamlyn v Houston and Co. (1905)

Facts:

An aspect of the defendant's business was to obtain commercial information relating to its competitors. Houston, a partner of the firm, obtained confidential information on Hamlyn by bribing one of its employees. The activities associated with obtaining this information were contrary to the defendant's instructions. In a claim for damages for the losses sustained by Hamlyn, it sued the company rather than the partner at fault.

→

Authority for:

The defendant company was held jointly vicariously liable for Houston's actions. The obtaining of information through lawful means was part of Houston's role at the firm and thus, accordingly, gathering the information through unlawful means was also within this scope of his authority.

This means that if one partner commits a tort or crime in the course of the business, the partnership will be liable (including each partner) if this was within the offending partner's actual or apparent authority.

Dubai Aluminium Co. Ltd v Salaam (2003)

Facts:

A solicitor was alleged to have been involved in dishonest practice in the drafting of documents. As a result, damages were sought not only from him but his fellow partners.

Authority for:

It was held that as the (dishonest) actions of the solicitor were so closely connected with those he would be expected to undertake in his ordinary role, they must be considered to have been undertaken in the ordinary course of his business. The other partners were thus jointly liable. Nothing in the Partnership Act 1890 excluded liability for acts in torts or deceit.

This results in the partners being held responsible for any losses incurred whilst they are partners. If the partnership owes a debt to a creditor and there are no resources of the organization to pay this, then under the concept of unlimited liability, the partners have to satisfy the shortfall from their own resources. This liability will be shared equally between the partners based on their respective percentage ownership. However, if one partner has resources and the other partner(s) does not have the resources to satisfy the debt, the partner with funds is responsible for the full debt (Partnership Act 1890, s. 9). They then have the responsibility/option to seek the money owed from the defaulting partner(s). This liability cannot be imposed on a partner for acts that occurred before they entered the partnership (Partnership Act 1890, s. 17). However, the liability continues even when the partner has left the partnership for acts conducted whilst they were a partner. It is therefore important to be aware of the person(s) who may become partners and there are several express and implied terms (obligations) on partners as to information they must disclose to potential partners.

- *Forming a partnership:* Establishing a partnership is very simple and can amount to an agreement between like-minded people to form a business with a common goal. It is always preferable, however, when forming an agreement that has the potential implications for the partners as identified above, to create a contractually binding agreement. This is referred to as the 'partnership agreement' and identifies for what purpose the partnership is being established, for how long (if a time is identified) the partnership should remain in existence, the names of the partners, the business address where official documentation is to be sent, the percentage ownership and distribution of profits of each partner, the authority for participating in the management of the partnership (if sleeping partners are included), and the responsibilities of each partner.

If new partners are to be included in the partnership (to increase expertise, introduce money, and so on), there has to be agreement between the existing partners for this to take effect (s. 24(7) and (8)). This right does not apply to partners who are retiring and its aim is simply to ensure that due to the unlimited liability nature of the business, and the need for the firm to work to a common goal (not to mention the duties on partners that will affect the working relationships of the partners), the new partners are accepted by all other partners who may be affected by their actions.

14.3.2.1   Duties on partners

There exists in partnerships a fiduciary duty for the partners to act with loyalty to the partnership and in 'good faith'. The Partnership Act 1890 also creates duties on the partners in the following ways:

* *Duty of disclosure:* Section 28 obligates partners to submit full information to the other partners or their legal representatives in matters affecting the organization and to submit true accounts.
* *Duty to account:* Section 29 obligates partners to account for any benefit they have obtained without consent from any transaction on behalf of the firm.

Bentley v Craven (1853)

Facts:

Mr Craven was a partner along with three others in a sugar refinery business. He was responsible for purchasing and, on his own account, bought sugar which he later sold to the partnership at the market price. He failed to declare his interest in the contract to the other partners.

Authority for:

Craven was liable to account to the other partners for the profits made on the contract.

---

* *Duty not to enter into competition with the organization:* Section 30 obligates a partner, who is competing with the partnership without the consent of the other partners, to account to those partners for any profits or benefit produced in the course of that business.
* *Relationship based on good faith:* The partnership agreement is a contract based on the utmost good faith. As such, partners must disclose relevant details to other partners (and prospective partners) that could affect the partnership. Therefore, a person's silence can amount to a misrepresentation.

14.3.2.2 The rights of partners

The Partnership Act 1890 provides the following rights (unless expressed to the contrary in the partnership agreement):

- the right to share equally in the capital and profits of the firm;
- the right to be indemnified by the firm for any liabilities or losses made in the normal course of business;
- the right to take a role in the management of the firm (but not 'sleeping partners');
- an entitlement to inspect the partnership's accounts and to have these available when requested;
- the right to veto the entry of a new partner to the partnership or to change the partnership's business.

14.3.2.3 Bringing the partnership to an end

The partnership may be dissolved on the agreement of the partners (s. 32(c)), or on lapse of time (s. 32(a)), or when a specific task for which the partnership was created has been completed (s. 32(b)). It may also be dissolved on the death or bankruptcy (s. 33(1)) of any partner or where there has been illegality on behalf of the partnership (s. 34). Illegality can occur where the nature of the business was unlawful (such as *Everet v Williams*); and where the partners cannot form a partnership to conduct an otherwise lawful action (such as the case of a solicitor allowing their practice certificate to lapse).

Everet v Williams (1725)

Facts:

The parties were highwaymen who entered into a partnership to share the proceeds from their criminal activities. An argument arose between the two regarding the share of the proceeds and this led Everet to bring a claim for damages against Williams.

Authority for:

Here the action for damages was dismissed due to its basis being on the criminal activities of the parties. Further, the court fined the lawyers representing the parties and required them to pay the court costs for having brought such a case.

The Partnership Act 1890 continues to identify events affecting the partners that lead to the partnership being brought to an end. These include if a partner becomes a patient under the Mental Capacity Act 2005, if they suffer some permanent form of incapacity (s. 35(b)), if the partner wilfully or persistently breaches the partnership agreement (s. 35(d)), where the business can only be continued at a loss (s. 35(e)), and where it is just and equitable to end the partnership (s. 35(f)). When the business has been brought to an end and the property owned by the partnership is realized, the resources are used to first pay any liabilities, then the partners who have loaned money to the firm are paid back, the capital contribution of the partners is paid, and the remainder is shared on the basis of the percentage of the partnership which each partner 'owned'.

If a partner decides to leave a solvent partnership that intends to continue trading, upon their leaving, the partner will be entitled to their share of the partnership, and the remaining partner(s) will have to generate the money to provide the settlement. This is often a key concern and disadvantage of partnerships as partners may die, and they often disagree about the business and might feel compelled to leave.

14.3.3 Limited Liability Partnerships

As noted, the partners in simple partnerships (unless in limited partnerships) have unlimited liability for the debts of the firm. The enactment of the Limited Liability Partnerships Act 2000 changed this situation, and a partnership created under the Act will be considered a separate legal entity, with its own legal personality. The LLP must be registered with the Registrar of Companies and whilst it has unlimited liability for any debts and liabilities, the individual partners of the LLP have limited liability. This will result in the partners losing any investment into the LLP if it is wound up and insolvent, but they will not be liable for losses beyond this contribution.

As the LLP has its own legal personality, contracts and obligations will be created with the LLP rather than the individual partners. The property of the LLP will also belong to the partnership instead of to the partners. This situation has further advantages over the simple partnership model. As partnerships have to contain at least two individuals, if, in a simple partnership of two partners, one was to die, then the partnership would come to an end (or a new partner(s) has to be found). With LLPs, the partnership will continue despite changes to its internal membership and it will continue until formally wound up. Typically, professional firms have taken the opportunity to become LLPs where the nature of their profession involves the risk of liability claims (such as negligence) that may expose the partners to risk, if the partnership could not settle any award.

The LLP is required to file its audited accounts and tax returns to the Registrar of Companies and the incorporation document must identify 'designated members' who will administer these and other matters on behalf of the LLP. The taxation of the partners will be based on the simple partnership model, and the individual partners are responsible for their 'share' of the tax due, rather than this being placed on the LLP itself. The partners will have to disclose their proportion of the profits in the annual returns to the Registrar (Limited Liability Partnerships Regulations 2001).

* *Forming an LLP:* To form an LLP, the incorporation document and a statement of compliance must be filed with the Registrar of Companies, who will then issue a certificate of incorporation if the documentary requirements have been satisfied. Having received this certificate, the LLP can begin to trade, although, to do so before the certificate is issued may result in the partners being held liable as they would under the Partnership Act 1890. The Registrar must be informed of the members of the LLP, who will maintain a register, and the Registrar must also be informed when new members join and others leave.

It is imperative when forming the LLP that the partners establish an agreement that incorporates issues regarding the purpose of the business, the capital in the firm and how profit and losses are to be distributed between the members, the requirements of meetings and voting rights, how new members will be allowed to join, the procedures for the retirement of members, and so on. The requirement for an agreement is even more prominent when it is remembered that LLPs are regulated somewhat similarly to companies, only there is no default standard set of 'model articles' that exist for companies under CA 2006.

This document is private, is not subject to public scrutiny, and does not need to be sent to the Registrar of Companies. Hence, those who are trading with the LLP have no actual mechanism (beyond asking to see the agreement) to identify the internal structure of the members' responsibilities and rights.

*   *Bringing the LLP to an end:* The LLP continues in existence until it is formally dissolved, as it possesses its own legal personality irrespective of its members. LLPs can be wound up through their insolvency and, as such, procedures may be established for voluntary arrangements, administration orders, receivership, and liquidation. Section 214A of the Insolvency Act 1986 has been beneficial to creditors to the LLP in that members who have made withdrawals in the previous two years before the winding-up may be requested to return these sums if during that period the member knew, or ought reasonably to have known, that the LLP would become insolvent. Section 74 of the Act ensures that members of the LLP and those members that have left, and who had established an agreement to contribute to the LLP upon dissolution, will contribute to the assets of the firm.

14.3.4 **Formation of a Company**

This section considers the types of companies and the methods of formation (or incorporation) that have to be satisfied. Due to the complexity of the topic, this introductory chapter identifies some important features that will be considered in greater depth in **Chapters 15–17**.

*   *The Registrar of Companies and Companies House:* The Department for Business, Innovation & Skills is the department where most of the laws relating to businesses generally will be considered, consulted upon, and advanced through Parliament. It has a section dealing with the registration of companies and it ensures compliance with the requirements established under legislation, including CA 2006, and is called Companies House. This is where the public can find out information regarding companies and their directors (details are available for public inspection), and the 'Registrar of Companies' heads this department. The Registrar is responsible for the issuing of certificates of incorporation when a company is registered, when the company's name is changed, and where the company is re-registered. It lists the details of all registered companies, limited partnerships, and LLPs; holds the annual returns and accounts submitted by companies as required by law; and maintains the details of charges over company property. It may strike companies off the register when dissolved, holds the register of a company's special and extraordinary resolutions, and publishes details of the companies and the receipt of documents in the London Gazette (this is the weekly supplement of the publication of The Stationery Office that identifies public notices such as bankruptcies and liquidations of corporations).

*   *Unlimited companies:* Very few companies are registered as unlimited companies as the members of the company have unlimited liability, and this significant protection for the members through incorporation is lost. An advantage of trading as an unlimited company is that its accounts are not made public and do not have to be submitted to the Registrar of Companies. However, these are somewhat weak reasons to establish the corporation on this basis, particularly in respect of the deregulation of limited companies through CA 2006. The liability of members exists in situations where the company is wound up, rather than to the company's creditors. Clearly though, where

the company does not have sufficient funds to satisfy its debts, the company will be wound up and the members of the company are liable on the basis of the nominal value of the shares held. If no share capital is held, then the members will be liable on an equal basis, and held jointly and severally liable.

• *Limited companies:* This is a very popular form of business enterprise and the changes introduced in CA 2006 remove many of the administrative procedures that were required under the Companies Act 1985. The two main types of limited companies are private limited companies and public limited companies, and this will be identified upon registration through the memorandum of association. It may be thought that only large organizations are corporations, but of course the majority are small and medium-sized enterprises, with just a few shareholders. The majority of companies formed are limited by shares and this identifies that the members of the company (the shareholders) are responsible for the nominal/par value of the shares they own if the company is wound up. The second example of a limited company is one that is limited by guarantee (usually a method chosen by charitable institutions rather than 'businesses'). The 'guarantee' in this respect is a determined amount, established in the memorandum (and possibly in the articles as well), which is to be paid when the company is wound up. Upon being wound up, the sums guaranteed have to be paid to satisfy the company's debts, and where this amount is insufficient in relation to the debt, those members that left within a year of the company's winding-up can be requested to contribute their guarantee in relation to the debts that occurred whilst they were members.

• *Corporations sole:* The very nature of a company, when compared to a sole trader for example, is that it conjures images of a number of persons joining together to run a business. Whilst this may be the case, a corporation may involve just one person (member). This was typically seen where the bishop or vicar of a parish had a vested interest in the church land, but when he died, the land technically had no owner until the clergyman's successor was found. In response to this, it was established by common law that the office of the bishop/vicar was a corporation with the present incumbent the sole member. Consequently, when the clergyman died, this did not affect the status of the corporation; the land still belonged to the corporation, and the next bishop/vicar simply became the new 'sole member'.

Consider

Abebi has not incorporated her second business before entering a contract with Gaagle plc. Is it possible to trade under the company name prior to its incorporation? Are directors allowed to ratify an agreement made prior to the company's existence?

14.3.5 Features of a Limited Company

When determining the form of business organization, a corporation, being a separate entity from its members, provides advantages to those members, and also empowers the company to take actions, accept liabilities, and so on, that other business organizations may not. Therefore, some of its more important features are identified below:

- *Limited liability:* Always remember that the 'limited' element of this type of organization refers to the potential liability of members of the company—the shareholders. The company itself has unlimited liability and therefore must satisfy any debts to creditors. If there are insufficient funds and assets to pay the creditors when the debts are called in, the money that is available in the company (its money, property, stock, and so on) will be made available to creditors depending upon their status. The shareholders have their liability for any debts of the company limited to the value they paid for the shares (which will become worthless as the company will be wound up) or the money they owe on any shares (shares do not necessarily have to be fully paid for when issued). It provides protection for the shareholders as to the liability they are exposing themselves to, but also imposes a risk for those trading with the limited company that they may not be able to seek owed money from those who ran or owned the business.

- *Perpetual succession:* One of the drawbacks with trading as a sole trader is that when the sole trader dies, the business may die with them. With a partnership of two people, where one dies another partner has to be found or the firm wound up or run as a sole trader/registered as a corporation. The advantage to the limited company is that once established, it will remain in existence until it is legally wound up, regardless of who owns or runs the company. Therefore, when shareholders leave the company, a director dies/leaves the organization, and so on, this has no effect on the company's assets or ability to continue trading. As businesses invest time and resources establishing a reputation (trustworthy image, reputation for a quality service/products, and so on), the ability to continue this 'brand image' when the company is sold or other directors take charge of its operation and direction is a significant advantage.

- *Raising finance:* It has been argued that a limited company may be able to raise capital investment and finance more easily than can a sole trader and a partnership. The sole trader and partnership will generally have to secure loans from a lending institution through a charge over the assets (providing collateral). Due to the increased regulation and reporting duties imposed on limited companies, and the controlled use of funds, lenders may be more willing to make loans to improve a business. There is the further benefit of being able to transfer/sell shares to generate income that may be used, and, unlike a loan, this does not have to be paid back.

- *Contractual capacity:* (Due to its separate legal personality) the company may establish contracts in its own right and enforce contracts when the other party is in breach, although a director of the company must physically undertake this.

- *Taxation:* Taxation of companies' profits may be more beneficial than personal income tax. This, evidently, is a simplification of a very complex area, and requires greater detailed examination than can be provided in this text, but tax has to be paid on taxable profits. Income tax (applicable to sole traders and partnerships) is charged (for 2017/18) at 20 per cent (the starting rate after exceeding the 'personal allowance'), rising to 40 per cent (the higher rate) where the person's income is in the band £33,500–150,000, and 45 per cent (the additional rate) for incomes over £150,000. The main corporation tax is charged at 19 per cent. Hence, it may prove advantageous to trade as a limited company to benefit from the levels of taxation.

- *Administration:* Whereas the sole trader and partnership are largely accountable to themselves, their partners (where relevant), the client/customer, and HMRC, the limited company has much greater administrative burdens that are required through CA

2006. This may include submitting company accounts to Companies House as required and holding an Annual General Meeting (AGM) (although this is not required for private companies). These are not applicable to sole traders/partnerships and as such they are a more 'simple' way of trading.

- *The ability to own property:* A company has the ability to own property irrespective of the composition of the shareholders. The person who forms the company may introduce property to it (e.g. houses in a property rental business). If the person owns this property in their own right, and then 'gives' it to the company, they are owed the money of the value of the property passed over to the company and, whilst stamp duty may be applicable, the person who formed the company will be able to receive the value of the property back from the company. However, the property is no longer owned by the person who gave/sold it to the company; rather it legally belongs to the company. Such assets may be used to raise finance.

- *Commit criminal offences:* It is possible for a company to commit a criminal offence (through the criminal intent (*mens rea*) of the directors).

R v ICR Haulage Ltd (1944)

Facts:

The managing director and the haulage company had committed offences and were convicted of conspiracy to defraud. However, the defendants had argued that the company should not be convicted of an offence which required *mens rea*.

Authority for:

That the actions in the case emanated from the company's managing director, as he was effectively the company's 'directing mind', the company was equally responsible with its managing director.

This has particularly been effective in cases of the manslaughter of persons, where the directors of companies may be convicted and imprisoned on the basis of their actions (health and safety laws are instrumental in this aspect of the law). See the online resources for a discussion of the Corporate Manslaughter and Corporate Homicide Act 2007 regarding the criminal actions of directors and organizations.

14.3.6 Distinctions Between Public and Private Companies

A Public Limited Company (PLC) is entitled to offer its shares and debentures for sale to the public and it may be listed on the London Stock Market (although due to the rules in which companies may be listed this is only applicable to the largest organizations). A private company is prohibited from offering its shares to the public (CA 2006, s. 755). Shares do not have to be paid for in full on allocation but, with a PLC, the shares must be paid for when requested (such as upon its winding-up). This must be in the form of money or assets, but when assets are provided, the value must be independently assessed by an auditor to ensure they represent the value of the owed amount and that a fraud is not being committed on the business. **Table 14.1** sets out the advantages and disadvantages

Table 14.1 The advantages/disadvantages of the trading structures

Business organization	Advantages	Disadvantages
Sole trader	It is simple to establish	The sole trader has unlimited liability
	The sole trader is responsible to their customers	Succession. The sole trader often trades under their own name; however, when the sole trader dies, their business may also die
	The sole trader has autonomy in how they run the business, when they work, and how profits are disposed of (subject to HMRC rules)	They have complete responsibility for the business—to fulfil contracts, to invest money into the business, to employee replacement if they are ill or on holiday, and so on
	They can begin trading immediately	
Partnership	Partners often 'buy into' a partnership, therefore capital is often introduced	Partnerships have unlimited liability and the partners' personal assets may be at risk for debts/losses
	Partners may offer expertise in an area or provide the ability to enter into new markets	Partners may create liabilities for the other partners and the firm
	Partners may share the work of the business and share the liabilities	Partners share in the profits of the firm, therefore the individual partner's share may be reduced
	Partners have several legal advantages including the ease of formation and it can be quickly dissolved, and it may provide tax advantages in certain circumstances	Partners may be jointly and severally liable for losses
Limited Liability Partnership	The LLP has its own legal personality and limits the liability of its members	It is subject to registration procedures with the Registrar of Companies
	The partnership continues despite changes in the internal membership of the firm	It must file accounts and tax returns to the Registrar
		It has many features in common with limited companies, some of these are positive to the members and many have negative implications
Limited companies	Limited liability for the members	It has much greater administration requirements than other forms of business organizations
	It has perpetual succession and only 'dies' when formally wound up	It is subject to external and internal regulation
	It is generally easier to raise finance than through a sole trader/partnership business organization	There is no automatic right to participate in the management of the company

(Continued)

Table 14.1 The advantages/disadvantages of the trading structures (cont.)

Business organization	Advantages	Disadvantages
	It can make contracts in its own right	
	Tax benefits are available for corporations compared to other business organizations	
	The company may offer fixed/floating charges over property	
	Companies may be formed in the belief that the 'status' of a limited company provides an advantage over operating as a sole trader	

of the various trading structures and **Table 14.2** shows a comparison between private and public companies.

The private company has become much less regulated and hence more favourable to those who run businesses than before. For example, there is no statutory requirement for a private company to hold any general meeting; there is no limit on the private company's share capital; and it need only have one shareholder, with no need for a company secretary. Private companies may also pass written resolutions without the need to hold a meeting. A PLC also only requires one member, but it does require a secretary and they must be qualified for the position (a solicitor, accountant, or someone who has three years'

Table 14.2 Comparison of private and public companies

Private company	Public company
Its name must end with the words 'Ltd' or 'Limited'	Its name must end with the words 'Public Limited Company' or 'PLC'
A private company is prohibited from offering its shares to the public (CA 2006, s. 755)	A PLC is entitled to offer its shares and debentures for sale to the public and it may be listed on the London Stock Exchange (although due to the Exchange's rules about which companies may be listed this is only applicable to the largest organizations)
A private company is not required to have a secretary (and if a private company chooses to have one they do not have to be qualified)	A PLC requires a secretary and they must be qualified for the position
There is no necessity to hold an AGM	The PLC must hold an AGM each calendar year
'No minimum share capital is prescribed'	The PLC must have an allotted share capital of £50,000 (one quarter of the value of which must have been paid up)
Only one director is required	At least two directors are required
It can pass written resolutions	It cannot pass written resolutions

experience of being a public company secretary). The PLC may not be unlimited and must have an allotted share capital of £50,000 (one-quarter of the value of which must have been paid up—most shares are paid for in full as soon as they are bought but this is not always required, although on winding-up, any outstanding money must be paid) and this information has to be sent to the Registrar. Without this information a trading certificate will not be issued and if one is not requested within one year of incorporation, an application may be made for its compulsory winding-up. Without a trading certificate, the company may not trade, but if it does, the directors of the company may be held liable (on the same basis as with a partnership) for any debts/liabilities incurred. The PLC must hold an AGM each calendar year.

- *Size of the company:* Companies are identified on their size and this has implications for the documents to be submitted to the Registrar. Companies identified as small have to satisfy two or more of the following requirements in a financial year (as amended by S.I. 2008/393):

  - a turnover of not more than £10.2 million;
  - a balance sheet total of not more than £5.1 million;
  - not more than 50 employees (as a weekly/monthly average).

However, the small companies regime does not apply to PLCs or a company that is an authorized insurance company, a banking company, an e-money issuer, a MiFID (S.I. 2007/2932) investment firm, an UCTIS management company, or a member of an ineligible group. The small company regime allows for abridged accounts to be submitted to the Registrar (although members have the right to be provided with full accounts but may agree to be sent 'summary of financial statements' instead (s. 426)). The advantage of this provision is that sensitive information, such as the salaries of directors, the directors' report, and a profit and loss account, need not be submitted.

A medium-sized company has similar rights to submit abridged accounts where it satisfies two of the three following requirements in a financial year:

- a turnover of not more than £36 million;
- a balance sheet total of not more than £18 million;
- not more than 250 employees (as a weekly/monthly average).

14.3.7 Establishing the Limited Company

There are three methods of establishing the limited company—either through Royal Charter, statute, or (most commonly and applicable to this text) through registration.

- *Royal Charter:* This is a mechanism for establishing companies, but as one can imagine, it will not be established for the means of trading (where registration under the Companies Act is more relevant). Examples of the Royal Charter being used to establish a company can be seen in the British Broadcasting Corporation, and universities such as Oxford and Cambridge. The Privy Council is the body that would establish a company in this manner.

- *Statute:* Statutes have been used to create corporations, such as the utilities, where, upon privatization, their status had to be altered as they were no longer owned by the State and did not possess the powers that the State did in relation to the purchase of land and so on. As such, these bodies were registered as PLCs. Statute has also been used to establish bodies such as the Health and Safety Executive, which regulates health and safety inspections and was established through the Health and Safety at Work etc. Act 1974.

* *Registration:* The most common and, in relation to the three forms available, the simplest way to form a company is through registration with the Registrar of Companies.

14.3.8 Procedures of Registration

When a company is formed in the UK, the Registrar of Companies must be sent the memorandum of association, the articles of association, and a completed Form IN01, along with the appropriate registration fee (£12 for online applications and £40 for paper-based applications), by the founding member(s) (also known as the **subscribers**). If the Registrar is satisfied the documents are correct, a certificate of incorporation is issued, identifying the company with its registered number, and the new company will be noted in the *London Gazette*. If the registrar is not satisfied that the documents are correct, or suspects the company is being established for some unlawful means, they can refuse to register the company, and the subscribers have an opportunity to appeal the decision.

14.3.8.1 The memorandum

The memorandum is a document available for public inspection and its aim is to identify the features of the company. It is not intended to form part of the company's constitution as it previously had, but rather to identify the company when it was formed. Essentially, this was an attempt to simplify the provision of company law and to provide the details of the constitution of companies in one document. Hence, the memorandum is almost supplementary to the articles of association (s. 28) and unless the company specifically restricts the remit of the objects of the company, its objects are unrestricted (s. 31(1)). The elements that establish the memorandum include:

* *Its name:* There are restrictions on the choice of business name that a company may use, and the use of words and symbols in the name (CA 2006 provides in s. 57 for the Secretary of State to prohibit the use of words that may make the tracing of a company difficult), and guidance is provided through Companies House. From 1 September 2011, Companies House will no longer accept company names on documents that contain minor variations and/or typographical errors. A list of acceptable abbreviations is provided on its website. Evidently, a company may not choose the same name as another company (a directory exists for the purposes of checking); nor may a name be used that is likely to cause offence, or one that infers a connection with local or central government. When a name is selected, it is registered on a 'first come, first served' basis and therefore names cannot be saved (as such it is recommended that electronic copies of forms be submitted to speed up the process). The name must end in Ltd or Limited where it refers to a private limited company (or its Welsh equivalent if the company is based there) or PLC (or the Welsh equivalent) in relation to a public limited company, and this must be published on company documents. This name must be displayed outside of the registered office, and placed on all company stationary, invoices, receipts, and so on (these materials must also include the company's registration number). The name of the company may be changed through a special resolution, or through a written resolution of a private company, or other means provided for in the articles (CA 2006, s. 77). The Registrar must be informed of such changes and will then issue a new certificate of incorporation.

* *The registered office:* The company must identify an address where correspondence from the Registrar and from Companies House may be sent. There is no requirement over the use of an address insofar as it is based in England or Wales, and the address is effective for delivering documents, to ensure that unnecessary delays can be avoided.

The memorandum and articles may be obtained from a company formation agent or a law stationer. Companies House will supply the new-style memorandum and a limited company will be able to use the relevant model articles where it wishes (CA 2006, s. 20).

14.3.8.2 The articles

The articles refer to the constitution of the company and how it may run its affairs. This is the contractual agreement between the parties and the company, and may be established on the basis of a bespoke set of articles, or the company will use the default model articles included in CA 2006. The articles of a company may be altered at a later date through a special resolution (s. 21) and s. 22 allows for the entrenchment of articles to enable the amendment or repeal of specified provisions in the articles where conditions are met, or procedures are complied with that are more restrictive than those applicable in cases of a special resolution.

14.3.8.3 Form IN01

'Form IN01' identifies (among others) the first director(s) and their personal details including their age, occupation, and details of previous directorships held in the previous five years; the secretary of the company, who can be both a director and secretary where there are two or more members of the company (where there is only one member, they must have another person to act as secretary); the company's registered office, and must again be authenticated by the subscribers.

The Registrar of Companies maintains the documents and makes them available for public inspection.

14.3.8.4 The certificate of incorporation

The company is established when the Registrar of Companies issues the certificate of incorporation. This document formally establishes the existence of the company and it will only 'die' when it is formally wound up. The certificate provides the company with its legal status and personality that will enable it to trade and establish the contracts that enable the 'business' to begin.

> **Consider**
>
> Abebi has established the contract with Gaagle before the company is incorporated. As such, the company cannot enforce the contract, but she will have the rights under it to seek fulfilment. Further, given the nature of the product, which remedy would be most suited to her claim (see **Chapter 10**)?

If the promoters of the company establish contracts on behalf of the company before the certificate is provided, they may be held personally liable and they will not obtain the protection from the limited liability status of the organization (s. 51(1)). However, the individual will be in a position to enforce the contract on their own behalf, in the case of a breach. This is where the promoter of the company has not informed the other party of the lack of incorporated status.

Braymist Ltd v Wise Finance Co. Ltd (2002)

Facts:

The claimant was establishing a company whilst at the same time selling land. The contract for the sale was signed by solicitors of the purported company but which, at the time, had not been incorporated. The respondent was unaware of the non-incorporation of the company.

Authority for:

The solicitors were personally liable for the contract as it was made in their name and could not be in the name of a company which, at the time, did not exist. It did also, however, give rights to the solicitors to enforce the contract.

Section 51(1) provides that the person is liable 'subject to any agreement to the contrary' and therefore if this is specifically identified to the other party and this party accepts that upon the certificate being provided the company will ratify the agreement, then the company may be subsequently bound (assuming the other party could be convinced to agree to this!).

14.3.8.5 Re-registration of the company

The private company and PLC may choose to re-register between the two statuses, and once completed a new certificate of incorporation is issued. The company will thereafter be subject to the rules applicable to the newly formed business. For the private company to re-register as a PLC, a special resolution must be passed through s. 90 to enable a change in the articles and memorandum to comply with the requirement to incorporate to a PLC. The documents outlined earlier have to be submitted to the Registrar, with the request for the change in status, and a report by the private company's auditors that the amounts of capital are as required under CA 2006.

A PLC may re-register as a private company through a special resolution. Section 97 of CA 2006 requires that all of the company's members have assented to its being so re-registered. Due to the nature of the PLC and the requirement for protection of the minority shareholders, s. 98 provides that shareholders with a minimum of 5 per cent of the nominal value of the issued share capital, or if the company is not limited by shares, by a minimum of 5 per cent of its members, or a minimum of 50 members, may apply within 28 days of the resolution, to a court to have the special resolution terminated and become unenforceable as they were not in favour. It is for the court to determine whether the resolution should be enforced or not.

14.3.8.6 Buying an off-the-shelf company

Due to the perceived problems that some people may have in completing the relevant forms and keeping up to date with the changes in company law and submitting the required documents, a simpler option may be to purchase a company from an agent. Such agencies are quite common and their service is to issue a company that has already been registered and they may also (for additional costs) act as company secretary for a given period of time to ensure all the necessary paperwork and documents are filed with Companies House. The agent that has established the company will sell this company to the purchaser and then resign as director/secretary and inform Companies House of this matter (having appointed the purchaser as the new director/secretary). This is undoubtedly a quick method of establishing the company, but there are issues to be considered. This may be a 'recycled' company and if the company has previously traded, any bad credit and so on will be passed on to the purchaser (as the company number originally issued will remain). This could have serious implications for future credit and financial matters. Hence, they should be used with caution.

Consider

Had Abebi purchased an off-the-shelf company and established the agreement with Gaagle plc it would have been enforceable by Eyesecure Ltd. As seen above, contracts may only be established and/or retrospectively ratified by the company where the company exists at the time of the agreement. It is not possible for Eyesecure Ltd to ratify Abebi's contract with Gaagle plc even if the board of directors agree—any contract, and its enforcement, would be between Abebi and Gaagle plc (CA 2006, s. 51).

14.3.8.7 Passing-off

This is an important issue to recognize when determining the implications of a company's name (for general information regarding this tort see **24.5.5**). The tort occurs where the company is given a name that is very similar to an existing business and it gives the (misleading) impression that the two companies are connected. As noted earlier, businesses often rely on their name and brand image to promote confidence to customers and retain and win new customers, therefore a company that is formed to take (unfair) advantage of this name may have to change its name (and be faced with a possible tort action for damages). An objection can be raised with the Registrar regarding the names of the companies and only the Registrar can decide whether the name should be changed (this is not a decision of the courts).

Halifax Plc v Halifax Repossessions Ltd (2004)

Facts:

The respondent company had been using a name similar to that of the claimant. In an action to prevent the respondent from infringing their trademark, the claimant was successful. The court ordered the respondent to refrain from using the trademark name, which it did, but the respondent did not change its company name. The claimant attempted to enforce the ruling, which was granted by the court, through an order to the Registrar of Companies to make the respondent remove the word 'Halifax' from its name.

→

Authority for:

The court did not have the authority to make such an order. The Registrar may only act within the confines of the statute (now the CA 2006) and, were a court allowed to make this order, it may have more serious and widespread consequences than those addressed in the issue heard before that court.

Whilst the motive of the subscriber of the company is not the primary concern in the issue of whether the company name should be changed, if they have acted to deliberately mislead customers into thinking the company is linked with another with a similar name, this will be negatively viewed by the courts.

Croft v Day (1843)

Facts:

A very famous firm that made boot polish (Day & Martin) had been established and named after the founders (who by the time of this case were deceased). Their business was bought by Mr Croft, who continued trading under the same name. Soon after, a Mr Day and Mr Martin started a business in the same profession and established the same business name on the basis of convincing (and misleading) potential buyers that the company was the same as the original. The court held that the new entrants to the market had attempted to pass the business off as the original, and granted Croft an injunction to prohibit the use of the new business's name.

Authority for:

Where a business name is already in existence, the use of the same/very similar name by others in an attempt to confuse or mislead the public as to believing they are dealing with the original will be considered a breach of 'passing off'. (This is the rule insofar as the requirements for breach of that tort are satisfied.)

In relation to a misleading registered company name, a complaint may be made by a person who possesses the goodwill in a name, adversely affected by the misleading company name, to the Company Names Adjudicator, who can order that the name be changed (CA 2006, s. 69. This has been supplemented by the Company Names Adjudicator Rules 2008 (S.I. 1738/2008)).

14.3.8.8 Bringing the company to an end

As the text continues with issues such as the winding-up of the company and the methods that may be adopted to achieve this, bringing the company to an end is considered in **15.7**.

CONCLUSION

This chapter has begun the process of considering the forms of business organization available and the implications of trading as each. The sole trader and partnerships are relatively simple organizations and hence they will not be investigated further. However, as corporations are complex, with detailed rules regarding how they are administered and governed, this will form the majority of the consideration of the remainder of this part of the text. This has been a deliberately introductory chapter and the text continues to detail the internal structures of companies, and how they operate.

SUMMARY OF MAIN POINTS

Legal personality

- Natural persons and businesses established as corporations possess their own legal personality.
- The legal personality of a company exists irrespective of the members or directors who carry out its functions.
- The legal personality of a company separates the company from those who own it. However, the courts may lift this 'veil' (reluctantly) to identify the true nature of the business.

Sole traders

- There is no legal distinction between the sole trader as an individual and the person running the business.
- The sole trader is a very simple business organization with very little internal or external regulation.
- The sole trader business can be formed and dissolved easily, and it does not require any special formalities other than informing the relevant government departments.

Partnerships

- A partnership involves two or more people coming together to establish a business.
- A partnership can be 'simple', 'limited', or a 'Limited Liability Partnership'.
- Partners may be 'typical/general', 'salaried', or a partner by estoppel.
- Many rights and obligations exist for partners in simple and limited partnerships including good faith, disclosure, and to account.
- Partners generally have the right to participate in the management of the firm and may bind the partnership through the exercise of actual or apparent authority.
- Bringing a partnership to an end is a relatively simple procedure, and the Partnership Act 1890 identifies specific reasons for its dissolution.

Limited liability partnerships

- Unlike sole traders and simple partnerships, LLPs have a separate legal personality and limited liability for members.
- They are regulated in similar ways to a company and are subject to some aspects of CA 2006.

Companies

- Companies are artificial things that have their own legal personality.
- Companies may be limited or unlimited.
- PLCs require a minimum of £50,000 allotted share capital on registration.

- There are exemptions from certain administrative duties for small/medium-sized companies.
- Limited companies may be formed by Royal Charter, statute, but most commonly through registration.
- The subscribers to a limited company must submit the memorandum, articles, and Form IN01 to the Registrar of Companies.
- Companies can be re-registered to reflect changes in their circumstances.
- Rather than forming the limited company, one may be bought 'off-the-shelf' through an agency.
- Regulations exist regarding the choice of business name.
- Businesses must ensure the name of the company is not too similar/the same as another company or they may be guilty of the tort of 'passing-off'.

 ## SUMMARY QUESTIONS

Essay questions

1. '*Salomon v Salomon* was wrongly decided. Its implications have allowed corporations to defraud innocent customers and suppliers, and it has facilitated the creation of sham companies with the protection afforded by the veil of incorporation. Corporations should not possess a legal personality distinct from those who subscribe to it.'

   Critically assess the above statement.

2. Identify the rights and duties imposed on partners, and assess how effective they are in maintaining trust and good faith.

Problem questions

1. Delia Smythe runs a small catering service from her home, providing hot lunches for the management of three firms in Sheffield. She has two employees—a driver and an assistant cook. She would like to bid for catering contracts at more firms and possibly expand into catering for private dinner parties, but could not do all this from her home. She is worried about how she would manage the operation. One of her worries is that she has no experience beyond institutional catering.

   Advise Ms Smythe about alternative forms of business organization available to her, explaining the advantages and disadvantages as they apply to her situation. Which form of business would you advise her to adopt? (Visit the online resources where a completed IN01 form is provided if Ms Smythe intended to form a private limited company.)

2. Paula has been approached by Jackson and Taylor Estates to join the partnership operating a property development and rental business. Jeffrey (Jackson), one of the partners, speaks with Paula about the offer and Paula agrees. She does not invest money into the business, but rather she says that she has expertise of negotiating good deals with builders, and has 'contacts' in the local Council which will assist on development applications, and advance knowledge of policies and plans likely to be adopted by the Council. Both existing partners—Jeffrey and Barbara (Taylor)—welcome Paula to the partnership and amend the partnership agreement to account for her addition to the business.

   Sometime after her arrival, Paula approaches her fellow partners with a business opportunity. There is a somewhat dilapidated building which would be prime for development and she has heard from her contacts that once developed, the Council would provide permission to convert its use to residential accommodation. This would dramatically increase its value, but a quick sale was essential to obtain the premises for fear the owner could decide against selling. The partners agree and the property is purchased. It transpires that the property is in very poor repair, to such an extent that it is dangerous. It contains a structural fault so severe that no valuation expert will provide a quote as to its insurable value. Further, unknown to Jeffrey or Barbara, Paula owns the property, she knew of its condition, and had been trying (unsuccessfully) to sell it for years.

When approached, the Council refuse permission to convert the building to residential accommodation. This has nothing to do with its condition or repair, but simply that any such application in that area would be refused. Paula had essentially misled the partners as to her 'contacts'—which is actually a receptionist on the front desk who occasionally hears gossip (usually about members of staff rather than secret plans or policies).

Finally, when the partnership applies for a loan to fund the purchase of the property, they are refused due to failing a credit check. They had never experienced this before Paula's introduction, and upon further investigation, they discover Paula has County Court Judgments against her and some quite serious criminal convictions. Paula never disclosed this information because 'she was never asked'.

Advise the parties as to their legal rights and duties under partnership law.

 You will find guidance about how to answer these questions online at www.oup.com/uk/marson5e/.

 FURTHER READING

Books and articles

Bourne, N. (2016) 'Bourne on Company Law' (7th Edition) Routledge-Cavendish: London.

Hawkey, J. (2005) 'Sale or Succession? How to Plan for a Successful Business Exit' How to Books: Oxford.

Whittaker, J. and Machell, J. (2016) 'The Law of Limited Liability Partnerships' (4th Edition) Bloomsbury Professional: Haywards Heath.

Websites, Twitter links, and YouTube channels

https://www.gov.uk/government/organisations/companies-house
@CompaniesHouse

https://www.youtube.com/user/TheCompaniesHouse
Information regarding the establishing of business organizations, forms to speed up the process, and general company advice.

http://legislation.gov.uk/ukpga/Vict/53-54/39/contents
The Partnership Act 1890.

http://www.legislation.gov.uk/ukpga/2006/46/contents
The Companies Act 2006.

http://www.legislation.gov.uk/ukpga/2000/12/contents
The Limited Liability Partnerships Act 2000.

 ONLINE RESOURCES

www.oup.com/uk/marson5e/

For further resources relating to this chapter, including self-test questions, an interactive glossary, and key case flashcards.

15 CORPORATE ADMINISTRATION

The members of a company, whilst delegating the day-to-day management of the business to directors and possessing no automatic rights of management themselves, can play a significant role in the company's administration. Depending on the shares held and the rights attached, shareholders may attend meetings, vote on resolutions, and even seek to remove directors or wind up the company. The members can therefore seek to protect their interests and hold the directors to account. The method of bringing a company to an end is also particularly important to the members and creditors of a company. Take, for example, Northern Rock Plc, which in 2008 had to be nationalized, adversely affecting the shareholders. Therefore, this chapter identifies the rights of members in the decision-making of the company and how the company, its members, and creditors may protect themselves from severe losses when the company may be in financial difficulties. Investing in a company involves risk, but with vigilant administration, these risks can, at least in part, be minimized.

Business Scenario 15

In March 2014, Carlos and Roman incorporated a company (Ecclesall FC Ltd) that specialised in selling football products, including technology such as player body-cameras and boots which contain microchips linked to the players' smart phones. They were the only directors of the company, and jointly own the ordinary shares in the company. Karen owns 25 preference shares in Ecclesall FC Ltd. In June 2017, having enjoyed a period of financial success, Ecclesall FC Ltd began to struggle when a new entrant to the market began to take some of the contracts Ecclesall FC Ltd had previously enjoyed exclusivity over. Carlos and Roman approached the company's bank for an overdraft facility and were granted £500,000 with the bank securing this through a floating charge over the company's assets.

At a recent general meeting, a resolution was notified to subdivide each current ordinary share into 10 shares with a nominal value of 10p. All shareholders were present at the meeting and both Carlos and Roman voted in favour of this ordinary resolution, whilst Karen voted against it.

In November 2017, following continued poor sales due to the lack of take-up of these technology-related products, Carlos and Roman were informed by the company's auditor that the company was in severe financial trouble. This would result in the company's insolvent liquidation and they were to cease trading immediately. Carlos and Roman disagreed and thought that if they had a good Christmas trading quarter, they could revive the failing company. However, the attempt failed and in March 2018 the company was wound up.

→

The liquidator has identified the following facts:

- Prior to the passing of the resolution, Carlos and Roman each owned 100 £1 shares;
- The preference shares have a nominal value of £1 each;
- The company owed the bank £500,000;
- The company owed £40,000 in wages to employees;
- In January 2018, Carlos and Roman agreed for the company to repay to Carlos £15,000 which he had loaned to the company, and this loan was unsecured;
- The liquidator's fees are £6,000;
- The company had £350,000 in assets.

Learning Outcomes

- Identify when a company acquires the capacity to begin trading (15.3)
- Understand the rights of members to oblige the company to call a meeting and circulate details and information of the resolutions to be moved (15.4–15.4.5)
- Explain the various resolutions that may be moved at meetings and the procedures involved (15.5)
- Explain the significance of a written resolution procedure and which business may not be moved through this mechanism (15.5–15.5.3)
- Identify the requirements for the recording and maintenance of these records of the business at meetings, and of resolutions moved (15.6)
- Explain the mechanisms for a company being wound up and the procedures involved (15.7–15.7.2.1).

15.1 INTRODUCTION

Having outlined the various forms of business organization available and the mechanisms for establishing each, this chapter begins the process of explaining the mechanisms for the company's administration. This is due to the regulation that is placed on companies through the legislation, including the Companies Act (CA) 2006. Companies have to register with Companies House in order to obtain a trading certificate, regulation exists with regard to the activities of a company's directors, members of the company have the right to participate in meetings and vote on resolutions that are to be moved, procedures must be followed when moving resolutions, and board meetings have to be conducted in accordance with rules and procedures required by statute.

15.2 THE COMPANIES ACT 2006

CA 2006 was a major reform to the laws governing companies and their relations with third parties and the members of the company. Whilst the law codified many of the existing laws (approximately one-third of the legislation), much of it was new and as such it may be some years before the issues are fully tested and analysed through the courts. However, this is a major piece of legislation, the largest single Act ever enacted, but it is hoped that it will make the provisions of governance of companies more accessible, less bureaucratic, and simpler to understand.

15.3 CAPACITY TO TRADE

Whilst a private company has the capacity to trade immediately upon incorporation, a public company that has been newly formed must receive a trading certificate from the Registrar of Companies before it may begin trading and other activities involved in a business (such as borrowing money—CA 2006, s. 761). This certificate is only provided where the Registrar is satisfied that the public company's nominal value of allotted share capital is not less than the authorized minimum of £50,000 (or the prescribed euro equivalent—CA 2006, s. 763, although the currency used may later be changed if required). For the purposes of this section of the Act, the company must have at least one-quarter of the nominal value of the share capital plus the whole of any premium paid up (not including shares allotted under an employees' share scheme unless one-quarter of the nominal value is paid up). The application for the certificate must include details of the costs in establishing the company and a statement of compliance with the requirements of the Act. When these formalities are completed, the Registrar will issue the certificate, and publish the receipt of the details in the *London Gazette*. This certificate provides the company with the authority to begin trading. Where it trades without the certificate (and in breach of s. 761), the company and every officer who is in default commit an offence, and they are subject to a fine. However, a contravention of trading before the certificate is granted does not invalidate the transaction, but the directors are jointly and severally liable to indemnify any other party to the transaction in respect of any loss or damage suffered by the company's failure to comply with its obligations (CA 2006, s. 767).

15.4 COMPANY MEETINGS

Whilst the members of the company delegate the powers of the management of the company to the directors, who themselves conduct decision-making through powers granted to them and through their own board meetings, the members themselves take responsibility for moving resolutions of the company. These resolutions are used to perform functions of the company, and some are more onerous to move than others due to the nature of what the resolution intends to achieve. These are discussed in **15.5**. However, the meetings of the members are conducted as follows.

There exist two types of meeting that a company may call: the Annual General Meeting (AGM) and general meetings. Private companies have the option of not holding AGMs but they must hold meetings where required by the members; the courts; or where, for example, directors or auditors are to be removed. Public companies are required to hold an AGM every financial year (but have the option of holding more than this minimum requirement where it is deemed appropriate). In order to move resolutions that will be considered effective, CA 2006 identifies several procedures that must be fulfilled to ensure that the business conducted at general meetings is fair to the members. Resolutions may be moved at general meetings insofar as notice of the meeting and the resolution is given to the members of the company. Further, the meeting must be held and conducted in accordance with CA 2006 and the company's articles (CA 2006, s. 301). The calling of these meetings is a power granted to the directors of a company (CA 2006, s. 302); however, where the director(s) does not call a meeting and the members wish one to take place these members have the power to require the directors to take this action (CA 2006, s. 303).

15.4.1 The Request for a Meeting

The directors are required to call the meeting in either of the following circumstances:

1. where they have received the request from members representing at least the required percentage of the paid-up capital of the company as carries the right of voting at general meetings; or

2. in the case of a company not having a share capital, members who represent at least the required percentage of the total voting rights of all members possessing the right to vote at general meetings. The percentages required are identified in s. 303 as 10 per cent unless, in the case of a private company, more than 12 months has elapsed since the end of the last general meeting—called in pursuance of a requirement under this section of the Act. Or in relation to which any members of the company had rights with respect to the circulation of a resolution, no less extensive than they would have had if the meeting had been so called at their request. In these cases the required percentage is 5 per cent.

The request has to identify the general nature of the business to be dealt with and it may include the text of a resolution that is intended to be (properly) moved at the meeting. This request may be in hard copy or electronic form but it must be authenticated by the person(s) making it. 'Properly' means a resolution that may be passed at a meeting unless to do so would be ineffective (such as against the constitution of the company), is defamatory of any person, or is frivolous or vexatious.

15.4.2 The Directors' Obligation to Call the Meeting

Where a meeting has been properly requested, s. 304 requires the director(s) to call a meeting within 21 days from the date on which they became subject to the requirement, and this must be held not more than 28 days after the date of the notice convening the meeting. Further, where the request has identified a resolution intended to be moved at the meeting, details of this resolution must accompany the notice. Where such a resolution is a special resolution, the directors must follow the requirements provided in s. 283 by giving the appropriate notice and so on.

- *Where the directors fail to call the meeting:* Where the requirements of s. 303 have been complied with and the directors fail to call the meeting, the members who requested the meeting, or any of them representing more than half of the total voting rights of all of them, may themselves call a general meeting and do so at the company's expense (limited to reasonable expenses—CA 2006, s. 305). The meeting must be called for a date not more than three months after the date on which the directors became subject to the requirement to call the meeting, and it must be called in as similar a manner as possible as other meetings called by the directors.

- *Power of a court to order a meeting:* It may be the case that with smaller companies the shareholder may have disagreements with the directors to such an extent that, for example, the shareholder(s) will not attend the meetings to allow for resolutions to be moved. Where it is impractical to call a meeting in a manner which it would normally be called, or as required by the company's articles, or CA 2006, a court may through its own motion or through an application of a director of the company, or a member of the company who would be entitled to vote, order for a meeting to be called, held, and conducted in any manner the court thinks fit (and when conducted in this way, the meeting will be considered for all purposes to have been duly called, held, and conducted—CA 2006, s. 306). Such power also extends to the court giving directions as it deems expedient, such as providing that one member of a company present at the meeting be deemed to constitute a quorum. The court will not, however, give a member a voting power that the member does not possess under the company's constitution. Note that this procedure is not intended to resolve petty squabbles between the equal members of a company.

Ross v Telford (1998)

Facts:

The case involved the two equal shareholders of a company. They had been husband and wife but had divorced acrimoniously and would not cooperate with each other regarding matters, including convening the company's meetings. The articles of the company required a quorum of two for the meetings and as this could not be practicably achieved, the husband requested a court to order a meeting with just one of the shareholders present to lawfully conclude the business required. This was initially granted but was stopped when the case was heard at the Court of Appeal, which held the provision of the Companies Act was not designed for this purpose. If the husband had been a majority shareholder and the minority shareholder had been deliberately attempting to prevent the business of the company being conducted, then the Companies Act would have been correctly used.

Authority for:

An interpretation of the relevant section of CA 1985 (s. 371) was that Parliament did not intend for it to be interpreted by the courts as a means to break a deadlock between equal shareholders. In so doing, the courts have no power to regulate the affairs of a company in this way (shifting the balance of power between shareholders where they agreed to share power equally).

15.4.3 Notice of Meetings

A general meeting of a private company must be called by giving notice of at least 14 days (notice can be given in hard copy, electronic form, through a website, or by a combination of these—CA 2006, s. 308). A general meeting of a public company must be called giving notice of at least 21 days for an AGM, or of at least 14 days' notice for other general meetings. These periods are provided for in CA 2006, s. 306, but the section allows the companies to provide for longer or shorter periods if agreed by the members. For the shorter period the agreement of members must be a majority of those members possessing the right to attend and vote, who together hold not less than the required percentage in nominal value of the shares giving a right to attend and vote. Where the company does not have a share capital, the members together represent not less than the required percentage of the total voting rights at that meeting of all the members (these do not apply to an AGM of a public company—CA 2006, s. 307).

This required percentage is, in private companies, 90 per cent or such higher percentage (not exceeding 95 per cent) as may be specified in the company's articles; or in the case of public companies, 95 per cent. For the members to reduce the notice period for an AGM of a public company there must be a unanimous agreement to the resolution (CA 2006, s. 377).

Where CA 2006 requires special notice to be given for a resolution, the resolution is not effective until notice of the intention to move the resolution at least 28 days before the meeting has been provided (CA 2006, s. 312). However, where this is not practicable, the company must give its members notice at least 14 days before the meeting through an advertisement in a newspaper having an appropriate circulation, or other manner specified in the company's articles.

- *Notification details:* Notice of a general meeting must be sent to every member and director of the company (CA 2006, s. 310). This notification, for general meetings, must include the time and date of the meeting, the meeting's location, the nature of the business to be dealt with at the meeting, and any other requirements subject to the company's articles (CA 2006, s. 311). In situations of accidental failure to notify of a resolution or general meeting, any accidental failure to give notice to one or more persons is disregarded for the purpose of determining whether notice of the meeting or resolution is duly given (with the exception of the requirements under ss. 304, 305, and 339 of CA 2006). The accidental failure provisions of CA 2006 are subject to any provisions of the company's articles.

15.4.4 Procedures at Meetings

CA 2006 provides details of how the companies must conduct meetings to ensure that the resolutions moved are lawful. This section of the Act initially considers the quorum at the meeting (the minimum numbers of the company's members who need to be present to allow resolutions to be effectively moved). A company limited by shares or by guarantee and having only one member will have reached a quorum when one qualifying person is present at a meeting. In other cases, and subject to the company's articles, two qualifying persons present at the meeting are a quorum unless the qualifying persons are the representatives of the same corporation or the persons are the proxies of the same member (CA 2006, s. 318). For the purposes of the Act, a qualifying person is an individual who is a member of the company, a person authorized to act as the representative of a corporation in relation to the meeting, or a person appointed as a proxy of a member.

A member may be elected to be the chairperson (including a proxy—CA 2006, s. 328) of the general meeting by a resolution of the company, but this is subject to the company's articles as to who may or may not be chairperson (CA 2006, s. 319). In the case of voting, the company's articles must allow the right for a vote through poll at a general meeting on any question other than the election of the chairperson or the adjournment of the meeting (CA 2006, s. 321). Where a vote on a resolution is by a show of hands, once the chairperson has made a declaration that it has either passed (or passed with a majority) or not, this is conclusive evidence of the fact without proof of the numbers or proportion of votes recorded either in favour or against the resolution (CA 2006, s. 320). However, as a safeguard this authority does not have any effect if a poll is demanded in respect of the resolution. This demand may be made by not less than five members having the right to vote on the resolution, or by a member(s) representing not less than 10 per cent of the total voting rights, or by a member(s) holding shares conferring a right to vote with not less than 10 per cent of the paid-up capital (CA 2006, s. 321). The chairperson's role at meetings is to ensure proper conduct and to oversee the proceedings, and in doing so to act fairly between the members' rights and the company's best interests.

When a member wishes to exercise their right to vote on a poll taken at a general meeting, a member with more than one vote has the right not to use their votes in the same way (CA 2006, s. 322). This may be achieved by appointing more than one proxy to vote at the meeting. CA 2006 provides the member with the right to appoint another person (the proxy) to exercise any or all of their rights to attend, speak, and vote at a meeting of the company (CA 2006, s. 324). Where the company has a share capital, the member may appoint more than one proxy where they are to exercise the rights attached to different share(s) held by them or to a different £10, or multiple of £10, of stock held by them. The notice provided to the member of the meeting must include information regarding their rights under s. 324, and any more extensive rights conferred by the company's articles to appoint more than one proxy (CA 2006, s. 325). However, any provision of the company's articles is void if it would have the effect of requiring any appointment of proxies or document(s) to be received by the company or another person earlier than 48 hours before the time of the meeting (or an adjourned meeting); and in the case of a poll, not more than 48 hours after it was demanded (this does not include anything other than working days—CA 2006, s. 327). These rights are the minimum required by CA 2006, but they do not prevent a company from conferring more extensive rights on the members or proxies (CA 2006, s. 331).

15.4.5 **General Meetings**

Every public company must hold an AGM within six months of its financial year-end (CA 2006, s. 336). The company must state that the meeting is an AGM, and notice must be provided that such a meeting is to be called (CA 2006, s. 337). Whilst the company must provide 21 days' notice of an AGM and 14 days' notice of all other meetings (CA 2006, s. 307), an AGM may be called by a shorter notice period than that in CA 2006 or the company's articles if all the members entitled to attend and vote agree to the shorter notice. The members of the company may require the circulation of resolutions to be moved (or intended to be moved) at the AGM. This must comprise members representing at least 5 per cent of the total voting rights of all the members who have a right to vote on the resolution; or at least 100 members who have the right to vote on the resolution and who hold shares on which the paid-up average per member is at least £100. Such a resolution may be properly moved unless it would, if passed, be ineffective (such as being inconsistent with the company's constitution), defamatory of any person, or if it were frivolous or vexatious (CA 2006, s. 338). Such a request may be made in hard copy or electronic form and it must identify the resolution of which notice has been given; it must be authenticated by the person(s) making it; and it must be received by the company not later than six weeks before the AGM to which the request relates or, if later, the time at which the notice is given of that meeting. Being in receipt of a valid request, the company is required to send a copy of the resolution to each member of the company entitled to receive notice of the AGM.

Additional responsibilities rest with '**quoted companies**' (defined under CA 2006, ss. 361 and 385), beyond those identified in the preceding paragraphs in relation to public companies. Quoted companies are those having a listing (through a decision of the

Financial Services Authority) and its shares may be traded on a stock exchange. Where a poll is taken at a general meeting of a quoted company, the company must ensure that the following information is made available on a website: the date of the meeting; the text of the resolution or a description of the subject matter of the poll; and the numbers of votes in favour of, and against, the resolution/subject matter (CA 2006, s. 341). Where the company fails to comply with this requirement, an offence is committed by every officer of the company in default but it does not affect the validity of the poll or the business or resolution to which the poll relates. The members of the quoted company may require its directors to obtain an independent report on any poll taken, or to be taken, at a general meeting. The directors are obliged to obtain the report where the request is from members representing not less than 5 per cent of the total voting rights of all the members entitled to vote on the matter to which the poll relates (excluding those with treasury shares); or not less than 100 members who possess the right to vote on the matter and who hold shares with an average paid-up sum of not less than £100 each (CA 2006, s. 342). This request may be in hard copy or electronic form, it must identify the poll(s) to which the request relates, it must be authenticated by the person(s) making it, and it must be received by the company not later than one week after the date on which the poll is taken.

Where the directors are required under s. 342 to obtain an independent report on a poll(s), they must appoint an appropriate person (known as an independent assessor) to prepare the report. This appointment must be made within one week after the company is required to obtain the report (CA 2006, s. 343). The independent assessor cannot be appointed if they are an officer or employee of the company (or associated company), or a partner or employee of such a person, or a partnership of which such a person is a partner. The assessor in this role is entitled to attend the meeting at which the poll may be taken and any subsequent proceedings in connection with the poll. These rights are to be exercised to the extent that the assessor considers necessary for the preparation of the report (CA 2006, s. 348). They are also entitled to company records relating to the poll or the meeting at which the poll may be, or was, taken (CA 2006, s. 349). Where the independent assessor has been appointed in compliance with this section of CA 2006, the company must ensure that the following information is made available on a website: the fact of the appointment; the assessor's identity; the text of the resolution, or a description of the subject matter of the poll to which their appointment relates; and a copy of the report (CA 2006, s. 351). The report must be kept available for two years, beginning with the date on which it was first made available on a website (CA 2006, s. 353).

The report will contain information regarding the appropriateness of the procedures followed in relation to the poll; whether the correct notice periods were provided; the nature of the voting and whether, in the assessor's opinion, they were cast fairly and recorded correctly; and whether the votes of proxies were assessed. If the assessor is unable to provide an opinion, they must give the reasons why.

15.5 RESOLUTIONS AT MEETINGS

Resolutions are the decisions made at the company meetings. There are various categories of resolution that may be moved by a company. With reference to the resolutions that may be moved by a private company, a written resolution or one moved at a meeting of the company's members are available (CA 2006, s. 281). The benefit of moving a written resolution is that there is no necessity of a meeting of the members, they are sent the resolution and they sign this resolution if they are in agreement.

A public company must move resolutions at a meeting of the members (or a class of members) and it may not move written resolutions by a majority using the procedure in CA 2006, ss. 288–300. However, at common law, such resolutions can be passed if unanimous. Where CA 2006 requires a resolution of a company, or of the members (or a class of members), and the type of resolution required is not specified, it is assumed that an ordinary resolution is required unless the company's articles requires a higher majority or unanimity. Whilst this does provide the company with some flexibility or control over the resolutions to be moved, there are protections in CA 2006 to prevent, for example, a director being removed before the expiry of their term of office through a written resolution because CA 2006 provides for important safeguards against potential abuse.

15.5.1 **Ordinary Resolutions**

CA 2006, s. 282 identifies ordinary resolutions as those passed, by a private company, by the members (or a class of the members) with a simple majority (over 50 per cent of the vote). An ordinary resolution can be passed as a written resolution if it is passed by members representing a simple majority of the total voting rights of eligible members. Further, a resolution to be moved at a meeting by a show of hands is passed by a simple majority where it is agreed to be passed in this way by members in person or through duly appointed proxies. Where a resolution is to be moved through a poll taken at the meeting, it is passed through a simple majority of members representing a simple majority of the total voting rights of the members entitled to vote in person (or through proxy) on the resolution. The section concludes that anything done by an ordinary resolution can also be done through a special resolution.

15.5.2 **Special Resolutions**

CA 2006, s. 283 identifies special resolutions. These are required for certain business to be taken by the company such as to alter the company's articles (CA 2006, s. 21); alter its name (CA 2006, s. 77); re-register the company from an unlimited to a private limited (CA 2006, s. 105), private to public (CA 2006, s. 90), or public to private (CA 2006, s. 97); reduce the company's share capital (CA 2006, s. 641); authorize the terms on which to make an off-market purchase of its own shares (CA 2006, s. 694); and so on. A special resolution of the members (or class of members) means a resolution passed by a majority of not less than 75 per cent. A written resolution is passed by a majority of not less than 75 per cent if it is passed by members representing not less than 75 per cent of the total voting rights of eligible members. Such a written resolution of a private company is not a special resolution unless it is stated as being moved as a special resolution and, if stated, it may only be moved as a special resolution. Where the resolution is to be moved by a show of hands, it is passed by a majority of not less than 75 per cent where not less than 75 per cent of the members (or the duly appointed proxies) who are entitled to vote do so in favour of the resolution. A resolution moved on a poll at a meeting is passed by a majority of not less than 75 per cent if passed by members representing not less than 75 per cent of the total voting rights of eligible members voting in favour of the resolution in person or through their proxies. Where a company wishes to move a special resolution, it may only do so by following these procedures and giving notice of the meeting, the text of the resolution wishing to be moved, and by passing it in the form required of a special resolution.

Consider

Karen had 25 of 225 shares in the company. Following the subdivision she owns 25 of 2025 shares. Has this led to a varying of a class right? Shares can be subdivided, but this requires notification (which has been complied with). However, approval of the resolution needs to be achieved through agreement of the class affected (which has seemingly been breached) However, giving proportional voting rights to a class of shareholders is not a variation to the rights of the other class of shareholders—but consider a petition under CA 2006, s. 994 (see **17.4.1**). Further, CA 2006, s. 630(4) requires a special resolution to be moved to achieve the subdivision and this has not been complied with.

15.5.3 Written Resolutions

A private company may propose and move a written resolution in accordance with the requirements laid out in CA 2006 (CA 2006, s. 288). However, such a resolution may not be used to remove either a director (CA 2006, s. 168) or an auditor (CA 2006, s. 510) before the expiration of their period of office. The resolution may be proposed by the directors of the private company or its (eligible) members (carrying not less than 5 per cent of the total voting rights) and has effect where it is moved by a company in a general meeting or a resolution of a meeting of a class of members of the company. The eligible members are those who would have been entitled to vote on the resolution on the circulation date of the resolution (CA 2006, s. 289). The circulation date is the date on which copies of the resolution are sent or submitted to the members (or if the copies/submissions are made on different days it is the first of those days—CA 2006, s. 290).

Where the company wishes to move a written resolution proposed by the directors, the company must send/submit a copy of the resolution to every eligible member at the same time (where reasonably practicable), in hard copy, electronic form, or by means of a website. The copy of the resolution must also be accompanied by a statement informing the member how to signify their agreement, and the date by which the resolution must be moved for it not to lapse (CA 2006, s. 291). Where these procedures are not complied with, an offence is committed by every officer in default, but this does not affect the validity of the resolution moved. The members of a private company may require the company to circulate a written resolution unless it would, if moved, be ineffective, defamatory of any person, or frivolous or vexatious (CA 2006, s. 292). The members (representing not less than 5 per cent of the total voting rights of all members entitled to vote on the resolution—unless the articles enable a lower percentage to be used) may also require the company to circulate the resolution with a statement of not more than 1,000 words on the subject matter of the resolution. Where this request is properly made, the company must circulate it (and the statement) to every eligible member within 21 days of the application of s. 292 (CA 2006, s. 293). This copy must also be accompanied by guidance as to how the recipient signifies agreement to the resolution, and the date that it will lapse if not moved. Importantly, those members that requested the circulation of the resolution must pay any expenses incurred by the company in compliance with s. 293, and the company may require a deposit to be paid in this regard (CA 2006, s. 294). It is also possible for the company (or another person claiming to be aggrieved) to apply to a court preventing the requirement of circulating a members' statement where it is claimed the right under s. 292 is being abused (CA 2006, s. 295).

A written resolution is moved when the required majority of eligible members have signified their agreement to it, and it will not be passed if the resolution lapses. This may occur when the time exceeds the period provided for in the company's articles; or in the absence of any articles to this effect, 28 days beginning with the circulation date. Any agreement signified after this date will be ineffective (CA 2006, s. 297).

15.6 RECORDING BUSINESS AT MEETINGS AND OF RESOLUTIONS

Every company is required to maintain records comprising copies of all resolutions of members moved otherwise than at general meetings, minutes of all proceedings of general meetings, and details provided to the company in relation to decisions of companies with a sole member (CA 2006, s. 355). These records must be kept for at least 10 years from the date of the resolution, meeting, or decision, and failure to comply will result in every officer in default being liable to a fine, and a daily fine for continued contravention. Where a resolution has been moved otherwise than at a general meeting, a record of it as well as it having been signed by a director (or the company secretary), is evidence of the resolution being passed. Where there is a record of a written resolution of a private company, the resolution will be deemed to have complied with the requirements of CA 2006 unless the contrary is proven (CA 2006, s. 356). The minutes of proceedings of a general meeting signed by the chairperson, or by the chairperson at the next general meeting will be evidence of the proceedings at the meeting. This record proves the meeting is deemed duly held and convened, all the proceedings at the meeting are deemed to have duly taken place, and all appointments at the meeting are deemed valid unless the contrary is proven.

Where the company has only one member and the company is limited by shares or by guarantee, and that member takes any decision that may be taken by the company in a general meeting, and has effect as if agreed by the company in the meeting, they must (unless taken in the form of a written resolution) provide the company with details of that decision (CA 2006, s. 357).

15.7 WINDING-UP OF COMPANIES

Chapter 14 identified the various forms of business enterprise and outlined the registration procedure that subscribers use to establish the corporation. This section considers how those corporations are legally brought to an end. It will be remembered that due to a corporation's perpetual succession, the company does not 'die' when the person(s) running it dies (or where the sole trader/partner is made bankrupt), but rather it will only cease to exist when formally wound up. Liquidation is considered in detail but many companies are wound up due to inactivity (non-trading).

15.7.1 Liquidation

A company being wound up and being liquidated essentially refers to the company ceasing to exist. Liquidation may take effect either through a petition to a court for the compulsory liquidation of the company (under the Insolvency Act 1986, s. 124A); or the members seeking the voluntary liquidation of the business.

15.7.1.1 Liquidation by a court

Liquidation through the court can be made by any of the following petitioning the court (the Insolvency Act (IA) 1986, s. 124):

- the company, the directors, or any creditor(s) (including prospective creditors);
- a contributory (who is a person who may have to contribute upon the company's liquidation, including a shareholder with fully paid-up shares);
- a liquidator appointed in proceedings, or a temporary **administrator**;
- the Secretary of State where a public company has not been issued with its trading certificate;
- (in the event of a company being voluntarily wound up) the **Official Receiver** where the court is satisfied that the **winding-up** cannot be continued with due regard to the interests of the creditors or contributories;
- or by all or any of those parties, together or separately.

Note: a contributory is not entitled to present a winding-up petition unless either the number of members is reduced below two, or the shares in respect of which they are a contributory, or some of them, either were originally allotted to them, or have been held by them, and registered in their name, for at least six of the 18 months before the commencement of the winding-up, or have devolved on him through the death of a former holder.

The court, when faced with such a petition, has the option to make the order for winding-up, or it may refuse. Importantly, the court may also appoint a provisional liquidator (who may or may not be the Official Receiver) where it is considered likely that the directors may attempt to remove assets of the company. The appointment is made as an interim measure before the substantive hearing of the petition.

The Insolvency Act (IA) 1986 identifies the grounds upon which an order for compulsory liquidation of a company may be made. Under s. 122, these are listed as:

(a) the company has by special resolution resolved that the company be wound up by the court;

(b) being a public company which was registered as such on its original incorporation, the company has not been issued with a trading certificate and more than a year has expired since it was so registered;

(c) it is an old public company, within the meaning of the Consequential Provisions Act;

(d) the company does not commence its business within a year from its incorporation or suspends its business for a whole year;

(e) except in the case of a private company limited by shares or by guarantee, the number of members is reduced below two;

(f) the company is unable to pay its debts;

(fa) at the time at which a moratorium for the company under section 1A comes to an end, no voluntary arrangement approved under Part I has effect in relation to the company [added by IA 2000, Sch. 1, para. 6];

(g) the court is of the opinion that it is just and equitable that the company should be wound up.

Therefore, a company may move a special resolution to effect that the company be wound up by the court under (a); and it will be remembered that the moving of a special resolution requires that three-quarters of the votes are in favour of the resolution. As such, where a smaller proportion of the members (and even just one member) wishes to have the company wound up, under (g) a petition to the court can be made that it is just and equitable to have the company wound up. This procedure also allows creditors and the directors of the company to petition the court on this ground. What will constitute a 'just and equitable' ground is a matter for the court looking at the facts of each case, and it has broad discretion in this area; however, examples have been provided. Where, particularly in small businesses, the directors who manage the company have severe disagreements that make its management practically impossible, this may lead to the court ordering its winding-up.

Re Yenidje Tobacco Co. Ltd (1916)

Facts:

The company was established by two tobacco manufacturers whose relationship broke down to such an extent that they stopped communicating or allowing any business to be carried on. Despite the profitability of the business, the court was petitioned to have the company wound up.

Authority for:

In winding up the company, the court referred to matters such as the refusal of the directors to meet on matters of business and that the company was in such a state of animosity that all reasonable hope of cooperation between the directors was lost. This did not involve the gross misconduct of a director, nor was the situation caused by one of the individuals attempting to take advantage of the situation.

The company may have been established for a fraudulent purpose:

Re Thomas Edward Brinsmead and Sons (1897)

Facts:

Three former employees of John Brinsmead & Sons (a well-known piano maker) formed a company to manufacture pianos with the aim of passing them off as of the established business. An injunction was obtained to prevent the company from selling the pianos but during this time the company's shares had been made available to the public and many thousands of pounds had been raised through subscribers. An application for the winding-up of the company was sought.

Authority for:

The Court of Appeal held the second company to have been established to commit a fraud and as such it was just and equitable for the company to be wound up.

. . . or the members may have (justifiably) no faith or confidence in the company's management:

Loch v John Blackwood (1924)

Facts:

The case involved the beneficiaries of a will which granted shares in the company to the claimant. These were not allocated according to the deceased's will. The claimant petitioned the court to have the company wound up citing several reasons including the failure to hold general meetings, non-submission of balance sheet, profit and loss accounts and non-compliance with the audit. Further, it appeared the directors were attempting to keep the shareholders in a state of ignorance of the company's finances with the aim of acquiring the shares at an under value.

Authority for:

A company may be wound up where a considerable proportion of the shareholders had a real lack of confidence in the directors and those directors had significant power. It was in the public interest to wind up the company on this just and equitable ground.

In each situation the courts have ordered the winding-up of the company. In order for the petitioner to succeed in this application they must have some genuine interest in the company being wound up, as a winding-up petition has very serious consequences for the company, its members, and any creditors; and where the company is still trading and being successful in its undertaking, the courts will be considerably more reluctant to make the winding-up order.

A winding-up petition may also be made under (f) regarding the company's inability to pay its debts. It is important to note that even where it has been proved to the court's satisfaction that the company cannot pay its debts, this does not automatically result in the court ordering its winding-up. The court may initially convene a meeting of the company's creditors (including consideration of the debts owed to each creditor) and contributories (taking into account the number of votes conferred on each contributory from CA 2006 or the articles) to identify their submissions on the petition, and then make a decision (IA 1986, s. 195). Only the views of the creditors will be taken into account if the company is insolvent. If a decision is made to wind up the company, the court will order for the appointment of a liquidator. The court may, for example after having heard from the creditors, determine that the company that owes a creditor a sum that would allow a winding-up order should not be wound up. Other creditors may consider that allowing the company to continue to trade would be in the best interests of all the parties. Such actions are much less common, however, with the availability of the administration procedure.

15.7.1.2 The winding-up order

Where the court orders the company to be wound up, the company's liquidation is effective from the date of the petition to the court and, until another liquidator is appointed, the Official Receiver assumes this position. Once the order has been given, notice of the order (and a copy) must be provided to the Registrar, who will then publish this in the *London Gazette*.

The role of the Official Receiver, when appointed, is to identify the state of the company's affairs with regard to its assets, debts, and other liabilities. The persons listed in IA 1986, s. 131 (may if requested) have to provide the Receiver with the following information that is verified by affidavit:

(a) the particulars of the company's assets, debts, and liabilities;

(b) the names and addresses of the company's creditors;

(c) the securities held by them, respectively;

(d) the dates when the securities were respectively given;

(e) such further or other information as may be prescribed or as the official receiver may require.

The persons required to provide such information are:

(a) those who are or have been officers of the company;

(b) those who have taken part in the formation of the company at any time within one year before the relevant date;

(c) those who are in the company's employment, or have been in its employment within that year, and are in the official receiver's opinion capable of giving the information required;

(d) those who are or have been within that year officers of, or in the employment of, a company which is, or within that year was, an officer of the company.

Where the requirement for the statement is made, those persons have to do so within 21 days after the day of the notice being given to them by the Receiver. Any person who fails to comply with such a request will, upon conviction, be subject to a fine, and continued daily fines until the contravention is ended. This information may prove valuable to the Receiver as IA 1986, s. 132 requires the Receiver to investigate (if the company failed) the causes of the failure; the promotion, formation, business, dealings, and affairs of the company; and to make the report to the court if they consider appropriate (IA 1986, s. 132).

To further assist in the investigation, the Receiver may undertake a public examination of the company's officers following a successful application to the court. This includes anyone who is or has been an officer of the company; has acted as a liquidator or administrator of the company or a manager or receiver; or a person (not identified in the previous examples) who is, or has taken part, in the promotion, formation, or management of the company (IA 1986, s. 133). The Receiver must also make an application to the court to perform this investigation if requested by one-half, in value, of the company's creditors, or three-quarters in value of the company's contributors. Further to the powers and duties of the Receiver above, upon winding-up, the company's assets may not be disposed of, and shares may not be transferred or altered, unless a court authorizes such actions (IA 1986, s. 127). Any actions for recovering debts are stopped, and the responsibilities for the management of the company transfer from the directors to the Receiver/liquidator. Any floating charges that were granted over assets are deemed to crystallize (see **16.13.1**).

15.7.1.3 **Voluntary liquidation**

Under IA 1986, a voluntary winding-up of a company may be achieved through an action by the company's members (who must involve the company's creditors if it is insolvent). A special resolution is required to be moved. Where the members wish to have the company

wound up, they would seek to have a special resolution moved, and then appoint a liquidator at a general meeting (this may be an option where the company is still solvent and
the members may wish to gain something from the remaining assets of the company—although ordinary shareholders are low on the list of creditors when a company is wound
up (and are at risk of getting little return on their investment in the company)).

Consider

The liquidator is engaged to gather the assets of the company and to pay its debts.
Where money remains in the company after this dispersal, it is distributed according
to the hierarchy identified in **Table 15.1**. This will require consideration of the repayment of the loan to Carlos; the floating charge to the bank; the employees' owed
wages; and the liquidator's fees.

The liquidator (and there may be more than one appointed) is appointed for the purpose
of winding up the company's affairs and distributing its assets (IA 1986, s. 91). If the
winding-up of the company takes longer than one year, the liquidator will call a general
meeting in each successive year and account for their acts and dealings, and the conduct
of the winding-up (IA 1986, s. 93). When the company's affairs are fully wound up, the
liquidator calls a general meeting to lay before it their account, how the company's property has been disposed, and so on, and provide an explanation for the actions. Notice of
the meeting is advertised in the *London Gazette* at least one month prior to it (IA 1986,
s. 94). Within one week following the meeting, the liquidator will send a copy of the
account and the details of the meeting to the Registrar.

In the event that the liquidator is of the opinion that the company will be unable to pay
its debts in full (including any interest at the official rate) within the period of the directors' declaration of solvency under s. 89, the liquidator will call a meeting of the creditors
within 28 days of forming this opinion (IA 1986, s. 95). The liquidator will preside at the
meeting, setting out in the prescribed form the affairs of the company. Following the
day of this meeting, IA 1986 holds that the winding-up becomes a creditors' voluntary
winding-up (IA 1986, s. 96). In the event that a member's winding-up becomes a creditors'
winding-up, ss. 98 and 99 do not apply. The procedure, as described in this paragraph and
the last, is only effective where the directors have made a declaration of solvency under
IA 1986, s. 89. Where they have not, the creditors' meeting procedure must be followed.

IA 1986, s. 98 provides for a meeting of the creditors to be summoned within 14 days
after the day of the company meeting where a resolution for the winding-up of the company is to be proposed. Notification of the meeting must be given to the creditors by post
not less than seven days before the meeting and be advertised in the *London Gazette* and
in two newspapers. The directors of the company will lay a statement of affairs before the
creditors, and it is the duty of the directors to choose one of them to preside over the meeting (IA 1986, s. 99). The creditors will be able to choose the liquidator and make arrangements for the remuneration to be paid (IA 1986, s. 100). The creditors are also empowered
to appoint a liquidation committee of not more than five persons to exercise the functions
of the liquidator (IA 1986, s. 101).

The same restrictions on the company's ability to trade and a restriction on the disposal
of assets are imposed in the same way as where the winding-up is performed by the court.

15.7.1.4 **The liquidator**

The liquidator, who must be a qualified insolvency practitioner, is appointed to wind up the company and to dispose of its assets in the best interests of the creditors and formally remove the company's registration at Companies House. The liquidator will seek to collect any assets that are owed to the company and then dispose of these to realize any capital. Having realized these assets, the proceeds are then distributed to the creditors, and having settled its debts (where possible), any remaining proceeds are distributed to the company's members. A very significant power is provided through IA 1986, s. 178, which gives the liquidator the power to disclaim onerous property so as to cease the company from completing unprofitable contracts. The third party would then have to bring an action for breach against the company but they would be considered to be an unsecured creditor.

Where the liquidator believes that a person should make some contribution to the company's assets, they may make an application to the court (IA 1986, s. 214). If, in the course of the winding-up of a company, it appears that a person who was or is an officer of the company; a liquidator or administrative receiver of the company; or has been or is concerned in the promotion, formation, or management of the company, has misapplied or retained money or property of the company, or is guilty of any misfeasance or in breach of any other fiduciary duty, the court may, on the application of the Official Receiver, liquidator, or any creditor or contributory, examine the person's conduct. Following this investigation, the court may compel them to repay, restore, or account for the money or property or any part of it (including interest at a rate the court thinks fit—IA 1986, s. 212).

Consider

Roman and Carlos have repaid a loan from Carlos to the company. This has occurred two months before the company was wound up insolvent. Given the IA 1986, s. 239, the liquidator is entitled to apply for a restorative order to make Carlos pay back this money and for him to join the other unsecured creditors when all the assets and duties of the company have been satisfied.

Where the company has gone into liquidation, and at some time before the commencement the person knew, or ought reasonably had known, that there was no reasonable prospect of the company avoiding the liquidation, and that person was a director/shadow director at the time, they shall be guilty of wrongful trading if they did not take reasonable steps to minimize any potential loses to the creditors (IA 1986, s. 214).

Consider

The company's auditor had informed Carlos and Roman in November 2017 to cease trading, yet they continued trading until the company was wound-up in March 2018. Therefore, as directors, they 'knew, or ought to have concluded' about the lack of a reasonable prospect of the company avoiding insolvency. Their optimism of trading out of financial trouble is no excuse and they will be personally liable for the amount of the assets depleted from the company by their decision to continue to trade.

15.7.1.5 **Effect of charges on winding-up**

Where a fixed charge has been applied to an asset(s), when the company is wound up the charge holder may take control of the asset and dispose of it to obtain monies owed (any surplus being paid back to the company). In respect of floating charges, the priority of the charge depends upon when it was made (and this is important where the company has insufficient funds to satisfy its debts). Prior to 15 September 2003, any affected floating charge holder could appoint an administrative receiver. They received money owed following the payment of the liquidator and the debts having been paid of the preferential creditors (see **16.13.3**). Following these payments, and those made to floating charge holders, unsecured creditors were paid and then the members in accordance with the articles.

Consider

A floating charge will generally allow the holder to take possession of the assets and recover owed money on crystallization. However, an important issue has happened in the scenario which requires attention and may change your answer. The Insolvency Act 1986, s. 245 must be considered. Where such a charge is granted to a person unconnected to the company within 12 months of it becoming insolvent, the charge will be invalidated. This does not stop the company owing the money to the bank, simply that the secured status of the loan is lost and the bank is now an unsecured creditor.

Table 15.1 identifies the priority of charges/liabilities when correctly registered.

For those floating charges made after 15 September 2003 the payments are in the same order insofar as the liquidator makes a provision called 'top-slicing', which will establish assets that will be distributed after the preferential creditors are paid and before the floating charge holders are. Further, these charges after 2003 only entitle the holder to appoint an administrator, rather than an administrative receiver.

Top-slicing is a term that relates to the obligation on the liquidator to set aside a proportion of the assets that would otherwise have been paid straight to the holder of a floating charge and maintain this in respect of the unsecured creditors. This amount is 50 per cent of the company's property, having paid the costs and any money owed to preferential creditors, up to £10,000. If the value of the company's property is less than £10,000, the

Table 15.1 Priority of charges

Priority	Type of charge	Rank
1	Fixed charge holders	Rank higher than existing floating charges unless the existing floating charge has made provision against this (fixed charges have effect from the time they are created)
2	Preferential creditors	Take priority over the holders of floating charges, but not over fixed charges. Preferential creditors include employees
3	Floating charge holders	(Takes effect when it crystallizes.) Has priority when the charge was created (hence the first floating charge will have priority over the last one created over the same asset, unless this is stated to the contrary)

liquidator has discretion not to distribute these funds to unsecured creditors where to do so would produce unreasonable costs. Where the property is in excess of the £10,000 figure, a further 20 per cent, up to £600,000, is retained for the purpose of top-slicing.

Evidently, business with companies involves risk and where goods are being supplied to companies on credit, it may be prudent to include a reservation of title clause (known as a Romalpa clause—see **9.2.1**) in the contracts so that upon liquidation, where the supplier has not been paid, these goods do not belong to the company and may not be disposed of and added to the company's funds.

Consider

Following the winding-up of the company and the liquidator realizing its assets, the distribution will be as follows—the liquidator will be paid their expenses; preferential debts will be paid (here it is the owed wages); payment of a (valid) floating charge—but the bank's floating charge is not such; unsecured debts will then be paid. As the company does not have sufficient assets to fulfil its obligations, unsecured creditors are paid on a *pari passu* basis. There will be no money left to distribute to the members of Ecclesall FC Ltd.

15.7.2 Administration

As opposed to appointing a liquidator to govern the winding-up of the company, IA 1986 introduced a mechanism for the appointment of an administrator to manage its affairs (this is often seen with professional football teams such as Leeds United Football Club Ltd in 2007). The powers of the administrator are contained in IA 1986 (as amended) and in exercising these they are acting as the company's agent. The administrator must also be qualified to act as an insolvency practitioner (IA 1986, Sch. B1, para. 6). The administrator is appointed either by the administration order of the court, by the holder of a floating charge, or by the company or its directors (IA 1986, Sch. B1, para. 2). The purpose of the administrator is to perform their functions with the objective of rescuing the company as a going concern (unless the administrator does not think it is reasonably practicable to achieve this), achieving a better result for the company's creditors as a whole than would be likely if the company was wound up, or realizing property in order to make a distribution to one or more secured or preferential creditors (IA 1986, Sch. B1, para. 3). A court will make an order for administration if it is satisfied that the company is unable, or is likely to become unable, to pay its debts and the order will be likely to achieve the aims as established in Sch. B1, para. 3 (IA 1986, Sch. B1, para. 11). On administration the company is restricted from going into liquidation and being wound up, save for the provisions identified in Sch. B1, para. 42.

15.7.2.1 Administrative receivership

Those holders of floating charges made before 15 September 2003 may appoint a receiver to realize the company's property and obtain owed money. If the charges relate to a majority or all of the company's assets then this appointment will be of an administrative receiver. This position provides the administrative receiver with the authority to dispose of the assets to which the floating charge relates, and having provided for the costs in realizing these assets, and the preferential creditors being paid, the monies will be distributed to the charge holders.

CONCLUSION

This chapter has identified the administrative requirements of a company, from the regulation of the company's meetings, and the interaction of the members with the company, and how the various resolutions may be moved. The chapter has also considered the main mechanisms for bringing a company to an end and the procedures involved for the directors, members, and creditors. The following chapter considers the regulation of the company's finances and maintenance of capital to protect the members and creditors, and (hopefully) to ensure the company need not face financial difficulties that require its winding-up.

SUMMARY OF MAIN POINTS

Capacity to trade

*   Public companies must possess a share capital of not less than £50,000.

*   Having supplied the required documents to the Registrar, a public company will be issued with a trading certificate that allows a company to begin trading. Private companies have this immediate capacity.

*   Procedures exist for the re-registration of companies.

Company meetings

*   Companies may, and in some cases must, hold Annual General Meetings (AGMs) and general meetings.

*   Public companies must hold AGMs but private companies need not.

*   Members of a private company, with the required minimum paid-up capital, can require the directors to call a meeting.

*   On application, a court can also require a meeting of the company and for it to be conducted as it sees fit.

*   A private company must give at least 14 days' notice of a general meeting.

*   A public company must give 14 days' notice of general meetings other than an AGM, which requires 21 days' notice.

*   Details of the meeting must be sent to the members and directors of the company.

*   Members holding the required percentage of voting rights may oblige the company to circulate details of the meetings and the resolutions to be moved (but not exceeding 1,000 words).

*   The meetings must be presided over by a chairperson, and a quorum of members must be present to lawfully move resolutions.

Resolutions

*   Resolutions are decisions made at company meetings.

*   There are various types of resolutions and they are used depending on the nature of the decision to be taken. Resolutions may be ordinary, special, or written.

*   The company must maintain records of its decisions taken at meetings and the resolutions moved.

Winding-up of companies

*   To bring a company to an end it must be legally wound up.

*   Courts have the power to wind up a company on petition.

- A petition may be presented by the company, the directors, the members, or a creditor(s), and there is also provision for the Secretary of State to petition the court.

- When the company is wound up, fixed charges allow the holder to dispose of those assets (with any additional revenue being returned to the company).

- Upon winding-up, any floating charges 'crystallize' and employees are dismissed.

- Winding-up may be achieved through the members' moving a special resolution and the appointing of a liquidator. The directors must be in a position to file a declaration of solvency if they wish to avoid summoning a creditors' meeting that could overrule their choice of liquidator.

- The creditors of a company are entitled to meet and overrule the members' choice of liquidator where the directors have not made the declaration of insolvency.

- Administrators are appointed to continue to run the business, whilst a liquidator is appointed to oversee the company's winding-up.

- Following the liquidation of the company, the creditors are paid according to a hierarchy, beginning with preferential creditors and ending with the members of the company.

- Since 15 September 2003, top-slicing has been introduced, which requires the liquidator to retain a proportion of the company's property (subject to a floating charge) to pay unsecured creditors.

 SUMMARY QUESTIONS

Essay questions

1. How may the members of the company engage in the management of the company at general meetings? Explain the rights of the members and how they directly affect the decision-making through the moving of resolutions.

2. Assess the role of a liquidator appointed to oversee the winding-up of a company. Explain the powers granted to the liquidator and how they may deal with the directors and creditors of the company.

Problem questions

1. All Bright Consumables (ABC) Ltd was a successful company, operating primarily a business of developing and selling technology products. It supplied goods to customers directly, but had a particularly lucrative contract to supply its touch screen computers to a sales company (Sign'em Up Quick Plc (SUQ)).

   As the recession hit the UK, ABC Ltd found it difficult to maintain its standards and started using inferior technology in its products. It entered into an agreement with HTD to supply these products and granted a charge over its factory for LCD displays supplied by HTD and used in the manufacture of the screens. Soon after using HTD's screens, and with continued complaints regarding reliability and durability, SUQ exercised its right to bring the relationship of supply with ABC Ltd to an end.

   Due to the loss of its contract, ABC Ltd found itself in financial difficulties. It could not maintain repayments to HTD for the supply of the screens. ABC Ltd owed HTD £30,000 for the screens supplied, it had means to satisfy this debt, and asked for the advice of its accountants. The accountants suggested that the company should cease trading immediately and be wound up. However, the directors, eager to rescue the business, continued trading but just continued getting into ever more debt.

Advise HTD as to proceedings it may take to have the company wound up. Would any responsibility be placed on the directors of ABC Ltd for not taking the accountants' advice on ceasing trading?

2. Raz is a minority shareholder (he holds 5 per cent of the shares) of Happy Harry's Bottles Ltd and is concerned by the actions of the directors. The directors are also majority shareholders (holding, jointly, 62 per cent of the shares) who refuse to hold a general meeting when asked to in order to discuss their actions and the future direction of the company. Raz would also like to put a resolution to the meeting and needs information on how, if at all, this may be achieved.

Prepare a report for Raz outlining the rules regarding a company meeting being called, and how many shareholders are needed to require a meeting called for to be held.

 You will find guidance about how to answer these questions online at www.oup.com/uk/marson5e/.

FURTHER READING

Books and articles

Cockerill, A. (2008) 'Floating Charges Hit the Rocks Again' *Solicitors Journal*, Vol. 152, No. 11, p. 22.

Mokal, R. J. (2005) 'Corporate Insolvency Law: Theory and Application' Oxford University Press: Oxford.

Wheeler, S. (1994) 'Empty Rhetoric and Empty Promises: The Creditors' Meeting' *Journal of Law and Society*, Vol. 21, No. 3, p. 350.

Websites, Twitter links, and YouTube channels

http://www.theqca.com
This is a not-for-profit organization that represents the interests, particularly, of smaller quoted companies (those outside of the FTSE 350).

http://www.fca.org.uk
@TheFCA

https://www.youtube.com/user/thefcatv
The Financial Conduct Authority regulates the financial services industry in the UK, by protecting consumers through ensuring healthy competition between financial services providers. It has rule-making, investigatory, and enforcement powers.

http://www.legislation.gov.uk/ukpga/1986/45/contents
The Insolvency Act 1986.

ONLINE RESOURCES

www.oup.com/uk/marson5e/

For further resources relating to this chapter, including self-test questions, an interactive glossary, and key case flashcards.

16 MAINTENANCE OF FINANCE AND CAPITAL

Companies have to adhere to the requirements of the Companies Act (CA) 2006 when issuing shares, altering and reducing their share capital, and granting charges to creditors. Detailed regulation exists and directors who fail in certain duties in these areas may be fined, and even imprisoned on conviction. Those who are lending money (creditors) to the company may wish to secure the loan through a charge over its assets. This ensures that the creditor can take control of the assets subject to the charge if the company is in default. Registration of charges is required to secure them and whilst failure may lead to the director(s) in default being subject to a fine, for the creditor such a situation will result in the loss of the charge and secured creditor status. Hence, the chapter contains vital information for directors, members, and creditors.

Business Scenario 16

Jimmy, Andy, and Ollie operate a business named Jimmy's Pizzeria Ltd. The business was incorporated in January 2015 and its shares, with a nominal value of £1 each, are distributed as follows. Jimmy, Andy, and Ollie (the company's only directors) own 1,000 shares each, Bob owns 3,000 shares and the remaining 1,200 shares are owned by several investors. The following events have occurred:

- Jimmy's Pizzeria Ltd has never declared a profit and consequently no dividends have been issued. This has continually angered Bob. Bob is unaware of whether this is a deliberate choice by the directors or simply a lack of ability on their behalf. Bob has sought to change the directors of the company but has been blocked by the current directors at general meetings.

- Bob attempts to secretly purchase shares from the other investors in order to gain the majority needed to replace the directors. When Jimmy, Andy, and Ollie discover this fact, they cause the company to issue 2,000 more shares and offer these to Jimmy's friend Jack. Jack, they believe, will be favourable to the directors and vote in their favour.

- Jack has a cash flow problem and thus offers to pay £1,300 in cash and has used his boat as consideration for the remaining £800. The boat is not valued and this matter is not referred to the members of the company.

Learning Outcomes

- Explain the nature and characteristics of a share and the different types of shares (16.2–16.6)
- Understand the requirement of the necessity of maintaining capital (16.4.2–16.4.2.1)
- Identify the procedures involved in issuing shares (16.9)

- Explain the nature of a company obtaining secured and unsecured loans (16.12–16.13.1)
- Explain the registration procedure process for charges applied to company assets (16.13.2–16.13.3).

16.1 INTRODUCTION

This chapter continues from the discussion of the administration of the company to consider the broad issue of corporate governance. It identifies how a company may raise capital, and considers the obligations placed on the directors to protect and maintain the capital of the company for its members. There are rules regarding the issuing of shares and granting of **debentures** to protect the company and the creditors from abuse; how **dividends** are to be agreed and provided to shareholders; and these must be understood to appreciate the effects of CA 2006 on companies, and to ensure these rules are not (innocently, negligently, or fraudulently) transgressed.

16.2 SHARES

A share is a bundle of rights and duties that the holder possesses in relation to the company and the other members. Under CA 2006, s. 540 a share means a share in the company's share capital which includes rights to attend meetings, vote, and/or receive a dividend. The share also provides liabilities to the owner to contribute the amount of capital required to be paid when called up by the company (if the shares, for instance, had not been fully paid for—The Companies (Model Articles) Regulations 2008, Art. 21). However, shareholders are only liable for this investment and do not have to contribute more if the company cannot satisfy its debts. This is the concept of the shareholders' limited liability. Shares are considered as personal property (and are not in the nature of real estate—CA 2006, s. 541), and as such the shares of any member may be transferred in accordance with the company's articles (CA 2006, s. 544). The share must have a fixed nominal value (or it is void) and each share must be distinguished by its appropriate number except when the shares are fully paid up and rank without preference (**pari passu**), or all the issued shares of a particular class are fully paid up and rank *pari passu* for all purposes (CA 2006, s. 543).

16.3 SHAREHOLDERS

CA 2006 refers to a company's members, but essentially this refers, in this instance, to the shareholders of the company. The shareholders are deemed to 'own' the company because they will have made an investment, such as by purchasing shares, and whilst this will be performed in the expectation of a return on their investment (such as through dividends or an increase in the value of the shares) they are entrusting their investment to a body with its own legal personality. Despite 'ownership', each of the shareholders could not expect to play an active role in the company's day-to-day management. As such, the members delegate the task of management to directors who are answerable (to varying degrees) to the shareholders. However, whilst the powers of the directors may be very broad and can bind the company into contracts and provide and take loans on the company's behalf, the role and powers possessed by shareholders must not be underestimated.

16.4 SHARE CAPITAL

When the company limited by shares is formed, the subscribers identify the amount of capital received from the share issue. The nature of limited companies, and hence the limit to the personal liability of its members, is very important to those doing business with the organization. The identification of the share capital reassures the company's creditors that sufficient funds (capital) are present in the event that the business fails and that the company will be in a position to satisfy its debts. It is for this reason that there are detailed provisions on how a company may alter or reduce its share capital.

A company having a share capital is considered under CA 2006 to possess a power under its constitution to issue shares (CA 2006, s. 545). These shares are required to have a nominal value (CA 2006, s. 542), identified in Sterling, euros, or some other nominated currency. This nominal value is the amount that the company and the purchaser have agreed as the purchase price for the share and this value may not be lowered (or this would constitute a fraud on the company). This nominal value is the lowest price that the share will be sold for. However, it may be possible (and indeed could prove advantageous) for the share to be transferred at a higher value than this, and this value is the share premium. It must be noted that when a company manages to receive a premium on the shares issued, this must be transferred into a share premium account and not distributed to the members as dividends. The money in the share premium account cannot be used to write off expenses such as when debentures are issued or for any costs incurred in forming the company, although it may be used to offset expenses incurred in the issuing of the shares involved (CA 2006, s. 610). This figure is then treated for the purposes of the company as capital and would be included in the company's balance sheet at the end of the year.

Shares are usually issued to raise capital and the most common form is in money (although some companies issue shares in return for assets or work completed and part of the payment is in the issue of shares—although this is subject to strict rules). The issue of raising capital in this manner is particularly important. Whereas loans taken by the company (and possibly secured on the company's assets) have to be repaid in accordance with the loan agreement, shares that are issued for an investment of capital do not involve any loan, and despite the dilution of the percentage of their shareholding of the major shareholder(s) by issuing shares to others, there is no right to a dividend on the shares held unless this is agreed at the general meeting (and from the company's profits). Loans have to be repaid whether the company has dispersible profits or not.

A company's share capital may be considered under the following headings.

16.4.1 Share Capital

This refers to the amount of capital that the company was registered with (the share capital may be raised by the decision of the directors (unless the articles provide otherwise) or through a resolution at a later date if required—CA 2006, s. 617). For example, a public company with a minimum £50,000 of share capital may have this divided into 50,000 £1 shares, and these will be distributed as the subscribers see fit.

- *Issued share capital:* Issued share capital refers to the amount of the authorized share capital that has been issued (a company does not have to issue all of its shares in the authorized share capital—CA 2006, s. 546). This relates to the funding that the company has received from the members. To continue the example above, that the company has the power to issue 50,000 shares does not mean that they have all been issued at the formation of the company. The company may have issued 40,000 of the £1 shares and hence it has an authorized share capital of £50,000, but an issued share capital of £40,000. It is this fund that the creditors will go to in the event of the company's insolvency.

- *Allotted share capital:* Allotted share capital naturally refers to shares that have been allotted. Both issued and allotted shares include those taken on the formation of the company by the subscribers to the company's memorandum (CA 2006, s. 546). Shares are allotted when a person acquires an unconditional right to be included in the company's register of members in respect of the shares (CA 2006, s. 558). A person who has been allotted shares may not necessarily take up these shares personally and may choose to transfer their right to others. However, the directors can (and at some time will) call up any payment owing on the shares because the subscribers, when forming the company, enter into a contract with it regarding the shares and their willingness to take these (and pay the nominal value).

- *Paid-up share capital:* The paid-up share capital is the amount of the nominal share capital that has been paid for by the company members (albeit that any premium paid does not count in this calculation). In the earlier example, when shares are allotted to the members it may not, at that time, require payment in full. The £1 shares remain at £1 but the company may have only required 50 pence per share to be paid. Hence, of the £40,000 issued share capital, the paid-up capital is £20,000.

- *Called-up share capital:* This refers to the share capital that the directors have 'called-up', including any share capital paid up without being called, and any share capital to be paid up on a specified future date under the articles. It includes the terms of allotment of the relevant shares or any other arrangements for payment of those shares (CA 2006, s. 547).

16.4.2 Alteration of Share Capital

Whilst a private company is not required to have any prescribed amount of share capital, compared with a public company's requirement of £50,000, it will identify its share capital on formation but may, at a later date, wish to vary this amount in light of its changing circumstances. Whilst generally it is prevented from doing so (CA 2006, s. 617) there are exceptions where the company wishes to increase its share capital by:

- allotting new shares, reduce its share capital in accordance with Chapter 10 of CA 2006, where it wishes to subdivide (e.g. to change 100 £1 shares to 1,000 10p shares) or consolidate (e.g. to change the existing shares to a smaller number of shares—1000 10p shares to 100 £1 shares) all or any of its shares, where it wishes to reconvert stock into shares (however, CA 2006, s. 620 prevents shares from being converted into stock, unless they were converted into stock before the Act—where they can be reconverted), or where it wishes to redenominate any or all of its shares (e.g. to convert the shares from one currency to another).

Where a company wishes to allot new shares, a contract has to be established between the parties that identifies the important information such as the amount of capital involved, when this capital is to be contributed, the nature and class of the shares to be allotted, and when the shares will provide the allottee with their rights attached to the shares. Chapter 2 of CA 2006 governs the allotment of shares and identifies the authority of directors to allot (CA 2006, s. 549). Where a private company has only one class of share, the director(s) is empowered to allot shares in the company unless the articles prevent this

(CA 2006, s. 550). Where a company has more than one class of share, or the company is a PLC, there must be authority provided by the company's articles or through a resolution of the company (a resolution of a company to give, vary, revoke, or renew authorization under this section may be an ordinary resolution, even though it amends the company's articles—CA 2006, s. 551). This authority may be conditional or unconditional, and it must state the maximum amount of shares that may be allotted, and specify the date on which the power will expire (which must not be more than five years from the date of incorporation (where the power is from the company's articles) or the date that the resolution was passed). This power may be extended for a period not exceeding five years. Having received the authority to allot shares, any further resolution will identify the maximum amount of shares to be allotted and identify the expiry date of the power. To maintain the company's capital, it is not permitted to issue the shares at a discount (CA 2006, s. 552), although the company may pay the subscriber a commission for their subscribing or agreeing to subscribe (CA 2006, s. 553). Having allotted shares, the company must inform the Registrar (of Companies) as soon as practicable and in any event within two months after the date of allotment (CA 2006, s. 554), and within one month of making the allotment, the company must deliver to the Registrar a return of allotment detailing the statement of capital (CA 2006, s. 555).

Shares may be consolidated for convenience by altering shares that were issued in small denominations into larger amounts. This does not change the percentage of the total number of shares. Subdividing is the contrary situation and involves the shares being 'reduced' into smaller denominations because, for example, in their current division the price is too great to attract investors. In relation to subdividing and consolidating shares, the proportion between the amount paid and the amount unpaid (if any) on each share must be the same as it was from the share from which it derived (CA 2006, s. 618). The company is empowered to make such a change where the members pass an ordinary resolution to that effect (although the company's articles may require a higher majority or may exclude or restrict any power conferred by CA 2006). If the company does make such a change, it must inform the Registrar within one month of having made the change along with a statement of capital (detailing the total number of shares of the company, their nominal value, the amounts of paid and unpaid shares, and so on—CA 2006, s. 619).

Where the shares are to be redenominated, the company's articles may impose restrictions and the members must pass a resolution authorizing this (which may specify conditions that must be met before the redenomination takes effect—CA 2006, s. 622). This will include details such as the exchange rate utilized, and the redenomination must take place within 28 days, ending on the day before the resolution was passed. Following the redenomination, the company must notify the Registrar of the changes within one month of doing so (CA 2006, s. 625), including a statement of capital and, within 15 days of the resolution being passed, a copy of the resolution. It is also important to note that redenomination does not affect any rights or obligations of the members under the company's constitution, or any restrictions affecting members (CA 2006, s. 624).

16.4.2.1 Reduction of share capital

A company may seek to reduce its share capital because its assets have permanently decreased in value, it may be a tactic to eliminate book debts (this is an uncollected debt owed to a company), or to return capital to shareholders where the capital involved is surplus to the company's requirements, and so on. A private company may achieve a reduction in the share capital by a special resolution supported by a **solvency statement**. However, the reduction must still leave at least one member with a share(s) (and one that is not a redeemable share—CA 2006, s. 641). Private and public companies may, through a special resolution confirmed by the court, reduce their share capital. However, the company may have provisions in the articles that restrict or prohibit such a reduction. The private company that wishes to reduce its share capital, supported by a statement of solvency, requires the directors of the company to make the statement not more than 15 days before the date on which the resolution is passed, and the resolution and the statement are registered in accordance with s. 644 (CA 2006, s. 642). The statement must identify, with respect to the company's share capital as reduced by the resolution, the total number of shares of the company, the aggregate nominal value of those shares, the amount paid up, and the amount (if any) unpaid on each share; and for each class of share, the rights attached to the shares, the total number of shares of that class, and the aggregate nominal value of shares of that class. The validity of a resolution is not affected by a failure to deliver the documents required, but an offence is committed and is punishable by a fine of the company and every officer of the company who is in default.

Where the resolution is proposed as a written resolution, a copy of the solvency statement must be sent or submitted to every eligible member at or before the time the proposed resolution is sent or submitted. Where the resolution is proposed at a general meeting, a copy of the solvency statement must be made available for inspection by the members of the company throughout that meeting. The validity of the resolution is not affected by a failure to comply with these sections of the Act (CA 2006, s. 642). The solvency statement requires the directors to have formed the opinion, with regard to the company's situation at the date of the statement, that there is no ground on which the company could then be found to be unable to pay (or otherwise discharge) its debts. Further, the directors must have formed the opinion that if it is intended to commence the winding-up of the company within 12 months of that date, that the company will be able to pay (or otherwise discharge) its debts in full within 12 months of the commencement of the winding-up, or in any other case that the company will be able to pay (or otherwise discharge its debts) as they fall due during the year immediately following that date. The resolution for the reduction is effective when the documents are registered with the Registrar.

Where a company has sought to reduce its share capital through a special resolution as noted earlier, it may have this confirmed by the court. If this proposed reduction of capital involves a diminution of liability in respect of unpaid share capital or the payment to a shareholder of any paid-up share capital, s. 646 allows the creditors to object to the reduction unless the court directs otherwise (CA 2006, s. 645). If the court does not disapply the provision of s. 645, every creditor of the company who is entitled to any debt or claim is entitled to object to the reduction of capital (CA 2006, s. 646). In practice, the company will provide the court with evidence that all the creditors have consented to the action, producing guarantees where necessary. Where an officer of the company intentionally or recklessly conceals the name of a creditor entitled to object to the reduction or they misrepresent the nature or amount of the debt or claim of a creditor, or where they are knowingly concerned in any such concealment or misrepresentation, they commit an offence punishable by a fine (CA 2006, s. 647).

The court may make an order confirming the reduction of capital on such terms and conditions as it thinks fit. Where it confirms the reduction, the court may order the company to publish the reasons for the reduction, or other information that it thinks fit to give proper information to the public. It may also require the company, where special reasons exist, to add to its name the words 'and reduced' during a period specified in the court's order (CA 2006, s. 648). When the court has provided its order confirming the reduction, the Registrar will register the order and the statement of capital (CA 2006, s. 649).

16.5 SHARE CERTIFICATE

A share certificate that is correctly issued is evidence of the holder's legal title to the shares identified in the certificate (CA 2006, s. 768). The nature of such a document enables the holder to use the ownership as a form of collateral/security. The company must issue certificates on allotment within two months unless the issue provides otherwise; the allotment is to a financial institution; or if, following the allotment, the company has issued a share warrant in respect of the shares (CA 2006, s. 769).

16.6 TYPES OF SHARE

Due to the nature of shares and the fact that companies may issue shares to generate capital, the company must ensure that as many of the shares issued are taken up to realize the investment of capital required. The shares provide rights and impose duties on the shareholders but a company has an ability to issue different types of share, with different rights attached to them, depending on what shares it considers investors will wish to purchase and so on. The articles of the company may provide the company with authority to issue different classes of shares. The Companies (Model Articles) Regulations 2008 provide for the right to issue different classes of share subject to the provisions of CA 2006, and where not to prejudice the rights of existing shareholders. Where different types of share are issued, these are placed in identifiable 'classes' and the 'class rights' that attach to the shares will ensure the shareholders have knowledge of the class and their rights under this class. This is important as the classes of shares may, for example, entitle the holder to more votes per share in company meetings, to preferential treatment when dividends are announced, and so on. When the company issues shares of different classes, this will be identified in the articles of association or the articles may be amended for this purpose through an ordinary resolution, and the details of the different shares and the rights attached have to be sent to the Registrar.

There are a variety of shares that a company may issue but the most commonly used are ordinary and preference shares, and these may or may not be redeemed by the company at a later date.

* *Ordinary shares:* These are the most common form of shares, and unless different classes of shares exist, all shares will be ordinary shares. When compared with preference shares the ordinary shares have a lesser status and the holders are more at risk if problems affect the company's ability to pay dividends or its solvency. The ordinary shareholders have the right to vote at general meetings and the right to receive a dividend if one is declared. However, they are only entitled to a dividend after preference shareholders receive theirs, and there may also be provision for the preference shareholders to receive a share from the company's remaining assets before ordinary shareholders in the event of the company being wound up.
* *Preference shares:* The nature of the distinction between ordinary shares and preference shares relates to the rights that attach to the shareholders of each class. The preference shareholder's main benefit over ordinary shareholders is in the right to a fixed dividend ahead of any dividend payment made to any other class of shares. However, as with any other dividend, this may only be paid from the company's profits and hence there is no guarantee to a payment being declared. The company will fix the amount of the dividend and this may be on a cumulative or non-cumulative basis.

Cumulative preference shares provide the right for a fixed dividend, but if there are insufficient profits in the given year then there is no payment made. However, the dividend cumulates to the next year and is added to the dividend that is applicable to that year. For example, if a company issues James with 100 £1 preference shares with a fixed dividend of 5 per cent, and at the end of the first year that James has held these shares the company has insufficient funds to issue a dividend, James gets nothing. Next year, the company has profits to distribute as dividends and as James' situation has not changed: he is entitled to 5 per cent of the profits for the current year (£5) and 5 per cent of the dividends owed for last year (£5). As a consequence, James receives £10 in dividends.

- Preference shares may also be non-cumulative, and in this situation, the holder is entitled to a fixed dividend from the company's profits, but where no profits are available, no dividend is paid. In the subsequent years, where there are profits and the company can issue dividends, the holders of preference shares are entitled to their fixed dividend. Further, where the company is wound up but is still solvent after paying the creditors, the preference shareholders may have the right to claim repayment of capital ahead of the ordinary shareholders.

- Where preference shareholders may be at a disadvantage compared with ordinary shareholders is that the company may not provide the holders of preference shares with the right to vote at general meetings (unless their dividends are in arrears). As such they have no right to influence the company in its decision-making. They are also unable to share in any surplus of the company that has been wound up and still solvent. When the creditors and other liabilities have been paid, if there is money left over, the ordinary shareholders will share in this distribution and the preference shareholders will not (however, of course, this is rather unlikely).

- *Redeemable shares:* A limited company that has a share capital has the power to issue shares that are to be redeemed or are liable to be redeemed at the option of the company or the shareholder (CA 2006, s. 684). A private limited company may exclude this right through its articles and does not require any express authorization to do so, but a public limited company may only issue redeemable shares if its articles authorize such an action. Redeemable shares may be issued only where other shares are in issue that are not redeemable (CA 2006, s. 684(4)). This ensures that a company does not issue only redeemable shares and, once redeemed, only the directors of the company remain with no members.

- A private limited company is only able to redeem shares out of capital in accordance with Chapter 5 of CA 2006, but specifically from distributable profits of the company or the proceeds of a fresh issue of shares made for the purposes of the redemption (CA 2006, s. 687). Having redeemed the shares, they are to be treated as cancelled and the amount of the company's issued share capital is diminished according to the nominal value of the redeemed shares (CA 2006, s. 688).

16.7 CHANGING CLASS RIGHTS

Where the company has just one class of share that carries with it the same rights, duties, and liabilities, then this is identified in the articles and all the members are in the same position with regard to votes at meetings, dividends, and so on (CA 2006, s. 629). However, the company may decide that it wishes to have different classes of shares, and with these different rights and liabilities. To achieve this change the company must look to its articles to identify any specific requirements that must take place for an alteration, and if none exist, then the shareholders of the class of share to be altered have to provide their consent (CA 2006, s. 630). The consent is provided through the holders of at least three-quarters of the nominal value of the issued shares of that class giving their written approval. Further, the company may gain the consent through the passing of a special resolution at a general meeting of the holders of that class of shares sanctioning the variation. These are minimum requirements required by CA 2006 and the company's articles may insist on more onerous requirements if it sees fit. Having successfully varied the class of shares, the company must inform the Registrar of the particulars of the variation within one month of so doing (CA 2006, s. 637).

Where the company has varied the class of shares as noted above, there is a provision for holders of not less than 15 per cent of the issued shares of the class in question (and who did not consent or vote in favour of the special resolution) to apply to a court to have the variation cancelled (CA 2006, s. 633). Where an application is made, the variation will not take effect until the court confirms the variation, and a variation may be refused by the court where to allow it would unfairly prejudice the holders of the shares concerned (CA 2006, s. 633).

16.8 THE COMPANY'S PURCHASE OF ITS OWN SHARES

A general rule exists that a limited company is prevented from acquiring its own shares, whether by purchase, subscription, or otherwise, except in accordance with Chapter 1, Part 18 of CA 2006. Contravention of this rule by the company and its directors in default is punishable on conviction on indictment for a term of up to two years' imprisonment (CA 2006, s. 658). Exceptions exist because it may lead to greater investment where venture capitalists may be willing to purchase shares if permitted to sell the shares back to the company; shareholdings in smaller companies (such as those which are completely family-owned) may be more easily managed if a shareholder wished to sell shares but no other member was in a position to purchase them and they could simply sell them to the company and so on. Therefore, CA 2006 makes provision for such sales.

A limited company that has a share capital may purchase its own shares (including redeemable shares—CA 2006, s. 690), subject to Chapter 4 of CA 2006 and any restrictions in the company's articles. The limited company is prevented from purchasing its own shares where to do so would result in there no longer being any issued shares of the company other than redeemable shares or shares held as treasury shares. The company may not purchase its own shares unless they are fully paid for, and the company, as purchaser, pays for them on purchase (and as such it cannot purchase unissued shares—CA 2006, s. 691). The authority for the company's purchase of its shares requires the agreement by the seller, and the appropriate authority for the company to act in this way. The company may finance the purchase only through distributable profits or the proceeds of a fresh issue of shares made for the purpose of financing the purchase; and any premium paid for its own shares must be paid out of distributable profits. However, this premium may only be paid in this circumstance up to an amount equal to the lesser of the aggregate of the premiums received by the company on the issue of the shares purchased; or the current amount of the company's share premium account (CA 2006, s. 692).

16.9 **SHARE ISSUE**

A company may wish to issue shares. These shares can be purchased from the company directly, they may be bought and transferred from an existing member, or they may be transferred by an operation of law (such as where shares have been inherited on the death of a member). This information will be provided through the company's annual return.

Shares relate to a company's share capital, and references to shares in CA 2006 include stock, unless a distinction between them is expressed or may be implied (CA 2006, s. 540). When a decision is taken to issue shares or to grant rights to subscribe for, or to convert any security into shares (of more than one class) by the directors of the company, the express authorization of the members must be secured (CA 2006, s. 549). This, however, does not apply to the allotment of (or right to subscribe for) shares under an employees' share scheme. The CA 2006, s. 558 provides: 'For the purposes of the Companies Acts shares in a company are taken to be allotted when a person acquires the unconditional right to be included in the company's register of members in respect of the shares.' Any director who knowingly contravenes or permits/authorizes such a contravention commits an offence under the Act and is subject to a fine on conviction. CA 2006, s. 550 continues that in private companies with only one class of shares, a director may exercise their power to allot shares of that class; grant rights to subscribe for shares; or convert any security into such shares, except where they are prohibited from doing so by the company's articles. A director(s) may exercise the power to allot shares if they are authorized to do so by the articles of association or by a resolution of the company (CA 2006, s. 551). The issue must be for a 'proper purpose' and not, for instance, to prevent a take-over by another person. Such an authorization is usually provided by an ordinary resolution at a general meeting and may take the form of a general power to allot shares (with a stated maximum amount of shares to be allotted under the authorization) or authorization for the specific shares being allotted. The power is provided in this respect for a fixed period of five years but may be renewed at such intervals. This authority may be revoked or varied by an ordinary resolution where the power has not been exercised. As soon as practicable after the allotment (or in any event no later than two months following the date of allotment) the company must register this fact unless the company has issued a share warrant in respect of the shares (CA 2006, s. 554). A company limited by shares may, if authorized by its articles, issue in relation to any fully paid shares a warrant providing the bearer with entitlement to the shares specified on it. The company may, if authorized by its articles, provide for the payment of future dividends on shares included in the warrant (CA 2006, s. 779). An offence, subject to a fine on conviction, is committed where a company fails to comply with the registration requirement.

Consider

The shares offered to Jack will affect the shareholdings of the other members of the company. Dilution of shareholdings is an issue and existing shareholders have pre-emption rights. This does not invalidate the issue, but means the directors responsible may have to compensate the shareholders who could have benefitted from the offer—such as Bob.

- *Pre-emption rights:* Where shares are being issued under CA 2006, s. 549, in both public and private companies, and hence the members have provided their authority for this action, the company is obliged to offer ordinary shares (in CA 2006, s. 561 these are referred to as equity securities), but not necessarily preference shares, to the existing members on a proportionate basis to their existing number of shares held (known as a right of **pre-emption**—CA 2006, s. 561). This is a requirement to ensure that existing shareholders do not have their stake in the company reduced (diluted) without the opportunity to purchase a proportion of the new issue. Where this obligation is contravened, the company and every officer of it who knowingly authorized or permitted it are jointly and severally liable to compensate any person to whom the offer should have been made, in accordance with those provisions for any loss, damage, costs, or expenses which the person has sustained because of the contravention (CA 2006, s. 563). There is a provision to exclude this obligation to offer shares to existing members. A private company may achieve this through making an additional clause to its articles (CA 2006, s. 567), specifically removing the pre-emption rights, although this position can be varied through a special/written resolution altering the articles (CA 2006, s. 571), or if the private company ceases to be a private company (this is a permanent measure). The private company may also use a written resolution to dispense with the pre-emption rights for a particular allotment or a general restriction of the rights for a period of five years (which is renewable). Public companies may remove pre-emption rights through a special resolution that can apply to a particular allotment or a general provision (although, as with private companies, this must be renewed every five years). Where the company is listed on the stock exchange, Listing Rules insist that only 5 per cent of the company's securities can be issued to persons other than existing shareholders in any year. The pre-emption rights do not apply to bonus issues (CA 2006, s. 564), shares issued and to be paid up wholly or partly otherwise than in cash (CA 2006, s. 565), or shares held under an employees' share scheme (CA 2006, s. 566).

- *Directors' duties on share issue:* The directors of a company who possess authority to allot shares are obliged to do so in an equitable manner and CA 2006 codifies existing common law requirements and wider duties to the company (CA 2006, s. 170). Therefore, when allotting shares, directors must refrain from basing the allotment on promoting persons favourable to themselves (such as those sympathetic to the directors and who would follow their decisions in the control and direction of the company). The members have some control in authorizing the allotment of shares and decisions to extend this allotment to persons outside the company (non-existing members).

16.10 PAYMENT

To reiterate the point, shares must not be offered at a discount. Where they are, the allottee is liable to pay the company an amount equal to the amount of the discount and any interest owing (at an appropriate rate—CA 2006, s. 580). The shares that are issued or allotted have to be paid for; however, this does not necessarily mean that such payment must be in cash (CA 2006, s. 582; s. 583 defines the meaning of 'cash').

Consider

Jack has not paid in cash for the full value of the shares. Whilst this is not problematic, an issue regarding the value of the boat needs addressing. Could this constitute offering shares at a discount? Also, the value of the boat has not been independently assessed and, though this is a requirement for public companies, private companies are not subject to the same requirement. For where private companies accept non-cash consideration for shares, the directors must act in good faith. However, *Re Wragg Ltd* [1897] limits the possibility of Bob seeking a remedy in the absence of fraud.

Typically, where companies purchase shares or another corporation they may pay for these through the allocation of shares from their own company or through providing assets. With a private company, the equalization of the value of the items traded for the shares will be a matter for the company.

Re Wragg Ltd (1897)

Facts:

Assets belonging to a business were sold to a company below their real value. A part of this consideration for the business was paid in shares. When the company was wound up, the liquidator pursued the directors, seeking a payment for the shares above their value to reflect the lower value of the assets.

Authority for:

It was for the company and the seller to determine the price for the business—but they must do so honestly. The extent, however, is to whether the non-cash consideration was based on fraud. In its absence, the value of services or property may not be inquired into.

However, with public companies, the shares may only be sold for cash (CA 2006, s. 584). Where the shares are traded for, say, assets (but not for work or services performed for the company—CA 2006, s. 585), the value of the non-cash items must be independently valued to ensure they represent an equivalent value and consequently ensure that the shares have been fully paid up. An auditor (or a person appointed by the auditor) must conduct, independently, the valuation in these circumstances (CA 2006, s. 593). Where non-cash consideration has been accepted for the shares, the contract to this effect must be sent to the Registrar within one month, and the public companies must enclose the valuation report with this contract (CA 2006, s. 597). Having received the information, the Registrar publishes the notice in the London Gazette.

16.11 DIVIDEND PAYMENTS

When an investment is made in a company, there is the hope (if not expectation) that a return will be provided and that may be through a rise in the premium of the shares held, but also on dividends in respect of the shares held. As stated previously, dividends may only be paid from the company's distributable profits (and in cash unless otherwise stated in the articles) as to do otherwise would be to reduce the company's capital. A profit available for distribution is defined as 'its accumulated, realized profits [these are the amounts of income produced through sales of assets that exceed its expenses], so far as not previously utilized by distribution or capitalization, less its accumulated, realized losses [these are the amounts of expenses that exceed the income generated through the sales of its assets], so far as not previously written off in a reduction or reorganization of capital duly made' (CA 2006, s. 830). Whilst it is expected that a company will generate profits and at least a proportion of these will be returned to the members in dividends, there is no automatic right to receive a dividend. Indeed, a company will wish to retain certain monies to enable growth, reinvestment, and a safeguard for certain unexpected costs. This would simply be evidence of prudent management of the company. However, the company must also ensure that the members receive some form of return or else these investors may take their money to another business.

The company's directors recommend a dividend and the amount is contained in the directors' report, and is declared by the members at a general meeting (for a public company). Only public companies have to hold a meeting to declare a dividend. The members have to agree to the amount of the dividend, and they may require the amount to be reduced (but have no right to increase the dividend). Where a director(s) refuses to reduce the dividend, the members can move to have the director(s) concerned removed from office. Creditors have no rights to prevent a dividend being paid to the members. The company's articles may also give the directors the power to pay an interim dividend. Where a dividend is declared but is not paid, then the member(s) affected has up to 12 years in which to bring an action against the company to realize the money owed. This is, however, a contentious point and it will be interesting to see if the courts follow this interpretation of the limitation period or follow the pre-CA 2006 position of limiting claims to six years.

Consider

As no profits are declared, the directors may not issue a dividend. Bob may be angered by this, but the directors are restricted by the CA 2006 from making an issue.

16.12 LOAN CAPITAL

When a company is formed, the members will contribute money to the business, but at some stage the company may have to borrow money to buy stock, invest in technology or premises, and so on. Due to the company's separate legal personality, it has the right to enter into contracts (such as to obtain goods on credit and loan money from banks) and the rights to raise finance are usually contained in the memorandum. These are express rights but the company may have implied rights if it is a trading company. A trading company has the power to buy and sell items as part of its functions, and implicitly to borrow money, and issue its assets as part of security for the loan.

The nature of loan capital is that money is borrowed on the basis of offering some form of security (collateral). With sole traders and simple partnerships, they may raise finance on loans through, for example, providing a bank with a charge over property they own. This may be their own personal property or business property, but a charge is placed on it and it is at risk if the person securing the loan cannot repay. Rather than place a charge over land or property, a company and a Limited Liability Partnership have the ability to provide a 'floating charge' over their assets (such as stock) to the lender, whilst sole traders and partnerships are unable to do so.

The company seeking to borrow money may contact a lending institution that is willing to provide this service, but evidently the lender will require certain formalities to be followed to ensure it will have any loaned money returned. To secure a loan, the company may issue the lender with a debenture.

16.12.1 **Debentures**

A debenture is a document produced in the form of a deed that secures a loan through granting the lender (such as a bank) the right to take control over assets and the business. Therefore, the lender is established as a creditor with the authority to appoint an administrator in the event of non-repayment of the debt. A debenture includes debenture stock, bonds, and any other securities of a company, whether or not constituting a charge on the assets of the company (CA 2006, s. 738). A contract with a company to take up and pay for debentures of the company may be enforced through the courts by an order for specific performance (CA 2006, s. 740).

- *Debenture stock:* Situations involving debenture stock are those where the public have been offered to invest in the company and receive stock certificates rather than investing in shares (and receiving share certificates). These certificates are maintained by the company through a registration process, and the certificates may be transferred in a similar manner to share certificates. Due to the nature of such a way of distributing the assets of the company, and that these debenture holders are 'creditors' of the company (albeit with no contract with the company), there has to be regulation of the company's actions. As such, the creditors enter into a trust deed with trustees who act for the debenture holders, and the trustees possess a charge over the company's assets and may appoint a receiver or administrative receiver when required. A private company limited by shares or by guarantee is not permitted to issue debenture stock to the public, but an offer not made to the public, to a financial institution for example, would be permitted (CA 2006, s. 755). The debenture stock is somewhat different from shares in that whilst it would constitute a fraud to issue shares below their issue value, debentures may be issued at a discount (CA 2006, s. 100).

- *Registration of charges:* When a debenture has been issued or a charge to secure a debenture, it must be registered with the Registrar (CA 2006, s. 860). The reason for registration is that this is a public document and those interested parties may consult the register before deciding to do business with the company. The company is also required to maintain its own copy of the register of charges at its registered office or other suitable place (CA 2006, s. 869), and this must be made freely available for inspection by the company's creditors or members (CA 2006, s. 877). If the company does not register the charge in its register the officers of the company are liable to be fined (CA 2006, s. 876(4)), although lack of such registration does not make the charge invalid. As the registration process is a requirement of law, failure to comply with the obligation to register the charge within 21 days of its creation (CA 2006, s. 870) will result in the charge being void if the company is wound up (and a liquidator appointed) or if an administrator is appointed. This has the effect that the lender does not possess secured creditor status (and hence they lose the protection of possessing a right over the property the company charged against the loan). However, this does not mean that the company does not continue to owe the lender the sum involved, and this will become repayable on request. Due to this potential problem of failure to register, and the concern and problems lack of registration brings, those lenders who are securing a loan on secured debentures may require the forms to be completed by the officers of the company and they take the responsibility to send these to Companies House. Where the 21-day registration period has been missed, a court may approve the registration and the charge will be given effect from the date of this registration. The charge will be satisfied and released through application to the Registrar that the debt relating to the charge has been paid or satisfied, or the property or undertaking charged has been released from the charge or has ceased to form part of the company's property or undertaking. This process will remove the charge from the register (through the issue of a memorandum of satisfaction, a copy of which is sent to the company), and will then enable the company, if it wishes, to secure loans on the property again (CA 2006, s. 872).

16.13 CHARGES

A charge is a contractual agreement in the form of security (on certain assets) for a loan. The borrower agrees to allow the rights over property to be transferred to the lender on the basis that if the loan is unpaid, the lender will be able to dispose of the property and secure the return of the loan. If such a charge is not made, the issue of limited liability may remove the shareholders' personal responsibility to contribute, beyond the value of the shares or any guarantees made, and the lender, if the borrower (e.g. a company) has insufficient funds to repay all of its debts, will have to join the remaining creditors and may not realize all of the money it is owed. Hence, charges are a valuable way of ensuring, as far as possible, that loans are secured on tangible property.

Faced with a situation where the borrower does not repay the debt, the lender with a charge over property may choose to bring an action for breach of contract, or they may choose to dispose of the assets to which they possess a charge. If, in this disposal, there is more money generated than is owed, then following deductions for expenses in selling the property, it must be returned to the borrower.

16.13.1 Types of Charges

As the charge involves a security over assets, it may be that the lender wishes to secure (fix) this on business premises (such as a factory) to ensure that a valuation can be made, and hence the loan be determined that will ensure the lender's position is secure. Whilst such a charge in this respect is commonplace (providing a mortgage over property) this is not the only method, and there is the second type of charge that is not attached to any particular asset. These are known as 'floating' charges as they float over given assets (such as stock). There are advantages to both and it is for the borrower and lender to identify the most suitable in the circumstances.

- *Fixed charges:* The nature of a fixed charge is that it is 'fixed' to a particular asset owned by the borrower, which may be real property or personal property, and it provides the lender with a proprietary interest over the asset. Real property consists of items such as property and land and whilst a charge rests over the property, there is no requirement to transfer the title to the goods to the lender. This leaves the ownership of the property with the borrower, although the Law of Property Act 1925 provides that the lender with a relevant charge is empowered to sell it without the permission or assistance of the title-holder. Personal property includes equipment and requires the borrower to assign the ownership of the property to the lender to ensure the borrower has the power to dispose of the property in the event of non-repayment.

- The benefit of the fixed charge for the lender, and a reason why they may pursue such a charge in determining whether to loan money, is the control over the property. It therefore represents the best form of security. The borrower may be prevented from selling the property that is subject to the charge until the loan is repaid, and the charge remains until the loan is fully repaid. Further, a lender with a fixed charge is generally considered to rank higher than preferential creditors and creditors who possess floating charges.

- *Floating charges:* A fixed charge, therefore, may involve (e.g.) a bank providing a loan to a company on the basis that it holds a charge over the company's factory. The company may use the factory, although it cannot sell it without the bank's authorization, and insofar as the company continues to make the required repayments, the bank will take no further action.

As opposed to a charge that is fixed to a particular asset, the borrower may apply the charge to a group of assets (such as the stock with which the company trades). The benefit for the borrower in this scenario is that they are free to trade in the goods/assets subject to the floating charge, and in the event of non-payment of the loan when it is due, the charge becomes fixed or 'crystallizes' over them. At this stage, the lender has the ability to dispose of the goods in the same way as someone with a fixed charge.

Buchler and Another v Talbot and Another (2004)

Facts:

The case involved a company granting a debenture to another to secure a loan and incorporating a floating charge. When the company went into voluntary liquidation, the liquidator's costs were to exceed the amount realized and they sought a declaration that their expenses should come from the assets of the company, including those subject to the floating charge.

Authority for:

The case related to the priority of claims in a company's liquidation. The House of Lords held there was no priority for the liquidator's expenses. The proceeds of the realization of a floating charge are held for the debenture holder. The other funds realized are available for the company's unsecured creditors.

Crystallization occurs where a receiver is appointed, if the company goes into administration or is wound up, or where an event that was provided for in the contract establishing the floating charge occurs. Once crystallization occurs and the assets are traded after this event, the holder of the charge may bring an action against the party to whom they were transferred.

Clearly, unlike a fixed charge where the charge is applied to a specific asset, the floating charge, by its nature, does not apply to a specific asset. As such, the borrower appears to be in possession of the assets and may appear to be more creditworthy than they actually are. To prevent fraud, and perhaps a situation of the borrower attempting to obtain loans on the assets subject to the floating charge, protection is afforded through a system of registration.

- *Potential difficulties:* What would occur where the parties identify a charge as a fixed charge, when in reality (and legally) it is a floating charge? A lender may wish to obtain a fixed charge, over a floating charge, due to the increased security it provides. However, a company may not have the property available to provide a fixed charge and, further, book debts may represent the company's largest asset. Book debts by their nature involve the company being owed money; that money is then brought into the company (and deposited in the bank) and then the book debt is reintroduced. It therefore appears that as an asset that is traded rather than being 'fixed' to a specific item, it must be a floating charge. This point was considered in the following case.

Siebe Gorman and Co. Ltd v Barclays Bank Ltd (1979)

Facts:

Here the bank attempted to protect its interests by identifying the proceeds of the company's book debts as a fixed, rather than a floating charge. The bank contracted for such an asset to be a fixed charge and as such it allowed the company to collect money owed.

Authority for:

Concerns were raised about the nature of the decision and how such an asset could in reality constitute a fixed charge. In answer to this, the company was required to place the proceeds into a specific bank account and it was not free to draw on the account even when in credit. It was this level of control that gave the appearance of it being a fixed charge.

It took 25 years but eventually the issue was addressed and finalized by the House of Lords in *National Westminster Bank Plc v Spectrum Plus Ltd.*

National Westminster Bank Plc v Spectrum Plus Ltd (2005)

Facts:

In a similar situation to *Siebe* involving the bank lending money with the requirement of establishing the company's book debts as a fixed charge, it was held that such charges were to be considered as floating, not fixed.

Authority for:

This involved a charge over the book debts, a requirement to pay the proceeds into a designated bank account, but the third element is crucial in determining its status. Here, there was a restriction on the disposal of the debts to any other party without the agreement of the lender (the bank). However, unless the bank blocks the account to prevent the lender from having access to the funds, this would not be a fixed charge. Where a company is free to deal with the item (in this case the proceeds of the book debt), its transferable nature signifies the existence of a floating charge and this is how the Lords held.

16.13.2 **Registration of Charges**

Similarly with debentures, a charge must be registered with the Registrar within 21 days of its creation (CA 2006, s. 870). The company is obliged to provide the Registrar with this information but it is also possible for the person interested in the registration to register it. The Registrar will then issue a certificate of registration and include details as to its particulars (CA 2006, s. 869). This is because where a charge is not registered, it will be invalid and it will not allow the creditor to have the right to dispose of the assets to which the charge was to relate. This does not mean that the creditor would be unable to bring an action against the company on the debt owed, but they would lose the security that the charge provides. Remember, a creditor without a charge over assets is an unsecured creditor, and on the basis of the company being wound up and unable to settle its debts, this creditor will join the rest in attempting to obtain the money it is owed. A secured creditor will have a greater opportunity (and priority) to have debts owed satisfied. However, it is possible to state that a fixed charge will rank below an existing floating charge, and hence it will rank below such creditors and behind preferential creditors. It is also possible to grant more than one fixed charge over assets (particularly where the asset has significantly grown in value and hence could accommodate such charges). More than one charge may also be made over a floating charge; however, when this occurs, they rank in the order that they were created (hence preventing the company establishing a fraud on the previous creditors through subsequent actions).

By 18 June 2010, the Government ended its period of consultation regarding reform of the process of registration of charges by companies and Limited Liability Partnerships. Its aim was to 'address the many imperfections of the present system' by implementing a system of electronic registration of charges (in force since 6 April 2013). An example provided in the consultation document was that 'charges are now commonly granted over expected future income from major projects while charges to secure issues of debentures are not'. These do not come under the remit of registration as required by CA 2006.

16.13.3 **Priority of Charges**

If the charges have been correctly registered, they rank in priority as follows. A fixed charge will rank higher than existing floating charges unless the existing floating charge has made provision against this. Fixed charges also have effect from the time they are created. The next level of charge is a floating charge and this takes effect when it crystallizes and attaches to the assets in the agreement. They will also have priority according to when the charge was created (hence the first floating charge will have priority over the last one created over the same asset, unless this is stated to the contrary).

Finally, preferential creditors take priority over the holders of floating charges, but not over fixed charges. Preferential creditors include employees who are owed wages (although limited to £800 per employee earned in the previous four months) and any loan taken to pay the employees' wages. The company will also have to pay any holiday pay due to employees and any loans from third parties taken for the purpose of paying such costs. The costs of the company's contributions to any occupational pension scheme are included. However, payments to the government are no longer included in the list of preferential creditors (following enactment of the Enterprise Act 2002). Preferential creditors are paid monies owed before other creditors are paid from the company's assets (if solvent when wound up). Where insufficient funds exist to satisfy these debts, they will each receive a proportion of the debts owed and they rank equally with each other.

CONCLUSION

This chapter has included details of the various obligations on companies that wish to issue and allot shares, provide debentures and charges over the company's assets, and guidance on the maintenance of the company's finances. As the company's directors often make such decisions (followed by the consent of the company's members), the role played by directors and their duties to the company is crucial. These issues are discussed in **Chapter 17**.

SUMMARY OF MAIN POINTS

Shares

- CA 2006 refers to members of a company and these are, in the case of a company limited by shares, those who have subscribed to the memorandum and taken shares. They are entered into the register of members.

- A share is a bundle of rights and duties, and it imposes liabilities on the holder.

- Shareholders have no automatic right of management in the company although, through attendance and the right to vote at meetings, they may have influence over the business conducted (such as the moving of resolutions).

- Shares may be ordinary or preference, and may also be redeemable by the company.

- Preference shares are so called because of the right to dividends before ordinary shareholders (these may be cumulative or non-cumulative).

- A company may purchase its own shares in accordance with CA 2006 if authorized to do so through its articles.

Share capital

- The company will identify its share capital when formed.

- The share capital may include the following factors: authorized share capital; issued, allotted, paid-up, and called-up aspects of the share capital depending on the actions of the directors and the requirements of the allotment/issue.

- Public companies must have at least £50,000 of allotted share capital to receive a trading certificate.

Alteration of share capital

- Companies are restricted from altering their share capital but may do so when following the rules prescribed in CA 2006.

- Such an alteration may include allotting new shares, consolidating and subdividing existing shares, redenominating shares, or reducing the share capital.

- Public and private companies may reduce the share capital through passing a special resolution that is confirmed by a court.

Share issue

- Shares may be issued to generate revenue for the company, and in the case of ordinary shares, the existing members have the right to be offered the opportunity to purchase such shares as equivalent to their existing holding before the shares are offered to non-members.

- Shares may not be offered at a discount.

- Shares in private companies may not be offered to the public.

Dividends

- Shareholders may only be paid dividends from distributable profits.
- The directors declare the dividends (and the shareholders must agree). Shareholders may require the dividend to be reduced but cannot increase it.
- There is no automatic right for a shareholder to receive a dividend.

Loan capital

- Companies may wish to obtain a loan and to do so may offer a charge over assets or offer a debenture.
- The charges that are provided over assets must be registered in accordance with CA 2006.
- Charges may be fixed or floating.
- Fixed charges apply to fixed assets (such as a mortgage over a company's factory).
- A floating charge is a security over a class of assets (such as the stock of the company). The charge becomes fixed (crystallizes) on the default of the company.
- Charges must be registered with the Registrar of Companies.

SUMMARY QUESTIONS

Essay questions

1. What are the various charges that a lender may require to be provided by the company that wishes to borrow money? Explain the nature of each, their priority, and their effect in the event of the company being wound up.

2. Explain the process of a company altering its share capital. Provide examples of why a company may wish to make such an alteration and how the creditors of the company are protected against abuse of this provision.

Problem questions

1. Michelle and Raj operate a bistro business called Café Culture Ltd in Manchester. They have run the business largely by attempting to build solid foundations through paying themselves a relatively small salary and reinvesting any profits back into the business. The business was originally a partnership, but the two owners later incorporated as a private limited company, with Michelle owning 60 per cent of the shares and Raj 40 per cent (and both are directors). Despite their initial introduction of capital, Michelle and Raj wish to increase the growth of the business and so allow Charlie to purchase 20 per cent of Café Culture Ltd's shares (with a reduction of Michelle's and Raj's shareholding by 10 per cent each).

   Upon taking a shareholding in the company Charlie stated that she had no wish to become a director but she did expect to receive an income from the dividends paid to shareholders. Café Culture Ltd makes a profit each year and it has substantial sums in its account (some £400,000) but the directors choose, for the third consecutive year, not to declare a dividend. However, the directors pay themselves fees and have voted for themselves an 'achievement bonus'. Charlie is concerned that this is a policy of the business and that dividends will never be declared. She is concerned that her stake in the business will continue to go unrecognized and unrewarded.

   Advise the parties as to their rights and obligations in this matter.

2. Jackson's Paints Ltd is a company in financial trouble and has experienced the following situations and requires advice on, among other things, the validity of the charges applied to its property and how to proceed.

Jackson's Paints Ltd decided to attempt to raise funds through the directors' decision to issue debentures.

A. One loan of £100,000 was made by Chloe, the wife of one of the directors, and this loan was secured through the issuing of a fixed charge over the property where the company sells its product (paint) to the public. The property was valued at £150,000.

B. A further loan of £20,000 was made by the company's bank by the issuing of a floating charge over the company's entire stock.

C. A final loan of £30,000 was obtained from Dale but the fixed charge issued to him in relation to this loan was over the same property as provided to Chloe.

The company's articles of association require that all loan agreements are first approved by the board of directors before they can take effect. The fixed charge provided to Chloe was not agreed by the board of directors and it was not registered. The floating charge issued to the bank was agreed by the board and was correctly registered. The fixed charge provided to Dale was correctly registered.

Having obtained the loans, Jackson's Paints Ltd failed to make repayments as they became due to the bank or to pay its staff their wages. Further evidence has come to light that before any of these loans were agreed, the auditors of the company had advised the directors of Jackson's Paints Ltd that the company was insolvent and should be wound up. Some of the directors are still of the opinion that the company can trade out of these problems when the economic downturn improves.

Advise:

a. Jackson's Paints Ltd on the validity of the charges it has purported to create over its property;

b. the directors on the potential personal liability for the debts of the company;

c. the options available to a secured creditor when faced with a company unable to pay its debts, and how such a creditor may petition for a company to be wound up;

d. the directors on granting charges when under notice that the company was insolvent.

 You will find guidance about how to answer these questions online at www.oup.com/uk/marson5e/.

 FURTHER READING

Books and articles

Chiu, I. H. Y. (2006) 'Replacing the Default Priority Rule for Secured Creditors—Some Reservations' *Journal of Business Law*, Oct., p. 644.

Goldring, J. (2006) 'Floating Charges—The Awakening' *Insolvency Intelligence*, Vol. 19, No. 5, p. 68.

Ho, L. H. (2006) 'Reversing *Buchler v Talbot*—The Doctrinal Dimension of Liquidation Expenses Priority' *Butterworths Journal of International Banking & Financial Law*, Vol. 21, No. 3, p. 104.

Nolan, R. C. (2006) 'The Continuing Evolution of Shareholder Governance' *Cambridge Law Journal*, Vol. 65, No. 1, p. 92.

Websites and Twitter links

https://www.gov.uk/government/organisations/insolvency-service
@insolvencygovuk

> The Insolvency Service operates mainly with matters to do with the Insolvency Acts 1986 and 2000, and the Company Directors Disqualifications Act 1986. Among its roles are providing information and assistance to administer and investigate the affairs of bankrupts and companies wound up by the courts, acting as a trustee/liquidator where no private sector insolvency practitioner is appointed, and authorizing and regulating the insolvency profession.

http://www.london-gazette.co.uk
@London_Gazette

> The *London Gazette* is the official newspaper of record for the UK, provided electronically to disseminate and record official, regulatory, and legal information.

http://www.legislation.gov.uk/ukpga/2006/46/contents
The Companies Act 2006.

 ONLINE RESOURCES

www.oup.com/uk/marson5e/

For further resources relating to this chapter, including self-test questions, an interactive glossary, and key case flashcards.

17 CORPORATE MANAGEMENT

The director and the company secretary are two major roles performed in the management of a corporation. The Companies Act (CA) 2006 identifies the powers and duties on these office holders, and it identifies, where relevant, any specific qualifications that must be held to fill the role. Whilst most companies have shareholders (although of course CA 2006 calls such people 'members' as companies need not have shareholders) who 'own' the company, it is the directors who 'run' the company, based on the powers conferred upon them, along with the secretary, who may perform many of the daily administrative tasks that are required. As every company must have at least one director who is a natural person, knowledge of their role in the company is of crucial significance, as are the protections available to the shareholders to ensure they are not unfairly prejudiced by the directors' actions.

Business Scenario 17

Vertigo plc is a company involved in property development. Its main objectives are in the residential sector but occasionally it acquires and develops land for commercial and leisure projects. Its board of directors comprises Faith, Godfrey, and Tafadzwa, and the following events have affected the company:

Godfrey owns a 20 per cent stake in Duracello plc, a company that provides power supply systems for commercial buildings. When the board of Vertigo plc agree a new contract with Duracello plc, which Godfrey voted in favour of, he failed to declare his interest.

Vertigo plc has decided at the latest board meeting to move the sourcing of its mobile solutions (phones and tablets) from Germany to Taiwan. These items are made to Vertigo plc's specifications and then shipped to the UK. The decision was made based on costs and no consideration was made to the environmental impact or the longer-term effect of the decision.

Tafadzwa entered into an agreement with Ritblat plc where he personally receives a 15 per cent 'commission' on the basis of orders from Vertigo plc for the purchase of kitchen units used in Vertigo's developments. In the past eight months, Tafadzwa has received £150,000 in commissions from Ritblat plc without declaring this information to the board.

Horizons plc is another property development company which has had previous dealings with Vertigo plc. Horizons plc offered to sell a plot of land to Vertigo plc for £800,000 but that offer was declined at a board meeting due to finance issues. However, Faith, seeing the opportunity for development of the plot, formed her own company (New Ventures plc) which purchased the land for the asking price. Later, when Vertigo plc had the finances in place, it wished to purchase the land offered by Horizons plc. It is approached by New Ventures plc which offers the land for a price of £1.2 million. Vertigo plc agrees the purchase.

The shareholders have recently discovered these facts.

- Explain the appointment process of a director and secretary of a company (17.2.3; 17.5)
- Identify the duties imposed on directors and how the Companies Act 2006 has added to the obligations established through the common law (17.2.7–17.2.8)
- Explain how a director may lose their directorship and the consequences of the disqualification of the director from a company (17.2.9; 17.2.12–17.2.13)
- Identify the protection of shareholders and the powers they possess in a company (17.4–17.4.3)
- Explain the responsibilities of a company secretary and the limitations of their authority (17.5–17.5.1).

17.1 INTRODUCTION

This chapter considers corporate management and focuses on the regulation of those who govern the company, and the protection of the shareholders (who have no automatic right of management). The actual 'running' of the company is left to the directors, a relatively small number of persons who may take individual responsibility for aspects of the company's business, or may oversee the company as a whole. Directors have significant powers when acting for the company, and whilst a corporation possesses its own separate legal personality, independent of those who manage it, the actions of the company are performed, under authority provided by statute and the company's constitution, by its directors. The chapter identifies the appointment of directors and their duties (codified from the common law into the Companies Act 2006), and the provisions for removing a director. It further identifies another officer of significance—the company secretary. Under CA 2006 private companies are no longer required to have a company secretary, although public companies must still have such an officer. They are of importance in corporate governance, and may provide a beneficial service to any company.

The governance of a company will also include consideration of the protection of the companies' shareholders and their rights in relation to the company. This includes their powers to appoint or remove directors, voting at meetings and other rights in the exercise of power with regard to the direction and control of the company, and also how protection may be sought, particularly in relation to minority shareholders who may be exposed to risk through the powers granted to directors.

17.2 DIRECTORS OF A COMPANY

The nature of a company is predicated on the concept of it possessing its own legal personality and this being independent of the person(s) who exercise the power to take the decisions of the company. These specific tasks, whilst performed in the company's name and on its behalf, have to be exercised by people. Therefore, CA 2006 requires that, upon formation, the company submits numerous documents to the Registrar of Companies, including the articles of association that identifies, *inter alia*, the nature of the company, what it intends to do, and other matters regarding the powers of those who 'run' the company. These positions are then filled by the directors. Directors possess the authority to act as the company's agent and perform the tasks required. As the shareholders may consist (although not necessarily so) of a large and diverse population, it would be impractical for each to have a management capacity and hence they appoint the directors who may exercise the powers conferred on the position by the company. They may also wish to remove the director from the position and hence they are provided with the mechanisms to achieve this.

Automatic Self-Cleansing Filter Syndicate Co. Ltd v Cuninghame (1906)

Facts:

The claimant held 1202 of the company's 2700 shares. He wished for the company to sell assets to another company and managed to persuade members totalling 1502 shares to vote in favour of his resolution. The directors were opposed to the resolution and this led to the claim, in the name of the company, against the directors, including Cuninghame.

Authority for:

The constitution of the company gave the general power of its management to the directors, it provided for a three-quarter majority of votes to remove a director, but was silent as to the ability of shareholders to issue directions to directors. The Court of Appeal held accordingly that the directors were entitled to reject this instruction.

When the registration documents are submitted to the Registrar, these must include who will hold the position of director (as companies cannot be registered in the absence of directors). It should also be recognized at this stage that the director of a company might be (and very often is) a shareholder of the company, although there is no requirement for this. The position of director is defined in CA 2006 so as to ensure that the relevant powers and obligations associated with this position are recognized and applied despite any alternative title that the officer of the company may have (such as manager): 'It does not matter much what you call them, so long as you understand what their true position is, which is that they are merely commercial men, managing a trading concern for the benefit of themselves, and all other shareholders in it.' (Jessel MR, *Re Arthur Average Association for British, Foreign and Colonial Ships* [1875]).

17.2.1 **Types of Director**

There are different types of director of companies and they are often described with reference to their position and their responsibilities to the company. Directors can be executive and non-executive directors. An executive director is so called due to their activities and because they undertake special responsibilities in the company. For example, a company may have an operations director, managing director, and a finance director. These directors take charge over the aspect or function of the company (although there is no legal requirement to have such 'executive' directors and, whilst unlikely, the board could delegate these functions to the company's employees). The non-executive directors have no specific function over an area of the business or take an active part in the company's management; rather they perform tasks such as attending meetings, taking a constructive part in the board's decision-making, or they may 'lend' their name to the business to increase its standing with customers. Therefore, the executive directors have both executive and non-executive functions.

Companies may also appoint 'shadow directors' who are defined as 'a person in accordance with whose directions the directors of the company are accustomed to act' (CA 2006, s. 251). This position will not extend to those who give their advice to the board in a professional capacity (such as a lawyer) and may include, for example, a major shareholder upon whose advice the directors would act.

17.2.2 Number of Directors

Companies are required under CA 2006 to have at least one director in the case of private companies, and two directors in the case of public companies (CA 2006, s. 154). At least one of the directors of the company must be a natural person (as companies may hold directorships of other companies—CA 2006, s. 155).

17.2.3 Appointment of Directors

The company's promoters include the details of the directors for the company with the registration documents. These documents include the details of the company's first directors, and the articles will include the company's provisions for the appointment and removal of future directors of the company. Such appointments will occur, for example, when existing directors leave, or additional directors are appointed to supplement the company's responsibilities or to add expertise to the company's management. The articles of association allow for the appointment of directors and authority for such action is usually through an ordinary resolution at a general meeting, although other mechanisms such as a written procedure may be equally valid. (For a director's removal a written resolution is not an appropriate instrument.)

A director must be at least 16 years of age, although this does not affect the validity of an appointment that is not to take effect until the person reaches this age (CA 2006, s. 157). Any appointment in contravention of this section is void, although this does not affect the liability of a person who purports to act as a director or acts as a shadow director. Where an existing director is under the age of 16 when these provisions came into force, s. 159 provides that the person will cease to be a director and the company will be required to make any consequential changes necessary in the register of directors, although notice of the change need not be given to the Registrar.

When a public company intends to appoint a director(s), it may not appoint two or more directors at a general meeting through a single resolution, unless a resolution that it should be made has been unanimously agreed (CA 2006, s. 160). This requirement must be followed, as any resolution that is passed in contravention of this section is void even if no one voted against the appointment of the directors.

The appointment of directors will usually result in one director taking charge for the whole company rather than its constituent parts (where relevant) and this person has traditionally been called the managing director. Due to the nature of the position, its significance, and the authority it bestows, the appointment is controlled through the articles and is made by the board (although the board can vary and curtail any powers associated with the position). The rationale for a managing director's appointment is simply that it is often convenient for the company to have a director who can take executive leadership.

17.2.4 Registration of Directors

Every company is required to maintain a register of its directors and contain the information required under ss. 163, 164, and 166 of CA 2006 (CA 2006, s. 162). This register must be available for inspection at the company's registered office or at another location as provided under s. 1136. Inspection by any member of the company must be available without charge, or to any other person on payment of a fee. Failure to comply with these requirements constitutes an offence by the company and every company officer (including shadow directors). A court is also empowered to order the register for inspection where there has been a refusal of inspection.

CA 2006, Part 10, Chapter 8 has added protection to directors from having to disclose their residential address on these documents (as they are available for public inspection). These details are considered 'protected information' (CA 2006, s. 240) and this duty to protect such information extends to the company (preventing its disclosure except for communicating with the director or in order to ensure compliance with CA 2006, s. 241) and to the Registrar in disclosing the materials unless these need to be stated (CA 2006, s. 242). Also, note that a court can make an order for disclosure of protected material where there is evidence that the service address is not effective to bring matters to the notice of the director or it is necessary for information provided in connection with the enforcement of a court order, and the court is satisfied that the order is appropriate (CA 2006, s. 244).

17.2.5 Directors' Pay and Contracts

It is not required that a director receives pay (remuneration) for their activities as a director. For example, a non-executive director is not necessarily paid for their services. Where payment is provided this is generally done through a contract between the company and the director, and due to the fiduciary relationship between the director and the company, the director is not permitted to make any profit that has not been expressly identified in the agreement. Fees and expenses may be paid, but in relation to executive directors, payment is traditionally made through a contract of service (an employee) and as such, it is a contract that must be personally performed by the post-holder (CA 2006, s. 227). Hence the delegation of these tasks is not permitted. The payment could be included in the articles of the company, and this would be more applicable where a non-executive director is provided with a fee for their services. However, it should not be assumed that a director is an employee of the company and there must be an agreement to this status. In terms of the payments made under a contract of service, CA 2006 requires that a copy of the contract is maintained at the company's registered address or other place specified under s. 1136, for every directors' service contract, and whilst this need not be in writing, the very least that is required is a written memorandum setting out the terms of the contract (CA 2006, s. 228).

In June 2012, following a period of consultation, the Business Secretary announced the Government's intention to introduce legislation to empower shareholders to engage more effectively with companies regarding pay. The intention is to:

- give shareholders binding votes on pay policy and exit payments (to enable them to hold companies to account and prevent rewards for failure);
- boost transparency so that what people are paid is easily understood and the link between pay and performance is clearly drawn.

These measures were incorporated into the Enterprise and Regulatory Reform Act 2013.

17.2.6 Directors' Duties

CA 2006 had a significant impact on the duties imposed on directors through codification and extension of duties that, prior to the enactment of CA 2006, had been developed through the common law. The provisions under Part 10A of CA 2006 (other than the issues of conflict of interest, the directors' residential addresses, and age of the directors) came into effect on 1 October 2007.

17.2.7 Directors' Duties Under the Companies Act 2006

Chapter 2 of CA 2006 identifies the duties of the directors and that the duties under ss. 171–177 (see **Table 17.1**) are owed by the director to the company (rather than those outside of the company). It provides instructions as to how these sections are to be interpreted when the director ceases to be a director of the company, such as the duty to avoid conflicts of interest (CA 2006, s. 175) and the duty not to accept benefits from third parties, which continues after the director has left office. Section 170 continues that these general duties imposed on directors are to be interpreted and applied in the same way as the common law rules and equitable principles on which they were based. Therefore, some of the previous cases are identified, but as these were decided under the common law it is important to be vigilant for case law derived specifically from the legislation. These duties also apply to shadow directors where the corresponding common duties and equitable principles apply to them.

17.2.7.1 Duty to act within their powers

The director must act in accordance with the company's constitution (now the articles of association rather than the memorandum—CA 2006, s. 171) and only exercise powers for the purposes for which they had been conferred. As such, where authority is provided for a specific purpose, the power must only be used for this purpose and will not be extended (even if the director acted in good faith and in the best interests of the company).

17.2.7.2 Duty to promote the success of the company

This was based on the common law duty of the director acting in good faith (CA 2006, s. 172). The Act requires the director to fulfil this requirement in the way they consider would be most likely to promote the success of the company for the benefit of its members as a whole. In so doing the director must have regard to the likely consequences of

Table 17.1 Duties of directors

Directors' duties	CA 2006
To act within their powers	s. 171
To promote the success of the company	s. 172
To exercise independent judgement	s. 173
To exercise reasonable care, skill, and diligence	s. 174
To avoid conflicts of interest	s. 175
Not to accept benefits from third parties	s. 176
To declare interest in proposed transaction or arrangement	s. 177
To disclose interests in existing transaction/arrangement	s. 182

decisions in the long term; the interests of the company's employees, the need to foster relationships with outside organizations (suppliers/customers and so on), the impact of the company's operations on the community and environment, the company's reputation, and the need to act fairly as between the members of the company.

Note; this is not an exhaustive list but provides examples of the requirements the section of the Act places on the director.

Consider

A director is under a duty to promote the success of the company. It appears that each of the directors involved in the scenario has breached this duty.

This section of the CA 2006 goes further than the common law upon which it is based and places a positive duty on the director not only to act in the interests of the members, but also, in certain circumstances, to consider or act in the interests of the company's creditors (and taking into account others beyond the members, such as the company's employees). Therefore, the company should ensure that evidence may be produced to demonstrate that at meetings and where decisions are made, regard had been taken of such groups.

This requirement may serve to instil an obligation of more strategic thinking on the part of directors, who will consider the wider implications of their actions for the company's stakeholders, and consider the folly of short-term decision-making compared with taking a long-term view of the company's actions. For example, the shareholders may wish to gain dividends from the profits, or seek for products to be sourced from the cheapest suppliers with a disregard as to the wider effects that this may have to their relations with suppliers, the environmental impact of the actions, and the long-term viability and sustainability of such measures. This section of CA 2006 may actually serve to protect the directors when making difficult decisions and assist in justifying these to the shareholders. (Although it should be thought that a requirement of considering the social and environmental impact of decisions should not override the directors' duties to the company.) Clearly these considerations will have a greater influence on large companies with regard to, for example, the 'carbon footprint' of their activities, and will depend on the infrastructure of the company to obtain relevant materials to identify the consequences of decisions. They are, however, a means to require greater thought and consideration of the wider consequences of business decisions, and there is no distinction in the legislation between the requirements placed on large and small companies. A small company that cannot afford to obtain research and documentation on its actions, and how this affects the environment, will still be obliged to provide its most accurate and best informed assessment.

To facilitate compliance in this area it may be wise for the board to ensure each director (and non-executive director) is aware of the responsibilities under this section of the Act, and those under the company's constitution. The director should have the knowledge of the requirements for the full consideration of s. 172 of CA 2006 and establish practices for decision-making subject to these obligations. This may also require establishing a review process to provide for transparency of decisions and analysis of how/why the director acted in the way they did. If failings are discovered, then a system of review and action is also a prudent step.

The case of *Hellard and Others v Carvalho* demonstrates how the interpretation of ss. 171–172 of CA 2006 will be given effect in the courts.

Hellard and Others v Carvalho (2013)

Facts:

Here, the liquidators of an insolvent company, which had been run by Mr Carvalho (as the company's Principal Director), brought an action against Carvalho on the basis of misfeasance due to payments he made between November 2005 and October 2008. The payments included the repayment of debts to creditors such as Carvalho's father, himself, companies under his control, and it also included a Christmas bonus to a key employee.

The case surrounded the rationale to make these payments, which were of Carvalho's own decision-making without any regard to the best interests of the company. Carvalho, as a director, was under a duty (articulated in s. 172) to act in good faith in a way that would promote the success of the company and should have known, or realistically appreciated, that the company was insolvent or may become unable to repay its debts. Carvalho was found to be in breach of s. 172 in failing to keep adequate records and was judged according to a director in his position. Simply because he failed to maintain records and operate his management in an informal manner did not allow the assessment of his directorship to be at a lower standard as may exist for other directors (e.g. more junior directors or those without the power of a principal director). He was, further, in breach of s. 171 in failing to exercise the powers as a director for the purposes in which they were given and was ordered to repay substantial sums to the company.

Authority for:

This case readily demonstrates the necessity of effective management, paper trails and evidence of decision-making, and continued vigilance of the company's affairs—especially when in financial difficulties.

Consider

The directors have not recorded their compliance with CA 2006, s. 172. Nothing was recorded in the minutes. Whilst the section is sufficiently broad so as not, necessarily, to have constituted a breach by the directors' disregard for purchasing goods from Taiwan and shipping them to the UK, it should be remarked that the directors have thought of the environmental impact of this decision. This action, along with the other potential breaches, should be recorded in the board meetings to demonstrate compliance with the duty.

17.2.7.3 Duty to exercise independent judgement

The director has an obligation to exercise independent judgement, although this will not be infringed by their acting in accordance with an agreement entered into with the company that restricts the future exercise of discretion by its directors, or in a way authorized by the constitution of the company (CA 2006, s. 173). As such, this is a further example of the law codifying existing requirements in the common law, but it reinforces the director's duty to act for the best interests of the company, and not necessarily follow the instructions of shareholders, whose interests may be selfish and not concerned for the company. This situation comes to prominence, as the shareholders appoint the director, and where this appointment has been made on a personal basis, the director must remain independent of the person(s) that made the appointment.

17.2.7.4 Duty to exercise reasonable care, skill, and diligence

The director has to exercise reasonable care, skill, and diligence (CA 2006, s. 174). This duty is based on what a reasonably diligent person with the general knowledge, skills, and experience for carrying out the functions required of the director to the company would consider, and the general knowledge, skill, and experience possessed by the specific director.

Re Brazilian Rubber Plantations and Estates Ltd (1911)

Facts:

Due to the directors' lack of qualifications and business acumen, the company lost a substantial amount of money following a poor investment in rubber plantations in Brazil. The directors were sued for their negligence.

Authority for:

The court held that the directors were to be held to a subjective test of their duty to exercise care and skill. A director need only exercise the care and skill that could be reasonably expected of them in terms of their knowledge and experience.

As such, where the director purports to possess special skills or knowledge, then this will be the standard against which they are assessed. Where no such special skills/knowledge are claimed, the standard test of how a 'reasonable' director would have acted will be applied. Therefore, a directorship (whether executive or non-executive) of a company is a very important role involving significant responsibilities, and it should not be accepted without consideration of the implications of the position and the obligations to the company—with reference made to CA 2006 and the company's constitution. Diligence was already a common law duty and requires the director to be vigilant for acts that require appropriate investigations to be made and questions to be answered. A director will fail in their duty by not taking the appropriate steps when faced with such scenarios.

> ### Re Railway and General Light Improvement Co., Marzetti's Case (1880)
>
> **Facts:**
>
> A director had been signing cheques without knowing what the money was for.
>
> **Authority for:**
>
> The court found a director negligent for signing cheques without knowing what the money was for and without making inquiries which a person in his position would have made.

17.2.7.5 Duty to avoid conflicts of interest

A director has an obligation to avoid situations where they have, or can have, a direct or indirect interest that conflicts (or has the potential to conflict) with the interests of the company (CA 2006, s. 175).

> ### Consider
>
> How does the fact that New Ventures plc is agreeing the sale affect the duties on Faith? Does the company having a separate legal personality remove any obligations on Faith under CA 2006, ss. 175 and 177? No—unless this is authorized by the directors and Faith is not to have any part of the discussion nor should she vote on the measure.

This duty applies particularly to the exploitation of any property, information, or opportunity and it is immaterial whether or not the company could take advantage of the property, information, or opportunity. However, there are limits to this duty and it does not apply in relation to a transaction or arrangement between the director and the company itself. Further, the duty is not infringed if the situation cannot reasonably be regarded as likely to give rise to a conflict or if the matter has been authorized by the directors. Such authorization may be given by the directors where:

1. the company is a private company (and nothing in the company's constitution invalidates such authorization) by the matter being proposed to and authorized by the directors; or
2. the company is a public company (and its constitution includes provision enabling the directors to authorize the matter) by the matter being proposed to, and authorized by, them in accordance with the constitution.

The authorization is only effective if any requirement as to the quorum at the meeting (where the matter is considered) is met without the director in question or any other director, and the matter was agreed to without their voting (or would have been agreed if their votes had not been counted). This section of the Act, with reference to a conflict of interest, includes conflicts of duty. Where the duty may become problematic is where a director holds directorships with several companies who may trade, or be in some other way involved with the business of the company in question. Separating the director's duty in such examples may be a challenging undertaking and the exercise of care will be needed to ensure adequate (but complete) disclosure is provided. As such, this section extends the requirements of the common law by imposing a positive duty on the director to avoid any unauthorized conflicts of interest, and it makes authorization of any conflict to be determined by the company's directors rather than the shareholders.

Consider

There is a possible breach of CA 2006, s. 175 where Faith has a conflict of interest with Vertigo plc. She has exploited or taken advantage of an opportunity which has become available due to her being a director of the company. Further, it is no defence to argue that as Vertigo plc could or did not take advantage of this, she is free to do so.

17.2.7.6 Duty not to accept benefits from third parties

A director of a company is not allowed to accept a benefit from a third party that is due to them being a director of the company and their acts or omissions as a director (CA 2006, s. 176). 'Third party' is interpreted as a person other than the company itself, an associated body corporate, or a person acting on behalf of the company or an associated body corporate. However, the duty is not infringed where the acceptance of a benefit 'cannot reasonably be regarded as likely to give rise to a conflict of interest'. This is an area of the law that will likely produce case law of significance on how to interpret the element and extent of what 'cannot reasonably be regarded as'.

The conflict of interest here, as with s. 175, includes a conflict of duties. This duty will be concerned with benefits such as bribes (in cash or in kind) that will impact on the impartiality of the director in acting for the company. Where a benefit is provided to the director and not the company, the director's objectivity may be compromised. This provides an obligation on the director not to accept bribes, but this was a duty long established in the common law, and what the Act requires is for the director to consult with the company's constitution to determine those actions that are acceptable, and those that are not. This is likely to be a particularly interesting aspect of the directors' duties under CA 2006, but for the affected director, transparency of any gifts provided and how decisions were made may ensure they do not transgress their obligations in this area.

Consider

Tafadzwa, in receiving commission payments, is in breach of CA 2006, s. 176. This action constitutes a benefit from a third party and will be a breach of this duty unless the payment could not reasonably be considered as likely to raise a conflict of interests. The result is that Tafadzwa will have to account to the company for any benefit received.

17.2.7.7 Duty to declare interest in proposed transaction or arrangement

The director has a duty if in any way, directly or indirectly, they have an interest in a proposed transaction or arrangement with the company (CA 2006, s. 177). This interest must be declared to the other directors with specific regard to the nature and extent of the interest. The declaration may be made in the following way, although others may be used:

1. at a meeting of the directors; or
2. by notice to the directors in accordance with s. 184 (notice in writing) or s. 185 (general notice).

The declaration must be complete and accurate and if it proves to be, or subsequently becomes, incomplete and/or inaccurate, then a further declaration is required. There are limits placed on this obligation and the director need not declare an interest where it cannot be reasonably regarded as likely to give rise to a conflict of interest; where the other directors are already aware (or ought reasonably to be aware) of the conflict; or where it concerns terms of the director's service contract that have been, or are to be, considered by a meeting of the directors, or by a committee of directors appointed for the purpose under the company's constitution.

Consider

Godfrey has a 20 per cent shareholding in another company, Duracello plc. CA 2006, s. 177 requires directors with an interest in a proposed contract to declare this to the members of the board. This must occur prior to the agreement being concluded, therefore Godfrey can avoid a breach of his duty if either the other directors knew of his relationship with Duracello plc, or Godfrey informs them prior to any contract being entered.

17.2.8 Duty of the Director to Disclose Interests in Contracts

Beyond the codification of the common law duties imposed on directors, CA 2006 imposes duties of disclosure on the director who has an interest (direct or indirect) in a contract or proposed contract with the company (CA 2006, s. 182). This disclosure must be made as soon as is reasonably practicable (such as where the matter is first discussed by the board) and include the nature and extent of the interest, and be made at a meeting of the directors; or by notice in writing; or by general notice. The provisions of such disclosures apply to loans, quasi-loans, and credit transactions and arrangements.

17.2.9 Civil Consequences of a Breach of the Duties

Where there is a breach (or threatened breach) of the duties identified in ss. 171–177, the consequences are the same as provided in the common law rules or equitable principles (CA 2006, s. 178). Further, the duties under s. 174 regarding reasonable care, skill, and diligence are enforceable, as are the other fiduciary duties that a director owes the company. Except where otherwise provided, more than one of the general duties may apply in any given case (CA 2006, s. 179).

Where the director has transgressed the requirements under this part of the Act, they may be liable to compensate the company for any losses sustained due to the director's breach. This may be the case even where the director had acted in good faith and where they believed the actions were taken in the company's best interests. This may be particularly so where the director has, for example, disregarded the consequences of their actions to the environmental impact which has led to the company being held liable for the consequential damage. The company will have a responsibility for any costs but may seek to reclaim these from the director's breach of their statutory duty (see **13.9**). It must also be remembered that even beyond the responsibilities of the director to the company and any imposition of responsibility through CA 2006, a director who disregards these duties may suffer a disqualification if they appear unfit to fulfil the role of director (Company Directors Disqualification Act 1986).

It is also possible for the members of the company to provide their consent, approval, or authorization of the director's actions (CA 2006, s. 180). Where the duty to avoid conflicts of interest is complied with through the authorization of the directors (CA 2006, s. 175); and the duty to declare an interest in a proposed transaction or arrangement is complied with, the transaction or arrangement is not liable to be set aside by virtue of any common law rule or equitable principle requiring the consent or approval of the company's members (CA 2006, s. 177). This is subject to provisions of the company's constitution that may require such consent or approval (CA 2006, s. 180). The compliance with these general rules does not remove the requirement of approval of the provisions of Chapter 4 of CA 2006 (regarding transactions requiring the approval of members).

17.2.10 The Meetings of Directors

The board of directors' meetings are where important decisions affecting the company can be addressed. Each of the directors of the company must be given notice of the meeting, and the directors are empowered to call a meeting when necessary. Every company is required to record the minutes of the meetings and these records must be maintained for 10 years (CA 2006, s. 248). The minutes of the meetings are an important record of the proceedings and where authenticated by the chairperson, they may be used as evidence of the proceedings at that meeting regarding the validity of appointments, that the proceedings are deemed to have duly taken place, and so on (CA 2006, s. 249). The decisions taken at the meetings are based on a voting system and it is assumed that each director has one vote, unless the articles of the company provide differently, and the resolution is passed with a majority. Where the votes are split, the chairperson has the option to exercise their vote in favour of the resolution and it will be deemed that the resolution has been passed, or not and the resolution will fail.

17.2.11 Indemnifying the Directors

The enactment of the Companies (Audit Investigation and Community Enterprises) Act 2004 introduced provisions for the **indemnity** of directors. Whilst they were given effect on 6 April 2005, they have now been included in CA 2006 and appear in ss. 232–239. These protections assist the directors by providing that the company will repay any costs incurred (in certain circumstances) by the director in the course of their duties.

> **Consider**
>
> The shareholders have the ability to ratify the breaches of the directors due to the power conferred in CA 2006, s. 239. This ratification, however, cannot involve the director using their vote as a member of the company.

A key element of indemnification is that not only can the company protect the director, but also even where it is unable to excuse the director from liability in cases of negligence, default, breach of duty, or breach of trust, the High Court or County Court possess this power under s. 1157. The section states that where the officer of the company or a person employed as an auditor (whether an officer of the company or not) appears to be liable, but they acted honestly and reasonably, and having regard to all the circumstances of the case they ought fairly to be excused, the court may relieve them wholly or in part from this liability as it thinks fit. The officer/person may apply to the court for relief where they believe a claim may be made against them (on the instances listed earlier). The court may, if it is being tried by a judge with a jury, and they are satisfied that the defendant should be able to rely on the relief provided under s. 1157, withdraw the case from the jury and enter a judgment, including costs, as it thinks proper.

17.2.12 Removal of a Director

Directors may leave office for numerous reasons. They may die in office or may resign (although once a resignation has been accepted the director cannot retract it); and on the dissolution of the company the directors are automatically dismissed.

> **Glossop v Glossop (1907)**
>
> **Facts:**
>
> A director provided notice of resignation. The question for the court was whether this could be withdrawn.
>
> **Authority for:**
>
> Once a director has provided their notice of resignation, it may not be withdrawn except with the consent of the board. However, if the articles of the company so provide, a resignation which is only effective by the consent of the board may allow it to be withdrawn before its acceptance.

The articles of the company may provide for a proportion or number of directors to retire annually (retirement by rotation) and these directors may then be replaced or re-elected to office. However, the company, through the other directors' action or the members, may wish to remove a director before their term of office has expired.

A director may be removed from office through an ordinary resolution to that effect. Special notice is to be provided of 28 days to the company secretary of the resolution and the meeting at which the resolution is to be passed must be called with at least 21 days' notice. There are many reasons why the shareholders may wish for a director to be re-moved and CA 2006 provides for the procedure of such a decision. The company may achieve this through an ordinary resolution at a meeting to remove the director before the director's term of office was due to expire (CA 2006, s. 168). However, as a director may also be a shareholder with voting rights, their removal may prove to be problematic.

Bushell v Faith (1970)

Facts:

A company had 300 shares split equally between a brother and his two sisters who were the company's directors. When the sisters wished to remove the brother as director they issued a resolution to this effect. However, the articles of association provided that where a director was to be removed from office, in the vote to move this resolution, the affected director's shares should carry three votes per share. This was perfectly legal and hence following the vote the two sisters' votes accounted for 200 votes, whilst the brother's 100 shares accounted for 300 votes. The House of Lords held therefore that the vote to remove the director had been defeated. It should be noted that it is possible to provide for this arrangement of voting, but also the articles of the company may be changed through a special resolution to circumvent this problem of entrenching a director.

Authority for:

It is perfectly legal to include a clause into the articles that affords protection to a director/minority shareholder from early removal from office. However, it is also possible to later alter this clause in accordance with the articles.

When the director is removed, this section of the Act is not to be taken as depriving the removed person of any compensation or damages payable in respect of the termination of the appointment. A director removed in this way may protest and upon receipt of the notice of an intended resolution to remove them from office, the company must send a copy as soon as is reasonably practicable to the director concerned (CA 2006, s. 169). CA 2006 also provides the director with the right to be heard on the resolution at the meeting. They may also, upon this notice, provide a written representation to the company (not exceeding a reasonable length) and request that this is notified to the members of the company. If the use of this procedure would be to abuse the rights provided in s. 169, the representations need not be sent out.

Beyond the use of CA 2006 for this removal, there may be provision in the company's articles to achieve the same result. For example, the company may incorporate a clause into the articles that the director could be removed with a majority vote by the board by notice in writing. The main use of a removal through the articles rather than through s. 168 is simply that in the case of subsidiary companies, a holding company is not entitled to use s. 168 to remove directors of the subsidiary, but it is achievable through the articles.

17.2.13 Disqualification of Directors

The legislation used to prevent a director holding office is the Company Directors Disqualification Act 1986 and it may be applied to both natural persons and to corporations that hold directorships. When the person is subject to a disqualification order, they are prevented from taking any part in the management of a company, they may not promote a company, and they are prevented from acting as an insolvency practitioner. To ensure that persons dealing with companies are protected, Companies House maintains a register of all disqualification orders and this is freely available to members of the public.

Examples of the offences that may lead to disqualification include the conviction of an indictable offence in connection with the promotion, formation, management, or liquidation of a company, or with the management or receivership of the company's property (s. 2). Orders made on this ground at a Magistrates' Court last for five years. Where the director has been persistently in default in providing the required annual returns or accounts to the Registrar, they may be subject to an order lasting no longer than five years (s. 3). Three convictions in a five-year period satisfies the requirement of a persistent breach. If an officer or receiver of a company in liquidation has been guilty of fraud in relation to the company, or has breached their directors' duties, or committed an offence of knowingly being a party to fraudulent trading, the court may issue an order for a maximum term of up to 15 years (s. 4). Note that these offences do not need to be supported with a criminal conviction for the order to be imposed. If the person acting as a director (or shadow director) had been engaged in conduct that led to a company becoming insolvent and it is considered they are unfit to act in a management capacity, an order may be made (for not less than two years—s. 6). The action that leads to a person being disqualified for unfitness is not restricted to actions taken in the United Kingdom—its jurisdiction is much broader (*Re Seagull Manufacturing Co. (No. 2)* [1994]). It is also possible for the articles to establish grounds for the disqualification of a director.

17.3 DIRECTORS' LIABILITY TO SHAREHOLDERS

The directors of a company and the company secretary owe duties to the company as a whole rather than to the individual shareholders (who make up the company) and as such the shareholders are unlikely to be able to claim directly against the director based on their conduct. Exceptions to this rule exist, for example where the director has made a contract between themself and the shareholders, and this may establish an agency relationship, with the consequent liability for breach of duty.

Allen v Hyatt (1914)

Facts:

The directors of the company induced its shareholders to provide to them options to purchase their shares. This was proposed on the basis of the directors negotiating the sale to another company. However, rather than selling the shares directly to this other company, the directors used the options to purchase the shares personally and then to sell them to the company.

Authority for:

The directors had made themselves agents for the shareholders and therefore had to account to them for the profits they made on the sales.

There appears to be a potential problem then between the decisions taken by the directors and the amount of influence that can be exerted by the shareholders, and this may be even more marked where the shareholders are in a minority—who or what mechanism protects their interests?

17.4 MINORITY PROTECTION

Shareholders have the right, and the company is obliged in certain circumstances, to place a resolution at a general meeting and have this voted upon by the members (the shareholders). However, directors may also be shareholders and they may form a majority and hence would find it relatively easy to pass through the resolutions that require a simple majority, or even those requiring a 75 per cent majority. This problem led to the famous case of *Foss v Harbottle*.

Foss v Harbottle (1843)

Facts:

Two directors sold part of their own land to the company. Following this was a claim by minority shareholders that the price paid by the company was too high. These affected shareholders brought a claim against the directors concerned but the court refused to hear the action. It held that the interest in the case belonged to the company, and if the company believed the directors had acted wrongfully, then it should determine whether to bring the action—not the minority shareholders.

Authority for:

This is known as a derivative claim, where one party attempts to sue another party on the basis of losses suffered by a third party (CA 2006, s. 260). The claim failed in *Foss*, but there have been many advances since the case was heard, with many exceptions to the general rule established that, whilst it remains 'good law', its usefulness has been significantly curtailed.

CA 2006 has introduced protections for minority shareholders where a shareholder may initiate proceedings against a director on the company's behalf, (a derivative claim) in respect of a cause of action arising from an actual or proposed act or omission involving negligence, default, breach of duty, or breach of trust by a director of the company (this also includes a former director and a shadow director). However, as this is a claim through the shareholders on the company's behalf, any award will be provided to the company, albeit that the shareholder claimant will be able to recover any expenses incurred in the action.

In order to use this procedure, CA 2006 identifies requirements that must be satisfied. The first is that the member must obtain the court's permission to proceed with their action (CA 2006, s. 261). This first stage is used to determine whether a prima facie case exists against the director. Where this is satisfied, the case continues and the court may give directions as to the evidence to be provided by the company, and at the hearing the court may give permission for the claim to continue on the terms it sees fit, refuse permission and dismiss the claim, or adjourn proceedings and give any directions it thinks fit.

Section 263 identifies situations where permission must be refused, and these occur where the court is satisfied that:

1. a person acting in accordance with s. 172 (duty to promote the success of the company) would not seek to continue the claim; or

2. where the cause of action arises from an act or omission that is yet to occur, the act or omission has been authorized by the company; or

3. where the cause of action arises from an act or omission that has already occurred, the act or omission (i) was authorized by the company before it occurred, or (ii) has been ratified by the company since it occurred.

Another area of protection available to the minority shareholder, rather than a derivative claim, is a claim that their rights have been 'unfairly prejudiced' by the way in which the company is being run.

17.4.1 Unfair Prejudice

The protection of members against unfair prejudice is contained in Part 30 of CA 2006 and provides a right for members to petition a court that the company's affairs are being conducted in a manner that is likely to unfairly prejudice the interests of members generally, or some part of its members (including at least themself). The member may also petition on the basis that an actual or proposed act or omission of the company is or would be so prejudicial (CA 2006, s. 994). This section of the Act also applies to a person who is not a member of the company but to whom shares in it have been transferred as they apply to a member of a company. CA 2006 also provides a right for the Secretary of State to exercise powers to petition the court where they believe the rights of members are being unfairly prejudiced (CA 2006, s. 995). Where the court is satisfied that the petition is well founded, it is empowered (CA 2006, s. 996(2)):

(a) to order as it thinks fit relief in respect of the matters complained of such as to regulate the conduct of the company's affairs in the future, such as altering the articles to prevent future abuses.

Re HR Harmer (1959)

Facts:

Mr Harmer established a stamp business. Later he established a company and sold the business to it. The directors were Harmer and his two sons, and Harmer and his wife (who would vote in accordance with her husband's instructions) held over 75 per cent of the shares. Harmer was a poor director, he would ignore the views of his other directors, he established a business in Australia which faltered whilst selling another successful business based in the US. Given the history of bullying and poor management, his sons petitioned the court for unfair prejudice.

Authority for:

The court ordered Harmer to have no further interference with the running of the company, he was granted the title 'president' but possessed no powers, and the company was to purchase his shares.

It is also important to note that under this section, the court having changed the articles will not enable the company to change them again through a special resolution—it will be necessary to request the court's permission to alter them again (s. 996(2)(d));

(b) (i) to require the company to refrain from doing or continuing an act complained of (e.g. to stop directors' unusually high salaries that are preventing dividends being provided to the shareholders);

(ii) to require the company to do an act that the petitioner has complained it has omitted to do (e.g. to adhere to resolutions of the board);

(c) to authorize civil proceedings to be brought in the name of (and on behalf of) the company by such person(s) and on such terms as the court may direct (e.g. to avoid the *Foss* situation and enable a claim in the company's name, rather than the shareholder);

(d) to provide for the purchase of shares of any members of the company by other members (or by the company itself); and in the case of purchase by the company, the reduction of the company's share capital accordingly.

This section of CA 2006 restates the law that had already been included in CA 1985 and incorporates a wide range of activities likely to adversely affect shareholders, particularly minority shareholders. The directors may be negligent in their management of the company that may, if the facts support it, lead to unfair prejudice; the directors may pay themselves salaries that reduce or remove entirely the members' dividends . . .

Re Sam Weller & Sons Ltd (1989)

Facts:

Shareholders who were not involved in the management of the company were dissatisfied with the dividend which had remained at the same level for 37 years.

Authority for:

The court established that this situation could amount to conduct unfairly prejudicial to the interest of those shareholders who did not participate in management. It also noted that this position should not be construed so that a shareholder who does not receive any other benefits from the company (besides the dividends) is automatically entitled to comply, but the claim must be founded on unfairly prejudicial conduct.

. . . and shares could be provided to directors on much more favourable terms than available to members; and so on. Many of the cases based on the unfair prejudice principle have focused on where a major shareholder has been refused a management role with the company or removed from the board of directors.

Ebrahimi v Westbourne Galleries (1972)

Facts:

Mr Ebrahimi and business partner transferred their successful partnership to a company which they formed. They were the only directors and each held 500 £1 shares. Later, the

→

son of the business partner was made the third director and issued with 100 shares from the other directors' shareholdings. The directors were paid from the profits and thus no dividends were paid. Later, the other directors removed Ebrahimi as a director and, whilst holding 400 shares, no dividends were paid and his holding was seen as worthless. He petitioned the court to have the company wound up so he could recover his share of the assets of the company.

Authority for:

Despite the removal of the director from his office in accordance with the Companies Act, it was considered a just and equitable ground to wind up the company. The company was established on the basis of the original business relationship and it was understood that this relationship, with regards the management of the company, would continue.

Where a director (and shareholder) of a company has been removed so that they can no longer take an active part in its management, the court has often ruled that the majority shareholders must purchase the shares of the removed director (but not necessarily a director who has not been removed and simply disagrees with the direction of the company), to allow the affected director to invest their money in another company, although such rulings do not prevent a petition for the winding-up of the company on just and equitable grounds.

O'Neill v Phillips (1999)

Facts:

Mr Philips was the sole owner of 100 £1 shares in a company and he hired Mr O'Neill as a manual worker. O'Neill impressed Philips so much that he was promoted and soon was made a director with a 25 per cent holding of the company's shares. O'Neill was informed that on Philips' retirement, he would take over the running of the company and receive 50 per cent of the profits. After Philips' retirement, O'Neill did become the sole director but after a period of financial decline, Philips used his majority voting rights to appoint himself managing director. O'Neill was not to receive 50 per cent of the profits— rather he would receive his salary and dividends for his 25 per cent shareholding. O'Neill claimed unfair prejudice on the part of Philips.

Authority for:

The House of Lords concluded that this was not a case of unfair prejudice. O'Neill had not been excluded from the business and the promise of 50 per cent of the profits of the company was not contractually binding. Even though O'Neill had lost trust in Philips, this was not a ground for concluding unfairly prejudicial conduct.

17.4.2 Property Transactions by the Company

Protection is provided through Part 10, Chapter 4 of CA 2006 regarding the members' approval of substantial property transactions. A company may not enter into an arrangement (not restricted to legally binding contractual agreements) under which a director (including shadow directors) of the company or of its holding company, or a person connected with the director, acquires or is to acquire from the company (whether directly or indirectly) a substantial non-cash asset (meaning an asset whose value exceeds 10 per cent of the company's asset value and is more than £5,000; or it exceeds £100,000—CA 2006, s. 191). The company is also prevented from entering into an agreement for it to acquire a substantial non-cash asset from a director or person connected with them. In both of these situations, the transaction is only allowed where it has been approved by the members through passing an ordinary resolution at a general meeting, or is conditional on such approval being obtained. Therefore, arrangements can be made that will proceed if and when the formal approval of the members has been realized. Where the transaction has been entered into in contravention of s. 190, but within a reasonable time it is affirmed by a resolution of the members, then the transaction or arrangement may not be avoided.

17.4.3 Loans, Quasi-loans, and Credit Transactions

CA 2006 continues from outlining where a substantial property transfer will or will not be permitted to identify the regulation of a company providing directors with loans and credit. This provision used to be prohibited, but CA 2006 allows for such transactions insofar as they are supported by the members of the company through an ordinary or written resolution.

A quasi-loan is a transaction under which one party (the creditor) agrees to pay, or pays, a sum for another (the borrower); or they agree to reimburse (or do reimburse), otherwise than in pursuance of an agreement, expenditure incurred by another party for another (the borrower—CA 2006, s. 199). This, essentially, can be interpreted as the company agreeing to pay a director's personal expenses, where the director agrees to pay the money back at a later date. This can involve personal loans where the nature of the item is purely for the director's personal consumption or it could be a loan associated with a cost that the director incurs as part of their work (such as travel costs that are not considered expenses reclaimable under the contract of service). A credit transaction (CA 2006, s. 202) is where a creditor supplies or sells under hire-purchase goods or land for their personal use and allows for deferred payments over a given period of time. Section 197 outlines the criteria for allowing such a loan.

17.5 THE SECRETARY

CA 2006 made an important change to the previous requirements under the Companies Acts by removing the requirement for private (but not public) companies to have a secretary. However, even though a private company is not required to have a secretary (CA 2006, s. 270), the powers and duties attributable to a director and a secretary cannot be performed by one person (a sole director) acting in both capacities as director and secretary. As a consequence, whilst the company may legally have just one member, it is required to have at least two officers of director and secretary. The secretary is also considered to be an employee of the company and this must be taken into account with regard to the rights of employees and the duties on employers (see Part 7), and also if the company is wound up this employment status has implications for the payments of creditors.

17.5.1 Appointment

A private company is entitled to make an appointment of a secretary, and where it chooses to do so, that officer of the company has to undertake statutory duties and those imposed through the articles, and they have authorization to perform various functions on the company's behalf. The board of directors will choose the secretary (a power usually authorized in the company's articles) and will usually determine the terms and conditions upon which the appointment is to be made, including the term of office. This decision is usually made at a general meeting and passed through an ordinary resolution. The company secretary does not take part in the management of the company (although they do have responsibilities for the company) but the position does provide certain powers (these are generally restricted to administrative tasks).

A public company must have a secretary (CA 2006, s. 271). Unlike a secretary for a private company, a public secretary must have the qualifications required to hold such a position (CA 2006, s. 273):

1. they have held the office of secretary of a public company for at least three of the five years immediately preceding their appointment as secretary;

2. they are a member of any of the bodies specified in subsection (3)—bodies representing the many chartered institutes of accountants;

3. they are a barrister, advocate, or solicitor called or admitted in any part of the United Kingdom;

4. they are a person who, by virtue of their holding or having held any other position or their being a member of any other body, appears to the directors to be capable of discharging the functions of secretary of the company.

It is also a requirement under CA 2006 that the company maintains a register of company secretaries and not simply include them in the Register of Directors, as was the previous practice (CA 2006, s. 275). This must be kept at the company's registered office or another specified place under s. 1136 and the company must inform the Registrar of where it is being held.

In the absence of a company secretary, the duties that would have previously been undertaken by this officer may be carried out by any other person that the company's board of directors so wish (so in essence the company has a secretary, but just not in name). It is possible for a company to occupy the position of secretary, but this will not be allowed where it is acting as secretary of a company run by a sole director and this sole director is also the sole director or secretary of the other company. Where there is no secretary because of some temporary vacancy or the secretary is incapable of acting in this capacity, an assistant, deputy secretary, or some other person such as a director may be authorized by the directors to fulfil this role (CA 2006, s. 274).

The main role of the secretary is to undertake many of the administrative burdens that a limited company has to comply with as a result of its members enjoying limited liability status. The secretary completes these documents, signs them, and returns them on the company's behalf. These include maintaining the company's registers, arranging the company's meetings and forwarding the notices of these meetings and any resolutions to be moved to the members, and submitting the company's annual return.

The secretary has the power to bind the company in contracts, even in the absence of any authority in this respect, where this relates to administrative proceedings such as employing staff and hiring transport. This power is associated with the usual authority of such a position (under agency) and will only extend that far. Where the secretary attempts to bind the company on issues which would be obviously beyond their authority such as taking loans on the company's behalf and registering the transfer of the company's shares, as these would be powers vested in the directors rather than the secretary, the secretary enjoys no powers in this respect. However, the law of agency applies in these situations and the company must ensure that third parties are not misled as to the authority possessed by the secretary.

Panorama Developments (Guildford) Ltd v Fidelis Furnishing Fabrics Ltd (1971)

Facts:

The secretary of a company was required to hire cars as part of the business of the company. They further used their position to order the use of cars for personal business. When the company discovered this fact, it wished to avoid having to settle the bill and considered the secretary liable.

Authority for:

The court held the company was liable. The company secretary was not a mere clerk and had the apparent authority to enter into such contracts.

CONCLUSION

This chapter has sought to identify the nature of a director's role in a company, the powers they possess, where these powers derive, and the obligations imposed on the director by the enactment of CA 2006. The secretary of the company is also an important position, and whilst there is no longer an obligation on private companies to have a secretary, public companies still have such a duty and there are specific qualifications that are required to be satisfied where a public company employs a secretary.

SUMMARY OF MAIN POINTS

Directors

- Directors exercise the specific tasks in the running of the company.
- The members (such as shareholders) 'own' the company but have no automatic rights of management.
- Directors may or may not be shareholders of the company.

Types of director

- Directors may be executive, non-executive, and shadow.

Number of directors

- A private company is required to have at least one director.
- A public company is required to have at least two directors.

Appointment

- Directors may be the promoter(s) of the company when it is first registered.
- Directors may be added to the company to increase expertise to the company's management or where additional responsibilities have to be performed.
- Directors may be appointed in accordance with the company's articles, usually through an ordinary resolution at a general meeting, but other mechanisms such as a written procedure may be valid.
- Directors must be over the age of 16 to be appointed to hold the position.
- A public company may not appoint two or more directors at a general meeting through a single resolution unless a resolution that it should be made has been unanimously agreed.
- Whilst corporations may be a director, every company must have at least one director who is a natural person.

Registration

- Every company is required to maintain a register of the directors which is available for inspection.

Directors' pay and contracts

- Directors may not necessarily receive remuneration but where pay is given the details must be maintained by the company and be available for inspection.
- Directors' length of contract, over a fixed term of two years' duration or more, may be terminated by providing reasonable notice.

Directors' duties

- The common law duties have been codified and expanded through CA 2006.
- The duties include:
  - to act within their powers;
  - to promote the success of the company;
  - to exercise independent judgement;
  - to exercise reasonable care, skill, and diligence;
  - to avoid conflicts of interest;
  - not to accept benefits from third parties.
- Directors must declare an interest in proposed transactions or arrangements that do, or may, cause a conflict.

Meetings of directors

- Each of the directors must be given notice of the meetings.
- The company must keep the minutes of the proceedings at the meeting, and maintain those for at least 10 years.
- Decisions at meetings are based on a voting system.

Indemnifying directors

- A company may indemnify a director when it concerns the provision of insurance, a qualifying third-party indemnity provision, or a qualifying pension scheme indemnity provision.

- Fines imposed through the criminal law or civil fines by regulatory authorities will not be indemnified.

Removal of a director

- Directors may retire annually (retirement by rotation) or through resignation, or through being removed before the expiration of their term of office.
- The director may be removed through an ordinary resolution and special notice of the resolution where it is provided to the company 28 days before the meeting (and where 21 days' notice is given of the meeting).

Disqualification

- The Company Directors Disqualification Act 1986 applies to both natural persons and corporations that hold directorships.
- Once disqualified the person may not take part in the management of a company for the period of disqualification.

Directors' liability to shareholders

- Directors are responsible to the company as a whole, not to individual shareholders.
- Minority protection is provided through CA 2006 to restrict directors' acts that may adversely affect their position. Shareholders may bring a claim against directors in the company's name (a derivative claim) or may claim that a directors' acts or omission would be unfairly prejudicial to the shareholder.

The company secretary

- Private companies are no longer required to have a company secretary, although a sole director cannot also be the company secretary.
- Public companies must have a company secretary and this officer must satisfy statutory requirements in relation to their qualifications.
- The board of directors are usually empowered to appoint the secretary.
- Companies are required to maintain a separate Register of Secretaries.
- The secretary undertakes many of the administrative burdens of the company, signing documents and returning them to the Registrar as required by law.

SUMMARY QUESTIONS

Essay questions

1. Discuss the implications for directors' duties to the company since the enactment of the Companies Act 2006. Explain where the statute has expanded the duties previously established through the common law, and what steps the company should take to ensure compliance with the Act.

2. How may members of a company remove a director before the expiry of their term of office? What protection is afforded to directors when faced with such a resolution?

Problem questions

1. John is the managing director of Widgets and Gadgets Plc and is aware that the company is the target of a takeover by Build 'em up, Knock 'em down Plc. John does not believe that

such a takeover would be in the best interests of the company and therefore a board decision is made to increase the allotment of shares under an employee share scheme. This will increase the shareholding of the company and prevent the takeover.

Advise Widgets and Gadgets Plc on the implications of this action.

2. Sarah is the company secretary of Picture Perfect Ltd, an advertising agency. The company regularly hires limousines to collect important clients from their offices and airports. Without authorization from the company, Sarah hires several cars to transport herself and her friends on nights out on the company's business account with the hire firm. When the company receives the invoice, Sarah's actions are discovered and the company refuses to pay the bill.

Advise the parties of their rights and obligations.

 You will find guidance about how to answer these questions online at www.oup.com/uk/marson5e/.

FURTHER READING

Books and articles

Almadani, M. (2009) 'Derivative Action: Does the Companies Act 2006 Offer a Way Forward?' *Company Lawyer*, Vol. 30, No. 5, p. 131.

Cheung, R. (2008) 'Corporate Wrongs Litigated in the Context of Unfair Prejudice Claims: Reforming the Unfair Prejudice Remedy for the Redress of Corporate Wrongs' *Company Lawyer*, Vol. 29, No. 4, p. 98.

Hadjinestoros, M. (2008) 'Exploitation of Business Opportunities: How the UK Courts Ensure that Directors Remain Loyal to Their Companies' *International Company and Commercial Law Review*, Vol. 19, No. 2, p. 70.

Keay, A. (2007) 'Company Directors Behaving Poorly: Disciplinary Options for Shareholders' *Journal of Business Law*, Sept., p. 656.

Websites, Twitter, and YouTube channels

http://www.bitc.org.uk
@BITC1

https://www.youtube.com/user/1BITC
This governmental organization (Business in the Community) enables companies to become members and share practices of effective corporate values, translating these into models of management that are applicable in modern business.

http://www.companieshouse.gov.uk
@CompaniesHouse

https://www.youtube.com/user/TheCompaniesHouse
Information regarding the establishing of business organizations, forms to speed up the process, the requirements for returning documents to the Registrar, other information of interest to companies and their members, and general company advice.

https://www.gov.uk/limited-company-formation/directors-and-company-secretaries
Government website providing details on appointing a company secretary and the role and duties of this officer.

http://www.iod.com
@The_IoD

https://www.youtube.com/user/iodchannel
The Institute of Directors is a body that supports and represents individual private directors.

http://www.legislation.gov.uk/ukpga/2006/46/contents
The Companies Act 2006.

 ONLINE RESOURCES

www.oup.com/uk/marson5e/

For further resources relating to this chapter, including self-test questions, an interactive glossary, and key case flashcards.

PART 6
AGENCY LAW

A great many business transactions take place between the third party and an agent acting on behalf of the principal. For instance, when a customer (the third party) purchases a coffee from a high-street coffee shop chain (the principal), they enter this transaction with the member of staff at the counter (the agent). Duties and responsibilities exist for both the principal and agent, and this chapter outlines the most important whilst also identifying how such a relationship may be brought to an end.

18 AGENCY

It is essential to recognize that in a commercial world, many business transactions are completed through an agency relationship. An agent creates contracts between the person they are acting for (the principal) and the other (third) party. This contract is binding on the third party and will allow them to enforce the contract. An agent can gain authority to act for the principal implicitly, or through express agreements, and their actions can bind the principal in such contracts. The agent has responsibilities and rights through agreements to act for the principal, and it is necessary to appreciate how these are defined and limited by the courts and by statute.

Business Scenario 18

Rob owns a company operating under the name 'Robert's Burgers Ltd' which employs ten part-time and casual staff. The company trades from a mobile burger van which has a weekly pitch at markets in Leeds, Bradford, and Wakefield, Yorkshire. However, the company makes the majority of its annual income from the sale of burgers at summer festivals held nationally.

Nine months ago, Rob decided to employ one particular part-time employee, Hugo Hamperman on a full-time basis. The aim of the appointment was that Rob would buy a second burger van which Hugo would manage. Accordingly, Rob purchased a van and for the last three months Hugo has been managing this side of the business which includes a responsibility of Hugo to purchase the raw ingredients to make the burgers for sale through the van. Rob issued to Hugo a list of suppliers with which he has had regular dealings. Further, one month later Rob imposed on Hugo a spending limit of £500 per week for raw ingredients.

Hugo purchased burger buns and condiments from Conway Meats plc, one of the suppliers on the list, at a total cost of £300. During the same week he then went to another supplier on the list, Conway Meats Ltd, but they had run out of the standard burger meat he usually bought. This meant Hugo was forced to buy premium quality burger meat from Pesto Meats Ltd at a cost of £420. Robert's Burgers Ltd is refusing to honour the contract with Pesto Meats Ltd.

Last month, on his way to a festival in Gloucestershire, Hugo realized that a freezer containing the raw burger patties was no longer working. He sent Rob a text message informing him of the situation and asking what he should do. After two hours and having received no response, Hugo sold all the burger patties to a local fast food restaurant at a loss.

Learning Outcomes

- Identify in which situations an agency agreement will be established (18.3)
- Explain the various forms of authority an agent may possess (18.3.1–18.3.4)
- Identify the duties and obligations imposed on an agent in relation to the principal (18.4–18.4.4)
- Explain where liability will be imposed on an agent in contracts made with authority (18.5)
- Explain the rights of agents when acting in their capacity (18.6)
- Explain the implications of the Commercial Agents (Council Directive) Regulations 1993 to agency contracts and the parties involved (18.8–18.8.3)
- Identify the procedures in terminating an agency relationship (18.7; 18.8.3).

18.1 INTRODUCTION

Agency is the relationship which exists between two persons when one, called the agent, is considered in law to represent the other, called the principal, in such a way as to be able to affect the principal's legal position in respect of strangers to the relationship by the making of contracts or the disposition of property (Fridman, G. H. L. (1996) 'The Law of Agency' (7th Edition) Butterworths: London).

The law in this area applies to many relationships and is frequently seen in commercial enterprises, including high street retailers, between partners, and the directors of a corporation. The agent's role is to act on the principal's behalf, in establishing contracts, for example; and when the agent has the required authority to act in this way, the contract will not be considered to bind the agent and the third party, but rather will bind the principal and the third party. By way of example, in retailing, the person who works as a 'shop assistant' is essentially acting as the agent of the shop's owner. When goods are sold at the retailer's establishment, the shop assistant is not personally trading the goods, but rather they are given the authority to complete the transaction for the sale, and the money paid is to the owner of the shop, not the shop assistant. With regard to this authority, where the third party has paid for the goods, and passed their money to the shop assistant, agency provides that even where the shop assistant fails to pass this money to the owner of the shop, it will be considered that the third party has paid for the goods and has good title to them, even though the shop assistant has not fulfilled their obligation to the owner. The agent has the authority to complete such transactions on behalf of the principal, and the third party has conducted their business on the basis of this authority. It is in this way that many (obvious) forms of agency are seen—the agent having authority to buy and sell goods.

18.2 TYPES OF AGENT

There are several forms of agreement in which an agent may have authority to bind the principal, and simply because the word 'agent' is used, this does not create a situation where their actions will bind the principal. For example, an estate agent is a term in common usage, but it does not establish the legal implications and rights of an agent in its legal sense.

> **Consider**
>
> The first issue to consider is the type of agent Hugo is.

Agents may take the following forms:

- *General agent:* This is the most common type of agency agreement, where the agent has the authority to act for the principal in the ordinary course of their business.
- *Special agent:* Denotes a similar form of agency agreement but the agent is only authorized to perform a particular act.
- *Commercial agent:* This is an agent, provided for under an EU Directive, which allows the agent greater protection (through the statute) than exists under the common law.
- *Commission agent:* This agent has the authority to buy and sell on the principal's behalf, but they are not authorized to establish privity of contract with the third party (see **6.3**).
- Del Credere *Agent:* Here the agent binds the principal, but they are provided with an additional sum that guarantees that the agent will indemnify the principal in the event that the third party fails to pay money owed under the contract (e.g. when goods are sold on credit).

18.3 CREATION OF AGENCY

Agency agreements are very easy to establish (see **Table 18.1**).

As there is no compulsion on agents to register with a governmental body to demonstrate their status as agents, or to work under a set of clear guidelines, the common law has assisted in identifying the powers of an agent. However, before the rights and duties

Table 18.1 Creating an agency

Through a contract (although in most situations this is not necessary)

Through verbal agreement

Where an agent is appointed to execute a deed (and have a 'power of attorney'), under common law, they must be appointed by deed

Implicitly where the intentions of the parties provide guidance as to the true relationship (see *Chaudhry v Prabhakar*)

and

Agency may be imposed on the parties by statute (e.g. Consumer Credit Act 1974, s. 56(2)), through necessity, and through cohabitation

---

of the agent and principal are considered, the source and implications of the form of authority that the agent possesses must be identified. Such authority may be based on 'actual' authority provided (either expressly or through implication); it may be 'apparent' through a representation made to the third party; it may exist through the principal's subsequent '**ratification**' of the contract; or the authority may have derived through 'necessity'. Note that the classic principle, that to create obligations under agency required the representation of this relationship to have derived from the principal and not the agent has been weakened, especially through the concept of apparent authority. Where the agent has authority from the principal to contract, the third party may rely on this in their enforcement of a contract.

Chaudhry v Prabhakar (1988)

Facts:

The claimant was accompanied by her friend to inspect a used car with the intention of purchasing it. Despite obvious damage to the car's bonnet, the friend recommended the purchase on the advice that it 'was in good condition'. After the purchase it transpires the car was not in good condition and this led to the claimant's action against the friend.

Authority for:

Even where a friend volunteers time and advice to help another person, an objective duty of care is imposed. The friend was aware that their opinion was to be relied on. However, similarly with contract law, the relationship between the parties is a material factor and opinions of friends in these circumstances (a social and domestic relationship) will not establish a duty of care.

18.3.1 Actual Authority

When expressed, there is an agreement between the principal and the agent as to the powers that the agent will have to bind the principal (e.g. the owner of a shop may inform the shop assistant that they have the right to sell the goods in the shop for the price identified on the ticket with no discretion for discounts). As with other types of express agreements, this can be established in words or writing (through a contract; and this may be preferable to clearly identify the extent of any authority).

Consider

Does Hugo have express actual authority? If so, how does the prohibition of spending more than £500 per week affect the actual authority? Further, as Hugo has the ability to go and trade with companies as provided for by Robert, would this amount to apparent authority?

There also exist situations where the authority may have been provided through implication due to the relationship/conduct between the agent and principal. Typical situations, relating to business, may occur where a director of a company may have been appointed incorrectly, or where they have not been appointed to a specific post (such as managing director), but the company has not made attempts to remove the authority or deny this authority to third parties. Implied authority may work in providing, in its entirety, the binding agreement between the agent and principal.

Hely-Hutchinson v Brayhead Ltd (1968)

Facts:

A company allowed its chairman to act in the way, and with the powers of, a managing director, without engaging him to this position. A managing director of a company would be assumed to have the authority to bind the company in most contractual dealings, and in this instance the chairman would not. The chairman established a contract that sought to bind the company and the Court of Appeal held the chairman had the implied authority to do this. It was the actions of the company that allowed for the chairman to act in this way, and hence it should be treated as if he had been given the position of managing director from the board of directors.

Authority for:

Actual authority and apparent (ostensible) authority often overlap. Where the board invest the chairman (using the facts of the case as an example) with the actual authority of that position but also with apparent authority to act with the authority of a managing director, this apparent authority can exceed the actual authority. It seeks to protect innocent third parties who are unaware of the limitation of authority placed by the principal on the agent.

Implied authority may also have the effect of broadening existing powers.

Waugh v HB Clifford and Sons Ltd (1982)

Facts:

A firm of solicitors were engaged by builders who required representation to protect against any legal action after they had negligently built houses. They expressly instructed the solicitor not to compromise on the basis of a substantial compensation payment. However, the solicitors disregarded the builders' instruction. It was common to allow solicitors in these situations to compromise on behalf of the principal. In the resultant action by the builders against the firm, the Court of Appeal held that as the builders had provided clear instructions not to compromise, and that express terms in a contract override implied terms (such as allowing the solicitors to compromise on the principal's behalf), the solicitors were in breach.

→

Authority for:

The authority between the agent and the third party is different to that between the agent and the principal. Where express instructions are given from a principal to the agent, this removes the implied nature of any authority in contradiction of the express agreement.

18.3.1.1 Usual authority

An unusual situation involving agency agreements occurred in *Watteau v Fenwick*.

Watteau v Fenwick (1893)

Facts:

The owner of a public house sold the property (and business), but was hired to be its manager. In his position as manager, he was provided with the authority to purchase bottled drinks on behalf of the new owner (the principal), but was expressly instructed not to purchase tobacco products on credit on the principal's behalf. The manager did purchase such goods from a salesman who had previous dealings with the manager (in his capacity as owner) and who was unaware of the change in management/ownership structure of the business (termed as an undisclosed principal). When the manager was unable to pay for the goods on credit he asserted that the principal was bound. It was held that the actions of the manager bound the principal.

Authority for:

This was a strange decision as the manager had no actual authority to act to bind the principal in this way; it could not be said there was apparent authority as the representation as to the agent's authority must move from the principal; the undisclosed principal was held liable for the actions of the agent, and hence the decision has been criticized. As such, it falls somewhere between actual and apparent authority, and has been termed 'usual' authority.

The reasoning for the decision was based on the manager being the previous owner and still having his name above the door (as required of licensed premises). He had not identified to the salesmen/traders in the area who had previous contact with the manager as to the change in organizational structure (and the change in authority), and as such it could be considered that the manager had authority to act, and the third party required protection. Despite the principal being bound by the agent's actions, this does not prevent him taking action against the agent for the breach.

18.3.2 Apparent Authority

Apparent authority (or ostensible authority, as it is referred to in some legal texts) exists outside of the actual authority previously identified. Whereas express and implied authority derives from the agreement between the principal and agent, apparent authority is applicable where the principal (or someone acting for them) has represented to the third party that the agent has the authority to act on their behalf. The consequence is that where the third party has been given this impression of authority of the agent, an agreement that is subsequently concluded between the agent and third party may bind the principal, who is unable to deny the representation made.

Therefore, to establish apparent authority, the following criteria must be demonstrated:

1. there must have been a representation regarding the person as an agent;
2. the principal must have conveyed this representation (or someone acting on their behalf);
3. the third party must have acted based on this representation.

An example of the effects of apparent authority was demonstrated in the previously discussed case of *Hely-Hutchinson* (as apparent and actual authority often overlap).

This point was made in the following case:

Freeman & Lockyer v Buckhurst Park Properties Ltd (1964)

Facts:

A director was given authority to act in the manner expected of a managing director, and in this capacity he engaged a firm of architects to act for the company. The company refused to pay the firm for the work on the basis that the director who had agreed the contract lacked the (actual) authority to bind the company. The Court of Appeal held that there was a contract between the firm and the company.

Authority for:

There had been an impression that the director had the authority to bind the company in the agreement, and therefore the principal was liable under the contract established on its behalf. The representation, moving from the principal, is usually provided (in the case of corporations) by the company's board of directors.

And again:

First Energy (UK) Ltd v Hungarian International Bank Ltd (1993)

Facts:

The claimants had sought credit from the bank and in negotiating on this matter had dealt with a senior manager. During the negotiations the manager disclaimed any right that he may have to bind the bank as he lacked the actual authority to guarantee credit. However, later the manager wrote to the claimants stating that the credit requested by the claimants had been authorized by the bank, even though this was not the case. The Court of Appeal held that the bank was bound under the offer made by the manager. Whilst the Court accepted that the manager had informed the claimants of his lack of capacity to contract on behalf of the bank, he did possess the authority to communicate matters

→

from the bank to clients. As such, the bank had represented that the manager had authority to pass on decisions made by it, and the claimants could rely on this decision.

Authority for:

Businesses contract through the use of agents. As such, third parties dealing with them
must be enabled to rely on their appearance (here as an authorized agent of the bank).

It must be noted that where the agent acts on apparent authority, but in fact does not possess actual authority, they may be held liable if the principal decides to bring an action
against them for disobeying the principal's instructions. If, on the other hand the agent
had actual authority to take the actions that bound the principal, no claim is allowed by
the principal against the agent (and the agent would be entitled to any payment under
this agency agreement).

18.3.3 Authority Through Ratification

An agent who purports to act for the principal may enter into a contract that they were
unauthorized to make. At this stage it may not bind the principal but when the principal
is aware of the contract established by the agent on their behalf, and the principal accepts the agreement, they will be bound by it. The ratification must be given within a
reasonable time of the agreement. Ratification allows for the retrospective acceptance of
a contract and it will entitle the principal to all the rights and obligations provided under
a contractual agreement. As such, they are empowered to compel the completion of the
contract even where the third party no longer wishes to be bound.

Re Tiedemann and Ledermann Freres (1899)

Facts:

An agent used the principal's name to enter into a contract but he did so to avail himself
of the benefits of the agreement. On discovery of the truth, the third party attempted to
end the contract due to a misrepresentation.

Authority for:

Where the principal ratifies the contract, the third party is bound.

Bolton Partners v Lambert (1889)

Facts:

The defendant had communicated to the managing director of a company his offer to purchase the company. Following this communication, on 13 December 1886, a committee

decided that it would accept the offer (even though the committee had no such power to accept) and this was in return communicated to the defendant. In January the defendant attempted to revoke the offer, but the company sought to enforce this through an action for specific performance. The Court of Appeal held that as the board of the company had ratified the agreement, its effect was to bind the parties following the acceptance of the offer. The acceptance of the company was retrospectively applied to the December meeting of the committee and hence the defendant's attempted revocation in January was too late and consequently ineffective.

Authority for:

Ratification by a principal of acts done by an assumed agent is 'thrown back' to the date of the act done, and the agent is put in the same position as if they had authority to do that act.

The steps required to enable ratification are outlined in **Figure 18.1**.

- *The agent must be acting for the principal:* Because of the nature of ratification, and the requirement for the agent to be acting for the principal, the third party must be aware that a principal exists. Without such knowledge, the third party will assume they are contracting with the agent and the agent will be bound by the agreement. This is vitally important as an undisclosed principal cannot later ratify, even if the parties want this.

Keighly Maxted & Co. v Durrant (1901)

Facts:

An agent had made a contract for wheat based at a higher price for the principal than had been agreed. The principal agreed to ratify the contract.

Authority for:

The House of Lords prevented the ratification as the agent had not informed the third party of the principal's existence at the time of contracting.

Figure 18.1   Steps to enable ratification

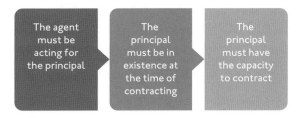

- *The principal must be in existence at the time of the contract:* This aspect applies particularly to companies that have been newly formed. Where the promoters of the company (its 'agents') have entered into a contract before the company has completed the registration process and been granted the certificate of incorporation, the agents are personally liable and the company may not, once it has been formed, later ratify the agreement.

- *The principal must have the capacity to contract:* The capacity to contract refers to elements such as whether the principal would have been able to enter into the contract that the agent actually formed. For example, corporations may lack the ability (capacity) to enter into the type of contract relevant to the claim, and hence there is no possibility of ratification. To avoid situations where ratification may cause problems between the parties, the agreement may be stated as being 'subject to ratification' and hence enable a withdrawal from the contract before ratification takes place.

18.3.4 **Authority Through Necessity**

Where the agent acts in relation to necessity (e.g. protecting property owned by the principal), then the courts may bind the principal in the actions of the agent even though they have no actual or apparent authority to act in the particular way. These cases have often occurred in emergencies at sea or where perishable goods are involved.

Consider

Consider Hugo's express actual authority and how this may have been affected by the availability of the meat. The operation of the law of necessity and the criteria required should be assessed. Significantly, the fact that Hugo must be unable to communicate with Robert should be applied to this situation to identify if such an authority could be established.

The requirements to bind the principal in this way involve satisfying the following criteria:

1. the agent must have had responsibility for the control over the property belonging to the principal;
2. it was not possible for the agent to discuss the issue with the principal and gain their instructions as to the action to be taken;
3. the situation must be considered an emergency;
4. the agent must have acted in good faith.

Springer v Great Western Railway (1921)

Facts:

The agent was not permitted to sell tomatoes (when engaged to carry these). However, due to weather and transport problems the agent did sell the goods on behalf of the

→

principal as the tomatoes were perishing in the heat. This had occurred on land and it was possible and reasonable for the carriers to contact the principal and obtain his instructions before taking the action.

Authority for:

It was held that such a situation did not amount to an emergency and was an unauthorized act.

18.4 DUTIES OF THE AGENT

Due to the nature of the agreement between the agent and principal, and the fact that the agent is given authority to act on the principal's behalf, trust and confidence are paramount in such dealings. The agent must respect the instructions of the principal and act in their best interests.

Consider

Hugo is subject to contractual duties which he has breached—in particular, the duty of performance of the undertaking and the duty to obey reasonable instructions need to be considered.

Duties that have been imposed on agents include:

- *An obligation to obey lawful instructions:* An agent may have agreed with the principal the parameters of the (actual) authority, and these may have been established in a contract. Where this is so, a failure on the side of the agent to follow the requirements of the contract will amount to a breach, even if this was performed in good faith. Therefore, even if, in not following instructions, the agent considered their actions to be the most appropriate course for the principal, a breach is still committed.

- *Non-delegation of duties:* There is a general duty that the agent should not delegate (and in essence this would amount to sub-delegation) the principal's authority, and should perform the task personally. However, this general duty will be removed where the principal expressly agrees for the agent to delegate, where such authority to delegate may be implied from the circumstances of the case, and if the delegation is required due to some unforeseen event.

- *To exercise care and skill:* When conducting the business of the principal, the agent must use the appropriate care and skill in the execution of their duties (based on the nature of the task and the skills they profess to hold. The most common examples of the nature of care and skill in professional occupations include agents in solicitors and accountancy practices—see *Chaudhry v Prabhakar* at **18.3**).

- *Fiduciary duties:* The **fiduciary duties** are imposed due to the nature of the relationship between the agent and principal, and the authority the agent exercises for the principal. If a breach of the duty is discovered, the principal may seek to recover any secret profit made by the agent, and/or any bribe that has been paid. In such a situation the principal may seek damages for the fraud committed. The principal may have the option to refuse to pay the commission or salary of the agent. The agent's contract with the principal may be terminated, and the agreement with the third party may be rescinded. The use of these options is determined by the courts depending on the actions of the parties and what is fair and reasonable in the circumstances.

The examples of fiduciary duties given at **18.4.1–18.4.4** are artificially separated in this section for ease of reference, and they frequently overlap.

18.4.1 Duty Not to Take Bribes

One of the most important duties placed on an agent is to ensure that they do not take bribes in the exercise of the authority for the principal. Clearly, good faith requires that the agent acts in the best interest of the principal, and for their, rather than the agent's benefit. As such, a bribe to, for example, secure the award of a contract would place the agent's motives and the best interests of the principal in conflict. It is this element of inducement that may give rise to accusations of accepting bribes, and this may not be confined to money, but could include free samples for the agent, the agent being invited to hospitality events, or any other gift in kind. Where the principal discovers the bribe they may terminate the arrangement with the agent and recover any commission paid, recover the bribe provided, consider the bribe to be held by the agent on trust, recover damages from the third party that provided the bribe for any losses attributable (rather than recovering the bribe), and they may rescind the contract between the principal and the third party.

Attorney General for Hong Kong v Reid (1994)

Facts:

Mr Reid, during his career at the legal service of the Government of Hong Kong, accepted bribes in breach of his fiduciary duties. He used the money to buy properties which had gained in value. The properties were deemed to be held in trust for the Government.

Authority for:

When a bribe is accepted by a fiduciary (the agent) in breach of their duty, the bribe is held on trust for the person to whom the duty is owed (the principal).

As can be observed, the effects of bribes can be catastrophic to the relationship between all the parties.

18.4.2 **Secret Profits**

The agent must ensure that the profits accrued from the agreement(s) with the third party are agreed between the agent and principal. The agent should not make a profit that has not been previously agreed (such as the agent's commission/salary). This may be particularly so when the agent is asked to dispose of goods and they do so at a higher price than requested by the principal (and the agent retains the 'extra' amount), or the agent uses the principal's property for their own purposes. It is important to remember that such situations do not have to cause the principal any loss, but it is the abuse of the position of trust and authority that is at issue. Where an agent has made a secret profit but has not been dishonest the court will usually award the principal with the profit rather than impose more harsh penalties.

18.4.3 **Avoid a Conflict of Interest**

In the same way as a duty exists to prevent the agent making a secret profit when acting for the principal, the agent must also not allow their own interests to conflict with those of the principal. The agency agreement is predicated on the basis of the agent acting in the best interests of the principal, and this is the case even where an agent acts, but not with the intention to defraud or mislead the principal, and there is the appearance of a conflict. As such, where a conflict of interest may arise, the agent should offer a full disclosure to the principal so an informed choice may be made.

Armstrong v Jackson (1917)

Facts:

The agent was a stockbroker. The principal wished to purchase shares in a particular company, and the agent obtained these shares (but they were in reality his own). The agent had informed the principal that he had purchased the shares, whilst the real situation was that the stockbroker was a promoter of the company when it was formed. When this fact was later discovered, the principal was successful in having the contract set aside.

Authority for:

The court held that the agent had a duty to disclose this potential conflict to the principal and had breached his duty in not so doing.

18.4.4 **Duty to Account**

The agent must maintain adequate records of their dealings on behalf of the principal and make these available for inspection when requested. As agents may work under the authority of several principals it is their duty to maintain records in a manner that allows for the separation of the principals' accounts. This is the case where information is maintained in computer form (e.g. on a database) and the principal is entitled to view their own accounts. Where the agent cannot separate the principal's accounts, the principal is entitled to see all of the accounts held by the agent. This further has an impact on the agent's duty of confidentiality, and the continuing nature of this obligation following the cessation of the agency agreement.

Bolkiah v KPMG (1999)

Facts:

KPMG had confidential information regarding Prince Bolkiah (a former client) which may have been relevant to an investigation about the use of assets which, it was suggested, Bolkiah had used for his personal benefit. The investigation was being undertaken by the Brunei Investment Agency (BIA) who had instructed KPMG to act for it.

Authority for:

The House of Lords granted an injunction against KPMG from acting for the BIA. A fiduciary cannot act for and against a client at the same time. A duty exists which goes beyond mere non-deliberate disclosure to ensure a client is not put at risk.

18.5 LIABILITY OF THE AGENT

In situations where it has been established that the agent acted beyond their authority and therefore did not bind the principal, it has to be determined what happens to the agreement with the third party. The third party has entered into an agreement and is entitled to have the other party (the agent) honour their side of the bargain. Where the agent has identified themselves as such, and established the contract on the principal's behalf, then the contract is between the principal and the third party, and the agent has no liability. If, on the other hand, the agent has not disclosed that they were acting for a principal, then the contract will exist between the agent and the third party and the usual rights and liabilities in a contractual agreement will apply. When the agent discloses the principal to the third party, and the agent was acting under actual authority, liability of the third party to the agent ceases and is transferred to the principal, but the agent and the principal will be jointly liable to the third party. The third party may then choose to enforce the contract against the agent or principal, but once the decision is made it cannot be changed. In a situation where the agent acted without actual authority, the principal will not be bound by the agreement.

Situations exist where an agent has not disclosed the existence of a principal and the principal is then prohibited from concluding the contract. Where the principal was not disclosed, and if they had been, the third party would not have agreed to the contract, this will prevent the principal from acting on it. Such a situation requires some 'personal element' in the decision (e.g. it may be permissible to prevent a reviewer who has had previous negative dealings with the third party from procuring a ticket to provide a review of the third party's production, but may not be so in the sale of land, which lacks this personal element). Clearly, the contract will not be enforced where the third party specifically asks the agent to identify the principal and they withhold this information or misrepresent the position.

Archer v Stone (1898)

Facts:

The defendant had asked the claimant if he was acting for a certain third party and was informed that he was not. This was untrue.

Authority for:

The contract was induced through a misrepresentation and as such, the party who told the lie cannot enforce the contract.

The principal cannot enforce the contract if it identifies that a contract under agency is excluded. Further, if the third party establishes the contract with the agent personally, rather than wishing to contract with a principal, this will stop the principal from acting on the contract.

- *Rights of the undisclosed principal:* Guidance was provided in *Siu Yin Kwan v Eastern Insurance Co.* regarding situations where an agent has failed to disclose the principal to a third party.

Siu Yin Kwan v Eastern Insurance Co. (1994)

Facts:

The third party intended to claim on the insurance of an agent company. However, the company was wound up before the claim could be made. The court had to determine whether such a claim was possible against an undisclosed principal.

Authority for:

Where an agent fails to disclose the principal to a third party, the agent who possessed actual authority to contract will enable the principal to enforce the contract (and the principal will also be subject to claims against them). The agent will also be allowed to sue and be sued as to the terms of the contract. Any defences available to the third party against the agent would be exercisable against the principal. The agent must have intended to act for the principal when establishing the contract, and the contract may stipulate that the principal has no right to enforce the contract, or be sued under the contract.

18.6 RIGHTS OF AN AGENT

Having identified the obligations and duties that are placed on the agent, and their potential liability when acting without, or in excess of, authority, this section identifies the protection to which agents are entitled.

- *Indemnity:* The agent is entitled to indemnity from the principal with regard to any liability or for the costs associated in acting for the principal (to have any expenses repaid), unless this is specifically excluded in the agreement. Therefore, this provides protection for the agent where they may be exposed to costs or losses. However, this protection may be lost where the agent exceeds their authority or is liable for their own negligence.

- *Payment:* The agency agreement often involves a service being provided by the agent for the principal and this business transaction would involve the agent receiving some form of remuneration. This may be included in the contract between the parties as to the rate of remuneration and when payment will take place. In the absence of an express agreement to remuneration, this may be implied through the same mechanisms as it is with other contractual agreements, such as through the parties' conduct and what the court considers were the true intentions of the parties. The implied terms are important, but it is important to note that as with other implied terms, an express term will take precedence over inconsistent implied terms, even if this leads to unfairness.

- *To maintain the goods (lien):* An agent who is owed money from the principal or some other unsatisfied claim may maintain control over the property (or possess a lien over the goods) until the debt is satisfied. This right entitles the agent to the possession of the goods that they have lawfully come into possession of, but the right does not extend to disposing of the goods to realize the money owed.

This particular right is restricted to the goods/transactions relating to the debt owed and they must be in the agent's possession. Further, a lien exists where there is no exclusion to the right in the contract, and if the agent acts to waive their right (such as allowing the principal or their agent to take possession of the goods) then the agent loses the lien.

18.7 TERMINATION AT COMMON LAW

An agency agreement may be terminated through many eventualities, including the death of either party, the mutual agreement of the parties, the fixed-term agreement coming to an end, the purpose of the agency having been completed, through frustration, and issues concerning bankruptcy. If the contract is silent on the period of notice to be given, and the agent is not an employee and subject to the statutory minimum period, then a reasonable period of notice is due. This is determined on the facts of the case.

Whilst the statutory provisions of the Commercial Agents Regulations (**18.8**) provide for minimum periods of notice to bring the agency agreement to an end, at common law the agent acts for the principal under their authority. If the principal chooses to withdraw this authority, then the agency agreement ceases. When the principal chooses to terminate the agreement, it is prudent to inform third parties who may have had dealings with the agent acting for the principal to ensure that contracts under apparent authority are not established. However, where the agency agreement has been established through a contract, the terms of the contract, such as notice periods, must be adhered to or the principal may be liable for breach.

Commercial agency is a potentially very complex area and requires the parties to establish clear contractual terms and conditions to prevent problems.

Claramoda Limited v Zoomphase Limited (t/a Jenny Packham) (2009)

Facts:

An agency continued to be held as a commercial agent beyond the point to which it had authority to negotiate, in accordance with the definition provided in the Commercial Agents Regulations 1993. Simon J held that an agency contract does not necessarily end when the agent stops negotiating sales on the principal's behalf.

Authority for:

An intermediary must not conclude contracts in their own name (rather than that of the principal) or they will not be an agent for the purposes of the Commercial Agents Regulations.

18.8 THE COMMERCIAL AGENTS (COUNCIL DIRECTIVE) REGULATIONS 1993

The Regulations (as amended by S.I. 1993/3173) were established and brought into effect on 1 January 2004 to transpose Directive 86/653/EEC to harmonize legislation throughout the EU regarding contracts between commercial agents and principals, and to give additional protection to the status of agents in these relationships. The Regulations identify commercial agents as self-employed intermediaries (hence they do not apply to employee agents, but could apply to companies and partnerships) who have continuing authority to negotiate the sale or purchase of goods on behalf of/in the name of the principal (reg. 2(1)). The Regulations affected all agency contracts; however, the rights and obligations under this legislation are restricted to goods, rather than any services that an agent may provide. The Regulations also only protect those agents who are paid rather than volunteer their services (reg. 2).

The Regulations imposed duties onto commercial agents to act dutifully and in good faith for the principal, and to act in their interest. The Regulations codify the duties as outlined in **18.4** and require the agent to make proper efforts to 'negotiate, and where appropriate, conclude transactions that he is instructed to take care of; to communicate all necessary information to the principal; and to comply with reasonable instructions given by the principal' (reg. 3). The principal is obliged to act dutifully and in good faith in relation to the agent and in so doing must provide the agent with all necessary documentation relating to the goods; the principal must obtain for the agent information necessary for the performance of the contract, and (where appropriate) identify to the agent, within a reasonable period, once they anticipate that the volume of commercial transactions will be significantly lower than could reasonably have been expected; and the principal shall inform the agent within a reasonable time of their acceptance or refusal (or any non-execution) of a commercial transaction procured for the principal by the agent (reg. 4). Further, it is unlawful to attempt to contract out of these duties (reg. 5(1)).

The Regulations identify the rights of agents to remuneration in the absence of any agreement between the parties. The level of remuneration in such a circumstance shall be determined on the customary allowances in the locality of where the agent's activities are situated, and where no customary practice is present, this will be based on an assessment of reasonableness in relation to all aspects of the transaction (reg. 6(1)).

18.8.1 Indemnity and Compensation

The Regulations provide for indemnity or compensation payments on the termination of the contract (regs. 17 and 18) and the indemnity will not prevent the agent from seeking damages (reg. 17(5)). Indemnity is provided where the agent has brought the principal new customers or significantly increased the volume of business with the existing customers (reg. 17(3)(a)). The payment is equitable, having regard to all the circumstances and, in particular, the commission lost by the commercial agent on the business transacted with such customers (reg. 17(3)(b)). The amount of indemnity cannot be in excess of a figure equivalent to an indemnity for one year, calculated by reference to the agent's actual pay over the previous five years or, where five years' work has not been completed, such time as has been worked (reg. 17(4)).

The compensation available is based on the damage suffered by the agent as a result (but not necessarily the fault of the principal) of the termination of the relations with the principal (reg. 17(6)). Damage is deemed to occur particularly when termination takes place in either or both of the following circumstances: those that deprive the agent of the commission that proper performance of the contract would have procured for them whilst providing the principal with substantial benefits; or those that have not enabled the agent to recoup (amortize) the costs and expense that they have incurred in the performance of the contract on the advice of the principal (reg. 17(7)(a) and (b)). Further, in relation to compensation payable, the House of Lords held in *Lonsdale v Howard and Hallam Ltd* [2007] that courts should look to the value of the income stream that the agency would have produced in assessing damages. In achieving this, expert testimony and elements such as the price that the agent could have achieved in selling the business will dictate the award of compensation.

These rights may not be waived by the agent through any agreement to their detriment (reg. 19), but the rights may be lost if the agent fails to inform the principal within one year of the termination of the agency contract that the agent intends to pursue the entitlement (reg. 17(9)).

18.8.2 Excluding the Right to Indemnity and Compensation

Regulation 19 states that the parties may not derogate from regs. 17 and 18 to the detriment of the agent before the contract expires. Regulation 18 provides where the compensation identified in reg. 17 shall not be payable. This situation exists where:

1. the principal has terminated the agency contract, justifiably, in relation to a breach of the contract identified in reg. 16;

2. the agent has terminated the contract (unless this termination is justified on circumstances attributable to the principal; or on grounds of the age, infirmity, or illness of the agent in consequence of which they cannot reasonably be required to continue his activities); or

3. the agent, with agreement from the principal, assigns their rights and duties under the contract to another person.

18.8.3 Termination of the Agency Under the Regulations

An agency contract may be justifiably terminated and the Regulations will not apply where one of the parties has failed to carry out all or part of their obligations under the contract (or in the case of exceptional circumstances—reg. 16). Where the contract is not a fixed-term agreement, the Regulations provide for minimum notice periods of one month in the first year of the agency, two months' notice in the second year, and three months' notice after two years of the contract. As such, these are minimum periods that the parties must adhere to, although they are free to negotiate longer terms if deemed appropriate and insofar as they are equal to both parties (reg. 15). Where a fixed-term contract continues beyond the term of the agreement, reg. 14 states that the contract is to be considered as an indefinite contract that is subject to reg. 15 procedures.

CONCLUSION

The chapter has identified agency relationships, their prevalence in business, and how the agency exists to bind the principal in contracts with third parties made on their behalf. Due to the nature of the agreement, obligations, potential liabilities, and rights exist for both the agent and the principal. It is essential that these are recognized, along with the statutory rights provided through the Commercial Agents (Council Directive) Regulations 1993, to minimize risk to the parties and to ensure the relationship is monitored and the authority of the agent is controlled. Contractual agreements specifically outlining the rights and limitations of the parties can assist in protecting all parties in agency.

The book continues by considering the various trading structures that may be formed to operate a business, and it offers a critique of the advantages and disadvantages each structure holds for the members.

SUMMARY OF MAIN POINTS

- Agency involves relationships between an agent, representing the principal in a way that may affect the principal's legal position, and third parties.
- Agency can apply to and affect the sole trader, partnerships, and corporations.
- Several types of agent exist depending upon their authority and how they may bind the principal.

Creation of agency

- Agency agreements are easy to establish and may be formed through a contract, an agreement, by statute, through necessity, and through cohabitation.

Authority of the agent

Actual authority
- An express agreement may be formed to establish the authority of the agent to bind the principal.
- Authority may be provided through implication.

Apparent authority
- This occurs where the principal (or someone on their behalf) represents to the third party that the agent possesses the authority to act for the principal.
- To establish apparent authority there must have been a representation identifying the person as an agent; the principal, or someone on their behalf must have conveyed this representation; and the third party must have acted on the basis of it.

Ratification

- Where the agent (acting for the principal) has acted beyond their authority in establishing a contract with a third party, the principal may subsequently ratify the agreement.
- The agent must have been acting on the principal's behalf, the principal must have been in existence at the time of the contract being established, and the principal must possess the capacity to contract.

Necessity

- Where an agent has responsibility for the control of the principal's property, and in a situation involving an emergency, the agent may have the power to act and bind the principal where the agent does not possess actual or apparent authority. For this situation to take place the agent must have acted in good faith and it must have been impossible to communicate with the principal regarding the emergency and to gain their instructions.

Duties of the agent

- The agent must:
  - obey lawful instructions;
  - not delegate the duty without authorization;
  - exercise reasonable care and skill.
- The agent's fiduciary duties include:
  - not to take bribes;
  - not to make secret profits;
  - to avoid conflicts of interests;
  - to account to the principal.

Liability of the agent

- If the agent has acted beyond their authority, the third party is entitled to have the other party honour their side of the contract.
- Generally, where the agent identifies they are working for the principal and establishes a contract on the principal's behalf, the agent has no liability under the contract with the third party.
- Where the agent has not identified the existence of the principal in the contract with the third party, the principal is prohibited from concluding the contract.

Rights of the agent

- The agent, in acting for the principal under the relevant authority, has the right to:
  - indemnity;
  - payment;
  - maintain goods (lien).

The Commercial Agents Regulations 1993

- The Regulations give rights and place obligations on commercial agents.
- The agent has to make proper efforts to negotiate and conclude the transactions required of them, to communicate relevant information to the principal, and to comply with the reasonable instructions of the principal.
- The principal is obliged to act in good faith to the agent in providing relevant information, the volume of commercial transactions if these are likely to be lower than anticipated, and their acceptance or otherwise of transactions procured by the agent.
- The Regulations identify issues of remuneration, indemnity, and compensation payable.

Termination of the agency

- At common law, the agreement may be terminated in compliance with the contract, or where the parties are no longer able to carry out their duties; in cases of bankruptcy; frustration; and so on.

- The termination of a commercial agency agreement is protected through the Commercial Agents (Council Directive) Regulations 1993.

- The Regulations provide for a minimum of one months' notice of termination in the first year of the agreement, two months' notice in the second year, and three months' notice after two years (although the parties can apply longer periods applicable to each other).

? SUMMARY QUESTIONS

Essay questions

1. 'The fiduciary and contractual duties implied into the contract of an agent are fair, albeit they are demanding.'

   Discuss.

2. 'The creation of agency by operation of the rules of common law are dated but still are considered good law.'

   Discuss the above in relation to necessity and cohabitation.

Problem questions

1. James operates a business, All Bright Consumables (ABC), which trades in DIY goods to electricians and traders. As James is expanding his business in other areas and has become too busy to manage ABC personally, he appoints Brenda to manage the operation. Brenda is engaged on a three-year fixed-term contract with payment by commission of 7 per cent of the sales the business makes. One stipulation James makes as part of the agreement with Brenda is that Brenda does not deal with ABC's major rival business, XYZ.

   At the beginning of the engagement, all parties are happy as business is good. However, soon afterwards the economy begins to move into recession and business slows. The result is Brenda's commission from sales is dramatically reduced and despite her pleas to James to increase her rate of commission, James refuses. Brenda is soon approached by XYZ who offer her a business opportunity. If she agrees to sell XYZ's electric shower for them to ABC customers, they will deliver the showers to the customers directly from XYZ's warehouse. As this will be 'their little secret', James need never know and XYZ will give Brenda 30 per cent of the profits from the sales.

   Sometime later, James is at a trade event where he is approached by an acquaintance who expresses to James his disappointment at the quality of the showers they are now selling. Further, he informs James that due to this choice of poor quality components he has had to suggest to his customers that they do not purchase from ABC. When James enquires about his acquaintance's concerns, he is shocked to discover that the showers are from XYZ. James immediately challenges Brenda about the truth of this situation, which she confirms. Brenda also says that she has had several customers return the showers as being of very poor quality and wanting a refund as they purchased them from the ABC store. Further, XYZ are refusing to accept any returns.

   Explain the legal position of the parties using agency law.

2. ABC Ltd operates a business of selling specialist cars and difficult-to-source car spares to customers and at auctions. It manages this through engaging representatives for regions around the UK who source the goods on behalf of ABC Ltd. ABC Ltd appoint Billy as its representative for the North West of England, on contractual terms of a three-year irrevocable

engagement, where he will receive a commission of 35 per cent of the profits made by ABC Ltd on the sale of the goods he acquires. An important aspect of the contract is that Billy is instructed not to obtain Ford cars or spare parts as these can prove difficult to sell. Billy is issued with a letter of introduction from ABC Ltd identifying him as the company's 'associate for the North West.'

Two months after his engagement began (on 5 July), Billy was approached by Stock-Cars who informed him that they had a mint-condition 1967 Ford Mustang, which was currently on display at the National Museum of American History until 2 November, which he could buy for £25,000. In the negotiations with Stock-Cars, Billy identified that he was acting on behalf of 'a specialist car-buying company' and that 'his principal will wait until the conclusion of the exhibition before taking delivery of the vehicle'. Billy and Stock-Cars agree that payment in full will be made within 30 days of 2 November when the vehicle is available. Having concluded the deal, on 8 July Billy reaches an agreement to sell the vehicle to Jack Vegas, a specialist car enthusiast, for £40,000, with delivery being made on 5 November. Billy intends to keep the profit made as 'a perk' by not informing ABC Ltd of the deal.

Soon after the meeting on the 8 July, Jack Vegas spoke with Stock-Cars about another vehicle he was interested in, and mentioned the car he had agreed to buy from Billy. Stock-Cars thus realized that they had sold the Ford Mustang too cheaply, and having investigated Billy and found that the 'specialist car-buying company' he worked for was ABC Ltd, they informed ABC that they would not proceed with the sale. On 9 July, in an attempt to secure the profitable sale to Jack Vegas, ABC Ltd informed Stock-Cars that they refuse the repudiation of the contract made with Billy, and insist on delivery as agreed.

In relation to the agency principles applicable to the problem, identify the rights of the parties.

 You will find guidance about how to answer these questions online at www.oup.com/uk/marson5e/.

 ## FURTHER READING

Books and articles

Baskind, E., Osborne, G., and Roach, L. (2016) 'Commercial Law' (2nd Edition) Oxford University Press: Oxford.

Fridman, G. H. L. (1996) 'The Law of Agency' (7th Edition) Butterworths: London.

Korotana, M. S. (2002) 'Privity of Contract and the Law of Agency: A Sub-agent's Accountability to the Principal' *Business Law Review*, Vol. 23, p. 73.

Munday, R. (2016) 'Agency: Law and Principles' (3rd Edition) Oxford University Press: Oxford.

Websites

http://www.legislation.gov.uk/uksi/1993/3053/contents/made
The Commercial Agents (Council Directive) Regulations 1993.

 ## ONLINE RESOURCES

www.oup.com/uk/marson5e/

For further resources relating to this chapter, including self-test questions, an interactive glossary, and key case flashcards.

PART 7
EMPLOYMENT

This part of the book details the employment relationship. Employment law is heavily regulated through national and EU law and outlines rights, obligations, and remedies available to the parties. Businesses will employ individuals to perform duties for the firm and the nature of the employment relationship will determine many important factors for the individual and the employer. Therefore, we begin this part with an outline of employment status and contractual terms.

EMPLOYMENT STATUS AND THE TERMS FORMING THE CONTRACT

The status of individuals at work is vitally significant to both the individual and to the employer. Whether the individual is an 'employee', 'worker', 'independent contractor', or 'employee shareholder' determines rights and obligations. For example, only individuals with the employment status of 'employee' are eligible to claim a remedy for unfair dismissal or redundancy. Employees are also subject to implied terms in the employment contract—such as fidelity (the employee must give their loyalty and faithful service to their primary employer). It is important to remember from the outset that employment status is merely a gateway to another right or duty—courts and tribunals will not determine the employment status of the individual unless there is, first, disagreement between the parties, and secondly, the right or duty being applied requires 'employee' status.

The parties may, for example, attempt to label the individual (such as in a contract of employment) as an 'employee', but the courts and tribunals look beyond the wording of the contract. They study the actual working relationship and terms of employment in reaching their conclusion as to employment status (*Weight Watchers (UK) Ltd v Her Majesty's Revenue and Customs*). For this reason, careful consideration of the case law is essential to identify the true status of individuals, and thereby the obligations on the parties.

Business Scenario 19

Yeo works as a driver for the company 'Super' which operates an online transportation network business. Super arranges its business through engagement of individuals as independent contractors and views itself as a technology company. Through its 'App', via which drivers may register, the drivers are connected with passengers who require a taxi service to their chosen destination. Super exercises the following controls over the drivers' roles: It interviews all drivers prior to engagement; requires the drivers to provide details of passengers and the travel provided; it may unilaterally end any contract with a driver; it approves the choice of vehicle used by the drivers; it operates a complaint mechanism and uses a rating system (akin to a system of performance management); and the drivers are subject to disciplinary rules operated by Super (drivers may be forced to log off the App if they cancel taxi requests or fail to accept a sufficient number of trips). Super advertises itself as connecting 'Super drivers' with 'Super passengers' and requires strict rules of conduct between the drivers and their fare-paying passengers (such as not allowing personal information to be shared between them). The drivers, finally, are prohibited from publicly criticizing Super or publishing any information (on social media for instance) which may be construed as being negative about the company or the drivers' experiences of it.

Super identifies the drivers as self-employed with each driver constituting a separate business. When Yeo wishes to enforce a right to be paid the national living wage he is refused as Super refer him to their terms and conditions of service which identify drivers clearly as a self-employed independent contractors.

The scenario will be referred to throughout the course of the chapter but at this stage do you think Yeo is an employee, a worker, or an independent contractor?

Learning Outcomes

* Explain why the distinction of employment status is important (**19.2**)
* Distinguish between an employee and an independent contractor, through the evolution of the common law tests (**19.3–19.3.4**)
* Identify the status of employee shareholders (**19.4**)
* Identify the contractual terms employees are entitled to be notified of when commencing employment (**19.5**)
* Identify the implied terms applicable to employees (**19.6.1**)
* Identify the implied terms applicable to employers (**19.6.2**).

19.1 INTRODUCTION

This chapter begins the consideration of the regulation of the employment relationship. It identifies the tests to establish the employment status of individuals, and why the distinction between an employee and **independent contractor** is so significant. The three common law tests that have been used to determine **employee** status (control, integration, and mixed/economic reality) are identified, but when applying the tests it is most appropriate to begin with those established in *Montgomery v Johnson Underwood* (see **19.3.4**), and then proceed to the final question in *Ready Mixed Concrete* (see **19.3.4**).

The chapter also identifies the terms implied into contracts of employment and the obligations these place on the parties. Awareness of employment status is crucial when the further chapters involving dismissals and discrimination are considered and enable the reader to identify which type of 'worker' may qualify under specific legislation and those who will be ineligible to make a claim.

19.2 THE REASON FOR THE DISTINCTION

Employees are subject to greater control and to the application of implied terms in their contract than are independent contractors. For an employer, they are responsible for paying the employee's tax and national insurance contributions, they may be responsible for torts committed by an employee (under vicarious liability), they have responsibilities for employees' health and safety at work, and may have to provide compensation in cases of unfair dismissal and redundancy (to name but a few). Employers also have the advantage of an employee's fidelity to the employer, employees have ob-ligations to cooperate, adapt to new working conditions, and obey the lawful orders of the employer. Consequently, determining employment status is crucial for an employer and the individual to appreciate their obligations and responsibilities in the working relationship.

The protective employment rights applicable to employees are the most extensive. The following is a non-exhaustive list but provides an overview of the distinction between the rights enjoyed by individuals with the following employment status:

Employee:

- Unfair dismissal (Employment Rights Act (ERA) 1996, s. 94);
- Redundancy (ERA 1996, s. 135);
- A written statement of particulars of employment (ERA 1996, s. 1);
- Request to work flexibly (ERA 1996, s. 80F);
- Maternity leave (ERA 1996, s. 71)/adoption leave (ERA 1996, s. 75A)/paternity leave (ERA 1996, s. 76)—and associated pay (Social Security and Benefits Act 1992, s. 164);
- Protection through an employer's insurance scheme (Employers' Liability (Compulsory Insurance) Act 1969, s. 1);
- Employer's vicarious liability for torts committed in the course of employment (Equality Act (EA) 2010, s. 109);
- Time off to perform public duties (ERA 1996, s. 50); and

all of the rights enjoyed by workers as outlined below.

Workers:

- Right not to be discriminated (EA 2010, s. 13) against and to equal pay through the Equality Act 2010 (EA 2010, s. 66);
- Right not to suffer a detriment on the grounds related to union membership or activities/non-membership of a trade union (Trade Union and Labour Relations (Consolidation) Act 1992, s. 146);
- Maternity, paternity, and adoption pay (but not leave);
- To be paid the national minimum wage (The National Minimum Wage Act 1998); paid holiday leave (Working Time Regulations 1998, reg. 13); and to be given rest breaks (Working Time Regulations 1998, reg. 12);
- Statutory sick pay (Social Security Contributions and Benefits Act 1992, s. 151);
- Protection against a detriment due to a worker making a protected disclosures (whistleblowing—the Public Interest Disclosure Act 1998, s. 2);
- Right to be automatically enrolled in a pension scheme (Pensions Act 2008, s. 3);
- Right not to be treated less favourably where the individual works part-time (The Part-time Workers (Prevention of Less Favourable Treatment) Regulations 2000, reg. 5); and protection of health and safety (Health and Safety at Work etc. Act 1974, s. 3 and more widely though the Management of Health and Safety at Work Regulations 1999, reg. 3, the Control of Substances Hazardous to Health Regulations 2002 (as amended), reg. 3, and the Control of Major Accident Hazards Regulations 1999, reg. 4).

The genuinely self-employed:

• Right not to be discriminated against through membership/non-membership of a trade union (The Trade Union and Labour Relations (Consolidation) Act 1992, s. 296); and

• Protection under the Health and Safety at Work etc Act 1974.

19.3 TESTS TO ESTABLISH THE EMPLOYMENT RELATIONSHIP

Being the highest form of law, the most obvious place to search in establishing how to identify an individual's employment status is statute. The Employment Rights Act (ERA) 1996 contains many of the laws relating to employment and under s. 230(1) an employee is classed as 'an individual who has entered into or works under (or, where the employment has ceased, worked under) a contract of employment' (similar definitions exist in the Trade Union and Labour Relations (Consolidation) Act 1992, s. 295(1) and the Equality Act 2010, s. 83(2)). The term 'a contract of employment' is defined under s. 230(2), which reads ' . . . "contract of employment" means a contract of service or apprenticeship, whether express or implied, and (if it is express) whether oral or in writing.' Ultimately, the legislation is unhelpful and very broad and requires reference to case law to extract the determining factors of employment status. As a consequence, the common law tests have evolved from 'control' and 'integration' to the modern 'mixed/economic reality' test.

It is important to recognize before the tests are discussed that no one test is conclusive and the courts and tribunals make the decision of the employment status based on mixed law and fact—the employment laws established from statute and the courts (through precedent) and the individual facts of the case. Indeed, Griffiths LJ commented that determining employment status 'has proved to be a most elusive question and despite a plethora of authorities the courts have not been able to devise a single test that will conclusively point to the distinction in all cases' (*Lee Ting Sang v Chung Chi-Keung*, see **19.3.4**). Also, note that in employment law, perhaps more than many other areas of law, social and political policy affects the decisions made by tribunals.

Figure 19.1 identifies the evolution of the common law tests in establishing employment status. These are considered in greater detail in this chapter.

19.3.1 The Control Test

This initial test of employment status occurred through the master and servant distinction, where the master held control over the servant who was subservient to him/her. One of the first cases demonstrating the importance of control in establishing employment status was that of *Yewens v Noakes*, where Bramwell LJ stated: 'A servant [employee] is a person subject to the command of his master [employer] as to the manner in which he shall do his work.' This degree of control was easily seen in employment relationships where the employer exercised complete control over the actions of the individual. However, soon after the test had been established the nature of the control in employment relationships began to change.

Figure 19.1 Common law test in establishing employment status

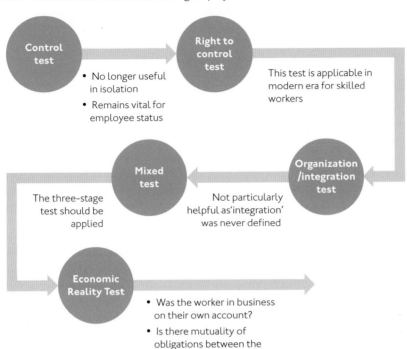

19.3.2 The Right to Control

The control test necessarily evolved with the advent of an increasingly skilled workforce who did not require the level of control as seen when the test was established. This test has been applied to a surgeon:

Cassidy v Ministry of Health (1951)

Facts:

The claimant attended the hospital with a broken wrist. It was incorrectly set and consequently did not heal. He brought an action for damages and it had to be determined whether the hospital was liable for the actions of the medical professionals involved in the actual work of setting the wrist in plaster.

Authority for:

Given that the surgeon involved was an integral part of the organization and he was controlled not as how to do the work—he was a skilled worker—but rather when and where he was working, there was sufficient control in existence to make him an employee. The hospital was therefore vicariously liable for the actions of this employee.

Another example of an individual exercising a high degree of independence in completing the tasks set by the employer is with a professional footballer.

Walker v Crystal Palace Football Club (1910)

Facts:

Mr Walker was a professional football player engaged through a written agreement to serve Crystal Palace Football Club. The agreement was for a term of one year in which Walker was obliged to attend regular training sessions and observe the general instructions of the club. On 17 October 1908 Walker suffered an accident in a match that damaged his knee and this led to his inability to play any further part in the completion of the agreement. Crystal Palace paid his wages until the end of the agreement but declined to re-engage him afterwards. Walker claimed compensation for permanent incapacity due to his inability to earn wages from any suitable employment. The ability to claim was determinant upon Walker being considered a 'workman' (an employee). Crystal Palace contended that Walker could not be an employee due to lack of control exercisable by the employer. The Court of Appeal held there was evidence of control exercised by the football club and hence Walker was an employee. The employer obliged Walker to attend training sessions and follow instruction, and he had to play when ordered to. The fact that the football club did not control how he played, when he passed the ball or decided to shoot at goal or not, was not inconsistent as Walker was a skilled individual.

Authority for:

The control test used to establish an individual's employment status evolved to the 'right to control' test which was more applicable for skilled individuals.

The case established how, even at this early stage, the control test was evolving. With skilled individuals, the test is 'Does the employer have the right to control the individual?' The employer does not have to control the method in which tasks are completed (essentially how the individual works), but rather to control the individual as to when they work, where they work, the order in which tasks are to be completed, and so on.

Control was a useful test when it was first established. However, with modern working practices this was of limited usefulness when applied in isolation. Per Griffiths LJ in *Lee Ting Sang v Chung Chi-Keung and Another*: ' . . . control will no doubt always have to be considered, although it can no longer be regarded as the sole determining factor'. Individuals increasingly are skilled and are employed away from the direct control of the employer. For example, if the manager of an airline employs a pilot, it may be unlikely that the employer can tell the pilot how to fly the aircraft. The pilot is employed as a skilled individual who can work under their own initiative and skill, making the control test an increasingly unrealistic isolated test. Many employers employ graduates or those with practical qualifications on the basis that these individuals already possess skills that require little supervision. Such individuals are provided with tasks and they utilize their skills in the completion of these, with little guidance or direct control exercised by the employer. Further, contracts of employment are considered to be contracts of personal service. This means that an employee has to perform the work personally and if they have the ability to subcontract the work or can provide a substitute, then it will be more likely that the individual will be held an independent contractor.

Express and Echo v Tanton (1999)

Facts:

Mr Tanton was engaged as a self-employed driver. His contract identified the relationship as one between a contractor and client rather than employer and employee. There were elements of his contract which pointed towards him being an employee, but a clause in the contract allowed Tanton, if he was unwilling or unable to perform his duties, to substitute his duties by him employing another person for the task. This he did on a few occasions and for a longer period when he was ill for a six-month period.

Authority for:

The Court of Appeal held that the delegation of duties to a substitute resulted in the individual being considered an independent contractor. An unfettered right to substitute the individual's work with someone else means the individual cannot be called an 'employee.'

The essential element of employment status is that an employee is synonymous with a contract of personal service.

James v Redcats (2007)

Facts:

Ms James was a courier delivering parcels for the defendant. James used her own car for the deliveries and was allowed to work for other employers/businesses. However, James was subject to deadlines for deliveries and was provided with detailed instructions as to the manner in which her duties were to be carried out.

Authority for:

In a claim regarding access to the National Minimum Wage, the Employment Appeal Tribunal identified where a tribunal should consider an individual as a worker. The essential question is 'whether the obligation for personal service is the dominant feature of the contractual relationship or not. If it is, then the contract lies in the employment field.'

Therefore, with the limitation of the control test, wider consideration of the employment relationship had to be undertaken. This led to the integration/organization test.

Consider

What level of control exists over the drivers of Super? Does Super have the right to control the drivers to a sufficient degree to make Super their 'master'? These are skilled individuals, but Yeo and his colleagues get their passengers through registration via the App, they have to ensure their vehicles comply with standards set by Super, and they are not allowed to share information—such as the driver issuing the passenger with their phone number (essentially facilitating solicitation of customers). It appears that there is a significant level of control exercisable by Super over Yeo.

19.3.3 The Integration/Organization Test

Due to the problems encountered in utilizing the control test in isolation, the courts began to extend the mechanisms and tests to identify employment status. Lord Denning, who had been instrumental in developing contract law in his judgments, had an opportunity to consider employee status:

Stevenson, Jordan and Harrison v Macdonald and Evans (1952)

Facts:

Mr Evans-Hemming had been employed as an accountant with Macdonald and Evans and following his employment ending, he produced a textbook on business management that consisted of lectures based on his experiences with the firm. He then purported to assign the copyright to the book to a publishing firm. Stevenson, Jordan & Harrison were the publishers to whom Mr Evans-Hemming had submitted the book and Macdonald and Evans brought an action to restrain its publication. It did so on the basis that the contents of the book infringed confidential information, and that the copyright belonged to Macdonald and Evans not Mr Evans-Hemming. It was to be decided if Mr Evans-Hemming was an employee or not at the time of the writing of the text to conclude ownership of the copyright. In determining the employment status Denning LJ considered that:

> One feature which seems to run through the instances is that, under a contract of service a man is employed as part of the business and his work is done as an integral part of the business; whereas, under a contract for services, his work, although done for the business, is not integrated into it but only accessory to it.

This definition uses common sense and its logic will be obvious to all, but it is unfortunate that Denning did not define the word 'integrated' to assist in identifying where the demarcation between employee and independent contractor lay. Integration can be interpreted widely and this even prompted Denning later in the judgment to state: 'It is often easy to recognize a contract of service [employee] when you see it, but difficult to say wherein the difference lies. A ship's master, a chauffeur, and a reporter on the staff of a newspaper are all employed under a contract of service; but a ship's pilot, a taximan, and a newspaper contributor are employed under a contract for services.' This enabled lawyers, the judiciary (e.g. Mackenna J in *Ready Mixed Concrete (South East) Ltd v Minister of Pensions & National Insurance*, discussed later), and academic commentators to differ on the usefulness of the test as a precedent. Given this limitation, the case law continued with the development of the mixed/economic reality test.

Authority for:

The greater an individual's integration into the workforce, the more likely they are to be held an employee. The more that the individual is on the periphery of the workforce, the more likely they are to be an independent contractor. This case was of limited use as a precedent however.

19.3.4 The Mixed/Economic Reality Test

The previous tests of control and integration had limitations in enabling individuals, employers, and indeed the tribunals to assess, with any real certainty, employment status. Therefore, these tests were extended through the following cases that began establishing the mixed test, utilizing the previous tests and addressing new and relevant questions to be asked to help establish employment status. A very important case in the development of the law in this area was *Ready Mixed Concrete*, which established three questions that a tribunal should seek to answer in reaching its conclusion:

Ready Mixed Concrete v Minister of Pensions and National Insurance (1968)

Facts:

Ready Mixed Concrete carried on a business of making and selling ready mixed concrete and similar materials. It separated the business of manufacturing and delivering the concrete and introduced a scheme of owner-drivers who would provide the service. The drivers did not have set hours, they did not have fixed meal breaks, they did have an obligation to follow directions given to them by the company as to loading and parking of the lorries, holidays had to be arranged with the firm to ensure no more than one owner-driver was on holiday at a time, they had to wear the company's uniform, they had to carry out all reasonable orders from any competent servant of the company, they could not alter the lorry in any way, and they had to maintain the lorry and keep it painted in the company's colours.

Following a query regarding responsibility for tax payments from one of the drivers, it had to be determined whether the contracts established employee status, or whether the firm was correct and the drivers were independent contractors. Mackenna J considered the facts and established three conditions that would identify the existence of a contract of service:

1. The servant agrees that, in consideration of a wage or other remuneration, he will provide his own work and skill in the performance of some service for his master (this was essentially the requirement of 'mutuality of obligations').

2. He agrees, expressly or impliedly, that in the performance of that service he will be subject to the other's control in a sufficient degree to make that other master (the right to control test).

3. Other provisions of the contract that are inconsistent with its being a contract of service (a negative question requiring determination of examples of factors which would point towards status as an independent contractor—e.g. whether the person performing the services provides their own equipment, whether they hire their own helpers, the existence of their financial risk, the degree of responsibility for investment and management, whether they have an opportunity of profiting from sound management in the performance of their task, and payment of expenses).

In the application of these tests it was held that the owner-driver subject to the case was an independent contractor. This was due to the lack of control and the inconsistencies of employee status such as his ownership of the lorry, his duty to maintain the lorry, he was not obliged to take any work, he had no set hours or instruction as to how to complete the jobs undertaken, and he could send a substitute.

Authority for:

The three-stage test identified in the case has been used to establish employment status. Having answered the two tests as provided in the *Montgomery* (discussed later) case in the affirmative, the third test in *Ready Mixed Concrete* is applied.

In applying the third element of the *Ready Mixed* tests, it may be worthwhile making a physical list of consistent and inconsistent features to assist in determining employment status. **Figure 19.2** demonstrates this approach with the facts of the case.

Consider

We have already observed that a level of control exists over Yeo. If we follow the authority in *Ready Mixed Concrete* we can see that features of an employment contract do exist. The drivers provide their own vehicles, they have to maintain these to standards set by Super, they are subject to common disciplinary rules, and the drivers have to provide details of fares and passengers to the company. Drawing up a physical list, we would be able to see there are more consistent features with this being a contract of employment than inconsistent features.

Figure 19.2 Determining employment status

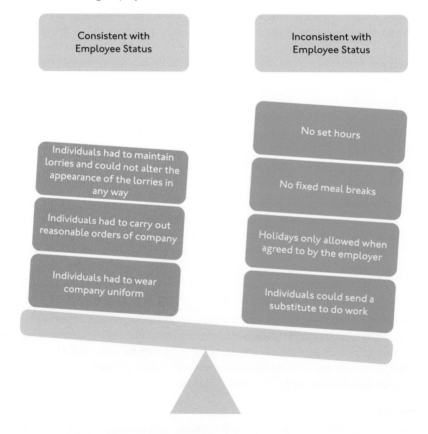

A further essential factor to consider and be addressed in establishing the employment status of an employee is **mutuality of obligations**.

Carmichael v National Power Plc (1999)

Facts:

The claimant was a guide at the Blythe power station between 1989 and 1995. The contract expressed that the engagement was on a 'casual as required basis.' When the claimant queried her employment status the tribunal remarked that her case 'founders on the rock of absence of mutuality'.

Authority for:

When the claimant was not working for the power company there was no contractual relationship between the parties. She was merely employed when necessary by the company and there was no obligation on it to offer any further work, or indeed for it to be accepted by the claimant. Hence, there was no mutuality of obligations between the parties.

More recently the UK courts and tribunals have been influenced by the American jurisprudence of the 'economic reality' of the employment relationship. Independent contractors are considered to be in business on their own account, employees are not. The following case identified the moving definition and test of who is an employee.

Market Investigations Ltd v Minister of Social Security (1969)

Facts:

The claimant research company had engaged groups of individuals on full-time and part-time bases to conduct interviews. The part-time workers (subject to a significant aspect of the case) were not provided with sick or holiday pay, they could work for other employers, they were not obliged to accept work offered, and there was mutual recognition of the contract being one for services.

Authority for:

The most significant question to ask regarding an individual's employment status is whether they are in business on their own account. Per Cooke J 'If the answer to that question is "yes", then the contract is a contract for services. If the answer is "no", then the contract is a contract of service.'

Whether someone is in business on their own account may be evidenced through a series of questions raised in the following case:

Lee Ting Sang v Chung Chi-Keung (1990)

Facts:

The claimant worked at a building site, on a casual basis, for a sub-contractor. He was injured at work and argued he was an employee in order to recover compensation.

→

Authority for:

The Privy Council approved Cooke J's test regarding the necessity of control in determining status as an employee, but further held that it could no longer be considered a sole determining factor. Other questions to be considered include:

1. whether the man performing the services provides his own equipment;
2. whether he hires his own helpers;
3. what degree of financial risk he takes;
4. what degree of responsibility for investment and management he has;
5. whether and how far he has an opportunity of profiting from sound management in the performance of his task.

However, it is essential to note that in *Hall v Lorimer* the court stated that the (increasing) tests developed in the case law should not be proceeded through mechanically.

Hall v Lorimer (1993)

Facts:

Mr Lorimer was a vision-mixer who, in 1985, left his current job to become a freelance contractor (seemingly to avail himself of tax benefits available to independent contractors—a 25 per cent deduction of business expenses from his total turnover). He enjoyed a successful career for the first three years of this trade with approximately 20 clients. He used equipment provided by the studios where he worked and he had no formal conditions of employment with the clients.

Authority for:

In a claim for unfair dismissal the Court of Appeal held that he was self-employed, even though he did not own the equipment used for the work. Where an individual has several clients, it was not available to them to simply pick one and argue successfully that it has employed the claimant. That Lorimer had claimed the business expenses as tax deductions was a significant factor in the court's reasoning.

Tribunals have the discretion to come to their own conclusions, and attach whatever weight they wish to the factors present. For example, if the tribunal believes that the employer deducting the individual's tax and National Insurance at source is indicative of employee status, as the tribunal has heard all of the evidence, it should be in the best position to reach such a conclusion. However, the tests noted earlier should be used as they provide an effective indication as to the direction the tribunals will take in determining employment status.

Consider

Super formed its business model on ensuring it appeared that the drivers were in business on their own account. Yeo and his colleagues had to supply their own vehicle, pay for their fuel and licences, they did not have to wear any uniform, and the drivers were responsible for their own tax and National Insurance contributions. What is problematic for Super is that it interviews the drivers prior to engagement, refers to them as 'Super drivers' and ranks them through performance review systems. It does not allow the drivers to solicit customers (and cut Super out of any arrangement for travel). Further, the fact that the drivers pay their own tax and national insurance is largely irrelevant to the realities of their employment relationship with Super—the label of the drivers being 'self-employed' is just that, a label—nothing more!

The cases identified in the mixed test section provide a list of questions that can be used in assessing employment status. Two final cases must be addressed as the most recent (and leading) authorities in this area.

Montgomery v Johnson Underwood (2001)

Facts:

An individual had found work through an employment agency and remained in the same employment on placement with a customer for more than two years. When the placement ended the claimant argued she was an employee and entitled to seek a remedy for unfair dismissal.

Authority for:

To establish employment status the individual must demonstrate an element of control exercisable by the employer (although this could amount to a general idea of how the work is done rather than control over how the work is done). Secondly there must be an irreducible minimum of mutual obligations. Where these fundamental factors are satisfied, the tribunal may then proceed to consider the other factors of an employment relationship.

These questions should always be considered in light of whether the individual truly is in business on their own account (see **Table 19.1** for an overview). If not, they are more likely to be considered an employee. The essential features of employment status are identified in **Table 19.1**.

Table 19.1 Features of the employment relationship

Features of the employment relationship						
Employment status	Control exercisable by the employer (*essential*)	Integrated into the business	A contract of personal service (e.g. no ability to subcontract)	On business on own account (*fundamental*)	Mutuality of obligations (*essential*)	Tax and NI taken at source (*indicative not conclusive*)
Employee	Yes	Yes (but difficult to define)	Yes	No	Yes	Yes
Independent Contractor	No	Not necessarily	No	Yes	No	No

In the following case the Court of Appeal identifies and distinguishes the previous authorities and explains these in relation to the business model adopted by the employer.

Pimlico Plumbers & Charlie Mullins v Gary Smith (2017)

Facts:

Mr Smith was a plumber and carried out plumbing duties for the appellant between 2005 and 2011. Following him suffering a heart attack in 2011, Smith claims he was unfairly or wrongfully dismissed on 3 May 2011. The appellant had 75 office staff and 125 people like Smith carrying out plumbing and maintenance work on their behalf. In an agreement signed in 2005, Smith was labelled a 'sub-contracted employee'.

Authority for:

Holding Smith as a worker and not a self-employed contractor, the Master of the Rolls commented: 'This case puts a spotlight on a business model under which operatives are intended to appear to clients of the business as working for the business, but at the same time the business itself seeks to maintain that . . . there is a legal relationship of . . . independent contractor rather than employer and employee or worker.'

Consider

Whether mutuality of obligations exists between the parties is crucial for status as an employee. However, the right that Yeo is seeking to engage—to be paid the national minimum wage—is applicable to those with the status of a worker. Therefore in the case of Yeo, whilst there does not appear to be any guarantees of work for him or for him to accept work offered (although this may be evident through a longer working relationship), this is not as crucial as it would be if he were seeking status as an employee. Yeo, being subject to the interview and performance reviews evidently has to perform the job personally, and this is a significant guide to his status as a worker.

19.4 **EMPLOYEE SHAREHOLDERS**

On 1 September 2013 a fourth form of employment status was introduced. Remember we had the existing status of employee, worker, and independent contractor each of which provide rights to the individual and impose obligations on the employer to varying degrees. As the case law has demonstrated, there are often disputes between the individual and the employer as to the status of that individual and this is always predicated on the basis of the rights to which the individual is seeking to avail themself.

Many employers began to offer incentives to individuals to engage as independent contractors on the basis that the individual would relinquish certain employment rights and in return be given benefits—such as tax relief. This situation often ended in dispute; it was a possibility that employers could abuse their position by asking an individual to reassign their employment status without the individual fully understanding the ramifications, and therefore the government decided that the employment status of employee shareholder would be formed (ERA 1996, s. 205A).

The individual will work under an employment contract identifying him/her as an employee shareholder with either the employer's company or the employer's parent company. The important aspect of this employment status is that the individual must be provided with shares in the company with a minimum value of £2,000 (this relates to the market value of the shares per the Taxation of Chargeable Gains Act 1992, ss. 272–273). There is no set upper limit to the value of the shares that may be offered in return for the individual occupying this employment status (The Growth and Infrastructure Act 2013, s. 31—in force since 1 September 2013 by the Growth and Infrastructure Act 2013 (Commencement No. 3 and Savings) Order 2013 (S.I. 2013/1766)). It is possible to offer this status to existing employees/workers or to offer it to new recruits; however, no existing individual employed may be forced to transfer to this new status (ERA 1996, s. 104G) or to suffer a detriment for refusing (ERA 1996, s. 47G).

The rationale for establishing employee shareholders is to enable businesses, in a competitive labour market, to incentivize individuals who will be rewarded for their work not only through the normal salary and bonus structure operated by many businesses, but further as a shareholder who will be entitled to the rights associated with that class of shares held. This, it is argued, may lead to the individual feeling a greater affinity with the company, working harder, and being more productive as they will obtain a direct benefit in relation to dividend payments (if provided) and increases in the value of the shares held (the sale of which may be exempt from some elements of capital gains tax—essentially the 'profit' derived in its rise in value). However, the value of the shares may go down as well as up!

Of course there is a downside to this status that is very significant. Employee shareholders will legally waive their rights to protections in the following areas:

1. unfair dismissal (ERA 1996, s. 94) (unless the dismissal is on the basis of an automatically unfair reason, is in breach of the Equality Act 2010, or is to do with a health and safety ground)—ERA 1996, s. 108(2);

2. statutory redundancy payment (assuming they qualify in the same way as currently exists—ERA 1996, s. 135). (These are two of the most significant protections at work and it must be clear to the individual that whilst being provided with £2,000 worth of shares in the business may be a useful incentive, they are much more vulnerable when the employment relationship is terminated.);

3. the statutory right to request flexible working (except in the two-week period following the return from parental leave—ERA 1996, s. 80F);

4. statutory rights relating to requests for time off to undertake training (ERA 1996, s. 63D).

Where the employee shareholder wishes to return to work early from either maternity (The Maternity and Parental Leave etc. Regulations 1999 (S.I. 1999/3312) reg. 11), additional paternity (The Additional Paternity Leave Regulations 2010 (S.I. 2010/1055), reg. 30), or adoption leave (The Paternity and Adoption Leave Regulations 2002 (S.I. 2002/2788), reg. 25), they will be required to provide 16 weeks' notice to the employer.

It is not a legal requirement to remove these rights, and indeed employers may wish to offer more generous contractual rights in order to attract the very best individuals. It would seem, however, that most employers choosing to engage an individual as an employee shareholder would do so on the basis of the payment in the form of shares to remove certain statutory rights. To alleviate any fears that individuals could be engaged as employee shareholders without understanding the full implications, the following criteria are required to be satisfied. Possibly the most important of these criteria is the necessity for the individual to be given independent advice clearly outlining the employment protections to which they are waiving:

1. there must be an explicit agreement between the individual and the employer, of the individual's employment status as 'employee shareholder';

2. the employer must provide the individual with the £2,000 of fully paid-up shares—and there can be no payment for the shares in any form from the individual;

3. section 1 of ERA 1996 must still be satisfied and the employer therefore has to provide the written statement of employment particulars to the individual, which, among other things, will include the employment status. It will also identify any voting rights attached to the shares, any rights to dividends, the class of shares (if more than one class of shares exists), whether the shares are redeemable and if so at whose option, any restrictions on the transfer of the shares (and details if relevant), any pre-emption rights or exclusions (The Companies Act 2006, ss. 561–562), and rights where the individual will be a minority shareholder—these specific features of the written statement of particulars are identified in ERA 1996, s. 205A(5);

4. the individual must be provided with independent advice regarding the status of employee shareholder and this must be paid by the employer. This payment is provided regardless of whether the individual accepts or declines the offer of employment. Independent advice may be provided only by a qualified lawyer (but not the company's in-house lawyer or a lawyer who has previously acted for the company/employer); an officer, official, employee, or member of a trade union where the trade union is certified as competent to provide the advice; a person working in an advice centre where that person has been certified as competent to give the advice; and any person authorized to give the legal advice by the Secretary of State (at the time of writing a person occupying the position of Fellow of the Institute of Executives employed by a legal firm)—ERA 1996, s. 203;

5. a seven-day period must pass until the individual can accept or agree to employment under the status of employee shareholder. This seven-day period does not commence until after the independent advice has been received.

Failure to follow these conditions will result in the employment status of employee shareholder being declared void. In such a situation, the individual will have the rights and benefits which their employment status (as determined by an employment tribunal) attracts.

In its Autumn 2016 statement the government announced that the Finance Bill 2017 will withdraw the Capital Gains Tax exemption and the Income Tax reliefs in respect of shares received when entering into most Employee Shareholder Status agreements. The draft Bill was published on 5 December 2016 and will result in agreements entered into before 1 December 2016, or before 2 December 2016 (where the independent advice was received before 1.30pm on 23 November 2016) retaining the tax benefits. As such, there will be no newly created employee shareholders—although existing employee shareholders will continue to enjoy the benefits of that status.

19.5 THE WRITTEN STATEMENT OF PARTICULARS

The employer has an obligation, under ERA 1996, s. 1, to provide employees with a copy of the written particulars of the employment. This must be provided within two months of the start of the employment. Note, however, that this document is not a contract of employment or a substitute for it. In *Systems Floors v Daniel* the EAT held that whilst the written particulars is not a replacement for a written contract, 'it provides very strong *prima facie* evidence of what were the contracts between the parties'. The written particulars provide important information that attempts to clarify many of the important terms in the contract. Section 1 includes the following information as admissible evidence before an Employment Tribunal:

(3) (a) the names of the employer and employee,

   (b) the date when the employment began, and

   (c) the date on which the employee's period of continuous employment began.

(4) (a) the scale or rate of remuneration or the method of calculating remuneration,

   (b) the intervals at which remuneration is paid (that is, weekly, monthly or other specified intervals),

   (c) any terms and conditions relating to hours of work.

   (d) any terms and conditions relating to any of the following—

     (i) entitlement to holidays, including public holidays, and holiday pay,

     (ii) incapacity for work due to sickness or injury, including any provision for sick pay, and

     (iii) pensions and pension schemes,

   (e) the length of notice which the employee is obliged to give and entitled to receive to terminate his contract of employment,

   (f) the title of the job which the employee is employed to do or a brief description of the work for which he is employed,

   (g) where the employment is not intended to be permanent, the period for which it is expected to continue or, if it is for a fixed term, the date when it is to end,

   (h) either the place of work or, where the employee is required or permitted to work at various places, an indication of that and of the address of the employer,

   (j) any collective agreements which directly affect the terms and conditions of the employment including, where the employer is not a party, the persons by whom they were made.

These terms are essential evidence for many of the statutory-based claims under which employees may seek protection. Outlining when the contract of employment began (due to the fact that unfair dismissal and redundancy have minimum periods of service before qualification is gained; and the levels of compensation are calculated on the number of years in service), the notice period that is required (particularly relevant for wrongful dismissal claims on fixed-term contracts), the sources of obligations and terms (such as through works handbooks and collective agreements), and payments for illness or absences from work each help the parties to identify their rights and obligations. When these terms are missing, as the document or the contract outlining the terms of the employment have not been provided, it makes it considerably more difficult to raise claims against an employer. The Employment Act 2002, s. 38 provides that in cases of unfair dismissal, redundancy, or discrimination, if no written statement of particulars had been provided by the start of the proceedings, then a minimum of two weeks' wages, and a maximum of four weeks' wages (currently capped at £479 per week) is awarded.

19.6 IMPLIED TERMS IN CONTRACTS OF EMPLOYMENT

Implied terms in contract law were considered in **Chapter 8**. They are present in employment law, and can have a fundamental effect on the obligations to both the employer and employee. As implied terms, they are part of the contract between the parties, and of course by being implied, they are by necessity never written in the employment contract or spoken in the negotiations. Such implied terms are just one reason why the document provided to employees under s. 1 of ERA 1996, is not the contract of employment, although many of the provisions will overlap. It is vital to be aware of the location of the implied terms. Some will derive from *statutes* (such as a pay equality clause in employment through the Equality Act 2010); and *custom* in a particular employment may provide terms. For example, the courts may imply terms where the practice is notorious and reasonable.

Sagar v Ridehalgh (1931)

Facts:

A mill owner in Lancashire deducted wages from an employee for cloth that had been damaged due to poor workmanship. This was the practice of the mill owner and thus, claimed the employer, implied into the contract.

Authority for:

The implication of the term was held as fair, was common practice in the locality and for that trade. Therefore it was implied into the employee's contract.

Works handbooks are also a common source for implied terms as the employer can establish terms that are to affect a large number of individuals, and instead of incorporating these terms into each employee's contract, they are maintained in the document, which can be accessed by the employees at their convenience. This does not mean that employees can rely completely on this document to identify their obligations and the employer may unilaterally modify the terms contained within if this is reasonable.

Dryden v Greater Glasgow Health Board (1992)

Facts:

The employer introduced a new no-smoking policy and the claimant argued that its introduction was a breach of contract and breached the trust and confidence between the parties. Dryden used this argument to resign and claim constructive dismissal.

→

Authority for:

The EAT held the new policy as a 'works rule' which had no contractual effect (and thus could not be a breach of the employment contract). Employers were entitled to make rules which impacted on the conduct of employees and, beyond this not being a contractual term, there was also no implied term that employees were permitted to smoke at the workplace.

However, terms are present in the contract that are relevant and may assist the employee in establishing claims to protect their rights.

Christopher Keeley v Fosroc International Ltd (2006)

Facts:

The claimant was made redundant. According to the works handbook, employees with his continuous service were entitled to receive an enhanced redundancy payment (above the statutory minimum). He did not receive the enhanced payment and brought his claim for breach of contract. The argument presented in the first case was that such provisions in the handbook are aspirational or procedural, but not contractual.

Authority for:

The Court of Appeal considered that redundancy provisions are by their nature apt for incorporation into the contract. This applies where employers mention enhanced redundancy payments in works handbooks and, in the event that these payments are discretionary, the employer should ensure this is made clear.

19.6.1 Implied Terms on the Employee

The contract of employment, the details in the written particulars provided to the employee, and the negotiations between the parties before the employment relationship is established each include express terms. However, it is of vital importance that it is recognized that contracts of employment are supplemented by many implied terms that have significant effects on the rights and duties of the parties. There are many implied terms imposed on employees and these have been developed and extended through the common law. There are too many to include in this text and those included here do not constitute an exhaustive list, but the more important examples include mutual trust and confidence.

Donovan v Invicta Airways Ltd (1970)

Facts:

The claimant was an airline pilot. He was asked to fly an aircraft in conditions which he considered to be unsafe and, further, was subject to abusive action from the employer.

Authority for:

Following the claimant's resignation and action for constructive dismissal it was held that the employer's conduct had fundamentally breached the trust and confidence between them. Continued employment was impossible, justifying Donovan accepting the employer's breach.

Note that whilst trust and confidence embodies respect between the parties, that does not prevent criticism of either. The High Court has held a Board of Directors may talk in negative terms about an employee, but extending this to a campaign of vilification of an employee will breach the mutual trust and confidence between the parties. If the breach is sufficiently serious, it may amount to a repudiatory breach, for which the employee is entitled to accept, resign, and seek damages. For the employee to gain protection against a repudiatory breach by the employer it is important for the employee not to have breached the same term, or they will lose the right to claim constructive dismissal.

RDF Media Group Plc v Clements (2007)

Facts:

An employee resigned from his employment and the employer, invoking a restraint of trade clause, placed the employee on 'garden leave' during the resignation period. Negative comments about the employee were leaked to the press and amounted to a prima facie breach of trust and confidence. However, prior to this the employee had divulged confidential corporate information to a competitor he was intending to work for.

Authority for:

The employee's claim of constructive dismissal failed. An employee cannot rely on a subsequent breach of the contract to justify a constructive dismissal if he has already breached that trust and confidence between the parties.

There is an obligation of fidelity (faithful service) where the employee must not work in competition with the employer and they must give their faithfulness to the employer. This restricts the employee from taking on other employment, without express permission, if it may interfere with their employment with the first employer.

Hivac Ltd v Park Royal Scientific Instruments Co. (1946)

Facts:

Five employees engaged by Hivac began working, on Sundays—a non-working day—for its only competitor. Despite this work being conducted in the employees' own time, Hivac sought an injunction to prevent them from continuing with this work.

Authority for:

The employees were subject to the implied term of fidelity. It was inconsistent with their contracts of employment that they would take action which could potentially conflict and cause considerable harm to their employer's business. This extended to action taken in their spare time.

Fidelity has caused problems in the employment relationship when employees have followed the exact terms of their contract, yet their actions were held to be breaching the duty of faithful service.

Secretary of State for Employment v ASLEF (No. 2) (1972)

Facts:

Following a dispute between workers and the employer, the trade union ASLEF advised its members to follow the exact instructions for workers as included in the works handbook. This included refusing to work overtime or on their designated rest-day. This is often referred to as 'working to rule' and is a form of industrial action.

Authority for:

The Court of Appeal held that even though the workers were following the contract, this action was not to fulfil a health and safety requirement, rather it was designed to disrupt the employer's work. It continued that if the union and the workers wished to take part in lawful industrial action, specific formalities were available and had to be followed. This action was a breach of the workers' obligation to serve their employer faithfully.

The issue of faithful service has extended to ensure that the employee does not steal from the employer, take other employees or customers when they leave to establish a new business, and they must not solicit bribes.

Boston Deep Sea Fishing and Ice Co. v Ansell (1888)

Facts:

The managing director of the company received secret commissions when placing orders for new boats and provided business to corporations in which he held shares.

Authority for:

The Court of Appeal held such actions to be against the implied duties on the director to give faithful service to his employer. Where a potential conflict of interest is evident, the employee should inform their employer of this fact and thus enable the employer to take the most appropriate action.

Employees who are fiduciaries have the duty to disclose the misdeeds of others (*Sybrom Corporation v Rochem Ltd*). This places an obligation on such an employee to inform the employer if they are aware or have knowledge of wrongful actions by colleagues.

Sybrom Corporation v Rochem Ltd (1983)

Facts:

Mr Roques was employed as the manager of Sybron's European zone. During his employment he, along with other senior employees, was part of a conspiracy to establish competing companies—including Rochem. This resulted in them directing contracts meant for Sybrom to these newly formed companies. The fraud was only discovered following Roques' retirement and the claimant sought to recover the pension and other benefits acquired by Roques.

Authority for:

The defence presented was that Roques was under no duty to disclose his own misconduct. This was clarified in *Tesco Stores Ltd v Pook* (2004) and *Item Software (UK) Ltd v Fassihi* (2004) where the Court of Appeal held that a director/senior manager *was* under such a duty. Individuals under a fiduciary duty (such as managing directors) are subject to an implied term of volunteering and disclosing the misdeeds of others to which they are aware.

Employees are under a duty of cooperation (see *Secretary of State for Employment v ASLEF (No. 2)* discussed earlier) and must work with their employer in the best interests of the business. Even if the employee dogmatically adheres to the textual reading of the contract of employment, if this is used to cause harm to the employer, the employee will breach their obligation to cooperate.

Employees must exercise reasonable skill and judgement in their employment so as not to endanger colleagues and clients. This extends beyond the issue of health and safety.

Janata Bank v Ahmed (1981)

Facts:

Mr Ahmed was engaged as a bank manager and in the course of his duties he agreed loans and mortgages to customers who were 'bad risks'. This led to loses of nearly £35,000 which the bank sought to recover.

Authority for:

The court held that Ahmed had breached the implied term of exercising reasonable care, skill, and judgement. He was ordered to repay the money.

Employees have a duty to obey lawful orders from the employer.

Pepper v Webb (1969)

Facts:

A gardener was employed by the defendant and towards the end of his employment his work and attitude had recently diminished. When asked to undertake some planting duties he responded to the employer 'I couldn't care less about your bloody greenhouse and your sodding garden.' Consequently he was summarily dismissed.

Authority for:

The Court of Appeal agreed with the employer's decision to dismiss. They had given the gardener a reasonable and lawful order, and his willful disobedience was a fundamental breach of the contract.

The duty exists even if this extends beyond their actual job description.

Macari v Celtic Football and Athletic Co. (1999)

Facts:

The claimant was the manager of the football club. His contract required him to live within a 40-mile radius of the city where the club was based (Glasgow). In fact he lived further away and following the appointment of a new managing director, the claimant was warned that he must adhere to this term and also to report to the managing director on a weekly basis. The claimant did not relocate and following his arranging a five-week holiday without the consent of the managing director was summarily dismissed.

Authority for:

The employer had made a lawful and reasonable instruction of its employee and the non-compliance amounted to a repudiation which permitted the employer to treat as a fundamental breach. The employer's motives may be considered in such an event, but this did not release the employee from having to follow their obligations under the contract.

Lawful orders can include mobility clauses in the contract.

United Kingdom Atomic Energy Authority v Claydon (1974)

Facts:

The employee was provided with an instruction to work in another base in the UK and he refused, despite a mobility clause being included in his contract of employment.

Authority for:

The employee was in breach of contract for refusing this lawful order. The court did say, however, that any express mobility clause is subject to an implied term that it must be used reasonably.

The employee may be expected to go beyond the exact scope of their contract, and this may amount to covering for an absent member of staff (*Sim v Rotherham Metropolitan Borough Council*). The 'lawful' element of the employee's duty does not extend to situations where by doing so they would endanger themself.

Ottoman Bank v Chakarian (1930)

Facts:

An employee, an American Turkish national, was asked, as part of his employment duties, to return to Turkey to work. However, he feared that if he did go to Turkey he was at risk of being murdered.

Authority for:

His fear was based on genuine grounds, his employer knew of the risk to his safety and therefore Chakarian's refusal was considered not to breach the implied term.

Neither does the term require the employee to follow an employer's instruction that would be to commit a criminal act.

Morrish v Henleys (1973)

Facts:

The employee was dismissed when he refused to falsify the company's accounts over the quantities of petrol assigned to his vehicle.

Authority for:

The dismissal was considered unfair. The employee was not in breach for his refusal to become involved in such unlawful action and agree to the changes made by the employer to the records. The implied term is for employees to follow an employer's lawful order—this does not extend to unlawful orders.

There also exists the duty to adapt to new working conditions.

Cresswell v Board of Inland Revenue (1984)

Facts:

The Inland Revenue transferred its method of working from a manual system to a computerized one (this was before the prevalence of home computers and people's familiarity with them). Cresswell and other individuals did not wish to use these and sought a declaration from the court that the employer could not force the change in systems as this was not provided for under the contract of employment.

→

Authority for:

There was an implied term allowing the change in working systems and the employer's unilateral right to alter the terms of the contract in light of this change. Walton J remarked on the expectation of an employee to adapt to new working conditions. Further, the obligation on the employer in such a situation is to provide adequate training for the employees and to give them time to adapt to the changes.

19.6.2 Implied Terms on the Employer

Again, this is by no means an exhaustive list, but a relevant example of an obligation imposed on employers has been the duty to *pay wages*.

Devonald v Rosser & Sons (1906)

Facts:

The employer closed the workplace due to lack of business. Two weeks later the employer gave all employees one month's notice of the termination of the contract. Devonald claimed pay for the two weeks before the notice was given.

Authority for:

The pay was granted because there was an implied duty that the employer would pay the employee.

This is often where the amount in wages or the frequency of the payments has not been agreed between the employee and employer. If no express agreement is made the employee should be paid a reasonable wage and within a reasonable time. (Payment should be made after the first week. The latest the employee should be paid is by the end of the first month, and then in monthly increments thereafter.) The employer also has the duty to pay a fair proportion of wages if industrial action is accepted (*Royle v Trafford Metropolitan Borough Council*). In *Miles v Wakefield MDC* the House of Lords held that where the superintendent registrar of births, deaths, and marriages took industrial action by refusing to work on Saturday mornings, the employer was entitled to withhold 3/37ths of his wages as Mr Miles was unavailable for work. The employer must pay wages in money, rather than a previous practice of paying in tokens redeemable in the employer's business, and no unlawful deductions can be made against the wages paid to the employee.

There is generally no obligation on the employer to provide work for the employee (*Collier v Sunday Referee Publishing Ltd*). As long as they provide the wages agreed then the employer may ask the employee to stay away from the place of employment (in examples where there is a decline in orders and there is no work for the employee to do). However, the exception to this is where the nature of the job requires work then the employer must provide it. Examples include those employees who get paid by the piece, those working on commission who require work to earn money, those employment situations where the skills of the employee must be maintained (such as doctors/surgeons), and where publicity is required (such as professional musicians/actors). In *Clayton & Waller v Oliver* an actor who had been given the lead role in a musical production, and was then removed from the role and offered a substantially inferior one, was entitled to seek damages due to the employer's actions, which had damaged his reputation.

The employer has an obligation to maintain the health and safety of their workers and this means the appropriate training of all staff, and safe systems of work to be put in place (*MacWilliams v Sir William Arrol & Co. Ltd*). As part of the requirements to protect employees' health at work, the employer must take out insurance for the benefit of employees working in the United Kingdom, under the Employer's Liability (Compulsory Insurance) Act 1969. This insurance protects employees in the event of an accident at work, or from illnesses that are attributable to their employment, and ensures that in the event that an employer is unable to compensate the employee, the insurance will.

Employers generally have no obligation to provide employees with a *reference* when leaving the employment and seeking a new position (unless an implied term is applicable or there is an express clause to the contrary). Some employers are reluctant to provide a reference due to the fact that what they say may not be very complimentary and they do not wish to fall victim of the law of defamation. Also, the employer may not wish to be regarded as having provided an inaccurate reference that amounts to a negligent misstatement and be subject to a liability claim. In *Spring v Guardian Assurance Plc* the House of Lords held that a reference that gave a poor impression of the former employee, even though these were beliefs genuinely held by the employer, was negligent as it was likely to cause the employee economic loss. There was an implied term in the employment to take reasonable care and skill in preparing a reference. Note that it is not uncommon for an employer to provide a poor employee with a particularly good reference simply to 'get rid' of the employee. Such tactics should, consequently, be adopted with caution. It should also be noted that there may be implied into the contract a duty to provide a reference where it has been provided for other employees, or if it has been agreed as part of a settlement issue in a grievance dispute.

As its name suggests, employers, like employees, also have the obligation to maintain mutual trust and confidence and to not take action likely to destroy it.

Isle of Wight Tourist Board v Coombes (1976)

Facts:

1 March 1976 was a Monday. On this day Mrs Coombes, who had worked for the Isle of Wight Tourist Board for 15 years and was now personal secretary to its director, was asked to undertake work which was not part of her general duties and, when she complained to the director, a colleague of Coombes ventured an opinion on the matter. Coombes told the colleague to keep out of it and at this point the director turned to the colleague, in the presence of Coombes and stated 'Don't worry about her. She's always an intolerable bitch on a Monday morning'.

Authority for:

The comment of the director was inappropriate and was a fundamental breach of the contract, destroying as it did the trust and confidence between them. Mrs Coombes was successful in her action for constructive dismissal.

An example of an extension of the term, albeit very fact specific and which, as held by the House of Lords, does not create a general right was seen in the following case.

Malik v Bank of Credit and Commerce International (1997)

Facts:

The Bank (the BCCI) was embroiled in one of the first major banking scandals in the UK and caused the collapse of the bank. Thousands of people lost their jobs as a result. This included the claimant. Beyond losing their job, the claimant argued he was entitled to damages due to the breach of trust and confidence of the directors in running a fraudulent business. This had caused them hardship in finding future employment due to their involvement with the BCCI (a 'stigma' head of loss).

Authority for:

The House of Lords held that an employer must not 'without reasonable and proper cause, conduct itself in a manner calculated or likely to destroy or seriously damage the relationship of confidence and trust between the employer and employee.'

Mutual trust imposes obligations on the employer to prevent actions including bullying:

Waters v Commissioner of Police for the Metropolis (2000)

Facts:

A female police officer made a complaint of serious sexual assault against a fellow officer and was subject to retaliatory action. She complained that the Commissioner had failed in their duty to protect her.

Authority for:

The House of Lords remarked: 'If an employer knows that acts being done by employees during their employment may cause physical or mental harm to a particular fellow employee and he does nothing to supervise or prevent such acts, when it is in his power to do so, it is clearly arguable that he may be in breach of his duty to that employee. It seems to me that he may also be in breach of that duty if he can foresee that such acts may happen and, if they do, that physical or mental harm may be caused to an individual.'

and stress faced by an employee (e.g. through an unreasonable workload):

Barber v Somerset County Council (2004)

Facts:

The claimant had been employed as a head of department in a school. Following changes made at the school he found the changes and an increase in hours very stressful. He

→

raised these concerns to his employer but they did nothing to relieve the stress and the claimant became ill and eventually suffered a nervous breakdown.

Authority for:

Employers may generally operate on the assumption that an employee is up to the requirements of their job. However, the House of Lords identified that an employer may have a duty to the employee to identify any steps that may be taken to assist them when the employee is having difficulty coping with their responsibilities. The employer had failed in this respect and was liable in negligence to the claimant.

If these are left unattended they may lead to successful claims for constructive dismissal and also possible tort actions against the employer for damages.

Consider

Yeo and other 'Super drivers' are subject to confidentiality clauses in their agreement with Super and are prohibited from speaking negatively about the company. This is evidence of an implied term not to breach the trust and confidence between the parties. This is a term which is more akin to employee status than an independent contractor as such terms do not, generally, apply to the self-employed.

CONCLUSION

The chapter has outlined the fundamental distinction between individuals who are employees and those who are independent contractors. The tests have been developed through the common law and have demonstrated that the current method is to begin with the tests identified in *Montgomery v Johnson Underwood*, and then if these questions are answered in the affirmative, to continue and apply the third question provided in *Ready Mixed Concrete* (and issues raised in *Market Investigations*). Whilst many employment rights are being introduced that affect 'workers' (such as the National Minimum Wage Act 1998, the Working Time Regulations 1998, and the Equality Act 2010) not simply employees, there are still many areas of employment law where rights and obligations fall on the employee and not the independent contractor. The independent contractor gains tax advantages, the ability to work for many different employers, and can deduct expenses incurred in their employment, which employees cannot. They are, however, excluded from many protections through statutory rights that may leave them vulnerable if they are dismissed, made redundant, injured at work, or become pregnant. These factors are considered in the following chapters.

SUMMARY OF MAIN POINTS

Employment status

- The Employment Rights Act, s. 230 defines employment status where 'an individual who has entered into or works under (or, where the employment has ceased, worked under) a contract of employment'.

- As the statute is deliberately broad in scope the courts have developed the following tests:
  - *Control test*: This continues to be a vital element of establishing employee status; it cannot, however, be used in isolation, and must form part of the wider range of questions established in *Montgomery, Ready Mixed Concrete*, and *Market Investigations*.
  - *Integration/organization test*: Here, the more the individual was integrated into the organization the more likely they would be considered an employee. This test was not often used following the decision.
  - *Mixed/economic reality test*: This test uses the criteria from *Ready Mixed Concrete, Lee v Chung, Market Investigations*, and *Montgomery* in establishing employment status.
- Since 2013, the status of 'employee shareholder' was introduced, which provides the individual with shares in the (employer/employer's parent) company in return for him/her waiving certain protective employment rights.

Reason for the distinction

- The following are examples of why it is important to differentiate between employees and independent contractors: the rate of income tax and responsibility for National Insurance payments; the statutory rights of unfair dismissal, redundancy, and various maternity rights, which are only available to employees; and the employer having potential liability for the torts committed by their employees in the course of their employment.

Written particulars

- This is not the contract of employment, although similar information may be contained in the document.
- This document must be provided within two months of the employee starting employment.
- It contains important information regarding the parties; the terms of the employment including duties, sources of obligations, and pay; whether the employment is for a fixed time or permanent; and pension details (among others).

Terms implied into the contract

- Due to the problems of attempting to include all the terms of the employment relationship into a single document, terms have been implied into the contract through the courts, customs, and statutes.
- Duties and obligations on the employee include mutual trust and confidence, fidelity, duty to disclose the misdeeds of others, cooperation, to use reasonable skill and judgement, obey lawful orders, and to adapt to new working conditions.
- Duties and obligations on the employer include to pay wages; in the case of industrial action being accepted by the employer, to pay a fair proportion of wages; to provide work for the employee; to maintain the health and safety of their workers; and employers also have the obligation to maintain mutual trust and confidence in the employment relationship.

 ## SUMMARY QUESTIONS

Essay questions

1. 'Through the last one hundred years, legislative and common law initiatives have failed to establish a single definitive test to establish the employment status of individuals.'

   Critically assess the above statement and identify reforms in the law that you deem expedient.

2. Lord Slynn, in *Spring v Guardian Assurance Plc* [1994], observed that 'the changes which have taken place in the employer/employee relationship . . . [have seen] . . . far greater duties imposed on the employer than in the past, whether by statute or by judicial decision, to care for the physical, financial or even psychological welfare of the employees.'

    Discuss the above statement in relation to the development of implied terms in contracts of employment.

Problem questions

1. Jennifer has been employed by All Bright Consumables (ABC) Ltd for the past two years. ABC retails electronic home entertainment equipment. Her tasks include offering sales advice, stock-taking duties, restocking the shelves, and accepting deliveries from suppliers. Jennifer works 40 hours per week and is entitled to six weeks paid holidays each year; however, these must be agreed in advance with her manager and she cannot take her holiday if another member of staff is on holiday at the same time.

    She is occasionally required to work in other regional branches when necessary, although Jennifer may claim expenses for the travel involved. Jennifer's contract identifies her as an independent contractor, and it also contains a restraint of trade clause. She is responsible for paying her own income tax and National Insurance.

    Following a disagreement with her employer regarding stock irregularities, Jennifer has been dismissed from work. She would like to know her employment status in order to identify if she may pursue a claim of unfair dismissal.

    With reference to appropriate case law, identify how a tribunal may decide the employment status of Jennifer.

2. Enzo is a maintenance engineer for ABC in its electronic gadgets department (servicing burglar alarms). Enzo is engaged to service the products sold by ABC to its customers in the customers' own premises. Enzo is provided with a list of customers and the priority of those jobs, but he is otherwise left to determine his workload and when he completes the jobs in the day. Following the completion of each job, Enzo obtains a signature from the customer and passes this back to ABC as proof of him completing the job. ABC then invoices the customer directly.

    Enzo uses his own vehicle to make the visits to the customers' premises and he is paid without any deduction of income tax or National Insurance contributions. ABC considers that Enzo will make his own arrangements with HM Revenue and Customs personally.

    Yesterday, whilst on a call to one of ABC's major customer's, Enzo was involved in an accident at work. The accident occurred as the customer had alarms placed in particularly difficult to reach locations. The ladders provided by ABC to Enzo did not reach these locations. Enzo contacted ABC about this but was told that this was a very important customer, and he must complete the service at that visit. As such, whilst attempting to do so, he fell and sustained a serious injury to his arm and shoulder.

    The result of the accident has left Enzo hospitalized for four weeks and he is unlikely to return to work for at least six months. ABC has informed Enzo that as he is an independent contractor he is not eligible to claim from its insurers, nor is he able to claim sick pay.

    Advise Enzo as to his employment status and any claim he may make for his losses against ABC.

 www.oup.com/uk/marson5e/

For further resources relating to this chapter, including self-test questions, an interactive glossary, and key case flashcards.

FURTHER READING

Books and articles

Anderman, S. (2000) 'The Interpretation of Protective Employment Statutes and Contracts of Employment' *Industrial Law Journal*, Vol. 29, No. 3, p. 223.

Boyle, M. (2007) 'The Relational Principle of Trust and Confidence' *Oxford Journal of Legal Studies*, Vol. 27, No. 4, p. 633.

Brodie, D. (2004) 'Health and Safety, Trust and Confidence and *Barber v Somerset County Council*: Some Further Questions' *Industrial Law Journal*, Vol. 33, No. 3, p. 261.

Clarke, L. (2000) 'Mutuality of Obligations and the Contract of Employment: *Carmichael and Another v National Power PLC*' *Modern Law Review*, Vol. 63, No. 5, p. 757.

Davidov, G. (2005) 'Who is a Worker?' *Industrial Law Journal*, Vol. 34, No. 1, p. 57.

Davies, A. C. L. (2007) 'The Contract of Intermittent Employment' *Industrial Law Journal*, Vol. 36, No. 1, p. 102.

Marson, J. (2013) 'Anatomy of an Employee' *European Journal of Current Legal Issues*, Vol. 19, No. 3.

Taylor, S. and Emir, A. (2015) 'Employment Law: An Introduction' (4th Edition) Oxford University Press: Oxford and New York.

Websites and Twitter links

http://www.danielbarnett.co.uk
@daniel_barnett

Daniel Barnett is a barrister specializing in employment law. This resource includes commentary on legislative reforms, and case law materials, often from the lawyers involved in the case. The service is free and is an excellent source of information—I highly recommend you sign up for the mailing service.

http://www.legislation.gov.uk/ukpga/1996/18/contents
The Employment Rights Act 1996.

http://www.justice.gov.uk/tribunals/employment
Employment Tribunals.

https://www.gov.uk/employment-tribunal-decisions
The Ministry of Justice site of Employment Tribunal decisions available online. Note, this is seen as a matter of transparency and a positive step. However, there has been criticism that it may enable employers to use the resource as a system to identify if a potential recruit has previously taken an employer to a tribunal and use that information negatively.

https://www.tax.service.gov.uk/check-employment-status-for-tax/setup
A website established by the tax office to determine the employment status of the user. This is different to how employment status is identified for employment law purposes, but is quite an interesting and useful tool.

#ukemplaw
A very useful source of discussion and commentary on topical employment issues in the UK.

ONLINE RESOURCES

www.oup.com/uk/marson5e/

For further resources relating to this chapter, including self-test questions, an interactive glossary, and key case flashcards.

20 DISMISSAL AT COMMON LAW; REDUNDANCY AND THE TRANSFER OF UNDERTAKINGS

At some point, the employment relationship will come to an end. There are various reasons for this—at the employer's will (giving notice); the individual may wish to leave and explore other opportunities (resignation); the task for which employment was established may have been completed; the individual may become redundant; or there may be some 'outside' factor where the employment cannot continue (including frustration). Whilst these are merely a few examples, the mechanisms that will enable a termination of the employment relationship without transgressing the law are clearly of importance. When a business (an undertaking) is sold (its ownership transferred), obligations exist for both the transferor and transferee to respect and protect the terms and conditions of employment of the affected individuals. By adhering to the legal requirements and adopting the correct approach to dismissal/transfer procedures, not only may court/tribunal action be avoided, but it will assist in maintaining good working relations, which are essential to promote trust, respect, and productivity.

Business Scenario 20

Wilko Co. Ltd has branches throughout the UK. It recently experienced financial difficulties and provided a warning to all employees that redundancies may have to be made.

Xiu has worked as a check-out assistant for Wilko's for five years before being informed that the branch where she worked was to be closed. Following this notice Xiu was offered employment, on the same terms and conditions, at a branch six miles away. She refused the offer due to travel difficulties—Xiu would have had to catch an earlier bus into work.

Robin sold garden furniture at a stand in several stores, and was paid on a commission basis. He worked at other branches in the local area and following Wilko's threat of possible redundancies, he resigned when offered employment at a rival firm.

Sasha, who had worked at Wilko for the previous six years, was employed in a department of the firm which was subject to a reorganization. Consequently, Sasha was regraded, subject to a variation in the terms of her contract, and suffered a loss in pay and status. Sasha refused to accept the variation and has resigned.

Jin was area manager in Sheffield for 10 years. He was told that fewer managers were required in Sheffield but was offered a position as a district manager in Surrey. Jin refused the offer as his children had only recently started school in Sheffield.

Learning Outcomes

- Explain the common law mechanism of seeking damages for the wrongful termination of employment (**20.3.2–20.3.6**)

- Compare and contrast the remedies of wrongful dismissal and unfair dismissal (**20.3.6 (Table 20.1)**)

- Identify when an employee may claim protection under redundancy (**20.4–20.4.8**)

- Identify the factors that will make the selection process for redundancies fair and unfair (**20.4.3–20.4.4**)

- Explain the obligations on the employer to consult with the employees (and/or their representatives) over planned redundancies (**20.4.5–20.4.5.2**)

- Explicate the obligations of an employer who wishes to transfer the undertaking, and the requirements on the transferee to protect the transferred workforce's continuity, and terms, of employment (**20.5–20.5.5**).

20.1 INTRODUCTION

Before the increasingly broad and complex legislative provisions governing employment relationships began to take effect with great pace from the 1960s, contracts of employment were largely dealt with by the 'normal' rules of contract law. Indeed, a claim for wrongful dismissal is a breach of contract claim (albeit a contract of employment), and is (often) heard by courts that hear contractual disputes. This chapter identifies the remedy for termination of the contract of employment through the common law claim of wrongful dismissal. The statutory measures of unfair (and constructive unfair) dismissal are discussed in **Chapter 21**. The chapter also addresses situations of redundancy, and the rights of individuals and obligations on employers when the business is transferred to a new owner. Each of these measures offer protection to employees, and employers should understand the nature of these rights, the qualifications necessary for each mechanism, and the remedies available, to ensure they select the most appropriate mechanism to bring the employment relationship to an end.

20.2 TERMINATION OF EMPLOYMENT

It is important to recognize from the outset that there are various ways of bringing an employment relationship to an end. Some of these may amount to a dismissal that may enable a claim for wrongful or unfair dismissal. There are also terminations that do not, at common law, constitute a dismissal.

20.2.1 Terminations not Establishing a Dismissal at Common Law

The following is a non-exhaustive list of situations where the employment relationship has ended, but no (common law) claim is available:

- *The mutual agreement of the parties:* There is a situation where the parties may simply no longer wish to continue with the contract of employment and as such release each other from any further obligations. However, the courts are suspicious of such arrangements and will look to see if the worker was provided with any inducement from the employer to end the contract (such as a financial inducement) that could lead to a common sense belief of mutual agreement. Where a termination is instigated by the employer, it will be held as a dismissal not mutual agreement.

Francis v Pertemps Recruitment (2013)

Facts:

Mr Francis was employed by the recruitment agency and placed with a client. At the end of that engagement Pertemps offered him one of two options. Francis could either be paid two weeks' notice plus redundancy pay. Or, he could choose to be paid two weeks' notice whilst the agency kept him on its books and looked for engagement with a new client. He chose the latter, then asked to change to the first offer. On this basis the employer wrote informing Francis of his right to an appeal 'against the decision to terminate your employment'. Francis appealed, unsuccessfully, and then brought an action for unfair dismissal.

Authority for:

The employer's argument that this was not a dismissal claim but one of mutual agreement was rejected by the EAT. Where the employer terminates the contract, as evidenced here by the language used in the communications, it will be accepted as such. This does not, however, reflect the fairness or otherwise of that decision.

If the individual was coerced into resigning due to a threat by the employer (such as a threat of dismissal), then this will not amount to an agreement.

Martin v MBS Fastenings (Glynwed) Distribution Ltd (1983)

Facts:

Martin had been involved in an incident at work where one of the company's vehicles was badly damaged. Following an investigation Martin was invited to attend a meeting to discuss the matter. He was approached before the meeting and told that the company had concluded he was at fault and at the conclusion of the meeting he would be dismissed. Informally, he was advised it would be better for him to resign and therefore would avoid a dismissal on his employment record. Martin's resignation at the meeting was accepted by the employer. However, later he complained of unfair dismissal.

Authority for:

The Court of Appeal held that a resignation had to have been voluntarily issued to be considered as such. Here, there was no voluntary resignation and thus it must be considered a dismissal.

---

* *Frustration of the contract:* Claims of frustration have been invoked in situations where the individual was conscripted to the armed forces under national service; where the individual becomes ill and cannot continue with the contract (*Condor v The Barron Knights*—see **10.2.3**); or where injury prevents the continuity of the contract.

GF Sharp & Co Ltd v McMillan (1998)

Facts:

McMillan was employed by GF Sharp as a joiner and suffered a serious injury to his left hand in October 1994. This left him permanently incapable of working again as a joiner. Following a meeting later in the same year with the company's managing director it was agreed that GF Sharp would keep McMillan 'on the books' despite not working because McMillan could draw more generous pension benefits if he remained in employment until after his 60th birthday (31 March 1996). In August 1996 McMillan made an application for a redundancy payment and GF Sharp refused arguing that, due to his injury, McMillan's contract of employment was frustrated and ended with effect from 22 November 1996.

Authority for:

The EAT held that a contract of employment is frustrated when, without default of either party, a contractual obligation had become incapable of being performed. As such, following his injury, McMillan could no longer continue with his employment and the contract was frustrated.

The courts will not readily accept an assertion that the contract is frustrated as this would negate the remedies provided under the statutory provisions and common law.

Williams v Watson Luxury Coaches Ltd (1990)

Facts:

Ms Williams was employed as a part-time typist and sustained an injury at work. As a consequence she was absent from work for a period of some 18 months. During this time the employer's business was sold and when Williams declared herself available for work, the employer informed her that there was no work available for her to do. On her claim that she had been unfairly dismissed, the tribunal rejected her argument as the contract had been frustrated due to the length of her absence.

Authority for:

Frustration of contract is a doctrine of last resort and this makes its application to sickness quite difficult to identify. Here the tribunal identified the factors to be considered when drawing conclusions: the nature of the job; the employee's length of service prior to the illness; the nature of the illness, its severity, and how long it may last; the prospect of recovery; the requirement for cover by another person; the length of the employment foreseeable; the employer's conduct; whether another reasonable employer would have chosen to terminate the contract or would have waited longer to see if the employee could return to work; and whether the employee had been paid wages/sick pay during the absence.

Remember, a finding of frustration means the employee cannot recover any benefits available through protective dismissal laws.

- *The expiry of a fixed-term contract:* When a contract has reached the end of its term, the relationship under that contract is complete and no claim may be made under the common law. However, this does not mean that there is no claim under the statutory provisions and, indeed, non-renewal of a fixed-term contract may enable a claim for unfair dismissal.

- *Non-return following child birth:* Under the common law, there is no breach for an employer refusing to allow a woman to return to her job following a period of absence following the birth of her child. However, the ERA 1996, ss. 96 and 137 establishes that such a refusal will be treated as a dismissal for the purposes of that Act.

20.3 WRONGFUL DISMISSAL (THE COMMON LAW ROUTE)

Under the governance of contract law, the contract of employment may have included a term regarding the period of notice required for each of the parties to terminate the agreement (although see *Autoclenz Ltd v Belcher & Others* for judicial comment on the distinctions between 'general' contracts and contracts of employment). Even in the absence of such a clause, statute establishes the minimum notice period that has to be provided. If this notice period is not adhered to, in the absence of a justifiable reason, then the termination will be in breach of contract and, in this circumstance, may amount to a **wrongful dismissal**. As this is a contractual dispute, the damages will attempt to place the injured party in the position they would have been had the contract not been breached.

20.3.1 The Notice Period

The contract of employment will possibly identify the notice period that is required of each party (and these periods may be different between the individual and employer). In the absence of any notice period ERA 1996, s. 86 states that employees who have worked between one month and two years continuously for the same employer are entitled to one week's notice. This notice period extends by one week for every year that is worked to a maximum of 12 weeks' notice (see **Table 20.1**).

Table 20.1 Notice periods

Period of employment	Notice period applicable
Less than one month	None
More than one month but less than 2 years	1 week
More than 2 years but less than 12 years	Maximum of 12 weeks (one week for every year worked)
More than 12 years	12 weeks

20.3.2 What May Be Claimed

In the event that the employer dismisses the individual contrary to the terms of the contract or the statutory minimum, the claimant is entitled to damages for their losses.

This will be assessed on the standard principles of contract law and will provide the lost income for the notice period that should have been provided, or in the case of a fixed-term contract, the balance of the contract.

Addis v Gramophone Co Ltd (1909)

Facts:

The employee was paid a relatively small salary with the remainder of his pay based on the commission he received from sales. A period of six months' notice on termination was included in the contract. When the employer issued Addis with this notice, he was provided with his salary for the term but he was prevented from working. Therefore he was prevented from an opportunity to earn the commission.

Authority for:

The House of Lords held that a wrongful dismissal had taken place. Addis was entitled to claim a reasonable commission, based, for example, on the earnings of his replacement.

However, claims may not be made for the manner of the dismissal. Being a wrongful dismissal, there may be an element of distress, even humiliation in the nature of such terminations, but these are not recoverable in respect of the '*Johnson* exclusion area'.

Edwards v Chesterfield Royal Hospital NHS Foundation Trust (2011)

Facts:

The claimant was employed as a consultant trauma and orthopedic surgeon whose contract of employment included a three months' notice of termination clause. Further, it identified the disciplinary procedure that was to be followed in the event of alleged misconduct. Subsequent to a dismissal for misconduct, Edwards argued that his dismissal was unfair as the procedures were not followed. Further, that as the contract was breached the normal remedies available in contract that flow from the breach—loss of reputation future earnings etc.—should also be available (above those allowed in the Employment Rights Act 1996 which governs unfair dismissal).

Authority for:

The claim for contractual damages failed. In the case *Johnson v Unisys Ltd* [2001] an employee was not allowed to recover damages for breach of trust and confidence where the circumstances giving rise to the breach related only to the manner in which the employee had been dismissed. This became known as the '*Johnson* exclusion area' and applied in Edwards' case.

The predominant remedy for wrongful dismissal claims is damages, but the courts have been increasingly inclined to make use of injunctions to prevent a dismissal, or to prevent a dismissal that attempts to circumvent a statutory right.

Irani v South West Hampshire Health Authority (1985)

Facts:

Mr Irani was employed by the Health Authority as an ophthalmologist. He and a more senior colleague had a disagreement resulting in the Authority convening an ad hoc panel to discuss the matter. The conclusion was that the differences between the employees were irreconcilable and as Irani was the more junior he should be dismissed. The contract of employment outlined disciplinary and grievance procedures that the Authority was required to follow. When these were breached Irani sought an interim injunction to stop the application of the dismissal, and to compel the Health Authority to fulfil its obligation under the contract.

Authority for:

As the procedures had not been applied properly an injunction was granted to stop the effect of the dismissal pending the correct application of the grievance procedures.

Note that specific performance is not available in contracts of personal service, but in *Irani*, the court followed the ruling in *Hill v CA Parsons* regarding when an injunction should be awarded:

1. there must still exist between the parties mutual trust and confidence so that the employment relationship has not irreconcilably broken down;
2. the claimant was seeking protection of statutory rights;
3. damages would not have been an adequate remedy in the case.

20.3.3 Duty to Mitigate

Having suffered a wrongful dismissal, the injured party must take reasonable steps to avoid further damages accruing and as such they must attempt to mitigate their losses. This does not require the affected individual to accept any job that is offered, or to take up employment at a much lower level than had been enjoyed whilst employed. The courts will expect evidence that alternative work has been sought. As in the case of seeking damages for breach of contract, it would be contrary to public policy to allow the injured party to sit back and allow any damages to mount if they could have minimized these losses through alternative employment.

Brace v Calder (1895)

Facts:

Mr Brace had entered a contract with Calder to serve it (consisting of four partners) for a term of two years. Before the two years had expired, two of the partners retired although the remaining partners were to continue running the business. Consequently Calder offered Brace to continue to serve the new firm for the remainder of the contract on the same terms and at the same rate of pay. He refused and claimed wrongful dismissal.

→

Authority for:

The Court of Appeal held there was a wrongful dismissal on the dissolution of the partnership, but Brace was only entitled to nominal damages (£50). He had been offered a suitable alternative which was fair and reasonable in the circumstances, and by refusing he had failed to mitigate his losses.

20.3.4 After Discovered Reasons

It may be the case that following an employer's decision to terminate the individual's contract, for example, on suspicion of breach of contract (such as for **gross misconduct** or **gross negligence**), after the dismissal evidence is gained that proves (or disproves) the employer's assertion. This is called 'after discovered reasons' as the evidence is only identified following the action taken by the employer. Whilst in situations of unfair dismissal these will not subsequently make an unfair dismissal fair, they will be allowed to enable the employer to mount a defence against a wrongful dismissal claim. Hence, after discovered reasons can make an otherwise wrongful dismissal a lawful dismissal. As such, it may be wise for an employer to continue their investigation, even following a dismissal, to gather whatever evidence is available to defeat a possible wrongful dismissal claim.

Boston Deep Sea Fishing and Ice Co. v Ansell (1888)

Facts:

Ansell had been employed as managing director of the firm and was dismissed on suspicion of dishonest practice (in the absence of tangible evidence that supported the employer's allegations). The employer continued to investigate the matter and in the course of this investigation discovered that Ansell had been taking bribes when awarding contracts to suppliers.

Authority for:

In defence to the wrongful dismissal claim, this after discovered evidence was presented and the court accepted that Ansell had breached the fundamental implied term of trust and confidence. Ansell had committed a repudiatory breach of the contract and the employer's actions were justified in bringing the employment to an end.

20.3.5 Time Limit for Claims

As this is a breach of contract case, the claimant can bring a claim for wrongful dismissal up to six years following the notice of the contract being ended.

20.3.6 Who May Claim

As this is an action for breach of contract, any individual who contracts to personally undertake the work can claim the remedy of wrongful dismissal. Therefore, unlike the statutory route of unfair dismissal, the status of employee is not required and this opens up the route for claimants who might otherwise not qualify under unfair dismissal. Further, there is no requirement for a period of continuous employment (**Table 20.2** on p. 508).

Table 20.2 Comparison: unfair dismissal and wrongful dismissal

	Unfair dismissal	Wrongful dismissal
Source of the right	Statutory (ERA 1996)	Common law (contract)
Who may claim	Only available to employees	Anyone with a contract
Minimum period of continuous employment required to access the right	Two years	Immediate from the commencement of the contract
Time limit within which a claim must be lodged	Three months	Six years
Where the claim is heard	Employment Tribunal	County Court; High Court. A claim may be heard at an Employment Tribunal where the claim does not exceed £25,000
Basis of the award	Compensation includes a basic award and a compensatory award to reflect ongoing and future losses	Only covers the loss incurred for breach of the relevant notice period, or the balance of a fixed-term contract with no early termination clause
Reasons for dismissal	s. 98 ERA 1996 outlines potentially fair reasons for dismissal. The statute also identifies reasons for dismissal that will be automatically unfair	The employer can choose any reason for dismissal. The stipulation is adherence to the notice period required under the contract
Costs	Legal costs incurred in the action are rarely awarded to the successful party	Costs are more readily awarded in the County Court and High Court
Remedies available	Reinstatement; re-engagement; or compensation	Damages (although injunctions may also be available)
Discipline/dismissal procedures	The procedures identified in the ACAS Code must be complied with or the tribunal may reduce any award by up to 25 per cent. The claimant must have engaged with the ACAS Early Conciliation Scheme prior to lodging a tribunal claim	Any procedures provided by the employer in the contract must be adhered to
After discovered reasons	Cannot make an unfair dismissal fair, but it may reduce any compensation awarded to a successful employee	These may justify a dismissal, and if accepted by the court, will make a wrongful dismissal a fair dismissal
Damages awarded	This is subject to a statutory-imposed cap (updated annually)	As this is a breach of contract claim there is no ceiling to the award of damages. It depends on the breach and the value of the contract

20.4 **REDUNDANCY**

There are many occasions where a business may become unprofitable, or a part of the business may have to be closed. In these events, employees will be affected and the employer may no longer require their services. In these circumstances the employees may be eligible for compensation in the form of a redundancy payment. There are criteria established to determine who is eligible to claim, and the amount of any award to be made. By possessing this information, the employer will recognize the steps to be taken, particularly in terms of consultation with the employees' representatives, and may avoid unfair selection procedures that will provide the employee with a right to claim unfair dismissal.

Redundancy is a complex issue of which there may have been many factors in the changes to, or decline of, the business that has necessitated the employer taking the decision to dismiss individuals. The law seeks to protect employees who are affected by this event, but also provide sufficient flexibility to enable an employer to carry on the business, or sell the undertaking to another buyer that may have the resources to 'save' it (for example). As such the law provides guidance on how this process may be undertaken to be as fair as possible to all parties.

Redundancy involves two broad scenarios. The employer may be closing the business and hence there is no work for the employee to do; or the employee may be surplus to the employer's requirements following, for example, a **reorganization** or refocus to the business.

Note; the tribunal is not allowed to assess the business need or rationale for the employer ending the business (*Moon v Homeworthy Furniture*).

Redundancy is one of the potentially fair reasons to dismiss, but unlike most of the other categories identified in ERA 1996, s. 98, it does not relate to the capability or the misconduct of the employee and in essence is a 'no fault' termination.

20.4.1 **The Definition of Redundancy**

The definition of redundancy is contained in ERA 1996, s. 139:

For the purposes of this Act, an employee who is dismissed shall be taken to be dismissed by reason of redundancy if the dismissal is attributable wholly or mainly to:

(a) the fact that his employer has ceased, or intends to cease:

(i) to carry on the business for the purposes of which the employee was employed by him; or

(ii) to carry on that business in the place where the employee was so employed; or

(b) the fact that the requirements of that business:

(i) for employees to carry out work of a particular kind; or

(ii) for employees to carry out work of a particular kind in the place where the employee was so employed by the employer, have ceased or diminished or are expected to cease or diminish.

When the employer decides to dismiss due to redundancy, the tribunal is not in a position to ascertain the business rationale behind the decision but rather limits the inquiry to determine whether redundancy was the reason for the dismissal, or whether redundancy was merely a 'smokescreen' for some other reason.

Consider

Xiu's redundancy is due to the branch where she has been employed closing. As such it is a redundancy under s. 139(a)(ii). However, for Sasha and Jin, it is a potentially more complex situation if it is the work of the particular kind which is diminishing (and in Sasha's case leading to her regrading). This means that instead of ceasing to carry on the business, there may be a need for fewer employees to do the work that they perform. For Jin, the work is diminishing. However, for Sasha, if her regrading is due to a change in the nature of her work and a reduction in the requirements on the employer to carry out that work, she will have been made redundant. Alternatively, if the regrading is simply a cost-reducing measure and the particular work undertaken has not diminished, there will be no redundancy. Application of the tests developed in *Safeway Stores v Burrell* is required here (see **20.4.1.1**).

20.4.1.1 **Work of a particular kind**

In the first definition of redundancy above (s. 139(a)), it is quite easy to identify a redundancy situation as the business is being closed and the entire workforce is being made redundant. However, if another firm is taking over the business (under a transfer of the undertaking) and the business is being sold as a going concern, the employees' contracts will be transferred to the new owner and no redundancies will be established.

Where the situation becomes more complicated is in the assessment under s. 139(b) as the statute requires a diminution in the number of employees required to perform 'work of a particular kind', rather than a diminution in the work itself. If the employer is reducing the workforce but the work required remains the same or is increasing then a redundancy situation will occur (*Johnson v Peabody Trust*), whereas if the employer, in the same circumstances, has reorganized the business and still requires the same number of employees, then no redundancy has taken place. The courts will look to the reason for the dismissal instead. Such an example may be seen in *Vaux & Associated Breweries Ltd v Ward* where an older woman was replaced in the public house by a much younger woman (to do the same job) on the basis of establishing a younger image for the premises. Ms Ward was not made redundant in this circumstance.

In s. 139(a)(ii) where the business that the employees had previously been employed is ceasing, the question to be asked is 'Where is the 'particular' place of work?' *Rank Xerox Ltd v Churchill* placed the interpretation of 'place of work' on the contract between the parties. Hence if a mobility clause was included in the contract, this interpretation was to be where the employer could require the employee to work, rather than looking at where the work was actually taking place. In *Bass Leisure Ltd v Thomas* the EAT addressed previous authorities such as *Rank Xerox* and held that where a woman had been informed that her position with the employer, based in Coventry, was moving to another plant some

20 miles away, despite the fact that her contract contained a mobility clause, the focus for redundancy was a geographical test. The woman worked in Coventry and when this employment ceased she was in effect made redundant, even though alternative work was offered 20 miles away.

The questions to be asked when determining if a redundancy situation has occurred were outlined by the EAT in *Safeway Stores v Burrell*:

1. Was the employee dismissed?

2. If answered in the affirmative, had the requirements of the business for the employees to carry out work of a particular kind ceased or diminished, or were they expected to cease or diminish?

3. If so, was the dismissal caused wholly or mainly by that cessation or diminution of work?

Consider

The staff who are subject to redundancy (Xiu, Robin, Sasha, and Jin) must qualify for the right to seek a remedy under this aspect of the law. Being governed by statute, these criteria are strictly applied and where any one is missing, the individual would have to seek a remedy in another legal area (if available).

20.4.2 Qualifications to the Right

As with unfair dismissal, qualification criteria exist that restrict the remedy only to an individual who:

- has 'employee' status;
- was continuously employed by the same employer for two years before the relevant date of the redundancy;
- is not in one of the excluded categories;
- was dismissed;
- was dismissed on the basis of redundancy.

20.4.2.1 Employee status and continuous employment

The test for employee status is assessed in the same way as it is for unfair dismissal and the particulars of employment will give evidence of the two years' continuous service.

20.4.2.2 Excluded categories

Certain categories of individual do not have the ability to bring a redundancy claim. These include share fishermen; employees of the Crown; and those individuals who were employed as a domestic servant of a relative. Access to the right is also restricted to those individuals who were dismissed for misconduct or for involvement in industrial action, and if the individual had been offered suitable alternative employment having been informed of the redundancy and unreasonably declined this, they will be ineligible to claim.

Consider

Robin has left the firm due to the threat of redundancy. However, significantly, his contract had not been terminated by reason of redundancy—he left the firm and took up employment with a rival firm. This will mean he does not qualify for a redundancy payment. Sasha has resigned due to the employer's unilateral variation of the contract. Could this amount to a constructive dismissal (see ERA 1996, s. 136(1)) which would satisfy the requirement that the employee has been subject to a dismissal? Xiu and Jin have been offered alternative employment with the firm—whether this is suitable will determine whether they have been dismissed for the purposes of redundancy law.

20.4.2.3 Dismissal

The employee's claim can only be made if the tribunal finds they have been dismissed for the reason of redundancy.

The employee is dismissed by reason of redundancy if:

* the contract under which they were employed has been terminated by the employer;
* the contract was for a limited term and the contract terminates by virtue of the limiting event without being renewed under the same contract; or
* the employee terminates the contract in circumstances in which they are entitled to terminate it without notice by reason of the employer's conduct (ERA 1996, s. 136).

For a dismissal to be effective in a redundancy claim the employee must have been given a specific date on which their employment will cease (termed 'being put under notice of dismissal'). The dismissal for the purposes of redundancy must be the actual notice of dismissal and not some future intention of the employer.

Morton Sundour Fabrics v Shaw (1966)

Facts:

Mr Shaw had worked for the company for a number of years as foreman and was entitled to 28 days' notice of termination of his employment. In March 1966 Shaw was informed that the department where he worked would have to be closed down at a date in the near future (although that date was not specified). Within days of being so informed, Shaw secured alternative employment and tendered his resignation. Later he claimed a redundancy payment.

Authority for:

Shaw had not been made redundant. In order to terminate a contract of employment for redundancy the notice must specify the date on which the employment was to come to an end. Alternatively, it must contain facts from which that date was ascertainable. The mere issuing of a warning is insufficient.

There is an exception to the above rule whereby an employee may leave the employment before the redundancy becomes effective (ERA 1996, s. 142). If the employee serves the employer with a 'counter-claim' within the statutory notice period of their intention to leave the employment early, and this is accepted by the employer, then the employee's right to claim a redundancy payment is protected. On the event of the employer refusing this request, they may provide a 'counter-notice' to the employee's claim. If the employee decides to leave the employment without serving the notice period and brings a redundancy claim, the tribunal will decide whether to enable the claim to proceed and the level of compensation (if any) to be awarded.

The dismissal is effective when notice of it has been received, not when it is delivered.

Newcastle Upon Tyne NHS Foundation Trust v Haywood (2017)

Facts:

Ms Haywood was informed in April 2011 that she was at risk of redundancy. On 20 July of that year she would turn 50 years old and be entitled to an increased pension if still in employment. Her contract identified that she was entitled to 12 weeks' notice of termination of her employment but was silent as to how the notice was to be provided. Haywood went on holiday on 19 April 2011 and returned home on 27 April. On 20 April the employer had sent a notice of termination to her home address and also this information via email (to her husband's email address). Haywood read the notice on her return from holiday.

Authority for:

The contractual notice period was deemed effective when it had been received and not on its delivery. Hence the effective date was 27 April and thus Haywood's dismissal occurred after her 50th birthday. She was thereby entitled to the more generous pension payment.

ERA 1996, s. 163(2) assists the employee by presuming redundancy is the reason for the dismissal and placing the burden on the employer to disprove this. The employee will not be held to have been dismissed if they are offered a renewal of the contract or re-engagement with the employer; if offered 'suitable' employment with an associated company of the employer; or where the business has been transferred under the TUPE 2006 Regulations.

Consider

Sasha has had her pay and status reduced following a reorganization of the department where she was employed. Whether this amounts to selection for redundancy is a matter of debate. However, if the employer's requirements for that particular role have not diminished, a tribunal will not hold Sasha to have been made redundant. In this circumstance, consider her remedies for an unfair dismissal due to the unilateral and fundamental change (breach?) of her contract.

20.4.3 The Employer's Selection of Employees for Redundancy

When the business is going to continue trading, but the reorganization involves making redundancies from certain departments, or it applies to groups of employees, the law provides guidance on how to establish fair selection procedures. There are many instances where an employer's decision, albeit innocently made, will in fact amount to a discriminatory or unfair selection. This enables a claim for unfair dismissal if the tribunal holds that there was discrimination in the selection procedure, therefore communication and consultation with the employees, trades unions and employees' representatives, in accordance with policies allowed under the legislation, will lessen the chances of claims being brought against the employer. As much warning of the possibility of redundancies as possible should be provided to the employees and their representatives to enable alternative courses of action to be taken. The employer should also identify any suitable alternative work that may be available in the organization for those selected for redundancy. Such transparency will also assist in maintaining good industrial relations during a very tense period in the business. See *Williams v Compair Maxam Ltd* for an example of how not to carry out the selection process for redundancy.

20.4.4 Automatically Unfair Selection for Redundancy

Just as with unfair dismissal, there are categories of employees who, when selected for redundancy because of their membership of that category, will be held to have been unfairly selected. Selections from the following categories will be held automatically unfair:

* membership or non-membership of a trade union, or activities connected with the membership (Trade Union and Labour Relations (Consolidation) Act 1992, s. 153);
* pregnancy or childbirth, or if the employee has asserted statutory rights or made complaints under health and safety legislation (ERA 1996, s. 105);
* selection due to the discriminatory policy or its non-application (*Williams v Compair Maxam*).

20.4.5 Obligation to Consult

When the employer is planning redundancies involving 20 or more employees at one establishment, there is an obligation, following the EU Directive on Collective Dismissals (75/129/EEC) (as amended by Council Directive 98/59/EC), and brought into effect in the UK through the Trade Union and Labour Relations (Consolidation) Act (TULRCA) 1992, ss. 188–198, to consult with the recognized trade union or other employee representatives. The appropriate representatives are identified in TULRCA 1992, s. 188(1B), although where an employer does not recognize a union, or has fewer than 10 employees, information and consultation may take place with the whole workforce. There is no requirement to hold elections and establish an employee representative group. The requirement is to begin the consultation process when the employer is 'contemplating' redundancies, which implies that the consultation is to begin as soon as is reasonably practicable. In *R v British Coal Corporation, ex parte Vardy* this was held to be when the employer first believes they may need to make redundancies. This was furthered by the Court of Justice in *Junk v Kuhnel*, where it was held that the consultation should take place when the employer intends to make redundancies rather than wait until the notices of dismissal are sent to the employees. However, TULRCA 1992, s. 188(1A) provides that consultation must take place:

- where between 20–99 employees are to be made redundant—the minimum consultation period is a period of 30 days before the first dismissal;
- where over 100 employees are to be made redundant—the minimum period is 45 days before the first dismissal (Trade Union and Labour Relations (Consolidation) Act 1992 (Amendment) Order 2013 (S.I. 763/2013)).

20.4.5.1 Purpose of the consultation

Evidently, the rationale for requiring a period of consultation with the affected employees' representatives is to enable possible alternatives to redundancies (such as reductions in hours, overtime bans, and so on) to be explored. These may be agreed which will affect all employees but may reduce the necessity of dismissals. Even if these negotiations do not produce a situation that prevents dismissals, agreements can be reached on the selection procedures to be used. The EAT has also held that the consultation places a duty on employers to identify the reason for the redundancies (*UK Coal Mining Ltd v National Union of Mineworkers*).

When an employee has been informed they are to be made redundant, they are entitled to time off work to attend training courses to increase their skills for new work and attend interviews for new employment (ERA 1996, s. 52).

20.4.5.2 Failure to follow the consultation requirements

A failure to consult with the employees' representatives before redundancies are announced may lead to a claim for compensation. The employer is required to explain why the consultations did not take place, and if no answer is provided, or the tribunal does not accept the employer's response, then the tribunal may make a declaration to that effect. The tribunal may also make a 'protective award' to compensate the employees who have been, or are about to be made redundant, which may be made for a period of up to 45 days (the protected period). The pay, following *Susie Radin Ltd v GMB* (see **20.5.5**), should be to deter future employers from failing to follow the consultation requirements (as confirmed in *Sweetin v Coral Racing*). The tribunal will make the award based on the seriousness of the employer's default and on the basis of what is 'just and equitable' in the circumstances. The award is calculated on the basis of one week's pay for each week in the protective period, and the maximum (if this figure is exceeded) is established on the same basis as is for unfair dismissal/redundancy claims (as of 6 April 2018—£508).

There may exist circumstances where the consultation period cannot practicably be held in the time limits identified above. TULRCA 1992, s. 189(6) provides for 'special circumstances' to exist where the employer should not be subjected to the protective award on the basis of this failure (*USDAW v Leancut Bacon Ltd (in liquidation)*).

20.4.5.3 Requirement to inform

Employers that are proposing to dismiss more than 100 employees are required, under TULRCA 1992, s. 193, to inform the Department for Business, Energy & Industrial Strategy at least 90 days before the first redundancy takes place. If there are more than 20 (but less than 100) employees being made redundant, the information requirement is at least 30 days before notice is provided of the termination of employment. Failure to follow the requirements results in a criminal offence being committed that may be punished with a fine (TULRCA 1992, s. 194).

20.4.6 Calculation of the Payment

The remedy that is provided in the case of redundancy is compensation. The ERA 1996, s. 135(1) states that an employer shall pay their employee a redundancy payment if the employee is:

- dismissed by the employer due to redundancy; or
- is eligible for a redundancy payment due to being 'laid off' or the employment constituting short-time.

The payment is subject to a maximum figure identified in the statute (in the same way as unfair dismissal payments are subject to a maximum) (see **21.4.3**)—note, years in employment whilst under the age of 18 are not included in the calculation. However, this statutorily imposed figure will not prevent an employer from establishing its own payments in excess of this amount (which is usually through an enhanced redundancy scheme that reflects the employees' length of service with the firm).

Note that if the employee claims both redundancy and unfair dismissal, and is successful in each, then any awards will be offset so as not to compensate the claimant twice.

> **Consider**
>
> Both Xiu and Jin have been offered alternative work following the notice of redundancy. In each case, the key issue is whether the alternative work is suitable and whether any employee's refusal is reasonable. In Xiu's case, it would appear she has been unreasonable in the refusal—taking an earlier bus into work would not seem (on face value at least) unreasonable. Sasha has been offered alternative employment, yet it is following a regrading which has adversely affected her terms and conditions of employment. Is this suitable and reasonable? If the tribunal holds the offer is suitable and her refusal unreasonable, Sasha will not be considered to have been made redundant. Jin's case is different. Moving hundreds of miles, particularly when the employee has a family settled in the existing area, may be unreasonable unless the employer could offer a substantial inducement to accept (which is, of course, unlikely in cases of redundancy).

20.4.7 Offer of Alternative Employment

As noted earlier, during the employer's procedure for handling the redundancy they should consider if the employee may be suitable for alternative work. This will assist both the employer in not having to make a redundancy payment, and the employee will move to alternative work without having to find employment (which may be difficult). The offer must begin within four weeks of the previous employment ceasing to avoid having to make a redundancy payment (ERA 1996, s. 141(1)). Whilst the employee is not obliged to accept this offer of employment, if they unreasonably refuse an offer of alternative employment they will lose the right to claim a redundancy payment. In *Bainbridge v Westinghouse Brake & Signal Co. Ltd*, an employee who had been based for the previous five years of his employment in Newcastle, and was offered posts in Glasgow and then in Leeds, was not unreasonable in a refusal to accept these offers. His children were situated in local schools, were to undertake examinations, and these issues were taken into consideration when determining reasonableness.

The tribunal will enquire:

1. whether a 'suitable' offer of alternative employment was made (e.g. *Taylor v Kent CC* where a headmaster was offered alternative work in a pool of substitute/mobile teachers (with his pay frozen at his existing level). This was held not to be suitable alternative work.);

2. if this question is answered in the affirmative, was the employee unreasonable in their refusal? (Compare *Rawe v Power Gas Corporation* and *Fuller v Stephanie Bowman (Sales) Co. Ltd.*)

20.4.8 Trial Period of Employment

An employee who accepts the offer of alternative employment is entitled to a trial period to ascertain if the work will be suitable. This trial period may last up to four weeks (ERA 1996, s. 138) and if the employee is dismissed from this position within this trial period, the dismissal will be held as being due to redundancy.

20.5 TRANSFER OF UNDERTAKINGS

When an employer decides to sell part or all of a business, the business (or 'undertaking') and its workforce transfer to the purchaser. The relevant legislation was enacted due to the UK's membership of the European Union, and was first brought into effect in 1981, with an update to the Regulations in 2001, and the most recent legislation (the Transfer of Undertakings (Protection of Employment) Regulations 2006 (TUPE)) taking effect from 6 April 2006. These Regulations were transposed from the Acquired Rights Directive (Council Directive 77/187/EEC) (ARD) that sought to preserve employees' rights and continuity of employment when a business was transferred to a new owner.

As TUPE 2006 is the UK's transposition of the EU Directive (ARD) it covers transfers in the UK. However, the EAT has held that TUPE 2006 may also affect transfers outside of the UK. In *Hollis Metal Industries v GMB and Newell Ltd* involving the transfer of part of a curtain-making business to a new employer in Israel, it was held that the transfer could fall under the TUPE 2006 Regulations, although the EAT did note the potential difficulties in the enforcement of any awards under the law. It has essentially been held that TUPE 2006 would apply in this respect as the transferor was based in the UK and hence this gave the domestic tribunals jurisdiction over the matter.

When the business is transferred to a new owner, and TUPE 2006 is applicable, those employees who were employed 'immediately prior to the transfer' automatically become the employees of the new owner, and they are employed on the same terms and conditions as they held before the transfer (*Litster v Forth Dry Dock and Engineering*). The new employer takes on the obligations and rights of these individuals and any of the collective agreements that had been agreed with the previous employer. Not only are the rights and conditions of the contracts of employment preserved, but any dismissal of an employee (regardless of whether this occurs before or following the transfer) where the sole or principal reason is due to the transfer, is automatically unfair (inserted through The Collective Redundancies and Transfer of Undertakings (Protection of Employment) (Amendment) Regulations 2014, reg. 8(1)(1)). The exception to the finding of an automatically unfair reason for dismissal is where an 'economic, technical or organizational' (ETO) reason exists—consequently, a dismissal in these circumstances may be fair, insofar as the decision is reasonable. The ETO must be the actual reason for the dismissal. If the dismissal is simply connected to the transfer, TUPE will be invoked making the dismissal automatically unfair. See *Manchester College v Hazel*.

20.5.1 A Relevant Transfer

TUPE 2006 preserves the rights of individuals, and continuity of employment, where a relevant transfer has taken place. A relevant transfer consists of two broad categories, the first being of *a transfer of an economic entity that retains its identity* (an 'economic entity' is defined as an 'organized grouping of resources' that has the objective of pursuing an economic activity—reg. 3). This is what may be considered a 'standard' business transfer involving the transfer of the business between the current owner (the transferor) and the new owner (the transferee). An organized grouping must facilitate the exercise of an economic activity which pursues a specific objective—see *Lom Management Ltd v Sweeney*. Further, the grouping must be a conscious/deliberate effort of the employer to put the employees to work on a specific contract for a client, not simply a matter of 'happenstance'—*Seawell Ltd v Cava*.

Hence, from this Regulation, there must be a transfer of a business activity from one owner to the next, and it must consist of the business, or an identifiable part of the business. It is also necessary, for TUPE 2006 to be effective, that the transfer includes a stable economic entity. In assessing these criteria, the business transferred must be likely to continue in the same or some similar aspect of economic activity that was in existence under the previous ownership (*Securicor Guarding Ltd v Fraser Security Services Ltd*). In *Rygaard v Dansk Arbejdsgiverforening* the Court of Justice of the European Union (Court of Justice) identified that this involved some aspect of permanence to the business. TUPE 2006 also includes the transfer of a lease or franchise and in *Daddy's Dance Hall* (see **20.5.3**) the transfer of a lease for a bar and restaurant was still subject to the Regulations. Whilst TUPE 2006 does not apply to transfers of shares (*Brookes and Others v Borough Care Services and CLS Care Services Ltd*), in *Millam v The Print Factory (London) 1991 Ltd* the Court of Appeal held that the two entities must be maintained as separate legal entities to avoid invoking TUPE.

The second form of transfer was added through TUPE 2006, reg. 3, and provides for *changes of service provider* (including organizations such as firms of accountants, lawyers, and so on).

For a transfer of a service to come under the remit of TUPE 2006, the following requirements must be met:

1. there must be an organized grouping of employees;
2. the service must not be a short-term or one-off contract;
3. the client must remain the same;
4. the activities must remain (be fundamentally) the same—they must not become fragmented.

The Regulations consolidate the case law of the Court of Justice to widen the concept of relevant transfer and which take the form of:

1. contracting-out/outsourcing (such as where a service previously undertaken by the client is awarded to a new contractor);
2. re-tendering (such as where a contract for a service is awarded to a new contractor);
3. contracting-in/in-sourcing (such as where a contract with the previous contractor is performed 'in-house').

This is a very interesting aspect of the law as it provides a new dimension to transfers of an undertaking.

> ### Hunt v Storm Communications, Wild Card Public Relations and Brown Brothers Wines (2007)
>
> **Facts:**
>
> Storm (a public relations consultancy firm) was employed to manage the public relations of the firm Brown Brothers Wines (Europe). Ms Hunt was employed by Storm as the account manager and spent approximately 70 per cent of her working hours devoted to the Brown Brothers account. Brown Brothers wished to transfer the account to another firm (Wild Card Public Relations) and informed Storm of this decision in June 2006. On the transfer of the account Storm informed Ms Hunt that she had been transferred to Wild Card under TUPE 2006. Wild Card Public Relations did not agree or wish for Ms Hunt to transfer to its business and claimed she had not been 'dedicated' to the business of Brown Brothers. However, the tribunal held that Ms Hunt was designated an 'organized grouping of resources' under TUPE 2006 and her principal purpose was acting on behalf of the client company. As such the effect of the transfer of the service was that Ms Hunt would transfer to the new firm taking over the Brown Brothers account under the TUPE 2006 Regulations.
>
> **Authority for:**
>
> The case was heard in a tribunal and therefore does not establish a precedent, but it does indicate the implications of the extension of TUPE to service provisions—outsourcing.

20.5.2 The Effect of the Transfer on Contracts of Employment

Upon a relevant transfer, the employees take their contractual rights and continuity of service with them when the transfer is completed. Whilst the transferee has to provide the same rights and continuity to the workers, they are also responsible for any liabilities or claims against the previous employer. Hence employment claims under, for example, equality laws will transfer to the new owner (*DJM International v Nicholas*), as will claims under torts (for example, personal injury—*Bernadine v Pall Mall Services Group Ltd*). As such, reg. 11 of TUPE 2006 places an obligation on the transferor to provide the prospective owner (the transferee) with 'employee liability information' (which following The Collective Redundancies and Transfer of Undertakings (Protection of Employment) (Amendment) Regulations 2014, must be provided at least 28 days before the transfer (reg. 10)) which includes details such as the ages of the employees, the contracts of employment and written particulars, and the firm's grievance procedure and disciplinary details. The transfer of the business also includes the transfer of collective bargaining agreements that had existed before the transfer (reg. 5) and any trade union that had been recognized by the employer before the transfer must also be recognized by the incoming employer (reg. 6).

20.5.2.1 When an employee does not want to transfer

TUPE 2006 protects an employee's terms and conditions of employment. However, there may be situations where the employee does not wish to have their contract transferred to the new employer, and they do not wish to work for the incoming owner. In *Katsikas v Konstantinidis* the Court of Justice held that employees could not be compelled to transfer to a new employer against their will. Regulation 4(7) of TUPE 2006 enables an employee, upon the knowledge of the transfer and the new owner, to inform the transferor or transferee, before the transfer, (and this has been extended to after the transfer—*New ISG Ltd v Vernon*) that they do not wish to transfer. Upon making this statement of their intention not to transfer, the employee's contract of employment ends (although without dismissal), and they cannot claim any remedy connected with a dismissal. There is an exception to this rule regarding refusals not amounting to dismissals. Where the employee refuses to transfer to the new employer under the belief that their conditions of employment will be changed with a resulting detriment being suffered, they may refuse to transfer (resign) and then claim constructive dismissal (*University of Oxford v Humphreys*).

Consider

With regards to Sasha, would your answer change if the reorganization she was affected by was a consequence of a sale of the business to a new owner? Consider changes to the terms of a contract in a redundancy situation compared with similar changes following a TUPE transfer.

20.5.3 Dismissal or Variation to the Contractual Terms and Conditions

The transferee has to recognize the rights of the contract that the employee was subject to prior to the transfer (reg. 5(1)). This has also been held by the Court of Appeal in *Computershare Investor Services v Jackson* to restrict the employees' terms and conditions to those at the time of the transfer, so they did not have access to beneficial terms of the new employer. Employees are entitled to benefits conferred at the date of a transfer and not from the start of their continuous employment. In *Daddy's Dance Hall* it was held that employees cannot be bound by agreements to vary the terms and conditions of employment if the transfer was the reason of the change. This included unilateral changes and those that were agreed by the transferee and the employees (although this is questionable following the Court of Appeal's decision in *Regent Security Services v Power* where it was held that an employee was entitled to rely on changes to their terms and conditions of employment following a transfer). The EAT has also identified that whilst the principle established in *Daddy's Dance Hall* remains, changes to employees' detriment are void, but those to their benefit are allowed (*Power v Regent Security Services Ltd*). This has been included in reg. 4(4) of TUPE 2006, unless there is an 'economic, technical or organizational' reason for the variation—which renders such changes or variations 'not void'. Changes/variations in contracts are not void where they are unrelated to the transfer; where the contract permits a variation; where there is an economic, technical, or organizational reason for the change; and where at least a year has passed since the transfer, the terms which have been varied are contained in a collective agreement, and overall, the changes are no less favourable to the employees.

Regulation 7 of TUPE 2006 also deems dismissals unfair if the sole or principal reason is the transfer itself. There is, again, an exception to this rule if the dismissal was due to an economic, technical, or organizational reason.

Important changes have been made since the enactment of The Collective Redundancies and Transfer of Undertakings (Protection of Employment) (Amendment) Regulations (CRATUPEAR) 2014 which took effect to transfers following 1 January 2014. In relation to collective agreements, whereby the terms and conditions of work affecting individuals could be regulated and agreed between the employer and, for example, a recognized body such as a trade union, the following provisions were applicable. The collective agreement could be established to operate for a given period—such as a five-year term, or it may cease to operate on any given event—such as upon derecognition of the trade union. Importantly in relation to TUPE, the transferee was not allowed to change these terms or the agreement. CRATUPEAR 2014 has amended this situation, first, by making the agreement static after the TUPE transfer, and secondly by enabling the transferee to renegotiate collective agreements which were in operation before (and effective with) the transfer, one year after this transfer (CRATUPEAR 2014, reg. 6), insofar as overall the changes are no less favourable to the affected employees. This simply means that the transferee is bound by the agreement as it stood on the date by which the transfer was concluded—if at a later date (but before ownership passes from the transferor to the transferee) the old employer (the transferor) changes the collective agreement, the new employer (the transferee) is not bound by such changes (CRATUPEAR 2014, reg. 6(2)).

20.5.4 An Economic, Technical, or Organizational Reason

Under reg. 7(3), an otherwise unfair dismissal connected to the transfer may be justified by the new employer if it is due to an economic, technical, or organizational (ETO) reason. Many transfers occur because the business that is the subject of the transfer is not performing as well as it could, or is in financial difficulties. Even if this is not the case, a new employer may have ideas regarding streamlining the business and improving its profitability. As such, there is some scope for them making changes to the organizational structure. Note, however, that this provides the employer with a 'potentially' fair reason to dismiss and they will have to convince the tribunal that the reason was fair. The Regulations do not offer much guidance on how to interpret the ETO, but there is latitude for the new employer to dismiss employees if the business is not profitable with the existing numbers of staff (this would constitute an economic reason) and a most frequent ETO is redundancies (*Gorictree Ltd v Jenkinson*). The new employer may choose to reorganize the management structure of the firm to increase its profitability/viability (an organizational reason), or they may decide that aspects in the production/manufacturing process require alteration (a technical reason) and so on. Following from CRATUPEAR 2014, a redundancy situation (a dismissal) involving the change of location of a business, which used to be held as an unfair dismissal, will now be included as an ETO (although it must still be explained and consulted upon by the employer). What this means for employees is that where the employee refuses to move to a new 'base'/location, this no longer constitutes an automatically unfair dismissal.

20.5.5 The Obligation to Consult Regarding the Transfer

TUPE 2006 does not stipulate any minimum consultation periods, albeit for requiring that consultation occurs (reg. 13). It requires that the employer consults with the affected employees' representatives as to the transfer, its date, and the reason for it; any legal, economic, and social implications for the affected employees; any measures that are to be taken by the employer; and any measures (if there are any) that the new employer will take that may impact on the affected employees (reg. 13(2)). If the employer fails in the duty to consult, both transferor and transferee will be held jointly and severally liable (reg. 15(9)), and if no justification for this failure is presented, the employees or the employee representatives (such as a trade union) may complain to a tribunal and be awarded compensation of up to 13 weeks' pay (TULRCA 1992, s. 189 and TUPE 2006, reg. 16(3)). This award of compensation should be sufficient to deter future employers from disregarding the law (as upheld in *Sweetin v Coral Racing*).

Susie Radin Ltd v GMB (2004)

Facts:

In March 2000 the Union was informed by the employer that the factory may close. In April 2000 letters of redundancy were issued to the employees. Conversations between the employer and the Union were held in June, but the factory closed in July 2000. A claim was made against the employer for protective awards for the affected employees as no meaningful consultation took place.

Authority for:

The Court of Appeal agreed with both the tribunal and EAT that the employer had breached the requirement to consult with the Union prior to any redundancy notices. The level of the award will be based on the seriousness of the employer's breach and it is no defence that consultation would have made no difference to the final result.

There exists a defence for the employer who does not consult due to 'special circumstances' that makes consultation not reasonably practicable (TULRCA 1992, s. 188(7) and TUPE 2006, reg. 15(2)). It should be noted that special circumstances may involve, for example, a sudden or unforeseen reason for the employer's insolvency, but would not be accepted as a reason simply because the employer attempted (unsuccessfully) to trade out of the financial difficulties before going into insolvency.

Clarks of Hove Ltd v Bakers' Union (1978)

Facts:

The employer summarily dismissed 368 of its employees (the majority of its workforce) for the reason of redundancy. On the same day the company ceased trading and appointed a receiver. As no consultations had been conducted with the recognized trade union, the union complained to the tribunal.

Authority for:

The insolvency of an organization will not, of itself, amount to 'special circumstances' for the purpose of excluding the requirement of consultation established in the TULRCA 1992, s. 188.

Employees have the right to request information from their employer regarding changes to terms and conditions of employment, information regarding the business's economic situation, and, of relevance to this section, when the business is involved in a transfer of the undertaking or there is the prospect of redundancies. The Information and Consultation of Employees Regulations 2004 provide that for organizations with 50 or more employees (from 6 April 2008), and where at least 10 per cent of these employees make a valid request, the employer has to set out an agreement as to how and when consultation over the matter will take place (which requires at least 15 employees and a maximum of 2,500 employees). If the employer fails in this request the Central Arbitration Committee can make a declaration that the Regulations have been breached, and they also provide for a penalty payment of up to £75,000 (enforceable in the EAT). In *Amicus v Macmillan Publishers* the EAT made its first judgment imposing a penalty under the Regulations (in this case £55,000) for the employer's 'significant' failure at 'almost every stage of the proceedings'.

CONCLUSION

This chapter has considered issues surrounding ending the employment relationship. When read in conjunction with **Chapter 21**, the individual and employer will be in a position to identify where terminations of employment are lawful, and those situations in which a termination may lead to a claim for breach of contract and/or of statute. **Chapters 20** and **21** should be read together to gain an overview of how the common law and statutory dismissal regulations interact, and to understand employers' responsibilities when the business is being sold. These laws are not simplistic, but neither are they particularly onerous, and awareness enables effective strategies for dismissal to be implemented enabling claims to be avoided; time and money lost (or wasted) in defending a dismissal can be reduced; and poor strategies for dismissals can lead, potentially, to a damaged reputation with the consequential negative impact on industrial relations.

SUMMARY OF MAIN POINTS

Termination

- There are many instances of the employment relationship ending but they will not always amount to a dismissal that would enable a claim for wrongful dismissal. Note, however, that these may give rise to a dismissal and claim under statute.

Wrongful dismissal

- Dismissals with the correct notice period provided, or in response to an individual's breach of the contract, are fair at common law.

- Wrongful dismissal occurs where (e.g.) the employer terminates the contract in breach of the required notice period and without a valid reason.

- To enable a lawful dismissal, the employer must adhere to the contractual notice period. In the absence of any contractual term, the bare statutory minimum applies.

- An employer is only permitted to substitute the notice period with a payment in lieu of notice where the contract allows this through an express term.

- An employer is entitled to dismiss without notice (a **summary dismissal**) where the individual has committed some fundamental breach of the contract.

- The claimant may wish to claim through wrongful dismissal rather than unfair dismissal due to there being fewer qualification criteria (a contract to perform the employment personally is required) and there is no maximum limit to the damages that may be awarded.

- The remedy for wrongful dismissal does not include reinstatement or re-engagement (as with unfair dismissal) but injunctions are available to prevent the employer from breaching the contract of employment.

- An individual dismissed in breach of the contract will be expected to mitigate their losses.

- Contrary to unfair dismissal, after discovered reasons may be used in wrongful dismissal to justify a dismissal.

Redundancy

- Redundancy may involve the employer ceasing to trade or the employee may be surplus to the requirements of the business.

- To qualify, the claimant must have 'employee' status; have been continuously employed with the same employer for at least two years; have been dismissed (and the reason being redundancy); and must not be in one of the excluded categories.

- The employer's redundancy selection policy must be fair and this can be assisted through negotiation with the employees' representatives/the recognized trade union. The policy should follow the ACAS Code of Practice wherever possible.

- There are automatically unfair reasons to dismiss for redundancy that include (e.g.) pregnancy; trade union membership and activities, and so on.

- The employer is obliged to consult with the employees or their representatives over any planned redundancies and the reasons for these.

- To be deemed fair, the employer should consider the employee for any suitable alternative work. If this is offered within four weeks of the redundancy this will prevent any payment having to be made (if the reasonable offer of employment is accepted).

- Employees who take up the offer of alternative work are entitled to a four-week trial period to assess whether the work is actually 'suitable'.

TUPE Regulations

- When businesses are transferred, individuals may have their employment preserved and their contractual rights maintained following the TUPE 2006 Regulations and CRATUPEAR 2014.

- Individuals must have been employed 'immediately prior to the transfer' and there must have been a 'relevant transfer'.

- A relevant transfer requires the transfer of a stable economic entity that retains its identity, with an 'organized grouping of resources'. TUPE 2006 also includes changes of service provider to protect those involved in outsourcing; re-tendering; and in-sourcing.

- The new employer (transferee) becomes liable for any claims/liabilities against the former employer by employees.

- The employee is entitled to refuse to transfer to the new employer and by doing so brings to an end their contract (and hence any application of a restraint of trade clause), but does not amount to a dismissal.

- The employee who has transferred may not be subject to worse terms imposed by the new employer but can benefit from more favourable terms introduced by it.

- A dismissal due to a relevant transfer will be unfair unless the transfer is due to an economic, technical, or organizational reason. This enables the new employer to justify the dismissal as being 'potentially' fair.

- Employers are obliged to consult with employees and their representatives regarding planned redundancies and transfers, unless there exist 'special circumstances' for not consulting.

? SUMMARY QUESTIONS

Essay questions

1. 'The statutory action for unfair dismissal is far superior to a common law action for wrongful dismissal. As such, wrongful dismissal can safely be ignored for all practical purposes.'

   Critically assess the above statement.

2. In the case of *Allen v Flood* (1898) Lord Davey pronounced 'an employer may refuse to employ from the most mistaken, capricious, malicious or morally reprehensible motives imaginable, yet a worker has no right of action. . . . no right to be employed by any particular employer.'

   To what extent does this statement continue to represent the law?

Problem questions

1. Redmount Borough Council (RBC) has an Adult Education Department which has had rising costs over the past few years. Given the budgetary restraints imposed by central government RBC has decided to take measures to reduce its overheads. Part of these measures has resulted in the catering and cleaning functions being transferred to an outside company—'Cleaneasiest Ltd'. There were 10 existing members of the catering and cleaning division of the Adult Education Department and these were transferred to the employment of Cleaneasiest Ltd, although the employees were transferred on a lower hourly rate of pay than enjoyed with RBC.

   Two months into the transfer, RBC were very unhappy with the quality of the service provided by Cleaneasiest Ltd and as such invoked an early termination clause in the contract (which they were entitled to do) and cancelled the contract. The Adult Education Department now wishes to replace Cleaneasiest Ltd with another company Clean-You-Out Ltd. However, Clean-You-Out Ltd is unwilling to take on any of the 10 original employees.

   Advise the employees and their trade union of any rights they may have in relation to the Transfer of Undertakings (Protection of Employment) Regulations 2006.

2. Joshua has been working at (the fictitious) Greenfingers Garden Centres Ltd for eight months. Without any warning he is called into the manager's office and told he is being dismissed immediately for misconduct due to his poor timekeeping. Joshua had been late to work for the two previous mornings but had made the time up during his lunch break and he had not been informed by anyone that his employer was unhappy with his work or his conduct.

   Unknown to the employer, Joshua had been stealing shrubs from Greenfingers and selling these to his friends.

   Advise the parties as to their legal position.

 You will find guidance about how to answer these questions online at www.oup.com/uk/marson5e/.

FURTHER READING

Books and articles

Hall, M. (2005) 'Assessing the Information and Consultation of Employees Regulations' *Industrial Law Journal*, Vol. 34, No. 2, p. 103.

McMullen, J. (2006) 'An Analysis of the Transfer of Undertakings (Protection of Employment) Regulations 2006' *Industrial Law Journal*, Vol. 35, No. 2, p. 113.

Prassl, J. (2013) 'Employee Shareholder 'Status': Dismantling the Contract of Employment' *Industrial Law Journal*, Vol. 42, No. 4, p. 307.

Taylor, S. and Emir, E. (2015) 'Employment Law: An Introduction' (4th Edition) Oxford University Press: Oxford and New York.

Williams, E. (2006) 'TUPE 2006—Mission Accomplished or Mission Impossible?' *Business Law Review*, Vol. 27, No. 7, p. 178.

Websites

https://www.gov.uk/browse/employing-people
The Government's website detailing updates and policy discussions relating to employment matters.

http://www.legislation.gov.uk/ukpga/1992/52/contents
The Trade Union and Labour Relations (Consolidation) Act 1992.

http://www.legislation.gov.uk/uksi/2006/246/contents/made
The Transfer of Undertakings (Protection of Employment) Regulations 2006.

 ONLINE RESOURCES

www.oup.com/uk/marson5e/

For further resources relating to this chapter, including self-test questions, an interactive glossary, and key case flashcards.

21 UNFAIR DISMISSAL AND CONSTRUCTIVE DISMISSAL

Whilst there are numerous potentially fair reasons for an employer to bring an employment relationship to an end, it is possible that an employer may dismiss a qualifying employee in a way the law holds unfair. Such dismissals may be unfair because of the reason used by an employer (substantially unfair) and/or the dismissal may have been handled contrary to legal requirements and hence the employer has failed to follow the correct procedure (procedurally unfair). It is also possible that the employer may fundamentally breach the contract of employment. Where the employee accepts the breach, they may resign and claim unfair dismissal (even though the employee has not been 'dismissed' by the employer). Defending unfair dismissal actions can be expensive for employers, as can be the awards of compensation to the employee. This chapter identifies the correct methods for (fairly) dismissing an employee.

Business Scenario 21

Arjun is the manager of a clothing manufacturer 'Fancy Pants plc'. He learns from the firm's computer records that there have been a number of unauthorized searches of the computer files overnight. There are six employees working the nightshift who have had access to the computer and Arjun believes that at least one of them must have made the searches. None of the six have had legitimate reasons to use the computer, and importantly to Arjun, the files searched contained confidential company information regarding both commercial and personnel details.

The computer system and it files are password protected and none of the six should have known about the password. Company security is very important to Arjun and he views unauthorized access as very serious. Arjun interviews the six, but each deny responsibility and knowledge of who may have accessed the computer. Arjun suspects that these workers are lying, and further that some or all of them must have seen or heard something.

The six have worked for the firm for 10 years and one of them, Paul, has recently been promoted because of his exemplary service. During his enquiries into the unauthorized computer access Arjun discovers that another of the six, John, lives with Mana the daytime computer operator. Mana is currently working under a 36-month fixed-term contract, of which she has completed two years, and Arjun believes that she may have provided John with the password. On this belief, Arjun dismisses Mana immediately.

Arjun seeks your advice as he wishes to dismiss everyone except Paul, and he is particularly suspicious of John. Arjun also brings along a copy of Mana's contract which does not contain any provision for early termination.

- Explain what is meant by the term 'unfair dismissal' **(21.2)**

- Apply the tests for qualification for protection against unfair dismissal **(21.2.2–21.2.2.4)**

- Explain the potentially fair reasons to justify dismissal under the Employment Rights Act 1996 **(21.2.3–21.2.3.5)**

- Identify the automatically unfair reasons to dismiss an employee **(21.2.4)**

- Explain the use and application of the ACAS Code on dismissal and grievance procedures **(21.2.5.2)**

- Determine how a tribunal assesses the reasonableness of an employer's decision to dismiss **(21.2.6)**

- Explain the concept of constructive unfair dismissal **(21.3)**

- Identify and apply the remedies of compensation, reinstatement, and re-engagement following a successful unfair dismissal claim **(21.4–21.4.3.3)**.

21.1 INTRODUCTION

Having identified the tests adopted by the courts and tribunals to establish employment status, and having considered the common law rights when an employment relationship is ended, this chapter continues by considering the termination of employment. Termination of employment is governed by statutory measures (**unfair dismissal**) and the common law (wrongful dismissal), and each of these provisions outline important factors when the contract is to be ended. Being aware of the procedures involved in each of these areas of law will ensure terminations can take effect without unnecessary recourse to court/tribunal action, saving time and money.

21.2 UNFAIR DISMISSAL (THE STATUTORY ROUTE)

Before 1971 there was no statutory right to protection against unfair dismissal. In 1971 the Industrial Relations Act was enacted, and before then an employer could dismiss an individual for any reason and the only protections available were those established in the contract and enforced through the common law. Unlike wrongful dismissal claims that are predominately heard in the courts, unfair dismissal claims are heard exclusively in Employment Tribunals. However, Employment Tribunals may also hear wrongful dismissal actions involving claims of up to £25,000 in compensation (Employment Tribunals Act 1996, s. 3).

Unfair dismissal is largely governed by the Employment Rights Act 1996 (ERA), and specifically under this Act, s. 94(1) provides the right not to be unfairly dismissed. ERA 1996 establishes the qualifications that the individual must satisfy before they have the right to protection under the Act; the 'potentially fair' reasons to justify a dismissal; the 'automatically unfair' reasons to dismiss; and how awards are to be assessed following a successful claim for unfair dismissal. A flow chart of the process of unfair dismissal claims is contained in **Figure 21.1**.

Figure 21.1 Process of unfair dismissal claims

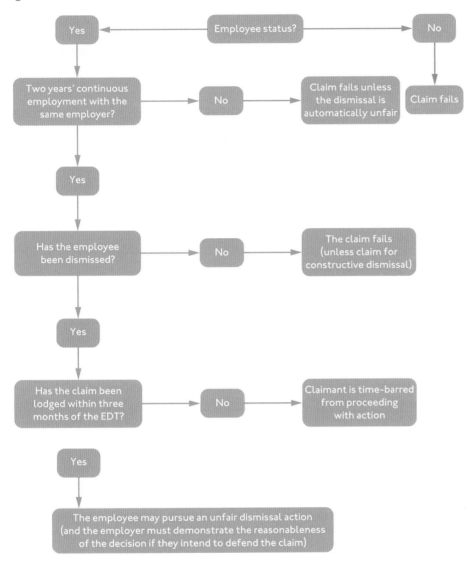

21.2.1 Excluded Groups from Unfair Dismissal Protection

Only an individual with 'employee' status is entitled to bring a claim for unfair dismissal. Those without this status (such as independent contractors), but whose contract of employment has been terminated may (if the contract has been breached) pursue a claim for wrongful dismissal. There are also groups of individuals who are not entitled to claim, and these include share fishermen (s. 199(2)); employees in the police service (s. 200); and persons excluded for reasons of national security (s. 193—see *Council of Civil Service Unions v Minister for the Civil Service* regarding the right to join a trade union).

21.2.2 Qualifications for Protection under Unfair Dismissal

ERA 1996 establishes who qualifies for protection under the Act. These qualifications have to be strictly adhered to and are only removed in situations involving 'automatically' unfair reasons to dismiss. If the individual does not qualify then there is no point in pursuing a claim under unfair dismissal:

1. the individual must have 'employee' status;
2. they must have been continuously employed by the same employer for at least two years;
3. they must have been dismissed (unfairly);
4. the claim must be submitted to a tribunal within three months of the Effective Date of Termination.

It should also be noted that, as part of the Government's initiative towards alternative forms of dispute resolution, the case may be heard by an arbitrator under the ACAS Arbitration Scheme, as opposed to the case proceeding to a tribunal.

21.2.2.1 Employee status

If there is no disagreement between the individual and the employer that the individual is an employee, then this test is satisfied and the issue of qualification continues to the next stage. If, however, there is disagreement, then **Chapter 19** demonstrates the methods used to determine employment status.

21.2.2.2 Continuously employed for at least two years

ERA 1996 identifies what will amount to 'continuous' service, and under s. 212(1): 'Any week during the whole or part of which an employee's relations with his employer are governed by a contract of employment counts in computing the employee's period of employment.' If the employee fails to work for the employer for at least one week or more, then the period of continuous service is broken. There are, however, exceptions to this rule. If the individual is absent due wholly or partially to childbirth or pregnancy and she later returns to work, these weeks count towards continuous employment (s. 212(2)); if the individual is incapable of work as a consequence of illness or injury (s. 212(3)(a)— to a maximum of 26 weeks), if they are absent due to a temporary cessation of work (s. 212(3)(b)), and if they are absent in circumstances that, by arrangement or custom, are regarded as continuing in the employment of the employer, then these weeks will also contribute to 'continuous employment'.

The employee does not have to work at the same physical location or necessarily in the same capacity throughout this period; the test is that there is a continuous contract of employment between the parties.

21.2.2.3 The employee must have been dismissed

The law requires that for a successful claim of unfair dismissal, it is the duty of the employee to demonstrate they have been dismissed. Under ERA 1996, s. 95, dismissal occurs in the following circumstances: the contract of employment is terminated (with or without notice) ((1)(a)); a fixed-term contract has expired and not been renewed ((1)(b)); or the employee ends the contract due to an act of **constructive dismissal** by the employer ((1)(c)). In *Futty v Brekkes* the employer told his employee to 'fuck off' which the employee interpreted as his notice of dismissal. Generally, the words used to constitute a dismissal will be interpreted as how a 'reasonable employee' would have understood them—see *Tanner v Kean* for a discussion of this point.

21.2.2.4 The effective date of termination

Determining the Effective Date of Termination (EDT) of the contract, which is clearly applicable to the rule that claims must be submitted to the tribunal within three months of this date, is outlined in s. 97 of ERA 1996.

Miller v Community Links Trust Ltd (2007)

Facts:

Mr Miller was submitting his claim for unfair dismissal and did so via the Employment Tribunal Service website. A disclaimer on the website identified that only where a receipt email is received would the ET1 claim form be considered as 'submitted'. Miller's claim was sent at 23:59:59 on the final day of the three-month limit and the confirmation email was received at 00:00:08 the next day.

Authority for:

The employer argued the claimant was time-barred from having the claim heard and the tribunal agreed. The submission was nine seconds late and as it was reasonably practicable for the submission to be sent on time, there was no justification for extending the period. The EAT agreed with the tribunal. Allowing the claim to be heard in these circumstances would cause delay and prejudice, and there was a public interest in conducting cases expeditiously.

The date of dismissal is assessed objectively on the facts of the case, and it is not permissible for the parties to reach an agreement between themselves as to the date (*Fitzgerald v University of Kent at Canterbury*). If a period of notice is given, the EDT will take effect when the notice period ends, not when the notice was given ((1)(a)). If no notice is provided, the EDT takes effect from the date on which termination was effective ((1)(b)); and for those employed under a fixed-term contract, if this is not renewed, the EDT is effective from the date on which the term expires (1(c)). Where the contract expressly allows for a payment in lieu of notice, the EDT will be considered to be effective from the last day worked (*Leech v Preston BC*).

21.2.3 Justification for Dismissal: Potentially Fair Reasons to Dismiss

Having established that the employee qualifies for protection under the Act, s. 98 of ERA 1996 outlines the reasons in which it may be acceptable, if reasonable on the facts, for the employer to dismiss the employee. The employer may explain the decision for dismissal as being potentially fair if the reason or, on the basis of more than one reason being presented the principal reason, is due to:

- the capability or qualifications of the employee (s. 98(2)(a));
- the conduct of the employee (s. 98(2)(b));
- that the employee was made redundant (s. 98(2)(c));

- that to continue the employment would amount to a contravention of a statute (s. 98(2)(d));
- some other substantial reason of a kind to justify dismissal (s. 98(1)(b));

Section 92 of ERA 1996 provides that a dismissed employee may request for the reason for the dismissal to be provided in writing. This will assist the employee in attempting to establish a defence based on the employer's assertion under s. 98. If the employer refuses, or fails to respond, then the tribunal may award the employee two weeks' pay. The employer may select as many of the reasons under s. 98 as they wish. However, the more that are chosen, the more evidence that will have to be provided to ensure the dismissal is fair. Indeed, in *Smith v City of Glasgow Council*, the employer offered three reasons for the employee's dismissal due to incapability, but as one of them could not be proven, the House of Lords held that the employee was unfairly dismissed. It was not possible for the court to distinguish if this reason was any less or more serious than the other two submitted.

21.2.3.1 Capability/qualifications

ERA 1996 identifies that the issue of capability should have regard to 'skill, aptitude, health or any other physical or mental quality' (s. 98(3)), and qualifications are ' . . . any degree, diploma or other academic, technical or professional qualification relevant to the position held'. It is necessary to look to the contract of employment and to what tasks the employee actually performed at work, and then consider the general standard of performance required, whether that standard was being met, and if not, how similar employees were treated.

Capability, as a reason for dismissal, generally focuses on whether the employee becomes ill and cannot perform their tasks, or if the employee is incompetent (or 'becomes' incompetent—perhaps by being promoted to a management position and not having the skills to adequately perform the job). This also involves the employer's belief of incapability rather than proof—per Denning LJ: 'Whenever a man is dismissed for incapacity or incompetence it is sufficient that the employer honestly believes on reasonable grounds that the man is incapable or incompetent. It is not necessary for the employer to prove that he is in fact incapable or incompetent.'

Alidair Ltd v Taylor (1978)

Facts:

Taylor was engaged as a pilot for the airline. On landing, he forgot to lower the landing gear and this caused the plane to crash. The employer dismissed him on the grounds of capability.

Authority for:

The Court of Appeal held that although this was one offence committed by the pilot who had an otherwise unblemished career, this 'spectacular' error was sufficiently serious to justify a dismissal.

Importantly, when considering the fairness of a dismissal, the tribunal will be looking at whether the employer raised any complaints or concerns with the employee to enable them to either change their practices or identify problems they had. The use of warnings,

> **Consider**
>
> Arjun suspects that one of the six members of staff have accessed the computer system. He has no proof of this, therefore he suspects one or more of them is guilty of misconduct. In the next section, consider how the law will allow Arjun to fairly investigate his suspicions.

following consultation regarding areas of difficulty, enables the employee to take appropriate action, but also ensures good industrial relations. It enables the employee to be aware of the employer's concern without simply being called into a disciplinary/dismissal meeting. Such discussions may be useful to identify a lack of appropriate skill or merely a lack of effort, and all alternatives to a dismissal should be explored.

21.2.3.2 Conduct

Here the issue is the misconduct of the employee and it can pose many problems for an employer in determining the facts surrounding the incident, and deciding how to react to it. Typical examples include fighting, stealing, misuse of company property (examples of *gross* misconduct), and poor timekeeping, unauthorized absences from work, or general disregard for instructions given fairly and lawfully by the employer (misconduct). Gross misconduct generally refers to a one-off serious offence that may of itself justify a dismissal, whereas misconduct may be a 'lesser' offence when considered in isolation, but when this culminates over a period of time it becomes sufficiently serious to (potentially) justify a termination of the contract. Gross misconduct may be closely aligned with gross negligence and can involve inaction as well as conduct itself.

> ### *Adesokan v Sainsbury's Supermarkets Ltd (2017)*
>
> **Facts:**
>
> The claimant was a regional manager for Sainsbury's. He received information that a manager in the organization's human resources department had issued an email with the intention of negatively interfering with a significant management consultation. Whilst he knew of the email, he took no action. As a result, and following a disciplinary hearing, his (in)action was considered to be grossly negligent, and was 'tantamount to gross misconduct'. As such, he was dismissed.
>
> **Authority for:**
>
> In an action for breach of contract the Court of Appeal agreed with the assessment in the High Court that although this was a case of inaction, it was so serious as to breach the trust and confidence between the parties. The Court of Appeal continued that whilst courts should not easily conclude that a failure to act will establish gross misconduct, the facts here were of a person in a senior position and this justified a dismissal.

To ensure that the employer conducts meetings and disciplinary hearings in a correct manner and in a way that is likely to be accepted by the tribunal, it is wise to follow the

ACAS Code of Practice 1 on Disciplinary and Grievance Procedures (2009). This is not 'law', but tribunals refer to it and it is good industrial practice to follow the guidance. If the employer identifies that the procedures as set out in the Code will be followed in circumstances involving dismissal/disciplinary action, and this is made clear to the workforce and any representative organizations, then concerns and ill-feeling may be avoided. The Code states that disciplinary procedures should be provided in writing and made available to the workforce (perhaps in a works handbook, human resources department accessible by the workers, and so on); it should clearly identify to whom the procedures apply and what sanctions are available to the employer; it should identify who in the organization is competent to decide and apply any sanctions; it should identify the investigatory procedures to be adopted in misconduct cases; it should ensure the employee is aware of their right to attend a disciplinary meeting and to be accompanied (Employment Relations Act 1999, s. 10); and it should enable an employee to appeal against decisions. These steps are not particularly onerous, and by following them all parties are aware of how a situation/allegation of misconduct will be investigated and how any decision will be determined.

Under the common law, a gross misconduct justifies a summary dismissal, but it is perhaps advisable for an employer to investigate the incident, follow ACAS and contractual procedures, and then conclude with a decision as to dismissal or disciplinary action short of dismissal. This process may not take as long as it may be thought, and it ensures that all available evidence is gathered and the relevant investigation is conducted. Further, it ensures that the employer has proof of their reasonable belief that led to the action against an employee. This is a particularly important aspect of misconduct.

Consider

The employer need not *prove* that the employee is guilty of the alleged misconduct, but rather the employer need only demonstrate that they had reasonable grounds on which to hold/maintain belief of misconduct. Insofar as Arjun follows the rules laid down in *BHS v Burchell*, he does not require actual proof of the employees committing the unauthorized access.

British Home Stores v Burchell (1978)

Facts:

The case involved an employee who had been dismissed on the employer's suspicion that theft from the store had been taken place. There was a lack of firm evidence of the theft and the tribunal found for the claimant, who was then reinstated. The employer appealed against the finding and the Employment Appeal Tribunal (EAT) established the points that became known as the 'Burchell principles'.

Authority for:

The Burchell principles provide that due to the nature of employment relationships and the trust necessary between the parties, an employer need not necessarily have concrete

→

evidence of an employee's alleged wrongdoing to justify a dismissal, but rather reasonable grounds for holding the belief.

As such, to ensure the employer can demonstrate that they did hold reasonable grounds for honestly believing the employee was guilty of the alleged offence they must:

1. honestly believe the employee is guilty;
2. have reasonable grounds on which to hold this belief;
3. have carried out as much investigation into the matter as was reasonable in all the circumstances of the case (per Arnold J in *BHS v Burchell*).

These tests are particularly apt in cases involving an allegation of misconduct such as in *Burchell*, but may be less strictly adhered to when the facts of the issue are not in dispute.

What is the situation where more than one employee may have been involved in a misconduct? The following cases demonstrate the options available to an employer with guidance from the courts.

Monie v Coral Racing Ltd (1980)

Facts:

The claimant worked as an area manager of 19 betting shops owned by the employer. Only the manager and his assistant had access to the company's safe, which held considerable amounts of money. The manager was on annual leave when his assistant discovered there was a substantial sum of money missing. The employer conducted an investigation revealing no evidence of a break-in to the property or that the safe had been forcibly opened (indicative of theft). Therefore, as neither the manager nor his assistant accepted responsibility or could be identified as the perpetrator of the offence, it was held that both could be dismissed for misconduct.

Authority for:

It was reasonable for an employer to dismiss two workers for suspicion of theft where there existed solid and sensible grounds on which the employer could reasonably suspect dishonesty; and the employer did not attempt to subsequently rely on a different reason for the dismissal.

Consider

There exist situations, as with Arjun's staff, where a group of employees may be considered to have been involved in misconduct. In cases where it is reasonable for the employer to assume that all or one of them were involved, yet following an investigation identification of the actual perpetrator(s) cannot be achieved, all of the group may be dismissed. Arjun would, following *Parr v Whitbread*, be able to dismiss all six employees given the circumstances presented in the scenario.

Parr v Whitbread (1990)

Facts:

Parr was employed as a branch manager of the firm and was dismissed, along with three other employees, when £4,600 was stolen from the employer's shop. It was concluded from an investigation that the theft indicated an 'inside job' and all of the employees were interviewed. They were given the opportunity to admit the offence, but declined to do so, and hence, by being unable to identify the actual culprit (indeed if there was just one), the employer decided to dismiss all four. The EAT held that the dismissals were fair as the act of theft amounted to a gross misconduct.

Authority for:

Where a group of employees could have a committed a particular offence, the tribunal will find the dismissal of all the group fair where:

1. a dismissal for that offence would have been justified;
2. the employer conducted a reasonable investigation and held a proper procedure;
3. the employer reasonably believed the offence could have been committed by more than one person;
4. the employer has reasonably identified those who could have committed the act;
5. the employer cannot reasonably identify the perpetrator.

Note that potential problems may exist where an employer cannot identify which of the employees has committed an offence, but decides to dismiss members of the group selectively. When one or more of the employees in the group are retained or re-hired despite the investigation not identifying the employee(s) responsible, there must exist solid and sensible grounds for the retention or re-hiring of certain members.

What will amount to a reasonable investigation will depend on the individual circumstances of the case, but factors such as the interviewing of any identifiable witnesses; the collation of documents and their assessment; and providing the employee with an opportunity to answer any charges put to them, and to genuinely consider their responses before any decision is made, will point towards a reasonable investigation. Of course, in situations involving theft or other activities with a criminal element, the tribunals have held that the employer may treat a guilty verdict in a court as proof that the employee did commit the offence (*P v Nottinghamshire CC*).

21.2.3.3 Redundancy

Redundancy, whilst covered under its own legislation, is included in ERA 1996, s. 98 as another form of dismissal. It enables a claim under unfair dismissal legislation where the employee considers that they have been unfairly selected for redundancy; where no warning or consultation had taken place; or where redeployment had not been considered. Unfair selection may occur where one or more employees have been selected for redundancy in breach of a customary or agreed procedure (e.g. an agreement between an employer and trade union to use a selection process such as 'last in, first out'; voluntary agreements, and so on); or if the employee was selected in connection with trade union membership. When choosing the employees for redundancy without the cessation of the business, the employer is strongly advised to draw up objective criteria to be applied and which could be used to defend a claim of unfair selection.

21.2.3.4 Contravention of a statute

A further potentially fair reason to dismiss is where to continue to employ the employee would be to break the law. In such a situation, the contract could be frustrated due to a subsequent law (such as the enactment of legislation prohibiting the employment of foreign nationals) or a change in the employee's situation that makes continued employment in the same capacity contrary to legislation.

Four Seasons Healthcare Ltd v Maughan (2005)

Facts:

A care home nurse was suspended regarding an alleged assault on a resident.

Authority for:

The EAT held that under the circumstances, the employer had the option to dismiss the employee for gross misconduct. It chose not to and decided instead to suspend them while on bail. Employers in this situation could select to suspend or dismiss because of reg. 19 of the Care Homes Regulations 2001 where either the employer or a criminal court held the employee not to be 'fit to work'. When suspending an employee pending criminal investigation, wages had to be paid.

Dismissal may be more likely to be due to some action by the employee rather than legislative changes. There are many situations that could lead to this potentially fair reason to dismiss, but a common example is where the employee has a driving element as part of their duties and they receive a driving ban. As such, to allow the employee to drive without a licence on the employer's engagement would be to contravene the law.

21.2.3.5 Some other substantial reason

In the absence of a reason fitting into one of the previous categories, s. 98 provides for 'some other substantial reason [(SOSR)] of a kind such as to justify the dismissal of an employee holding the position which the employee held' to be forwarded as a reason for the dismissal. There has been a very wide interpretation of the concept of what would amount to SOSR. In the past, tribunals have held that an employee whose spouse was an employee of one of the employer's competitors permitted a dismissal; a homosexual man was dismissed from his job at a residential holiday camp due to a potentially negative reaction from parents on discovering his sexuality (*Saunders v Scottish National Camps Association*); and an employee's refusal to agree to the inclusion of a restraint of trade clause in his employment contract was deemed SOSR.

RS Components v Irwin (1973)

Facts:

Mr Irwin was an electronic component salesman who was asked to agree to a new contract which included a restrictive covenant. Irwin was threatened with dismissal if he refused to agree to the new term. Following his dismissal, Irwin claimed this was unfair.

→

> **Authority for:**
>
> The employer argued the dismissal was fair for 'some other substantial reason' and this was accepted at appeal. The employer had been subject to several ex-employees leaving the business with valuable proprietary information and they were entitled to protect this through a reasonable restrictive covenant (also referred to as a restraint of trade clause).

In *Scott v Richardson* the EAT held that the tribunal did not have to be satisfied that the commercial decision of the employer was sound, but rather the test was whether the employer believed it to be so.

SOSR may also amount to a situation where an employee is dismissed because their attitude at work is sufficiently unpleasant and disruptive that it breaches the implied duty of trust and confidence (*Perkin v St George's Healthcare NHS Trust*). As noted earlier, non-renewal of a fixed-term contract will be deemed a dismissal for the purposes of ERA 1996. However, such a non-renewal may be justified on the basis of SOSR if the employer can demonstrate (e.g.) a business reason for the non-renewal, and that they acted fairly in the circumstances (*Terry v East Sussex CC*).

21.2.4 Automatically Unfair Reasons to Dismiss

The qualification of two years' continuous service to gain access to unfair dismissal protection is removed in certain circumstances that the legislators considered should be protected from the moment the employee begins work. Whilst this is not an exhaustive list (if for no other reason than the list changes depending on the public policy rationale of the Government) some of the most significant include:

- dismissals due to the pregnancy of the worker or any related illness (ERA 1996, s. 99);
- dismissals due to a spent conviction under the Rehabilitation of Offenders Act 1974;
- dismissals due to trade union membership or activities (TULRCA 1992, s. 238A(2));
- dismissal on transfer of an undertaking (TUPE 2006, reg. 7);
- dismissal because the employee took steps to avert danger to health and safety at work (ERA 1996, s. 100);
- dismissal through an unfair selection for redundancy (ERA 1996, s. 105);
- dismissal in connection with the employee asserting a statutory right (ERA 1996, s. 104);
- dismissals where the employee has made a protected public interest disclosure (ERA 1996, s. 103A), as provided through the Public Interest Disclosure Act 1998.

21.2.5 The Procedures for a Fair Dismissal

Unfair dismissal legislation outlines the procedures that have to be followed in order to enable a 'fair' dismissal. The legislators did not want, and realistically could not create, a situation where an employer had to continue employing an individual against their will. The legislation provides for a series of reasons (potentially fair reasons to dismiss) that the employer can utilize in deciding when to dismiss (substantially fair reasons).

The legislation, through increasing intervention by Parliament, has provided for the use of correct procedures that will promote fairness and 'natural justice', and lead to the resolution of disputes in the workplace with recourse to tribunals. An employer that fails to follow these procedures may have to pay compensation (unnecessarily) to the employee, or it may even lead to a successful claim against them for dismissal (procedurally unfair reasons).

Consider

Has Arjun followed the correct procedure when investigating the incident of unauthorized computer access? A dismissal can be either (or indeed both) substantially unfair or procedurally unfair. Therefore Arjun needs to follow the ACAS procedural rules and to recognize the employee's right to be accompanied at a disciplinary/dismissal meeting.

21.2.5.1 The right to be accompanied at grievance and disciplinary hearings

On the basis of an allegation against the employee that may lead to disciplinary action or a dismissal (in a matter in which there is duty by the employer in relation to the worker—s. 13(5)), the employer is required to investigate the facts before taking action. A disciplinary hearing is defined under s. 13(4) as (a) the administration of a formal warning to a worker by his employer; (b) the taking of some other action in respect of a worker by his employer; or (c) the confirmation of a warning issued or some other action taken. Part of this action may involve interviewing the employee to ascertain the facts surrounding the incident in question. If this is part of a fact-finding exercise, then the employer can request the employee to attend alone. However, the legislative provisions apply when the situation escalates to the possibility of issuing a warning or some other form of discipline.

London Underground Ltd v Ferenc-Batchelor (2003)

Facts:

Ms Ferenc-Batchelor alleged a failure by the employer to allow her to be accompanied to a disciplinary hearing which could have led to an informal oral warning. She had been involved in an incident where she had incorrectly allowed a train into a station after going through a red light. When she asked to be allowed to be accompanied at the meeting, Ferenc-Batchelor was told that 'trade union representation was not allowed at this level'.

Authority for:

The nature of the 'informal oral warning' hearing was not in reality anything other than a formal warning hearing. The findings of it would be confirmed in writing and have effect on an employee's record for 12 months. As such, the employer breached the Employment Relations Act 1999 when denying the employee the right to be accompanied.

The Employment Relations Act 1999, ss. 10–13, as amended, introduced the right of a 'worker' to be accompanied to such meetings by a colleague (s. 10(3)(c)) or a trades union official (even if they are not employed by the same employer as the interviewee—10(3)(a) and (b)). This colleague or trades union official has increased rights to represent the employee, such as establishing the employee's case and presenting points, but is restricted from answering direct questions to the employee (10(2)(b)), who must address these questions personally. However, despite a narrow interpretation of this requirement, the ability to have a colleague or trades union official accompany the worker is a minimum, not an exhaustive list. There may be advantages for an employer, when requesting an individual to attend a disciplinary meeting, to allow that individual to be accompanied by, for example, their parent or a friend. Following an employer's failure (or threat of failure) to comply with the requirement for the individual to be accompanied, a tribunal may award up to two weeks' pay as compensation (£1016 (6 April 2018)—s. 11(3)).

21.2.5.2 The ACAS code on disciplinary and dismissal procedures

ACAS, the Advisory, Conciliation and Arbitration Service, produced a code of practice and procedural fairness (Code of Practice 1—Disciplinary and Grievance Procedures) identifying how the employer and employee should conduct themselves during grievance/disciplinary matters. The code is not law, but it is referred to by tribunals when assessing the reasonableness of an employer's decision to dismiss.

Features to be considered by the parties in the event of disciplinary/grievance matters are:

* The parties should raise issues quickly and these should be dealt with in a prompt manner—with no unreasonable delays.
* The employer should carry out a reasonable investigation to ascertain the facts.
* The employer should present their concerns to the employee and give them an opportunity to respond before a decision is made.
* The employer should follow the Employment Relations Act 1999, ss. 10–13 regarding the right of the employee to be accompanied at formal disciplinary/grievance meetings by a colleague/trades union official.
* An appeal against the decision of the employer should be offered to the affected employee.

21.2.5.3 Failure to follow the code

The tribunal will consider whether the parties followed the code in determining the reasonableness of any action taken in such proceedings. The tribunal will be able to raise or lower any award by up to 25 per cent for an unreasonable failure to follow the code. The procedures apply to situations involving disciplinary measures and dismissals, and as such, if the employee unreasonably failed to participate in the proceedings, and they are held to have been unfairly dismissed, any award of compensation may be reduced by 25 per cent.

The early conciliation process

Given the austerity measures introduced in the legal system of England and Wales in 2010 which began the process of introducing fees and reducing legal aid for many employment-related disputes, claims by an employee alleging unfair dismissal are prohibitively expensive and often involve considerable stress on the employee. Through ACAS, the early conciliation process was established to enable the employee to avoid the costs and associated expenses of taking the issue to be heard before an employment tribunal (The Employment Tribunals (Early Conciliation: Exemptions and Rules of Procedure) (Amendment) Regulations 2014

(S.I. No. 847)). The intention of the scheme is for the parties to agree a settlement without the need for the matter to be resolved by a tribunal. Available since 6 April 2014, and mandatory (ACAS must be notified of the dispute before a claim is lodged at a tribunal) since 6 May 2014, it has become a legal requirement that the employee and employer attempt to resolve the matter which has led to the dismissal through conciliation before allowing the employee to lodge the claim at an employment tribunal. On the basis that:

- the employee refuses to enter into conciliation; or
- the employee wishes to enter into conciliation but the employer refuses;
- the employee and employer cannot reach an agreement; or
- the employer is insolvent

the employee is required to obtain a certificate from ACAS to enable the employee to lodge the claim at an employment tribunal.

Both parties, initially, have a period of up to one calendar month to explore a resolution to the dispute with the aid of an ACAS conciliator who attempts to assist the parties in reaching an amicable resolution to the dispute. It is important to note that where there exists more than one respondent, the claimant employee is required only to submit one early conciliation form naming one respondent. Additional respondents may be added later without the requirement to submit another form(s).

Employees may be concerned that time spent involved with conciliation will affect the three months' time limit for the employee to lodge their claim at the employment tribunal following the dismissal. However, this time limit is suspended during the conciliation process and indeed the employee may contact ACAS to begin the conciliation process at any time following the dismissal until the point where the case is heard at the tribunal. The service is independent, free, and applies to many employment disputes including unfair dismissal, discrimination and equal pay, redundancy, and associated selection procedures.

21.2.6 Reasonableness of a Dismissal

The employer may present a potentially fair reason, as outlined in s. 98 of ERA 1996, to justify the dismissal. However, it is necessary for the employer to demonstrate that they acted fairly in deciding to dismiss the employee. This burden of demonstrating reasonableness is neutral between the parties and, under s. 98(4) ERA 1996, the tribunal will hear the evidence and determine, taking into account all relevant circumstances, the issue of reasonableness. Reasonableness will include aspects such as the size of the business and the employer's access to assistance in the administration of discipline and investigations. It is absolutely essential to remember that in determining reasonableness, the tribunal must not consider what action it would have taken, and if the employer's action fell outside of this, subsequently to hold it as unreasonable. Hence the tribunal will assess the evidence forwarded by the employer and consider the employer's response to this and whether their action fell into the band of reasonable responses.

Iceland Frozen Foods Ltd v Jones (1982)

Facts:

Mr Jones, a nightshift foreman, was dismissed for failing to operate the company's security system and for attempting to deceive the company into making additional overtime payments.

→

Authority for:

The EAT identified the correct test of the reasonableness of an employer's decision to dismiss. It is whether the decision is within the band of reasonable responses to the employee's conduct which a reasonable employer would adopt.

The employer's disciplinary procedures are important as they enable the parties to have an awareness of how decisions will be taken in the event of the employer considering the dismissal of an employee. This sometimes caused problems when the procedure was not used (even before the advent of the Employment Act 2002), even though ACAS has frequently produced codes of practice that tribunals used in their deliberations on the reasonableness of an employer's actions. The EAT considered that in cases where following the procedure would have made no material difference to the decision of the employer in dismissing an employee, a failure to follow the procedure would not necessarily render the dismissal unfair. However, this has been changed following the House of Lord's judgment in the seminal case of *Polkey v AE Dayton Services*.

Polkey v AE Dayton Services Ltd (1987)

Facts:

Dayton Services decided to make three of its four van drivers redundant and informed Mr Polkey he was one of the three. Polkey complained of unfair dismissal as the employers had failed in their duty to consult before making the decision.

Authority for:

The House of Lords considered that the key issue is the employer's reason for the dismissal and whether this was sufficient to justify a dismissal. This was an unfair dismissal because of the (procedural) failures, but a reduction in the compensatory award would be made if the employer's decision would not have altered had the correct procedures been followed.

The Lords decided that whether the employer had acted reasonably should be determined on the facts that they had available when the decision was made—assuming, of course, that the employer had conducted a reasonable investigation and attempted to gather all the facts surrounding the issue. Without the procedure being followed, the facts would probably be incomplete and the decision of the employer would be flawed.

Consider

Imagine that Arjun, following a further period of investigation, discovers that Mana did give the password to John to access the computer system. As this occurred after the termination of her contract, how does the law of unfair dismissal affect Mana's claim?

21.2.7 After Discovered Reasons

When an employee is dismissed, and claims that the dismissal was unfair under the relevant legislation, the employer has to identify what evidence they possessed at the time of making the decision that would enable one of the potentially fair reasons under s. 98 of ERA 1996 to be invoked. The employer will, however, only be able to produce the evidence they had at the time of deciding to dismiss that can justify the decision and enable it to fall into one of the bands of reasonable responses. Facts that surface after the decision *cannot* be used in justification. These are often referred to as after discovered reasons and whilst, if presented at the tribunal, may lead to a reduction in any damages awarded, they cannot make an unfair dismissal fair.

W Devis & Sons Ltd v Atkins (1977)

Facts:

Mr Atkins was the manager at the employer's abattoir and was dismissed for failing to observe their purchasing policy. He was offered a £6,000 ex gratia payment but before he could accept, it was withdrawn. The employer informed Atkins that they became aware of his misconduct (of which they were unaware prior to their dismissal of him).

Authority for:

The House of Lords held that an employer may not justify misconduct of an employee which is only identified after the decision to dismiss is made. However, it would be relevant when the tribunal assesses the compensatory amount.

21.3 CONSTRUCTIVE UNFAIR DISMISSAL

Consider

Arjun is considering dismissing all the staff who were working the nightshift and who could have accessed the computer system. However, if his actions were procedurally unfair and if this amounted to a fundamental breach of the contract of employment, the affected employees are allowed to treat the breach as a repudiation, resign, and claim constructive unfair dismissal without an actual 'dismissal' having taken place. Constructive dismissal further applies to situations of employers unilaterally changing a contract of employment or affecting terms and conditions.

It should be borne in mind that constructive dismissal is a mechanism that enables a claim under unfair dismissal (see **Figure 21.2** on p. 544 for a flow chart of the process of a claim). As noted earlier, one of the qualifications to claim under the statutory protection of unfair dismissal is for the claimant to demonstrate that they were dismissed

Figure 21.2 Process of a claim

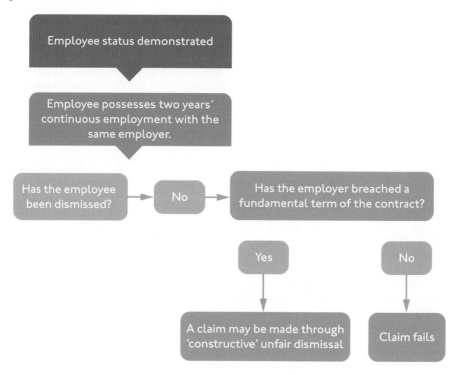

(and unfairly). The drafters of the legislation recognized that a tactic by recalcitrant employers would be to 'coerce' employees to resign by, for example, making their job unreasonably unpleasant or onerous. The test established in *Malik v Bank of Credit and Commerce International* (see **19.6.2**) from the House of Lords was whether the employer's action was to destroy or very likely severely damage the relationship between the employee and employer. If the individual resigned, there would be no dismissal and therefore no right to claim unfair dismissal—hence the legislation would have been circumvented. Constructive dismissal allows an employee to accept the employer's repudiation of the contract and claim unfair dismissal (ss. 95(1)(c) and 136(1)(c) of ERA 1996).

Section 95(1)(c) outlines the right to claim constructive dismissal:

> For the purposes of this Part an employee is dismissed by his employer if . . . —
> (c) the employee terminates the contract under which he is employed (with or without notice) in circumstances in which he is entitled to terminate it without notice by reason of the employer's conduct.

Examples of situations where an essential/fundamental term of the contract was breached include unilaterally reducing an employee's pay (*Industrial Rubber Products v Gillon*), and a failure to provide a safe and suitable working environment (*Waltons and Morse v Dorrington*). Breaches enabling a constructive dismissal claim have extended to a failure to adequately investigate allegations of sexual harassment.

Bracebridge Engineering Ltd v Darby (1990)

Facts:

Ms Darby made a complaint to her office manager that she had been a victim of a sexual assault committed by two colleagues. The manager took no action and Darby resigned.

Authority for:

The EAT held that as the actions occurred in the context of Darby's employment, the employer's failure to investigate and take seriously the allegations, and to take action was a fundamental breach of the contract. This justified Darby's claim of constructive dismissal.

Whilst in *Bracebridge* the breach was of a statutory right (the Sex Discrimination Act 1975), if the action of the employer was to breach a fundamental implied term in the contract, such as mutual trust and confidence, then this may also give the employee a right to resign and claim. This could include an unreasonable accusation of theft (*Robinson v Crompton Parkinson*) and may even lead to claims in an area which is forming an increasing number of claims for unfair dismissal (and other actions such as sex discrimination)—the harassment and bullying of workers (*Reed v Stedman*). Further, if the employer imposes a disciplinary penalty out of proportion to the offence that had been committed, the employee would be able to accept this as a breach of such significance that it would enable a constructive dismissal action.

BBC v Beckett (1983)

Facts:

Mr Beckett was a scenic carpenter. His employer informed him that he had left his working area in a dangerous condition and that due to this, he was given notice of his dismissal although he could appeal the decision. Beckett appealed and the employer offered him alternative employment (which was a demotion).

Authority for:

The EAT held that whilst Beckett's contract allowed for the employer's action, the demotion was sufficiently severe given Beckett's actions to amount to a fundamental breach.

It must also be considered that whilst the examples above demonstrate a serious (or gross) breach of the contract, relatively minor breaches of the contract, such as in the case of harassment, may cumulate into a 'last straw' action that enables the employee to accept the repudiation and claim constructive dismissal (*Woods v WM Car Services*). However, the underlying principle is that there was a breach of a fundamental term of the contract that enables a constructive dismissal claim.

Western Excavating v Sharp (1978)

Facts:

Mr Sharp had taken unofficial leave from work and his employer responded by suspending him from work for five days. This led to Sharp having lost his income and he approached his employer for either a loan or an advance on his holiday pay. The employer refused both requests and Sharp, considering this a breach of his contract, resigned and claimed constructive dismissal.

Authority for:

The Court of Appeal held there was no contractual obligation (either express or implied) for the employer to make a loan or to advance wages to an employee. It further identified the criteria by which constructive dismissal would be assessed. These were:

- the employer must have breached a term (express or implied), or had clearly established that they would not be bound by the contract;
- the term breached must have been an essential or fundamental term;
- the employee must have accepted the breach of the contract by the employer and acted to end the employment within a reasonable time.

21.3.1 Affirming the Breach

There is a requirement for the employee to make some outward sign that they do not accept the breach by the employer. If the employee says nothing in dispute to the employer's action, then it may be considered that they have waived the right to claim by 'affirming' the change in contract and will have lost their right to bring an action against it. Insofar as they make an outward sign of not accepting the variation, they may continue to work under the new conditions, until, for example, alternative employment is secured, and then they may leave and claim constructive dismissal. This is known as 'working under protest'. However, once the employee has agreed to work to the changed contract 'under protest', an employee who subsequently refuses to work under the new conditions may be dismissed as refusing to obey lawful and reasonable instructions (*Robinson v Tescom Corp.*). Under constructive dismissal, the employee has to claim within a reasonable time, having informed the employer that they were leaving *because* of the employer's action.

Holland v Glendale Industries Ltd (1998)

Facts:

Mr Holland had been engaged as a parks foreman by the local authority for approximately 11 years. At this point the parks and gardens operation was contracted to an outside agency and Holland remained in employment for a further five years. A new employer took over and Holland was informed that he would no longer receive the additional payments that had previously been made to him and that his job was being offered to 'a younger man.' Sometime later Holland was subject to a staff assessment and consequently informed the employer he was leaving and retiring early. However, he claimed constructive dismissal.

→

Authority for:

The EAT held that the ordinary contractual principles applied to constructive dismissal and where a party repudiated the contract, and the other party wished to rely on this and to accept it, this must be clear by words or action. (Essentially, Holland should have told Glendale he was leaving because of the alleged breach of contract.) As he had not done so, his claim for constructive dismissal could not succeed.

21.4 REMEDIES FOR UNFAIR DISMISSAL

Where an employee has been unfairly dismissed, the tribunal has to assess how to compensate the dismissed employee. The three remedies available are reinstatement; re-engagement; and compensation (ERA 1996, s. 112). These remedies are initially explained to the claimant and the tribunal identifies whether the employee wishes to be reinstated to their previous job. At this stage the employer has no say in what should happen next, and it is the tribunal's decision, having considered the case, the relationship between the parties, and what is in the best interests of the employee. It is important to note that if the employee does not wish to return to the employment then this would not be ordered, but if the tribunal considers that re-engagement may be available and the employee unreasonably refuses to accept this, then the award of compensation may be reduced. Employees who have, however, been somewhat at fault in the dismissal will not ordinarily be awarded reinstatement or re-engagement.

21.4.1 Reinstatement

This remedy is provided at the discretion of the tribunal where the dismissed employee is reinstated to their previous job. Both the employer and employee must agree to this remedy, and as can be imagined, it is quite rarely complied with. In such an instance where the employer refuses to reinstate the employee, the tribunal will increase the damages awarded to the employee, but it cannot compel the employer to restore the employee to their previous job as specific performance will not be awarded in cases involving contracts of personal service.

21.4.2 Re-engagement

As there may be several months (at least) from when the employee is dismissed to when a tribunal may have heard the case and provided its award, the employee's previous position with the employer may have been taken by another individual. Instead of ordering reinstatement, due to the practical problems that this may cause, ERA 1996 provides for the employee to return to the employment as close to the same job (in terms of pay, requirements, seniority, and responsibility) as is possible.

21.4.3 Compensation

Compensation is provided by the tribunal on the basis of two elements—a basic award and a compensatory award. Under this section the tribunal will award a conventional sum of £250 as way of compensation for loss of a statutory right (ERA 1996, s. 123(1)).

21.4.3.1 The basic award

ERA 1996 provides for the method of calculation of this element of the remedy. The current rate of a week's pay is established at a maximum of £508 and the age of the claimant and their length of continuous service governs the level of the award provided. It is the element of the award that is designed to reflect the employee's loss of pay between the time of the dismissal and the date of the tribunal's decision.

The calculation is based on the *Employee's Age* × the *Length of Service* × the *Weekly Gross Pay* (to the relevant maximum).

This calculation is further subject to a multiplier based on the employee's age. Where the employee is below the age of 22, any period of service is multiplied by .5; between the age of 22 and 41 the figure is multiplied by 1; and for workers over the age of 41 the figure is multiplied by 1.5.

The maximum amount provided under the basic award is £15,240—applicable 6 April 2018. The level of compensation may be reduced if the employee contributed to the dismissal through their conduct; if they received any redundancy payment; or if they unreasonably refused reinstatement.

21.4.3.2 The compensatory award

This element of the award is not calculated to a strict formula as is the case with the basic element and the tribunal has wide scope for assessing what is just and equitable in the circumstances. The maximum award under the compensatory element is the lower of £83,682 —applicable 6 April 6 2018—(although, of course, the majority of cases do not reach this figure) or 12 months' gross pay (which figure excludes pension contributions, benefits paid by the employer, and any discretionary bonuses. Where the employee has been dismissed for whistle blowing, some health and safety related reasons or where the dismissal is due to unlawful discrimination, the compensation remains uncapped). The award includes compensation for losses of overtime payments, tips, future losses, loss of accrued rights, and so on.

The ERA 1996, s. 123 restricts a tribunal to award financial losses only. The award may not include damages for 'distress, humiliation, and damage to reputation in the community or to family life'.

Dunnachie v Kingston upon Hull City Council (2004)

Facts:

Mr Dunnachie had been employed as an Environmental Health Officer and who, the tribunal found, had been driven from his employment due to a campaign of workplace bullying. This action involved Dunnachie's manager who also failed to take appropriate action when a complaint was made. As a result, Dunnachie left the employment and obtained another (lower paid) job.

Authority for:

The House of Lords agreed that Dunnachie had been constructively dismissed, but confirmed that damages for his non-economic losses (the stress, humiliation, and so on) were not recoverable in an unfair dismissal claim.

Tribunals were provided with guidance as to how to assess this element of damages in *Norton Tool Co. Ltd v Tewson* so as to include: any immediate loss of earnings; any calculation of future losses; the figure to include a loss of a statutory right; any losses of rights under a pension; and any expenses incurred in obtaining another job. Future loses cannot be too remote and may identify losses attributed to the employee gaining alternative employment. It will also impact on an employee who had already obtained another job at a similar rate of pay or better pay than had been provided by the employer subject to the claim.

As with the basic award, the compensation may be reduced where there was a contributory fault by the employee, or where the employee failed to mitigate their losses.

21.4.3.3 The additional award

ERA 1996, s. 117 provides for the additional compensation where the tribunal has ordered reinstatement or re-engagement and the employer has unreasonably refused to agree to the order. This award will be based on between 26 and 52 weeks' pay (at the tribunal's discretion). The rates applicable from 6 April 2018 are: a minimum of £13,208 and a maximum of £26,416.

Based on the calculations as noted earlier, the maximum award that is available under compensation for unfair dismissal is, from 6 April 2018, £98,922 (i.e. £83,682 plus 30 x £508).

CONCLUSION

The chapter has aimed to demonstrate the nature of unfair dismissal legislation: who qualifies for the right; the procedures that the parties are required to follow; and the remedies available. It also identified where the statutory protection is available for dismissals that are considered automatically unfair.

The unfair dismissal legislation provides a greater range of protection to those who qualify than does the common law remedy of wrongful dismissal. Claims may be made under both sources of law, but any remedy received in one claim would be off-set in a remedy under the other jurisdiction.

SUMMARY OF MAIN POINTS

Unfair dismissal

- Unfair dismissal is governed by statute law and most of the rules applicable to this jurisdiction of law are contained in the Employment Rights Act (ERA) 1996.

- To qualify the individual must have employee status; have been continuously employed with the employer for at least two years; they must have been dismissed (and unfairly); and must have submitted their claim to an employment tribunal within three months of the Effective Date of Termination (EDT).

- The employer must allow the employee to be accompanied at grievance and disciplinary hearings.

- The tribunal will assess the reasonableness of an employer's decision to dismiss based on their reasonable grounds for holding a belief/suspicion; the investigations into the matter that were conducted; and whether another 'reasonable employer' would have acted in the same way.

- There are five potentially fair reasons to dismiss an employee. These are the capability/qualifications of the employee; conduct; redundancy; contravention of a statute; and some other substantial reason.

- There exist automatically unfair reasons to dismiss an employee (which results in the requirement for two year's continuous employment being dispensed with). These include dismissals on the grounds of pregnancy; membership of a trade union or trade union activities; dismissal for asserting a statutory right; and so on.

Constructive dismissal

- Constructive unfair dismissal enables an employee to claim unfair dismissal even where they have not been 'dismissed'. The employer must have breached a fundamental term of the contract and the employee must have accepted this repudiation.

- A fundamental term includes actions such as a unilateral reduction in pay and failure to provide a safe system of work or suitable working environment.

- The employee must claim within 'a reasonable time' of the breach to gain protection from constructive dismissal or they run the risk of having affirmed the contractual change.

- The affected employee must inform the employer of their non-acceptance of the contractual change before resigning and claiming constructive dismissal.

Remedies

- There are three remedies available to a tribunal when an employee has been unfairly dismissed. These are reinstatement, re-engagement, and compensation.

 SUMMARY QUESTIONS

Essay questions

1. The potentially fair reasons to dismiss under the Employment Rights Act 1996 are far too broad and enable an employer to dismiss an employee very easily. They should be narrowed and the test of reasonableness of an employer's action made more robust if the legislation is to have any impact on the abusive exercise of managerial prerogative.

   Discuss.

2. The statutory dismissal procedures, intended to resolve employment disputes 'in-house' without recourse to tribunal, were replaced in April 2009 with a system based on alternative forms of dispute resolution. Why did these statutory procedures fail and what is the likely success of the ACAS Code reducing such action? What lessons can be learned from the Gibbons review?

Problem questions

1. Kate runs a clothing manufacturing firm employing several workers. One day Kate comes into work and sees what she thinks is a fight between John and Tom. Therefore Kate sacks both of them on the spot. What has really happened is that Tom has been attacked by John because John has never liked Tom due to his exemplary service and being a 'goody two shoes'.

   Tom was actually working on a fixed-term contract, which he had worked for two years out of a three-year contract. Tom's contract does not state anything about early termination and he earns £20,000 per year.

   Kate later appoints Sarah on maternity leave cover for an eight-month contract. Once appointed, Sarah announces that she is pregnant, and Kate is disgusted by this revelation and immediately dismisses Sarah due to her pregnant status.

Advise the parties of the legal issues and their rights.

(Visit the online resources where there are completed claim (ET1) and answer (ET3) forms relating to this question, and a completed employment contract to demonstrate the reality of this dismissal scenario.)

2. Calvin is a designer working for a large fashion house. Calvin is an employee at the firm and has worked there for four years. His employer Donna arrives at work on Monday morning and finds Calvin acting suspiciously. Donna checks the petty cash box and discovers that £100 is missing. Despite the fact that four other employees were in the vicinity at the time Donna came into the room she dismisses Calvin without any notice saying she 'would not have a thief like Calvin working there any more'.

Advise Calvin of any rights under unfair dismissal and wrongful dismissal protections.

 You will find guidance about how to answer these questions online at www.oup.com/uk/marson5e/.

 FURTHER READING

Books and articles

Brodie, D. (2002) 'Fair Dealing and the Dismissal Process' *Industrial Law Journal*, Vol. 31, No. 3, p. 294.

Davidov, G. and Eshet, E. (2015) 'Intermediate Approaches to Unfair Dismissal Protection' *Industrial Law Journal*, Vol. 44, No. 2, p. 167.

Learmond-Criqui, J. and Costly, J. (2001) 'Arbitration in Employment Disputes' *Business Law Review*, October, p. 222.

Marson, J. (2013) 'The End of the Opportunistic Breach of Contract! The Elective Theory of Repudiatory Breach Prevails: Societe Generale, London Branch v Geys [2012] UKSC 63' *European Journal of Current Legal Issues*, Vol. 19, No. 2.

Parrott, G. and Potbury, T. (2007) 'Unfair Dismissal: The Polkey Principle Laid Bare' *Employment Law Journal*, Vol. 79, April, p. 5.

Taylor, S. and Emir, A. (2015) 'Employment Law: An Introduction' (4th Edition) Oxford University Press: Oxford.

Websites, Twitter, and YouTube channels

http://www.acas.org.uk
@acasorguk

http://www.youtube.com/user/acasorguk
The Advisory, Conciliation and Arbitration Service provides a wealth of practical information for employers and workers on their rights and responsibilities at work.

https://www.gov.uk/browse/working/redundancies-dismissals
Information from Direct Gov, an organization established to provide information and guidance from various government agencies and departments. It offers practical advice on, amongst other things, employment and termination matters.

https://www.citizensadvice.org.uk/work/leaving-a-job/dismissal/check-if-your-dismissal-is-fair/
@CitizensAdvice

http://www.youtube.com/user/CitizensAdvice
The Citizens Advice Bureau website provides information on rights at work, making claims, and so on.

http://www.justice.gov.uk/tribunals/employment
Employment Tribunals.

http://www.legislation.gov.uk/ukpga/1996/18/contents
The Employment Rights Act 1996.

ONLINE RESOURCES

www.oup.com/uk/marson5e/

For further resources relating to this chapter, including self-test questions, an interactive glossary, and key case flashcards.

22 EQUALITY IN THE WORKPLACE AND PARENTAL RIGHTS

Does an employer have to take action to prevent an employee from telling rude jokes at work? What responsibility does an employer have with regards to unwanted conduct perpetrated by or to their employee? How many times must an employee complain to the employer about this unwanted conduct before it becomes actionable? Do you know the 'protected characteristics' that are protected against prohibited conduct by the Equality Act 2010? Do you as an employer/does your business have policies in place to reflect the changes in equality law that took effect from 1 October 2010? If you answered 'no/don't know' to any or indeed all of the above questions you are exposing you and your business to potentially very expensive claims, poor industrial relations, and potential damage to your reputation as an employer. Equality law has changed, it will continue to develop over the coming years, and ignorance is likely to be a costly error.

Business Scenario 22

Clara and Chitra work as silver service waitresses in a hotel. Their duties include entering the kitchen to collect courses of dinner to be served and assisting the kitchen staff with general catering duties such as cleaning surfaces, collecting and distributing deliveries, and so on. The hotel has a policy where female staff who have been trained as providing 'silver service' are required to wear skirts instead of trousers. The male staff are required to wear trousers, white shirt, and black tie when providing the silver service. Clara has requested that in the interests of safety she and her colleagues should be permitted to choose to wear either a skirt or trousers. The management of the hotel refuse this request. During a particularly busy shift when the work in the kitchen was chaotic, hot fat from the fryers was accidentally spilt onto Clara's legs. She is badly injured as a result, and it is later confirmed that she would not have been injured had she been wearing the trousers requested.

Chitra injured her back whilst moving a delivery of potatoes and required several weeks' leave to recover. During a conversation with her doctor, Chitra was advised that she should not return to her role as a waitress or her back problem would recur. In the opinion of the doctor, Chitra should not return to a job involving lifting and/or standing for long periods. Chitra contacted her line manager about the news who promised to provide Chitra with alternative work. However, when the general manager of the hotel discovered this arrangement he requested that Chitra resign from her position as she is unfit for work. Chitra thinks that if she does not resign she will be dismissed.

Learning Outcomes

- Explain the development of the Equality Act 2010 in relation to its main aims and the legislation it replaced (**22.2–22.3**)
- Identify the groups of workers protected by the Act through the use of 'protected characteristics' (**22.4–22.5**)
- Explain the codification of the previously discriminatory behaviour and identify where the law has added new protection against 'prohibited conduct' (**22.6**)
- Consider the extent of protection against prohibited conduct of an individual with a protected characteristic (**22.5**)
- Identify the 'heads' under which an equal pay claim may be made, and apply these in problem scenarios (**22.12.4–22.12.4.3**)
- Explain the protection against discrimination based on sex and race in employment (**22.6–22.6.6.2**)
- Identify the protection against discrimination in employment of those working under part-time and fixed-term contracts (**22.15–22.16**)
- Identify the rights at work of pregnant employees and biological and adopting parents, including the right to request flexible working and family-friendly policies (**22.18–22.18.5**).

22.1 INTRODUCTION

From 1 October 2010 much of the previous equality law developed through the common law, statute, and the United Kingdom's membership of the European Union has been codified in the Equality Act (EA) 2010. There have been many changes adopted following the enactment of this legislation. The Act is relevant for businesses as it imposes obligations to provide a safe system of work, including regulating the activities of management, colleagues, and third parties. This is an area of law that will evolve over the coming years, and whilst much of the previous case law is applicable to this Act, new judgments will likely expand and clarify the extent of equality law.

22.2 THE EQUALITY ACT 2010

According to the Government Equalities Office:

> The Equality Act 2010 is intended to provide a new cross-cutting legislative framework to protect the rights of individuals and advance equality of opportunity for all; to update, simplify and strengthen the previous legislation; and to deliver a simple, modern and accessible framework of discrimination law which protects individuals from unfair treatment and promotes a fair and more equal society.

Previous anti-discrimination and equality laws were spread over many pieces of legislation, statutory instruments, and case law. It was unwieldy to identify the relevant laws applicable to employers, employees, workers, third parties, organizations, and so on. It had also developed different approaches to the application of these laws through the various amendments and decisions of the EU and the Court of Justice of the European Union. Therefore, EA 2010 was enacted to harmonize these complex areas of law, apply consistent approaches to the interpretation and application of the provisions, and to take the opportunity to extend rights to the new 'protected charac-teristics'. The body with the responsibility for overseeing EA 2010 is the Government Equality Office.

Previous equality legislation provided for the establishment of the Commission for Equality and Human Rights (merging the Equal Opportunities Commission, the Com-mission for Racial Equality, and the Disability Rights Commission). The Commission took the previous powers enjoyed by these Commissions and consolidated their experience in promoting equality and respect for human rights, and enforcing legislation against transgressors. The Act was significant in placing a duty on public authorities to promote equal opportunities between men and women, and prohibiting sex discrimination in the exercise of public functions.

A further, significant, introduction in EA 2010 was explicit reference to allowing posi-tive action policies to be adopted by organizations (in recruitment and promotion). Posi-tive action enables an employer to pursue a policy of appointing applicants where there is an under-representation of persons from the specific group in the organization; or where they suffer a disadvantage associated with that characteristic (EA 2010, s. 159). This has been incorporated into EA 2010, but it is at present applicable where the employer volun-tarily adopts the policies—it is not a legal requirement.

22.3 PREVIOUS ANTI-DISCRIMINATION LAW REPEALED

EA 2010 formally repeals/revokes and changes much of the previous legislation (in its attempt to simplify and codify the provisions contained in the plethora of statutes). The following have been repealed in their entirety (note this list is not exhaustive and refers to those statutes relevant for this section of the text):

1. The Equal Pay Act 1970
2. The Sex Discrimination Act 1975
3. The Race Relations Act 1976
4. The Sex Discrimination Act 1986
5. The Disability Discrimination Act 1995
6. The Employment Equality (Religion or Belief) Regulations 2003
7. The Employment Equality (Sexual Orientation) Regulations 2003
8. The Equality Act (Sexual Orientation) Regulations 2007.

22.4 GROUPS AFFECTED BY THE ACT

This Part of the text is focused on employment laws, and hence this chapter considers the effects of EA 2010 on employers, employees, and workers. But these are not the only groups who will be affected by the Act. Former employees, agency workers, self-employed workers, consumers, and providers of goods and services are each subject to provisions of EA 2010 and should be aware of how it affects them. Further, there are increasing obliga-tions on employers in the public sector regarding disclosure of pay details and greater transparency, with the consequent need for effective policies to be established to avoid transgression of the Act.

Consider

For Clara and Chitra to have protection under the Equality Act 2010 they must have been discriminated against on the basis of a recognized protected characteristic and they must have experienced prohibited conduct.

22.5 THE PROTECTED CHARACTERISTICS (GROUPS)

The previous anti-discrimination laws (the Equal Pay Act 1970, the Sex Discrimination Act 1975, the Race Relations Act 1976, and so on) each identified groups who were protected from the discriminatory acts contained within the remit of the particular piece of legislation. In its attempt to simplify and harmonize equality laws, EA 2010 identifies the following as being 'protected characteristics'—a method of explaining which groups are protected from discrimination and who will be part of these groups—and hence possess a characteristic that is protected under this legislation (ss. 4–12 and 72–76). They are as follows:

- age (s. 5);
- disability (s. 6);
- gender reassignment (s. 7);
- marriage and civil partnership (s. 8)—single people are not covered;
- pregnancy and maternity (ss. 72–76);
- race (s. 9);
- religion or belief (s. 10);
- sex (s. 11);
- sexual orientation (s. 12).

22.6 PROHIBITED CONDUCT

EA 2010 outlines the forms of conduct that the Act seeks to prohibit (ss. 13–27). These harmonize the definitions of actions such as **direct and indirect discrimination, harassment,** and **victimization** which the previous anti-discrimination laws defined. The forms of conduct, to which of the protected characteristics they apply, and where changes have been made from the previous legislation are contained in the following paragraphs.

Consider

Clara has experienced discrimination based on her sex and thus this will be direct discrimination. A key issue is whether the employer's action falls into the category of an exception—an occupational requirement (remember, direct discrimination on the basis of sex cannot be justified).

22.6.1 Direct Discrimination

22.6.1.1 The protected characteristics

There are no changes to this form of discrimination (from the legislation it replaced) and it covers all the protected characteristics.

22.6.1.2 Application of the law

Direct discrimination occurs when a person treats another less favourably because of their protected characteristic than they would a person without the characteristic. The less favourable treatment has been extended in EA 2010 in the following ways. A person is treated less favourably than another due to:

1. a protected characteristic they possess; or
2. a protected characteristic it is thought they possess (this amounts to perceptive discrimination); or
3. their association with someone who has a protected characteristic (this amounts to associative discrimination) (s. 13).

Therefore, perceptive and associative forms of discrimination are included in the Act (these are covered in the following sections).

In relation to pregnancy and maternity, the test is not whether the claimant was subject to less favourable treatment, but whether the treatment was unfavourable. This is because there is no need for the claimant to compare her treatment with other workers.

To determine whether the claimant has been a victim of direct discrimination the test is to identify if an act of discrimination had been committed; and if so, would, but for the claimant's protected characteristic, they have been treated more favourably.

James v Eastleigh BC (1990)

Facts:

The Council gave free entry to its swimming pools to people of pensionable age. Women reached that age at 60 whilst the retirement age for men was 65. A 61-year old man claimed this was discriminatory.

Authority for:

This action was direct discrimination as it treated one sex (men) less favourably than the other. The Council's benign motive was irrelevant.

When discrimination occurs between groups of workers, the claim requires the discrimination is on the basis of the protected characteristic and not on matters that are materially different.

Bullock v Alice Ottley School (1993)

Facts:

A school had a policy of requiring academic staff to retire at 60 whilst the gardening staff had to retire at 65.

→

Authority for:

In a claim of direct discrimination, the Court of Appeal held that this was discrimination on the basis of the jobs and not on the sex of the workers. Just because the academic staff tended to be female and the gardening staff male, did not stop women becoming members of the gardening staff and being subject to the retirement policy at 65.

Direct sex discrimination cannot be justified on the basis of the motives of the employer.

Hafeez v Richmond School (1981)

Facts:

A job at the school required the successful applicant to teach English and the students had expressed their opinions that they would rather be taught by an English teacher. The claimant's application to work in the school was rejected on the basis that he was not English.

Authority for:

Regardless that the employer did not mean to discriminate, the rejection on the basis of the race of the claimant was unlawful.

However, exceptions do exist. In relation to the protected characteristic of age, less favourable treatment may be justified if it is a proportionate means of achieving a legitimate aim. A disabled person may be treated more favourably than a non-disabled person; and justification for direct discrimination may be evidenced through the **occupational requirements** of the job.

22.6.1.3 Occupational requirements

Due to the nature of certain types of employment, or by necessity, the role to be filled may require a person from a specific protected characteristic group.

Note; this will not extend to a policy of only employing women in a female clothes retailer (*Etam Plc v Rowan*) and the same argument applies to men's fashion retailers (*Wiley v Dee and Co. (Menswear) Ltd*).

As such, EA 2010 provides for exceptions to acts that would otherwise amount to direct discrimination. This is merely an option and a claim cannot be raised that the employer could/should have restricted the post to (e.g.) a particular gender (*Williams v Dyfed CC*).

It is important that EA 2010 identifies the Occupational Requirement (OR) to be a proportionate means of achieving a legitimate aim and there exists a link between the requirement and the job (hence it is not a sham).

Discrimination laws provide for the following ORs:

* Where the essential nature of the job calls for a man for reasons of physiology (excluding physical strength or stamina—*Barker v Goodwave Security*), or in dramatic

performances (e.g. a leading man in a film), or for authenticity (e.g. the role of playing Othello). The OR of authenticity has been used to prevent a male applicant for a job on a 'chat line' that was advertised as 'live girls . . . 1–2–1 chat'. The nature of the employment was restricted to female applicants (*Cropper v UK Express Ltd*).

- The job needs to be held by a man to preserve decency or privacy (*Lasertop Ltd v Webster*). This has been applied to employment situations where, whilst being in a state of undress is not of itself a requirement of the job, it was reasonably incidental to it (*Sisley v Britannia Security Systems*), or the job involved entering women's toilets to carry out maintenance work. It was quite foreseeable in these circumstances that women may object to a man carrying out such functions (*Carlton v Personnel Hygiene Services*).

- The nature or location of the establishment makes it impracticable for the holder of the job to live elsewhere than in the premises provided by the employer; and separate living accommodation/sanitary facilities for women are unavailable. Where an employer would be unable, reasonably, to make provisions to adapt the available accommodation to allow members of the opposite sex to take up a post, this will satisfy the OR. However, where the employer simply does not wish to make an adaptation, and this would be reasonable to do so, the defence will not be accepted (*Wallace v Peninsular and Oriental Steam Navigation Company*).

- The holder of the job provides individuals with personal services promoting their welfare or education (or similar services) that can be most effectively provided by (e.g.) a man; or a person of a particular race. In *Tottenham Green Under Fives Centre v Marshall (No. 2)* the case involved a day care centre where 84 per cent of the children at the centre were of Afro-Caribbean descent. The previous nursery worker (who was of Afro-Caribbean descent) left the employment and it was considered by the Centre's committee to appoint a replacement of the same ethnic origin. Mr Marshall (a white man) applied for the position and when it was discovered that he was not of the required ethnicity, his application was rejected. It was held by the EAT that this requirement was included under the Race Relations Act (RRA) 1976, s. 5(2)(d) (the previous applicable legislation) as the ability to read and speak in dialect was an OR.

- The job is required to be held by a man because it is likely to involve the performance of the duties outside the UK in a country whose laws/customs mean that the job could not, or could not effectively, be performed by a woman.

- The job involves participation as an artist's or photographic model in the production of a work of art, in which a person of that racial group is required for authenticity.

Consider

From the above list does it appear that wearing a skirt rather than trousers is an occupational requirement? How do dress codes affect individuals at work when they apply on the basis of sex?

22.6.2 Associative Discrimination

22.6.2.1 The protected characteristics

In relation to race, religion and belief, and sexual orientation the law remains the same as each is covered.

In age, disability, gender reassignment, and sex this is a new right to protection.

It does *not* apply to the marriage and civil partnership, and pregnancy and maternity protected characteristics.

22.6.2.2 Application of the law

When a person is directly discriminated against due to their association with another person who has a protected characteristic. This has the potential to provide substantial benefits and protection to workers. For example, where an employee is refused promotion due to her having a disabled spouse and the employer believes the employee will have to spend time away from work to care for that person, this is now an act of discrimination. It is evidently not based on a disability which the employee (claimant) has, but rather someone associated with her.

22.6.3 Perception Discrimination

22.6.3.1 The protected characteristics

In relation to age, race, religion or belief, and sexual orientation each remains covered by EA 2010.

The protected characteristics of disability, gender reassignment, and sex are now protected through EA 2010.

Marriage and civil partnership, and pregnancy and maternity are *not* covered in previous legislation or under EA 2010.

22.6.3.2 Application of the law

A person is directly discriminated against when those discriminating believe they possess a particular protected characteristic (even if in fact the person discriminated against does not actually possess that protected characteristic).

22.6.4 Indirect Discrimination

22.6.4.1 The protected characteristics

Age, race, religion and belief, sex, sexual orientation, and marriage and civil partnership remain covered under EA 2010.

Disability and gender reassignment are now covered as protected characteristics.

The protected characteristics of pregnancy and maternity are *not* covered (although in pregnancy and maternity indirect sex discrimination may still apply).

22.6.4.2 Application of the law

Following enactment of EA 2010, there is a common definition of what will amount to indirect discrimination. Indirect discrimination is a seemingly neutral provision, criterion, or practice (PCP) that is applied to everyone but it particularly affects people who share a protected characteristic and it puts them (or would put them) at a particular disadvantage. A simplistic example of indirect effect is if a university, in recruiting lecturers, stated that the applicants had to be 6ft tall or over. This criterion has no discriminatory element as it is applied to all applicants. However, the reality is that a greater proportion of men than women can comply with it. Hence, it may be discriminatory unless the employer can objectively justify its inclusion as a proportionate legitimate aim (s. 19). Further, EA 2010, s. 19 requires that the claimant has suffered a disadvantage due to the application of the PCP, but the wording 'or would put them' (s. 19(2)(b)) enables a challenge to a PCP which has not yet been applied but whose effect would be discriminatory if it were.

To justify discrimination, the following two-stage test should be adopted to establish an 'objective justification':

1. Is the aim legitimate? Therefore is the rule/practice non-discriminatory and one that represents a real and objective consideration?

2. If the aim satisfies the test of being legitimate, is it necessary in the circumstances (is it proportionate)?

A legitimate aim must constitute a genuine, objective need, which can include business/economic needs, but should not be based solely on (e.g.) reducing costs.

The disadvantage to be suffered by the claimant is not defined in the Act, but it may include denial of a promotion or imposition of a dress code. However, dress codes in particular may be justified for a broader, objectively justified reason. In *Panesar v Nestle Ltd* the workers at the confectionary factory were prohibited from wearing beards or their hair long. The provision was discriminatory against members of the Sikh religion who suffered a detriment, as they could not comply with the provision. However, this did not constitute a breach of the law (RRA 1976), as it was a provision in fulfillment of health and safety legislation and in the interests of hygiene (similar findings to *Singh v British Rail Engineering Ltd* involving a requirement to wear protective headgear).

Establishing the link between the disadvantage with the PCP may be possible through the use of statistics.

- *Provision, criterion, or practice:* The tribunal will assess the employer's provision, criterion, or practice in an objective manner to assess whether there may be a justification for its imposition. The objective nature of the examination removes the employer's beliefs or understandings of the need of the business but rather will require tangible grounds that would make such a provision acceptable. The test considers the prima facie evidence of discrimination that is established by the claimant, and has previously included a requirement to work from an office location (*Lockwood v Crawley Warren Group Ltd*), a provision of working full-time (*Home Office v Holmes*), or the necessity of the inclusion of a mobility clause in the contract (*Meade-Hill and National Union of Civil and Public Servants v British Council*). Having established that there does exist a provision in the requirements of employment, the next stage is to demonstrate that it has caused the claimant a disadvantage.

- *Disadvantage:* The claimant has to demonstrate that they had suffered a disadvantage, or would be put at a disadvantage, due to the provision to enable a claim to proceed. The requirement of 'being placed at a disadvantage' instils an element of *locus standi*, which stops 'busybodies' from taking offence at what they may see as discrimination and lodging claims against the employer. The disadvantage shows the claimant has suffered a loss and hence enables/justifies their action against the employer (*Home Office v Holmes*).

Note that the comparator in instances of indirect discrimination based on a worker's disability is not with *all* disabled people, but rather with people with the particular disability. Similarly, where the protected characteristic is race, the comparator may be persons of a specific race. In age-related indirect discrimination, the correct age group of persons disadvantaged is an important aspect in demonstrating discrimination.

However, does the claimant have to offer an explanation of the reasons why a PCP puts one group at a disadvantage when compared to others? The Supreme Court offered an answer to the question in the following case:

Essop and others v Home Office (UK Border Agency) and Naeem v Secretary of State for Justice (2017)

Facts:

Mr Essop was the lead claimant of a group of Home Office employees. He alleged that the use of a test for the purposes of career advancement was indirectly discriminatory on race and/or age. Statistics demonstrated that persons from BME backgrounds and those over 35 years old had a significantly lower pass rate than white and younger candidates. Naseem's case was that as a newly appointed Muslim chaplain at a prison, he was paid on the lowest pay band because there had been no such role prior to 2002. This was different for Christian chaplains and this led to a claim of indirect race/religious discrimination.

Authority for:

The cases are significant because the Supreme Court had to address the issue of indirect discrimination (direct discrimination, as provided by the EA 2010, being largely settled law). To succeed, it was not necessary to establish the reason for the particular disadvantage being applied to the group affected. The essential element in a claim on this basis is a causal connection between the PCP and the disadvantage suffered—not only by the group, but also the individual claimant.

22.6.5 Harassment

22.6.5.1 The protected characteristics

The protected characteristic of sex remains covered by EA 2010 (s. 26(5)).

The protected characteristics of age, disability, gender reassignment, race, religion or belief, and sexual orientation were already covered through existing legislation, which is now subject to EA 2010.

Marriage and civil partnership, and pregnancy and maternity are still *not* covered.

22.6.5.2 Application of the law

The types of harassment covered by s. 26 include:

1. harassment related to a person of a relevant protected characteristic;
2. sexual harassment;
3. less favourable treatment of a worker because of the sexual harassment or harassment related to sex or gender reassignment.

Harassment continues to be 'unwanted conduct' related to a protected characteristic, which has the purpose or effect of violating a person's dignity or creating an intimidating, hostile, degrading, humiliating, or offensive environment. The right gives employees the power to complain of offensive behaviour, even if not directed at them, and complainants also are not required to personally possess the protected characteristic. Employees are further protected from harassment due to association or perception (s. 26). The harassment may involve the harasser performing actions that gradually lead to a complaint, but if the action is sufficiently serious (*In Situ Cleaning v Heads*), a one-off act may enable a claim of harassment to be made (*Bracebridge Engineering Ltd v Darby*, see **21.3**).

The words 'purpose or effect' are important as they enable a claim for harassment even where the harasser did not intend for this to be the effect of their actions. For example, male workers may be downloading an image of a naked woman at work. A female colleague may know this is happening and may feel it is creating a hostile and humiliating environment. Therefore, she has a claim for harassment even though this was not the intention of the men. It is the perception of the worker (a subjective test) that is relevant— (EA 2010, s. 26(4)(a)), their personal circumstances (such as health or culture)—EA 2010, s. 26(4)(b), and whether it was reasonable that the conduct would have that effect on the worker (an objective test)—EA 2010, s. 26(4)(c). Hence, it may not be harassment if the claimant was deemed by the tribunal to be hypersensitive.

As noted earlier, unwanted conduct related to a protected characteristic affords protection due to the worker's own protected characteristic or a situation connected with a protected characteristic (associative discrimination or perceived discrimination). The issue of a 'connection with' the protected characteristic allows for protection against a broad range of discriminatory scenarios. For example, a worker subject to homophobic banter could have been harassed in relation to his sexual orientation, an employer racially abusing a black worker could lead to a white worker being offended and leading to a claim of racial discrimination, and a worker who has a disabled son whose colleagues make offensive remarks about the disability could lead to a claim of harassment related to disability.

There is no need for the claimant to establish a comparator in harassment cases.

22.6.6 Victimization

22.6.6.1 The protected characteristics

Each of the protected characteristics are subject to changes following enactment of EA 2010.

22.6.6.2 Application of the law

Where a worker is subjected to a detriment because they have performed a 'protected act' or because the employer believes that they have done, or will do a protected act in the future, they have a complaint under the Act (EA 2010, s. 27(1)) for victimization (*Aziz v Trinity Street Taxis Ltd*). A protected act includes:

1. initiating proceedings under EA 2010 (s. 27(2)(a));
2. providing evidence/information in relation to proceedings under EA 2010 (s. 27(2)(b));
3. doing anything related to the provisions of EA 2010 (s. 27(2)(c));
4. making an allegation that another person has done something in contravention of EA 2010 (s. 27(2)(d)); or
5. making/trying to obtain a 'relevant pay disclosure' from a colleague/former colleague (EA 2010, s. 77(3)).

564 Chapter 22 **Equality in the Workplace and Parental Rights**

The worker is not required to possess the protected characteristic personally to be protected under the Act. A detriment for the purposes of victimization may take many forms and can include a refusal to provide a reference to a former worker (*Coote v Granada Hospitality Ltd*), or if the employer applies unfair pressure and intimidation to prevent the pursuit of a claim (*St Helens Borough Council v Derbyshire and Others*).

An important change in EA 2010 is that the need for a comparator in such instances is no longer required. Where a complaint is made maliciously, or the employee supports a complaint they know is untrue, then protection under the legislation is lost (s. 27(3)).

22.7 LIABILITY FOR ACTS OF THIRD PARTIES

Under the (now repealed) Sex Discrimination Act 1975, an employer could be liable to an employee who was subject to unwanted conduct by a third party. A 'third party' is someone who is not under the control of the employer (such as another employee) but rather can be a customer, client, delivery driver, and so on (essentially a visitor to the premises).

The employer may be vicariously liable where the employee has been the victim of unwanted conduct and the employer has failed to take 'reasonable steps' to prevent it.

Despite the repeal of the third-party harassment liability of the employer (previously included in EA 2010, s. 40(2)), the affected employee may have an action under the Protection from Harassment Act 1997, with its six-year time limit to bring a claim and with the availability of awards of injunctions to prevent further acts of unwanted conduct. However, such claims are heard in the County Court and are subject to rules of evidence that are similar to a criminal proof of liability (a not insubstantial test) and subject to potential costs being awarded against the party who loses the case. EA 2010 requires claims of discrimination to be brought within a three-month time period, and as the claims are heard in the Employment Tribunal (ET), costs are rarely awarded.

22.8 AGE DISCRIMINATION

Age is one of the protected characteristics under EA 2010. However, it should be noted that some discrimination on the basis of age is allowed, and indeed age is the one protected characteristic that permits a justification of direct discrimination. This is allowed where the employer can successfully demonstrate that the less favourable treatment suffered by the claimant on the basis of their age is a proportionate means of achieving a legitimate aim (e.g. an employer's mandatory retirement age policy of 65 years old was held as appropriate and justified—*Seldon v Clarkson Wright and Jakes*). This is the 'objective justification test'.

Gorka Salaberria Sorondo v Academia Vasca de Policia y Emergencias (2017)

Facts:

The Basque Police and Emergency Services Academy required applicant police officers to be younger than 35 years old when applying to join the police force. Following a

→

question regarding the possible breach of age discrimination laws, the CJEU identified that there was no unlawful discrimination based on the facts of the case.

Authority for:

The policy did impact on workers' access to employment, but this was not unlawful as it was based on a genuine occupational requirement. The state had to be mindful of the physical requirements of the job, the consequences if the officers lacked the ability to use physical force, and it was not merely a question of looking at age at recruitment. The years of service that may be accomplished thereafter was a further factor to be considered.

Section 5 defines 'age' in reference to a person of a particular age group and persons of the same age group. All age groups are protected (hence not just 'old' people). Also, as evidenced above, age discrimination is interpreted in conformity with EU law and the jurisprudence of the CJEU.

Abercrombie & Fitch v Bordonaro (2017)

Facts:

Mr Bordonaro worked for Abercrombie & Fitch in Italy under a zero hours contract until he turned 25 years old. He was then excluded from the work schedule and was informed that, under Italian law, individuals under 25 years old and those over 45 years old may be employed on such contracts. Those in the 25–44 age group may only be so employed in limited circumstances. On the basis of an age discrimination claim by Bordonaro, the Italian court made a reference for clarification to the CJEU.

Authority for:

It is for national courts to determine discrimination and any objective justification presented by the employer. However, Advocate-General Bobek provided the following as factors to take into consideration when deciding on the potential for discrimination:

1. Less favourable treatment is determined according to a comprehensive assessment of the rule's impact;
2. Promoting a system which facilitates the recruitment of younger workers may be a legitimate aim;
3. The greater the number of 'legitimate aims' raised will become increasingly difficult to justify;
4. Justification of the aim requires specific evidence and cannot amount to generalizations; and
5. According to the Advocate-General, on the evidence provided he was not convinced that dismissing workers at the age of 25 was justified to allow younger workers to have access to employment opportunities.

> **Consider**
>
> Chitra has been injured at work and, according to her doctor, cannot continue in her employment undertaking the same duties. If this physical impairment affects her day-to-day activities it may be held as a disability and will place an obligation on the employer to take action to make reasonable adjustments.

22.9 DISABILITY DISCRIMINATION

Since the enactment and coming into force of the Disability Discrimination Act (DDA) 1995, employers (and a wider group of service providers—such as shops and businesses giving access to the public) have had to make reasonable adjustments to their businesses to ensure that those individuals with a disability are not discriminated against (this duty does not extend to an employee associated with a disabled person—see *Hainsworth v Ministry of Defence* regarding the interpretation of EA 2010 and the Equal Treatment Framework Directive, Art. 5). Since October 2004, all service providers/employers have been required to produce a Disability Equality Policy covering the delivery of services; an employment policy; training and education; consultation with disabled representatives; and access to buildings, information, and services.

EA 2010 provides a new definition of discrimination based on disability. This has been largely welcomed following the problems encountered after the judgment in *London Borough of Lewisham v Malcolm*.

> **London Borough of Lewisham v Malcolm (2008)**
>
> **Facts:**
>
> Mr Malcolm was a tenant of the Council. He had a disability (schizophrenia) and, as a result, had moved from his council accommodation and sublet it. This had continued for more than one year and as a long term tenant, Malcolm was exercising his right to buy the property. However, the sublet had ended his secure tenancy, the Council then served him with notice to quit and brought proceedings for possession. Malcolm argued that his disability had caused him to sublet the property and the Council, in taking the action, was breaching the Disability Discrimination Act 1995.
>
> **Authority for:**
>
> The House of Lords held there was no breach by the Council. The comparator in such a case was any other tenant who had sublet. Any defence related to disability discrimination required knowledge of the disability and this was not present here.

Section 15 provides:

A person (A) discriminates against a disabled person (B) if— (1) A treats B unfavourably because of something arising in consequence of B's disability, and (2) A cannot show that the treatment is a proportionate means of achieving a legitimate aim.

Subsection (1) does not apply if A shows that A did not know, and could not reasonably have been expected to know, that B had the disability.

Under EA 2010, s. 6 a person is defined as having a disability if they have a physical or mental impairment that:

has a substantial:

Foster v Hampshire Fire and Rescue Service (1998)

Facts:

Ms Foster was employed as a clerk for the Service who was dismissed for capability. In the latter years of her employment she had a poor attendance record and this was attributed to her suffering, although admittedly to a minor degree, from asthma and migraine.

Authority for:

The EAT upheld the decision of the tribunal that the claimant was not a disabled person within the meaning of the Disability Discrimination Act 1995. The EAT accepted that Foster had a physical impairment and this adversely affected her mobility, this was not 'substantial'.

. . . and long term

Rowley v Walkers Nonsuch Ltd (1997)

Facts:

Rowley sustained a back injury at work and had to take six months sick leave.

Authority for:

His injury did not satisfy the requirements of a disability as it did not have a long-term and adverse effect on his ability to carry out day-to-day activities.

. . . adverse effect on their ability to carry out normal day-to-day activities.

Law Hospital NHS Trust v Rush (2001)

Facts:

Ms Rush was employed as a staff nurse working night shifts. One evening whilst helping a patient she injured her back. This led to her taking sick leave for 14 months and, on her return, having been moved to a ward involving lighter duties. Rush no longer completed the duties which caused her injury and, following an assessment, she was identified as being 7 per cent disabled for life. She did, however, have to take medication to manage her pain. Nearly 12 years later Rush was dismissed and she complained of unlawful disability discrimination.

→

Authority for:

In holding that Rush was disabled in the meaning of the DDA 1995, the correct test is whether the employee can carry out their normal day-to-day activities rather than whether they can carry out the particular job properly.

DDA 1995 widened the scope of a disability and from 5 December 2005 it includes people with, or diagnosed with, cancer, HIV, and multiple sclerosis. The Act covers all employers (since 1 October 2004), regardless of size (with exceptions for recruitment to the armed services).

Taylor v Ladbrokes Betting & Gaming Ltd (2016)

Facts:

The claimant was dismissed and claimed that for the year before his dismissal he had been disabled due to his type 2 diabetes condition.

Authority for:

The EAT held that as type 2 diabetes is a progressive condition, it would amount to a disability even if it did not have a substantial adverse effect at that time. The important element for the tribunal was that it was likely to result in such a condition and hence was likely to result in an impairment.

An employer may not discriminate against a person due to their disability, or for a reason related to a disability, although the employer may provide an objective ground for any discrimination in this respect. In relation to service providers, objective reasons for discrimination may include where health and safety are at risk, where a person is incapable of entering a contract, and where a service provider is unable to provide that service to the public.

Consider

Does Chitra's back problem have a substantial effect (probably given that she cannot return work in the capacity of waitressing); is it long term (yes as it is not identified by the doctor as being for a number of weeks/months); and does it affect her day-to-day activities (again yes, and this is not limited to her job). As such, given she would be held to possess a disability of which she has informed her employer, the employer is required to make reasonable adjustments.

In an attempt to prevent discrimination to a person with a disability, the employer has to make reasonable adjustments to their premises, practices, or procedures to ensure disabled employees are not put at a substantial disadvantage compared with non-disabled employees (EA 2010, s. 212(1)—this is a disadvantage that is not minor or trivial and is assessed objectively on the facts of the case). This can include installing ramps/lifts to enable persons in wheelchairs to gain access, producing documents in Braille/large print/ or in audio format, and providing workers with speech recognition software for their computers. Where an employer fails to comply with the duty to make reasonable adjustments, the disabled person is discriminated against (EA 2010, s. 21(2)). EA 2010 identifies the following three steps as being reasonable to comply with the law:

1. avoid substantial disadvantage where a provision, criterion, or practice applied by or on behalf of the employers puts the disabled person at a substantial disadvantage compared with persons without the disability (EA 2010, s. 20(3));

2. remove or alter an existing physical feature (or provide the means to avoid it) where it puts the disabled person at a substantial disadvantage compared with persons without the disability (EA 2010, s. 20(4));

3. provide an auxiliary aid/service (EA 2010, s. 20(11)) where a disabled person would (but for this aid) be put at a substantial disadvantage compared with persons without the disability (EA 2010, s. 20(5)).

Reasonable adjustments are an essential feature of equality legislation as it imposes a requirement on employers to take positive steps to ensure people with a disability can have access to the job market and progress in their employment (EA 2010, s. 20).

Consider

Chitra's immediate line manager has changed her work to avoid causing problems to her back and enabling her to continue her employment. The general manager has disagreed and wishes for her to be dismissed or to resign—is this an actionable act of discrimination?

The key element here is for 'reasonable' adjustments. This will include facts such as the size of the employer, the resources available to them, and the needs of disabled persons coming into the business/and or premises. EA 2010 requires the employer to make reasonable adjustments for 'actual' persons with a disability rather than hypothetical persons, or to anticipate the needs of persons with disabilities. Therefore, the requirement is effective where the employer knew, or should have reasonably known of the existence of the disability, and where to take no action would likely have the effect of substantially disadvantaging the applicant to a job or an existing employee.

Ridout v TC Group (1998)

Facts:

Ms Ridout applied for a job with the defendant and was shortlisted to attend an interview. She disclosed on her application that she suffered from 'photosensitive epilepsy' and this was 'controlled by epilim'. The lighting in the room was problematic to her, a point she raised on entering the room, and it was suggested by the panel that she wear

→

her dark glasses if needed rather than to hold the interview in another room. When she failed to be appointed, Ridout brought her claim for breach of the DDA. The employer contested that Ridout had a very rare form of epilepsy which no reasonable employer could be expected to know without an explanation by the applicant.

Authority for:

The EAT remarked: 'It would be unsatisfactory to expect a disabled person to have to go into a great long explanation as to the effects that their disablement had on them merely to cause the employer to make adjustments, which he probably should have made in the first place. On the other hand, a balance must be struck. It is equally undesirable that an employer should be required to ask a number of questions about a person.'

In *HJ Heinz Co. Ltd v Kenrick* and *Rothwell v Pelikan Hardcopy Scotland Ltd* an employer's failure to enquire about an employee's medical condition that led to his dismissal on health grounds, constituted a breach. This provision is now contained in EA 2010, Sch. 8, para. 20(1)(a).

Employers are also under a duty to make reasonable adjustments in recruitment and the selection process for job applicants.

22.9.1 A Comparator

In instances of direct discrimination based on a person's disability, the use of a comparator is the same as the other types of direct discrimination. But, here the comparator must be a person who does not possess the same disability as the claimant, but who has the same abilities and skills. Hence, it is the circumstances relevant to the less favourable treatment that is the focus.

22.9.2 Pre-employment Health Questionnaire

EA 2010 provides limited conditions where health questions may be asked (by an employer or their agent or employees) of an applicant before a job offer is made (EA 2010, s. 60). This ensures persons with a physical/mental impairment are not discriminated against. However, common sense must prevail, and the exceptions noted below to the general rule about pre-employment health questionnaires being unlawful are to be construed narrowly. Consequently, questions regarding an applicant's health may be asked to determine the following:

1. any reasonable adjustments that may be required for the person to do that job/attend interviews (EA 2010, s. 60(6)(a));

2. an applicant's ability to perform an intrinsic aspect of the job (EA 2010, s. 60(6)(b));

3. to monitor equality and diversity information for the organization (EA 2010, s. 60(6)(c));

4. to enable a positive action policy to be pursued (EA 2010, s. 60(6)(d));

5. to demonstrate an occupational requirement of the person required for the job (EA 2010, s. 60(6)(e));

6. where such questions are necessary in relation to national security (EA 2010, s. 60(14)).

The 'pre-employment' element of the protection is important as, once the person has been offered employment, an employer *is* permitted to ask health questions. (Note that a person applying for a job does not have the right to complain to a tribunal if they believe a pre-employment health question was asked, but they may complain to the Equality and Human Rights Commission.)

22.10 DISCRIMINATION ON THE BASIS OF GENDER REASSIGNMENT

Under EA 2010, s. 7, gender reassignment refers to a person who is proposing to undergo, is undergoing, or has undergone a process (or part of a process) for the purpose of reassigning the person's sex by changing physiological or other attributes of sex (a transsexual person). The Act now protects a woman (e.g.) who wishes to live permanently as a man even though she does not intend to undergo any medical procedures (what used to be the medical supervision requirement for protection). Permanency is required, hence a cross-dresser would not be protected. Despite the change in gender, this will not allow the transsexual person to 'benefit' from their change in areas such as marriage, parenthood, social security benefits, succession, peerages, and sport. However, they will be recognized as being of the gender reassigned to, they will be issued with a new birth certificate, and be able to marry.

22.11 SEX, MARRIAGE/CIVIL PARTNERSHIP AND RACE DISCRIMINATION

EA 2010 prohibits discrimination on the basis of a person's sex or their marital/cohabitation status, or their race. In relation to the protected characteristic of sex, s. 11 identifies that a reference to a person who has this particular protected characteristic is a reference to a man or to a woman; or to persons of the same sex.

There are no changes to the protection already provided in relation to race. Section 9 defines race as including colour, nationality, and ethnic or national origins. The protected characteristic refers to a person of a particular racial group or persons of the same racial group. Section 8(4) continues that because a racial group comprises two or more distinct racial groups this does not prevent it from constituting a particular racial group. Section 8(5) is an important power granted to a Minister of the Crown to amend this section to provide for caste to be an aspect of race. The Enterprise and Regulatory Reform Act 2013 imposed a requirement on the Government to establish secondary legislation so as to include caste within the meaning of 'race' for the purposes of interpreting EA 2010. The Government commenced a consultation on the matter which ended in September 2017, and legislation is expected later in 2018.

EA 2010 provides protection against discrimination based on sex or race to a wide range of workers—those who carry out the employment personally. There is no qualification period necessary to qualify and, unlike claims for redundancy payments or unfair dismissal, there is no cap on the amount of damages that may be awarded. This has led to substantial sums being awarded to the victims of discrimination under the previous Acts.

Protection is afforded against each form of prohibited conduct. As such, and similarly to the previous legislation, acts of direct and indirect discrimination are outlawed, and claims for victimization suffered as a result of exercising rights or giving evidence in hearings also results in a breach, and for harassment suffered by a claimant are actionable. Direct discrimination can be demonstrated in the following case.

> ### Owen & Briggs v James (1982)
>
> **Facts:**
>
> Ms Owen, a black woman, applied, but was rejected, for the position of secretary. The successful applicant was a white woman with less experience and fewer qualifications. Evidence was deduced that the employers stated 'why should we appoint "coloured girls" when we could hire English applicants'.
>
> **Authority for:**
>
> The Court of Appeal held the employers had refused to hire Owens due to her race, and this was to her detriment.

Where an employer applies a requirement that a significantly smaller proportion of persons from one racial group can comply with, and not complying is to their detriment, an indirectly discriminatory breach is committed.

> ### Meer v London Borough of Tower Hamlets (1988)
>
> **Facts:**
>
> Mr Meer who is of Indian origin applied for the position as a solicitor and was subject to the respondent's use of selection criteria. One criterion was that the applicant had previous experience in Tower Hamlets which Meer claimed was indirectly discriminatory.
>
> **Authority for:**
>
> The tribunal and EAT held there had been no breach of the relevant law (the Race Relations Act 1976) as the criterion was not a requirement or condition. Thus, it was not a bar to his selection (adhering to the Court of Appeal's ruling in Perera v Civil Service Commission (No.2)).

22.11.1 Discrimination Before Employment

It is possible for employers to fall victim to discrimination laws even before they have employed the worker. In relation to sex and race discrimination, this typically occurs when the employer places an advertisement for a job, or in the interview/selection procedure.

* *Advertisements:* An employer may not publish or cause to be published an advertisement which indicates or might reasonably be understood to indicate an intention to sexually or racially discriminate. This clearly has implications when an employer uses words to describe a vacancy such as 'manager' (rather than manager/manageress), 'waitress' (rather than waiting staff), and so on (and for anyone who publishes it). This may be seen in terms of race discrimination where an employer states in an advert that the applicant must have 'English as their first language'. This may have been innocently included by the employer, to require high proficiency in the English language of the applicant, but its impact is to dissuade those members of groups from applying where English may not be their 'first' language. This, however, does not

mean that they are less than proficient in the language. Employers, therefore, should be careful to ensure that advertisements do not transgress the law. It does not mean that the employer cannot seek to hire members of one ethnic group, or one sex. Occupational Requirements exist that enable discrimination where this is a particular requirement of the job. However, the employer would be advised to state this in the advertisement to remove any doubt.

- *Interview/selection events:* An employer should not employ practices that are discriminatory, such as (e.g.) invoking a policy not to hire women of child-bearing age or people of ethnic groups. Such practices may be halted by the Equality and Human Rights Commission through the issuing of a non-discrimination notice.

It should be remembered that employers may not instruct someone else to perform the discriminatory practice on their behalf (a manager, human resources department, recruitment agency, and so on). They may not seek to influence someone to discriminate through, for example, bribes or threats, and it is unlawful to assist someone in the commission of discrimination.

22.11.2 **A Comparator**

To establish a claim of discrimination, the claimant must establish that they were discriminated on the basis of their sex, marital/cohabitation status, or race. Hence, they must have been a victim of less favourable treatment attributable to the protected characteristic; and this is evidenced when compared with how a member of the opposite sex, marital/cohabitation status, or race was or would be treated. As such, a hypothetical comparator may be used. Where a hypothetical comparator is used, this could be evidenced from several people in the same employment whose circumstances are somewhat similar to that of the claimant, but not the same. The Code of Practice provides for another way to approach the application of hypothetical comparators as 'but for the relevant protected characteristic, would the claimant have been treated in that way?'

Note that a comparator is not needed in cases of racial segregation (EA 2010 s. 13(1)). Employers must not seek to segregate workers based on their race, regardless of any policy reason surrounding this, or else they face falling victim to a potential claim for discrimination: *Pel Ltd v Modgill*).

Section 23(1) requires that (in relation to direct discrimination) there must be no material difference between the circumstances of the comparator and claimant. But this need not mean that the two people are identical, rather it is circumstances which are relevant to the treatment of the claimant and the comparator.

In direct discrimination in employment related to marriage/civil partnership, the direct discrimination only covers less favourable treatment because the worker is married or a civil partner. Single people or those in relationships outside of these protected characteristics are not protected.

22.12 **EQUALITY IN PAY**

EA 2010, s. 66 imposes an equality clause in the terms of a contract of employment, even where one is not included. The law relating to sex equality in pay (ss. 66–70) is based on a person employed on work that is equal to that of a comparator of the opposite sex. This ensures that (e.g.) a woman's terms of employment are no less favourable than a man's (the comparator). If the man's contract contains a term that benefits him, and it is not present in the contract of the woman, s. 66(2)(b) provides that the woman's contract is modified (equalized) to include this term (*Hayward v Cammell Laird Shipbuilders*). The legislation is applicable to workers regardless of age, there is no qualification period to gain protection, the law is applicable to those employed full-time and part-time, and there is no exemption for small businesses. See **Figure 22.1** for an overview of claims for sex discrimination in pay.

Figure 22.1   Claims for sex discrimination in pay

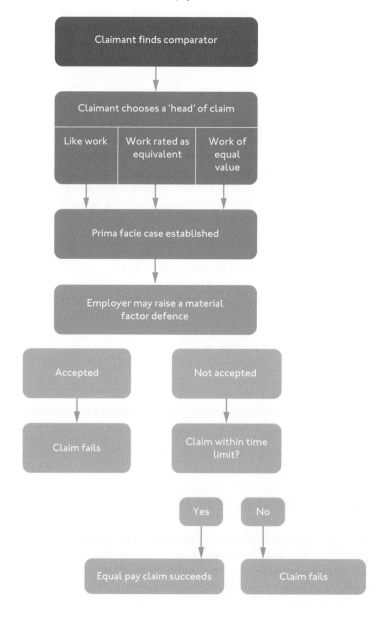

22.12.1 'Pay'

The term 'pay' has to be interpreted in conformity with EU law (The Equal Pay Directive and Art. 157 TFEU). Pay is defined in Art. 157 TFEU as any 'consideration whether in cash or in kind, which the worker receives directly or indirectly, in respect of his employment, from his employer'. It therefore not only includes wages, but all terms and conditions of pay in employment including occupational benefits (*Griffin v London Pension Fund Authority*), sick pay (*Rinner-Kühn v FWW Spezial-Gebäudereinigung GmbH*), bonus payments, pension contributions (*Barber v Guardian Royal Exchange Assurance Group*), and compensation for unfair dismissal (*R v Secretary of State for Employment ex p Seymour-Smith*).

The pay received by men and women must be equal in relation to the heads of claim identified at **22.12.4**. If pay is different between a man and woman, but this is due not because of the worker's gender but, perhaps, because of qualifications, length of service, or some other 'material factor' not applicable to gender, the difference may be objectively justified.

22.12.2 A Comparator

To establish an action of equal pay the claim must be that the reason for the difference in pay is due to the gender of the claimant. The legislation is not designed to give fair pay or enable the claimant to bring an action because someone in another job has better pay and the claimant believes they should be provided with the same. Rather, EA 2010 requires a claim between a woman and a man, and this involves establishing a comparison between workers. The previous law regulating sex equality in pay (the EPA 1970) required the claimant to produce an actual comparator of the opposite sex, working in the same employment as the claimant by the same employer, an associated employer, or at an establishment where common terms and conditions are observed (*British Coal Corporation v Smith*). The Court of Appeal has recently confirmed the meaning and extent of the concept of 'same employment'.

Asda Stores Ltd v Brierley and Others (2016)

Facts:

A case was brought on the basis of (predominantly female) retail store workers who wished to compare their pay with that of (predominantly male) distribution depot workers.

Authority for:

The tribunal held that in the specific facts of the case, in spite of some geographical and organizational distinctions between the two sets of workers, they were in the same employment for the purposes of the law and their pay could be compared. A single source was responsible for the alleged inequality and this was therefore able to remedy the treatment of the individuals affected.

Cases brought after 1 October 2010 involving direct gender pay discrimination may involve the use of a hypothetical comparator rather than an 'actual' comparator (and the problems associated with this). In all other instances, an actual comparator will still be required. Section 78 identifies that (apart from excluded groups) employers are required to publish information relating to the pay of employees for the purpose of showing whether, by reference to factors of such description as is prescribed, there are differences in the pay of male and female employees.

An actual comparator may consist of a person employed at the same time as the claimant, but not successors of the claimant.

Walton Centre for Neurology v Bewley (2008)

Facts:

Ms Bewley claimed equal pay and compared herself with male employees who were engaged after she had left the employer.

Authority for:

The EAT said that the tribunal had erroneously applied an aspect of the CJEU's ruling in *Macarthys Ltd v Smith* that a comparator could include the person who succeeds the claimant. The use of a successor was too speculative and enters the realm of hypothetical comparators.

However, predecessors may be used (as the time limits and extensions to back-pay enable greater access to claims)—*Macarthys Ltd v Smith*. A further improvement to equality effected through EA 2010 has been the introduction of pay transparency. EA 2010, s. 77 provides for discussions about pay. Where a person's contract of employment prohibits them from disclosing or seeking to disclose information about their terms of work, insofar as this relates to a relevant pay disclosure, such a term is unenforceable. This is an interesting step in promoting equality in pay. Previously, establishing the most appropriate comparator in equal pay claims was difficult as many workers (particularly those in the private sector) were subject to a confidentiality clause regarding their employment. It was possible for a potential claimant to require the employer to identify a comparator through an order for discovery (*Leverton v Clwyd County Council*), but this was difficult in practice. Indeed, one of the reasons for the general lack of success of the legislation in this area was often the practical problems associated in making a claim of sex discrimination in pay. EA 2010 should help alleviate some of these difficulties.

Having established an actual/hypothetical comparator who is paid more than the claimant, the next stage is to demonstrate which form the discrimination in pay takes: the claimant bases the claim for equal pay on one of the 'heads' of claim.

22.12.3 Preparing a Claim—Pay Disclosure

Where a worker wishes to bring an equal pay claim, due to the complexity in establishing such actions, advice from a trade union, or local not-for-profit advisory agency may be very beneficial. Section 77 requires that a term of a person's work that purports to prevent or restrict the person from disclosing or seeking to disclose information about the terms of their work is unenforceable against them in so far as the person makes or seeks to make a relevant pay disclosure. Colleagues and former colleagues may also seek a relevant pay disclosure (if made for the purpose of enabling the person who makes it, or the person to whom it is made, to find out whether or to what extent there is a connection between pay and having (or not having) a particular protected characteristic). The Act protects against victimization by protecting those who make, seek, or receive information disclosed in a relevant pay disclosure.

22.12.4 The Heads of Claim

The claimant has to select the most appropriate 'head' under which they are to base the claim. There are three heads—like work, work rated as equivalent, and work of equal value. The tribunal is not entitled to choose the head and it is important for the success of the claim that the claimant selects the most appropriate head based on their circumstances.

22.12.4.1 Like work

Section 65(1)(b) of EA 2010 identifies that a claimant is performing 'like work' with their comparator, if the work is the same, or broadly similar work. The work being undertaken does not have to be exactly the same, and any minor differences that are of no practical importance may be ignored (s. 65(2)(b))—*Electrolux Ltd v Hutchinson*. If the comparator is actually taking on additional duties that do differentiate the role performed by the claimant and the comparator, then this can justify a difference in pay and the 'like work' claim will fail (*Eaton Ltd v Nuttall*—the male workers had greater responsibility than their female colleagues and the consequences of losses occurring during their work would have been significantly more serious). However, EA 2010 requires regard to the frequency of differences between the claimant's and comparator's work in practice and the extent and nature of these. Even prior to EA 2010, the courts had looked to the roles of the claimant and comparator being undertaken at work, rather than focusing on the (stated) terms of the contract when determining their responsibilities and duties.

Shields v E Coomes (Holdings) Ltd (1978)

Facts:

Ms Shields was employed in a betting shop and compared herself with a male colleague being paid at a higher rate. The employer stated that, although the male and female workers performed largely the same role, the reason for the higher pay to the men was because they acted as a deterrent to the risk of attack on the premises.

Authority for:

The male employees had never had to act in the capacity identified by the employer. Therefore the women and men were performing like work and the claim for equal pay should succeed.

22.12.4.2 Work rated as equivalent

To avoid potential claims against the employer, and in the interests of transparency, the employer may perform a job evaluation study that seeks to rate the pay provided to workers on the basis of the roles and responsibilities that are undertaken (EA 2010, s. 65(1)(b)). However, an employer cannot be forced to conduct this study, but where they have, the claimant may use the findings in any claim (in the same way as the employer can use the findings to defend a claim). Clearly, to have any value the study must be appropriate and objective. It must not be based on a sex-specific system (s. 65(4)(b)) where values are set differently between men and women.

A fair rating system will satisfy the following:

1. it must be analytical;
2. the work undertaken must be objectively assessed (identifying the value of the work in terms of skill, responsibilities, and so on—factors such as strength may be discriminatory between male and female workers and hence should be avoided: *Rummler v Dato-Druck GmbH*);
3. both the claimant's and comparator's jobs must have been part of the study;
4. the study must have been conducted at the undertaking where the claimant is employed.

It should also be noted that even though a job evaluation study may rate a man's job as *lower* than that of a woman while the employer pays the man a higher wage, this will not prevent a successful claim from the woman, despite the fact that the legislation provides for a claim when the jobs are rated as 'equivalent' (*Bainbridge v Redcar and Cleveland BC*).

22.12.4.3 **Work of equal value**

In the past, employers often used to employ men and women in different jobs (therefore restricting claims under 'like work'), and they would refuse to undertake a job evaluation study (hence preventing 'work rated as equivalent' claims). The result was an impasse in successful actions on the basis of equal pay. As such, following action by the EU Commission that the UK was in breach of its EU law obligations, legislative action was taken to introduce a 'third head' of complaint of sex discrimination in pay—'work of equal value' (the Equal Pay (Amendment) Regulations 1983). This increased the possibility of claims and provided access to the right for many more claimants. Further, it was held in *Pickstone v Freemans Plc* that an equal value claim is possible even where a 'token' man is employed in the same job as the claimant. This prevents an employer from employing the tactic of hiring a man in order to prevent the claimant pleading under this section of the Act.

EA 2010, s. 65(1)(c) enables claims that (e.g.) a woman's work is equal to a man's (the comparator) where it is neither like the man's work, nor rated as equivalent to his, but it is nevertheless equal in terms of the demands made upon her by reference to factors such as effort, skill, and decision-making (EA 2010, s. 65(6)(b)).

The previous case law further requires that all of the individual terms and conditions of the contract have to be equalized, rather than looking at the broad aspects of the contracts of the claimant and comparator.

Hayward v Cammell Laird Shipbuilders (1988)

Facts:

The case involved a woman engaged as a cook at the shipyard who claimed equality in pay based on her assertion that her work was of equal value with comparators performing jobs as a painter, engineer, and joiner. The employer's defence was that when viewed

→

as a whole, the claimant's contract was as favourable as the comparators. The claimant's contract provided for better holiday pay and meal entitlements (among others) not enjoyed by the comparators, although her pay and overtime rates were lower. The House of Lords held that all the terms of the claimant's contract had to be as favourable as those of the comparator, including the pay.

Authority for:

A claimant who is engaged on work of equal value with the comparator is entitled to equality of pay in relation to each element of the contract.

When faced with a claim that, prima facie, demonstrates the claimant and comparator are being paid on different rates, and this is due to sex discrimination in pay, the employer may mount a defence of a genuine material difference justifying the difference.

22.12.5 Material Factor Defence

Once the claimant has established their claim under one of the previously discussed three heads, the employer may be in a position to avoid equalizing the pay between the claimant and the comparator under EA 2010 (s. 69). The employer is entitled to demonstrate that the difference in the pay is not based on the sex of the parties, but rather it is based on a **material factor**, that can be objectively justified on the needs of the business, and is a proportionate means of achieving that aim. For the factor to be 'material' it must be a material difference between the claimant's case and the comparator's. This argument is available to be pleaded at the preliminary or full hearing.

- *Responsibility:* An employer may attempt to justify differences in pay based on the additional responsibilities undertaken. Where this is relied on, the employer must demonstrate that the responsibilities are frequently required, and are based on the conduct of the parties rather than what is included in the contract (*Shields v E Coomes Ltd*— see **22.12.4.1**).
- *Market forces:* It may be necessary for an employer to provide pay at different rates between jobs, which would otherwise enable a 'work of equal value' claim, because of the nature of the market that the jobs are in (*Rainey v Greater Glasgow Health Board*).

Rainey v Greater Glasgow Health Board (1987)

Facts:

Ms Rainey was a prosthetist who worked under the control of the Health Board. Due to its expansion, the Health Board had to recruit more staff and due to shortages in the public sector, these recruits had to be selected from the private sector. Even though the new recruits had comparable skills and experience, they were paid approximately 40 per cent more than those recruited on the NHS scale. The new recruits were predominantly men which led to the claim for equal pay.

Authority for:

An employer can avoid a finding of discrimination on the basis of pay where the reason for the difference between the men and women is something other than sex. Here the 'material' difference in pay (which means the difference must be significant and relevant) was due to the sector from where the recruits were selected. Those from the private sector just happened to be men whilst those from the NHS happened to be women. Had women been recruited from the private sector to facilitate this expansion, they would have received the same pay as the men.

- *Collective bargaining agreements:* It may be possible for an employer to rely on agreements between workers' representatives and the employer regarding collective bargaining agreements or pay structures, although they cannot provide an automatic defence (*Enderby v Frenchay Health Authority*).

Enderby v Frenchay Health Authority (1994)

Facts:

Dr Enderby, a speech therapist, complained on the basis of equal pay when she compared the value of her work with that of (largely male) pharmacists and clinical psychologists employed in the NHS. The employers, denying that the comparators and Enderby were engaged in work of equal value, argued that the difference in pay was due to a collective bargaining agreement (a material factor which is not the difference of sex).

Authority for:

Following a reference to the CJEU it was held that even if the bargaining agreements were non-discriminatory this did not satisfy a sufficiently objective justification for the difference in pay between the roles of the men and women.

- *Experience:* The general rule has been that those workers who have longer service at an employer's business will, generally, be paid higher wages due to their seniority. The employer can (generally) justify this on the basis of rewarding loyalty, providing motivation to stay with the organization, reflecting experience, and so on.
- *Regional variations:* An employer may seek to justify differences in pay because the claimant and comparator's work exist in different locations (*NAAFI v Varley*).

NAAFI v Varley (1976)

Facts:

Ms Varley was employed in Nottingham on the same grade as a comparable male worker in NAFFI's London office although staff in Nottingham worked slightly longer hours than those in London. Varley argued her hours should be equalized with the male comparator to avoid discriminatory conduct by NAFFI.

Authority for:

In a claim to have her hours equalized with staff in London, the EAT refused. It held the variation to be otherwise than to do with the sex of the workers. It was a custom in London for workers to work shorter hours. On appeal, again it was held there was no discrimination on the basis of sex—it was simply one group of workers were based in Nottingham, the other in London, and region variations would exist.

- *Red-circle agreements:* A red-circle agreement is where an employer has performed, for example, a job evaluation study and the result of which has led to groups of workers being downgraded. The agreement protects the affected workers' salaries at the current rate, despite being moved to a lower grade. The agreement, and its application, must be performed in a non-discriminatory way—the employer's intentions are irrelevant (*Snoxell v Vauxhall Motors Ltd*).

22.12.6 Time Limits for a Claim

A claim for equal pay may be made at any time while the worker is employed under a 'stable employment relationship' (*Preston v Wolverhampton Healthcare NHS Trust*) although this can also include a succession of consecutive contracts (see the Court of Appeal ruling in *Slack and others v Cumbria County Council* and *Equality and Human Rights Commission sub nom Cumbria County Council v Dow (No. 2)*). If they do not wish to bring an action whilst working, they can wait until the employment is terminated, and bring a 'rolled up' claim within six months of leaving (as held by the Court of Justice). However, in circumstances where the employer has deliberately misled a worker or concealed facts that would have assisted with their claim, and the worker could not have been reasonably expected to be aware of this; or where the worker is suffering a disability during the six-month period when they left the employment where the claim would have been presented, the time period is extended. In cases of concealment, the six-month period does not begin until the worker discovered (or should have discovered) the concealment; and in cases of disability, the period begins when the worker is no longer under the disability.

Equal pay claims may be backdated for a six-year period.

22.12.7 'Good Practice'

Due to changes in the legislation, and in an attempt to assist employers in complying with their legal responsibilities, Codes of Practice have been created to offer practical help with implementing the provisions of EA 2010. The Codes (on equal pay; employment; and services, public functions, and associations) were laid before Parliament on 12 October 2010 and came into force on 6 April 2011 in the form of the Equality Act 2010 Codes of Practice (Services, Public Functions and Associations, Employment, and Equal Pay) Order 2011. Further, the Enterprise and Regulatory Reform Act 2013 has provided for an employer to be required to complete an equal pay audit, at the discretion of the Employment Tribunal, where an employer has breached equal pay laws on or after 1 October 2014. An employer can be required to publish the results of the audit on its website for a period of three years (unless it can justify that to do so would be to breach a legal obligation).

22.12.8 **Gender Pay Gap Reporting**

On 6 December 2016 the Government released the latest version of the Equality Act 2010 (Gender Pay Gap Information) Regulations 2017. In an attempt to allay fears and criticism of the previous drafts, this (probably final) draft has incorporated computational details regarding individuals' hourly pay, applicable bonus payments, working hours, and so on. The result is a very complex set of requirements to comply with the law.

22.12.8.1 **Who is covered**

The important aspects of the Regulations are: All employers in Great Britain with at least 250 employees will be required to publish information regarding differences in pay between male and female employees (some public authorities will be exempt from this requirement). The Equality Act 2010 (Specific Duties and Public Authorities) Regulations 2017 apply to public sector employers and these Regulations largely reflect The Equality Act 2010 (Gender Pay Gap Information) Regulations 2017 which apply to private sector employers. The main differences between the two Regulations are that the public sector duty takes effect as part of the existing public-sector equality duty. As such it does not establish a standalone requirement. Further, the pay information 'snapshot' date is 31 March for public sector employers and 5 April for those in the private sector. The reporting requirements will affect those individuals in 'employment' according to the definition provided in the Equality Act 2010—therefore employees, workers, casual workers, and the self-employed (where they provide the services personally) will be covered. An interesting exception to the reporting requirements is where the employer does not have, nor is it reasonably practicable for them to collect, those individuals who are required to personally complete the work (workers and some self-employed individuals).

22.12.8.2 **What information is reported**

Employers will be obliged to publish the following information:

- The mean and median pay differences between male and female 'full-time relevant employees'. This will exclude employees absent from work and not in receipt of their full pay.
- The proportion of male and female 'relevant employees' who received bonus pay. The time period for the calculation is difference in mean and median pay between male and female 'relevant employees' during the period of 12 months, ending with a snapshot on 5 April.
- The proportions of these 'relevant employees' in the lower, lower middle, upper middle, and upper quartile pay bands.
- Overtime payments will be excluded from the calculations.

22.12.8.3 **Compliance**

- The relevant information will have to be published within a 12-month period beginning with the 5 April snapshot date.
- The data will have to be signed off by a senior person in the organization and published on its website for a period of not less than three years. Further, the data will have to be uploaded to a government-sponsored website. This may incentivize employers to avoid the 'naming and shaming' that will likely be reported when this information enters the public domain.

- A failure to provide the data will be considered an 'unlawful act' and thereby enable the Equalities and Human Rights Commission to commence enforcement proceedings against the recalcitrant employer.

Finally, employers will be able to provide a narrative/commentary on any differences and the data presented generally. This may include details of any pay gap to put the information in context, explain any difference in pay, and if so, what the employer plans to do to remedy the difference.

22.13 DISCRIMINATION ON THE BASIS OF RELIGION OR BELIEF

Legislation to prevent discrimination based on an individual's religious belief was extended following the enactment of the Employment Equality (Religion or Belief) Regulations 2003. This legislation has been repealed following EA 2010 and its provisions are contained within that legislation.

EA 2010 protects workers against discrimination based on their choice of religion, religious beliefs (or non-belief), or other similar philosophical belief—be that a real or perceived belief. Section 10 identifies that religion means any religion and a lack of religion. Belief means any religious or philosophical belief or a lack of belief. There are no changes to this area of protection against discrimination; however, it is important to note that the discriminator and the person discriminated against may hold the same religion or belief.

Eweida and Others v UK (2013)

Facts:

This case was discussed at **2.7.2.2**.

Four cases were joined in issues surrounding Art. 9 of the European Convention on Human Rights which provides the right to freedom of thought, conscience and religion, and a qualified right to manifest one's religion or beliefs. The cases involved: 1) Ms Eweida who was employed by British Airways (BA) and 2) Ms Chaplin who was employed as a geriatric nurse. They both wished to wear a crucifix visible over their uniforms. This action was in breach of their employers' dress code; 3) Ms Ladele who was a registrar required to perform civil partnership ceremonies but refused to do so for same-sex couples; and 4) Mr McFarlane who was employed to provide counselling services for Relate (a relationship counselling service). He refused to provide sexual counselling for same-sex couples. In all the cases the question was whether the individuals had the right to manifest their religious views at work.

Authority for:

Regarding the dress codes in questions 1 and 2, BA's uniform policy was designed to establish an 'image' for its members of staff. However, as the nature of the crucifix was discreet and had not attracted any complaints or negative impact on the BA brand, a refusal to allow Eweida to wear it at work had breached Art. 9. Chaplin was lawfully refused to wear her crucifix as this was to do with hygiene rather than her religious freedom. In both 3 and 4 the refusal to perform the services required of their job due to discrimination on the basis of sexual orientation was not permitted.

The *Eweida* cases demonstrate the power of European Convention rights and how they may impact on employment policies. It also shows the difficulties employers may face when choosing to ban items of clothing, hairstyles, or displays of a person's faith. Any such ban must satisfy the test of being a proportionate means of achieving a legitimate aim.

The CJEU has also provided direction on the wearing of Islamic headscarves at work and the extent to which employers may seek to control their use.

Case C-157/15 Achbita, Centrum voor Gelijkheid van kansen en voor racismebestrijding v G4S Secure Solutions (2017)

Facts:

The case involved a reference from the Court of Cassation (Belgium). Samira Achbita worked as a receptionist for G4S. This is a private organization was there was an unwritten rule at the time of Achbita's employment that prohibited employees from wearing visible signs of their political, philosophical, or religious beliefs in the workplace. In April 2006, Achbita informed her employer that she intended to wear an Islamic headscarf at work, and the employer responded that such action would not be tolerated. Between April and June (including some time away for a period of sick leave) a conflict existed between the employer and Achbita, who insisted on wearing the headscarf. On 12 June 2006, Achbita was dismissed.

Authority for:

The Belgian court referred the matter to the CJEU as the matter raised the compatibility between the national law, the employer's actions, and the Equal Treatment in Employment and Occupation Directive (Council Directive 2000/78/EC). The CJEU held that there was no breach of EU law. Equal treatment, as a matter of EU law, means that there can be no direct or indirect discrimination on the grounds of religion. But, the employer's action was to promote a sense of neutrality of the organization with its customers and its rule did not introduce a difference of treatment that was directly based on religion or belief. This rule was justifiable by promoting a legitimate aim and the means of doing so were proportionate, appropriate, and necessary. A key aspect here was that Achbita interacted with customers, and this was directly associated with the purpose of achieving the aim of the employer.

The CJEU considered that the willingness of an employer to take into account the views of a customer who did not wish to interact with a worker wearing an Islamic headscarf would not amount to an occupational requirement. It would, however, avoid a finding of discrimination.

Case C-188/15 Bougnaoui and Association de défense des droits de l'homme (ADDH) v Micropole Univers (2017)

Facts:

Prior to her employment with the private sector company Micropole, Ms Bougnaoui had met with one its representatives at a student fair. The representative had said that her wearing

→

→

of an Islamic headscarf might pose a problem when she was in contact with customers of the company. During her internship, Bougnaoui wore a bandana but was subsequently hired and she wore an Islamic headscarf for work. This continued until a customer for whom Bougnaoui had been assigned complained about the headscarf. Micropole reaffirmed the need for neutrality when dealing with customers and when Bougnaoui objected to its instruction, she was dismissed. At her hearing, the French court referred questions to the CJEU as to the lawfulness of an employer taking into account the wishes of a customer and whether it constituted a 'genuine and determining occupational requirement'.

Authority for:

The CJEU remarked that it was not sure of the reasoning for the difference in treatment of Bougnaoui. If the dismissal was based on non-compliance with an internal rule prohibiting the visible wearing of signs of political, philosophical, or religious beliefs, the decision in *Achbita* should be followed. However, if the reason for the dismissal was the willingness of an employer to take account the wishes of a customer to have no dealings with a worker wearing an Islamic headscarf (and essentially dismissing her because of that reason), it would not be considered a genuine and determining occupational requirement within the meaning of the Directive.

Consider

Whether Clara can argue that the employer's dress code has disproportionately affected the female staff may be open to question. However, given the nature of the job, the safety implications of wearing trousers, and the employer's duty in relation to protecting the health and safety of their staff, it is likely she would succeed in an action for damages.

As with the other protections from discrimination outlined earlier, protection is afforded against direct and indirect forms of discrimination, against victimization, and against harassment.

22.13.1 Occupational Requirements

There exist situations where an otherwise directly discriminatory act is allowed, and hence not a transgression of EA 2010, where it is an OR for the job. In relation to where an employer has an ethos based on a religion or belief, the employer can rely on the OR if it can be demonstrated that, in relation to that ethos and the nature of the work to be undertaken:

1. the requirement of possessing that particular region or belief is an occupational requirement;
2. the application of the requirement is a proportionate means of achieving a legitimate aim;
3. the person (claimant) fails to meet the requirement or the employer possesses reasonable grounds to believe that they do not meet the requirement.

22.14 DISCRIMINATION ON THE BASIS OF SEXUAL ORIENTATION

A worker may not be discriminated against on the basis of their sexual orientation following the EU Framework Directive (Council Directive 2000/78/EC) that was transposed and given effect in the UK through the Employment Equality (Sexual Orientation) Regulations 2003 (now replaced by EA 2010, s. 12). An individual's sexual orientation is defined as their orientation towards persons of the same sex (homosexual), opposite sex (heterosexual), or both sexes (bisexual)—EA 2010, s. 12. EA 2010 prohibits unwanted conduct (either based on the individual's sexual orientation or on their perceived orientation). To exemplify, on a monetary basis at the very least, the importance of preventing discrimination based on a person's sexual orientation is the following case:

Ditton v CP Publishing Ltd (2007)

Facts:

The claimant, a gay man, was subject to offensive comments about his sexual orientation by a company director. This continued for the first eight days of his employment before he was dismissed.

Authority for:

The tribunal (in Scotland) held he had been discriminated against, he had been harassed, and as the employer had failed to follow the (then applicable) statutory dispute resolution procedures, the award was uplifted to £118,000.

EA 2010 allows for the OR defence of an employer where being of a particular sexual orientation is a genuine and determining occupational requirement (and it is proportionate to those ends); and in the case of organized religions where the sexual orientation contradicts the beliefs of the members of the particular religion.

22.15 DISCRIMINATION AGAINST PART-TIME WORKERS

Before the enactment of the Part-time Workers (Prevention of Less Favourable Treatment) Regulations 2000, a claimant who considered that they had been discriminated against due to their employment status had to initiate a convoluted claim under indirect sex discrimination. However, since July 2000, provision is provided for part-time workers not to be treated less favourably than their full-time counterparts. This may be with regard to the contracts of employment or being subjected to any other detriment through an employer's act or omission (reg. 5(1)).

The Regulations provide the part-time worker with the right to the relevant proportion of pay, access to pension schemes, holiday leave, sick leave, maternity leave, training, and access to promotion on a pro-rata basis, as are the full-time workers. There may be some difference between the full- (s. 2(1)) and part-time (s. 2(2)) workers with regard to overtime pay (the part-time workers would have to work beyond the 'normal' contracted hours of the full-time workers to benefit from this additional rate of pay).

It should be noted that whilst the Regulations protect part-time workers, the employer would only be acting unlawfully in treating the workers differently if this is due to the employment status. An employer may also treat the groups of workers differently if there is some objective reason for the distinction. However, reg. 6 enables an affected part-time worker to request from the employer a written statement regarding the reasons for any difference in the way the groups of workers are treated, and this information may be used in a tribunal against the employer.

The part-time worker may compare how they are treated with those working under full-time contracts, if the work is of 'broadly similar' nature so as to provide a fair comparison.

Matthews v Kent and Medway Towns Fire Authority (2006)

Facts:

Retained part-time firefighters argued that they were employed on the same or broadly similar work as their full-time colleagues (for the purposes of the Part-time Workers (Prevention of Less Favourable Treatment) Regulations 2000).

Authority for:

The issues raised were assessment of levels of qualification, skill, and experience when determining the similarity of the work undertaken. However, this is only relevant in respect to the actual job the person is engaged to perform. The test of similarity was one that had to be considered in light of the Directive and interpreted purposively.

Workers may compare each other's treatment to identify evidence of less favourable treatment where they are employed under the same type of contract; they are performing broadly similar work (and where relevant have similar levels of qualifications, skills, and experience); and the part-time worker and full-time worker are based at the same establishment; or, where no full-time worker is based at the establishment who satisfies the above criteria, works or is based at a different establishment, and satisfies the criteria (s. 2(4)).

22.16 DISCRIMINATION AGAINST WORKERS ON FIXED-TERM CONTRACTS

Those employees engaged on fixed-term contracts have been protected against discrimination based on their contracts (from July 2002) through the Fixed-term Employees (Prevention of Less Favourable Treatment) Regulations 2002. A worker employed on such a contract has the right not to be treated less favourably due to their status than a comparable employee on a permanent contract. Regulation 3(1) provides that the fixed-term employee should not be treated less favourably in relation to the terms of their contract, or through acts or omissions of the employer unless there exist objective grounds for such treatment. Affected employees can request a written statement from an employer where they have been treated less favourably and this information may be used in tribunal proceedings.

Less favourable treatment includes disadvantageous terms of the contract when compared to permanent employees. The Regulations further provide that following four years of successive fixed-term contracts, the contract will become permanent, and a breach of the Regulations enables a damages action for compensation. As with the protection of part-time workers, any attempt by the employer to dismiss a worker for using the Regulation's provisions, or dismissing an employee under a fixed-term contract due to this status, is automatically an unfair dismissal.

22.17 ENFORCEMENT AND REMEDIES FOR DISCRIMINATION CLAIMS

The claimant must bring their claim within three months of the discriminatory act (or within three months of the discrimination ending) for work-related claims (EA 2010, s. 123). The tribunal is empowered to extend the three-month period where it would be just and equitable to do so (EA 2010, s. 123(1)(b)), but before the claim is brought before a tribunal, a conciliation officer is appointed to attempt to resolve the matter between the employer and the claimant. However, if this attempt is unsuccessful, following a finding of discrimination the tribunal can provide the following remedies:

1. declare the rights of the complainant;

2. award damages;

3. make a recommendation that the employer eliminates/reduces the effect of the discrimination for all employees not just the claimant (EA 2010, s. 124). This does not apply to claims of sex discrimination in pay.

Consider

Clara has received physical injury because of the employer's potential breach of equalities law. Chitra will likely have sustained psychiatric injury in the way she has been treated. Are damages recoverable in each instance?

When awarding damages, the tribunal is entitled to compensate for injury to feelings:

O'Donoghue v Redcar Borough Council (2001)

Facts:

O'Donoghue was a barrister at the local authority who was dismissed. The tribunal held this to be unfair and to also constitute victimization. In assessing the quantum of damages, it awarded £8805 for the dismissal and included £2000 for injury to feelings. It stopped at these figures as the company established that it was going to (fairly) dismiss her within six months due to her very poor attitude at work.

Authority for:

The Court of Appeal upheld the award of damages but insisted that there is no 'cut off' point when determining awards for distress and humiliation due to victimization (as this would be a breach of the Sex Discrimination Act). Therefore, the award for injury to feelings was increased to £5000.

They may even extend to include damages for personal injury and psychiatric injury:

HM Prison Service v Salmon (2001)

Facts:

Ms Salmon was one of three women prison officers of 120 in total at a prison where male colleagues engaged in sexual harassment. This included openly reading pornographic materials, engaging in sexual conversations and banter, and ultimately writing offensive comments about Salmon in a dock book.

Authority for:

Salmon's claim was that this situation had led to her suffering from depression and retirement on medical grounds. The EAT agreed and awarded her damages in heads of a psychiatric injury, injury to feelings, and loss of earnings. It did note that future tribunals should be careful not to double compensate claimants in situations involving psychiatric injury and injury to feelings.

Note; in cases of discrimination there is no limit to the compensation that may be awarded, and interest is charged on compensation payments not made in the time of the order:

Marshall v Southampton and South West Hampshire Area Health Authority (No. 2) (1994)

Facts:

Ms Marshall had been employed by the Authority until, in 1980, she was dismissed due to her passing the (then) retirement age. The retirement age between men and women was different and, having successfully argued this was a breach of EU law, she claimed in the second case that the national limit on the compensation that may be awarded in sex discrimination cases was unlawful.

Authority for:

The national compensatory limit contravened the EU Directive. As such, the national law which limited the damages that may be awarded in sex discrimination cases was held unlawful as it breached superior EU law.

22.18 MATERNITY RIGHTS

A pregnant employee gains protection against discrimination on the basis of her pregnancy or childbirth (considered under ERA 1996 to be the birth of a child after 24 weeks of pregnancy (whether alive or dead)). To ensure she receives the protection, the employee must inform her employer of her pregnant state to enable them to comply with the relevant health and safety obligations, and she must also issue the employer with the certificate of pregnancy provided through the hospital or doctor. This identifies the employee's pregnancy, and may also be used by an employer to reclaim any Statutory Maternity Pay (SMP) issued to the employee.

Under health and safety legislation, an employer may have to suspend an employee from work if the job could endanger her or the unborn baby (as required by legislation, a code of practice, and so on). The employer must continue to pay the employee during this suspension, and her continuity of service and other benefits continue to accrue. However, the employer may offer the employee suitable alternative work. If the employee unreasonably refuses, then the employer may cease paying the wages.

Beyond the protection afforded to pregnant women, and those who have given birth, EA 2010 provides specific protection for pregnant employees, such as the right not to be dismissed, the right to attend doctor's appointments, and the right not to be treated less favourably because of pregnancy or maternity leave (EA 2010, s. 18). Section 55(1) of ERA 1996 specifically enables a pregnant employee to have paid time off work to attend the appointment—insofar as it was made on the advice of a doctor, registered midwife, or registered health worker. The protection afforded to women due to their protected characteristic of pregnancy or maternity leave begins when the woman becomes pregnant and continues until the end of her maternity leave or until she returns to work (if this is earlier)—the 'protected period' (EA 2010, s. 18(6)). Outside of these times, unfavourable treatment because of her pregnancy may be considered sex discrimination rather than pregnancy and maternity discrimination (EA 2010, s. 18(7)).

Lyons v DWP JobCentre Plus (2014)

Facts:

Miss Lyons had been employed for over 10 years and had a history of depression. Following the birth of her child in February 2010 Lyons was diagnosed with post-natal depression and she did not return to work. In March 2011 the employer dismissed her on the basis of capability and Lyons brought an action for unfair dismissal and discrimination on the grounds of pregnancy and sex.

Authority for:

The EAT dismissed Lyons's claim for discrimination although upheld the unfair dismissal. This was not a breach of either EA 2010, s. 18 (dismissal due to a pregnancy-related illness) as the unfavourable treatment occurred outside of the protected period, nor was it a breach of EA 2010, s. 13 (direct sex discrimination) as a pregnancy-related absence *after* maternity leave is judged according to how a comparable sick man would be treated (applying *Brown v Rentokil*).

Consequently, if the employer would have dismissed the man for (in)capability to do the job due to his illness, he may also treat a woman (once beyond the protected period) in a similar fashion.

There is further protection for pregnant workers through EU initiatives which prohibit, *inter alia*, the dismissal of pregnant workers/those on maternity leave, other than in exceptional circumstances not related to their pregnancy or maternity leave status (e.g. the Pregnant Workers Directive (92/85/EEC) and the Equal Treatment Directive (2006/54/EC)).

22.18.1 Breastfeeding

There is no obligation on an employer to give breastfeeding workers time off work to perform this activity, but employers are under a duty to reasonably accommodate such a request. A woman may provide the employer with written notice that she is breastfeeding and the employer may, where it is reasonable to do so, adjust the employee's conditions or hours of employment to comply. If this is not possible or would not avoid risks identified in a risk assessment conducted by the employer, the employer should suspend the employee for as long as is necessary to avoid the risk. Employers are under a duty to provide suitable facilities at work for women who are breastfeeding, and a refusal to allow a breastfeeding mother to breastfeed (through a change of her hours of work) or to express milk, may result in unlawful sex discrimination.

22.18.2 Parental Leave

The Maternity and Parental Leave Regulations 1999 allow all employees with one year's continuous employment, to take a period of leave to care for their children. Following this period, the employee may take 13 weeks' unpaid leave for each child insofar as this is taken before the child's fifth birthday (eighteenth birthday in respect of children with a disability). The employee must, as a minimum, give at least four weeks' notice before any leave is taken, and they must further provide double the notice period in relation to the time taken (up to the 13 weeks). An employer is entitled, where this is reasonable in relation to the needs of the business, to postpone the leave for a period of up to six months.

The employer must allow the employee to return to their job following the leave (or a similar job if more than four weeks of leave is taken) on the same basis and hours that are no less favourable than when they left. To enable the employer to run the business effectively and with certainty of staffing levels and so on, the Regulations require that employees may take leave in 'bundles' rather than one continuous block, but these must be in blocks of one week and not exceed four weeks' leave if taken in this manner.

22.18.3 Maternity and Paternity Leave

ERA 1996 provides pregnant employees with a right of 26 weeks of Ordinary Maternity Leave, and a further 26 weeks of Additional Maternity Leave. During the leave, the employee is entitled to receive any contractual benefits as if she were at work. Whilst the woman may take all of this period of leave, some may wish to return to work sooner. She is entitled to do so, following a period of two weeks' compulsory maternity leave (four weeks if she works in a factory) following the birth of the child, when she has provided the employer with at least eight weeks' notice of her wish to return. The woman must inform her employer no later than the fifteenth week before the expected due date of the child that she is pregnant, the expected due date of the child (evidenced through the maternity certificate called MATB1), (a specimen form is included with the online resources), and when she wishes to start maternity leave (and the employer should notify her, in response, of the date for the leave, within 28 days of the employee's notification). If the employer fails in this obligation the employee may have protection against any dismissal or less favourable treatment by not returning to work on time.

Where the employee has accrued one year's continuous employment before the eleventh week of the expected due date of the birth, she has the right on return to have her rights of employment intact. She is also entitled to the terms and conditions of her employment to accrue during the leave (such as pension contributions), except for her wages—and the employee is also bound by the terms of her contract during this period. A further extension to the employee's rights was the introduction of 'keep in touch' days where an employee on maternity leave can return to work (and be paid) for up to 10 days without losing her right to SMP. If the employee has taken more than four weeks of maternity leave, she is entitled to return to a suitable alternative position if it is not reasonably practicable for her to return to the same job she left. In *Blundell v St Andrew's Catholic Primary School* a primary school teacher was returned to a job teaching different pupils in a different year to when she left. The EAT stated that a consideration of returning to the same job involved consideration of the nature, capacity, and place of employment.

Whilst she is not entitled to be paid her wages during the leave (although many employers provide such a scheme—on varying bases), the employee will receive SMP for the first 39 weeks of the leave if she qualifies. To qualify the employee must have been employed by the same employer continuously for at least 26 weeks into the fifteenth week before the week of the due date (called the qualifying week); and be earning on average at least an amount equal to the lower earnings limit (for 2018–19 this is £116 per week/£503 per month/£6,032 per year). If the employee does not qualify for SMP, the employer must inform her of this, and the reasons, by issuing her an SMP1 form, which will help her to claim Maternity Allowance.

The Paternity and Adoption Leave Regulations 2002 provides the father of the child with the right to take one or two weeks' paid leave (although the two weeks' leave must be taken consecutively) to be taken within 56 days of the child's birth. The man's continuity of employment and other benefits continue to accrue during this time. In order to receive the leave the employee (the man) must have responsibility for the child's upbringing (or expect to have this responsibility), he must be the child's biological father or the husband/ partner of the child's mother, and he must have accrued 26 weeks' continuous employment 15 weeks before the expected due date. To qualify for the pay during the leave, the man must have been making NICs.

Fathers of children due on or after 3 April 2011 who satisfy the qualification criteria are entitled to Additional Paternity Leave (APL)—but this is to be abolished from 5 April 2015 given the introduction of the Children and Families Act 2014 discussed in the next section.

22.18.4 Extension of Rights to Parents Adopting Children

Rights for parents who are to adopt children were provided in the Paternity and Adoption Leave Regulations 2002. At the time of writing, the members of the couple seeking to access the rights provided in the Regulations must have worked for the employer continuously for at least 26 weeks and be 'newly matched' with a child through an adoption agency, and this can be a domestic adoption or an inter-country adoption following the Flexible Working (Eligibility, Complaints and Remedies) (Amendment) (No. 2) Regulations 2007. The 2007 Regulations extended the definition of an adoption agency to include private foster care and a residence order. However, as of April 2015, statutory adoption leave will apply from the first day of the employee's engagement with no qualifying criteria as above being required, and statutory adoption pay is being equalized with that of statutory maternity pay—90 per cent of the primary adopter's pay for the first six weeks of leave.

The Children and Families Act 2014 (along with several implementing statutory instruments) provides qualifying employees with several extensions to the right to request flexible working. These will make important changes to employment including:

- *Right to attend antenatal appointments:* With effect on or after 1 October 2014, the partner of the pregnant woman (the father-to-be) is allowed (unpaid) time away from work to attend up to two antenatal appointments with the woman.

- *Shared parental leave and pay:* Very significantly, and a genuine boost to combat the historic discrimination faced by women of childbearing age, with effect from 5 April 2015 (applying to babies born on or after this date), the right to 52 weeks' maternity leave (39 paid weeks) will remain for women but those with partners (defined as husband, partner, and same-sex civil partner), who have at least 26 weeks' continuous service by the fifteenth week of the expected week of confinement, will have the ability to end their maternity leave and share the remaining leave, and pay, with their partner as shared parental leave and pay. The expectation is for the leave to be taken in one continuous period of time, but the employee may request it to be taken over a period of shorter blocks of time (of at least one-week duration) with agreement of the employer. Following introduction of the shared parental leave provisions, ordinary paid paternity leave will continue but additional paternity leave and pay is to be abolished.

- Both parents are entitled to 20 keeping-in-touch days in addition to the existing 10 days that women on maternity leave currently have access to.

22.18.5 Family-Friendly Policies

When elected to government, the Labour Party sought to introduce protective rights for those at work and to cooperate with the EU in the extension of rights for workers. One such measure was to facilitate family-friendly working practices, and enable those with child care and other dependants' responsibilities to work, but also to be able to take leave or change their work when required. As such, employees may take reasonable time off work to provide assistance to a dependant (who may be a child, parent, spouse, or partner and extends to any other person who reasonably relies on the employee to make arrangements for the provision of care). ERA 1996, s. 57A provides the employee with a right to a 'reasonable' amount of (unpaid) time off to look after a dependant who is ill, has given birth or is injured, in relation to an unexpected incident at a school involving a child of the employee, due to unexpected problems in the provision of care for a dependant, or where a death occurs to an employee's dependant. An employee unreasonably denied the right to leave may claim within three months of the refusal to a tribunal, which can award compensation.

 CONCLUSION

This chapter has considered the enactment of the new legislation to promote equality in the workplace and beyond. EA 2010 has repealed and refocused previous legislative provisions, and in codifying the principles from the European and domestic courts, it has aimed to simplify equality laws. The increased rights of workers, extension of these to consumers, and new obligations on employers to promote equality at work will present interesting challenges in the future. Many trading partners and customers require businesses to be seen to be following equality laws as a symbol of their being a good and ethical employer and the type of firm with whom they wish to do business. Promoting equality is not just a legal requirement. Purposely adopted into an organization's culture, it can instil respect, transparency of decision-making, and a better working environment for all.

The book now continues to examine the regulations placed on employers through contracts of employment and statute, such as to protect the health and safety of workers.

 SUMMARY OF MAIN POINTS

Protected characteristics

- The protected characteristics in the codified Equality Act 2010 are age, disability, gender reassignment, marriage and civil partnership, pregnancy and maternity, race, religion or belief, sex, and sexual orientation.

Discrimination law

- EA 2010 prohibits discrimination in certain areas before employment (at advertising/interview stage), during employment, and following employment (providing/refusing to provide references, equal pay claims).
- Employers may be liable for acts of harassment against their employees by third parties.
- English law is subject to interpretation in conformity with EU laws and decisions of the Court of Justice.
- Discrimination may be 'direct' or 'indirect', involve victimization, and harassment.
- A comparator is required to establish a claim.
- Claims have to be lodged at a tribunal within three months of the last complained of act of discrimination.

Sex discrimination in pay

- All contracts of employment are deemed to include an equality clause. Claims have to be made on the basis of discrimination based on the claimant's sex.
- English law must be interpreted in conformity with EU laws and decisions of the Court of Justice of the European Union.
- The term 'pay' includes all consideration the worker receives from the employer.
- A claim must be made under one of three 'heads' of complaint—like work, work rated as equivalent, and work of equal value.
- Claims have to be made with reference to a comparator from the same employment and in claims of direct sex discrimination in pay, a hypothetical comparator may be used.
- Equal value claims can include a claimant who has been rated as performing 'higher' work (not equal work) than the comparator.
- The employer can raise a 'material factor' defence that a difference in pay is not due to the sex of the claimant but due to reasons such as responsibility, market forces, experience, and regional variations.

Pregnant workers

- Dismissal of a pregnant employee for anything to do with her pregnancy is automatically unfair dismissal.
- The woman has to demonstrate unfavourable treatment due to her pregnancy.
- The woman must inform her employer of her pregnancy and the employer is required to perform a risk assessment of the workplace to ensure it does not place the woman, or her unborn child, at risk.

Maternity rights

- Employees with one year's continuous employment may take 13 weeks' unpaid leave for each child (to be taken before the child's fifth birthday—eighteenth birthday where the child has a disability).

- An employee who has given birth has the right to 26 weeks of Ordinary Maternity Leave (OML) and a further 26 weeks of Additional Maternity Leave (AML).

- Statutory Maternity Pay, Maternity Allowance, Statutory Paternity Pay, and Statutory Adoption Pay are available where appropriate.

- The father, or employee with responsibility (or expected responsibility) for the child's upbringing, is entitled to take two weeks' Statutory Paternity Leave and may, after 5 April 2015, qualify to share the mother's (right to) paid leave.

- Rights to leave have been extended to adopting parents.

Family-friendly policies

- Employees may take reasonable time off from work to provide assistance to a dependant (child, spouse, parent, partner, or someone who relies on the employee for care); or to take time off when the dependant is ill, has given birth, been injured, has an unexpected problem relating to the dependant's care, or in the event of the death of a dependant.

SUMMARY QUESTIONS

Essay questions

1. The sex discrimination laws in the UK have offered increasing levels of protection to women workers. Some commentators have suggested that this is unfair and should be restricted, particularly in matters to do with pregnancy. With specific reference to the Equality Act 2010, explain how the law protects women workers and whether these Acts have been successful.

2. 'Despite a rather benign interpretation by the judiciary, and judicial development over the last 40 years, the practical impact of the Equal Pay legislation has been very disappointing in securing equality of pay between men and women.'

   Critically analyse the above statement.

Problem questions

1. All Bright Consumables (ABC) Ltd has placed an advertisement in the local newspaper for the recruitment of a new member of staff to act as assistant manager in a new shop it is opening. Due to the high proportion of immigrants from Poland living in the area, the advert specifies that the applicant must be able to speak Polish. Margaret, who has several years' experience in management, applies for the position but is rejected as she only speaks English. Despite this shortcoming, she satisfies each of the essential characteristics identified in the job specifications.

   Sofia also applies for the position of assistant manager at ABC. Sofia is a wheelchair user and is informed at the interview that whilst she satisfies the criteria for the position, the office where the management team are based is on the second floor of the building and the only access is via stairs. The toilets in the building are also located on the second floor and ABC has no plans to move either the office or the toilets. As such, Sofia's application is rejected.

Lena is appointed to the position of assistant manager having satisfied all the relevant criteria and performing well in the interview. She lives in a same-sex relationship with Carla. ABC has a policy of providing its staff with a travel discount for flights in Europe, and this extends to the spouse of the staff. When Lena claims the discount for herself and Carla she is informed that ABC only recognizes marriage or cohabitation between persons of the opposite sex, and therefore ABC refuses to provide the discount to Carla. Soon after this request, Lena begins to receive abusive notes on her desk and on the staff notice board about her sexuality. When she complains to senior management, Lena is told to 'grow thicker skin' and there is nothing ABC can do about it.

Advise each of the parties as to any legal rights they have.

2. Consider Redmount Borough Council's (RBC) potential liability in the following circumstances:

Benny applied for an advertised post in the parks department of RBC as a delivery operative. Following his rejected application for a post he considered himself to be qualified for, he asked RBC for the reason and any other feedback. Benny was informed that RBC had recently adopted a policy, following discovery of an under-representation in the workforce of women and persons from ethnic minority groups, that these groups would be given priority of appointment and promotion. Any person not from these groups would not be considered for the position.

Dora was recently appointed as a speech therapist for RBC. She was appointed at the top of the pay scale. Diego is employed by RBC as a consultant and is paid £10,000 per annum less than Dora although he considers his job as being of equal value to RBC as the speech therapists. Further, most of the speech therapists are women whilst most of the consultants are men. RBC state that the reason for the difference in pay is to facilitate the recruitment of speech therapists from the private sector where salaries are higher. There are very few speech therapists in the public sector so RBC has to match/improve on the salaries paid in the private sector to entice the therapists to work for the Council.

RBC employed Isa, a lesbian, five months ago as a care assistant at a home for delinquent girls which is under the control of the Council. When Isa's sexual orientation was discovered, she was dismissed as it was considered that she would be an 'inappropriate role model for troubled teenagers'. The dismissal letter to Isa read 'Given that these are highly impressionable girls, often from broken homes, your lifestyle choice makes you unsuitable for continued employment.'

Advise each of the parties as to their legal rights.

 You will find guidance about how to answer these questions online at www.oup.com/uk/marson5e/.

 FURTHER READING

Books and articles

Bennett, M., Roberts, S., and Davis, H. (2005) 'The Way Forward: Positive Discrimination or Positive Action?' *International Journal of Discrimination and the Law*, Vol. 6, No. 3, p. 223.

Oliver, H. (2004) 'Sexual Orientation Discrimination: Perceptions, Definitions and Genuine Occupational Requirements' *Industrial Law Journal*, Vol. 33, No. 1, p. 1.

Pigott, C. (2002) 'Knowledge and the Employer's Duty to Make Reasonable Adjustments' *New Law Journal*, No. 152, p. 1656.

Riley, R. and Glavina, J. (2006) 'Sexual Orientation Discrimination—Adequate Investigation of Employee Grievance' *Employer's Law*, November, p. 10.

Steele, I. (2010) 'Sex Discrimination and the Material Factor Defence under the Equal Pay Act 1970 and the Equality Act 2010' *Industrial Law Journal*, Vol. 39, No. 3, p. 264.

Useful websites, Twitter, and YouTube channels

http://www.acas.org.uk
@acasorguk

https://www.youtube.com/user/acasorguk
The website of the Advisory, Conciliation and Arbitration Service, which offers practical guidance and assistance on all forms of employment matters.

https://www.gov.uk/browse/business
Information, forms, and ideas for businesses to comply with the law, expand their business, develop networks with others in the locality, and so on. It is a national organization, but has information specific to regions throughout the UK to ensure relevance and the practical approach that many businesses want.

https://www.gov.uk/government/organisations/government-equalities-office
@Govt_Equality and @Govt_Women
Government Equalities Office is the body established to formulate the equality and legislative strategy of the Government. These are excellent sources of easily accessible materials and explanations of the legislation. The second Twitter link is the Government Equalities Office focusing on issues faced by, and specifically related to, women.

http://www.legislation.gov.uk/ukpga/2010/15/contents
The Equality Act 2010.
Telephone advice
ACAS runs a helpline for businesses of all sizes (whether in the public or private sector) providing practical help on equality and diversity issues. It is available on the following number: 0845 600 34 44.

 ONLINE RESOURCES

www.oup.com/uk/marson5e/

For further resources relating to this chapter, including self-test questions, an interactive glossary, and key case flashcards.

23 REGULATION OF THE CONDITIONS OF EMPLOYMENT

Legislation places many obligations on employers. Employers are required to protect their workers' health and safety in terms of safe systems of work; safety procedures, and instructions to colleagues regarding their conduct at work; and there are wider protections in terms of the workers' maximum working hours and rest/leave periods, and minimum rates of pay. If these are ignored the employer may face substantial damages claims, and there may also be criminal sanctions against the employer. Further, mechanisms exist to assist workers if the employer becomes insolvent and owes wages or other contractual benefits. The terms and conditions of employment provide the employer with an opportunity to protect their business by incorporating a restraint of trade clause into the contract or using 'garden leave' agreements to prevent unfair competition or exploitation of the employer's confidential information. Lack of adequate protection of a business's confidential information may be severely damaging hence the necessity of awareness of this area of law.

Business Scenario 23

Jianyu is employed as an estate agent for Top Homes Ltd. Jianyu's contract of employment include the following terms:

- he must work the hours required of him by his line manager;
- his employment duties may vary in respect of the needs of the company;
- he may only take holidays agreed six months in advance by his manager;
- following the termination of his contract, Jianyu may not establish his own business as an estate agent, nor work for another estate agency, within a five-mile radius of Top Homes Ltd's office for a period of one calendar year.

Jianyu is also required to inspect properties in the course of his duties. The (fictitious) Agents, Employees and Safety Act 1970 provides that all estate agents whose role includes property value and assessment must receive health and safety training. The Act does not, however, stipulate the content of the training or outline the regularity of the maintenance of the training.

Learning Outcomes

- Explain the scope of the Working Time Regulations 1998 and its application to the workforce (**23.2–23.2.6**)
- Identify how the maximum working week is calculated and workers' right to paid annual leave (**23.3–23.3.4**)
- Identify the employer's duty to protect workers' and visitors' health and safety, and the duty to maintain liability insurance (**23.4–23.4.2.5**)

- Describe the mechanism for incorporating a restraint of trade clause into a contract of employment and the scope of its protection to the confidential information of a business (**23.5–23.5.8**)
- Explain the protections to workers in the event of the insolvency of the employer (**23.6**).

23.1 INTRODUCTION

This chapter continues from the discussion of the obligations on employers to protect their workers from discrimination and harassment, to a wider consideration of the regulation of conditions of employment. Employers are increasingly subject to statutory controls that provide for a minimum wage to be paid to workers; for regulation as to the maximum number of hours workers may be required to work; and for the protection of workers' health and safety. In the event of an employer's insolvency, the rights of employees are identified, and finally, the mechanisms for employers to protect their business interests in the contract of employment are considered.

23.2 THE WORKING TIME REGULATIONS 1998

Prior to 1998, there was little regulation over working hours in the United Kingdom (UK). Whilst men were allowed to work as many hours as they could physically manage, regardless of the negative impact this may have on their health, women and children had been protected through the Factories Acts. In 1993, the EU passed the Working Time Directive that sought to regulate the maximum working hours in the EU, and the UK responded by enacting the Working Time Regulations 1998. The Regulations apply to 'workers' rather than just 'employees'. To qualify as a worker the individual has to perform their work or provide services personally (reg. 1), hence, it does not matter if they are self-employed, an agency worker, or a trainee.

It is important to recognize that whilst this text presents legal topics in isolation (where possible), the reality is that a breach of one area of law may lead to breaches of others. For example, a breach of the Working Time Regulations may lead to liability under these Regulations, but it may also result in an employee's stress and mental illness which could also lead to tortious liability. Insofar as these are reasonably foreseeable, an employer could face liability on each count.

Hone v Six Continents Retail (2005)

Facts:

The claimant pub manager was subject to an excessive workload that, he claimed, led him to suffer stress and this extended to a psychiatric injury. According to records maintained by Hone, he was working between 89–92 hours per week. Whilst the judge referred to planning issues which were in the control of Hone and could have alleviated the negative effects of his work, later in his employment key personnel left the business. This exacerbated his stress and he complained to the Operations Manager who failed to take appropriate action.

→

Authority for:

The meeting where Hone identified his stress levels and need for help established a reasonable foreseeability of harm. This was a plain indicator of impending harm to the claimant for which the employer was responsible.

However, given that reasonable foreseeability is often fact-specific, the decision in *Hone* should be compared with the following case:

Sayers v Cambridgeshire County Council (2006)

Facts:

Sayers was a Senior Operations Manager and working on average 50–60 hours per week. She had been observed at work showing manifest signs of distress (crying and visibly upset) but this was attributed to the nature of her work and the reaction to criticisms, work failures, and so on. She also had time away from work but at no point did Sayers refer to any stress or illness related to her workload. Even though three employees engaged in comparable positions as Sayers had suffered a psychiatric injury it was held that her illness and injury was not reasonably foreseeable.

Authority for:

It was in the claimant's deliberate concealment of her ill health and absences that the employer could not have reasonably foreseen the consequences suffered by Sayers. An understanding of some of the more obvious signs of stress is not necessarily sufficient to hold the employer liable when an employee becomes ill.

Whilst there was a failure to adhere to the Regulations, the employee's illness was not reasonably foreseeable and the employer's actions were reasonable in the circumstances.

Consider

Consider that Jianyu is required to, and regularly does, work in excess of 50–60 hours per week. However, as the business is going through a period of rapid expansion with the boom in the housing market, his employer has informed Jianyu that he needs to put in extra hours to meet demand (as per his contract). As such, Jianyu is currently working 80+ hours per week which is affecting his private life and his health. What regulations are applicable, can Jianyu opt-out of working such hours, and what are the responsibilities on Top Homes Ltd to ensure that it is acting in accordance with the law?

23.2.1 The Maximum Working Week

The Regulations provide that in a seven-day-week period, the worker should not exceed 48 working hours (reg. 4), assessed over a 17-week period. As a consequence, the worker may perform substantially longer hours in some weeks as long as the employment over this period averages out to no more than 48 hours per week. Also, the restriction is on a maximum *working* week, what then is work for the purposes of this calculation?

Landeshauptstadt Kiel v Jaeger (2004)

Facts:

A doctor was employed at a hospital in Germany. He would work at the hospital administering care. He would also undertake on-call duties which required him to be at the hospital although this was offset by granting him leave, providing some additional pay, and giving him a room and bed to rest when his services were not required. German law distinguished between 'readiness for work' and 'stand-by' which led to the doctor's query regarding what was considered work.

Authority for:

The Court of Justice of the European Union clarified the meaning of 'working time' as part of the Directive—and thereby the UK's interpretation of its Regulations. 'Work' means working at the employer's disposal, and carrying out the duties concerned with this work. Hence, those individuals who are on call as part of their working duties have this time included in the assessment if the work is performed at the employer's place of business but not if the 'on-call' duties involve the worker waiting away from the workplace.

Further guidance was provided by the EAT in 2017:

Focus Care Agency v Roberts (2017)

Facts:

Three cases involving individuals and whether their 'sleep-in' time counted as 'time work' for the purposes of the National Minimum Wage. The EAT considered that yes or no answers to this question was often not possible as such cases were very fact specific. However, it did state that merely because an individual was on the employer's premises, provided with accommodation or on-call did not automatically result in them being at 'work'.

Authority for:

At para. 44 the EAT identified four factors which will help determine whether an individual is working whilst being present:

I. Where the individual is present due to a regulatory or contractual requirement on the employer;

→

→

2. Any restrictions on the individual's activities—such as having to remain on the premises throughout the shift and may face disciplinary action if they leave (and do something else);

3. The degree of responsibility undertaken by the individual. For example, a distinction may be drawn between an individual sleeping at the employer's premises to alert emergency services on the basis of a fire or break-in; at the other end of this scale an individual may have to care for persons with a disability and thus have a heavier personal responsibility throughout the night; and

4. The immediacy of the requirement to provide services if something untoward occurs or an emergency arises. Hence, whether the individual is the person who decides to intervene and then intervenes when necessary, or whether the individual is woken as and when needed by another worker with immediate responsibility for intervening.

23.2.2 Opt-outs

The UK Government, during the negotiations for the Directive, was successful in obtaining an opt-out clause to the effect that individual workers could waive their rights to protection under the law. Workers cannot be forced to agree to the opt-out, but in practice many recognize this may be necessary to obtain employment. If a worker has opted out, they may change their mind and seek protection under the law if the employer is given seven days' notice (and this time is not beyond an agreement established with the employer for a longer period).

23.2.3 Enforcement

The workers who are not in the excluded categories are entitled to protection under the Regulations. If an employer refuses to allow a worker to gain access to these rights, or does not take reasonable steps to ensure compliance with the Regulations, they are guilty of a criminal offence. This is extended to an employer who dismisses or penalizes a worker for exercising, or attempting to exercise, their rights (ERA 1996, ss. 45A and 101A). It should be further noted that whilst there are limited obligations on the employer to hold anything other than 'general' records regarding workers' hours of work and written documentation, the Court of Justice of the European Union (Court of Justice) provided a strong recommendation that it may be in the employers' interest for employers to hold sufficient records to demonstrate that the opt-out was expressed, rather than implied, and was, along with any other contractual term, entered into freely.

Pfeiffer v Deutsches Rotes Kreuz Kreisverband Waldshut eV (2004)

Facts:

Workers, including Mr Pfeiffer, were engaged by the German Red Cross as emergency staff. They were subject to a collective agreement which set their weekly working hours

→

at 49. This was in breach of the Working Time Directive (although the employer claimed, unsuccessfully, that their work was exempt from the Directive).

Authority for:

The CJEU held that working hours could not be fairly set collectively and that each worker had the right to opt-out on an individual basis. In order to effectively operate a maximum working week a 'worker's consent must be given not only individually but also expressly and freely'.

23.2.4 Rest Breaks

Along with the maximum working week, the Regulations provide that adult workers are entitled to a 20-minute rest break if expected to work more than six hours at a stretch. Further, they are entitled to 11 hours' rest in each 24-hour period, and 12 hours' rest for young workers (reg. 10). For those workers employed on a shift pattern, these Regulations do not apply in this manner. However, they are entitled to an equivalent period of rest and a refusal will amount to a breach of the Regulations.

Grange v Abellio London (2016)

Facts:

The claimant was contracted to work for eight hours and thirty minutes and his shift included a thirty minute lunch break. His employer instructed him, however, that he should not take the lunch break. Rather, Grange was to work straight through and leave work early. He claimed this was a breach of reg. 10 on the basis that he had been refused a rest break.

Authority for:

The employer argued successfully at the tribunal that as Grange had not asked for a rest break he could not have been refused one. However the EAT held that the instruction to work through could be interpreted as a refusal. An explicit request was not needed.

23.2.5 Entitlement to Annual Leave

The Working Time Directive provides that workers are entitled to four weeks' paid leave. The Regulations provided for the introduction of a system of paid annual leave (reg. 13) that has resulted in entitlement to 5.6 weeks (28 days) to reflect 20 days of holidays and eight days of statutory bank holidays. This was a major increase to workers' rights, as many received less than this minimum when the Regulations were brought into effect. The employer is also obliged to clearly distinguish between 'normal' pay, and pay for leave as provided in lieu of holidays. It was a practice of employers to 'roll up' pay with pay in lieu and hence circumvent the requirement to allow workers to take their holidays (a particular concern of casual workers). The Court of Justice provided this clear identification of how the pay received by the worker was to be declared separately as pay for work, and pay for holiday entitlement.

Robinson-Steele v RD Retail Services Ltd (2006)

Facts:

A reference was made to the CJEU regarding the hours of work of the claimant employees and whether this expressly included an amount to cover annual leave (and thus was 'rolled up' holiday pay). The question was therefore did the employees have an entitlement to leave or had they been issued with additional pay to reflect that they were not taking holidays?

Authority for:

Including holiday pay in the payments to workers often occurs with temporary and casual staff. This simplifies a potentially complex situation for the employer. The CJEU held that rolling up holiday pay is unlawful. It must be clearly identifiable as a separate sum on a worker's pay form to comply with the Directive.

Recent case law from the Court of Justice has clarified the obligations imposed on employers when dealing with annual leave and holiday pay. In *Lock v British Gas Trading Ltd* the claimant, a sales consultant for British Gas, took two weeks' annual leave and was paid his normal (basic) salary without the commission he usually earned being added to this sum (his commission regularly accounted for 60 per cent of his salary). Despite the fact that the commission earned varied from month to month, it was sufficiently permanent and directly linked to his work and the payment of his salary, and there was an intrinsic link between the commission and the performance of the tasks of the worker's job. Hence the Court of Justice required it to be included in his holiday pay. To do otherwise would have been an incentive for the individual not to take annual leave, and the purpose of the Working Time Directive was to enable workers to take rest periods away from work as a health and safety measure. In *Lock and Another v British Gas Trading Ltd (No. 2)* the Court of Appeal, upholding the EAT's decision, found that the Regulations should be interpreted to require employers to include a worker's commission payments in calculations regarding their holiday pay. Of course, this ruling is based on the Working Time Directive (which provides four weeks of paid leave) rather than the additional 1.6 weeks' leave provided in the UK's Regulations. Also, in respect of the recovery of underpayments of holiday pay through unlawful deductions from wages, such claims must be made within a three-month time period of the alleged underpayment. There is a two-year cap on claims for backdated holiday pay, hence, employers will be looking forwards to ensuring they comply with wages and payments in the future.

Consider

If Jianyu had to give six months' notice to take paid annual leave, what would be the effect if he was too ill to take his holiday at the date when arranged? What would happen to his holiday entitlement if he died in service and was unable to have his holiday? Recent case authority from both national courts and the CJEU have helped to answer those questions.

In *ANGED v FASGA* the Court of Justice established that a worker who is sick during the year in which holiday entitlement accrues and cannot take leave is entitled for the leave to continue into the next year (of annual leave entitlement). This right to paid annual leave continues to accrue when the illness which has prevented the worker from taking the leave leads to their death.

Bollacke v Klass & Kock B.V. (2014)

Facts:

Mr Bollacke had been engaged by the employer for a period of 10 years before his health began to deteriorate. This led to absences in 2009 of eight months' leave, some absences in the first part of 2010, and then later in 2010 whilst on sick leave he died. His wife was his sole beneficiary and claimed for the holiday pay which her husband was unable to take whilst ill. In total, it transpires Mr Bollacke had accrued 140.5 days of unpaid leave.

Authority for:

The employer claimed that, in accordance with German law, an employee's contract died with them and therefore the employee cannot take any unused holiday leave whether entitled to it or not. The CJEU had already distinguished between holiday leave and sick leave in *ANGED*. It went further by confirming that the Directive was not to be interpreted so that the death of a worker relieves the employer of the duty to pay any outstanding leave. Nor could allowance for the leave be restricted to a prior application.

23.2.6 Night-shift Workers

The Regulations are applicable to those who work during the day, but are also applicable to, and perhaps even greater protection is required for, those workers employed on shift patterns and night work. This assessment is concerned with the regularity of the period of night work rather than whether it involves the majority of the work. Regulation 6 provides that night workers should not exceed eight hours in any 24-hour period (albeit that this is assessed over an average of 17 weeks). Night work is defined as work, under the normal course of the employment, of which at least three hours of the daily employment is performed during the night.

23.3 THE NATIONAL MINIMUM WAGE AND NATIONAL LIVING WAGE

Workers have the right to be paid, and their pay must be at least at the level established in the National Minimum Wage Act 1998 (NMW 1998) or the National Living Wage (The National Minimum Wage (Amendment) Regulations 2016). Since 1 April 2016 workers aged 25 or over (and not in the first year of an apprenticeship) are legally entitled to be paid at least the National Living Wage.

This is regardless of the size of the employer, and regardless of whether the worker is employed full- or part-time, paid on commission, or is a casual or agency worker. Employees are also entitled to an individual, written pay statement that identifies the gross pay, the deductions made, and the net pay provided to the worker. There are strict rules on the deductions that an employer may make to an employee's pay. The most obvious reason for a deduction involves those that are required by legislation (National Insurance Contributions and income tax for those subject to Pay As You Earn taxation). Deductions may also be identified in writing in the worker's contract and authorized by the worker or the relevant negotiating body. Finally, an employer, under certain circumstances, may be able to deduct up to 10 per cent of the gross pay of workers in the retail sector to reflect cash shortages or stock deficiencies. This last category is reviewable by an Employment Tribunal if the employee argues it has been applied unfairly.

NMW 1998 provided most workers over compulsory school age with the right to be paid the minimum wage established by that legislation and the subsequent increases as established under the Act. The Government takes recommendations from the Low Pay Commission with regard to the increases in the rate of the minimum wage. As of 1 April 2018 the rates were as follows:

- for adults aged 25 and over the National Living Wage is applicable: £7.83 per hour;
- for workers aged 21–24 and over: £7.38 per hour;
- for workers aged 18–20: £5.90 per hour;
- for young workers (16–17): £4.20 per hour;
- for apprentices (under 19 years old or 19 and over in the first year of their apprenticeship): £3.70 per hour.

23.3.1 **Worker**

The term 'worker' is defined in s. 54 as someone employed under a contract of employment or any other contract where the person performs the work or provides their services personally. This does not, however, include someone who is genuinely in business on their own account. Examples of workers who qualify include: agency workers; apprentices; foreign workers; piece workers; commission workers; and homeworkers. Examples of workers who do not qualify include: self-employed workers; volunteers; company directors; and those working for friends and family.

23.3.2 **Calculating the Pay**

As the legislation provides for a minimum level of hourly pay, and many workers are paid on a monthly or weekly basis, establishing that the minimum level of pay is being received requires a mechanism for calculation.

NMW 1998 provides that the minimum wage is based on the gross pay provided to the worker, but it does not include pension payments, redundancy pay, overtime pay (to ensure that workers do not have to work overtime in order to achieve the minimum wage), expenses, and so on. However, note the distinction in the following case:

Esparon t/a Middle West Residential Care Home v Slavikovska (2014)

Facts:

The claimant was a care worker engaged at the employer's residential care home. She was required to stay at the care home on night shifts for emergency purposes and as required by law. She claimed this was 'work' for the purposes of the NMW and she should be paid accordingly.

Authority for:

The EAT distinguished between an individual who undertakes a shift pattern involving sleeping at the employer's premises as required as part of the employer's legal obligations and staff generally being on call. The former will be entitled to pay for these hours under 'time work'. This applies even though the worker may essentially be doing no 'real' work during that period. Per HHJ Serota QC: 'An important consideration in determining whether an employee is carrying out time work by reason of presence at the respondent's premises "just in case" must be why the employer requires the employee to be on the premises. If he requires the employee to be on the premises pursuant to a statutory requirement . . . that would be a powerful indicator that the employee is . . . working regardless of whether work is actually carried out.'

The employer may include accommodation provided to the worker as part of their hourly pay (which would be offset against the minimum wage payments), but this is limited to a maximum of £7.00 per day. Bonuses paid by the employer and tips received due to service may be counted by the employer in calculating the minimum wage, as are any performance-related pay awards.

The period of work that is used in the calculation of the averaged hourly pay must not be more than one month. However, if the pay is provided on a weekly or monthly basis, this assessment (reference) period will be reduced (reg. 10). There are various forms of working practices that establish the calculation of the hours, and then a reduction of these hours down to the pay received (and hence the pay per hour) is possible. The methods available are:

- *Time work:* Here the work is paid according to the number of hours worked. The calculation simply consists of dividing the pay received by the worker by the number of hours worked to establish the hourly rate (reg. 3).

- *Salaried work:* Here the worker is paid an annual salary and the work is then reduced to a number of (basic) hours worked, with the pay reduced from this annual amount to a weekly (divided by 52) or monthly (divided by 12) rate (reg. 4).

- *Output work:* Here the work is paid when a task is completed (such as piecework or work on commission)—it depends upon the speed of the work by the worker that would determine how many hours were worked, and therefore the pay per hour (reg. 5).

- *Unmeasured work:* If the work does not fit into the above categories then it will be calculated under this measure. The minimum wage must be paid for each hour worked, or the pay must be determined according to a daily average.

23.3.3 Obligation to Maintain Records

Due to the nature of the minimum wage, an employer is obliged to maintain records of payments to their workers, and the hours worked, to ensure that evidence is produced and can be inspected. Her Majesty's Revenue & Customs (HMRC) may access these records to ensure compliance, but there is also a right for the workers to view their own records, and to obtain copies. Falsifying records is a criminal offence and may lead to an enforcement order against the employer.

23.3.4 Enforcement Proceedings

As the minimum wage is a right that ensures workers receive the minimum amount established by the legislation, it is only effective if it is enforceable. An aggrieved worker may bring an action to an Employment Tribunal to claim owed wages (and if they suffer any detrimental treatment such as a dismissal for bringing a claim they have an additional action for unfair dismissal). Here the worker establishes their claim, and as the employer is obliged to maintain adequate records, the burden is on the employer to demonstrate that the worker's claim is incorrect. The Government also established a penalty notice policy designed to further 'encourage' recalcitrant employers to fulfil their obligations. It provides HMRC with the authority to enforce NMW 1998 and as such a compliance officer may serve an enforcement notice on an employer which specifies the amount of money owed to the worker(s); the time limit in which the employer has to pay this sum; and the time limit in which payment has to be provided. A penalty of 200 per cent of the amount owed will be levied unless the arrears are paid within 14 days. A fine of up to a maximum of £20,000 may be imposed on an employer guilty of breaching the Regulations and an employer who fails to satisfy the fine will be disqualified from holding the office of a company director for a period of up to 15 years.

23.4 HEALTH AND SAFETY

Every employer owes their workers and visitors to their premises a duty to take reasonable care for their health and safety. The obligations on the employer apply to all workers and this primary responsibility for safety rests with the employer, even though the workers are legally obliged to assist in these matters. Health and safety requirements have bases in both the common law and through increasing legislative action, both domestically and from the EU. The Health and Safety Executive (HSE) provide statistics each year regarding injuries and deaths at workplaces. In 2016/17, 137 workers were killed at work and there were, according to the Labour Force Survey, 609,000 injuries at work. These reports highlight the dangers at work and seek to raise awareness (particularly of employers) of the need for appropriate actions, mechanisms, and policies to reduce incidence of accidents and to prevent injuries and illnesses.

The law regulates health and safety through legislative provisions and the common law (including criminal and civil law jurisdictions). They have different aims, and both may be used against an employer where an employee has suffered an injury or illness due to a negligent act or omission of the employer.

Consider

Could working 80+ hours per week adversely affect Jianyu's health? Assume that Jianyu had been a cooperative colleague with a pleasant demeanor who recently, following his working the extra hours required by Top Homes Ltd, has become withdrawn, aggressive, and exhibits other signs of stress. What obligations are imposed on Top Homes Ltd to protect Jianyu?

23.4.1 The Common Law

The health and safety of employees is a non-delegable duty on the employer. The employer may delegate the duty (in theory) but the presumption by the courts is that the employer may not escape responsibility if the duty has been delegated and then not performed correctly or as required.

McDermid v Nash Dredging & Reclamation (1986)

Facts:

A ship-hand was injured as a result of the captain's disregard of adhering to relevant safe systems of working. A question of vicarious liability was raised but ultimately rejected.

Authority for:

The House of Lords held that the duty to operate a safe system of work was non-delegable. Employers had a duty to devise the system and also had a responsibility to fulfil its application—it cannot be delegated to an employee for example.

In terms of health and safety, the duty of care has to be established specific to the employer's responsibility, rather than the broad test as outlined in the discussion of negligence. Workplaces may often involve dangerous machinery (e.g. in factories) or activities that place workers in circumstances where injury may occur. The test of establishing a duty of care involves the employer taking reasonable precautions and safety initiatives that are relevant and not unduly oppressive.

Paris v Stepney BC (1951)

Facts:

The full facts of this case are covered at 11.5.2.2. Mr Paris was blinded in the course of his work for the Council. The employer did not consider the job to be sufficiently serious to warrant the use of safety goggles.

Authority for:

The House of Lords held that due to the potential for injury, the employer did owe Mr Paris a duty of care to provide the correct safety equipment, and due to this failure, he was entitled to claim damages for his injury.

Breach of the duty to take care involves a cost/benefit analysis to be considered.

Watt v Hertfordshire CC (1954)

This case is also discussed at **11.5.2.2**.

Facts:

An emergency call was made to a fire station regarding a woman trapped under a lorry. The accident occurred approximately 200–300 yards from the fire station and the fire crew were requested to attend. A heavy lorry jack was required to be transported to the scene quickly and the usual vehicle for this purpose was unavailable. The chief ordered the claimant and his colleagues to use the fire engine to take the jack to its destination and to hold it secure during its journey. On route, when the fire engine had to brake, the jack fell onto the claimant and severely injured his leg.

Authority for:

There was no way to securely hold the jack in place during its transportation and this was an emergency situation involving life and death. Given the circumstances, the need for very prompt action and a balance between the benefit of the action compared with the need to take precautions, there was no breach of the duty of care. Denning LJ stated: 'It is well settled that in measuring due care you must balance the risk against the measures necessary to eliminate the risk. To that proposition there ought to be added this: you must balance the risk against the end to be achieved.' This is a balancing act between ensuring the employer takes precautions to prevent injury, and ensuring the preventative measures are reasonable and not excessive.

Therefore, a common-sense approach is adopted.

Latimer v AEC (1953)

Facts:

The full facts of this case are covered at **11.5.2.2**.

A storm flooded the factory where Mr Latimer worked. Though the employer spread sawdust to prevent workers from slipping, Mr Latimer fell in an unprotected area.

Authority for:

It was held that the employer did owe Mr Latimer a duty of care, but had not breached this and had done all that was reasonable. It was not reasonable for AEC to close the factory, but it should have attempted to prevent injuries through preventative actions, including the sawdust and instructions to workers. As this had been achieved, the claim for damages must fail.

The requirements under the common law attributable to employers, follows the House of Lords decision in *Wilsons and Clyde Coal Co. Ltd v English* (see **13.6.2**). Essentially employers are required to provide competent employees for the claimant, a safe system of work, safe equipment at work, and a safe workplace.

Consider

Today, Jianyu is visiting a dilapidated building to provide an assessment of the property and a valuation. This is the first property in such a condition that Jianyu has visited and he is doing so unaccompanied. Jianyu has not been provided with any health and safety instructions or training (as required per the Business Scenario at the start of this chapter). He therefore has not taken a flashlight/torch with him, he only has his office shoes to wear (rather than safety boots), and he has only informed the staff in the office that he is visiting the property at some point in the day rather than providing any details.

On entering the property Jianyu falls through a hole in the floorboards and breaks his arm. He is unable to move and, in the course of falling, he drops his briefcase which contains his mobile phone. In relation to the following sections, identify any potential breaches of health and safety law by Top Homes Ltd. Further, do you think Jianyu had any responsibility towards maintaining his own health and safety?

23.4.1.1 Competent employees

The employer is required to ensure that the colleagues of the claimant are competent and do not endanger other workers. Establishing mechanisms to avoid dangerous colleagues ensures that a policy of acceptable behaviour at work is created and applied. They are used to identify (and minimize) risks; and to facilitate necessary training and supervision of workers in matters of health and safety. Where the employer has employed someone who is not sufficiently competent to perform the tasks required of the position, the employer may be liable for any damages suffered as a result of this employee. For example in *Hawkins v Ian Ross (Castings) Ltd*, a worker was injured as a result of a 17 year old, who had only a rudimentary understanding of English, making an error and spilling molten steel.

The incompetence has to be foreseeable, but where the injury is due to the colleague being involved in practical jokes, if the employer is aware of such actions and has done nothing to prevent them, then consequent injuries may have to be compensated.

Hudson v Ridge Manufacturing Co Ltd (1957)

Facts:

The claimant was injured at work by a colleague who had a history and reputation of horseplay and engaging in pranks at work. Whilst the employer was aware of this and had reprimanded the colleague on several occasions, they did not take any formal action and it, evidently, did not prevent his continued actions.

Authority for:

The employer was liable for the injury to the claimant. The employer was aware of the source of danger and had failed to take adequate steps to prevent it.

However, where such action involves an unauthorized act that the employer could not have foreseen, the employer will not be liable.

Aldred v Nacanco (1987)

Facts:

The claimant was injured when a colleague tried to startle her by pushing an insecure washbasin in her direction. However, this action caused the claimant injury and she sought damages.

Authority for:

The claim failed as the colleague's action was not connected with her employment. Employers may be liable for authorized acts and the wrongful ways in which they are carried out. Where it is not reasonably foreseeable that injury would occur due to the actions of employees, the employer will not be in breach of their duty.

23.4.1.2 Safe system of work

The employer must ensure that their employees have systems in place to allow tasks to be conducted without any unreasonable risk of injury or illness attributable to carrying out this function. This requires the employer to provide adequate training, suitable equipment, and information and warning signs where appropriate. An employer has to inform the employee as to potential dangers when using equipment and how and when safety procedures have to be used. This is a requirement on the employer and they are obliged to ensure that safety systems are used, rather than simply to raise the issue of safety and allow employees' discretion as to when they wish to follow the instructions. This does not remove the employee's own use of common sense or for their own duty to protect themself, especially in minor matters.

O'Reilly v National Rail (1966)

Facts:

Workers employed in a scrap yard discovered an unexploded bomb and challenged Mr O'Reilly to hit the bomb with a hammer to see what would happen. The bomb exploded, injuring Mr O'Reilly. He claimed for damages against his employer.

Authority for:

The court held that there was no liability as the common sense of the employee was not to hit the unexploded bomb. The employer had not breached the duty to provide a safe system of work by failing to instruct the employee not to take the action.

Whilst physical injury is most commonly associated with ensuring a safe system of work, the employer is also responsible for ensuring the wellbeing of their employees, and in particular this has manifested itself in issues of stress and other psychological pressures.

This has been raised in **13.4**, but in relation to an employer's duty to their employees, the employer must take positive action to reduce the stress placed on workers where this would have a *foreseeable* negative impact on health (*Walker v Northumberland CC*). Figures awarded for stress at work can be substantial, and employers are increasingly settling the claim out of court in an attempt to avoid the admission of liability (although financial liabilities remain). In *McLeod v Test Valley BC* the claim was settled with a payment to the claimant of £200,000. Employers are entitled to assume that employees can reasonably withstand the 'normal' pressures of the job but it is where the employee asks for help or shows obvious signs of stress (e.g. the court will require expert evidence on what is an obvious sign of stress but there are behavioural and physical signs that may demonstrate that the employee is suffering and is in need of assistance) that the employer will be under a duty to act.

23.4.1.3 Safe equipment

The equipment that is provided to employees must be fit for its purpose and safe to use. This may involve ensuring the correct guards or protective screens are used on the equipment; ensuring that electrical equipment is subjected to regular safety checks; ensuring that appropriate safety apparel (goggles, clothes, footwear) is used; and so on. Each of these requirements will depend on the nature of the employer's business, the hazards that are faced by the employees, and the equipment that the employees are using or are exposed to.

23.4.1.4 Safe workplace

Employers have a duty to ensure that the correct heating, lighting, and ventilation are available in the workplace. The employer must provide washing and toilet facilities for employees. The employer must also ensure that the entrances and safety exits are correctly maintained, as are corridors and walkways. The employer is also required to ensure a safe workplace through maintenance of the property to a sufficiently safe standard (*Latimer v AEC*— see **11.5.2.2**), to maintain records for the reporting of accidents, to provide the appropriate first aid facilities, and to undertake appropriate risk assessments. Materials used at the workplace must be handled, stored, and used safely, and any potential hazards (chemicals, explosive, or flammable materials) should be brought to the attention of the employees.

Kennedy v Cordia (Services) LLP (2016)

Facts:

The claimant, a carer, slipped on an icy and snow-covered footpath whilst visiting a house-bound individual. She sought damages from her employer for injuries sustained to her wrist in the course of her employment.

Authority for:

The Supreme Court found that the employer had breached the EU health and safety directives (among other failures) regarding adequate risk assessments. The Supreme Court went further and considered that an employer's duty is not confined to taking precautions as commonly undertaken and an employer can be guilty of a negligent omission from a failure to seek knowledge of risks which are, of themselves, not obvious. This places a greater responsibility on employers to be proactive in their protection of individuals at work.

23.4.1.5 *Defences*

The employer may raise absolute and partial defences to a claim for damages due to an alleged breach of health and safety under negligence. These were identified in **11.6** and are applicable here.

23.4.2 **Statutory Provisions**

The main legislative provision covering health and safety in the workplace is the Health and Safety at Work etc. Act (HSWA) 1974, which identifies the requirements imposed on employers, and it also provides for the enactment of Regulations that 'flesh out' or extend the Act. Breach of the statute, as opposed to the common law route that involves an action for damages for the employer's breach of duty, may lead to a criminal act being committed and the employer being prosecuted for this infringement. Therefore a disregard for health and safety matters may lead to a criminal record and imprisonment.

23.4.2.1 **The Health And Safety At Work etc. Act 1974**

The Act places duties on employers, workers (employees and other workers such as independent contractors), and those with responsibilities in the workplace for ensuring that the required standards are maintained. Whereas the common law route allows an employee to seek compensation for their losses and enables them to initiate a claim, the employee is not entitled to bring an action against the employer for contravention of HSWA 1974, rather this is the task of the Health and Safety Executive (HSE).

   The employer has an obligation to ensure, as far as is reasonably practicable, the health, safety, and welfare of all of the employees (s. 2(1)). Whilst this is a general duty, s. 2(2) extends this in the following ways:

1. the provision and maintenance of safe plant and systems of work that are safe and without risk to health;

2. arrangements for ensuring the safe use, handling, storage, and transport of articles and substances;

3. providing the necessary information, training, and supervision to ensure the health and safety of the employees;

4. in places of work under the control of the employer, maintaining the workplace to a standard that is safe and without risks to health, and maintaining the entrances and exits to the workplace;

5. providing the facilities for a safe working environment for their employees, and maintaining these.

The employer has an obligation to adhere to the above duties, with the proviso that this obligation extends to what is 'reasonably practicable' for the employer. Consequently, where to exercise the duty would not be reasonably practicable, the employer is permitted to make this defence (albeit that the burden of proof of it not being reasonable rests with them).

Associated Dairies v Hartley (1979)

Facts:

The dairy supplied its workers with safety shoes but charged them £1 per week for their use. The claimant argued that this was in contravention of the employer's duty to provide safety equipment.

Authority for:

The Court of Appeal held the obligation to provide the shoes for free was not reasonably practicable and the cost to the workers was fair. The costs of providing the shoes, in relation to the benefit provided to the worker, and the relative low risk of minor injury to the worker, did not place the obligation on the employer to provide free shoes.

23.4.2.2 Responsibilities on the employer

Employers are also obliged, under HSWA 1974, s. 3(1), to conduct their undertaking in such a way as to ensure that non-employees (such as independent contractors) who may be affected by their actions, are not exposed to risk of their health and safety. The employer, further, is required to inform any non-employees of any potential risks to health and safety at the workplace.

R v Swan Hunter Shipbuilders (1982)

Facts:

Work was being carried out on the ship *HMS Glasgow*. A fire started in the ship during welding operations conducted by a sub-contractor, and this fire was exacerbated due to there being too much oxygen in the ship. This fire led to several deaths. It was discovered that Swan Hunter Shipbuilders had informed its employees of the dangers of working with oxygen in confined spaces with poor ventilation, but this information had not been provided to the sub-contractor. The Court of Appeal held that the company was in breach of its obligation under HSWA 1974, s. 3(1).

Authority for:

HSWA 1974, s. 3(1) imposes a duty on employers to inform non-employees of dangers present in the workplace.

Not only do employers have obligations to protect their employees and non-employees at work, s. 6 of HSWA 1974 imposes a duty on anyone who designs, manufactures, imports, or supplies any article that is used at work. This involves things done in the course of business or the particular trade, and it must relate to matters that are within the control of the individual on whom the duty is imposed. They must:

1. as far as is reasonably practicable, ensure the article is designed and constructed so as to be safe when it is being set, used, cleaned, and maintained by a person at work;

2. conduct, or make arrangements for there to be carried out, tests that are necessary to ensure adherence with (1);

3. ensure that the person supplied with an article is provided with the necessary information regarding the use for which it has been designed, and any information required to make its use safe;

4. where it is reasonably practicable, provide any revisions to information that are necessary to ensure adherence with the requirement in (3).

These duties are also replicated for the import or supply of any substance (s. 6(4)). HSWA 1974 also imposes an obligation on designers and manufacturers to conduct research and investigations with the aim of discovering any risks to health and safety and to implement procedures to remove any such risks (s. 6(2)). Section 6(3) imposes a duty on those who erect and install equipment at work to ensure that the manner in which this is achieved should not make the article unsafe or a risk to health and safety. This requirement is subject to the limitation of 'reasonable practicability'.

HSWA 1974 imposes many duties on the employer, as presented in this section of the chapter, but it also requires employees to ensure that they take care for their own safety and for others in the workplace (s. 7). In this respect, they must cooperate with their employer (and any other person) to enable them to comply with their duties (such as using the correct and supplied safety equipment). Section 8 provides a duty on every person in the workplace not to interfere or damage items provided as an aid to protecting health and safety (such as fire extinguishers)—whether this is intentional or reckless action.

23.4.2.3 Potential consequences for employers

If a person commits an offence under HSWA 1974 due to an act or default of some other individual, the other individual will be guilty of the offence (s. 36). This individual may be prosecuted even if the person who actually committed the offence has not faced legal proceedings. If a health and safety offence is committed with the consent of an employer (such as a director, manager, and so on), or with their connivance, or is due to their neglect, then the organization and that individual may be liable for prosecution under HSWA 1974, s. 37. Further, it is no defence for the employer to organize their business so as to leave themself ignorant of any risks or attempt to remove their obligations for the health and safety at the workplace.

If the employer is found guilty of any offence, they may face a fine or, in terms of gross negligence manslaughter, a sentence of life imprisonment. They may also be subject to disqualification from acting as the director of a company under the Company Directors Disqualification Act 1986, s. 2(1). Remember, these offences and punishments affect the individual employer and their business, so the employer cannot hide behind the corporate veil of the limited company. See the online resources for an extra chapter on corporate manslaughter.

23.4.2.4 Advancement of protection through the EU

Membership of the EU has led to the UK transposing Directives established under Art. 137 EC (now Art. 153 TFEU). The UK responded by enacting six sets of Regulations in 1992 (and subsequently amended) to protect health and safety at work. Whilst the reality is that they have not radically extended the protection afforded to those at work (perhaps merely codifying existing obligations), they ensure the employer is proactive in protecting their employees:

• *The Management of Health and Safety at Work Regulations 1999 (as amended 2006):* These impose requirements in relation to the cleanliness and maintenance of the workplace.

This legislation requires the employer to conduct a risk assessment of dangers facing employees and others likely to be affected by their work. If there are five or more employees in the organization then the employer must provide a written health and safety policy (s. 2(3)). This statement must also identify the periods in which inspections will be held, and which member of staff has responsibility for health and safety in the workplace. The employer further has an obligation to bring this information to the attention of the employees and to inform them of any changes to the document(s). The employer has a duty to consult with their employees over health and safety matters (Health and Safety (Consultation with Employees) Regulations 1996).

- *The Workplace (Health, Safety and Welfare) Regulations 1992:* The obligations required under ss. 2 and 4 of HSWA 1974 are extended through these Regulations to employers and occupiers of premises. The Regulations place a duty for the maintenance of the workplace, and its environment, in relation to lighting, heating, entrances, and exits, and to ensure that workplace equipment is in good working order. The employer has to identify any dangers to the employees, and mark any hazards.

- *The Provision and Use of Work Equipment Regulations 1998:* Machinery and other equipment used must be maintained and be in good working order. The Regulations reinforce s. 6 of HSWA 1974. The equipment must be safe to use and be routinely checked.

- *The Personal Protective Equipment at Work Regulations 2002:* Personal protective equipment must be supplied to employees where it is necessary. The employees must have training on the use of the equipment and the employer must maintain the equipment.

- *Manual Handling Operations Regulations 1992:* These require the protection of employees when handling items that may cause injury. The employee may have to lift or transport items as part of their duties, and could consequently sustain injury or be subject to an accident. As such, the employer should consider training, reducing the size/bulk of items, and other remedial action that is appropriate.

- *Health and Safety Display Screen Equipment Regulations 1992:* Training is required for employees who use such materials on its safe use, and regular eye tests must be provided if requested. Employees must also be given breaks (although this may be a change to the work conducted by the employee rather than a 'rest break'). Employees may suffer if their workstation is not correctly fitted (poor posture leads to back problems and so on). These risks must be effectively managed.

In additional to the many regulations that are passed to protect employees' health and safety, the Health and Safety Commission issue codes of practice that provide guidance as to how the regulations should be put into practice. This includes the Health and Safety (First Aid) Regulations 1981; Control of Substances Hazardous to Health Regulations 2002; Reporting of Injuries, Diseases and Dangerous Occurrences Regulations 1995; and so on. These codes are not 'law' but they will be used in the courts, and the employer will be asked whether they adhered to the provisions. If they have not, it is likely a criminal offence will have been committed.

23.4.2.5 Compulsory insurance

As part of their protection of workers' safety, most employers are obliged to carry appropriate insurance to protect against any injury or disease that may befall an employee in the course of their employment (employers in the nationalized industries; local authorities; the health services; family-only employers; and so on do not require employers' liability insurance). 'Course of employment' involves injuries or illness caused both at the employer's premises and off-site (although injuries caused through motoring accidents may be covered by the employer's or employee's own car insurance). The protection is also limited to those workers with 'employee' status.

The requirement is established through the Employers' Liability (Compulsory Insurance) Act 1969. The insurance company that provides the cover will issue a certificate establishing the relevant information regarding the coverage, and it is the employer's responsibility to display the certificate (who may be fined if they do not comply with this requirement). The certificate will identify the cover provided (a minimum of £5 million); which company/business is included in the policy; and the insurance company's details (that may be checked through the Prudential Regulation Authority and the Financial Conduct Authority (FCA) under the terms of the Financial Services Act 2012). Employers are also required to retain copies of their insurance certificates for at least 40 years (and these policies are generally renewed annually) to enable employees whose injury or illness was caused at work, but the symptoms or effects were not identified until sometime later, to establish the relevant insurer.

23.5 RESTRAINT OF TRADE CLAUSES

An employee is restricted from certain activities, either through implied terms or those expressed in their contract of employment, such as working in competition with the employer (the implied duty of fidelity). Once the employee has left the employment, they are, generally, free to work for whomever they wish, or to establish a business and work in competition against the former employer. In order to protect the employer from having an employee (or former employee) use information or knowledge of the employer's business against them, a **restraint of trade clause** may be included in the contract.

A restraint of trade clause is a post-contractual agreement that restricts the employee from working in competition with their previous employer for a certain duration and within a defined geographical/industrial distance. It must be remembered that this agreement limits the employee's right to undertake employment, or to trade in their own business, following termination of the employment relationship. For the employer, there are valid and economically necessary reasons and justifications for this contractual clause. Employers trust employees with significant access to information including (potentially) customers, suppliers, price lists, and trade secrets that could be of great value to a rival, or they may give an unfair advantage to an employee who 'abuses' this trust and sets up in competition with the employer. It is also against public policy for an employer to require agreement to a clause that restrains an employee after the contract of employment has ceased. Restricting employees from working in the area of their expertise, or in industries where they have skills, is not necessarily conducive to an enterprising economy.

Consider

Jianyu's contract prevents him from setting up his own business or working for a competitor for a period of one year and within a five-mile radius of the office of his employment. Assuming this clause has been incorporated to protect the legitimate valuable customer information held by Top Homes Ltd, would you consider this to be protection of an employer's legitimate proprietary interest? Further, given that the other estate agency firms are located within the five-mile radius, how do you think the courts would assess its reasonableness between the parties and in the public interest?

23.5.1 The Application of a Restraint of Trade

The following case established when a restraint of trade clause will be enforceable.

Herbert Morris v Saxelby (1916)

Facts:

A clause in Saxelby's contract prevented him from working in the same trade following the termination of employment. When his contract came to an end Saxelby pursued the same trade in France and his former employer sought to enforce the contract.

Authority for:

The employer's action for the clause to be enforced failed. It went beyond that what was required to protect their legitimate business interests and was held as unreasonable.

A clause will only be applicable if:

1. it seeks to protect the employer's legitimate proprietary interests (such as trade secrets and customer information);
2. it is reasonable between the parties and is in the public interest.

23.5.2 The Protection Afforded by the Clause

An employer may legitimately claim protection where an employee has acquired specialist knowledge such as the details of customers of the employer's business or confidential information. This is often referred to as a 'proprietary interest' rather than general know-how, which the courts would not allow to be included in a restraint of trade clause.

Examples of clauses restricting ex-employees from soliciting customers and clients have been demonstrated in *Allied Dunbar v Frank Weisinger* (involving a firm of solicitors) and in *AM Schoeder v Maccaulay* (involving hairdressing assistants). It is also contrary to a restraint of trade clause to copy an index of customer's names when the ex-employee enters into competition with the employer.

Roger Bullivant Ltd v Ellis (1987)

Facts:

Ellis was subject to a restraint of trade clause preventing him contacting any person with whom he had previous dealings and whose name was included on the employer's customer card index. The restraining clause applied for a limited period.

Authority for:

Ellis had removed the details on the customer index card when he established a business in competition with his former employer. This information did not warrant a trade secret, but his actions were in breach of his duty of good faith.

23.5.3 A Legitimate Proprietary Interest

> **Consider**
>
> The restraint of trade clause affecting Jianyu must protect the employer's legitimate proprietary interests, not restrict the general know-how he has picked up during his employment. However, what are proprietary interests that the courts will enable the employer to legitimately protect?

The identification of what amounts to a legitimate proprietary interest justifying the post-contractual restraint of trade was summed up by Lord Wilberforce in the following case:

> **Stenhouse Australia v Phillips (1974)**
>
> **Facts:**
>
> A five-year post contractual restriction on competition was included in the contract of the managing director of an insurance broking company.
>
> **Authority for:**
>
> The court upheld the application. 'The employer's claim for protection must be based upon the identification of some advantage or asset inherent in the business which can properly be regarded as, in a general sense, his property, and which it would be unjust to allow the employee to appropriate for his own purposes, even though he, the employee, may have contributed to its creation.' (Per Lord Wilberforce).

Therefore, confidential information (client lists, suppliers' details, and so on) and trade secrets (secret formulas and so on) will be included in the court's assessment of a proprietary interest. However, general information regarding the employer's business, or skills that have been gained whilst working for the employer, are not subject to protection.

23.5.4 Reasonableness

In order for the employer to be successful in arguing for the clause to be upheld, they must satisfy the court that the restrictions included are no greater than is 'reasonably' necessary for the protection of the employer's business. In assessing reasonableness, the court will consider the duration of the restraint, the geographical distance covered, the type of business the employer operates, and whether allowing a restraint is fair according to public policy. A clause may fail the reasonableness test if its terms are not sufficiently precise:

Commercial Plastics v Vincent (1964)

Facts:

Mr Vincent was the research and development coordinator for the firm. It had recently spent a large sum of money on producing plastic sheeting and had taken great precautions in ensuring this information remained secret. The bulk of the company's competitors and its sales were in the UK. A restraint of trade was included in Vincent's contract and this restricted his future employment with any of the employer's customers for a period of one year after leaving employment. Vincent did leave Commercial Plastics and began working with a competitor within this time period.

Authority for:

The clause was considered unreasonable. It was too broad to incorporate all the technical details needed to reproduce, and thereby breach, the employer's proprietary interests. Further, as it applied for a one-year period to all of the competitors, it was unenforceable as this went beyond what was required to protect the employer.

or where the clause is contrary to public policy:

Bull v Pitney Bowes (1967)

Facts:

Mr Bull had worked for the employer for 26 years and then left to work for a competitor. The defendant had a rule included in its pension scheme that employees would lose their pension rights if they left the employment for a rival firm.

Authority for:

The employer attempted to impose a restraint of trade through indirect means and this was held as against public policy. The rule was held void against Bull.

Where the extent of the restriction and its duration are excessive to the protection required, the clause also will unlikely be upheld (*Mason v Providence Clothing and Supply Co. Ltd*). Therefore, as a 'rule of thumb', the duration of the restriction and the area of its application are inversely proportional. The wider the area of the restriction, the shorter should be the duration; the smaller the area, a longer duration will be considered reasonable.

Fitch v Dewes (1921)

Facts:

A solicitor (27 years old) who had been working for his employer for a number of years, signed a contract which restricted his acting in competition with the employer within seven miles of Tamworth Town Hall for an unlimited time.

→

Authority for:

The employee complained of the nature and extent of the clause. It was held as reasonable given that the employer had taken him into their employment when he was 14 years old, they had trained him to be skilled in the position he held, and he was privy to their confidential information.

23.5.5 Repudiation of the Contract by the Employer

It should also be noted that the clause will only continue to have effect (as a post-contractual agreement) whilst the parties behaved reasonably with each other. If the employer repudiates the contract, for example by wrongfully dismissing the employee, then any restraint of trade clause becomes unenforceable.

General Billposting Co. Ltd v Atkinson (1909)

Facts:

The employers dismissed the employee who had been engaged as a manager. The manager had successfully won an action for wrongful dismissal and then set up his own business. His contract of employment included a restraint of trade clause for a two-year period after his engagement with the company ended and the company attempted to enforce that clause.

Authority for:

The action for enforcement failed as the company's repudiation through the wrongful dismissal absolved the employee from any further performance on his part. Therefore he was no longer bound by the covenant and was free to act in competition with his former employers.

This authority continues despite the fact that some employers attempt to draft contracts that provided for the continuation of restraint of trade clauses even if the employer breached the contract of employment.

Rock Refrigeration v Jones (1996)

Facts:

Following the promotion of the defendant from general engineering manager to industrial sales director a new restraint of trade clause was included in the contract. This sought to enforce the clause following the termination of the contract 'however so arising or occasioned'. Following his resignation and serving out his contract, the defendant took up work with the new employer. The previous employer attempted to enforce the clause.

Authority for:

It was held that the nature of the clause, in attempting to have application even if the employer repudiated the contract, was by its nature unlawful and therefore unenforceable. Phrases in a restraint of trade clause such as 'for any reason' or similar would be fatal to their enforceability.

Consider

If, on the assessment of the clause, the court considered either that the five-mile radius was too broad or that the one-year duration was too long, what options are available to amend such a cause?

23.5.6 Blue Penciling

This term is used to describe the options available to the courts when faced with a restraint of trade clause that goes beyond the necessary aims of protecting the employer's business. It enables the court to remove an offending passage or term of the clause, and if it still leaves the remainder making grammatical sense, and it is supported by consideration, then it may be held to be valid and enforceable. If the clause and its terms are part of an indivisible agreement, then even if it would be grammatically possible to separate or remove a passage or word(s), the court will refuse to do so.

Attwood v Lamont (1920)

Facts:

The employee had been employed as a tailor and was subject to a restraint of trade clause that prevented him from working as a tailor, dressmaker, milliner, hatter, haberdasher, or men's, women's or children's outfitter. This restriction was to apply within a 10-mile radius of the employer's premises.

Authority for:

The geographical area of the restriction was lawful but the noncompetition clause and its extent beyond that of a tailor (the employee's previous role with the employer) was unreasonable. The court further held that the clause must be read as one single restriction and therefore those parts of it which were unreasonable could not be severed.

The courts, as with any contractual term, will not rewrite a poorly drafted contract, and any clauses that are ambiguous will be subject to the *contra proferentem* rule (see **8.5.3**). The correct drafting and the arguments regarding the necessity for the clause remain the obligation of the employer. The tests were defined in *Sadler v Imperial Life Assurance of Canada* as requiring:

- the ability to remove the words without requiring the addition or alteration of the remaining aspects of the clause;
- the remaining clause continuing to make grammatical sense;
- the removal of the words not altering the nature of the original clause.

Consider

Given the power of blue penciling and, indeed, its limitations, what strategies would you devise in establishing a contractual restraint of trade which could be amended latterly by a court to at least preserve some of its features? Ultimately, compare the effectiveness of the restraint of trade clause with the greater certainty, albeit greater costs, of a garden leave arrangement.

23.5.7 Remedies

The claimant, if successful in convincing the court of the necessity of the restraint of trade, may seek damages to compensate for any losses incurred (such as the ex-employee having solicited clients away from the business) and they may seek an injunction to prevent any further activities that may be in contravention of the clause for its duration. An interim injunction may be granted to prevent the employee breaching the restraint of trade clause until the case is heard in court, where a final injunction may be granted following the conclusion of the hearing. In determining the grant of an interim injunction the court will consider the clause; whether damages are an appropriate remedy; and whether the employer's claim is likely to succeed at the full hearing.

23.5.8 Garden Leave Agreements

Due to potential problems of the courts refusing to uphold a restraint of trade clause, or if the employer has to terminate the employee's contract in advance of any agreed date, the employer may obtain the protection required if they are prepared to pay the employee's salary. The employer may include a long period of notice and in the event that the employee wishes to leave the employment, the employer simply enforces the notice period. Whilst an employee cannot be forced to work, they can be paid a salary with the employer knowing that the employee cannot start a business in competition or take up employment with a rival. This may be a more expensive proposition than relying on a restraint of trade clause, but it provides greater certainty of protection, and ensures that an employee cannot take important secrets or knowledge of the employer's business and use it in competition. Note that the courts will not allow an unusually long **garden leave** clause, and in *GFI Group Inc. v Eaglestone* a notice period of 20 weeks was reduced to 13 weeks as this was considered sufficient in order to protect the employer's proprietary interests.

23.6 THE INSOLVENCY OF THE EMPLOYER

Insolvency can affect an employer who is acting as an individual (in which circumstances the person becomes bankrupt or has entered into a voluntary agreement with creditors) or, for situations where the employer is a company (such as a private limited company or limited liability partnership). Insolvency includes administration, liquidation, receivership, or an agreement that has been entered into voluntarily with the creditors.

Insolvency occurs where the business does not have adequate funds to continue trading or to settle its debts (including, e.g., owed wages to employees). In such a situation, the employee may require assistance to claim what is owed to them, but there are limits to what may be claimed (from the National Insurance Fund—ERA 1996, s. 182), and the employer must be insolvent as defined under the legislation. Employees may recover arrears in pay for a period of at least one week, but this may not exceed eight weeks in total. Holiday pay for up to six weeks in the previous 12 months may be claimed. A failure by the employer to provide the correct statutory entitlement to notice (ERA 1996, s. 86), and the basic award granted under an unfair dismissal claim can also be claimed (including the basic amount of an award by an ACAS arbitrator under the ACAS Arbitration Scheme (Great Britain) Order 2004 (S.I. 2004/753)). The term 'pay' includes contractual payments and statutory payments such as maternity pay or payments ordered through an Employment Tribunal (such as under the information and consultation requirements). Payments are determined, for holiday pay and wages, from the date of insolvency, whereas redundancy and statutory notice pay are determined from either the date when the employer became officially insolvent or when the employment ended (whichever is later). To qualify for redundancy payments the claimant must have employee status; have been continuously employed by the employer for at least two years; and have made a written application to the employer or a tribunal within six months of the employment ending.

Upon insolvency, an insolvency practitioner such as a liquidator, receiver, administrator, supervisor (in voluntary agreements), or trustee (in bankruptcy) will take control over the business and the employee should apply to this person for the relevant forms. Once completed, these are forwarded on to the Redundancy Payments Office. Debts that remain following the payments from the National Insurance Fund are only available if there are sufficient funds in the employer's assets, but holiday pay and wages (to a current maximum, as of 6 April 2018, of £508 per week) are assigned 'preferential debt' status and may be paid out of the employer's remaining assets ahead of other debts.

CONCLUSION

This chapter has identified further obligations placed on employers to protect their employees' health and safety at work through offering a safe system of work; regulating their hours of work; and ensuring they have access to paid leave. Workers have the right to be paid at least the minimum wage and have the ability to seek owed pay if the employer becomes insolvent. Further, employers may seek to protect their legitimate proprietary interests through the insertion of restraint of trade clauses in the contracts of employment. Each of these elements offer protections and establish obligations on employers, and in many cases, compliance is not only necessary in the interests of the business, but necessary to comply with the law. Therefore, they are essential elements for a business employing labour.

SUMMARY OF MAIN POINTS

Working Time Regulations

- The Regulations were enacted to transpose the EU's Acquired Rights Directive.

- 'Workers' not just 'employees' are protected.

- The Regulations provide (in most circumstances) for a maximum working week of 48 hours, averaged over a 17-week period.

- Workers may opt out of the Regulations, although no worker can be forced to opt out, and the worker may opt in to gain protection from the Regulations if they choose.

- Workers are entitled to 11 hours' rest (12 hours for young workers) in each 24-hour period.

- Workers are entitled to 5.6 weeks' paid holiday leave.

- Employers must include commission payments in the calculation of the four weeks of paid leave.

- Night workers should not exceed eight hours' work in any 24-hour period (averaged over 17 weeks).

National Minimum Wage

- The National Minimum Wage Act 1998 (NMW 1998) and the National Living Wage (NLW) is applicable to workers, not just 'employees'.

- There are four levels of NMW and NLW depending on the age of the worker and these figures are regularly reviewed (each October) by the Government following recommendations from the Low Pay Commission.

- 'Pay' is the gross pay of the worker but this does not include pension payments, redundancy pay, overtime, or expenses.

- The employer is obliged to maintain records of the hours worked and payments made to workers.

- Workers can enforce the NMW and the NLW through Employment Tribunals and Her Majesty's Revenue & Customs can enforce the law against a recalcitrant employer.

Health and safety

- Employers owe a duty to take reasonable care of the health and safety of all workers.

- The common law obligations on employers enable an employee to claim for any injuries or damage suffered due to the employer's negligence.

- The statutory measures are largely covered by the Health and Safety at Work Act (HSWA) 1974 and the Regulations enacted following 1992.

- The general duties on employers include: providing safe plant and systems of work; the safe handling and use of articles and substances; providing the relevant and necessary information on health and safety matters to employees; and maintaining a safe working environment.

- A breach of HSWA 1974 may lead to an employer (director, manager, and so on) facing a fine or imprisonment.

Restraint of trade clauses

- Such a clause is a post-contractual agreement restraining the employee from working in competition with the employer for a defined duration and a defined geographical/industrial region.

- The clause must protect the employer's legitimate proprietary interests; it must be reasonable between the parties and be in the public interest.

- A wrongful dismissal/repudiation of the contract by the employer will prevent the application of a restraining clause.

- The courts may remove an offending aspect of the restraint clause to make it fair and enforceable (known as blue pencilling).

- A restraint clause may be enforced through the courts by the award of an injunction.

- Rather than using a restraint of trade clause, the employer may use a garden leave agreement whereby an extended notice period is included in the contract. This is more expensive to the employer, but is enforced with greater certainty than are restraint clauses.

Insolvency

- Where an employer becomes insolvent, the employee can claim for any owed wages and in the event that the employer lacks the resources to settle the claim, they may seek assistance through the National Insurance Fund.

SUMMARY QUESTIONS

Essay questions

1. Is it appropriate to have a national minimum wage? Given the differences in the cost of living throughout the country, and obliging the employer to pay an amount set by the State for employment when market forces may have been better able to regulate pay, evaluate the necessity for, and impact of, the National Minimum Wage Act 1998.

2. An employer is entitled to have their confidential information protected against unauthorized use by a rival. How have the courts determined what may be regarded as 'reasonable' in the award of this protection?

Problem questions

1. Clive works for Trusthouse Fifty, a chain of hotel and dining establishments. He was promoted to manager of the restaurant and bar department. He had not opted out of the Working Time Regulations, his contract provided that he was contracted to serve the employer for 42 hours per week, and he should endeavour to complete his work within this time.

   Despite this contract, Clive was told by the general manager at the establishment that he had responsibility for all aspects of the department. He hired the staff for the functions held there, he ensured the food was prepared to a sufficiently high standard, and he also had sales targets to meet regarding the quantity and price of wine that was sold. As a result, Clive was under great pressure and started to work 80 hours per week to complete his work.

   Clive did not complain to the general manager about this, but it was evident he was suffering health problems due to working excessive hours. After just six months in this job he had become very irritable, had been rude to employees, criticized their work, and had started drinking alcohol to excess. Clive exhibited none of these symptoms when first hired.

   When a concerned colleague (Zoe) informed the general manager of her concerns for Clive's health, she was told that Clive must complete his tasks, and the manager did not care how long it took him to achieve this. Further, it transpires that the general manager has not maintained any records of the time staff work at the establishment.

Clive has now suffered a breakdown and cannot work. Advise him on any claim he may have against the employer based on his statutory rights.

2. Devon is employed by All Bright Consumables (ABC) Ltd in the factory where it makes tablet computers. Devon is a senior manager and has responsibility for the production of the components and their assembly. He is also involved in senior planning meetings where strategies, including plans for patents, are discussed.

    Devon's contract provides for a restraint of trade where Devon will not compete with ABC Ltd either through establishing his own business or working for a competitor, in the technology field, in the UK, Germany, the USA, China, the Middle East, and Africa, for one year after ceasing to work there. A further clause restricts Devon from 'employing ABC Ltd staff, or poaching customers'.

    Some time later, Devon decides to leave ABC Ltd and establish his own company. It specializes in touch screen computers and he wishes to hire the chief designer and operations manager of ABC Ltd to help him in this new venture. Devon approaches both people with an offer to triple their current salary if they leave ABC Ltd with immediate effect. Devon is planning on developing and then marketing a new computer which uses 'gesture-based input' on both the front and back of the device. He was privy to this idea whilst working at ABC Ltd and he knows that ABC Ltd has not yet applied for a patent.

    Advise ABC Ltd on their likely arguments and success in preventing Devon competing with ABC Ltd, hiring the staff, and developing this new computer. How would your answer be developed if Devon said it was the company he established that had taken the actions when he left ABC Ltd?

 You will find guidance about how to answer these questions online at www.oup.com/uk/marson5e/.

 FURTHER READING

Books and articles

O'Reilly, T. (2008) 'Health and Safety for Small Businesses' Management Books: Cirencester.

Websites, Twitter, and YouTube channels

https://www.gov.uk/browse/working
A Government website specifically designed to provide employees with a comprehensive overview of their rights and responsibilities at work.

https://www.gov.uk/national-minimum-wage-rates
Information regarding the National Minimum Wage.

https://www.gov.uk/maximum-weekly-working-hours
Information regarding the Working Time Regulations.

https://www.gov.uk/government/organisations/insolvency-service
The Insolvency Service provides guidance and the relevant forms for affected workers to facilitate any claims.

https://www.gov.uk/government/organisations/low-pay-commission
The website of the Low Pay Commission, which makes recommendations on matters surrounding the national minimum wage.

http://www.legislation.gov.uk/uksi/1998/1833/regulation/4/made
The Working Time Regulations 1998.

http://www.legislation.gov.uk/ukpga/1998/39/contents
The National Minimum Wage Act 1998.

http://www.hmrc.gov.uk
Her Majesty's Revenue and Customs.

http://www.legislation.gov.uk/ukpga/1974/37
The Health and Safety at Work etc. Act 1974.

ONLINE RESOURCES

www.oup.com/uk/marson5e/

For further resources relating to this chapter, including self-test questions, an interactive glossary, and key case flashcards.

PART 8
INTELLECTUAL PROPERTY

Individuals and corporations may produce, buy, and possess property. This is often in a physical form but also the fruits of mental labour may be produced. This is called intellectual property and its worth can be substantial—such as an App for a computer or smartphone, a new design for a vacuum cleaner, a brand name etc. Intellectual property law governs the ownership, rights to exploit, and the ability to transfer rights of usage of ideas and inventions. It is important to understand how the law affects the right to safeguard these 'inventions' and how law in the UK and the EU operates together and independently to broaden the scope of protection.

24 INTELLECTUAL PROPERTY

Intellectual property is of vital importance to business. Most commonly seen in copyrighted materials, patents, and trademarks, businesses invest considerable resources in developing and acquiring brand images or the rights to materials. Hence, they are rightly protective over who has access to utilize the material and the control that they, as owners, can exert. If a business owns the copyright to a film or album, or where they have the right to use a trade name (Microsoft, Apple Inc.), and so on, it is easy to see the problems and concerns of unauthorized use of this material. Therefore, businesses need to know how to protect their intellectual property rights, and also how to ensure they do not, deliberately or innocently, infringe the intellectual property rights of another.

Business Scenario 24

Alexei is a rising star in Mixed Martial Arts and has proved increasingly popular since he joined the UPC fighting organization. On the basis of his rising popularity, Alexei was approached with a proposition. He could make use of his image rights in the form of a series of cartoons to be used to encourage children to be more active and engage in sporting activities. Alexei established a company 'Fighting Fit Alexei Ltd' which hired a cartoonist to produce the cartoon. Fighting Fit Alexei Ltd registered the trademark 'The Notorious Alexei' and sold t-shirts and other associated merchandise.

The cartoon series was very successful and given his increased publicity, Alexei secures a high profile and financially lucrative showcase boxing match with the former champion Floyd Pilgrim. Alexei's stardom seems likely to enable him and Fighting Fit Alexei Ltd to maximize his intellectual property rights.

The following events have transpired which require assessment. In each case, no permission has been sought or granted from either Alexei or Fighting Fit Alexei Ltd:

- The cartoon series involving Alexei has been posted to YouTube by several of their content creators. They are receiving revenue based on the advertising associated with the number of views.
- Alexei's old private school has begun an advertising campaign using his image of when he participated in school sports day events. The school is trying to entice parents to send their children to the fee-paying school in order to achieve the same guidance which made Alexei a sporting success.
- The individual who created the cartoon for the videos has begun reproducing the same images for sale directly to fans of Alexei through the internet. Further, he is invited to sporting goods stores where he draws caricatures of the patrons alongside the Alexei image and also prepares the image directly onto clothing sold in the stores. These are then sold as The Notorious Alexei Sportswear.

24.1 INTRODUCTION

This chapter considers some issues regarding a business's ownership of **intellectual property** (IP). Ownership of goods and the issues surrounding buying and selling of these have been identified in Part 3 of this text. Further, due to the constraints of this text, it is not possible to discuss issues regarding the ownership of land (although guidance for those interested in the topic is provided in the Further reading section at the end of this chapter). Rather, this chapter considers the issues surrounding the concept of IP and how this may be more difficult to determine than ownership of land. The intellectual creativity of persons can prove to be very valuable (consider the revenue generated from computer software, books, music recordings, and so on), and the common law and statutes have sought to offer protection to the owners of these creations. Without protection and enforcement of the owner's rights, the desire and impetus placed into creating these materials may be stifled, negatively impacting on society and the economy. Remember, protection of IP rights allows the owner to control the 'fruits of their labour' whilst also allowing the public to have access to it (and enjoy the benefits of this).

IP is a broad concept but may be most readily seen where businesses create a name, brand, product, process, and so on, and wish to protect against its unauthorized use. The UK Intellectual Property Office (UK-IPO) provides an example of the applicability of IP in terms of a mobile telephone where the ringtone would be covered through copyright, its shape is protected through a registered design, the name of the phone or associated logo could be protected through a registered trademark, and the processes used in its manufacture can be protected through patents (see **Figure 24.1**).

24.2 PROTECTING INTELLECTUAL PROPERTY

IP is a wide-ranging term, but essentially it is used to describe the patents to protect new inventions; trademarks that are used by businesses that may define brands, logos, and the shapes of products; design rights and registered designs; and copyright, which provides

Figure 24.1 Protection of intellectual property rights

the owner with protection against unauthorized use of their literary, artistic, and dramatic works, sound recordings, software and databases, and so on. There are regulations regarding the protections afforded and the mechanisms available to enforce rights, and these are identified in the following sections.

24.3 COPYRIGHT

The law relating to copyright is governed, through statute, by the Copyright, Designs and Patents Act (CDPA) 1988 (as amended by the Copyright and Related Rights Regulations 2003). The protection of copyright is afforded to anyone's creation of a literary, dramatic, musical, or artistic work or the creation by an employee who is contracted to create such works. Through this ownership, control may be exercised as to who may use the work and how permission will be granted (e.g. through licensing). Examples of the use of the copyrighted materials may include the publication of literary products (such as books and articles—although these may be written, spoken, or sung to qualify as literary works under s. 1(1) as is very broadly defined), the distribution and broadcast of films and music, the creation of databases, and the production of computer software. Section 3A(1) identifies a database as a collection of independent works, data, or other materials that are arranged in a systematic way and are individually accessible by electronic or other means. The copyright also crosses media, such as when a photograph is reproduced on a website it would still breach the owner's copyright even though they are in different mediums. Copyright need not be applied for, and claims can be made for the unauthorized use of the owner's copyright once the work has been fixed (such as being recorded and written down).

From 1 October 2014 the new Intellectual Property Act (IPA) 2014 commenced with the aim of modernizing copyright law and further helping those who design and hold patents to protect the valuable intellectual property that they produce. Copyright law was previously out of date and had not kept adequate pace with changes in technology or how people produce, access, and consume copyrighted materials—think of the use of ebooks, digital libraries (e.g. iTunes), and cloud-based computing services, and how each has changed the way people interact with copyrighted materials. IPA 2014 has led to small, but important, changes in the law which will not be fully realized until several years after the full commencement of the Act.

Further, the Act aims to simplify and strengthen the protection of the UK designs industry, which the Government estimates is worth in excess of £15 billion a year to the UK economy. It creates a criminal offence, which prior to the 2014 Act was merely a civil offence, for intentional copying of a registered design. It makes changes to research conducted at UK universities; it enables a system of webmarking, as opposed to greater detailed information, relating to a patent right; and it facilitates the expansion of dispute resolution relating to patents.

24.3.1 Who is Protected?

The copyright holder is entitled to protection where the work fulfils the following criteria:

1. the work is of a type that is protected under CDPA 1988;
2. it has been produced in some tangible form—written, recorded, and so on;
3. the work satisfies the requirement of originality;
4. the owner/creator is a British citizen and/or the work was first published in the UK.

The term 'original' does not refer to an idea or thought that is original, but rather it is the expression of the idea that must be original. For example, in preparing a textbook, the text will refer to other authors' work in books and journals, judgments, research reports, government documents, and so on. These will be 'owned' by the copyright holder in each case, and other textbooks may have already included similar materials, but if the way the ideas are expressed is original, and they have been expressed in some tangible form (referred to as being fixed—s. 3(2)), then copyright will exist for this 'original' work.

Consider

The YouTube uploaders may have infringed the rights of Fighting Fit Alexei Ltd as the first owners of the copyright—it hired the cartoonist. The cartoonist is not the legal owner of the image of Fighting Fit Alexei and is breaching copyright by drawing the image on pictures and clothing.

24.3.2 What is Protected?

Copyright affords the owner protection against breaches such as the unauthorized use of *original* material including (s. 1(1)):

- *Literary works:* This includes books, computer software programs, song lyrics, and even instruction manuals (s. 3);
- *Music and broadcasts:* Including films, videos, and radio shows (ss. 5 and 6);

Consider

The YouTube uploaders have breached the CDPA s. 5A—the protection for broadcasts due to the definition provided in that part of the Act.

- *Dramatic productions:* Including plays, dances, and sound recordings;
- *Artistic works:* This is wide-ranging and includes drawings, diagrams, logos, photographs, and sculptures (s. 4). As logos also may involve trademarks, it can be seen how IP rights are not restricted to one of the categories identified in this chapter.

Lucasfilm Limited v Ainsworth (2011)

Facts:

Mr Ainsworth contracted with Lucasfilm to make the iconic Stormtrooper helmet made famous in the Star Wars films. He was provided with a clay model from which to make the helmets. He produced the items for Lucasfilm and then proceeded to make more helmets from the model which he sold for personal gain over the internet. LucasFilm sought to assert copyright in the clay model and enforcement of their US copyright.

Authority for:

The clay model was an object with a functional purpose, not an artistic one. The Supreme Court concluded therefore that it was not a 'sculpture' within s. 4 of CDPA 1988. This meant that copyright did not subsist, and the issues on the availability of defences to copyright infringement were irrelevant.

- *Typological arrangements of published editions:* This involves the planning and establishing of type that may then be printed. Examples include sections of a newspaper and the layout of a book (s. 8).

It is not possible to claim copyright protection for ideas; names, phrases, and slogans (although they may be applicable to trademark protection); or products and manufacturing processes (although patents may be applicable). Use of the copyright without the owner's consent will enable enforcement proceedings to be initiated, with the possibility of an action in damages.

24.3.3 Rights Provided Through Copyright

- *Legal rights:* The owner's legal rights allow them to (s. 16):
  - copy and distribute copies of the work to the public;
  - issue copies to the public;
  - perform, show, or play the work in public (such as through various broadcast media);
  - broadcast the work or include it in a cable programme service;
  - make an adaptation of the work or do any of the above in relation to an adaptation;
  - sell a work; under the Artist's Resale Rights Regulations 2006, an artist has the right (resale right) to a percentage of the selling price (resale royalty) when they own the copyright and certain forms of art are sold.

- *Moral rights:* The owner has the legal rights to the work, but it must be recognized that they also hold the moral rights (beyond those economic rights—s. 77). These rights include:

  - protection against the distortion of the owner's work;

  - in relation to literary, dramatic, artistic, or musical works, that they have the right to be recognized as the author of the work whenever it is performed commercially or in public;

  - literary, dramatic, artistic, or musical works may not be falsely attributed to an author;

  - where an undertaking has been made to make a film or take photographs for private consumption, they may not show or broadcast this to the public.

Infection Control Enterprises Limited v Virrage Industries Ltd (2009)

Facts:

A question arose regarding the rights held by the owner of IP in the form of bespoke software.

Authority for:

In the event of IP being created in the form of bespoke software, a customer will only receive the minimum rights necessary unless they specifically provide for these in the negotiations. Here, the court rejected the argument of *Shirlaw v Southern Foundaries* (see **8.3.2**) that such a fact was omitted from the contract because it was 'so obvious' there was no need for it to be mentioned.

IPA 2014 allows for the reasonable copying of sound recordings, films, and broadcasts which are used for non-commercial research and private study, without the need for obtaining the permission of the copyright holder. This is particularly important for researchers at university and students who will have access to content, although copying and use of the material must be reasonable and fair.

24.3.4 Registration of Copyright

A significant protection afforded to the owners of copyright in the UK is that it is automatic and, unlike other protections of IP rights, there is no registration process. Because of the lack of formal registration, the owners of the property may be concerned as to how proof of ownership is established. Tactics have included sending a copy of the work in a dated and unopened package to oneself, or leaving a copy of the work with a solicitor. Further evidence of ownership may be supplemented through the use of the internationally recognized copyright symbol © followed by the owner's name and the year of the work's creation which identifies copyright and prevents others from infringing, intentionally or unintentionally, that copyright. As this symbol is internationally recognized, it transcends the jurisdiction of the UK, but whilst it is acknowledged elsewhere, many countries have their own rules on the enforcement of breaches of copyright, and the domestic laws of the relevant country will have to be used to enforce copyright ownership (which evidently differs as regards success rates depending upon where in the world the copyright is infringed). It is also important to note that simply because materials are available free of charge does not necessarily mean that they are free of copyright. Materials on the Internet may display the © but even if they do not, downloading or using materials may be infringing the owner's rights (the Copyright and Related Rights Regulations 2003 have harmonized the protections in this area through the European Union). This also applies to the peer-to-peer networks where copyrighted materials are made available for download without charge (unlike, e.g., iTunes, where legal downloads are permitted). The owners of copyright, particularly corporations, are often vigilant in enforcing their IP rights, and actions against children and their parents for illegal downloads of copyrighted materials (games, movies, music, and so on) are not uncommon.

24.3.5 Duration of Copyright Protection

The protection afforded under copyright differs depending on the nature of the work, the time at which it was created, and where the copyright was established. **Table 24.1** identifies the duration of copyright protection.

Table 24.1 Duration of copyright protection

Type of original works	Duration of copyright
Sound recordings	50 years
Broadcasts	50 years
Literary and dramatic works	The life of the creator plus 70 years
Typographical arrangements	25 years
Publication of a literary, dramatic, musical, or artistic work (previously unpublished) and commercially exploited	25 years
Databases	15 years

24.3.6 Primary and Secondary Infringement of Copyright

Infringement of copyright exists where a qualitatively substantial part of the work is copied. Primary infringement of copyright does not consider the perpetrator's motive or knowledge of the copyright's existence. Infringement occurs when one or more of the exclusive 'legal' rights of the owner as identified in **24.3.3** have been breached (hence performed/used without the permission of the owner—s. 16(2)).

However, a breach of a secondary infringement requires the perpetrator to know, or they should have known, of the existence of the copyright of the work being infringed. Further, this is for some other reason than for the person's own personal/domestic use (hence to exploit this infringement commercially), and the person does not have the owner's permission (licence)—s. 22. Secondary infringement occurs where the person, without the owner's permission:

- imports an article into the UK (s. 22);
- possesses an article in the course of business;

- sells or lets for hire; offers for sale or hire such an article;
- in the course of business exhibits in public or distributes an article; or
- otherwise than in the course of business, distributes an article to an extent that it prejudicially affects the owner of the copyright of the article (s. 23).

Further, where the person transmits the work by means of a telecommunications system (other than through broadcasting/cable programme service) without the owner's permission, knowing or having reason to believe that infringing copies of the work will be made by this means, this will constitute a secondary infringement (s. 24). CDPA 1988 also protects against secondary infringement where a means has been provided for making copies of work that would enable a breach of copyright (s. 24), where a person gives permission for a performance in a public place of literary, dramatic, or musical work that infringes copyright (s. 25), or where this is infringed through the public performance of copyrighted works (e.g. playing sound recordings or showing films—s. 26). Where such events have taken place in which the person knows, or should have been aware, that the owner's permission had not been granted, this will constitute infringement.

24.3.7 Enforcement of Copyright

Where the owner of a copyright considers their property rights are being infringed, the first step may be to inform the transgressor. This informal measure may be achieved through a letter, either personally drafted or through a solicitor, and many cases cease at this stage. However, where the other party does not respond, or may challenge the ownership of the copyright, then legal proceedings may have to be initiated. The penalties for infringing copyright may include civil and criminal liability.

24.3.7.1 Civil actions

Section 96 of CDPA 1988 provides that infringement of copyright is actionable by the owner and relief may be available through damages, injunctions, and the transgressor being held to account.

Consider

Enforcement of Fighting Fit Alexei Ltd's rights against the YouTubers could be somewhat problematic in practical terms—identifying and initiating the legal action itself. A complaint could be made to YouTube and its role in facilitating the infringement and the impact of the safe harbour provided to hosts of third-party content under the E-Commerce Directive could be effective. Note, an injunction would only need to be sought if YouTube ignored the notification of it hosting infringing material.

Whilst damages is an available remedy in cases of infringement, if the defendant can satisfy the court that at the time they were unaware (and did not have reasonable grounds to believe) that the copyright existed, an award of damages may be reduced or removed (s. 97). This is because the court will take all matters into consideration when determining if an award is to be made, including the flagrancy of the infringement and any benefit that accrued to the defendant. A more useful remedy, perhaps, than a damages action, is the availability of injunctions. Here the court orders the transgres-sor to stop infringing the copyright (through an interim order) until the full hearing, and a further injunction may be ordered following this hearing. A court is also em-powered to make an order for the delivery of the product infringing the copyright or its destruction (s. 99). Further, s. 100 provides for the owner or a person authorized by them to seize and detain work exposed or otherwise available for sale or hire (where an action would have been available under s. 99). However, the time and place of the proposed seizure must be given to the police, it must be public (but cannot be a per-manent or regular place of business), and the owner or the person authorized by them must not use any force.

An infringement of a moral right is actionable as a breach of statutory duty owed to the person entitled to the right. Where equitable, the court may grant an injunction to prevent further abuses (s. 103). However, while it is possible to assign copyright in its en-tirety, and parts of copyright (such as bequeathing it in a will—s. 95), it is not possible to assign moral rights (s. 94).

24.3.7.2 Criminal offences

Criminal offences may be committed by a person who:

- offers for sale or hire;
- imports in the UK otherwise than for their own private and domestic use; or
- possesses, in the course of business, with a view to committing an act infringing copyright, an article which is, or they have reason to believe is, infringing copyright of a work. The defendant, if found guilty, may be liable, on summary conviction, to imprisonment for a period not exceeding six months (s. 107).

Further, where goods are imported into the UK, the owner may give notice in writing to the Commissioners of Customs and Excise that they are the owner of the copyright in published literary, dramatic, or musical work; or the owner of copyright in a sound re-cording or film, and request that the Commissioners treat the copies as prohibited goods (s. 111). Other works may be physically protected from infringement through the use of technology (anti-copy DVDs, smart cards/decoders for satellite broadcasts).

In situations where the two parties have disagreements regarding the terms of an agree-ment, the Copyright Tribunal exists and can determine the facts and assist the parties in reaching a decision.

There are exceptions to breaches of copyright and in certain situations there is no need for permission. The user is granted limited use of the material that is used for non-commercial research or study (such as copying a section of a book), where the materials are used for reporting events/court proceedings, and if they are used in reviews. Previ-ously, exemptions under CDPA 1988 allowed for businesses to take copies of copyrighted materials for commercial research insofar as this was fair. The Copyright and Related Rights Regulations 2003 ended this exemption from breach of copyright.

24.3.8 Exceptions to Breach of Copyright

The following is a non-exhaustive list. The rules regarding copyright and the application of CDPA 1988 have already been discussed. IPA 2014 provides for certain situations where the use of another person's copyright material may be used without seeking the permis-sion of that owner:

- *Non-commercial research and private study*: This allows a non-owner of copyright to copy limited extracts of works when this is used for non-commercial research or private study and the amount of materials taken was reasonable and appropriate for those purposes (what is known as fair dealing). This exception has been included to facilitate researchers and students to make limited copies of all types of copyrighted works and the criterion to be applied is that the use of the copyrighted material must not have any significant financial impact on the owner. Where researchers use such materials, they must acknowledge the use and source of the material.

- *Criticism and review*: The fair dealing exception to copyright material extends to where the works have been used for criticism, review, or quotation. In respect of reporting current events, fair dealing applies to any type of copyright work except for a photograph. Again, acknowledgement of the source and ownership of the copyrighted material used in these exercises is necessary.

- *People with disabilities*: Two exceptions exist to copyright where these offer a benefit to disabled people (which may be a physical or mental impairment). The first is where the individual with the disability, or someone acting on their behalf, produces a copy of lawfully obtained copyright material in a format that helps the individual with the disability to access it. Making this accessible copy is permitted where the person with a disability lawfully owns or has the right to use the particular work, but the nature of the disability or impairment makes the work in its current format inaccessible; and producing a copy in the format accessible to that individual is not commercially available. The second exception enables educational establishments and charities to make accessible copyrighted materials on the behalf of persons with disabilities. Again, the exception will only apply where the newly formed accessible materials have not been available commercially. Where they are available in such format, the exception will be invalid, as will, in either situation, the person making the accessible copy profiting from this (this does not extend to charging a fee which has been incurred in producing the copy).

- *Time-shifting*: One of the problems with CDPA 1998, and a criticism often levelled against the domestic law, was that it was out of date and did not reflect adequately changes made to digital services and the way that individuals consume media. The time-shifting development enables individuals to record a broadcast which is intended for private and domestic use and can be viewed or listened to at a time convenient for that purpose.

- *Personal copy*: A remnant from the old legislation was that individuals were unable, lawfully, to copy materials such as CDs and DVDs. There is now a personal copying exception that permits individuals to copy such media, which they own, for the purpose of backing-up and in so doing, the individual is not breaching the owner's copyright. This may involve taking hard/electronic copies of CDs or perhaps 'ripping' CDs to include in digital libraries such as iTunes. The requirement here is that a copy is made for personal use and access; it is not lawful to make a copy and distribute it to friends and family, or to hire DVDs, for example, and to make copies or to download copyrighted materials from file-sharing websites.

- *Parody*: Some copyrighted materials may be used by individuals without the owner's permission for the purposes of parody, caricature, or pastiche. This is based on fair dealing and will enable an artist to make reference to films, songs, artworks, and so on.

24.4 DESIGN RIGHTS AND REGISTRATION

- *Design rights:* A business may have spent time and resources in developing a product's shape and design that makes its appearance stand out or may become synonymous with the business (e.g. consider the shape of a Coca-Cola bottle). A design right is established, and the period of protection begins when the work is first 'fixed' in design documents such as a drawing or when it is first made. The design must be original, and in demonstrating that it is not commonplace in a specific area (the UK, the EU, and certain other third countries which have established reciprocal arrangements with the UK), the owner should maintain their records of the design's development (such as in email communications, plans, and files). The specific areas are the UK, the EU, and certain other third countries which have established reciprocal arrangements with the UK. The issue of design rights assists a business as the design right of the product is an automatic right (like copyright) and it prevents others from copying the design for a period of 15 years. There is also an EU-based recognition of unregistered design rights, and this protects the product's shape and pattern for a three-year period (and throughout the EU). The copyright protection is effective where the design is artistic or involves plans and drawings, and the design is not intended to be mass-produced. Where the creator of the design wishes to gain further protection, not just of preventing the design being copied without permission, but also of controlling the exploitation of the design in any manufacturing of products, it must be registered. Protection under the Registered Designs Act (RDA) 1949 exists for a period of 25 years. **Table 24.2** identifies the duration of protection of a design right.

- Design rights are applicable to three-dimensional works only, but the unregistered community designs procedure (under EU law) does protect two-dimensional products. The main drawback when compared with the registered method is that the unregistered method gives protection for a shorter period of time, it is less likely that the threat of legal action here will be a deterrent as the owner has to prove they held the design right, and then that the person infringing the right has deliberately copied it, and demonstrating the right to sell or licence the use of the rights is considerably more difficult. It is important to recognize that in the final five years of the design right's period of protection, its owner is obliged to agree licensing terms with third parties who wish to use the design. Where no agreement can be reached, the terms are decided by the UK-IPO.

- *Registered designs:* Whilst the design right provides protection without any form of registration, as it is governed by Part III of CDPA 1988 (and may be considered closely related

Table 24.2 Duration of protection of a design right

Design right	Duration of protection
UK registered design	Five years from the date of filing (renewable in five-year periods to maximum of 25 years).
UK unregistered design	Automatic—10 years from the first marketing of the product or 15 years after the design's creation (whichever is earlier).
EU registered design	Five years from the date of filing (renewable in five-year periods to maximum of 25 years).
EU unregistered design	Three years from the date the design was first made available to the public.

to copyright), it must satisfy the requirements of originality of the design. However, great-er protection is afforded the owner if they register at the Patent Office (Designs Registry) under RDA 1949 (which is more closely related to patents). Whilst in the case where dam-ages are sought for infringement of the design right, there must have been an intentional decision to infringe the owner's rights, under the registration scheme, such intention need not be proved and damages may be awarded in cases of unintentional breach.

- To qualify for the right to register the design it must be a new design, and it must have characteristics that give its appearance an original look. This form of protection is often limited to the exterior of a product (rather than how it actually works—see pat-ents). Following the registration, the owner is granted exclusive rights to produce and use (in the UK) any product that incorporates the design and this right exists for five years, with renewals possible for further five-year periods to a maximum of 25 years. The registered design right includes two-and three-dimensional works. Due to its reg-istration and the confirmation that the IP belongs to the owner, selling or the licensed use of the design is more successful than unregistered designs. As the owner may use this as an income stream, the registration process, whilst incorporating expenses such as the registration fee, may be more advantageous than unregistered designs.

- The protection for registered designs only applies, and is enforceable, in the UK. As protection may be sought beyond the jurisdiction of the UK, a mechanism exists at the EU level where the registration rights apply throughout the Union and ensures that registration procedures are consistent throughout the EU. Registration is made to the Office for Harmonization in the Internal Market and following registration the design is published in the 'Community Designs Bulletin'. There has been further expansion to these rights following the agreement of the EU to join the World Intellectual Property Organization's (WIPO) Geneva Act of the Hague Agreement (and hence each of the 28 Member States of the EU are now included). Since 1 January 2008 designers in the EU can apply for international protection for their designs and this is applicable in all the countries that have signed up to the agreement. The Internal Market and Services Commissioner commented, 'European businesses will now be able to obtain and pro-tect their designs internationally in a simple, affordable and effective way. This should further stimulate trade and innovation, create new commercial opportunities and boost integration within the EU Internal Market.' Further, IPA 2014 is extending the interna-tional design registration by the UK joining the Hague system as a member in its own right (not simply being included as a Member State of the EU). Registration can be ef-fected just to the UK, rather than having to select the EU-wide registration as currently exists, and should lead to less expense incurred by the person seeking the registration.

- The registration process involves identifying the design, even simply through sam-ple drawings that show the work and how the design is to be applied. This design must be original and not simply a collection of other designs fashioned together to form something 'new'. Registration of a design that has been used in marketing may be made at any time up to 12 months after it was first marketed, but this should be performed as soon as possible to ensure protection. The UK-IPO website contains the relevant details and forms that must be submitted, including details of the regis-tration fee applicable, and these are sent to the UK-IPO Design Registry (more than one application may be made at the same time, and if so, only one registration fee is payable). The applications are generally examined within two months of submission, and on the basis that no objections are submitted, two to three months following the application the registration process should be complete.

24.4.1 Enforcement of a Design Right

With regard to businesses that may take 'inspiration' from the works they have seen and been influenced by in creating a design, it is important not to transgress another's design right. This can be embarrassing, show a lack of imagination or integrity, and it can also be very expensive (legal fees and damages actions may be the result). Therefore, it is prudent to identify whether the design has been registered through the UK-IPO. However, as some design holders may not register the work, the use of a specialist lawyer may assist in ensuring design rights have not been breached (The Chartered Institute of Patent Attorneys maintains details of relevant lawyers in the UK).

Where a possible infringement has taken place (such as the use of the design or the sale of designs belonging to the holder) it is typical to begin an informal route through communication with the other party, explaining the right and the consequences of further breaches. If both parties are still in dispute, and they agree, they may seek to use a mediator under a form of alternative dispute resolution (see **4.4**) to avoid the necessity of court action. If unsuccessful, then the holder of the right may be forced to commence a civil action to recover damages and seek the granting of an injunction to compel the transgressor to cease their activities. Clearly where the case involves an unregistered design, the claimant will have to demonstrate that they own the design right and the defendant had copied it. Where the design has been registered, following the unsuccessful attempt at preventing the breach through the communications between the parties, the holder may claim damages due to the defendant's work closely resembling the holder's design (rather than having 'copied' it).

If the situation arises where the alleged breach has occurred whilst in the process of registering the design, the UK-IPO may be contacted to request an urgent examination, and subsequent registration, of the design.

24.4.2 Changes to Design and Patent Law

The main changes which IPA 2014 will bring into effect are:

* *The ownership of design* (IPA 2014, ss. 2 and 6)*:* For designs that are created on or after 1 October 2014 or are the subject of contracts after this date, the owner of a commissioned design will be the designer and not the person who commissioned the work unless the contract provides otherwise. It is therefore vitally important that the parties are aware of this change in the legislation and act accordingly to prevent disputes at a later date. This does not simply include commercial contracts but rather should be a feature in contracts of employment (however, the current system whereby employees producing designs as part of their job and general employment duties do so on the basis that the design belongs to the employer, will continue).

* *Prior use* (IPA 2014, s. 7): In the event that a person uses a design in good faith (e.g. the design was not copied) which is subsequently registered by another person, protection will be available to them against infringement actions. The individual who is using the design but who subsequently finds that another person has registered that same design before they have, will be able to continue using the design on the basis only of how they have used it previously and will not be able to exploit the design—the exploitation of the design and its further use will belong to the person who first registered it.

* *Criminal offence* (IPA 2014, s. 13): Prior to IPA 2014 the intentional copying of a registered design was a civil offence. The 2014 Act now makes such action a criminal offence. The requirement necessary for the guilt of the individual is that they intentionally copied

the design without the consent of the owner and whilst knowing, or having reasonable belief, that the design was registered. Remember, accidental and incidental use of a copy design (essentially use in good faith) will not establish a criminal offence. Powers of enforcement will belong to Trading Standards officers in England and Wales and to the procurator fiscal in Scotland. Such a criminal offence carries the penalties already in existence for copyright and trademark violations—a fine and/or imprisonment of up to 10 years (although such a sentence would be passed in only the most serious instances).

* *Unregistered design right* (IPA 2014, s. 2): IPA 2014 has simplified the process of a person qualifying for an unregistered design right in the UK. Further, it restricts the ability of an individual to base a claim for copying on a cropped area of the unregistered design.

24.5 TRADEMARKS

A business has to protect its IP rights and by registering its trademark, the owner has the right to use the ® symbol to demonstrate ownership. It warns others who may otherwise have used it without authorization that legal consequences may follow for infringement. Without following the registration process, the owner must seek a remedy through the common law action of 'passing-off'.

A trademark is defined under the Trade Marks Act (TMA) 1994 as:

> any sign capable of being represented graphically which is capable of distinguishing goods or services of one undertaking from those of other undertakings. A trademark may, in particular, consist of words (including personal names), designs, letters, numerals or the shape of goods or their packaging (s. 1(1)).

A trademark (denoted by the ® symbol) identifies that the owner of the trademark has been registered, and it prevents others from using the same image (using the symbol without the required registration is an offence). A trademark may be applied to a name or logo that identifies a product or service, or it could further include a slogan used by a brand or even some sound.

Shield Mark BV v Joost Kist hodn Memex (Case C-283/01) (2003)

Facts:

Shield Mark BV, a Dutch company, had registered 14 sounds as trademarks to be used in computer systems, commercial communications, and so on. In four instances, the sounds included the first nine notes of a composition of Ludwig van Beethoven. A question was raised as to whether sounds could be registered as trademarks.

Authority for:

The European Court of Justice held that notes from a composition by Beethoven could constitute a trademark when used in an advertising campaign on the radio.

As such, they are often associated with a business, product, or brand, and are of significant advantage in assisting customers to recognize the company. McDonald's 'golden arches' and the Nike 'swoosh' are instantly recognizable symbols that the public associate with that company. Indeed, many Nike products, including hats and T-shirts, do not even contain the company's name, but merely that symbol, as it denotes the company. Following registration, the trademark provides the owner with exclusive use of the mark, and those who infringe the mark are subject to a civil action by the owner, but it also enables the police and/or Trading Standards to initiate criminal proceedings for breach (such as with counterfeiters). The law is governed by TMA 1994 (following the transposition of EU Directive 89/104/EEC). Once the registration process has been completed, infringement is committed where the trademark and the other item are confusingly similar to make the consumer (for instance) buy one good believing it to belong to the trademark holder.

Arsenal Football Club Plc v Reed (2003)

Facts:

The football club Arsenal FC brought an action against Reed who had sold souvenirs and other memorabilia bearing the club's name and its badge (for several years). It was claimed that Reed had infringed registered trademarks, but Reed's defence was that these products would be perceived as a badge of support rather than indicating trade origin. Following reference to the Court of Justice of the European Union (Court of Justice) it was held the trademarks, when applied to the goods in this instance, were purchased as badges of support, but this did not prevent the third party being liable to jeopardize the function of the trademark. Following this case, Arsenal changed its club badge to prevent potential further abuses.

Authority for:

A key issue regarding infringement of a trademark is whether the consumer would believe there was a link between the proprietor and the goods being sold.

24.5.1 Reasons to Refuse the Grant of a Trademark

TMA 1994 defines where an absolute refusal of registration will take place. Under s. 3 the following shall not be registered:

1. signs which do not satisfy the requirements of s. 1(1);
2. trademarks which are devoid of any distinctive character;
3. trademarks which consist exclusively of signs or indications which may serve, in trade, to designate the kind, quality, quantity, intended purpose, value, geographical origin, the time of production of goods or of rendering of services, or other characteristics of goods or services;
4. trademarks which consist exclusively of signs or indications which have become customary in the current language or in the bona fide and established practices of the trade;
5. the shape which results from the nature of the goods themselves, or where it is necessary to obtain a technical result, or which gives substantial value to the goods;
6. marks which are contrary to public policy or to accepted principles of morality, or are of such a nature as to deceive the public;

7. if or to the extent that its use is prohibited in the UK by any enactment or rule of law or by any provision of Community law; or

8. if the application is made in bad faith.

Having registered the trademark, it must be renewed every 10 years to remain effective (and may be renewed indefinitely), and where the owner has not registered it, the action to ensure protection against unauthorized use lies in the common law through an action under the tort of 'passing-off'. Whilst such a claim is possible, the costs and complexity of such actions must not be underestimated, and even though costs may be awarded against the party at fault, this is still a considerable undertaking that registration may have made easier. A registered trademark is enforceable throughout the UK, whereas unregistered marks may not be applicable to such an extent and may be confined to enforcement in restricted geographical areas. In the EU, a trademark that has not been genuinely used for more than five years in the country to which it was subject to the registration, or, in relation to an EU trademark, where it has not been used in the EU, may be revoked unless an accepted reason is presented for the non-use.

24.5.2 Registration of the Trademark

A trademark may be registered in the UK through the completion of form TM3 from the UK-IPO, along with the required fee, and submitting these to the UK-IPO Trademarks Registry. The applicant should conduct a search to ensure that the trademark is not registered or that another person has not applied for the same or similar mark. Since 1 October 2007, all trademark applications are subject to regulations with the effect that there will no longer be an automatic block of the registration of the mark if there is an earlier conflicting trademark (The Trade Marks (Amendment) Rules 2007, The Trade Marks (Fees) (Amendment) Rules 2007, and The Trade Marks (Relative Grounds) Order 2007). The application will result in an examination of the existing UK, EU, and international trademarks protected in the UK and the EU, and on the basis that the UK-IPO discovers a conflict with an earlier trademark, the applicant will be informed of this finding and given the choice to:

1. continue with the application and the UK-IPO will inform the owner of the previously registered trademark of this new application, enabling them to oppose the application based on specific times and procedures (note that licensees will not be given the right to object to an application);

2. change the application so that it is sufficiently different from a current trademark;

3. liaise with the owner of the existing trademark to allow the application to continue unopposed; or

4. withdraw the application.

As such, the role is to attempt to settle potential disputes at as early a stage as possible and reduce the instances of court actions. There has been a move by the courts to introduce alternative forms of dispute resolution, and this is extending more broadly to include legal jurisdictions such as IP.

Where the nature of the product requires protection beyond the territory of the UK, the registration process will have to be undertaken with the various international bodies. The process has been somewhat simplified in that rather than having to seek an application (individually) to each country, the applicant can register a Community Trade Mark

(CTM) through the Office for Harmonization in the Internal Market to have effectiveness throughout the EU. The CTM applies to any person resident in a Member State or a business that is based in a Member State, and includes any distinctive sign capable of graphical representation. The benefit of an EU-wide system of registration is that its application is throughout the EU and any injunctions used to enforce a right and prevent infringement have force in each of the Member States. It has a further advantage of lower costs and administrative burdens than applying to each country individually, but due to the size and composition of the EU, a single system of registration may be difficult to enforce and apply in practice.

A further registration system applicable to the entire world was developed through the Madrid System, and following registration in the UK, an application can be made to WIPO.

24.5.3 Rights Provided Through Registration

Registration is recommended in most cases as it provides access to TMA 1994 (as amended) and enables the injured party to seek remedies provided under that Act. Section 10(1) provides: 'A person infringes a registered trademark if he uses in the course of trade a sign which is identical with the trademark in relation to goods or services which are identical with those for which it is registered.' Further, infringement occurs where the identical sign is used in relation to goods and services similar to those for which the trademark is registered and there exists the likelihood of confusion on the part of the public (s. 10(2)), or where the identical sign is used not for similar goods and services, but the trademark has a reputation in the UK and its use takes advantage of, or is detrimental to, the distinctive character or the repute of the trademark (s. 10(3)).

Consider

The use of the name The Notorious Alexei Sportswear by the sports shops is a breach of the company's trademark. This action involves advertising merchandise which is similar/identical to that which is subject to a trademark.

TMA 1994 identifies that a sign, for the purposes of the Act, is used where it is fixed to goods or the packaging; exposes or offers the good for sale; imports or exports goods under the sign; or uses the sign on business papers and on advertising literature.

There are limits placed on the rights of a registered trademark, and as such s. 11 states that there will be no infringement where:

- the person uses their own name and address;
- it consists of the use of indications concerning the kind, quality, quantity, intended purpose, value, geographical origin, or other characteristics of goods and services;
- the use of the trademark is necessary to indicate the intended purpose of a product or service;
- it is used in the course of trade in a particular locality of an earlier right which applies only in that locality.

24.5.4 Enforcing a Registered Trademark

There exists an automatic right to enforce the trademark against a person infringing the owner's rights and the courts are empowered, as with the common law, to award damages and grant injunctive relief to the claimant. Where the trademark breach has involved a criminal offence, beyond the loss to the owner where a common law remedy is available, such as dealing in counterfeit goods, Trading Standards may initiate an action that could lead to imprisonment for a period of 10 years and/or an unlimited fine.

24.5.5 The Tort of Passing-off

'Passing-off' protects the holder of an unregistered trademark. At common law, where an individual or business attempts to pass itself as another business, or to pass goods off as being those of the other business, in an attempt to deceive or confuse the public, a tort of 'passing-off' may have been committed. It aims to prevent the infringement of the holder's right and to prevent the other person from benefiting from the holder's reputation.

Irvine v Talksport (2002)

Facts:

The defendants had used a distorted, but still recognizable image of Eddie Irvine (a famous F1 racing driver) to endorse their product. This led to his claim for damages for the tortious act of 'passing off.'

Authority for:

Irvine had a property right in his goodwill which could be protected from unlicensed use comprising of false claims of association or endorsement of a third party's business or goods. Irvine's claim of passing–off succeeded.

Therefore, it is concerned with the relationship between the holder of the trademark and the public.

Consider

The school may have fallen into the trap of false endorsement (see *Irvine v Talksport*). This involves the school passing-off its association with Alexei as an endorsement and may have the effect of negatively affecting Alexei's future commercial interests.

Trademark law is associated with the concept of goodwill, and this is established in business names, brand names, packaging of products, even a person's name (e.g. a professional football player's image rights), and so on. When considering the amount of money spent on advertising, contracting to have a sportsman/woman wear one manufacturer's brand of sporting goods, and so on, it is very clear why the holders of these rights want to protect their investment.

24.5.6 **Goodwill**

For infringement, the goods/services in question must have goodwill attached. This means that they exhibit particular identifying features which enable the public to associate with the good/service.

Pfizer Ltd v Eurofood Link (UK) Ltd (1999)

Facts:

The defendants had marketed a health food drink as 'Viagrene' and its properties had an aphrodisiac quality. It was a blue coloured liquid and the bottle contained a diamond shape. The claimant manufactured 'Viagra' the impotence treatment. It sold the drug in a quite distinctive blue, diamond-shaped tablet. Viagra had been registered under British and EU trademarks, and Pfizer argued that such a name was too similar to its product 'Viagra' and could be considered similar. The High Court held that the defendants had been passing-off the product as the claimant's drug.

Authority for:

The claim involved an action under s. 10(2) and (3) of TMA 1994. The judgment confirmed the Court of Justice decision that there was no requirement to prove confusion for a breach of s. 10(3). Viagra had an established reputation and there was a breach of goodwill that would amount to a misrepresentation. There was a potential to damage the claimant's reputation and therefore the tort of passing-off had been committed.

It is also important to recognize that passing-off is a strict liability tort. Therefore, the motive of the person infringing the right is irrelevant.

24.5.7 **Recognizing Infringement**

In order to mount such an action against a transgressor, it has to be established that the public associated the trademark with the claimant's product, and that the product of the other party was mistaken for that of the claimant, and in so doing has caused them loss/damage (such as reductions in sales).

As such the three elements may be seen as in **Figure 24.2** (see p. 652).

Be aware that whilst **Figure 24.2** identifies a quite simple outline of the process to establish a successful claim, the reality is of course very complex and open to interpretation. For instance, these tests have been established through the common law, not by statutory definition, and proving infringement of the holder's goodwill is very subjective. In the *Pfizer* case above, the judge outlined that the name 'Viagra', even though an anti-impotence drug, was actually a household name. As such, a similar named product claiming to relieve the symptoms of impotence would likely damage the goodwill of the drug company. In other situations, associating the damage or potential damage due to the association of the public with the good/service may be considerably more difficult.

Figure 24.2 Stages to establish a successful claim

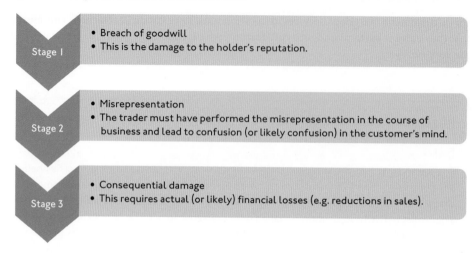

24.5.8 Defences Available

It is possible to defend an allegation of passing-off and the following are the most common defences:

1. the holder of the IP had given consent;
2. the holder's trademark (slogan, brand, and so on) was not distinctive;
3. the trademark is generic;
4. the defendant is using their name innocently.

24.5.9 Remedies

Following the successful finding of passing-off, the following remedies are available to the court:

1. damages or account of the defendant's profits (not double awards for both aspects);
2. delivery/destruction of the infringing goods;
3. injunctive relief;
4. an enquiry to establish loss.

24.6 PATENTS

A business may seek to protect its inventions, such as a new product, or its new way of making the product (a new process) that has an industrial application. An invention would constitute an inventive step where it would not have been obvious to someone with skill and experience in the area. To be considered as new, the invention must not form part of the **state of prior art** (this includes all factors that were publicly available prior to the invention). To be considered as having an industrial application, it must be capable of being used or made in any form of industry (with exceptions regarding medical treatment, diagnosis, and so on identified in s. 1(3) of the Patents Act (PA) 1977). It is important to recognize that a patent need not be a completely new item, but rather it could include a new way in which an item already in existence is produced (or other such examples). A typical example of a patent was that of the bagless vacuum cleaner developed by the Dyson company. When the Hoover company produced its own 'version' of such a cleaner, it was held that this was a breach of Dyson's patent (*Dyson Appliances Ltd v Hoover Ltd* [2001]).

By registering the patent, it prevents others from using or selling the same product without permission. The registration period lasts for five-year periods and must be renewed (up to a maximum of 20 years in total). The law in this jurisdiction is governed by the Patents Act (PA) 1977 and s. 1(1) provides that a patent may be granted if the following criteria are satisfied:

1. that the invention to be patented is new;

2. that there is an inventive step involved (not obvious to a person with knowledge and experience in the area);

3. that it is capable of industrial application (as such it is capable of being made or used);

4. that the granting of the patent is not to be excluded by ss. 1(2), 1 (3), or 4A of PA 1977.

Section 1(2) identifies that the following will not satisfy the requirements of 'inventions' and hence are incapable of patents being applied:

* scientific and mathematical discoveries, theories, or methods;

* works of an artistic, literary, dramatic, or musical nature;

* ways of performing a mental act, playing a game, or doing business;

* certain computer programs; or

* the presentation of information.

Section 1(3) continues that in certain circumstances, a patent should not be provided on the basis of it being contrary to public policy (against the law) or morality. Section 4A provides that a patent shall not be granted for the invention of a method of treatment of the human or animal body by surgery or therapy or a method of diagnosis practised on such bodies.

24.6.1 Exploitation of a Patent

The power of a patent is that it provides the owner with a monopoly right to control it, even where another person, acting independently of the owner of the patent, could have developed the same invention. (This is merely to recognize that whilst patenting an invention gives control of it to the owner, they will still be subject to rules governing its potential use. This is commonly seen where pharmaceutical companies develop drugs—these drugs still have to be licensed for use in the UK.) With the monopoly control, the owner may exploit the invention for commercial gain, and as this form of IP is identified as personal property, it is capable of being sold, licensed, used to raise finance (such as through a charge over it), or transferred to another party (through inheritance and so on). As this is property, it may also be owned by more than one person (as could other property such as land or a house), and such joint owners have rights over the property.

The patent provides the monopoly right, but this is subject to competition rules and the Comptroller-General may issue a compulsory licence where relevant (s. 48B). They will also determine the level of payment for the licence. Three years after the granting of the patent, any person may apply to the Comptroller for a licence if:

1. the invention is capable of being commercially worked in the UK, but is not being so worked (or not worked to the fullest extent that is reasonably practicable);

2. where the patent is a product, the demand for it is not being met on reasonable grounds, or is being met through importation from countries outside of the EU;

3. where the invention is capable of being commercially worked in the UK, it is being prevented or hindered from being worked through imports;

4. by reason of the refusal of the proprietor of the patent to grant a licence(s) on reasonable terms, the market for the export of the patented product is not being supplied, the working or efficient working in the UK of other patented inventions which make a substantial contribution to the art is prevented or hindered, or the establishment or development of commercial or industrial activities in the UK is unfairly prejudiced;

5. by reason of conditions imposed by the proprietor of the patent on the grant of licences under the patent, or on the disposal or use of the patented product or on the use of the patented process, the manufacture, use or disposal of material not protected by the patent, or the establishment or development of commercial or industrial activities in the UK, is unfairly prejudiced.

24.6.2 Application for a Patent

The Patent Office is the body that is responsible for granting patents with effect in the UK and is headed by the Comptroller-General. The applicant will identify what the invention is, details regarding its specifications (blueprints/schematics and so on), an abstract explaining the nature of the patent being applied for, and submission of the relevant fee. As the patents may be sought by persons in industry to protect against their inventions being used in an unauthorized way, the application process is essential and the Office will record this date of the application. The Patents Office will only officially record this date of filing where all the relevant documents have been submitted and the correct fee has been paid, and the applicant has specifically identified their request for a patent. Therefore, care must be taken when submitting documents.

The documents must be filed on the prescribed form and submitted in the prescribed manner (s. 14(1)(a)), it must contain sufficient detail to enable a person 'skilled in the art' to produce the invention (s. 14(3)) and as such include details on the matter for which the applicant seeks protection, be clear and concise, be supported by the description, and relate to one invention (or a group) to form a single inventive step (s. 14(5)). Having filed the appropriate forms, paid the fee, and submitted the necessary information, the submission is examined to ensure compliance with PA 1977. If the application passes this preliminary test, the next stage is the substantive test. Here, any anomalies in the application are identified and these are passed on to the applicant who is provided with the opportunity to respond (and change any elements of the application if necessary). Given that the changes made are to the satisfaction of the examiner, the application will be granted for the patent; if the changes are unsatisfactory, the application may be refused. Following the successful application process and the grant of the patent, this fact is published in the *Patents and Designs Journal*.

24.6.3 **Breach of a Patent**

A patent protects the owner who has control and a monopoly right over the invention. However, a breach/infringement of the patent will not occur where the 'breach' is performed for research/experimentation (s. 60(5)(b)), or where its use is for private rather than commercial purposes (s. 60(5)(a)). Infringement of a patent is determined on a decision as to whether or not a very similar product comes within the scope of the exclusive right.

> ### *Catnic Components Ltd v Hill & Sons Ltd (1982)*
>
> **Facts:**
>
> The claimant possessed a patent for a lintel. It provided that the rear face was vertical and the defendant relied on this description by making their lintel with a face with a 6-degree slant. The House of Lords held that a purposive rather than literal approach should be given to interpreting when an infringement occurs. A skilled person would interpret vertical to also include slightly-off vertical.
>
> **Authority for:**
>
> The traditional, certain literal approach of interpretation may assist the courts, parties, and third parties, but may enable deviation and hence evasion of infringement. A method with more 'common sense' is to adopt a purposive approach, but this leads to uncertainty and provides the patentee with greater protection than envisaged when filing the patent.

Situations where a person infringes a patent in force in the UK include (s. 60(1)):

1. where the invention is a product, the person makes, disposes of, offers to dispose of, uses or imports the product or keeps it whether for disposal or otherwise;

2. where the invention is a process, the person uses it, or offers it for use in the UK knowing (or reasonably ought to have known) that its use there without the consent of the proprietor would constitute an infringement; or

3. where the invention is a process, the person disposes of, offers to dispose of, uses, or imports any product obtained directly by means of that process or keeps any such product whether for disposal or otherwise.

Having established a breach, an injunction (which may also be awarded against the owner of a patent who brings unfounded claims against another that they have breached the patent) may be granted to prevent further infringements of the patent. Damages may be awarded if the defendant knew (or ought reasonably to have known) that the patent was in existence, there may be an order made to deliver any of the patented products, the defendant may have to account for any profits derived from their breach (but awards will not doubly compensate the claimant in respect of this head of claim and damages), and a declaration may be made that the patent is valid and had been infringed through the defendant's actions. Describing a product/process as a patent where no such grant has been made constitutes a criminal offence.

24.7 EMPLOYEES AND INTELLECTUAL PROPERTY

It is important to recognize that a business may be involved in creating products and works that may be commercially valuable (stories for a publishing company/drugs for the pharmaceutical industry and so on). Universities, for example, invest heavily in research and development in the attempt to further understanding, but also in the hope that such results will be commercially successful. There may be IP rights being created even when the employee is not hired in such a capacity. Developing databases, producing training manuals, and so on may also form a valuable IP. When an employee produces a valuable IP, who owns it?—the employee (who has been paid a salary), or the business that has engaged the employee?

Based on the 'general' rules of an employee's contract of employment (see **Chapter 20**), the creation by the employee of IP rights at work, clearly having benefited from, and had access to, the resources that the employer has made available, belongs to the employer. Whilst this is generally true, it is prudent to specifically state this in the employee's contract of employment (the contract may also state that the employee will be acknowledged in relation to the creation—the moral rights. This would be applicable to artistic, literary, musical, and dramatic rights). As IP rights are often very valuable to a business, an employer may wish to use a restraint of trade clause (see **23.5**) to restrict the employee's exploitation of such sensitive (and possibly lucrative) information. However, contract terms in contravention of the Patents Act 2004, regarding patents and their ownership, will be considered unenforceable.

In relation specifically to patents, PA 1977 provides at s. 39(1) that inventions created by employees will belong to an employer where they were created during the normal course of employment and relating to the employee's duties at work (and as such would be reasonably considered to be the result of carrying out those tasks). This is considered in light of the implied terms in employees' contracts (see **19.6.1**), and the fact that provision for the ownership of IP rights has not been drafted to include, for example, an obligation or expectation that inventions will be created, does not restrict the duty of fidelity providing the employer with a means to secure the ownership of the IP.

British Syphon Co. Ltd v Homewood (1956)

Facts:

Mr Homewood was employed as the chief technician for the claimant. During his employment, Homewood invented a soda water dispenser which he wanted to patent, having joined a rival company.

Authority for:

The invention belonged to Homewood's employer. He was an employee at the time of making the invention and thus the patent would be assigned to the employer.

The courts will look towards what tasks/duties are being undertaken in the course of employment that will establish the obligations on the employee, rather than simply reviewing a contract of employment and using the terms therein to determine ownership of IP.

Re Harris' Patent (1985)

Facts:

An employee had made an invention that was patentable. The fact that he was a salesman with no requirement or expectation to invent resulted in the invention belonging to him, not the employer.

Authority for:

An employer will generally be the owner of IP rights established by employees, unless the invention has no relation to their employment.

There has been a development to the law in this area and PA 2004 provides that in situations where an employee has created an invention for the employer and a patent has been granted, the employee is entitled to be compensated (determined by a court or the Comptroller-General. The court/Comptroller also has the authority to award compensation in situations where an employee has assigned the patent to the employer for less than it was worth). When determining whether compensation is to be payable and its amount (if any), the following will be taken into consideration: the size of the organization, whether the invention or its patent is of outstanding value to the employer, the nature of the employer's business, and so on, and then whether it is just and reasonable to award the employee compensation. The compensation awarded will reflect the employee's share of the benefit received (or expected to be received) by the employer.

24.8 INDEPENDENT CONTRACTORS AND INTELLECTUAL PROPERTY

The employer owns the employee's IP created at work because of the contract of employment and the distinctive feature of control exercisable by the employer (a fundamental feature of employee status). However, if an independent contractor/freelance worker is used by the employer to perform some task that creates an IP (which could include an advertising campaign, or the development of a firm's website), who owns this? Do not think that simply because a business has paid for a creation that has IP rights, that it will automatically have ownership of it to use, change, and sell however it chooses. Again, in general terms (and as such there may be exceptions) the employer has an implied right to use the IP created, as this will have formed part of the contract, but such rights must be assigned to the employer or the business otherwise they will not own the IP or be in a position to make further use of them. The key element is to establish at the contract stage who will possess ownership, and therefore control, over the created IP and this should also identify any moral rights to the creation.

In situations of copyright, for example, the creation by an employee will usually result in the work belonging to the employer. However, an independent contractor will, unless stated otherwise, retain control of the copyright. Legal advice to draft a secure contract may be money well spent in the longer term. Care must also be taken when a business begins negotiations to sell or license its product or work. Registering the design, trademark, and patent, and ensuring ownership of copyright is present through the techniques identified earlier will reduce the possibility of unauthorized use, and enable legal action to prevent infringements.

Beyond the use of contracts and restraint of trade and confidentiality clauses within contracts of employment, a business should restrict physical access to materials that have a valuable IP from those who could make unauthorized use of them. This is a simple technique, but it ensures that information does not get leaked and information is restricted to key individuals in a firm. Where tasks are outsourced to third parties, it may be wise not to provide information regarding the nature of wider projects that the materials are being designed for. For a very good example of ensuring confidentiality and secrecy in IP, investigate the Apple Corporation and consider how many actual leaks regarding new products come to the public domain before officially announced—relatively few. This is why that business has been growing successfully and is one of the most innovative organizations in the technology sector.

24.9 THE INTELLECTUAL PROPERTY (UNJUSTIFIED THREATS) ACT 2017

The law of IP is often complex and legal action can be daunting. Beyond the commonplace notion of 'patent trolls' who pursue legal action against those who, so the troll claims, has infringed their IP rights, as IP is frequently referred to as the fourth industrial revolution, its value to society and to its owners is significant—and worth defending. The oft faced problem with IP rights was the rights of the owners, their power and ability to intimidate alleged infringers with very costly and time consuming legal actions, and whether such actions amounted to unjustified threats and perpetuated, in some cases, monopoly controls which would have negative results for public policy and innovation.

The law, pre the Intellectual Property (Unjustified Threats) Act 2017 (the 2017 Act), allowed both rights holders and their legal representatives to be sued for issuing a threat of action against an alleged infringer. The rules relating to this right and the control of it were spread amongst common law principles and various legislative instruments. The result was a lack of clarity and consistent application depending upon the IP rights applicable. The 2017 Act seeks to address those points by clarifying and harmonizing the law by identifying what rights holders may do in the event of an alleged infringement of their rights without falling victim to a retaliatory threats claim.

The Intellectual Property (Unjustified Threats) Act 2017 received Royal Assent on 27 April 2017 and came into force on 1 October 2017. It stemmed from the Law Commission's consultation on the reform of the law and the existing common law provisions regarding unjustified/groundless threats. Whilst it began with the law of patents, it applies now to the majority of IP rights (patents, trademarks, registered, and unregistered designs) with the exception of copyright and the tort of passing-off. These provide alleged IP infringers with a standalone right of action where an IP owner threatens them with action for their IP infringement (see **Figure 24.3**).

24.9.1 What is a Threat?

A threat must relate to acts of infringement executed, or to be undertaken, in the UK with proceedings being brought in the UK. The threat may, however, originate from anywhere in the world.

A threat is demonstrated according to the test established in the case *Best Buy v Worldwide Sales Corp.* [2011] which is what a reasonable person, in receipt of the communication, would understand it (perceive it) to mean (the test incorporates both objective and subjective elements). The manner of the threat is not relevant. The threat may be in the form of a letter, communication through a lawyer, it may also be verbal. It does not have to be communicated directly from the infringer. The communication also needs to viewed at the time of its issuance and it may not preclude a future threat of action—hence still breaching the 2017 Act.

Figure 24.3 Steps to identify an actionable threat

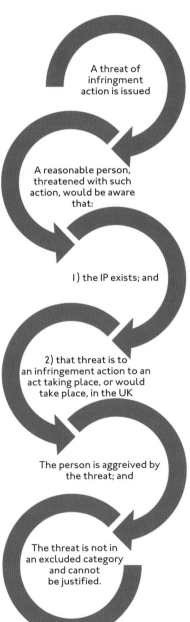

A threat of infringment action is issued

A reasonable person, threatened with such action, would be aware that:

1) the IP exists; and

2) that threat is to an infringement action to an act taking place, or would take place, in the UK

The person is aggreived by the threat; and

The threat is not in an excluded category and cannot be justified.

24.9.2 Exclusions Permitted

The Act will allow the rights holder to threaten primary infringers with any act of infringement—but in relation to patents specifically, a primary infringer may also be threatened with a claim for acts of secondary infringement.

The Act further allows for permitted communications based on 'permitted purposes' which the rights holder believes are true, and are:

- giving notice that a right exists;
- discovering the primary infringers; and
- any purpose which the court considers in the interest of justice to allow.

24.9.3 Justifying Threats

For all the rights it is a defence to an unjustified threat where, obviously, the threat can be justified (the holder can prove the right subsists and is being infringed).

24.9.4 Remedies

Damages, an injunction, and declaratory relief remain the same under the 2017 Act.

CONCLUSION

This chapter has identified the rights that owners of IP have over their creations and inventions. Whilst rights are provided, as recognized by law, in certain instances by simply being the creator of a work, there is far greater protection through the registration of the ownership of the IP and, where relevant, establishing with employees and contractors as to ownership of valuable IP. Due to the value of names, slogans, logos, and inventions to business, these matters should be of serious consideration when the business is established and throughout its creation of products. Whilst this chapter has identified, briefly, some important points, always refer to professionals when ensuring protection.

SUMMARY OF MAIN POINTS

Intellectual property

- IP is often a very valuable commercial asset that can be exclusively used by the owner, sold, and licensed. It may provide a significant revenue stream for businesses.

Copyright

- The law is governed by the Copyright, Designs and Patents Act 1988 and the Intellectual Property Act 2014, which protect the owner's original materials including literary, dramatic, musical, artistic works, and typographical arrangements.
- Copyright is an automatic right and need not be applied for (but proof may be needed to establish ownership).
- The copyright must be expressed and fixed (such as being written down) and as such ideas/ thoughts are not copyright protected.
- Legal rights (and in some cases moral rights) are attributed to copyright holders.
- Copyright exists for varying periods of time depending on its form.

- Enforcement takes place in the civil courts through the owner seeking a remedy against the transgressor(s).

Design rights

- Design rights protect the appearance/shapes of a product (such as the Coca-Cola bottle).
- The design must be fixed and original, not commonplace in a specific area (UK, EU, and selected third countries with reciprocal arrangements with the UK).
- There is an automatic right to the design right for 15 years but a registration process is available.
- Unregistered design rights exist for a shorter period than registered designs and the owner has to demonstrate that the transgressor deliberately copied the design (which can be difficult).
- Designs may be registered at the Patent Office (Designs Registry) under the Registered Designs Act 1949.
- The registered design allows the owner exclusive rights and use of the product in the UK. The exclusivity lasts for five years and may be renewed at five-year periods for up to 25 years.
- It covers two- and three-dimensional works.
- To claim for infringement of the registered design right, the owner merely has to show the transgressor's design is similar. They do not have to demonstrate intention to infringe the owner's right or direct copying of the design.
- Registration may be made to the Office of Harmonization in the Internal Market to give protection to the design throughout the EU. The protection only lasts for three years.

Trademarks

- The Trade Marks Act 1994 protects the owner of any sign capable of being represented graphically which is capable of distinguishing goods or services of one undertaking from those of another.
- Trademarks may consist of words, designs, numerals, or the shape of goods/packaging.
- A registered trademark provides its owner with exclusive use of the mark.
- Enforcement may take place through the civil and criminal jurisdictions.
- Since 1 October 2007 it is possible to register a mark that is similar or the same as an existing mark (unless there is an objection).
- Registration can also be made to the Community Trade Mark giving protection throughout the EU.

Passing-off

- A common law action exists where a business/individual attempts to pass themself or a product off as that of another business. Its aim must be to confuse/mislead the public.

Patents

- Protection is granted to inventions through a new way of making a product that has industrial application.
- Registration prevents others from using or selling the same product without permission. The protection lasts for five-year periods (to a maximum of 20 years).

- The owner of a patent is provided with a monopoly right to control the item.
- Mechanisms exist where a person may request from the Comptroller-General to license a patented invention (after three years following the grant of the patent).

Employees and independent contractors

- Generally, IP created by an employee in the course of employment will belong to the employer (although the employee may possess moral rights).
- IP created by an independent contractor/freelance worker is more complicated. The employer should establish an agreement with the contractor as to the ownership and exploitation of the IP.

SUMMARY QUESTIONS

Essay questions

1. Identify the ways in which the Trade Marks Act 1994 has liberalized obtaining a registered trademark? Are there any problems that remain?

2. Have the Patents Acts 1977 and 2004 effectively balanced the rights of the employer and employee in the ownership of inventions created by the employee?

Problem question

1. Sundeep has developed a new football boot that he considers to be a radical development and will improve players' performance. He seeks to protect his invention through a patent and seeks your advice on the registration process, the rights that registration will provide him, and how he may enforce the patent against transgressors.

2. You are approached by the following two parties for advice on possible breach of trademarks.

   a. Sweet Perfume Ltd wish to sell a new perfume which is aimed at the high end of the market. To appeal to these customers it intends to use a distinctive, fancy bottle, in the shape of a pyramid and with the product name 'Cleopatra'. Fearing imitators, Sweet Perfume Ltd has requested advice as to whether the chosen product name and bottle shape may be registered as trademarks.

   b. Super Quick Plc operates a national chain of replacement car tyre and exhaust centres. It trades under the registered name 'Super Quick'. Super Quick has noticed an announcement in the Trade Mark Journal that 'Rubbery Products Ltd' has applied to register the name 'Kwik-Fit' for a new brand of sheath contraceptives it is launching. Super Quick Plc wish to know whether this new application can be defeated.

   c. Advise both parties.

   You will find guidance about how to answer these questions online at www.oup.com/uk/marson5e/.

FURTHER READING

Books and articles

Property and land law

Clarke, S. and Greer, S. (2018) 'Land Law: Directions' (6th Edition) Oxford University Press: Oxford.

IP resources

Norman, H. (2014) 'Intellectual Property Law: Directions' (2nd Edition) Oxford University Press: Oxford.

Bergquist, J. and Curley, D. (2008) 'Shape Trade Marks and Fast-Moving Consumer Goods' *European Intellectual Property Review*, Vol. 30, No. 1, p. 17.

Intellectual Property Newsletter (1998) 'Intellectual Property when Transferring Businesses' *Intellectual Property News*, Vol. 21, No. 9, p. 5.

Jaeschke, L. (2008) 'The Quest for a Superior Registration System for Registered Trade Marks in the United Kingdom and the European Union: An Analysis of the Current Registration System in the United Kingdom, the Community Trade Mark Registration System and Coming Changes' *European Intellectual Property Review*, Vol. 30, No. 1, p. 25.

Swycher, N. and Luckman, M. (1991) 'Buying Businesses: Intellectual Property Investigations' *PLC Magazine*, Vol. 2, No. 2, p. 21.

Websites, Twitter, and YouTube channels

https://www.gov.uk/browse/business/intellectual-property
This Government website contains guidance on intellectual property rights relating to business.

http://www.ipo.gov.uk/home.htm/
@The_IPO

http://www.youtube.com/user/ipogovuk
The UK Intellectual Property Office. This is the government body responsible for registering IP rights in the UK and these resources contain valuable information regarding developments in the law, reports, newsletters, and so on.

http://www.itma.org.uk/intro/index.htm
@ITMAuk
  The Institute of Trade mark Attorneys. The institute seeks to ensure that all practising members possess the specialized knowledge and experience in trademark matters. It convenes lectures and seminars throughout Europe and provides details of recent cases and commentary on their implications.

http://www.wipo.int
@WIPO

https://www.youtube.com/user/wipo
The World Intellectual Property Organization is a specialist organization of the United Nations that promotes the effective use and protection of IP worldwide.

http://www.cipa.org.uk
@TheCIPA
  The Chartered Institute of Patent Agents is the professional and examining body for patent attorneys in the UK. The resources provide effective links to materials, advice, and educational development initiatives.

http://www.legislation.gov.uk/ukpga/1988/48/contents
The Copyright, Designs and Patents Act 1988.

http://www.legislation.gov.uk/ukpga/1994/26/contents
The Trade Marks Act 1994.

http://www.legislation.gov.uk/ukpga/1977/37
The Patents Act 1977.

ONLINE RESOURCES

www.oup.com/uk/marson5e/

For further resources relating to this chapter, including self-test questions, an interactive glossary, and key case flashcards.

GLOSSARY

On the online resources you will find an interactive glossary where you can test your understanding of these terms. www.oup.com/uk/marson5e/

Administrator An officer of the court (whether or not appointed by the court) appointed with the objective of rescuing the company as a going concern, achieving a better result for creditors than would be likely if the company were wound up, or to realize the company's property to make a distribution to secured and preferential creditors.

ADR Alternative forms of dispute resolution have been developed in an attempt to settle disputes between parties without recourse to litigation. The term is typically used when referring to mediation, conciliation, and arbitration techniques.

Agent A person who has the authority to act on another's (the principal) behalf, and will bind the principal in contracts as if the principal had personally made the agreement.

Automatically unfair reasons to dismiss Certain reasons used in choosing to dismiss (such as for pregnancy; trade union membership; enforcement of rights under health and safety legislation) are automatically unfair and as such the claimant is not required to satisfy the two years' continuous employment qualification.

Balance of probabilities The test used to establish liability/guilt in civil cases, which is a lesser test than of 'beyond reasonable doubt' used in criminal cases. The facts of the case and the evidence presented will be assessed to determine whether the court is satisfied that the claim has been proved.

Band of reasonable responses In determining whether an employer's decision to dismiss was a reasonable response to the alleged conduct, the tribunal will have regard to the Employment Appeal Tribunal's decision in *Iceland Frozen Foods v Jones* [1982] (see **21.2.6**).

Breach of contract When a party fails to complete their obligations under the contract, they may be in breach, allowing the injured party to seek a remedy.

Breach of statutory duty A statute may impose a duty but fail to mention any civil law sanctions. In order to claim under the statute, the claimant must demonstrate that Parliament intended liability in tort to follow from the breach.

Business Includes the activities of any government department or local or public authority.

Business efficacy This expression has been used when describing how the courts may imply terms in order to produce an intended or anticipated result in the contract.

Case law These are reports of cases that have been decided by the courts. You can 'identify' case law as the report contains the names of each of the parties (e.g. *Donoghue v Stevenson* [1932], see **11.5.1.1**).

Claimant/appellant The 'party' (person/body) bringing the action and is named first in the proceedings (e.g. Carlill in *Carlill v Carbolic Smoke Ball Co.* [1893], see **5.4.1**). Note that older cases refer to this party as the 'plaintiff' but from 26 October 1999 the term 'plaintiff' was replaced with 'claimant' under the Civil Procedure Rules 1999.

Collective ministerial responsibility Ministers with responsibility for government departments are members of the Cabinet. They have the ability, in Cabinet discussions, to contribute to policy. However, when the Cabinet collectively establishes a policy, each of the Ministers must follow this (or the convention is that if they cannot support the Government they must resign their Ministry).

Common law Law created through judicial decisions. It is a body of law that was being developed before a united system of government had been formed in England. Wrongful dismissal is governed by the common law, and hence the rules and remedies applicable with the common law are applied to the regulation of contracts of employment.

Comparator To found a claim of discrimination, the claimant must establish that they were discriminated on the basis of a protected characteristic. Therefore, they must have been a victim of less or (un)favourable treatment attributable to the protected characteristic; and this is evidenced when compared with how a person without the protected characteristic was or would be treated. Depending on the claim, a permissible comparator may be hypothetical, or in other instances a 'real' person may have to be used to demonstrate less favourable treatment.

Consensus ad idem This is the Latin term for an 'agreement as to the same thing' in English law, more commonly referred to as a 'meeting of minds' between the parties.

Consideration Simple contracts have to be a bargain rather than a gratuitous promise (that cannot be enforced). Consideration is something of value that makes the agreement a bargain 'the price paid for a promise'.

Constitution The constitution is a system defining the power of the State and State bodies, and regulating their actions, thereby ensuring accountability.

Constructive dismissal When an employer radically or fundamentally changes the contract to the employee's detriment, but has not dismissed the employee, the employee may treat this unilateral change as a repudiation, resign, and claim constructive dismissal. This may be best understood as a claim for unfair dismissal when the employee has not been dismissed.

Consultation Where an employer plans to transfer an undertaking they are required, under the TUPE 2006 Regulations, to consult with the employees and their representatives. A similar duty applies in cases of proposed redundancies.

Consumer Refers to an individual acting for purposes that are wholly or mainly outside of that individual's trade, business, craft, or profession. The significance of this definition is that it provides certainty and consistency between consumer protection legislation. Any trader who claims that the individual was not a consumer for the purposes of this law has the obligation to prove it. Such definitions remove the confusion present in the current/previous legislation relating to consumers and traders. The Unfair Contract Terms Act 1977, s. 12 sought to define what 'dealing as a consumer' and acting in 'the course of business' meant in real world scenarios.

Contra proferentem This is a rule whereby the courts, generally, will interpret an exclusion clause narrowly and against the party that is seeking to rely on it.

Corporation A legal entity, such as a company, that possesses its own legal personality separate from the members.

Course of employment For an employer to be held liable for the torts of an employee, the tort must have been committed in the working hours and/or under the responsibility of the employer. The common law has demonstrated many examples, and established rules, to identify what will constitute 'course of employment'.

Damages Compensation awarded by the court in the form of a monetary payment.

Debenture Written evidence of a secured loan given by the lender to the company. It has been described as 'a document which either creates a debt or acknowledges it'.

Defendant The party defending the claim.

Delegated legislation Laws that enable an individual/body to pass legislation under the authority and control of Parliament. These include Statutory Instruments, Orders in Council, and by-laws.

Direct applicability A concept of EU law where the Treaty Article/Regulation becomes part of national law immediately following its commencement. Thus, its provisions are capable of being relied upon in UK courts without any action being necessary on the part of the Member State.

Direct discrimination Direct discrimination occurs when a person treats another less or (un) favourably because of a protected characteristic than they would a person without the characteristic.

Discharge of contract The contract may be brought to an end through performance of the obligations, through agreement between the parties, through frustration of the contract, or through one of the parties' breach and this being accepted by the innocent party.

Dissolution This is the process of ending a business relationship (such as a company or partnership).

Dividend The distributable profits of a company to shareholders.

Doctrine This term is used to refer to a body of thought and is used in legal theory to identify a principle of law, such as those developed through the common law.

Duress Compelling a party to enter a contract on the basis of a threat, which makes the contract voidable.

Duty of care The rule that places an obligation to take reasonable care not to injure your 'neighbour' or damage property.

Economic, technical, and organizational reason Where there has been a transfer of an undertaking regulated by TUPE 2006, the employee is transferred to the transferee with the terms and conditions of employment preserved. These terms and conditions may be altered, and the employee may even be dismissed, if there is an economic, technical, or organizational reason connected with the transfer, to the satisfaction of the tribunal.

Effective Date of Termination A claim under unfair dismissal has to be lodged at a tribunal within three months of the Effective Date of Termination. The Employment Rights Act 1996 (ERA), ss. 97 and 145 identify the mechanism to determine the date.

Employee A person who works under a 'contract of service'. These individuals, who perform the contract personally, have greater obligations placed on them (such as implied terms) but also have greater protection in employment, including the right not to be unfairly dismissed and the right to compensation upon redundancy.

Employment Appeal Tribunal (EAT) This is not a tribunal (despite its name) but is the court that hears cases of appeals from Employment Tribunals.

Employment Tribunal Tribunals are established to hear employment law complaints between the employer and individual. These tribunals were previously known as Industrial Tribunals and they hear employment cases (dismissals; discrimination; cases involving other statutory rights; and so on). They are presided over by an Employment Judge (formally a chairperson) and are assisted by two lay members representing (generally, rather than specific to the case) both employers and workers. However, from 6 April 2012, Employment Judges may sit alone in cases of unfair dismissal.

Equitable remedy Discretionary remedies granted by the courts, generally where damages would not provide an adequate remedy. Examples of equitable remedies include injunctions, rescission, and specific performance.

Exclusion/exemption clause A term that attempts to exclude a party's liability which would otherwise exist. There are common law and statutory rules regulating the use of such clauses.

Executive A broad concept that, whilst generally attributed to the Government (and specifically the Cabinet), can include any organ that administers power.

Fiduciary duty A fiduciary has authority belonging to another person/body, and they are obliged to exercise this for the other party's benefit. An example of a relationship establishing fiduciary duties is between solicitor and their client.

Force majeure clauses This is an element of frustration in determining how to deal with events that are beyond the control of the parties (wars, acts of God, and so on).

Freedom of contract No one can be forced into an agreement, therefore the State did not regulate such agreements and allowed the parties to establish their own terms and conditions.

Frustration An event, that is neither party's fault, may render the contract impossible to perform or radically different from that agreed. This leads to the contract being frustrated (unable to be continued) and results in the parties being discharged from further responsibilities.

Garden leave agreements The employer may decide that instead of incorporating a restraint of trade clause and (possibly) having this rejected by the court, a 'safer' option may be to incorporate an extended period of notice where the employee, having given his/her notice or resignation, is paid to 'stay in the garden'—albeit that they cannot work in competition with the employer.

Gross misconduct The 'gross' element is a one-off, serious, event that would justify a summary dismissal such as theft, assaults, and so on.

Gross negligence To justify a summary dismissal this would involve a serious act of negligence such as endangering customers, colleagues, and so on.

Harassment Harassment involves 'unwanted conduct' related to a protected characteristic, which has the purpose or effect of violating a person's dignity or creating an intimidating, hostile, degrading, humiliating, or offensive environment.

Heads of claim For an action to succeed on the basis of direct sex discrimination in pay, the claimant must choose one of the three 'heads' of claim identified under the Act—like work, work rated as equivalent, or work of equal value.

Indemnity The Civil Procedure Rules define indemnity as a right of one party to recover from a third party the whole amount that they themselves are liable to pay. This is particularly apt in situations involving the liability of partners.

Independent contractor A person who works under a 'contract for services'. These individuals have the ability (and option) to work for several employers, and have better tax benefits, but lack many elements of employment protection that employees enjoy.

Indirect discrimination Indirect discrimination involves the application of a seemingly neutral provision, criterion, or practice that is applied to everyone. However, it particularly affects people who share a protected characteristic and it puts them (or would put them) at a particular disadvantage.

Individual ministerial responsibility A government Minister has responsibility for the actions of themselves, and their department.

Innominate/intermediate terms Where the parties attempt to identify in advance a term as a condition or warranty and this is impossible as it requires knowledge of the consequence of the breach.

Intellectual property This is a product of someone's intellect that has commercial value and may be exploited. It provides legal rights of ownership and control and is typified by copyright of artistic and literary works, patents, trademarks, and design rights.

Intention to create legal relations A legally enforceable contract must be one where the parties understand and accept that failure to fulfil obligations under the agreement may result in legal consequences.

Inter alia The Latin phrase meaning 'among other things'.

Judiciary The body of the judges. They interpret and apply the law. The 'judiciary' often refers to the senior judges in the Court of Appeal, the Supreme Court, and the judicial wing of the Privy Council.

Law reports Case law is reported in law reports, which identify the facts of a particular case and the rulings/judgment of the court. Those that are reported have some importance in developing precedent or identifying the interpretation of statutes and so on. These reports are published by commercial organizations and as such the case may be produced in any or all of the available reports including the Law Reports (Appeal Cases, Chancery Division, Family Division and Queen's Bench Division); the Weekly Law Reports; the All England Law Reports; and, increasingly, specialized reports for specific areas of law such as the Family Law Reports and Butterworths's Medico-Legal Reports.

Legal personality The rights attached to a natural person and/or an artificial thing, such as a corporation.

Legislation Law created through, or under the authority of, Parliament. It is the highest form of law and is not subject to challenge by the courts.

Legislature The body that passes legislation. In terms of the concept of separation of powers, this is generally Parliament.

Limitation clause This is often used to describe terms such as exclusion/exemption clauses that seek not to completely exclude any potential liability, but rather to limit or restrict a liability which would otherwise exist. For example, a clause could be included into a contract which provides that an individual/corporation is liable for specific loss or damage, but that this is restricted to a monetary award.

Liquidated damages These are damages that are determined in the contract in advance of a breach. They must be a pre-estimate of loss and not a penalty clause.

London Gazette This is the official newspaper that provides, in the context of this chapter, legal and regulatory information regarding companies, disqualification of directors' notices, and so on.

Material factor To defend an action against an equal pay claim, the employer may demonstrate that the difference in pay is not due to the sex of the individual, but is based on some objective, justifiable, reason (e.g. responsibility or qualifications).

Misrepresentation A false statement of fact inducing the innocent party to form the contract.

Mitigation In the event of a breach of contract, the injured party has an obligation to limit his/her losses as far as is reasonably possible.

Mutuality of obligations There is an obligation for the individual to offer their services to the employer (attend work) and there is a mutual obligation for the employer to provide work/pay. This is an essential component of 'employee' status.

Non-delegable duties Certain responsibilities are imposed by statute or the common law and they cannot be delegated to another body/person. For example, in an employment context duties exist and are applied to the employer who is unable to delegate these to sub-contractors, and the employer will remain responsible, jointly or severally, for any subsequent torts.

Nudum pactum This is a promise made with no consideration to support it.

Nuisance This is an unlawful interference that prevents an owner/occupier's enjoyment of their land.

Obiter dicta These are statements made by judges that are not part of the ratio, and hence are not part of the judgment of the case. They are not binding on lower courts but they are of persuasive authority and may be followed in future cases where the issue has been raised.

Occupational Requirement This provides a defence to a claim of discrimination where (e.g.) there is discrimination between men and women, but this is not due to their sex per se, but rather is necessitated by the nature of the employment.

Offeree The party(s) to whom an offer has been made.

Offeror The party making an offer and setting out the terms by which they are willing to be bound.

Official Receiver This is a civil servant of the Insolvency Service (part of the Department for Business, Innovation & Skills) and an officer of the court. They are appointed on a bankruptcy or winding-up order and administer the initial stages, and possibly a longer period, of the insolvency of the company.

Pari passu An interpretation from the Latin means 'with equal step' and can be considered as meaning shares that rank without preference.

Parliament Parliament consists of the House of Commons, the House of Lords at Westminster, and also the monarch. All three institutions are involved in the legislative system, and Parliament assists in scrutinizing the work of the Government and holding it to account.

Parliamentary supremacy Parliament at Westminster is where primary legislation is created. A key element of the constitution is that Parliament has the power to make or repeal any legislation, and it cannot bind successive (future) Parliaments. Therefore, tyranny and abuse of power is avoided, as the public may elect a new Parliament at a general election (which must be held within at least five years following the election of the Government).

Parol evidence This rule prevents extrinsic (outside) factors being introduced into a contract or being used to vary the written terms.

Penalty clause A clause which seeks to stop the other party from breaching the contract by imposing the threat of a penalty, which is not a genuine pre-estimate of loss, will be considered a penalty and be held void.

Precedent This is a system where the decisions of higher courts (through case law/common law) bind lower courts due to the hierarchical system of the court structure. Precedent is established from the *ratio decidendi* of the case. The judges in a case will spend time explaining, with reference to previous cases, how and why they have arrived at a decision, and whether the case establishing the precedent should be followed or distinguished.

Pre-emption rights This is the right of shareholders to be offered new issues of shares before they are made available to non-shareholders.

Primary victim A person who was not physically injured in an incident, but was in the zone of physical danger. Typically, this has been related to a claimant's fear for their personal safety that caused some psychiatric injury.

Principal The person who instructs the agent to work on their behalf.

Privy Council The Privy Council has a function as an appeal court used by some former Commonwealth countries.

Promisee The party to whom a promise is made.

Promisor The party making the promise.

Promissory estoppels A doctrine providing an equitable defence preventing a party who has made a promise to vary a contract for the other party's benefit from later reneging on it and attempting to enforce the original contract.

Proximity The close relationship between the parties to a negligence action which is essential to establish a duty of care.

Pure economic loss This is where the claimant's losses are not connected with any physical loss or damage. This is typically in the case of negligent advice or information provided to the claimant.

Quoted company This is a company whose equity share capital has been included in the Official List in accordance with the provisions of Part 6 of the Financial Services and Markets Act 2000, or is officially listed in an EEA state, or admitted for dealing on the New York Stock Exchange or Nasdaq.

Ratification Where the agent acts without the express or implied authorization of the principal, or in excess of this authority, the principal may ratify the contract and be bound by it as though authorization had been given from the start of the contract.

Ratio decidendi This is the part of the judicial decision that is binding on all lower courts. The judiciary explain the previous case law and establish the legal principle on which the case is being decided. The ratio is not identified as such, but rather it has to be 'found' through reading the judgment and identifying the salient factors leading to the decision.

Red-circle agreement An employer who has conducted a job evaluation study to make pay structures transparent may protect the pay of a group of affected workers where, following assessment, they are to be downgraded.

Redundancy This occurs when employment at the place of business has ceased or the nature of the business/industry has changed and the employee's role in the organization is surplus to requirements.

Reorganization of the business An employer has the ability to reorganize their business. This may be due to changes in competition; to respond to the needs of the organization, and so on. Such reorganization, if resulting in dismissals, may lead to claims for redundancy payments.

Representations Statements in the negotiations of a contract that do not amount to a term. Breach of a representation may lead to a claim for misrepresentation.

Repudiation To end or reject a contract, usually in response to the other party's breach.

Rescission An equitable remedy where the party misled has the option to set aside the contract.

Restraint of trade clause This is a contractual clause that prevents or restricts an employee from competing with the employer for a specific duration and a specific region/area of industry. To have the clause enforced the employer must demonstrate the necessity for the clause and that it protects the employer's legitimate proprietary interests.

Revocation An offer may be withdrawn (revoked) by the offeror before being accepted by the offeree.

Rule of law A theory that identifies fundamental principles which provide for a just and fair system of law, and which ensures tyranny and abuse is avoided. For example, everyone is equal before the law.

Secondary victim A person who was not injured physically in an incident or in fear of their own safety, but was closely related to a victim, which caused them psychiatric injury.

Secured loan This refers to a loan where the borrower provides the lender with some collateral (through charges over property).

Separation of powers To ensure too much power is not vested in one body, and a system of accountability through 'checks and balances' exists, the three elements of the State (the executive, the legislature, and the judiciary) must have clear demarcation between them. This ensures there is sufficient independence in these three branches of government.

Share warrant Companies may, where authorized by the articles, issue in respect of fully paid-up shares, a warrant that states the bearer is entitled to the shares specified in it.

Solvency statement The directors formally state that they have formed an opinion that the company will be able to repay its debts where the company wishes to reduce its share capital.

State of prior art In patent law, an invention may be refused a patent because it is not novel. Therefore, if it can be demonstrated that 'prior art' existed before the patent applied for (through documents and other evidence) then the patent will not be granted.

Statute A law created through Parliament, and also referred to as legislation.

Statutory interpretation The wording of legislation is precisely drafted but this still requires interpretation and application by the judiciary. There are various methods of interpreting these laws.

Strict liability Liability is imposed where, in the case of the Consumer Protection Act 1987, a product contained a defect. There is no requirement for the claimant to demonstrate negligence on the part of the defendant.

Subscriber When, in relation to company law, the subscriber is the person who has agreed to start the company and take a proportion of the original issue of shares.

Summary dismissal This is an immediate dismissal (without any notice).

Supreme Court The judicial function of the House of Lords became the Supreme Court on 1 October 2009. It more clearly separates the (previous) legislative and judicial functions held by the Lords.

Tortfeasor The party who has committed the tort.

Trader Refers to a person (both natural (human) and artificial (corporation)) acting for purposes relating to their trade, business, craft, or profession. The term trader applies whether they are acting personally or whether another person is acting in the trader's name or on their behalf.

Transposition A process by which the Member States give effect to a Directive by passing an implementation measure—such as an Act of Parliament. For example, the Working Time Directive was transposed into UK law through the Working Time Regulations. It is intended that following the correct transposition, individuals in the Member State will rely on the implementing law rather than the parent Directive.

Undue influence Where a party unfairly exploits its relationship with the other party to enter a contract, this may also render the contract voidable.

Unfair dismissal A statutory-based right. Legislation provides protection for employees against certain dismissals, and it establishes methods in which a dismissal must take place to be considered fair.

Unliquidated damages The court calculates an award of damages as they are incapable of being pre-determined.

Unsecured loan These are loans that are not secured on the company's property/assets.

Vicarious liability Holding another party (usually an employer/principal) jointly responsible/liable for the actions of the tortfeasor (usually an employee/agent).

Victimization The offence of victimization occurs where an individual has brought a claim under the Equality Act 2010 or they intended to claim under the Act(s); or gave evidence at a hearing and has suffered less favourable treatment from the employer as a result.

Void contract The law will not recognize the agreement and therefore it has no legal effect (such as an illegal contract or one established through mistake).

Voidable contract This is an agreement that can be a legally binding contract at the option of the injured party or which such party can have set aside (such as with contracts established under misrepresentation or duress).

Volenti non fit injuria The Latin phrase relating to a voluntary assumption of risk. Where a person engages in an event and agrees and accepts to the inherent risks, if injured, they are prevented from recovering damages.

Winding-up This is the process of bringing a company to an end. As a corporation possesses its own separate legal personality, it must be formally wound up to 'die'.

Written resolution This is a mechanism for the board of directors to make a decision without having to meet in person. The resolution is valid and effective as if it had been agreed and passed at a meeting, if signed by all the directors entitled to receive notice of it.

Wrongful dismissal (A claim under the common law.) This involves a breach of contract when, for example, insufficient notice is provided to the individual. As it is a contractual claim, it is, significantly, available to all workers rather than the strict criteria that must be satisfied to qualify for rights under the unfair dismissal protections.

INDEX